FUNDAMENTALS OF PHARMACOLOGY
(Volume – II)

Dr. K.G. BOTHARA
M.Pharm., Ph.D.
Principal, Sinhgad Institute of Pharmacy,
Narhe, Pune - 411041

Dr. K.K. BOTHARA
M.B.B.S.

FUNDAMENTALS OF PHARMACOLOGY (VOL-II)　　　　ISBN : 978-93-81595-12-1

First Edition : January 2012

© : Dr. K.G. Bothara

The text of this publication, or any part thereof, should not be reproduced or transmitted in any form or stored in any computer storage system or device for distribution including photocopy, recording, taping or information retrieval system or reproduced on any disc, tape, perforated media or other information storage device etc., without the written permission of Author with whom the rights are reserved. Breach of this condition is liable for legal action.

Every effort has been made to avoid errors or omissions in this publication. In spite of this, errors may have crept in. Any mistake, error or discrepancy so noted and shall be brought to our notice shall be taken care of in the next edition. It is notified that neither the publisher nor the author or seller shall be responsible for any damage or loss of action to any one, of any kind, in any manner, therefrom.

Published By :
NIRALI PRAKASHAN
Abhyudaya Pragati, 1312, Shivaji Nagar,
Off J.M. Road, PUNE – 411005
Tel - (020) 25512336/37/39, Fax - (020) 25511379
Email : niralipune@pragationline.com

Printed By :
Repro India Ltd.,
Mumbai.

DISTRIBUTION CENTRES

PUNE
Nirali Prakashan
119, Budhwar Peth, Jogeshwari Mandir Lane
Pune 411002, Maharashtra
Tel : (020) 2445 2044, 66022708
Fax : (020) 2445 1538
Email : bookorder@pragationline.com

MUMBAI
Nirali Prakashan
385, S.V.P. Road, Rasdhara Co-op. Hsg. Society Ltd.,
Girgaum, Mumbai 400004, Maharashtra
Tel : (022) 2385 6339 / 2386 9976,
Fax : (022) 2386 9976
Email : niralimumbai@pragationline.com

DISTRIBUTION BRANCHES

NAGPUR
Pratibha Book Distributors
Above Maratha Mandir, Shop No. 3, First Floor,
Rani Jhanshi Square, Sitabuldi, Nagpur 440012,
Maharashtra, Tel : (0712) 254 7129

BENGALURU
Pragati Book House
House No. 1,Sanjeevappa Lane, Avenue Road Cross,
Opp. Rice Church, Bengaluru – 560002.
Tel : (080) 64513344, 64513355,
Mob : 9880582331, 9845021552
Email:bharatsavla@yahoo.com

JALGAON
Nirali Prakashan
34, V. V. Golani Market, Navi Peth, Jalgaon 425001,
Maharashtra, Tel : (0257) 222 0395
Mob : 94234 91860

KOLHAPUR
Nirali Prakashan
New Mahadvar Road,
Kedar Plaza, 1st Floor Opp. IDBI Bank
Kolhapur 416 012, Maharashtra. Mob : 9855046155

CHENNAI
Pragati Books
9/1, Montieth Road, Behind Taas Mahal, Egmore,
Chennai 600008 Tamil Nadu, Tel : (044) 6518 3535,
Mob : 94440 01782 / 98450 21552 / 98805 82331
Email : bharatsavla@yahoo.com

RETAIL OUTLETS
PUNE

Pragati Book Centre
157, Budhwar Peth, Opp. Ratan Talkies,
Pune 411002, Maharashtra
Tel : (020) 2445 8887 / 6602 2707, Fax : (020) 2445 8887

Pragati Book Centre
Amber Chamber, 28/A, Budhwar Peth,
Appa Balwant Chowk, Pune : 411002, Maharashtra,
Tel : (020) 20240335 / 66281669
Email : pbcpune@pragationline.com

Pragati Book Centre
676/B, Budhwar Peth, Opp. Jogeshwari Mandir,
Pune 411002, Maharashtra
Tel : (020) 6601 7784 / 6602 0855
Email : pbcpune@pragationline.com

Pragati Book Centre
917/22, Sai Complex, F.C. Road, Opp. Hotel Roopali,
Shivajinagar, Pune 411004, Maharashtra
Tel : (020) 2566 3372 / 6602 2728

PBC Book Sellers & Stationers
152, Budhwar Peth, Pune 411002, Maharashtra
Tel : (020) 2445 2254 / 6609 2463

MUMBAI
Pragati Book Corner
Indira Niwas, 111 - A, Bhavani Shankar Road, Dadar (W), Mumbai 400028, Maharashtra
Tel : (022) 2422 3526 / 6662 5254
Email : pbcmumbai@pragationline.com

www.pragationline.com　　　　info@pragationline.com

PREFACE

Paul Ehrlich's concept that protozoal diseases could be cured by the administration of synthetic chemicals which selectively react with the target tissue of the protozoa rather than that of the host and Domagk's later expansion of this view to the treatment of bacterial diseases with the introduction of prontosil were the prominent landmarks in the birth of modern chemotherapy. The accuracy and the depth of clinical applications of these chemotherapeutic agents were further sharpened due to new inventions in the molecular biology which are increasingly involved to explain the mechanisms of action of many new chemotherapeutic agents. These broad area of pharmacology presented together with necessary data on the chemistry, absorption, excretion, tolerance and toxicity of the drugs are expected to provide a proper understanding of both, the value and limitations of the drug therapy.

In the last two decades, pharmacology attained a status of a basic medical science due to tremendous achievements in both, basic pharmacology and its clinical applications. Many of the changes in pharmacology are reflected in the new foundations and techniques which can be exploited in the synthesis of drugs as well as in their application to the clinical problems. We have incorporated this latest information available without growing appreciably in size. This is reflected particularly in the chapters on the treatment on cancer, organ transplantation and cardiovascular diseases.

Much progress has been achieved in cardiovascular therapy over the past 20 years. Extensive research, in which the academic community and the pharmaceutical industry co-operated with and stimulated each other, has resulted in the development of new drugs affecting cardio-vascular system. These phases of evolution can be witnessed in the chapters on the treatment of cardio-vascular diseases.

Many new drugs have been added to the list through many advances, especially on chemical front. Unfortunately the clinical complications and limitations of each such invented drug, often make the choice of the drug difficult, if the basic principles of pharmacology are not clear. Hence separate chapters (i.e., protein-binding; immuno-modulators) have been added in certain fields to better understand newer concepts or to correlate the relevant data.

The authors are greatly indebted to their colleagues for their generous help and criticism. We wish to place on record our sincere thanks to the publisher, Mr. D.K. Furia for his kind co-operation.

Suggestions from all corners of the profession are welcome. Authors are responsible for any deficiencies or errors that have remained and would be grateful if readers would call them to our attention.

AUTHORS

CONTENTS

1. General Principles — 1.1 to 1.8
    1.1   Introduction — 1.1
    1.2   Bacterial Cell-Wall — 1.3
    1.3   Drug Resistance — 1.7

2. Topical Anti-Infective Agents — 2.1 to 2.12
    2.1   Introduction — 2.1
    2.2   Classification — 2.3
    2.3   Urinary Tract Antiseptic Agents — 2.10
    2.4   Topical Comedolytic Agents — 2.11

3. Chemotherapy of Parasitic Diseases — 3.1 to 3.20
    3.1   Introduction — 3.1
    3.2   Antimalarial Drugs — 3.2
    3.3   Chemotherapy Of Malaria — 3.4
    3.4   Classification Of Antimalarial Agents — 3.5
    3.5   Drug Resistance — 3.11
    3.6   Amoebiasis — 3.12
    3.7   Chemotherapy — 3.13
    3.8   Leishmaniasis — 3.16
    3.9   Trypanosomiasis — 3.17
    3.10   Trichomoniasis — 3.19
    3.11   Giardiasis — 3.19
    3.12   Toxoplasmosis — 3.20
    3.13   Balantidiasis — 3.20

4. Sulphonamides and Urinary Tract Antiseptic Agents — 4.1 to 4.14
    4.1   Introduction — 4.1
    4.2   Nomenclature and Classification — 4.3
    4.3   Pharmacokinetic Features of Sulphonamides — 4.4
    4.4   Adverse Effects — 4.5
    4.5   Mechanism of Action — 4.6
    4.6   Bacterial Resistance — 4.7
    4.7   Therapeutic Uses — 4.8
    4.8   SAR Studies of Sulphonamides — 4.8
    4.9   Systemic Sulphonamides — 4.9

	4.10	Locally Acting Sulphonamides	4.10
	4.11	Topically Used Sulphonamides	4.10
	4.12	Trimethoprim-Sulphonamide Combination (Co-Trimoxazole)	4.11
	4.13	Urinary Tract Infections	4.12

5. Modes of Action of Antibiotics — 5.1 to 5.16

	5.1	Introduction	5.1
	5.2	Penicillin-Binding Proteins (PBP)	5.3
	5.3	Bacterial Resistance to the Antibiotics	5.4
	5.4	Pathogenic Microorganisms	5.7
	5.5	Classification of Antibiotics	5.7
	5.6	Mechanisms of Action of Antibiotics	5.8
	5.7	Nephrotoxic Reactions of Anti-Microbial Agents	5.12
	5.8	Novel β-Lactam Antibiotics	5.13
	5.9	β-Lactamase Inhibitors	5.13
	5.10	Synergistic Antibiotic Combinations	5.15
	5.11	Suprainfection (Superinfection)	5.15

6. β-Lactam Antibiotics — 6.1 to 6.22

	6.1	Introduction	6.1
	6.2	Degradation Products of Penicillins	6.2
	6.3	Classification	6.3
	6.4	Mechanism of Action	6.6
	6.5	Pharmacokinetic Properties	6.7
	6.6	Adverse Effects	6.8
	6.7	Hypersensitivity Reactions	6.8
	6.8	Therapeutic Uses	6.9
	6.9	Bacterial Resistance to β-Lactam Antibiotics	6.10
	6.10	Probenecid	6.11
	6.11	Cephalosporins	6.11
	6.12	Classification	6.12
	6.13	Pharmaco Kinetic Properties	6.13
	6.14	Adverse Effects	6.15
	6.15	Therapeutic Uses	6.15
	6.16	Moxalactam	6.16
	6.17	Other β-Lactam Analogs	6.16
	6.18	Peptide Antibiotics	6.19

7.	**Antibiotics That Affect Protein Synthesis**		**7.1 to 7.18**
	7.1	Aminoglycoside Antibiotics (Aminocyclitol Antibiotics)	7.1
	7.2	Classification	7.2
	7.3	Mechanism of Action	7.3
	7.4	Antibacterial Activity Spectra	7.3
	7.5	Pharmacokinetic Properties	7.3
	7.6	Adverse Effects	7.4
	7.7	Therapeutic Uses	7.4
	7.8	Bacterial Resistance	7.7
	7.9	Tetracycline Antibiotics	7.9
	7.10	Mechanism of Action	7.10
	7.11	Pharmacokinetic Properties	7.10
	7.12	Antimicrobial Activity Spectra	7.10
	7.13	Adverse Effects	7.11
	7.14	Therapeutic Uses	7.12
	7.15	Chloramphenicol	7.12
	7.16	Mechanism of Action	7.12
	7.17	Antimicrobial Activity Spectrum	7.13
	7.18	Pharmacokinetic Properties	7.13
	7.19	Adverse Effects	7.13
	7.20	Therapeutic Uses	7.14
	7.21	Macrolide Antibiotics	7.14
	7.22	Mechanism of Action	7.15
	7.23	Antimicrobial Activity Spectra	7.15
	7.24	Adverse Effects	7.16
	7.25	Therapeutic Uses	7.16
	7.26	Bacterial Resistance	7.16
	7.27	Lincomycins	7.17
	7.28	Adverse Effects	7.18
	7.29	Therapeutic Uses	7.18
8.	**Antibiotics That Interfere With Cytoplasmic Membrane Function**		**8.1 to 8.4**
	8.1	Introduction	8.1
	8.2	Polymyxin Antibiotics	8.1
	8.3	Polyene Antibiotics	8.3

9. Antibiotics Affecting Nucleic Acid Synthesis and Miscellaneous Antibiotics — 9.1 to 9.4
    9.1 Antibiotics that Act by Inhibiting Nucleic Acid Synthesis — 9.1
    9.2 Miscellaneous Antibiotics — 9.3

10. Antifungal Agents — 10.1 to 10.14
    10.1 Introduction — 10.1
    10.2 Classification — 10.5
    10.3 Natural Products — 10.14

11. Antiviral Agents — 11.1 to 11.12
    11.1 Introduction — 11.1
    11.2 Design of Antiviral Agents — 11.2
    11.3 Classification of Antiviral Agents — 11.4

12. Anti-Neoplastic Agents — 12.1 to 12.24
    12.1 Introduction — 12.1
    12.2 Causes of Cancer — 12.1
    12.3 Cell-Cycle Kinetics — 12.1
    12.4 Directive Principles of Rational Drug Design in Cancer Chemotherapy — 12.2
    12.5 Adverse Effects — 12.3
    12.6 Drug Resistance — 12.5
    12.7 Combination Therapy — 12.5
    12.8 Classification — 12.6
    12.9 Alkylating Agents — 12.7
    12.10 Anti-Metabolites — 12.13
    12.11 Antibiotics — 12.17
    12.12 Vinca Alkaloids — 12.19
    12.13 Enzymes — 12.19
    12.14 Hormonal Agents — 12.20
    12.15 Miscellaneous Agents — 12.22

13. Anti-Tuberculosis and Anti-Leprotic Agents — 13.1 to 13.12
    13.1 Introduction — 13.1
    13.2 First-Line Agents — 13.4
    13.3 Second-Line Agents — 13.6
    13.4 Anti-Leprotic Agents — 13.9

14. Adenohypophyseal Hormones — 14.1 to 14.16

- 14.1 Introduction — 14.1
- 14.2 Classification — 14.3
- 14.3 Mechanism of Action — 14.3
- 14.4 Therapeutic Applications — 14.5
- 14.5 Pituitary Hormones — 14.6
- 14.6 Hypothalamic Control of Adenohypophysis — 14.7
- 14.7 Pathological Endocrine Disorders — 14.9
- 14.8 Adenohypophyseal Hormones — 14.11
- 14.9 Neurohypophyseal Hormones — 14.15

15. Thyroid And Parathyroid Hormones — 15.1 to 15.14

- 15.1 Introduction — 15.1
- 15.2 Biosynthesis, Storage and Metabolism of Thyroid Hormones — 15.3
- 15.3 Pharmacokinetics — 15.5
- 15.4 Relationship Between the Growth Hormone and Thyroid Hormones — 15.6
- 15.5 Physiological Actions of Thyroid Hormones — 15.6
- 15.6 Mechanism of Action — 15.7
- 15.7 Therapeutic Uses — 15.7
- 15.8 Diseases of Thyroid Gland — 15.7
- 15.9 Drugs Used In the Therapy of Hyperthyroidism — 15.9
- 15.10 Parathyroid Hormones (Parathormones) — 15.11
- 15.11 Hyperparathyroidism — 15.13
- 15.12 Hypoparathyroidism — 15.13
- 15.13 Therapeutic Uses — 15.13
- 15.14 Calcitonin (Thyrocalcitonin) — 15.13

16. Sex Hormones — 16.1 to 16.28

- 16.1 Introduction — 16.1
- 16.2 Sex Hormones — 16.1
- 16.3 Estrogens — 16.5
- 16.4 Antiestrogens or Ovulation Stimulants — 16.9
- 16.5 Progesterone and its Analogs (Progestins) — 16.10
- 16.6 Androgens or Male Sex Hormones — 16.13
- 16.7 Antiandrogens — 16.15
- 16.8 Ovulation — 16.15
- 16.9 Gynaecological Diseases — 16.18
- 16.10 Oral Contraceptives — 16.20

16.11	Types of Oral Contraceptives	16.22
16.12	Pearl Index	16.26
16.13	Mechanism of Action	16.26
16.14	Adverse Effects	16.26

17. Adrenocorticoids — 17.1 to 17.12

17.1	Introduction	17.1
17.2	Adrenocortical Steroids	17.3
17.3	Mechanism of Action	17.8
17.4	Pharmacokinetics	17.8
17.5	Adverse Effects	17.9
17.6	Therapeutic Uses	17.9
17.7	Topical Anti-Inflammatory Steroidal Agents	17.9
17.8	Mineralocortico-Steroids	17.10
17.9	Diseases of Adrenal Cortex	17.11
17.10	Inhibitors of Biosynthesis of Adrenocorticosteroids	17.12
17.11	Addison's Disease	17.12

18. Insulin and Oral Hypoglycemic Agents — 18.1 to 18.18

18.1	Introduction	18.1
18.2	Types of Diabetes	18.3
18.3	Insulin and its Preparation	18.6
18.4	Biosynthesis of Insulin	18.8
18.5	Secretion of Insulin	18.8
18.6	Chemistry of Insulin	18.9
18.7	Physiological Functions of Insulin	18.10
18.8	Mechanism of Action	18.11
18.9	Insulin Deficiency	18.11
18.10	Adverse Effects	18.12
18.11	Insulin Resistant Diabetes	18.12
18.12	Insulin Preparations	18.13
18.13	Limitations of Insulin Therapy	18.14
18.14	Oral Hypoglycemic Agents	18.14
18.15	Mechanism of Action	18.16
18.16	Pharmacokinetics	18.17
18.17	Adverse Effects of Sulfonylureas	18.17
18.18	Glucagon	18.18

19. Diuretic Agents — 19.1 to 19.14
    19.1 Introduction — 19.1
    19.2 Classification — 19.3
    19.3 Anti-Diuretic Substances — 19.14

20. Drugs Acting on GIT — 20.1 to 20.28
    20.1 Introduction — 20.1
    20.2 Gastric Antacids — 20.1
    20.3 Treatment of Gastric Hyperacidity — 20.3
    20.4 H_2-Receptor Antagonists — 20.6
    20.5 Antimuscarinic Agents — 20.7
    20.6 Tricyclic Antidepressants — 20.7
    20.7 H^+-K^+-ATPase Inhibitors — 20.7
    20.8 Prostaglandins — 20.7
    20.9 Miscellaneous Agents — 20.8
    20.10 Ulcerative Colitis — 20.9
    20.11 Antispasmodics (Spasmolytic Agents) — 20.10
    20.12 Emetics and Antiemetics — 20.11
    20.13 Laxatives and Purgatives — 20.14
    20.14 Antidiarrhoeals — 20.17
    20.15 Sialagogues — 20.19
    20.16 Antisialagogues — 20.20
    20.17 Appetite Affecting Drugs — 20.20
    20.18 Carminatives — 20.21
    20.19 Digestants — 20.21
    20.20 Anthelmintic Agents — 20.22

21. Diagnostic Agents — 21.1 to 21.12
    21.1 Introduction — 21.1
    21.2 Classification — 21.1
    21.3 Radio-opaque Agents (Contrast Media) — 21.2
    21.4 Adverse Effects Associated With Contrast Media — 21.8
    21.5 Diagnostic Chemicals — 21.9

22. Drugs Acting on Blood — 22.1 to 22.28
    22.1 Introduction — 22.1
    22.2 Coagulants And Anticoagulants — 22.1
    22.3 Plasma Coagulation Factors — 22.2

22.4	Anticoagulants	22.6
22.5	Heparin (Parenteral Anticoagulant)	22.7
22.6	Oral Anticoagulants	22.9
22.7	Anti-Thrombotic Drugs	22.12
22.8	Plasma Expanders	22.12
22.9	Fibrinolytic Agents	22.14
22.10	Haematinics	22.15
22.11	Haemopoietic Vitamins	22.18
22.12	Lipid Lowering Agents	22.19
22.13	Types of Lipoproteins	22.19
22.14	Lipoprotein Transport Machinery	22.20
22.15	Hyperlipoproteinemia	22.22
22.16	Drug Therapy of Hyperlipoproteinemia	22.23

23. Myocardial Diseases — 23.1 to 23.10

23.1	Introduction	23.1
23.2	Myocardial Cell	23.2
23.3	Actin-Myosin Tension Generating System	23.3
23.4	Molecular Basis of Myocardial Contraction	23.3
23.5	Cardiovascular Diseases	23.6

24. Cardiac Glycosides — 24.1 to 24.20

24.1	Introduction	24.1
24.2	Pathophysiology of Heart Failure	24.2
24.3	Mechanism of Action	24.5
24.4	Other Effects of Digitalis Glycosides	24.6
24.5	Pharmacokinetic Parameters	24.7
24.6	Therapeutic Uses	24.8
24.7	Adverse Effects	24.8
24.8	Digitalis Intoxication	24.9
24.9	Treatment of Intoxication	24.10
24.10	Alternatives to Digitalis Therapy	24.10
24.11	Anti-Arrhythmic Agents	24.11
24.12	Anti-Anginal Drugs	24.15
24.13	Antihypertensive Agents (Hypotensive Agents)	24.16

25.	**Anti-Anginal Agents**	**25.1 to 25.10**
25.1	Introduction	25.1
25.2	Types of Angina Pectoris	25.2
25.3	Nitrites and Nitrates	25.3
25.4	β-Adrenoceptor Blocking Agents	25.5
25.5	Calcium Channel Blocking Agents	25.6
25.6	Other Antianginal Agents	25.9
25.7	Combination Therapy	25.9
25.8	General Measures	25.10
26.	**Anti-Arrhythmic Agents**	**26.1 to 26.18**
26.1	Introduction	26.1
26.2	Classification	26.5
26.3	Quinidine	26.7
26.4	Procainamide	26.9
26.5	Disopyramide	26.10
26.6	Lidocaine	26.11
26.7	Phenytoin	26.11
26.8	Mexiletine and Tocainide Hydrochloride	26.12
26.9	Encainide	26.13
26.10	Class 2 β-Adrenergic Blocking Agents	26.14
26.11	Class 3	26.15
26.12	Class 4	26.17
27.	**Anti-Hypertensive Agents**	**27.1 to 27.26**
27.1	Introduction	27.1
27.2	Etiology of Hypertension	27.5
27.3	Classification	27.6
27.4	General Considerations	27.6
27.5	Drugs Affecting Sympathetic Tone (Sympatholytics)	27.10
27.6	Vasodilators	27.18
27.7	Agents Acting on Renin-Angiotensin System	27.22
27.8	Diuretics	27.25
28.	**Fat-Soluble Vitamins**	**28.1 to 28.16**
28.1	Introduction	28.1
28.2	Classification	28.2
28.3	Vitamin A	28.3

28.4		Vitamin K	28.9
28.5		Vitamin D	28.11
28.6		Vitamin E	28.15

29. Water-Soluble Vitamins — 29.1 to 29.28

29.1		Introduction	29.1

30. Immuno-Modulators — 30.1 to 30.22

30.1		Introduction	30.1
30.2		Components of Immune System	30.3
30.3		Types of Immunity	30.5
30.4		Hypersensitivity Reactions	30.5
30.5		Immunomodulators	30.9
30.6		Drugs Affecting Immune Responses	30.10
30.7		Disorders of Immune System	30.18
30.8		Acquired Immunodeficiency Syndrome (Aids)	30.20

* **Index** — I.1 to I.12

❖❖❖

GENERAL PRINCIPLES

1.1 INTRODUCTION

Pathogens are microorganisms that can cause a disease condition both in man and animals. Not very long ago, at the beginning of this century, neither the causative agents of infective diseases nor the active ingredients of the traditional remedies which were used to cure the infections could be identified. With the introduction of the science of microbiology, it was soon possible to grow bacteria in culture. The scientific practice of organic chemistry and the rational application of microbiology resulted in the birth of various antimicrobial substances. The term, microbiology can be defined in various ways and it essentially includes the study of microorganisms. Bacteriology is the science that deals with the study of bacteria while mycology covers the study of fungi. These typical unicellular microscopic organisms are widely distributed in the air, water, soil, in the bodies of living plants and animals and in the dead organic matters. Some dermatophytes do not invade living tissues but they survive on the dead tissue structures of stratum corneum of the skin, hairs and the nails.

Mild endogenous defence line is provided by the secretion of sebum, sweat, mucous, saliva, tears, gastric and intestinal juices which helps to wash away the microorganisms from various body surfaces. Whereas the stronger defence mechanisms include inflammatory mechanisms (e.g. phagocytosis) and immunological responses. The immune response to infection, especially to viral infection may lead to significant damage to the cell or a tissue.

The first significant event reported in the history of chemotherapy was the introduction of magic antisyphilitic bullet, *salvarson* by **Paul Ehrlich** in 1909. It was followed by the report of synthesis and antibacterial activity of *prontosil* by **Domagk** in 1935. He reported the effect of *prontosil rubrum,* an azo dye, against streptococcal infection. The 'in-vivo' conversion of prontosil to the active sulphonamide moiety was later found to be responsible for its antibacterial activity. This observation then initiated the development of more safer and effective sulphonamides. In 1929, *Penicillium notatum*, a laboratory contaminant growing on agar plate was found to inhibit the growth of *Staphylococcus* growing in the same plate. With the isolation of penicillin from this fungus by Florey, China and coworkers, a new era of antibacterial agents was opened. Subsequently many natural and semisynthetic antibiotics were developed by changing the nature of the side-chain of the parent nucleus. This modification in the structure created variation in the antibacterial and pharmacokinetic parameters of the basic skeleton.

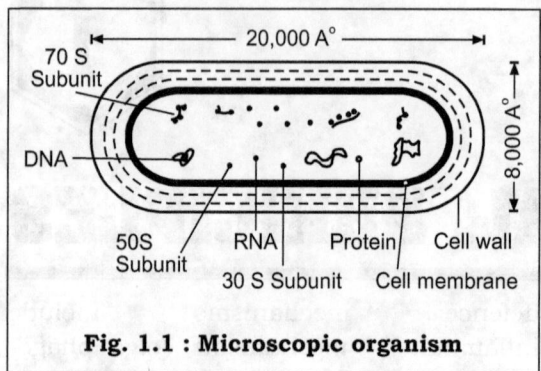

Fig. 1.1 : Microscopic organism

Microorganisms comprises algae, fungi, bacteria, viruses and protozoa. Bacteria and fungi are devoid of chlorophyll while it is present in algae. The main structural features of a microscopic organism are represented in above Fig. 1.1.

The major classes of microorganisms are as follows :

(i) Bacteria :

A bacterial cell consists of cell wall, cytoplasmic membrane, cytoplasm, flagella, capsule and fimbriae etc., which helps in carrying out various functions of the cell. The cytoplasmic membrane encloses the thick, viscous semifluid or almost jelly-like, colourless, transparent material which is known as protoplasm. Other structures visible in protoplasm are nucleus, vacuoles, mesosomes, mitochondria, ribosomes, polysaccharides, lipids, metachromatic granules etc. Although the vast majority of bacteria are harmless or beneficial, a few pathogenic bacteria can cause infectious diseases. The most common bacterial disease is tuberculosis, caused by the bacterium *Mycobacterium tuberculosis*. Besides this, pathogenic bacteria contribute to other globally important diseases, such as pneumonia (*streptococcus* and *pseudomonas*). They also cause some food born illinesses (*Shigella* sp. *Salmonella* sp.). Infections such as tetanus, typhoid fever, diptheria and syphilis are also initiated by bacteria.

(ii) Protozoa :

It can be differentiated from the remaining classes on the ground of morphological, physiological and nutritional characteristics.

(iii) Viruses :

Viruses are ultra-microscopic microorganisms ranging from 0.1 µ - 0.3 µ in diameter. They can be cultivated only in the living cells and are parasites of plants, animals or even bacteria. They just contain a nucleic acid core and a protein coat. They are rich in nucleic acid and possess only one type of nucleic acid, either RNA or DNA. They differ from other disease producing pathogens on the basis of their smaller size, simpler chemical composition, lack of metabolic enzymes, lack of protein synthetic machinery and a host cell dependent mechanism of multiplication. Infections such as smallpox, influenza, mumps, measles, chickenpox, ebola and rubella are some common infections caused by viruses.

(iv) Fungi :

These are usually multicellular plant organisms devoid of chlorophyll. They have different shapes and sizes. Fungi are the most common cause of disease in crops and other plants. Life threatening fungal infections in humans most often occur in immunocompromised patients or vulnerable people with a weakened immune system; although fungi are common problems in the immunocompromised population as the causative agents of skin, nail or hair infection. They range from single-cell microscopic yeast to giant multicellular mushrooms.

They includes :

(a) Actinomyces : These are anaerobic organisms that grow as thin branching filaments. Actinomycosis, a disease caused by actinomycetes affects lungs causing pneumonia.

(b) Yeast : These are spheroidal cells that reproduce by budding. They most frequently give rise to abcesses in the brain or lungs or to the meningitis.

(c) Yeast like fungi : They are normally present in the mouth, arms or vagina of healthy adult. They may cause pruritus ani, pruritus vulvae, thrust like condition in mouth, ophthalmic candidiasis or monilial stomatitis. Candidiasis is one such infection caused by an organism, *Candida albicans*. It thrives normally in alimentary tract and vagina of the healthy humans. Candidiasis also influences corticosteroid therapy.

(d) Filamentous fungi : *Microsporum, Trichophyton, Aspergillus* and *Penicillium* moulds are some examples of filamentous fungi. They are characterised by the presence of long filaments (i.e. hyphae) which are arranged in irregular triangles (i.e. mycelia). Aspergillosis caused by *Aspergillus* most frequently affects lungs but extrapulmonary systemic infection involving brain or kidney may also occur. Other infections like ringworm (tinea), tinea circinats (skin), tinea pedis (athlete's foot); tinea capitis (scalp) and onychomycosis (nails) are also caused by members of this group.

(e) Dimorphic fungi : This category includes *Histoplasma* (histoplasmosis or reticuloendothelial cytomycosis), *Sporotrichum* (e.g. sporotri-chosis) and *Blastomyces* (blastomycosis). Infections in humans usually occur by inhalation of infectious soilborne spores.

(v) Algae : Algae are relatively simple organisms. They may be unicellular (primitive type) or in some cases, are aggregation of similar cells. Algae are found most commonly in aquatic environments or in damp soil. Whatever may be the size or complexity, all algae cells contain chlorophyll and thus are capable of photosynthesis.

1.2 BACTERIAL CELL-WALL

The bacterial cell-wall is about 10-25µ in thickness. It is a porous and permeable structure that controls the flow of various solute molecules in and out of the bacterial cell. It encloses the cytoplasmic membrane that acts as a physicochemical barrier due to its semipermeable nature. It is about 5 - 10 mµ thick and consists of polymerizing enzymes that are involved in formation of cell-wall and other extracellular subunits. Cytoplasmic membrane encloses a thick, viscous semifluid or almost jelly-like, colourless transparent material known as 'protoplasm'. Other structures visible in protoplasm are nucleus, vacuoles, mesosomes, polysaccharides, lipids, ribosomes, metachromatic granules etc. The main function of cytoplasm is to synthesize enzymes and other proteins necessary for the functioning of bacterial cell. Many bacterial bodies contain granules rich in nucleoproteins, starch, stored glycogen, fats or lipids. A number of bacilli are motile due to presence of flagella, the organelles of locomotion.

Chemically, bacterial cell-wall is composed of diaminopimelic acid, muramic acid, teichoic acid, amino sugars, amino acids, carbohydrates and lipids.

In gram-positive bacteria, cell-wall is composed of a peptidoglycan (mucopeptide or glycopeptide or murein).

The peptidoglycan structure is made up of amino sugars (e.g. N-acetylglucosamine, N-acetylmuramic acid) and amino acids (e.g. L-alanine, D-alanine, D-glutamic acid, L-lysine, mesodiaminopimelic acid, glycine, L-serine, L-threonine, D-aspartic acid etc.). The peptidoglycan is composed of glycan chains which are linear strands of alternating units of N-acetyl glucosamine and N-acetylmuramic acid. These glycan chains are further cross-linked by peptide chains, the composition of which varies from species to species.

The cell-wall of gram-negative bacteria is considerably more complex in organization and composition. In gram-positive microorganisms, the cell-wall is 50 - 100 molecules thick but it is only one to two molecules thick in gram-negative bacteria. The cell-wall of gram-positive bacteria contains fewer amino acids than that of gram-negative bacteria. Since the major constituent of the gram-negative cell-wall is lipopolysaccharide, the lipid content of gram-negative bacteria is considerably higher than that of gram-positive bacteria.

As like gram-positive bacteria, the structure and composition of lipopolysaccharide is not uniform and similar in all species of gram-negative bacteria. Infact, a scheme of classification and identification between the species is proposed which mainly utilises the information about the cell-wall structure as a main criteria for differentiation.

The bacterial cell-wall is a rigid structure and is responsible for the form of a bacterial body. It offers protection to the intracellular bacterial components against mechanical damage and media of low osmotic strength. It also plays a fundamental role in the life activities of the cell. In more drastic and adverse conditions, an additional protection to the bacterial cell is provided by the process of spore formation.

Microorganisms release waste materials during the course of their metabolism. Pathogenicity thus can be defined as 'the reaction from the host side against these metabolic waste'. *Virulence* is the measure of pathogenicity of a microorganism. A microbial infection can be rapidly spread up in subarachnoid space because cerebrospinal fluid lacks potent antibacterial properties. Various enzymes present in the microorganisms were found to be responsible for potentiating the degree of virulence. For example, collagenases present in *Clostridium* species help to destroy collagen while streptokinases present in *Streptococci* causes lysis of fibrin. Similarly coagulases present in *Staphylococcus aureus* leads to plasma clotting.

In 1877, **Pasteur** and **Joubert** recorded for the first time the clinical potential of microorganisms. Thereafter the era of chemotherapy began. The term chemotherapy first coined by Paul Ehrlich can be defined as "*treatment of infection caused by pathogenic microorganisms by chemical substances leaving the host unaffected*". Microorganisms may get entry to the tissues of the body; may release poisonous substances (toxins); may establish themselves in the organs and may alarm fatal reactions in the host. The whole thing can be described as an infection. From the various gates of entry or sites of initial infection, organisms may pass into the circulating blood and accommodate themselves at suitable places to release their next generations.

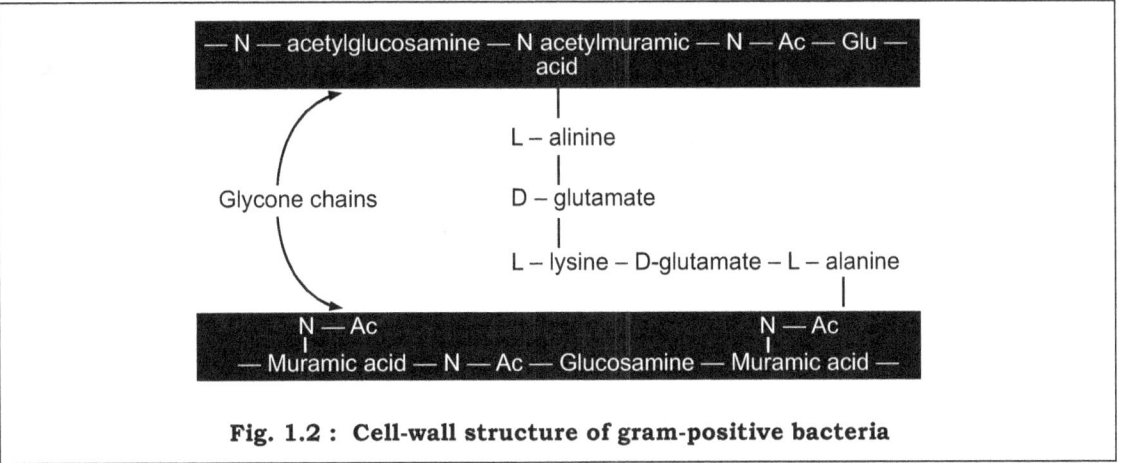

Fig. 1.2 : Cell-wall structure of gram-positive bacteria

Table 1.1 : Pathogenicity of microorganisms

Organ	Microorganism	Infection caused
1. Gastrointestinal tract	*Esch. coli, Proteus, Pseudomonas, Klebs. aerogenes.*	Pyelonephritis
	Salmonella, Campylobacter, Rotaviruses, Adenoviruses.	Gastroenteritis
	Myco. tuberculosis, C. trachomatis.	Cystisis
	Mumps virus, *Rubella* virus.	Pancreatitis
	T. pallidum, serum hepatitis virus.	Hepatitis
	Anaerobic cocci, *E. histolytica.*	Liver abscess
	Giardia lamblia.	Giardiasis
	Enterobius vermicularis.	Enterobiasis
	Ascaris lumbricoides	Ascariasis
	Trichurus trichiura	Trichuriasis
	Entamoeba histolytica	Amoebiasis
2. Respiratory tract	*Streptococcus pneumoniae.*	Pneumonia
	Corynebacterium diphtheriae.	Diphtheria
	Haemophilus influenzae.	Chronic bronchitis
	Streptococcus pneumoniae, Bordetella pertussis.	Whooping cough
	Mycobacterium tuberculosis.	Tuberculosis
	Rhinoviruses, Coronaviruses.	Common cold
	Pneumococci, Haemophilus influenzae, β-haemolytic streptococci.	Otitis media

contd...

3.	Cardiovascular system	*Strept. pyrogens, Brucella, Leptospira.*	Myocarditis
		Staph. aureus, Strept. pneumoniae, viruses.	Pericarditis
		Coliforms, Fungi, *Strept. mitis, Strept. faecalis.*	Endocarditis
		Streptococcus pyrogenes.	Rheumatic fever
		Plasmodium vivax, Plasmodium falciparum.	Malaria
4.	Genitourinary tract	*T. pallidum, C. albicans.*	Balanitis
		T. vaginalis, Coliforms,	
		T. pallidum, Mumps virus.	Orchitis
		Enterobacteria, Bacteroides,	Cervicitis
		N. gonorrhoeae, C. trachomatis	
		Treponema pallidum	Syphilis
		Neisseria gonorrhoeae	Gonorrhoea
		Strept. pyrogenes, Anaerobic cocci, *Staph. aureus, Mycoplasma*	Endometritis
		N. gonorrhoeae, Ureaplasma urealyticum, Trichomonas.	Urethritis
		N. gonorrhoeae, C. trachomatis, Coliforms.	Prostatitis
		Enterobacteria, Candida, Staph. aureus, Trichomonads, β-haemolytic streptococci.	Vaginitis
5.	Skin	*Staphylococcus aureus.*	Impetigo, folliculitis
		Corynebacterium diphtheriae.	Cutaneous diphtheria
		Haemophilus duccreyi.	Chancroid
		Candida albicans.	Cutaneous candidiasis
		M. canis, M. gypseum.	Tinea capitis
		Trichophyton rubrum	Tinea pedis
		Sarcoptes scabei.	Scabies
		M. leprae.	Leprosy
6.	Central Nervous System	*Cryptococcus neoformans, Listeria monocytogenes, Entero* viruses.	Meningitis

contd...

7. Miscellaneous	Brucella abortus	Brucellosis
	Staphylococcus aureus	Food infections
	Leishmania donovani	Leishmaniasis
	Bacillus anthracis	Anthrax
	Yersinia pestis	Plaque
	Rhabdovirus	Rabies
	Streptobacillus moniliformis	Ringworm
	Schistosoma japonicum	Schistosomiasis
	Trypanosoma spp.	Trypanosomiasis
	Corynebacterium acnes	Acne

In the early days, carbolic, iodine and heavy metal salts like silver nitrate and mercuric chloride were in clinical use. Later on mainly due to their toxicity problems, a search began for the agents having greater effectiveness, lower toxicity and improved pharmacological properties. Agents were required with selective toxicity against microorganisms and much reduced toxicity towards the host. Selective toxicity of the chemotherapeutic agents against pathogenic organisms could be achieved by just then exploiting this difference.

The modern era of the chemotherapy started with the clinical use of sulphonamides in 1936. The second channel of antibacterial substances came into existence in 1941 with the introduction of penicillin, a β - lactam antibiotic. Several hundreds of antimicrobial substances then isolated from the microbial cultures, were subjected to evaluation and standardization. Some of these substances were discarded due to high toxicities.

These antimicrobial agents are considered to be the metabolic products of the microorganisms. Clinical use of these antibiotics (from the word antibiosis, i.e. anti = against; biosis = life) was the outcome of an important observation that substances derived from one living organism may be used to prevent the growth (-static) or to kill (-cidal) another organism of the same type. Thus, antibiotic therapy is nothing but a further extension of all processes that occur naturally and continuously in soil, sewage, water or other natural habitats of microorganisms.

1.3 DRUG RESISTANCE

A new drug designed is expected to differentiate between the host (an infected person) and the pathogen (a microorganism). Biochemical differences were used to develop the selectivity of action. Drug developed with this philosophy was emerged in clinical practice with high activity profile. But hopes could not survive for long due to the development of drug-resistance in micro-organisms. This became a major limitation to the clinical use of antibiotics and synthetic antimicrobial agents.

In many cases, prolonged or repeated therapy and low dose suppressive antibacterial prophylaxis may induce drug resistance amongst bacteria. Bacteria may be naturally resistant to a particular antibiotic but they may also acquire resistance to the drugs either by mutation or gene transfer. A mutagenic cell, through repetitive multiplication, releases a totally new, drug-resistant bacterial strain. As a result, bacterial growth resumes and organism no longer shows susceptibility or sensitivity to the same drug concentration. Such drug-resistant strain when comes in contact with another drug-sensitive strain, latter also undergoes mutagenic changes to acquire the drug-resistance. Actual cell contact is necessary for the development of such cross-resistance.

Various mechanisms have been proposed to explain the phenomenon of drug-resistance. However the mechanism differs as per the mode of action of individual drug.

Thus, decreased response to the same drug concentration by the mutagenic cell culture may be related to :

(i) Decreased drug diffusion into the microbial cell due to altered cell permeability.

(ii) Change in the structure or/and function of drug-susceptible microbial enzymes.

(iii) Production of new enzymes that causes inactivation of the drug.

(iv) Even if drug enters into the cell, its action is terminated by formation of drug antagonistic metabolities.

(v) Other biochemical means may be searched for substitute drug-sensitive biochemical reaction.

(vi) Through mutagenic changes, receptor affinity for the drug is altered.

Combination therapy thus can be effectively utilised to prevent emergence of drug-resistant bacterial strain. For example, in the treatment of chloroquine-resistant malaria, pyrimethamine can be used either with dapsone or sulfadoxine. Another commonly used combination is co-trimoxazole (sulphamethoxazole and trimethoprim) where the synergism is an additional advantage. However, combination therapy also provides increased risk of drug toxicity and greater chances of superinfection because of broader overall activity spectrum. Certain antimicrobial drugs should be avoided during pregnancy, lactation and in the newborns where the drug handling is quite different from what happens in the healthy adult.

2

TOPICAL ANTI-INFECTIVE AGENTS

2.1 INTRODUCTION

Skin is the largest organ of the body. Hospital disinfection, sterilization of instruments and the surgical handwash are the general measures which are being routinely used to reduce the risk of hospital-acquired infections and to minimize the transfer of microorganisms to the susceptible patients. Topical anti-infective agents may be applied to intact cutaneous and mucous surfaces before surgery and to treat minor cuts, abrasions or burns. **Koch** (1865) had established the relationship between infection and microorganisms. The pathogenic manifestation may be limited to skin or systemic symptoms may also appear in some cases.

Until it was discovered that microorganisms cause the pathogenic conditions, the need for topical anti-infective agents was not realised. Thereafter, they are extensively used in surgical, public health, hospital and laboratory techniques to destroy both, pathogenic as well as non-pathogenic microorganisms. **Lister** was the first to employ phenolic solution to treat infections in surgery. Early attempts of disinfection relied largely on aromatic substances and on chemical deodorants which still continue today. Alcohols, cationic detergents or chlorine were the drugs of choice when only disinfection is desired. Besides this, U.V. radiation and heat are also preferred. For example, saturated steam at 2 atmospheric pressure (120°C) for 20 minutes is successfully used to destroy microorganisms, while for sterilization of heat-labile materials, β, γ and U.V. radiation can be used frequently.

Topical anti-infective agents may be categorised into following categories:

1. Keratolytic agents
2. Antiseptic agents
3. Disinfectants
4. Sanitizers, and
5. Germicides.

Keratolytic agents include sulfur (2 - 10 %), resorcinol (2 - 6%) and salicylic acid. They may be used alone or in combination with one another depending upon the situation. Salicylic acid is usually combined with sulfur to get synergistic effect. Pumice, aluminium oxide or polyethylene granules may also be employed for this action. Keratolytics act by removing surface oils and causing drying and peeling of surface skin. This results into suppression of the spread of skin lesions.

Antiseptic agents oppose the sepsis, putrefaction or decay of the damaged or exposed tissue by inhibiting microbial multiplication and their metabolic activities or by killing the pathogenic microorganisms. An ideal antiseptic should destroy bacteria, spores, fungi, viruses or any other infective agent without causing any harm to the tissues of the host. They can be applied to almost all tissues of the body and may be used in the form of mouth washes, soaps, deodorants, throat and nasal sprays and vaginal douches. In general, all antiseptics are protein denaturants and act on enzymes present. in the bacteria. This accounts for the reduced effectiveness of most antiseptics in serum, blood or pus. Out of so many antiseptic agents, only intestinal and urinary tract antiseptics are pharmacologically important.

Disinfectants are widely used for home and hospital sanitation. They are bactericidal and rapidly produce irreversible lethal effects. Disinfection may be accomplished by heat, irradiation or chemicals. They are non-selective and destroy non-pathogens as well. They are applied only to inanimate objects. These includes the substances which remove bacterial contaminants from dishes and bed pans or substances which are used in water treatment and public health sanitation. All disinfectant solutions undergo deterioration on prolonged storage and elevated temperature conditions.

Some powerful disinfectants are too irritant, corrosive or toxic to be applied to the skin or to tissues. The chemical disinfectants can be subclassified as,

(a) Solid disinfectants : e.g. bleaching powder,

(b) Liquid disinfectants : e.g. phenol, formalin, and

(c) Gaseous disinfectants : e.g. formaldehyde gas.

Disinfectants that are used to maintain general public health standards, are known as 'sanitizers'. Sanitation is the process commonly used in the restaurants and at similar places for cleaning the dishes. It is mainly concerned with cleaning or washing away the organic matter (e.g. saliva, mucous etc.). An infection may re-occur if the pathogenic organism is not killed. Hence the anti-infective agent used should have power to destroy (i.e. -cidal properties) the microorganisms. A germicidal agent may further be subcategorised as bactericide, fungicide, virucide or amebicide. Many agents at higher concentration exhibits germicidal activity.

An ideal germicide should possess following properties :

(1) The concentration of germicide used to destroy or eliminate pathogenic microorganism should not produce any local cellular damage.

(2) It should not interfere with the body defences or impair the healthy process.

(3) On topical application, if absorbed it should not produce any systemic toxicities.

The rate of germicidal action is dependent upon the concentration of the drug, local pH and temperature. The germicidal action of anti-infective agents is usually defined by the phenol coefficient of the agent. This parameter is obtained by following expression –

$$\left[\begin{array}{c}\text{Phenol}\\\text{coefficient}\end{array}\right] = \frac{\text{Dilution of chemical agent}}{\text{Dilution of phenol}}$$

It is a ratio between minimal effective concentrations of phenol and test compound under standardized conditions against bacteria usually *Salmonella typhi* and *Staphylococcus aureus*. If the coefficient is greater than 1, it is assumed that the substance is having better germicidal activity than phenol. The germicidal activity of these agents is brought about due to their ability to alter proteins through oxidation, alkylation, dehydration or by inactivation of the sulfhydryl group. They may also affect the bacterial cell permeability.

2.2 CLASSIFICATION

The topical anti-infective agents can be classified as follows on chemical basis :

(a) Alcohols
(b) Phenols
(c) 8-Hydroxyquinolines
(d) Aldehydes
(e) Acids
(f) Halogen-containing compounds
(g) Furan derivatives
(h) Oxidising agents
(i) Heavy metals
(j) Cationic surfactants
(k) Dyes
(l) Miscellaneous agents.

These agents can also be categorised on the basis of their mechanism of action :

1. Oxidizing agents : These include halogens, hydrogen peroxide, acids etc.

2. Dehydrating agents : These include alcohols.

3. Alkylating agents : These include formaldehyde, glutaraldehyde, ethylene oxide etc.

4. Sulfhydryl combining agents : These include silver nitrate.

5. Surface-active agents : These include benzalkonium chloride, cetylpyridinium chloride etc.

(a) Alcohols :

Alcohols have been used as an antiseptic agents in the dressing of the wounds. Germicidal potency in the aliphatic alcohol series runs parallel with its lipophilicity value. Branching and additional hydroxy groups results into decreased potency. Ethyl and isopropyl alcohols are most commonly used agents in the concentration range of 30 - 70%. Benzyl alcohol is also used as a bacteriostatic agent in a number of parenteral preparations.

The antibacterial action is due to their ability to denature the bacterial proteins. In addition to this, alcohols also inhibit phosphorylation systems. They give synergistic effect when used with chlorhexidine, iodine or hexachlorophene. Ethyl and isopropyl alcohols are also used as cleansers and rubefacients. They do not irritate the tissues. However, they lack antibacterial effect on spores. Ethanol may coagulate the proteins present in the wound that results in formation of a protective layer over microorganisms. Alcohols currently used for their anti-infective activity are ethanol, isopropyl alcohol, benzyl alcohol, chlorobutanol, phenylethyl alcohol etc.

(b) Phenols :

The first aseptic surgery was demonstrated by Lister in 1867 with the use of phenol. The bacteriostatic concentration of phenol is 0.5% while it is bactericidal in the concentration of 1.0%. It is fungicidal in the concentration of 1.5%. In fact, phenol coefficient is used as the parameter to judge the anti-infective activity of the new drugs. Although phenol is no longer used clinically, it still remains a component (0.1% - 4.5%) of various gels, liquids, ointments, throat sprays and lozenges. Because of its penetrability, it is used as an effective fecal disinfectant.

A large number of phenolic derivatives have been synthesized and are used as germicides. These include alkyl and aryl phenols, parabens, halophenols and bisphenols. In all these series, activity is related to the number of free hydroxy groups. Halogenation, especially para to the hydroxy group potentiates the activity.

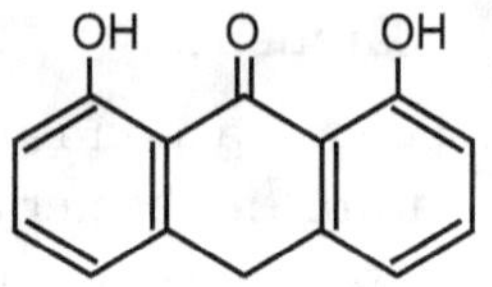

Anthralin

Phenols and their derivatives have antiseptic, anthelmintic, anesthetic, keratolytic, vesicant and protein precipitant properties. For example, thymol may be used as anthelmintic agent while hexylresorcinol is frequently used in throat lozenges due to its spreading and penetrating properties. It is also used in mouth washes and for cleaning the skin wounds. Parachlorometaxylenol is an effective bactericidal agent used for acne, seborrhea and ear infection. The antiseptic action of coal tar and coal tar solution is because of their various phenolic components. Hexachlorophene, a chlorinated bisphenol, is commonly used for hand washing by hospital personnel and for preoperative skin preparation. Anthralin is used in the treatment of psoriasis and other chronic skin diseases because of its antiseptic and a keratolytic properties.

Phenols exhibit germicidal activity mainly due to their ability to denature bacterial proteins. At higher concentration, phenols bring about lysis of cell-membrane.

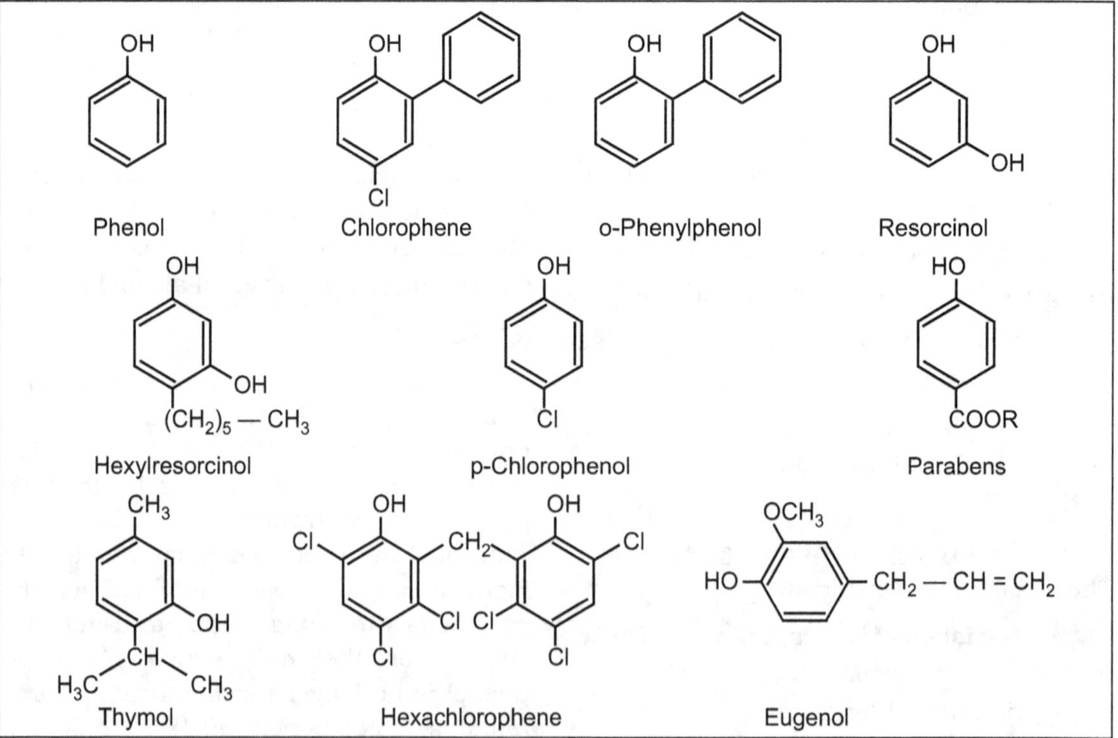

Phenol

Chlorophene

o-Phenylphenol

Resorcinol

Hexylresorcinol

p-Chlorophenol

Parabens

Thymol

Hexachlorophene

Eugenol

(c) 8-Hydroxyquinolines :

The members of this series have antibacterial, antifungal and antiamebic properties. The mechanism of their anti-infective action involves a transfer of iron or copper ions into bacterial cell via a chelation process. This leads to an interference in the normal bacterial enzyme functioning.

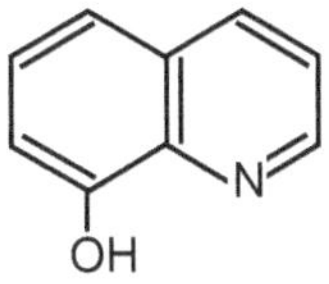

8-Hydroxyquinoline

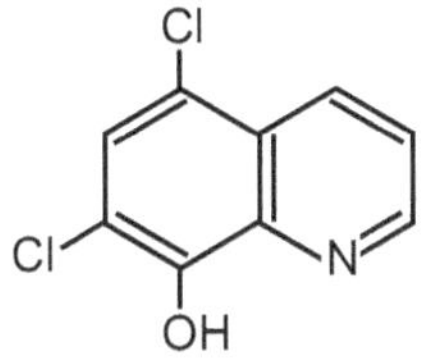

Chloroxine

(d) Aldehydes :

Several aldehydes possess bactericidal, sporicidal and virucidal activities. Following are some examples of effective anti-infective agents.

HCHO
Formaldehyde

$(CH_2O)_n$
Paraformaldehyde

$(CH_2)_6N_4$
Methenamine

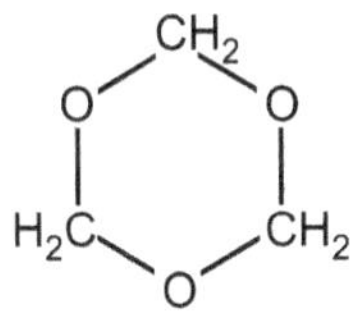

Trioxymethylene

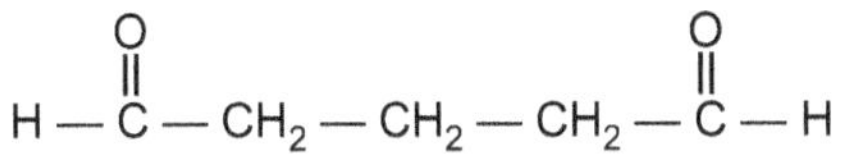

Glutaraldehyde

Formaldehyde is an excellent germicide but having unpleasant odour. It is highly effective antimicrobial agent and is used as a vapour or as a aqueous solution in the concentration range of 1 - 10%. Because of its irritant nature and poor penetrability in the tissues it can not be used as an antiseptic. Hence, it is widely used as a disinfectant for surface sterilization. For example, rooms can be sterilized using formaldehyde gas.

The mechanism of action involves denaturation of proteins by the replacement of labile H-atoms in amino, carboxyl, hydroxy or thiol groups of component amino acids. Ethylene oxide also acts as anti-infective agent by the same mechanism. It reacts with water and chloride to form ethylene glycol and ethylene chlorohydrin. Both are active germicides. Because of its explosive nature, ethylene oxide should not be used in the concentration above 3%. It is mainly used for sterilization of plastic equipments. It is mutagenic, carcinogenic and causes irritation to eyes and mucous membranes. Glutaraldehyde (Gluteral) is effective dialdehyde against almost all microorganisms when its 2% aqueous solution buffered at pH = 7.5 - 8.0 is employed. It has the broad spectrum antimicrobial and sporicidal activities. It is mainly used to sterilize equipments, surgical instruments and surfaces contaminated with hepatitis virus. Beside this, succinic dialdehyde is also sometimes used as a disinfectant.

(e) Acids :

Benzoic acid, undecylenic acid, mandelic acid, acetic acid and other organic acids and their ester forms are often used for their antiseptic, fungicidal and spermatocidal activities. Benzoic acid and its few derivatives (e.g. methyl paraben) are used extensively as preservative in food and drinks in a concentration of 0.1 %. It is also used to treat ringworm and other skin infections. Acetic acid exhibits bactericidal action against many microorganisms. While mandelic acid is used in the form of its sodium salt to treat urinary tract infection in the oral dose of 8 - 12 g per day.

Beside this, boric acid, lactic acid, propionic acid and salicylic acid also possess anti-microbial activity. However, the use of boric acid should be limited to only ophthalmic ointment.

(f) Halogen containing compounds :

Chlorine is well known for the sterilization of community water supplies and for other sanitation purposes. Halogen containing compounds include both, chlorine, iodine and their complexes with organic compounds (i.e. chlorophores and iodophores). They act by oxidizing sulfhydryl groups to S - S form and thereby affecting the protein structure and function. Bromine and fluorine are not used for this purpose.

(i) Elemental chlorine and chlorophores are the potent germicidal agents having broad spectrum of activity. When necessary, rooms can be sterilized by chlorine washing. Chlorine also has fungicidal and virucidal activities. Chlorophores serve as a depot from which free chlorine is slowly released. Chlorine and its derivatives are popularly used as disinfectants. Their bactericidal activity is due to the formation of hypochlorous acid (HOCl). The ease and extent of hypochlorous acid liberation determine the efficacy of chlorophores. Some examples of effective chlorophores include,

$$ClO_2$$

Chlorine dioxide (Chlorinated lime)

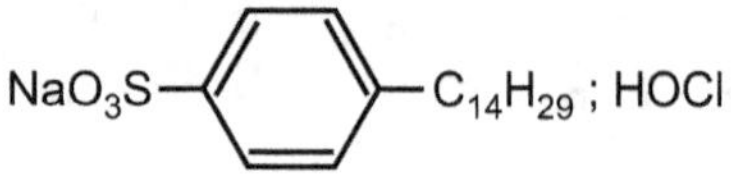

$$NaO_3S-\text{⟨benzene⟩}-C_{14}H_{29} \; ; \; HOCl$$

Oxychlorosene sodium

Chlorophores are usually less volatile, less irritant and longer-acting compounds. Chlorinated lime is an unstable form of chlorine that forms hypochlorite upon dissolution. While oxychlorosene is a mixture of alkyl benzene sulfonates and hypochlorous acid, from which the latter is slowly released to produce germicidal activity. All these chlorophores were thought to act by –

(i) releasing chlorine which then oxidizes the sulfhydryl groups of bacterial enzymes,

(ii) deactivating certain bacterial proteins, or

(iii) releasing HOCl which then generates nascent oxygen to destroy the vital cellular machinery of microorganism.

(ii) N-Chloramines : Chemically chloramines may be amines, amides or imides, containing N-chloro substituents.

In the presence of water, they decompose and release either hypochlorous acid or a free chlorine. Some examples of N-Chloramines : Chloramine-T, Dichloramine-T, Halazone, Dichloroisocyanuric acid, Chloroazodin.

Most effective chloramine is halazone. It is used for disinfection of drinking water and for sanitation. Since the activity of these chlorophores is due to the released chlorine or hypochlorous acid and not directly due to these agents, chloramines are sometimes called as "active chlorine".

(iii) Iodine : Elemental iodine and iodophores are broad spectrum antiseptics, effective against bacteria, fungi, protozoa and viruses. Its use as an antiseptic agent dates back to 1839. In the form of tincture and liniment, it still remains as one of the most valuable disinfectant of skin and fresh wound. It is effective over a wide pH range. Since the bactericidal activity is related to the amount of free iodine generated, the iodides and tri-iodide lack germicidal activity.

Iodine is thought to act by —
(a) oxidizing the vital sulfhydryl groups,
(b) formation of reversible complexes with proteins or bacterial enzymes, and
(c) direct iodination of saturated double bonds and tyrosine moieties.

However, iodine may cause severe idiosyncrasy and hypersensitivity reactions.

Iodine has been combined with various solubilizers, stabilizers or carriers buffered in the pH range of 3 to 4. The resulting complex when comes in contact with water, slowly releases iodine. Such complexes are known as 'iodophores' (i.e. sustained released depot of iodine). Generally non-ionic surfactants are employed as carriers for iodine. Examples include pluronic-188 (poloxameriodine), polyvinylpyrrolidone (povidone-iodine) and acylcolaminoformylmethyl pyridinium chloride (undecoylium chloride - iodine).

Povidone iodine is a non-toxic, non-volatile and non-staining antiseptic agent. It is used as a vaginal disinfectant for the treatment of Trichomonas and Gardinella infections.

(g) Furan derivatives :

Nitrofurazone (Furacin) is the most effective anti-infective agent in this class. The essential features of this class includes a nitro group at 5th position and an enamine group at 2nd position. The effective members of this class include :

1. Nitrofurazone,
2. Nifuroxime,
3. Furazolidone,
4. Nitrofurantoin

First studied in 1944, nitrofurazone is used topically in the form of a 0.2 % cream, solution, ointments and powder on superficial wounds and for surgical dressings. It is highly effective in the treatment of burns. It is effective against a wide variety of gram-positive and gram-negative bacteria and some protozoa. It lacks fungistatic properties. The bactericidal action of these furan derivatives may be due to –

(i) ceasation of cell-division due to the blockage of energy transfer processes,

(ii) inhibition of bacterial respiratory enzymes.

(h) Oxidising agents :

Oxidising agents mainly exhibit germicidal activity and are of great value in the treatment of infections caused by anaerobic microorganisms. They are also known for their wound cleanser and deodorant properties. Oxidation of the sulfhydryl group of bacterial enzymes and other vital groups present in the bacteria along with the lysis of bacterial cell-wall contribute to their germicidal activity.

Examples include, carbamide peroxide, benzoyl peroxide, hydrogen peroxide, sodium perborate; potassium permanganate and ozone.

In the concentration range of 2 - 3%, hydrogen peroxide is a good disinfectant and sterilant. It rapidly decomposes into oxygen and water. The liberated oxygen then mechanically loosens pus and tissue debris and kills bacteria. Its ability to generate free radicals adds further to its bactericidal activity. A 3% solution may be instilled in ears to loosen and remove cerumen.

Although hydrogen peroxide have a broad antibacterial spectrum, it is not stable and undergoes decomposition on storage. To overcome this problem, hydrogen peroxide is used in the form of carbamide peroxide and hydrous benzoyl peroxide. These preparations slowly release hydrogen peroxide when they come in contact with water. Carbamide peroxide is marketed as a 12.6% carbamide peroxide solution in anhydrous glycerin. Topical benzoyl peroxide is used mainly in the therapy of mild to moderate acne vulgaris. It also functions as exfoliant, sebostatic and comedolytic agent. It is available in 5 and 10% concentrations as creams, lotions and cleanser and in 5 to 10% concentration as washes and 2.5, 5 and 10% concentration as gels.

Sodium perborate releases oxygen when it comes in contact with tissues. As a 2% solution it is used as a mouth wash. A 40% suspension of zinc peroxide may also be used against anaerobic infections of oral cavity. Ozone and potassium permanganate solution are germicidal due to their oxidizing properties.

(i) Heavy metals :

Heavy metals are also known as sulfhydryl-combining agents due to their ability to react principally with –SH (sulfhydryl) group of bacterial enzyme. This results into bacterial enzymatic inactivation. These metals can be conveniently studied under the following heads :

(i) Mercurials : From early days, mercurials were used locally to treat skin infections and syphilis. They can be used as antiseptics, disinfectants and diuretics. Mercuric chloride was the first mercurial which was used as an antiseptic and disinfectant.

Mercurials are neither bactericidals nor sporicides. Due to the reversible nature of sulfhydryl group blockadge by these agents, they are only bacteriostatic and fungistatic. Hence, mercurial salts are less preferred. The currently used mercurials from this category include, merbromin, thiomersal, nitromersol and ammoniated mercury. Thiomersal is an organic complex that contains about 50% mercury. Though they are less toxic than the inorganic salts, they are potential contact allergents.

(ii) Silver compounds : Silver ions combine with sulfhydryl, carboxyl, phosphate and amino groups of the bacterial cell constituents. Hence silver salts are highly germicidal. Silver nitrate, at a concentration of 1% is often used to control gonococcal ophthalmia neonatorum. It may also be used in the treatment of extensive burns. However, it may stain tissue black due to the deposition of reduced form of silver upon exposure to sunlight. Similarly silver sulfadiazine, 1% cream may be used to treat burns and chronic pressure ulcers. Because of its ability to release silver and sulfadiazine, it effectively suppresses microbial flora. The colloidal silver preparations (e.g., mild silver protein) also act by slowly releasing the silver ions.

(iii) Zinc compounds : Zinc ions are effective antibacterials because of their astringent (i.e. precipitate the proteins) property. Inorganic zinc salts are mild antiseptic and may be used in eye and skin infections. Examples include zinc sulphate, zinc oxide, zinc stearate, zinc oleate and zinc pyrithione. Calamine powder consists of not less than 98% zinc oxide along with small amount of ferric oxide.

(j) Cationic surfactants :

The anionic surfactants (common soaps) exhibit activity only against gram-positive organisms, while gram-negative organisms are not affected. They emulsify the sebaceous matter and remove them alongwith dirt and microbes. Hence to increase the efficacy, other antiseptics like, phenols or mercuric iodide may be incorporated in the soaps. In comparison to anionic surfactants, cationic surfactants are more effective and have a broader antibacterial spectrum.

They are effective against a broad range of gram-positive and gram-negative bacteria, many fungi, lipid containing viruses and spermatozoa. However, they do not kill spores. They have been employed either as 10% solution or as 0.1% tincture for detergent, sanitizant, antiseptic and disinfectant purposes. They wet the surfaces, penetrate the skin and have emulsifying, keratolytic and detergent properties. In aqueous solution, these agents undergo ionization to form cations which then react with negatively charged phosphate groups on membrane phospholipids. This leads to an increase in the permeability of bacterial cell-membrane and a change in the cell-wall integrity.

Benzalkonium chloride is the prototype agent of quaternary ammonium compounds. It may be used to reduce infection in the wounds. Methylbenzethonium is a broad spectrum antiseptic that may be applied topically as dusting powder and as a rinse to prevent irritant contact dermatitis. Occasional allergic reactions are reported with the chronic use of these agents.

(k) Dyes :

Ehrlich was the first to notice the antimicrobial potential of dyes. Before 1930, they were employed topically for controlling various skin infections. These dyes can be categorised into :

(a) Azo dyes

(b) Thiazine dyes

(c) Triphenylmethane dyes, and

(d) Acridine dyes.

These dyes exert their bacteriostatic and bactericidal actions by enzyme inhibition and denaturation of proteins. Bacteria can not survive due to disfunctioning of important biological processes.

(l) Miscellaneous agents :

(i) Bis-biguanides : The biguanides are strongly basic compounds. They are very much similar to cationic surfactants in many aspects. Chlorhexidine is the most effective member of the series of antiseptic biguanides. This chlorophenyl biguanide has effectiveness against a broad range of gram-positive and gram-negative bacteria but it remains ineffective against some gram-negative bacilli, spores and viruses. Since last 25 years, it is being marketed in Europe. It is one of the three most important surgical antiseptics. At low concentrations, it disrupts cytoplasmic membrane of bacterial cells and causes cellular constituents to leak out from the cell. At high concentrations, it causes the precipitation of cell membrane and the cytoplasmic constituents. It is most commonly used as mouth wash, general sanitation, dental antiseptic and in the treatment of superficial infections. In the form of heat sterilized fresh solution of 0.1% in water, it can also be used to rinse the wounds.

The bactericidal concentration of chlorhexidine is estimated to be about 200 µg/ml. It is marketed in the form of 4 % aqueous emulsion and as a 0.5 % tincture in 70 % isopropyl alcohol.

(ii) Lactones : Among lactones, the most effective gaseous sterilizing agent is propiolactone. Chemically, it is a lactone of β-hydroxypropionic acid.

$$\begin{array}{c} H_2C - CH_2 \\ |\quad\quad\quad | \\ O - C = O \end{array}$$

β-propiolactone

The practical drawbacks of this agent include its toxicity and the lack of penetrating ability. It acts in a similar manner as that of ethylene oxide. The probable site of action is adenine in the DNA structure. Alkylation of adenine results in the death of the cell.

(iii) Sulfur : Sublimed sulfur, precipitated sulfur, and colloidal sulfur are the forms in which sulfur constitute the part of germicidal soaps, gels, lotions and creams. It is usually used in combination with other keratolytic agents in the treatment of cutaneous disorders.

(iv) Amides : Tribromsalan and dibromsalan are the examples of antibacterial amides. Both are the derivatives of salicylamide.

(v) Essential oils : Pine oil was extensively studied for its disinfectant property against many pathogens. Borneol, α-terpineol and fenchyl alcohol are amongst the main constituents of pine oil.

2.3 URINARY TRACT ANTISEPTIC AGENTS

In urinary tract infections, many drugs are used to kill or to inhibit the growth of pathogenic organisms in the urinary tract. These agents are retained in the renal tubules. They are effective antiseptics due to their localized actions in the urinary bladder, ureters and kidneys. The list of urinary antiseptics include mandelic acid, methenamine mandelate, nitrofurantoin, nalidixic acid and hexylresorcinol.

Introduced in 1962, Nalidixic acid was found to be highly active against gram-negative organisms. But the activity against gram-positive bacteria is almost nil. On metabolism, it gets converted into more active 7-hydroxy methyl metabolite. Further metabolism leads to formation of inactive glucuronide and 7-carboxylic acid metabolites.

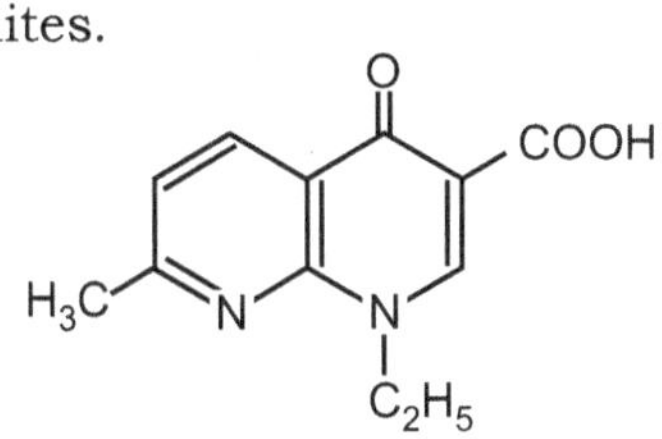

Nalidixic acid

2.4 TOPICAL COMEDOLYTIC AGENTS

Many compounds can be used as an antiacne agents because of their sebostatic, keratolytic and anti-infective properties. These include sulfur, resorcinol, salicylic acid, benzoyl peroxide, tretinoin (vitamin A acid), isotretinoin (i.e. 13 - cis retinoic acid) etc. Tretinoin is the most effective topical comedolytic agent available today. It is marketed as a 0.1 and 0.5% cream, 0.025 and 0.01% gel and 0.05% solution. A synthetic derivative of vitamin A is isotretinoin. Adverse effects of these agents include eye irritation, xerosis, pain, stiffness and arthralgia.

Table 2.1 : Mechanism of action of topical anti-infective agents

Sr. No.	Class	Mechanism of Action	Examples
1	Alcohols	Protein precipitation	Ethanol, Isopropyl alcohol
2	Alkylating agents (aldehydes)	Protein denaturation	Formaldehyde, Glutaraldehyde
3	Surface-active agents (Quaternary ammonium compounds)	Alteration of cellular membrane. Denaturation of lipoprotein membrane	Benzalkonium, Benzethonium Cetylpyridinium
4	Halogens	Coagulation of proteins Interference with enzyme action	Iodine solution, Povidone iodine, Halazone
5	Heavy metals	Denaturation of proteins Inactivation of SH group	Nitromersol, Thiomersol, Merbromin, Silver nitrate
6	Organic dyes	Denaturation of proteins, Enzyme inhibition	Gentian violet, Methylene blue

contd...

| 7 | Oxidizing compounds | Oxidation of organic matter | Hydrogen peroxide, Zinc peroxide, Potassium permanganate |
| 8 | Phenolic compounds | Protein precipitation | Phenol, Cresol, Resorcinol, Hexylresorcinol, Hexachlorophene, Methyl paraben, Thymol |

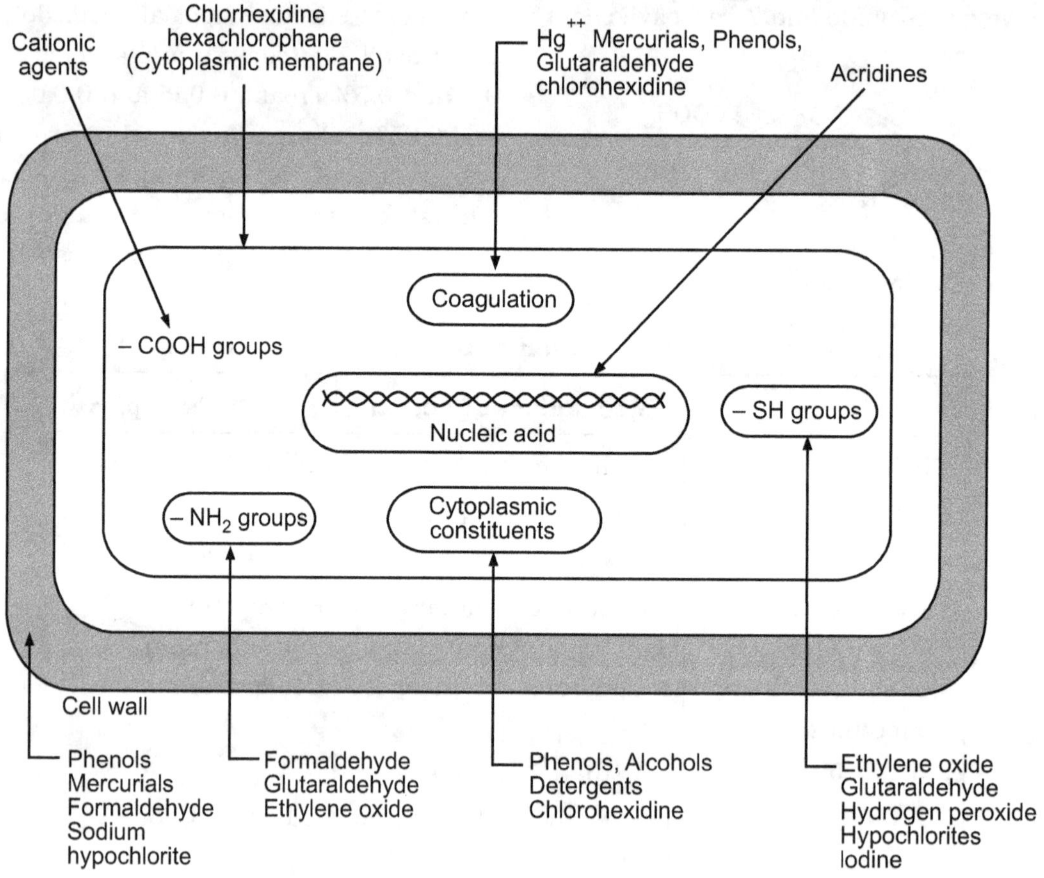

Fig. 2.1 : Sites of action of some topical anti-infective agents

CHEMOTHERAPY OF PARASITIC DISEASES

3.1 INTRODUCTION

Atleast 45,000 species of protozoa have been described, out of which many species are parasitic. Examples of such parasitic species include, a single celled protozoa, amoeba; helminthes etc. Parasitic infections pose a major world-wide health problem. Moreover, the development of resistance by these parasites to drugs and of mosquitoes to the insecticides, make the problem more complicated. Many factors contribute towards the spread of these parasitic diseases.

Table 3.1 : Commonly occurring parasitic diseases

	Infection	Parasitic protozoa	Effective drugs used
1.	Amoebiasis	*Entamoeba histolytica*	Chloroquine, emetine, iodoquinol, diiodohydroxyquine, metronidazole, dehydroemetine, diloxanide, tetracycline, paromomycin, nimorazole, tinidazole.
2.	Balantidiasis	*Balantidium coli*	Metronidazole, tetracycline, paromomycin.
3.	Giardiasis	*Giardia lamblia*	Metronidazole, nimorazole, quinacrine, tinidazole.
4.	Leishmaniasis	*Leishmonia donovali* *Leishmonia tropica*	Amphotericine B, sodium stibogluconate, meglumine antimoniate, pentamidine.
5.	Malaria	*Plasmodium falciparum* *Plasmodium vivax* *Plasmodium malariae* *Plasmodium ovale*	Amodiaquine, chlorguanide, chloroquine, primaquine, pyrimethamine, quinine, sulfadiazine, sulfisoxazole.
6.	Enterobiasis	*Enterobias vermicularis*	Mebendazole, piperazine, pyrantel, pyrvinium pamoate, thiabendazole.
7.	Pneumocystosis	*Pneumocystis*	Carinii pyrimethamine, sulfadiazine, sulfisoxazole, trimethoprim- sulfamethoxazole pentamidine.
8.	Trichomoniasis	*Trichomonas vaginalis*	Metronidazole, nimorazole, tinidazole.
9.	Trypanosomiasis	*Trypanosoma cruzi*	Melarsoprol, nifurtimox, pentamidine suramin sodium, diminazene aceturate.
10.	Ascariasis	*Ascaris lumbricoides*	Bephenium, mebendazole, piperazine, pyrantel pamoate, thiabendazole, levamisole.

Infections with helminthes and protozoa are the most common causes of human diseases. The occurrence of these infections is much more in the poor, undeveloped or developing countries than in developed countries. Population crowding, poor sanitation and negligence to provide health education are some of the important contributing factors. These diseases are prominently seen in tropical countries.

The parasitic diseases are easy to acquire, difficult to eradicate and are prone to relapse. Table 3.1 illustrates commonly occurring parasitic diseases.

3.2 ANTIMALARIAL DRUGS

In developing countries, the paramount needs are still related to nutrition, communicable diseases and poverty. The messianic call for "health for all by the year 2000", however emotionally attractive, is very difficult to achieve, in the surroundings of hard realities. Unhealthy economic system influences the standards of both, health and education in the country. Malaria is one of such diseases whose appearance may be related to the socio-economic status of the society. It is mainly a disease of tropic and sub-tropic countries. Though on large scale malaria eradication programme was initiated since from 1957, this disease still affects about 200 million people and causes atleast 2 million deaths per year.

Malaria in humans is caused by the infection with protozoan parasites of the genus, *Plasmodium*. These parasites spend an asexual phase in a man and a sexual phase in female *Anopheles* mosquitos. Out of several hundred known *Anopheles* species, four species infect man. These include :

1. *Plasmodium falciparum* :

It causes malignant tertian or subtertian form of malaria which may cause death by invading the CNS. About half of the cases of malaria are caused by this species. In this type, the attacks are more severe and relapses do not occur.

2. *Plasmodium vivax* :

It causes benign tertian malaria in which fever revisits patient every 48 hours or on the third day. About 40% of the cases of malaria are caused by this species.

3. *Plasmodium malariae* :

It is responsible for the occurrence of quartan malaria in which fever repeats after every 72 hours. It is a milder form of infection. *Plasmodium falciparum* and *P. malariae* do not persist within the liver cells after erythrocytes have become infected.

4. *Plasmodium ovale* :

It is responsible for the mild tertian malaria which is most commonly seen in West Africa.

Except *P. falciparum*, all three species of *Anopheles* have a secondary exo-erythrocytic stage. *Plasmodium vivax* and *P. ovale* do persist within the liver cells even after erythrocytes become infected and may produce true relapses, months or even years after.

Life-cycle of Malarial Parasite :

The female *Anopheles* mosquito feeds on vertebrate blood. Malaria infection is initiated through the bite of infected female *Anopheles* mosquito which releases motile sporozoites into the human blood stream. Within 1 - 2 hours the sporozoites get entry into the parenchyma cells of the host's liver. Through repeated nuclear divisions sporozoites multiply and develop into schizonts. After the period of 10 - 16 days, liver cells rupture due to multiple repeated divisions of schizonts. This results in the release of approximately 20,000 merozoites into circulation. This stage is known as pre-erythrocytic or exo-erythrocytic phase of infection.

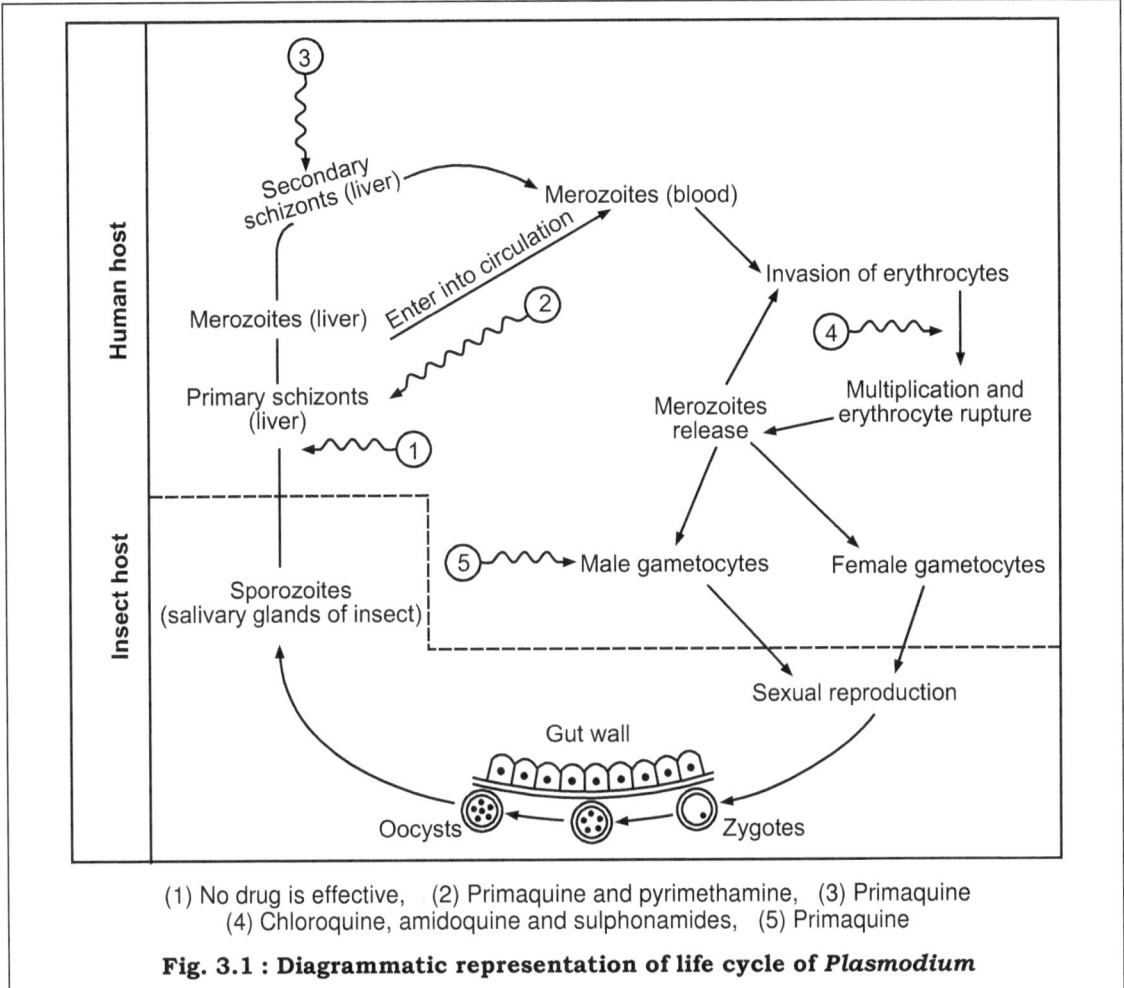

(1) No drug is effective, (2) Primaquine and pyrimethamine, (3) Primaquine
(4) Chloroquine, amidoquine and sulphonamides, (5) Primaquine

Fig. 3.1 : Diagrammatic representation of life cycle of *Plasmodium*

Merozoites now enter in the circulation and invade erythrocytes. Some merozoites invade fresh liver cells and repeat pre-erythrocytic cycle. Erythrocytes are invaded by merozoites for the following reasons :

(1) The plasma constituents and haemoglobin serve as a source of several amino acids necessary for the survival of the parasite.

(2) For rapid multiplication of merozoites, the purine bases (i.e. adenine and guanine) are obtained from erythrocytes which are then utilized to synthesize parasitic DNA and RNA molecules.

(3) Pentoses and phosphates are necessary for nucleic acid synthesis. The protozoal parasites do not have any means to get these raw materials. Obviously, it is the host who is going to suffer.

Inside erythrocytes, the merozoites continue to grow. In erythrocytes, the merozoites undergo asexual multiplication which results into formation of daughter cells, schizonts. Due to the repeated multiplication of the latter, erythrocyte ruptures and releases about 6-24 merozoites into the circulation. Each merozoit again invades fresh erythrocyte and the cycle of asexual multiplication is repeated again. This stage is known as schizogony phase of infection. It continues for 48-72 hours. Febrile clinical manifestations are witnessed due to schizogony phase.

After this phase, some of the erythrocytic merozoites develop into male and female gametocytes by some unidentified mechanisms. Such infected blood when ingested by female mosquito, the sexual forms (i.e. gametocytes) undergo reproduction within the gut of the insect. The resulting zygote, through various stages of development gives rise to the infective sporozoite. The latter gets localized in the salivary glands of the insect and enters the host's blood circulation when the infected mosquito bites a healthy person. The story thus goes on repeating.

Symptoms of Malaria :

The life-cycle of malarial protozoa is dependent on the erythrocytes of the human host, where the parasite undergoes main morphological changes. The symptoms of malaria however, are reported to occur about 12 - 16 days after the mosquito bite. It means that the pre-erythrocytic phase is free of any symptoms. It is the erythrocytic phase which is responsible for the occurance of various symptoms of malaria. These symptoms can be grouped together as :

(1) Symptoms like nausea, vomiting, severe chills, delirium and fever may reappear after every 3 to 4 days depending upon the species of protozoa and hence upon the type of malaria.

(2) As the erythrocytic phase continues, increasing number of erythrocytes undergo destruction, resulting into severe form of anaemia, and

(3) To provide necessary amino acids for the multiplication of parasite, haemoglobin undergoes breakdown process. If this process continues, it leads to jaundice because of accumulated bilirubin.

3.3 CHEMOTHERAPY OF MALARIA

Two different attempts have been made to design new or modern antimalarial drugs. After studying the life-style of malarial parasite in human, many drugs were designed and their target selectivity was tested for various phases of plasmodium life-cycle. For example,

(a) Drugs effective against primary tissue schizonts :

These drugs are also known as prophylactic agents. Since no drug is effective at this stage, true prophylaxis does not exist for malarial parasites.

(b) Drugs active against erythrocytic phase :

These drugs are also known as schizontocidal agents. Examples include amodiaquine, chloroquine, mefloquine, quinine, pyrimethamine etc.

(c) Drugs active against all malarial parasites :

These drugs are also known as gametocytocidal agents. Examples include primaquine. Gametocytes of *P. falciparum* may remain in the circulation for prolonged period, even after the patient receives the treatment with chloroquine. These gametocytes are rapidly killed by a single dose of 79 mg of primaquine phosphate.

In second approach, the host-parasite relationship was thoroughly examined to point out biochemical differences. For example, mammalian cells are capable of utilizing preformed folates while bacteria and protozoa are unable to do so. Hence they must synthesize folates of their own. Hence such drugs that selectively inhibit folate biosynthesis in the protozoa by blocking the enzymes involved therein, can be used for suppression or radical cure of malaria.

Certain antimalarial drugs are not capable of destroying plasmodium merozoites. They just inhibit the erythrocytic stage of development of malarial parasite and thus prevent the onset of symptoms. The treatment with such drugs is known as 'suppressive treatment'. It may be used to prevent maturation of the erythrocytic infection but it may not have any effect on the stages in liver cells. It serves as a prophylactic measure before entering the area susceptible to malarial infection. Drugs commonly employed in suppressive treatment are chloroquine, amodiaquine, pyrimethamine and proguanil. Some antimalarial drugs completely destroy the plasmodium merozoites and thus terminate the malarial attack. Such agents are said to provide clinical cure of the disease. Examples include, chloroquine, and amodiaquine. However, the patients treated with these agents may show the relapse of the disease due to the presence of gametocytes in the circulation for prolonged period even after the drug treatment. Radical cure is the third category in which a combination therapy is generally used to eradicate both, the developed parasites and those still developing in the erythrocytes, and other tissues. Generally, primaquine is used in combination with chloroquine or amodiaquine.

3.4 CLASSIFICATION OF ANTIMALARIAL AGENTS

Early discoveries of **Paul Ehrlich** with organic dyes and organoarsenicals gave new dimensions to the traditional methods of treating malaria. Presently available various antimalarials are the direct outcome of Ehrlich outstanding pioneering efforts. On the chemical basis, antimalarial drugs are classified as :

(1) Quinolines
    (a) *Cinchona* alkaloids,
    (b) 4-Aminoquinolines, and
    (c) 8-Aminoquinolines
(2) 9-Aminoacridines
(3) 2, 4-Diaminopyrimidines
(4) Biguanides
(5) Sulfones and sulphonamides, and
(6) Miscellaneous agents.

(1) Quinolines :

(a) *Cinchona* **alkaloids :** *Cinchona* bark contains a mixture of more than 20 alkaloids. Four major alkaloids are isolated from it, which are effective against erythrocytic merozoites and constitute a part of suppressive treatment of malaria. All four are derivatives of 4-quinoline methanol which is linked with a substituted quinuclidine moiety.

Cinchona alkaloids

1. Quinine :
    $R_1 = OCH_3$; $R_2 = -CH = CH_2$ (–) isomer
2. Quinidine :
    $R_1 = OCH_3$; $R_2 = -CH = CH_2$ (+) isomer
3. Cinchonine :
    $R_1 = H$; $R_2 = -CH = CH_2$ (+) isomer
4. Cinchonidine :

$R_1 = H$; $R_2 = -CH = CH_2$ (–) isomer

Quinine and its d-isomer, quinidine are the only *cinchona* alkaloids currently in the use. Quinine is the most active antimalarial ingredient of the *cinchona* bark and is present in highest concentration to the extent of about 5.0%. It is schizonticidal and gametocytocidal for *P. vivax* and *P. malariae*. It is orally active in the form of sulfate while quinine dihydrochloride may be used for intravenous administration. The antimalarial activity is mainly associated with the laevorotatory form. Subcutaneous or intramuscular administration is not usually recommended due to local tissue damage.

SAR studies of quinine nucleus revealed the importance of secondary alcohol group in the structure. The methoxy (R_1), vinyl (R_2) moieties were found to be not necessary for antimalarial activity.

About 70% of administered dose is bound to the plasma proteins. It has a plasma half-life of 12 hours. It undergoes extensive metabolism. Hydroxylated metabolites and other inactive metabolites appear in the urine alongwith 2 – 5% dose in unchanged form. Adverse effects include nausea, vomiting, abdominal pain, diarrhea, headache, tinnitus, vertigo, blurred vision, mydriasis, asthma, hypersensitivity reactions and hypotension.

It is extremely useful in treating chloroquine resistant *P. falciparum* infections. High doses of quinine may produce a quinidine like depressant effect on the heart. It causes vasodilation and may cause hypotension. Since it antagonises the actions of physostigmine on the skeletal muscles by exerting curare-like effect, it may be beneficial in the symptomatic relief of nocturnal muscle cramps or myotonia congenita. Toxic doses of quinine may induce abortion. It has analgesic, antipyretic and local anaesthetic properties.

Due to its low therapeutic index, quinine is not used alone. It can be used alongwith primaquine, pyrimethamine or a sulphonamide in the combination therapy.

(b) 4-Aminoquinolines : During the period 1940-1944, a limited number of antimalarials were available in the market. They were associated with a high toxicity profile and a low therapeutic index. To overcome this situation, 4-aminoquinolines were investigated in United States through a research programme. Chloroquine, hydroxy-chloroquine and amodiaquine are the most important members of this series.

Chloroquine is found to be concentrated in parasitized red cells where it binds to double-stranded DNA. This results into inhibition of the functions of DNA and RNA polymerases. It inhibits several enzyme systems and binds to lysosomes resulting into their stabilization. This exerts an inhibitory influence on the cell growth of bacteria and protozoa. However erythrocytes affected by chloroquine-resistant strains of *plasmodium*, are less permeable to the drug. Hence, chloroquine is accumulated less readily and to a lesser extent in such parasitized erythrocytes.

Chemically, chloroquine is 7 - Chloro - 4 (4 - diethylamino - 1-methylbutylamino) quinoline. Due to the presence of asymmetric carbon in the side-chain, it exists as isomers. The chemical name of amodiaquine is 7 - chloro - 4 - (3 - diethylamino - 4 - hydroxyanilino) quinoline. Both these drugs are effective against a sexual erythrocytic form of all four *plasmodium* species.

SAR studies indicated that 7 - Chloro group, the tertiary amine and diaminoalkyl side-chain are the essential features for antimalarial activity. Chloroquine phosphate is the orally effective form of this drug. About 65% of administered dose is bound to the plasma-proteins. It has plasma half-life of about 3 days. Principal metabolites include, desethyl-chloroquine, bisdesethylchloroquine and a carboxylic acid analog, which are excreted in the urine along with 52-53% dose in unchanged form.

Chloroquine and amodiaquine have some depressant effects on the bone marrow. Both these agents, cause hemolysis in patients with glucose-6-phosphate dehydrogenase deficiency. The toxicity profile of these agents is less severe and include nausea, vomiting, headache, blurred vision and dermatitis. Chloroquine is more prone to cause photoallergic dermatitis since it accumulates in the skin to a greater extent than amodiaquine. Hence, it must be used with caution in children.

Chloroquine also has anti-histaminic and anti-inflammatory properties. It is used to treat hepatic amebiasis, rheumatoid arthritis, discoid lupus erythematous, cutanea tarda, solar urticaria and polymorphous light erruptions. It is a drug of choice for the suppressive prophylaxis and for the treatment of acute clinical attacks in all types of malaria except chloroquine-resistant *falciparum* strains. For the treatment of chloroquine-resistant *falciparum* malaria, a combination therapy comprising of quinine, pyrimethamine and sulfadiazine may be given. The combination of a 2-day course of quinine and a single dose of mefloquine is even more effective.

In chloroquine sensitive strains, response in adults is rapid when 1.5 g of chloroquine is given over 2 days. If parenteral administration is required, the intramuscular route should be preferred. However, to prevent relapsing malaria, a single dose of 79 mg of primaquine phosphate may also be given to the patient. Amodiaquine hydrochloride and hydroxy chloroquine sulfate are other clinically used members of this group having uses and adverse effects similar to chloroquine.

(c) 8-Aminoquinolines : Primaquine was the first synthetic antimalarial agent to be introduced into the clinical practice in 1929. Principal agents from this class include primaquine, pamaquine and quinocide.

8 - Aminoquinolines

In contrast to 4-aminoquinolines, these agents lack activity against erythrocytic merozoites. In fact, they attack both, the pre-erythrocytic phase of the disease and also show gametocidal activity to some extent. Obviously then, if used alone, they can only be used for prophylactic purposes. They produce radical cure of *vivax* malaria when they are used alongwith chloroquine.

Their toxic effects are much more severe than those of 4-aminoquinolines and are related principally to the central nervous system and circulatory system. These includes, nausea, vomiting, anorexia, headache, hemolytic anaemia, leukopenia and methemoglobinemia. Because of its relative safety and lower toxicity, primaquine is the only member of this series which is clinically used.

In the form of its diphosphate, primaquine is completely absorbed by oral route. It is rapidly metabolized to various metabolites that include 5-hydroxyprimaquine, 5-hydroxy-6-desmethyl primaquine and 8 - (3 - carboxyl - 1 - methyl propylamino) - 6 - methoxyquinoline. They all appear in the urine along with small amount of unchanged drug. The parenteral form of primaquine is not available.

The antimalarial activity of primaquine is due to its ability to interfere with protein synthesis, with enzymes and with erythrocyte phospholipid metabolism in the parasites. It is usually given along with a 4-aminoquinoline schizontocide (e.g. chloroquine) to prevent relapses in *P. vivax* and *P. ovale* infections and to reduce the chances of development of chloroquine resistant strains of *plasmodium*. It may also be used against primary exo-erythrocytic forms of *P. falciparum*. Besides this, it also depresses myocardial excitability and possesses antiarrhythmic actions.

(2) 9 - Aminoacridines :

Quinacrine, acriquine and aminoacrichin are the clinically useful agents from this class.

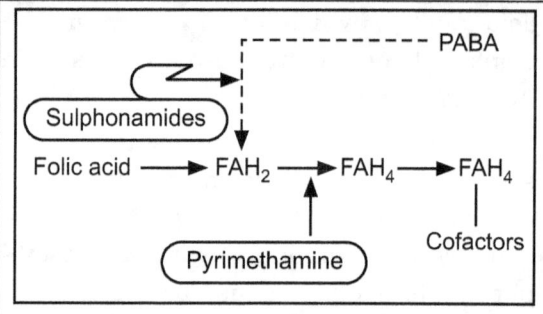

9 - Aminoacridines

Quinacrine is the most active compound of the series. In general, these derivatives pose a high degree of risk with low activity profile. Hence, after the development of 4-aminoquinolines, they are used rarely for the treatment of malaria.

Fig. 3.2 : Mechanism of action of Diaminopyrimidines

Yellow pigmentation of the skin and yellow colour appears in the urine during the treatment with quinacrine. These signs disappear with the discontinuation of therapy. Nausea, vomiting, headache, convulsions, aplastic anaemia and psychotomimetic reactions are the adverse effects associated with these drugs.

(3) 2, 4 - Diaminopyrimidines :

In this series, pyrimethamine and trimethoprim are the effective antimalarial agents. After establishing itself as a good antibacterial agent, trimethoprim secured a place in the chemotherapy of malaria. These derivatives are effective against both the exo-erythrocytic and erythrocytic phases of the disease.

Pyrimethamine is very effective in the chemoprophylaxis and treatment of chloroquineresistant *falciparum* malaria. It is also used in the treatment of toxoplasmosis and pneumocystosis.

Diaminopyrimidines, biguanides and dihydrotriazines are the drugs which are designed through the studies of biochemical differences between the host and parasites.

Tetrahydrofolate (FAH_4) is required for the biosynthesis of purines, pyrimidines and certain amino acids (needed for protozoal DNA synthesis). It is obtained by the reduction of dihydrofolate (FAH_2) catalyzed by the enzyme, dihydrofolate reductase. Mammalian cells are permeable to folates whereas bacteria and protozoa are unable to transport preformed folates. Hence, they must synthesize their own folates. Thus, any attempt to inhibit protozoal biosynthesis of FAH_2 (e.g. sulphonamide) or a selective inhibition of the protozoal enzyme, dihydrofolate reductase (e.g. pyrimethamine) leads to the disturbances in the protozoal DNA synthesis and subsequently death of protozoal cells.

Pyrimethamine inhibits malarial dihydrofolate reductase at concentration far lower than needed to inhibit the mammalian enzymes. Due to the structural similarity with part of FAH_2 structure, pyrimethamine competitively tries to block the action of dihydrofolate reductase enzyme. However, parasites can develop drug-resistance due to utilization of alternative metabolic pathways. Sulphonamides inhibit the conversion of folinic acid to dihydrofolate. Hence, the combination of pyrimethamine with a long acting sulpha drug (e.g. sulfadoxine, sulphamethoxazole etc.) gives a supradditive therapeutic effect and reduces the chances for developing drug-resistant strains. Pyrimethamine is more potent antimalarial agent than chloroguanide and has a much longer duration of action because of its slow rate of excretion.

Pyrimethamine possesses very low toxicity. Adverse effects include muscular weakness, emesis, diarrhea, dehydration, seizures and macrocytic anaemia. Most of these effects may be due to inhibition of mammalian enzymes involved in folic acid metabolism. Adverse effects may thus be minimized by concomitant administration of folinic acid to the patients receiving pyrimethamine.

(4) Biguanides :

A large number of biguanides and dihydrotriazines have been synthesized and tested for their antimalarial activity. Biguanides are largely prodrugs and are not active until they are metabolized *in-vivo* to the dihydrotriazine derivatives. Proguanil was first synthesized in Britain in 1945. Chloroguanil is metabolized to the active triazine ring compound, cycloguanil which is responsible for its antimalarial activity.

The antimalarial activity of cycloguanil is due to its structural and functional similarity with pyrimethamine. Due to this similarity, the parasites that are resistant to the action of pyrimethamine, also exhibit resistance to the action of chloroguanide. It inhibits dihydrofolate reductase enzyme and interferes in the folic acid metabolism. This leads to inhibition of nuclear division in malarial parasites. Cycloguanil has a duration of action of several weeks. The drug damages gametocytes so that they fail to complete their cycle in mosquito.

Chloroguanide acts slowly and is effective against susceptible strains of *Plasmodium*. However, the development of drug resistant strains limits its clinical utility. In the form of hydrochloride, it is used orally, while in the form of cycloguanil embonate or pamoate, it is used intramuscularly. It provides a longer duration of action.

SAR studies revealed the importance of halogen atom in the phenyl ring. An additional chloro-substitution in the proguanil structure (chloroproguanil) increases activity with simultaneous increase in toxicity.

The toxicity profile of biguanides is very mild. Proguanil is probably the least toxic of all clinically used antimalarial agents. If taken on an empty stomach, mild gastric disturbances like nausea, vomiting, diarrhea etc. may result.

(5) Sulphones and sulphonamides :

Though the antimalarial potency of sulphonamides was proved long back in 1943, they were neglected because of their low therapeutic index. Later on, due to the development of chloroquine resistant strains of *P. falciparum*, long acting sulphonamides were tried in combination with pyrimethamine or trimethoprim. Dapsone, in combination with pyrimethamine can also be effectively used as a chemoprophylactic agent against drug-resistant strains of malarial parasites. Effective members of this class are Sulphadiazine, Dapsone, Diacetyl dapsone.

Dapsone is found to possess mild toxicity and prolonged duration of action. Both, sulphonamides and sulphones are active only against erythrocytic stages of malarial parasite. They are ineffective in the treatment of *P. vivax* infections.

(6) Miscellaneous agents :

(a) Mefloquine : It bears some degree of structural similarity with quinine. Chemically it is a 4-quinoline-carbinolamine. It is marketed in the form of its racemic mixture where the erythro form is more active than threo-isomer. It is an orally active derivative of 4-quinoline - methanol. About 95 - 98% of administered dose is bound to be plasma-proteins. It has a plasma half-life of 17 days. Principal metabolites include, 2, 8 - bis - trifluoromethylquinoline - 4 - methanol and a carboxylic acid analog. They are excreted in the faeces. Presence of trifluoromethyl moiety at position 2, (see structure), lowers down the rate of metabolism and precludes the phototoxic effects commonly associated with other carbinolamines.

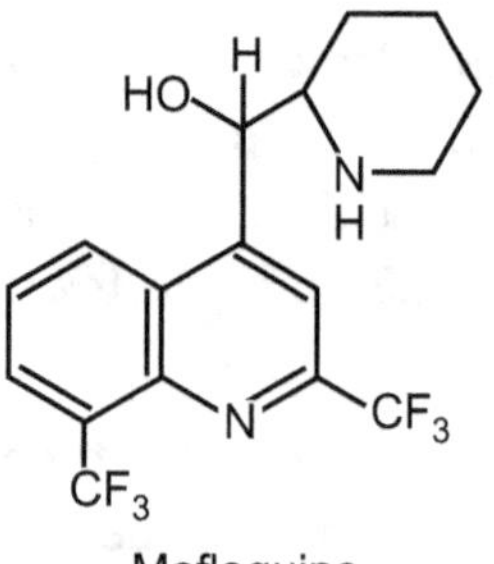

Mefloquine

Very little is known about its mechanism of action. It is predicted that it may be acting at erythrocytic stage in the life-cycle of *Plasmodium*. It may affect the ring stages of *P. falciparum* and *P. vivax* by inducing morphological changes. To potentiate its spectrum of activity it may also be used in combination with pyrimethamine, trimethoprim or sulfadoxine. However, it can not be used in infants, children and during pregnancy.

It can be used in both, chemo-suppressive and radical cure of infections caused by resistant strains of parasites. Adverse effects are mild and mainly include its effects on CVS and pulmonary systems.

(b) Other antibacterials like tetracyclines, clindamycin, lincomycin and chloramphenicol are found to possess antimalarial activity. A combination of quinine and tetracycline has been used to treat clinical attacks of chloroquine-resistant *P. falciparum* infection. However, the use of antibiotics produce antibiotic-resistant pathogenic bacteria, if continued for long-term.

Shortly after the discovery of mefloquine, a new drug, halofantrine has been developed as a promising alternative to mefloquine.

Inactivated, parasitized red blood cells or their fractions and more recently extracellular erythrocytic merozoites have been tested as vaccines in various forms of experimental procedures. In 1976, **Trager** and **Jensen** became successful in demonstrating immunogenicity of small amounts of merozoit antigen isolated in high yield and relative purity from cultured parasites. It was a milestone in the history of malariology.

Red blood cells however, are used for culture which exposes the risk of inclusion of red blood cells antigens in the vaccine. This may develop a severe autoimmune haemolytic anaemia in patients receiving this vaccine.

3.5 DRUG RESISTANCE

During 1941-46 over 16,000 agents were synthesized and tested for their antimalarial potential. Similarly, 250,000 compounds were screened out during the decade 1968-78. Due to the extensive and liberal use of currently available antimalarial drugs, resistance to most of these drugs has developed in the strains of *P. falciparum* (this species is responsible for about 85% cases of human malaria). The progressive development of drug-resistance in *Plasmodium* strains may overburden the research programmes to yield new synthetic antimalarials.

Beside the chloroquine resistant strains, incidences of resistance development to pyrimethamine-sulfadoxine combinations are also accumulating. The increased number of cases of appearance of multi-drug resistant strains of *P. falciparum* and failure of quinine to re-exhibit its clinical potency are the problems of severe concern. It is for this reason, mefloquine should be reserved only for the treatment of multi-drug resistant strains and it should not be over exposed. The parasites would not need much time to develop mefloquine-resistant strains, if misuse of this drug is permitted.

Unfortunately the underlying principles of acquired resistance to antimalarial drugs still remain unclear and demand further investigations.

3.6 AMOEBIASIS

Amoebiasis is an infection of the mucous membrane of the large intestine where *Entamoeba histolytica* is the causative organism. This organism occurs in the intestine in the form of trophozoites and cysts. In most infections, trophozoites (vegetative form) appear to feed on intestinal bacterial flora and multiply in the colonic lumen without causing any symptoms. But under certain circumstances, trophozoites may get activated and invade the intestinal mucosa, causing tissue lysis and producing dysentery or diarrhoea. Under unfavourable atmosphere however, trophozoites are encysted and the cyst form is excreted in the faeces. In majority of cases, the infected persons do not show any symptoms and excrete both cysts and trophozoites in the faeces. The cyst form of the organism is infective and the infection is acquired by ingestion of amoebic cysts in food or water contaminated due to handling by such asymptomatic infected person. Ingested cysts liberate trophozoites in the intestine and continue the process in the new host. The infection usually prevails in the areas of poor hygienic conditions and inadequate sanitation.

Amoebic dysentery : Amoeba can cause attacks of acute dysentery which is characterized by presence of blood and mucous in the stools and severe abdominal pain. This occurs when the amoebae invades the wall of intestine, multiplies and causes tissue damage, often forming ulcers. Later amoebae may invade the blood vessels and be carried to the liver and even to the brain. Death can occur from liver abscess which can perforate into the lung and elsewhere. Of the several species of amoebae that occur in the human intestinal tract, only *Entamoeba histolytica* is pathogenic.

Invasive intestinal amoebiasis may vary in its symptoms from a mild illness to severe amoebic dysentery with blood and mucous in the stool. Trophozoites may spread to the liver through portal vein and produce either an acute amoebic hepatitis or may encyst and produce amoebic liver abscess. The latter may be complicated by rupture or extension of infection to adjacent organs. It may be associated with chronic colonic dysfunction, acute colonic perforation, insidious peritonitis and amoebic granuloma.

Amoebic abscess of the liver is the most common extra-intestinal manifestation of invasive amoebiasis. It may be characterized by abdominal pain, anorexia, fever, weight loss and hepatomegaly. In the mild amoebiasis, the symptoms are mainly of intestinal origin which appear due to invasion of the intestinal wall by the multiplying trophozoites. In more severe form, other vital organs like liver, lungs, brain and genitourinary tract may get affected. This constitutes the cause of extra-intestinal symptoms.

3.7 CHEMOTHERAPY

Various drugs used in the treatment of amoebiasis can be categorised on the basis of their site of action :

(i) Luminal amoebicides :

These drugs are effective against the organism present in the bowel lumen. Most of them owe their effectiveness due to their poor oral absorption. This helps the drug to stay more time in the intestine. They are highly effective in eliminating cysts in asymptomatic carriers. Examples include, diloxanide furoate, iodoquinol, clioquinol etc.

(ii) Luminal trophozoitocidal agents :

These agents mainly attack intestinal trophozoites and are effectively used to treat invasive intestinal amoebiasis. Examples include metronidazole, tinidazole, paromomycin, tetracycline and erythromycin.

(iii) Systemic amoebicides :

As the name indicates, these drugs are not acting locally in the intestine. When trophozoites spread into liver, brain or lungs, these drugs may be used to treat extra-intestinal manifestations of invasive amoebiasis. Examples include metronidazole, tinidazole, chloroquine and dehydroemetine. Metronidazole and tinidazole not only eliminate trophozoites present in the intestine but are also effective at extra-intestinal sites.

In addition to the chemotherapeutic measures, the large liver abscesses may be aspirated percutaneously for better results.

(a) Diloxanide furoate :

It is a cheap, relatively non-toxic dichloroacetamide derivative, mainly used in the treatment of chronic amoebiasis. It is less effective in the treatment of acute intestinal amoebiasis. Studies of diloxanide ester showed that, in the form of furoate, the drug is less soluble and hence more effective locally. This ester undergoes hydrolysis in upper intestine to release diloxanide which is then absorbed. Major amount of drug is excreted in the urine in the form of its inactive glucuronide. About 4 - 10% dose appears unchanged in the faeces.

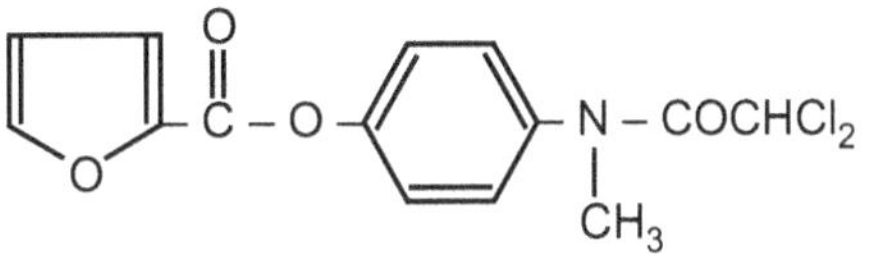

Diloxanide furoate

Adverse effects include vomiting, abdominal cramps, flatulence, diarrhoea, urticaria, and pruritus. It is contraindicated during pregnancy and in children under 2 years of age.

Little is known about its mechanism of action. It appears to interfere with protein synthesis and with the activity of some essential enzymes of protozoa. It is used in the treatment of cyst-passing patients. In the treatment of extra-intestinal amoebiasis, it may be used along with a systemic amoebicidal agent.

Teclozan and etofamide are other effective amoebicidal members of dichloroacetamide series.

(b) 8-Hydroxyquinolines :

Diiodohydroxyquin (iodoquinol), iodochlorohydroxyquin (clioquinol), dibromoquin, chiniofon and chloroquinaldol are examples of halogenated derivatives of 8-hydroxyquinoline having luminal amoebicidal activity.

They are used alone in the treatment of chronic intestinal amoebiasis. In acute amoebiasis they are generally used in combination with either emetine, metronidazole or carbarsone. Since the drug therapy increases plasma iodine levels, these agents must be used with caution in patients hypersensitive to iodine or with thyroid dysfunction. In long term therapy, these agents are reported to cause optic neuritis and thus may prove to be dangerous.

Iodoquinol is excreted mainly through the faeces. Adverse effects include nausea, vomiting, diarrhoea, stomach pain, blurred vision, optic atrophy, skin rashes, chills, muscle pain, weakness, headache and peripheral neuropathy.

It kills trophozoites and cysts in intestinal tract by chelating ferrous ions which are essential for the protozoal metabolism. As a luminal amoebicide, it is used in the dose of 2 g daily for 20 days.

(c) Nitroimidazole derivatives :

First report of study on nitroimidazole derivatives appeared in 1955 by **Nakamura** and coworkers. Four such active members of the series include, metronidazole, tinidazole, timorazole and ornidazole.

Out of these, metronidazole was introduced in 1959 for the systemic treatment of trichomonal infections of urinogenital tract. It has exhibited a high degree of activity against amoebiasis, trichomoniasis, giardiasis, balantidiasis and dracunculiasis. It has been found to possess extremely broad spectrum of both, antibacterial and antiprotozoal activities.

Its effectiveness is due to the presence of nitro group which participates in the endogenous reduction reaction as an electron acceptor. Since it has a redox potential lower than the proteins, ferredoxin, which is found in anaerobic organisms, its nitro group is reduced. This reduced form of metronidazole then causes interference in the carbohydrate metabolism and nucleic acid synthesis. It also binds with the cytoplasmic proteins of susceptible cells.

Metronidazole is an orally active drug. About 10% of administered dose is bound to the plasma proteins. It has a plasma half-life of 8.5 to 10.0 hours. The 2-hydroxy methyl metabolite and several inactive metabolites appear in the urine in the form of their glucoronides. Adverse effects include nausea, vomiting, anorexia, metallic taste, stomatitis, glossitis, vertigo, dizziness, flushing, neutropenia and thromboplebitis.

It is effectively used in the treatment of amoebiasis, giardiasis and trichomoniasis. However metronidazole alone, may not always eradicate the intestinal phase. Hence, it should be given along with diloxanide (a luminal amoebicide) in order to prevent recurrence. It is also effective against a number of anaerobic bacteria (e.g. *Bacteroides, Eubacterium, Clostridium, Fusobacterium, Peptococcus* etc.). It may sometimes be used with other antibiotics to control the infections caused by aerobic microorganisms. It is contraindicated in patients with blood dyscrasias and with alcoholic drinks (because of its disulfiram like effects). In children, a tasteless oral suspension of benzoyl metronidazole is usually preferred.

(d) Antibiotics :

Tetracycline, chlortetracycline, oxytetracycline, erythromycin and paromomycin are the examples of antibiotics which can be used in the treatment of amoebiasis. Since amoebicidal action is not their main activity, they are usually used in combination with other principal amoebicidal agents in the treatment of mild to severe stages of intestinal amoebiasis.

Most of the trophozoites present in the lumen, feed on the intestinal bacterial flora and then multiply. Except paromomycin, rest of the antibiotics exert an indirect trophozoitocidal action by destroying the enteric bacteria necessary for amoebic proliferation. Paromomycin is an aminoglycoside antibiotic obtained from *Streptomyces rimosus*. It has a direct effect on the amoebae present in the lumen. It interferes in the protozoal DNA and RNA synthesis and it is generally used as a supplementary therapy in amoebiasis and in the treatment of various tapeworm infections. Adverse effects include diarrhoea and anorexia.

(e) Carbarsone :

Carbarsone is an example of organic arsenicals. It may be used in combination with other amoebicides in the treatment of both acute and chronic intestinal amoebiasis. They are of no value in the treatment of systemic amoebiasis. Examples of drugs include carbarsone, glycobiarsol (a bismuth salt of phenylarsonic acid) and diphetarsone. They are effective antiamoebic agents due to the presence of arsenic in their structures. Arsenic exerts amoebicidal effect by non-specifically inactivating the enzymes containing sulfhydryl groups. They are less favoured due to severe toxicity associated with their use.

(f) Chloroquine :

Chloroquine is an effective agent in the treatment of systemic amoebiasis. It is used only in the cases where other drugs either fail or are contraindicated. It is highly effective drug when used alongwith quinine, in the treatment of hepatic amoebic abscesses or amoebic hepatitis because of its preferential localization in the liver. To achieve complete cure it is given along with intestinal amoebicide.

It is not much effective in the treatment of colonic amoebiasis in which its only function is to prevent development of liver abscesses.

(g) Ipecacuanha alkaloids :

These include emetine and dehydroemetine. The latter is a synthetic analog of emetine, an alkaloid obtained from the roots of *Ipecac* plant (*Cephaelis ipecacuanha*). Emetine is highly effective agent in systemic amoebiasis but it fails to act as luminal amoebicide because of poor concentration of the drug in that area. However, it may be used as luminal amoebicide in the form of emetine bismuth iodide which contains about 25% anhydrous emetine and 20% bismuth. It releases emetine slowly in the intestinal lumen.

Dehydroemetine is a better chemotherapeutic agent than emetine. Both are more effective against motile trophozoites than cysts. They affect protein synthesis by inhibiting the translocation of peptidyl-t RNA on ribosomes resulting in the inhibition of polypeptide chain elongation.

In severe cases of amoebiasis, emetine is used in combination with either chloroquine, tetracycline or paromomycine, while dehydroemetine may be used for rapid relief of symptoms in patients with severe amoebic dysentery. Emetine is not a safe drug. Administration of either drugs need close medical supervision. A number of adverse effects affecting gastrointestinal, neuro-muscular, cardiovascular systems are reported with their use. Dehydroemetine is less toxic than emetine.

(h) Miscellaneous agents :

Many compounds exhibit amoebicidal activity when used orally. Important examples of such clinically used agents includes chlorbetamide, chlorphenoxamine, chlorphenoxamine ethyl ether, phanquone and teclozan. These agents are used as luminal amoebicides.

3.8 LEISHMANIASIS

This infection is transmitted to the humans by the bites of infected female flies which are pre-infected by biting the cats, dogs or rodents, the non-human mammalian reservoirs. Depending upon the type of protozoa involved and the organ affected, leishmaniasis may be of three different types.

(a) Visceral leishmaniasis :

It is caused by *Leishmania donovani*. This protozoa parasitizes the reticuloendothelial cells that results into an enlargement of lymph nodes, liver and spleen. The main symptoms of the disease include fever, dysentery, severe anaemia and massive spleen.

(b) Cutaneous leishmaniasis :

It is caused by *Leishmania braziliensis* and involves ulceration of skin and formation of skin lesions. It is a form of localized and non-systemic infection.

(c) American leishmaniasis :

It is caused by *Leishmania tropica*. The infection is characterized by the ulceration of mucous membranes of nose, mouth and pharynx. Skin lesions may also appear.

Of all the types, visceral leishmaniasis (kala azar) is the commonly occurring form of infection while other two forms are rare. The occurrence of localized or systemic (kala azar) form of disease depends on the type of the infecting protozoa and the host immunological system.

Leishmania species occur intracellularly in the amastigate form in MPS (mononuclear phagocytic system) cells of the host, mainly in those of spleen, liver, bone marrow or lymph nodes in the visceral disease (kala-azar) and mainly in the skin and/or mucous membranes in the cutaneous diseases (tropical sore chiclero' ulcer, etc.). One cell may contain 10 or more organisms. The cytoplasm of organism may be vacuolated and the organism may occur in vacuoles in cytoplasm of host cell or simply in the continuity of cytoplasm.

Most of the drugs used in the treatment of leishmaniasis belong to pentavalent antimonial category. These include sodium stibogluconate, urea stibogluconate, ethyl stibamine, dihydroxy stibamidine isethionate and meglumine antimonate (i.e. N-methyl glucamine antimonate). These pentavalent antimonials get converted to trivalent antimonials *in-vivo*. The latter then inhibits phosphofructokinase, an enzyme that catalyses a rate limiting step in glycolysis. Hence the organisms whose growth is dependent upon the anaerobic metabolism of glucose, can not survive due to lack of energy source. Besides this, these agents are also reported to inhibit several enzyme systems of the protozoa. The effectiveness of sodium stibogluconate in the treatment of visceral leishmaniasis is due to its ability to concentrate in liver and spleen.

Orginally developed as an antimalarial agent, atovaquone is mainly used against Pneumocystosis infections as an alternative to trimethoprim/sulfamethoxazole therapy. Due to structural similarity, it acts as an antimetabolite to ubiquinone 6, an essential component of the mitochondrial electron transport chain in microorganisms.

Pentamidine isethionate is a poor orally absorbed aromatic diamidine having antiprotozoal and fungicidal activities. About 80% of administered dose is bound to the plasma proteins. It is excreted unchanged in the urine at much slow rate.

Adverse effects include nausea, vomiting, anorexia, headache, fever, rash, pancreatitis, leukopenia, thrombocytopenia, dizziness, confusion, hypotension and hypoglycemia.

It is used as a prophylactic agent in systemic blastomycosis, trypanosomiasis, cutaneous leishmaniasis and in pneumonia due to *P. carinii*. The latter infection may be associated with acquired immuno deficiency syndrome (AIDS).

Amphotericin B is also reported to be effective in the cases of leishmaniasis, not responding to other drugs.

3.9 TRYPANOSOMIASIS

Trypanosomes are mobile protozoan parasites that require two hosts including man (vertebrate) and insect (invertebrate). The parasites may be found in the blood and spinal fluid of the infected person. Some *trypanosomes* are non-pathogenic and live silently in the body of the host. Trypanosomiasis is of two types based upon the species of *trypanosomes* involved.

(a) African trypanosomiasis :

It is caused by the bite of the fly belonging to *Glossina* species. The infective protozoa is either *T. gambiense* or *T. rhodesiense*. The disease caused is known as sleeping sickness which is characterised by fever, headache, lymph node enlargement, drowsiness, lethargy, weakness and mental disturbances. Since the protozoan enter into the cerebrospinal fluid and CNS, the signs of mental disturbances are also seen.

(b) American trypanosomiasis (Chagas disease) :

It is caused by *T. cruzi* and is transmitted by kissing bugs.

(i) Suramin sodium : It is a non-metallic dye derivative having trypanocidal activity. Freshly prepared solution should always be used for i.v. administration. About 99% of administered dose is bound to the plasma-proteins. It has a plasma half life of 48 - 49 days. It does not undergo metabolism and is excreted slowly in urine in unchanged form over a period of months. Since a single injection provides adequate blood concentration for several months, it can be used in both, prophylaxis and treatment of African trypanosomiasis.

Because of its anionic nature, it binds with the cationic sites present in proteins and enzymes in glycolytic pathways and inhibits their functioning. Protozoa may die due to the lack of energy source. It does not readily penetrate mammalian cells. This explains its selectivity of action. It is effective in treatment of onchocerciasis either alone or along with arsenicals and is also effective in the prophylaxis of Rhodesian and Gambian trypanosomiasis.

(ii) Melarsoprol : It is a dimercaprol derivative of melarsen oxide used as antiprotozoal agent. Trimelarsan is a water soluble derivative of melarsoprol which may be used intra-muscularly. The activity is due to the arsenic content which inhibits the essential sulfhydryl group containing enzymes. This inhibitory action of arsenic is of non-specific and non-selective nature which explains the severe adverse effects associated with the use of this drug. Drug-resistant strain of protozoa are less permeable to the drug.

It is marketed as a 3.6 % w/v sterile-solution in propylene glycol. It is used to treat African trypanosomiasis involving CNS symptoms.

(iii) Tryparsamide : It is a pentavalent arsenical, once used in the treatment of advance cases of trypanosomiasis. It contains about 25% antimony and can be used along with suramin in the treatment of West African trypanosomiasis. Because of drug-induced optic nerve damage, it is a less preferred agent.

(iv) Nifurtimox : It is a nitrofuran derivative, effective specifically against *T. cruzi* infections and is an orally effective drug. It has a plasma half life of about 8 hours. Inactive metabolites appear in the urine along with 5% dose in unchanged form.

Adverse effects include nausea, vomiting, headache, weight loss, euphoria, tremors, insomnia, drowsiness, psychic disturbances and peripheral neuropathy.

The nitro group of nifurtimox is converted to nitro anion radical in the presence of pyridine nucleotides. This anion produces superoxide by reaction with molecular oxygen, resulting into regeneration of nifurtimox. This superoxide then may interfere with the synthesis of proteins and in the functioning of protozoal enzymes.

Nitrofurazone is a topical antibacterial agent effective against many gram-positive and gram-negative bacteria and some protozoa. It is used to treat special cases of American trypanosomiasis which are resistant to other drugs. The adult oral dose in the treatment of trypanosomiasis is 500 mg daily for 3 days and then 500 mg every 8 hours for a week. This dose schedule may be repeated thrice with a week's interval each time.

Eflornithine acts by inhibiting ornithine decarboxylase, an enzyme responsible for biosynthesis of polyamines essential for the regulation of DNA synthesis and cell proliferation in microorganisms. It is used to treat African trypanosomiasis.

3.10 TRICHOMONIASIS

Trichomonas are unicellular, flagellated protozoal parasites. Most of them are non-pathogenic in nature. In humans, the pathogenic parasites reside in the urinogenital tract. The pathogenic species include *Trichomonas vaginalis* in man and *T. foetus* in cattles.

Males are asymptomatic carriers but females often develop severe vaginitis and cervicitis. *T. vaginalis* infection in male appears as a symptom-free urethritis while in female, it occurs as vaginitis which is characterised by a frothy pale yellow discharge. Age of the female, pH at vaginal region and period of her menstrual cycle are some of the factors that affects her susceptibility to the infection. Since the transmission of disease is effected due to sexual contacts, the male sexual partner should be treated simultaneously to prevent occurrence of relapses in the female.

Aminitrozole, niridazole, acetarsol, furazolidone and nifurtimox are the agents which can be used in the treatment of vaginitis. Alongwith these agents, metronidazole, nimorazole, tinidazole, arsenicals, 8-hydroxyquinolines and certain polyene antibiotics (e.g. pimaricin and hachimycin) can also be used. A single dose of 2 g of either metronidazole or tinidazole has been shown to be effective, if the patient is not reinfected.

3.11 GIARDIASIS

Giardiasis is an intestinal protozoal infection caused by *Giardia lamblia*. Unhygienic conditions, low socio-economic status and homosexuality are some factors that contribute in the spread of giardiasis. The asymptomatic patients may release protozoal parasites in the form of cysts in the faeces. Transmission then occurs after ingestion of cysts in contaminated food or water. The main symptoms include diarrhoea, anorexia, bloating, flatulence and weight loss.

Though all amoebicidal drugs can be used in the treatment of giardiasis, metronidazole, tinidazole and quinacrine are more preferred agents.

(a) Quinacrine :

Though it is no longer used in the prophylaxis and treatment of malaria still it is used as an important agent in the treatment of giardiasis. It is an orally active, long acting acridine derivative which is very slowly excreted in the urine. The metabolic pathways for quinacrine are poorly understood.

Adverse effects include nausea, vomiting, anorexia, diarrhoea, headache, ocular toxicity, discolouration of nails, dizziness, anxiety, restlessness, blood dyscrasias and psychosis. It is contraindicated during pregnancy and in patients receiving antimalarial therapy with primaquine.

It acts by binding to DNA through an intercalation mechanism, and strongly inhibits DNA replication and RNA transcription process. It also interferes with protein synthesis and functioning of various enzyme systems. It is used as anticonvulsant agent in certain cases and exerts quinidine like effects on the heart.

It is a drug of choice in the treatment of giardiasis and is used orally in dose of 100 mg three times a day for 5 - 7 days. The dose-schedule can be repeated, if necessary, about 2 weeks later. Besides this, furazolidone and paromomycin can also be used in the treatment of giardiasis.

3.12 TOXOPLASMOSIS

It is caused by the ingestion of oocysts of *T. plasma gondii* from the faeces of infected cats or ingestion of cysts affected raw meat. Active ocular toxoplasmosis, systemic toxoplasmosis and congenital toxoplasmosis (in newborns) are the important types of this infection.

Drugs like pyrimethamine, sulfadiazine, and spiramycin (a macrolide antibiotic) can be used alone or in combination with corticosteroids in the treatment of infection. Folinic acid (Leukovorin calcium) may be concomittantly administered alongwith pyrimethamine to minimize the adverse effects of pyrimethamine on folic acid metabolism.

3.13 BALANTIDIASIS

This intestinal infection is caused by *Balantidium coli*, which is normally a parasite of pigs. Trophozoites may induce either a superficial necrosis or a deep ulceration in mucosa and submucosa of large intestine. This results into a variety of symptoms including nausea, vomiting, abdominal pain, diarrhoea or severe dysentery.

The infection can be treated by giving tetracycline, 500 mg four times daily for 10 days. Iodoquinol, 650 mg 3 times a day is also effective in the treatment of balantidiasis.

Other pathogenic intestinal protozoan infections include isosporiasis (*Isospora belli* and *I. hominis*) and *Pneumocystis carinii* infection. Both are treated with either pyrimethamine-sulphonamide or co-trimoxazole combination preparations. Pentamidine can be given intramuscularly to control pneumocystosis.

SULPHONAMIDES AND URINARY TRACT ANTISEPTIC AGENTS

4.1 INTRODUCTION

The modern chemotherapy and the concept of prodrug was successfully utilized with the introduction of sulphonamides. They were the first effective chemotherapeutic agents to be employed systemically.

Paul Ehrlich (1854 - 1915) is regarded as the father of modern chemotherapy due to his pioneering work in this field. He synthesized and successfully used Atoxyl in the treatment of sleeping sickness.

Atoxyl

The next major achievement in the field of chemotherapy is credited to **Gerhard Domagk**, a research director of Bayer laboratories, who in 1932, recognized the antibacterial activity of an azodye, Prontosil Red. It was found to be effective in the treatment of hemolytic streptococcal infections in the mice. For this work, he was awarded Nobel prize in Medicine in 1938. Though synthesized first in 1908, sulphonamides did not receive much attention till 1937 when it was proved by some workers at Pasteur Institute in France that prontosil is a prodrug and the active drug, sulfanilamide gets released into the body after *in-vivo* cleavage of the azo linkage.

This discovery led to the synthesis of atleast 5500 congeneric substances which are known as 'sulphonamides'. However, only few of them have retained the place in therapeutics. Sulphonamides are all white crystalline powders, mostly poorly soluble in water. Their sodium salts are usually used because of aqueous solubility. The solubility parameter is greatly influenced by the nature of the substituents on $-SO_2NH_2$ group. These substituents modify the chemical features of the molecule and hence, they play an important role in governing the rates of absorption and excretion of sulphonamides.

The term sulphonamide is usually employed as a generic name for the derivatives of para-amino benzene sulphonamides. Sulphonamides are bacteriostatic agents but in the rare circumstances where bacteria are exposed to thymineless medium, they may act as bactericidal. Sulfanilamide is the basic skeleton of this category. The successful exploitation of this lead nucleus opened up new avenues in the field of chemotherapy. Presence of free amino group (–NH$_2$) is essential for antibacterial activity. However, it can be replaced only by groups which can be reconverted in body to free amino group. Examples include acetamido (–NHCOCH$_3$), succinylamido and phthalylamido groups. The compounds in which these groups are present, may undergo metabolism to regenerate free amino functional group.

Pharmacologically, all sulphonamides exert similar actions. However, they differ from one another in solubility, rates of absorption, distribution, metabolism and excretion and in protein binding behaviour. Thus, all sulphonamides have same pharmacological action but different pharmacokinetic features. These differences served as the basis of their clinical classification. For example, relatively insoluble sulphonamides largely remain unabsorbed in GIT after oral administration. Hence, such agents may be of value in the treatment of GIT-infections, while the sulphonamides with rapid excretion feature may be used in the treatment of urinary tract infections.

Sulphonamides are less potent antibacterials than most antibiotics. Their antibacterial potential gradually drops by the presence of pus, tissue fluids and such drugs which contain para amino benzoic acid (PABA) as a basic skeleton (e.g. local anaesthetics). Moreover many *Staphylococci, Enterococci, Clostridia* and *Pseudomonas* species remain highly resistant to the sulphonamide action. The popularity of sulfonamides as antibacterial agents declined after 1945 because of following reasons :

(a) Publications of reports regarding sulphonamide toxicity in some patients.

(b) Development of sulphonamide-resistant bacterial strains, and

(c) Introduction of clinically more effective antibiotics.

However, the impression of the 'wonder drugs' created by penicillins in their early days unfortunately could not be maintained. Many factors contributed for their clinical devaluation. Acid-instability and microbial resistance were important amongst such factors. Attempts to synthesize new sulphonamides with improved qualities thus began in 1957 after realising clinical deficiencies associated with the use of antibiotics. The high clinical merits associated with the combination of trimethoprim and sulphamethoxazole reawakened the interest in sulphonamides. Many are still employed in the treatment of various bacterial, protozoal and viral infections.

4.2 NOMENCLATURE AND CLASSIFICATION

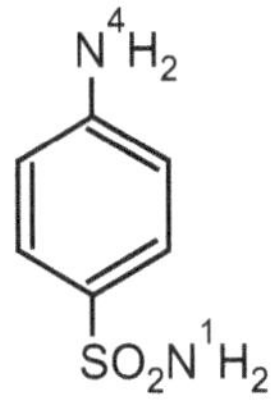

Sulphanilamide

Sulphonamides can be considered as the derivatives of para-amino benzene sulphonamide (i.e. sulphanilamide) skeleton. Since the sulphonamide ($-SO_2NH_2$) group is the most important moiety for the antibacterial activity of sulphonamides, the amide nitrogen is designated as N^1 while nitrogen of para amino functional group is designated as N^4. Most of the clinically used sulphonamides belong to the class of N^1-substituted sulphonamides.

A third but separate category is described by the term, sulphones where the basic nucleus is 4, 4'-diaminodiphenyl sulphone, rather than sulphanilamide.

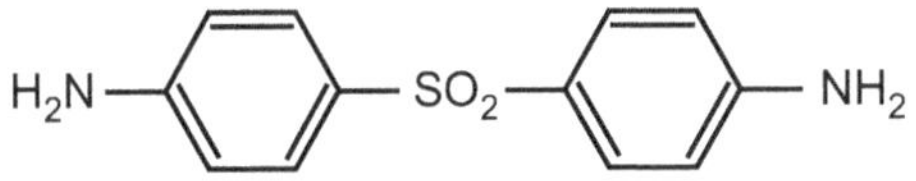

4, 4'-diaminodiphenyl sulphone

Sulphonamides can be classified in various ways. Many criteria can be utilized as the basis of their classification. These includes :

(a) On the basis of pharmacokinetic properties, they may be classified as:

(i) Agents which are rapidly absorbed and are rapidly excreted : They are also known as systemic sulphonamides. Examples include : sulphamethoxazole, sulfisoxazole, sulfapyridine, sulphadiazine.

(ii) Agents which are poorly absorbed in GIT : They are known as locally acting drugs. Their use is intended to exert local antibacterial effect in bowel lumen either to treat specific intestinal disease or to reduce luminal bacterial population prior to bowel surgery. This helps to reduce the changes of postoperative wound infection after colon surgery. Examples include sulphasalazine, phthalylsulfathiazole etc.

(iii) Agents which are employed topically : They are applied only in conjunctival sac, otic canal and vagina to treat bacterial infections. They may also be used topically to abolish bacterial colonization of burns. Examples include mafenide, sodium sulphacetamide and silver sulphadiazine.

(b) On the basis of chemical nature, they may be classified as :

(i) Agents carrying substituents on amino group : These are N^4-substituted sulphonamides which undergo metabolism in body to release free amino group. Hence, they may be considered as prodrugs. Examples include, prontosil, solucopticin.

(ii) Agents having substituents on amido group : These are N^1-substituted sulphonamides. Most of the clinically used sulphonamides belong to this category. Examples includes, sulphadiazine, sulphacetamide, sulphadimidine etc.

(iii) Agents having substituents at both, amino and amido nitrogens : They are also known as N^1, N^4 - disubstituted sulphonamides. Examples include succinyl sulphathiazole, phthalyl sulphathiazole etc.

(iv) Agents missing the amino functional group from the benzene nucleus : They are also known as non-anilino sulphonamides. Example includes mafenide.

(c) On the basis of pharmacological activity, sulphonamides can be categorized as :

(i) Antibacterial agents : Examples include sulphacetamide, sulphadiazine, sulphisoxazole etc.

(ii) Oral hypoglycemic agents : Example includes, tolbutamide.

(iii) Diuretics : Examples include, furosemide chlorthalidone, bumetanide etc.

(d) On the basis of duration of action, sulphonamides can be classified as :

(i) Long-acting sulphonamides : They have plasma half-life greater than 24 hours. They have a greater ability to cause hyper-sensitivity reactions. Examples include, sulfamethoxypyridazine, sulphamethoxy diazine, sulfadimethoxine.

(ii) Intermediate - acting sulphonamides : They have plasma half-life between 10 - 24 hours. Examples include sulphasomizole, sulphamethoxazole.

(iii) Short-acting sulphonamides : They have plasma half-life less than 10 hours. Examples include sulphamethizole, sulphasomidine, sulfisoxazole etc.

(iv) Ultra-longacting sulphonamides : These agents have plasma half-life greater than 50 hours. Examples include sulfalene, sulphormethoxine, sulphasalazine, sulfa-methopyrazine, sulfadoxine. (plasma half-life = 150 hours). These agents should never be used in patients with renal insufficiency. Recently a new broad spectrum sulpha drug, sulphaclomide has been introduced. It is found to achieve higher serum level than all presently available sulpha drugs.

4.3 PHARMACOKINETIC FEATURES OF SULPHONAMIDES

All sulphonamides in systemic use are well absorbed primarily in small intestine. On absorption, they are widely distributed to all organs and to pleural, peritoneal and articular body fluids. They are also able to cross placental barrier and are also found to appear in cerebrospinal fluid. These agents vary in their ability to bind with plasma-proteins. For example, sulphadiazine is poorly bound (20%) while sulphamerazine is 85% bound to the plasma-proteins. Usually acetylated derivatives are extensively bound to plasma-proteins. Protein binding of sulphonamides is directly proportional to plasma albumin concentration. Hence, renal adverse effects are more pronounced in patients having hypoalbuminea due to higher concentration of free drug in the plasma.

The main metabolic pathways for sulphonamides include acetylation and oxidation. Acetylated metabolites do not retain antibacterial activity. They are usually more toxic and less water-soluble than the parent drugs. The extent of acetylation for any sulphonamide is proportional to the duration of stay of that agent in the body.

Most of the metabolites and active drugs are excreted in the urine in free or glucuronidated form. Some loss may also occur in sweat, tears, saliva, milk and faeces. Sulphonamides accumulate in the patients suffering from renal failure.

4.4 ADVERSE EFFECTS

The toxicities of sulphonamides vary considerably and may have little relationship with the dose of the drug. Adverse effects of sulphonamides can be studied as per the organ involved. Below mentioned are some commonly encountered adverse effects :

(a) Gastro-intestinal tract : Adverse effects include nausea, vomiting, anorexia, diarrhoea, hepatitis etc.

(b) Urinary tract : More effective sulphonamides are usually less soluble in acidic urine. Moreover, acetylated metabolites of most of the sulphonamides are sparingly water-soluble. This leads to the deposition of crystalline aggregates of parent drug and/or its metabolites in the kidney, ureters or bladders. Oliguria, crystalluria and other renal complications may thus result. Such damage can result in epithelial irritability, bleeding and/or complete obstruction of kidneys.

The smooth excretion of drug is possible only when it is water soluble (ionized form). The water solubility of drug can be ensured by adjusting its pKa. Because urine pH is typically about 6, many sulpha drugs are designed to have pKa, closer to the pH of urine, for example, sulfamethoxazole (pKa = 6.1), sulfadiazine (pKa = 6.5) etc.

Crystal formation is dependent upon the solubility of sulphonamide, pH and volume of urine of the patient. Hence, patient undergoing sulphonamide therapy should consume adequate fluid so as to produce atleast 1.5 litres of urine per day. Chances of development of crystalluria may be minimized by :

(i) increasing the fluid intake and

(ii) keeping the pH of the urine in alkaline range by using alkalinizing agents (e.g. sodium salts of bicarbonate, lactate, acetate or citrate).

However, alkalinizing agents also lower down plasma sulphonamide concentration by enhancing its renal excretion.

(c) Nervous system : Effects on nervous system include headache, dizziness, confusion, mental depression, peripheral neuritis (motor and sensory neuropathy) and optic neuritis.

(d) Hematopoietic system : Effects include leukopenia, thrombocytopenia, agranulocytosis and marked decrease in erythrocytes and haemoglobin contents. Sulphonamides cause acute hemolytic anemia in patients with glucose - 6 phosphate dehydrogenase enzyme deficiency in their erythrocytes.

(e) Hypersensitivity reactions : These include, skin and mucous membrane eruptions, fever, headache, vascular lesions and serum sickness. Jaundice, hamaturia or sore throat are the indications to withdraw the drug immediately.

(f) Effects on foetus and neonate : Sulphonamides compete with bilirubin for the binding sites on plasma proteins (specifically on albumin). As a result, the unbound bilirubin concentration increases in patients under sulphonamide therapy. If sulphonamide is given to a pregnant woman, the unbound bilirubin may get deposited in basal ganglia and subthalamic nuclei in CNS of the foetus or newborn, causing kernicterus, a toxic encephalopathy. Hence, its use is contraindicated in case of newborns and pregnant women.

(g) Miscellaneous effects : These include conjunctivitis, porphyria, arthralgia and pulmonary eosinophilia. Sulphonamides also compete for binding sites on plasma albumin with many drugs like aspirin, phenylbutazone, coumarins and methotrexate. Hence, sulphonamides may cause sudden and unexpected rise in the plasma concentration of these drugs by displacing them from plasma-proteins. This results into the appearance of adverse effects characteristic of displaced drug.

Due to this reason sulphonamides should be carefully administered in individuals on above drug therapy.

4.5 MECHANISM OF ACTION

The therapeutic effect of sulphonamides is achieved by arresting the growth and multiplication of the infectious organism and thus allowing the host to eradicate the infection by its cellular and humoral defense mechanisms. Various folate derivatives like, folinic acid; N^5, N^{10}-methylenetetrahydrofolic acid and N^{10}-formyltetrahydrofolic acid act as coenzymes in transport of one-carbon units in several biochemical reactions in human and microorganisms. These one carbon transfer reactions are necessary for the synthesis of purines, thymidine and some amino acids.

One of the products of these folate dependent biochemical reactions is deoxy-thymidine monophosphate which is involved in nucleic acid synthesis. Sulphonamides block the biosynthesis of these folate coenzymes resulting into the arrest of bacterial growth and cell division.

Filds and **Woods** independently suggested in 1940, that the para-amino benzoic acid (PABA) is essential in the biosynthesis of various folate enzymes and cofactors. The structural similarity with PABA results into competitive inhibition of take-up of PABA in microorganisms by sulphonamides. Sulphonamides inhibit the incorporation of PABA in dihydropteroic acid which is a precursor of folic acid needed for the synthesis of DNA and 1-carbon fragments. Thus, by acting as antimetabolite, sulphonamides prevent the formation of pteroylglutamic acid (PGA) in microorganisms. Mammalian cells can utilize the preformed PGA present in the diet while bacterial cells can not utilise preformed PGA and they have to synthesize PGA from PABA. Hence, sulphonamides do not affect mammalian cells.

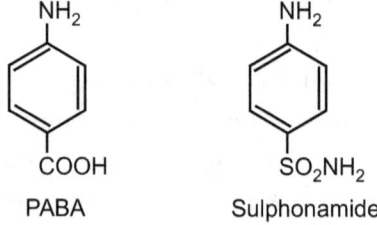

The antibacterial action of sulphonamides depends upon :

(i) the form (ionized/unionized) in which they are circulated in the body and

(ii) the dose of sulphonamide. Greater the concentration of drug in the plasma, greater will be the activity.

PABA has much greater affinity for the bacterial enzyme system. Since sulphonamide activity is based upon the principle of competitive antagonism, it is necessary to maintain always a high concentration of sulpha drug in the tissue to achieve the desired effect. Hence certain drugs having PABA as the basic skeleton (e.g. procaine) will antagonize the action of sulphonamides *in-vivo*.

Sulphonamides exert only bacteriostatic effect in the body. They possess a wide range of antimicrobial activity against both, gram-positive and gram-negative bacteria. These include, *Mycobacterium tuberculosis, Strep. pneumoniae, Haemophilus influenzae, Corynebacterium diphtheria, Nocardia, Actinomyces, E. Coli, Meningococci* etc. Sulphonamides are therefore used for treating tonsillitis, septicaemia, pneumonia, meningococcal meningitis, bacillary dysentery and a number of infections of urinary tract.

The conversion of dihydrofolic acid to tetrahydrofolic acid is catalyzed by the enzyme, dihydrofolate reductase. Trimethoprim is a potent and selective competitive inhibitor of this enzyme. It appears to be the most active agent that exerts a synergistic antibacterial activity when combined with a sulpha drug. Combination of sulpha drug with other bacteriostatic agent (e.g. tetracycline) may also give synergistic effect, while in antimalarial therapy, pyrimethamine and sulpha combination yields synergistic effect.

4.6 BACTERIAL RESISTANCE

Wide and non-selective use of sulpha drugs lead to the development of drug-resistant bacterial strains. First seen in *N. gonorrhoeae*, resistance to sulpha drugs then rapidly developed in the variety of *Staphylococci*, Hemolytic streptococci, meningococci, Pneumococci and *Shigellae*.

The bacterial resistance may be :

(1) Natural (intrinsic) resistance or

(2) Acquired resistance.

Bacterial resistance develops mainly due to mutation process. Bacterial plasmids can cause production of altered enzyme that can bypass the due affinity for sulphonamides. Other possible mechanisms of bacterial resistance include :

(a) An increased production of PABA in the bacterial cell,

(b) An increased ability of bacterial cell to destroy or inactivate the sulpha drug,

(c) Production of sulpha drug antagonist by the bacterial cell,

(d) Decreased bacterial permeability to sulpha drug,

(e) A production of an altered dihydrofolate reductase.

The development of drug resistance severely limits the therapeutic efficacy of the drug. If a microorganism is resistant to one sulphonamide, it develops resistance against all sulphonamides. Similarly, the sulphonamide-sensitive species may develop drug resistance when it comes in contact with a resistant bacterial species. Studies have shown that the use of trimethoprim with sulfamethoxazole may reduce development of resistance to sulpha drugs.

4.7 THERAPEUTIC USES

Depending upon the solubility, sulphonamides may be used systemically, topically or may be used orally for local effects.

Following are some principle uses of sulphonamides :

1. Uncomplicated urinary tract infections :
2. Intestinal infections :
   e.g. sulphaguanidine
3. Ophthalmic infections :
   e.g. sulphacetamide
4. Ulcerative colitis :
   e.g. salicylazosulfapyridine
5. Rheumatic fever :
   e.g. sulfadiazin, sulfisoxazole.
6. Nocardiosis :
   e.g. sulfadiazine, sulfisoxazole
7. Chancroid (a veneral infection caused by Haemophilus ducreyi) :
   e.g. sulfasalazine.
8. Toxoplasmosis : e.g. sulpha drug with pyrimethamine.
9. Respiratory tract infections :
   e.g. Cotrimoxazole.
10. Otitis media : sulpha drug is used in combination with erythromycin.
11. Dermatitis herpetiformis :
    e.g. sulfapyridine
12. Vaginal infections :
    e.g. sulfisoxazole diethanolamine.
13. Infected burns :
    e.g. silver sulfadiazine.
14. Meningococcal meningitis :
    e.g. sulfadiazine.
15. Trachoma and inclusion conjunctivitis : sulfisoxazole, sulfadiazine, sulfacetamide etc.

4.8 SAR STUDIES OF SULPHONAMIDES

Sulphonamide being an important chemical class, several thousand sulphonamides had been investigated for their activity on infective organisms. In antibacterial therapy, they are placed next to antibiotics, sometimes even preferred over the latter.

The major features of SAR of sulphonamides include :

(a) Sulphanilamide skeleton is the minimum structural requirement for antibacterial activity.

(b) Sulfur atom should be directly linked to the benzene ring.

(c) In N^1-substituted sulphonamides, activity varies with the nature of the substituent at amido group. With substituents, imparting electron rich character to SO_2 group, bacteriostatic activity increases. Heterocyclic substituents lead to highly potent derivatives. Sulphonamides that contain a single benzene ring at N^1- position, are considerably more toxic than heterocyclic ring analogs.

(d) The free aromatic amino group should reside para to the sulphonamido group. Its substitution at ortho or meta position results in compounds devoid of antibacterial activity.

$$H_2N-\underset{\text{Unionized}}{\underline{\bigcirc}}-SO_2NH_2 \rightleftharpoons H_2N-\underset{\text{Ionized}}{\underline{\bigcirc}}-SO_2-\overset{\ominus}{N}H + \overset{\oplus}{H}$$

(e) The presence of free amino group is very essential for the activity. Any substitution of amino group either results in prodrug nature or in the loss of activity.

(f) The active form of sulphonamides is the ionized form. Maximum activity is observed between the pKa values 6.6 to 7.4.

(g) Substitutions in the benzene ring of sulphonamides have also been tried. All attempts ended up in the formation of inactive compounds.

(h) Substitution of free sulfonic acid ($-SO_3H$) group for sulphonamido function, destroys the activity but replacement by a sulfinic acid group ($-SO_2H$) and acetylation of N^4-position retains the activity.

4.9 SYSTEMIC SULPHONAMIDES

These agents are rapidly absorbed into the circulation when given orally. They can also be given parenterally. They are readily excreted from the body by the efficient excretion process. Depending upon their duration of action, they can be further sub-divided into :

(i) short-acting sulphonamides,
(ii) intermediate-acting sulphonamides, and
(iii) long-acting sulphonamides.

Along with the therapy of systemic sulphonamides, an adequate fluid intake is necessary to minimize the risk of crystalluria. In certain cases, urinary alkalinizer may also be tried to help rapid excretion of the drug and/or its metabolites.

(a) Sulfisoxazole :

It is an example of short-acting sulphonamide. Other examples of this group include sulfamethizole, sulfacetamide, sulfamerazine, sulfamethazine, sulfisomidine and sulfadiazine. All these are capable of causing crystalluria. A mixture of sulfamerazine, sulfamethazine and sulphacetamide is marketed under the name of trisulfapyrimidine. It has an advantage of low potential to cause crystalluria.

Sulfisoxazole is an orally effective agent. About 91 - 93% of administered dose is bound to the plasma proteins. It has a plasma half-life of 7.0 hours. About 40 % dose appears unchanged in the urine along with 20-30% dose in acetylated form.

Adverse effects include nausea, vomiting, anorexia, diarrhoea, dizziness, hypersensitivity reactions, crystalluria and blood dyscrasias.

It is available in a fixed dose combination (sulfisoxazole, 500 mg and phenazopyridine, 50 mg) form which is used in the treatment of urinary tract infections caused by the susceptible strains of *E. Coli, Klebsiella, S. aureus, P. mirabilis* and *Proteus vulgaris*. It may also be used alongwith erythromycin ethyl succinate in the treatment of otitis media, specifically in children. Sulfisoxazole and sulfadiazine may be used prophylactically to control *streptococcal* infections in rheumatic fever patients who are hypersensitive to penicillins. It may be used as an alternative drug for the treatment of meliodiosis caused by *Pseudomonas pseudomallei* and for the infections caused by *Nocardiae*. It may also be used topically as a 10% cream in the treatment of infections of eye, ear, nose or vagina.

(b) Sulphadiazine :

It is an orally active sulphonamide used in the treatment of nocardiosis and other infections caused by *Chlamydia* and *Toxoplasma gondii*. Optimal antibacterial activity was probably achieved in 1908 with the introduction of this agent. About 54 - 58% of administered dose is bound to the plasma proteins. It has a plasma half-life of 7 - 10 hours. About 30 - 40% dose is acetylated during metabolism. It is excreted in the urine along with about 55 - 60% dose in unchanged form. Its relative insolubility in acidic urine exposes the patient to the high risk of crystalluria. Hence, adequate sodium bicarbonate (a urine alkalinizer) should be given.

It may be used intravenously in the therapy of meningitis and for prophylaxis against meningococcal meningitis if *Neisseria* is the basic cause. It is also used as an antimalarial agent when given in combination with pyrimethamine.

4.10 LOCALLY ACTING SULPHONAMIDES

These agents are poorly absorbed from GIT when they are given orally. Hence they are intended to be used for exerting local sterilizing effect on the bowel. Examples of such agents include, phthalylsulfathiazole, succinyl sulfathiazole, phthalylsulfacetamide and salicylazosulfapyridine. All these are the examples of N^1, N^4 - disubstituted sulphonamides in which an organic acid is conjugated at N^4-position.

Salicylazosulfapyridine (sulfasalazine) :

It is a poor orally absorbed sulphonamide that does not have antibacterial activity. It splits in the gut into sulfapyridine and 5-aminosalicylic acid moieties. The former is absorbed systemically and appears in the urine while the latter is excreted in the faeces. The enzymes responsible for splitting of sulfasalazine are azoreductases, amidases, and glycosidases.

Hence, it is effective in inflammatory bowel disease. Part of its effectiveness is attributed to anti-inflammatory effects of 5-aminosalicylate. It also inhibits prostaglandin synthesis.

Adverse effects include nausea, vomiting, anorexia, gastric distress, pancreatitis, headache, rashes, fever, arthralgia, anaemia, agranulocytosis and thrombocytopenia.

It is effective in the long-term treatment of ulcerative colitis, granulamatous colitis and regional enteritis. It may also be used in the therapy of malaria, conjunctivitis, meningococcal meningitis, nocardiosis, otitis media, toxoplasmosis and chancroid (a venereal infection caused by *Haemophilus ducreyi*).

4.11 TOPICALLY USED SULPHONAMIDES

These agents are extremely useful in decreasing the bacterial colonization of burnt skin and thereby preventing burn-wound sepsis. For antibacterial effect, they may also be applied topically to eye, ear, nose, and vagina. Examples include, mafenide, silver sulfadiazine, sulfapyridine, sulfisoxazole diethanolamine and sodium sulfacetamide.

(a) Mafenide acetate :

It is a sulphonamide antibacterial agent effective against *Pseudomonas aeruginosa*, an organism that colonizes the burns. It is effective in the presence of necrotic tissue and also inhibits other gram-positive and gram-negative bacteria. It is partly absorbed systemically upon topical application and is converted to p-carboxylbenzene sulphonamide. In the form of acetate, it may act as carbonic anhydrase inhibitor and cause either alkalosis or acidosis.

Adverse effects include skin rashes, eczema, urticaria, exfoliative dermatitis, metabolic acidosis, intense pain at the site of application and chances of superinfection with Candida.

It is available as a cream containing 85 mg/g of mafenide and is applied once or twice a day over burnt skin till desired response is obtained. Occasional cleansing of wound and removal of debris is necessary.

(b) Silver sulphadiazine :

Silver ions are especially effective against *Gonococci* and *Pseudomonas* species. Silver salts are highly germicidal. Silver sulphadiazine is available in microionized form. It may be used topically in the form of cream (10 mg/g) to inhibit the growth of most bacteria, yeast form of some fungi and herpes simplex. It is effectively used to treat extensive burns and burn infections.

Sulfapyridine is relatively toxic and less effective antibacterial agent. It may be of some value in the treatment of dermatitis herpetiformis. While in the form of eye-drops, sodium sulphacetamide may be used to treat blepharitis and conjuctivitis, and may also be used in prophylaxis against trachoma and inclusion conjuctivitis. It penetrates into the ocular tissues in high concentration, hence it is suitable for local management of ophthalmic infections.

4.12 TRIMETHOPRIM-SULPHONAMIDE COMBINATION (CO-TRIMOXAZOLE)

The synergistic effect achieved by the combination of trimethoprim and sulpha-methoxazole is recognized as the major advance in the field of chemotherapy.

Bacteriostatic activity is observed due to the inhibition of two prominent steps in bacterial enzymatic pathway involved in folate synthesis. Sulphamethoxazole inhibits utilisation of PABA in the formation of dihydrofolate, while trimethoprim is a potent and selective inhibitor of the enzyme that catalyzes the conversion of dihydrofolate to tetrahydrofolate. Thus, a synergistic antimicrobial effect is observed due to the double sequential effects on the bacterial metabolism.

Originally introduced as antimalarial agent, trimethoprim has also shown significant bacteriostatic activity. It is effective against most of the gram-positive and gram-negative organisms with exceptions of *P. aeruginosa* and *S. faecalis*.

Sulphamethoxazole was selected from systemic sulphonamide class on the basis that it has similar pharmacokinetic features (i.e. rates of absorption and elimination) to that of trimethoprim. It is hence co-administered with trimethoprim in a fixed dose ratio of 5 : 1. This dose ratio yields a fairly constant plasma concentration of sulphamethoxazole - trimethoprim as 20 : 1 ratio which is found to be the most effective concentration range for exhibiting synergistic effect against most of the pathogenic microorganisms.

Co-trimoxazole is thus effective against most gram-positive cocci and gram-negative bacteria. *Neisseria meningitidis* and *Gonococci* are also susceptible. It is used in the treatment of infections of urinary, intestinal and lower respiratory tracts. It is also effective in the treatment of acute otitis media, chronic bacterial prostatis, meningococcal infections, gonorrhea, nocardiosis and antibiotic resistant *Salmonellae* and *Shigellae* infections.

This combination preparation is preferably used in the treatment of acute and recurrent urinary tract infections, typhoid fever, brucellosis, endocarditis, salmonella sepsis, acute bacterial exacerbations of chronic bronchitis and pneumocystis.

Adverse effects of this combination arise as the summation of adverse effects of individual components. However, most of the adverse effects of cotrimoxazole are mainly due to sulphamethoxazole moiety. Trimethoprim just helps to intensify some of these (e.g. hematologic adverse effects) toxicities.

4.13 URINARY TRACT INFECTIONS

Many drugs are used to control urinary tract infections mainly because of their ability to develop enough concentration in urinary bladder which is adequate to inhibit the growth of infective organisms. Examples include nitrofurantoin, nalidixic acid, oxolinic acid, resoxacin, norfloxacin, cinoxacin and methenamine. Several other 4-quinolones, such as ciprofloxacin, amifloxacin, enoxacin etc. are under clinical investigations.

(a) Nitrofurantoin :

It is an orally active nitrofuran antibacterial agent effective against various strains of *E. coli*, *Klebsiella*, *Proteus* species and *S. faecalis*. Chemically it is N-(5-nitro-2-furfurylidine) - 1 - aminohydantoin.

The antibacterial activity is due to the presence of 5-nitro group which helps to generate the superoxide and other toxic oxygen compound by undergoing conversion to nitro anion. The latter undergoes interaction with molecular oxygen leading to formation of superoxide and the original nitro group. The former interferes with the carbohydrate metabolism in bacteria. It does not affect the functioning of human cell because of its low serum concentration and rapid rate of drug metabolism in liver. Antibacterial activity can be potentiated in acid pH range. Alkalinization of urine enhances the rate of excretion in urine and also lowers down its antibacterial efficacy. It is a bacteriostatic in low concentrations while exerts bactericidal effect at higher concentrations.

It exhibits antibacterial activity against most of the organisms causing lower urinary tract infections. It may also be used to prevent recurrences of these infections and it may also be used to prevent bacteriuria after prostatectomy. Resistance in bacteria may develop during the treatment. This may be because of formation of nitroso and hydroxyamine metabolites which act as mutagens. It is contraindicated in children below one month of age and in patients with pregnancy or renal dysfunction.

(b) Nalidixic acid :

It is an orally active antibacterial agent belonging to 4-quinolone series. Its introduction in 1962 was followed by development of other agents from this class. These include cinoxacin, oxolinic acid, resoxacin, norfloxacin, ciprofloxacin and amifloxacin. All these are found to be effective against most of gram-negative bacteria, *staphylococci* and *P. aeruginosa*.

Nalidixic acid is effective against *E.coli, P.mirabilis, Klebsiella, Enterobacter, Coliform* bacteria and some *Shigellae*. Hence, it is used as a bactericidal agent in the treatment of urinary tract infections caused by all the above gram-negative bacteria. It acts by inhibiting DNA - gyrase enzyme that is responsible for unwinding of supercoiled bacterial DNA prior to its replication and transcription. Bacteria, however can readily develop resistance to its action.

About 93 - 97 % of administered dose is bound to the plasma-proteins. It has a plasma half-life of 8 hours. Active hydroxynalidixic acid metabolite is excreted as conjugated form in the urine alongwith 2 - 3 % dose in unchanged form. About 4 - 5 % dose also appears unchanged in the faeces.

Adverse effects include nausea, vomiting, abdominal pain, urticaria, eosinophilia, photosensitivity, headache, vertigo, dizziness, weakness, drowsiness, visual disturbances, hallucinations, hemolytic anaemia, leukopenia and thrombocytopenia. It should not be used in infants under 3 months of age because of their inability to metabolize or excrete nalidixic acid efficiently.

It is also useful in the treatment of mild to moderate forms of gastroenteritis.

Cinoxacin is an orally active antibacterial agent having structural similarity with nalidixic acid. About 63% of administered dose is bound to the plasma proteins. It has a plasma half-life of 1.5 hours. About 60% dose appears in urine in unchanged form alongwith 30 - 40 % dose as inactive metabolites.

Oxolinic acid is yet another 4-quinolone having potent antibacterial activity. It is extensively metabolized in the liver. Inactive metabolites in the form of glucuronides appear in the urine alongwith 5% dose in unchanged form. Adverse effects and therapeutic uses are similar to those of nalidixic acid.

Ciprofloxacin and norfloxacin are the examples of other orally active quinolone antibacterial agents used in the treatment of urinary tract infections. Rosoxacin is the member of same class but it is not used in the treatment of urinary tract infections. It is extremely effective against penicillin-resistant strains and is preferred in the treatment of gonorrhoea.

(c) Methenamine (Hexamine or Hexamethylenetetramine) :

It is an orally active urinary tract antiseptic agent used in the form of either mandelate or hippurate. If administered in the form of normal tablet, a considerable amount (about 10–30%) of methenamine decomposes in the stomach due to acidic pH. Hence, it is to be supplied in the form of enteric coated tablet. In circulation it remains unmetabolized. In acidic urine of pH = 5.5 or lower, it spontaneously decomposes to ammonia and formaldehyde. The latter agent (alkylating agent) denatures bacterial protein and acts as a non-specific antibacterial agent effective against both gram-positive and gram-negative bacteria. Acidic urine is must for the liberation of formaldehyde. However, some bacteria (e.g., *Proteus* species) prevent normal urinary acidification by releasing ammonia from urea. Hence, methenamine is usually administered as a salt of mandelic, hippuric or ascorbic acid to impart acidic pH to the urine. Beside this function, all these acids also exerts antibacterial property.

Adverse effects include nausea, stomach upset, epigastric distress, bladder irritation, skin rash, pruritus, albuminurea, crystalluria and painful and frequent micturition. It is contraindicated in patients with renal insufficiency.

MODES OF ACTION OF ANTIBIOTICS

5.1 INTRODUCTION

The term chemotherapy can be defined as 'the treatment of diseases caused due to infective parasites or organisms' without causing destruction of their host cells'. Modern chemotherapy began with the work of **Paul Ehrlich** (1854 - 1915). Due to his pioneer discoveries in this field, he is regarded as 'Father of Chemotherapy'.

The second phase of revolution emerged in 1930's following the discovery of the British bacteriologist, **Alexander Fleming** when he tested the filtrate of a broth culture of a *Penicillium* mould for its antibacterial activity.

The term antibiotic has its origin in the word, antibiosis (i.e against life); the latter being first time used by **Vuillemin** in 1889 in an attempt to describe the concept of survival of the fittest. Although the discovery of penicillin is named after Sir Alexander Fleming in 1928, it was not until 1940 at Oxford that **Florey** and **Chain** and their associates isolated it and described its properties in detail and thus turning Fleming's discovery to practical significance. Among many attempts to define the term, antibiotic, the most appropriate one may be stated as *"Antibiotic is a chemical agent derived from or metabolically produced by microorganism and that in high dilution it antagonizes the growth and/or the survival of one or more species of microorganisms"*. The probable points of differences amongst antibiotics include physical, chemical and pharmacological properties, antibacterial spectra and mechanism of action.

Park et al in 1952, reported the isolation of first nucleotide linked precursor of peptidoglycan from *Staphylococcus aureus* grown in the presence of benzylpenicillin. They were later identified as uridine diphosphate-acetylmuramyl pentapeptide and its breakdown products like uridine - 5' - pyrophosphate and N-acetylmuramic acid. Park nucleotides as they are known, were already shown to be an integral part of the bacterial cell-wall structure. This key observation by Park, led the foundation of the concept that penicillin interfers in the biosynthesis of bacterial cell-wall.

In all bacteria, the cell-wall offers protection to the cytoplasmic membrane against changes in osmotic pressure. The cytoplasmic membrane is a fragile structure and is the site of most of the biological processes of the cell. Any defect in the cell-wall, therefore, may cause the lysis of cytoplasmic membrane and will indirectly impair protein synthesis in bacteria.

Table 5.1 : Landmarks in the field of antibacterial agents

Scientists	Discovery	Period
1. Paul Ehrlich	Father of chemotherapy	1854 - 1915
2. Sir Alexander Fleming	Penicillin	1929
3. Domagk	Prontosil and sulphonamides	1932 - 1935
4. Florey	Penicillin isolation	1939
5. Waksman	Streptomycin	1944
6. Steinberg	Amphotericin B	1956
7 Gentiles	Griseofulvin	1958
8. Prusoff	Clinical use of iodoxuridine	1959
9. Bauer	Clinical use of β-isatin thiosemicarbazone	1962

The walls of all bacteria contain peptidoglycan as their main structural components. This cell-wall polymer protects the bacterium from the lysis in a hypotonic environment. In gram-positive bacteria, peptidoglycan is the major constituent of the cell-wall and may account for as much as 80% of total weight of the wall. However, in gram-negative bacteria, it represents only a minor component of the cell-wall. Peptidoglycan is thus a vital component of bacterial cell wall which offers a network of high tensile strength and rigidity. It is formed by cross-linking of the glycan chains. Some glycan chains may remain uncross-linked and may get interspread through the peptidoglycan network.

Due to the simplified structure of gram-positive bacteria, they are highly susceptible to the action of β–lactam antibiotics due to the freely permeable nature of their cell-wall. The bacterial cell-lysis occurs due to the activation of autolytic peptidoglycan hydrolases by β-lactam antibiotics. In gram-negative bacteria, however, above the peptidoglycan, a complex outer membrane is present which contains lipoproteins (linked covalently with the peptidoglycan), phospholipids, lipopoly-saccharide and other components. Through its selective

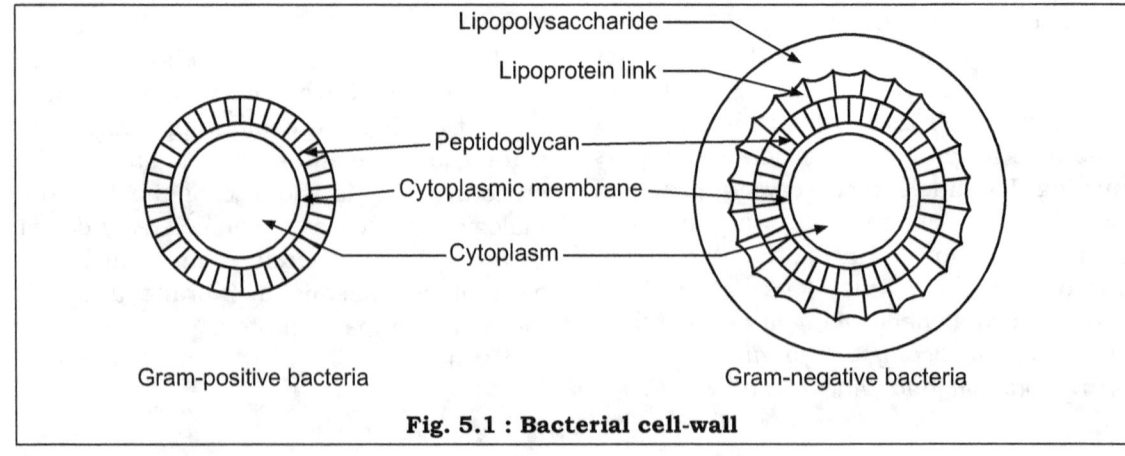

Fig. 5.1 : Bacterial cell-wall

permeable nature, the outer membrane effectively controls the composition of periplasmic fluid that lies between the outer membrane and the cytoplasmic membrane. The permeability of outer membrane greatly varies among gram-negative bacteria, being generally high in *Neisseria*, intermediate in *Enterobacteriaceae* and very low in *Pseudomonads*. Periplasmic fluid is the main site where the β-lactamase enzymes are present in the higher concentration and they decrease the ability of β-lactam antibiotic to enter the gram-negative bacteria. Thus, the selective permeability of the outer membrane and the presence of β-lactamases in the periplasmic fluid are the main factors that lowers the effectiveness of β-lactam antibiotics against gram-negative microorganisms.

5.2 PENICILLIN-BINDING PROTEINS (PBP)

The bacterial cell-wall consists of specific binding sites for β-lactam antibiotics. These membrane-associated binding sites for antibiotics are known as penicillin-binding proteins. These are nothing but the enzymes (i.e. transpeptidases and carboxypeptidases) which are actually involved in the terminal stages of peptidoglycan biosynthesis. Inactivation of these enzymes occurs mainly through the formation of penicilloyl ester linkages. This results into immediate biochemical defects in the synthesis of cell-wall peptidoglycan.

In gram-negative bacteria, penicillin binding proteins are present in the periplasmic fluid. Due to the high concentration of β-lactamases in this region, it becomes difficult for β-lactam antibiotic to bind with these proteins and to produce biochemical defects in the synthesis of cell-wall. Moreover, the impressive variety of β-lactamases that gram-negative bacteria are able to produce, helps the organism to hydrolyze both penicillin and cephalosporins. The highly permeable nature of gram-positive bacteria allows the easy passage of not only all β-lactam antibiotics but also the penetration of larger antibiotics (e.g. bacitracin, vancomycin etc.) which otherwise remain ineffective against gram-negative bacteria due to their poor penetration ability.

Most of the bacteria produce β-lactamase enzymes. These enzymes hydrolyze the β-lactam ring of different β-lactam antibiotics including penicillins and cephalosporins. It involves the formation of an acyl enzyme intermediate that is probably important in all β-lactamase reactions. Studies with several different β-lactamases have implicated a serine residue as a site for acetylation. After some time, deacetylation occurs to release hydrolyzed β-lactam molecule and a normal β-lactamase enzyme.

The number of penicillin-binding proteins present varies between 10^3 to 10^4 per bacterial cell. Depending upon the molecular weight, these proteins can be broadly catagorised as :

(i) abundant but relatively low molecular weight penicillin-binding proteins, and

(ii) less but relatively high molecular weight penicillin-binding proteins.

5.3 BACTERIAL RESISTANCE TO THE ANTIBIOTICS

The emergence of microbial strains that are resistant to the antibacterial agents obviously limits therapeutic value of these agents. Various mechanisms have been put forward to explain the development of resistant strains of micro-organisms.

(a) The production of β-lactamase enzymes will continue to be an extremely important mechanism of resistance to β–lactam antibiotics. The presence of β–lactamases lowers down the concentration of antibiotic and decreases the binding of antibiotic to the penicillin-binding proteins present in the bacterial cell-wall.

(b) Resistance to the antibiotic action also develops due to modifications in penicillin-binding proteins through the mutational-effects. This leads to reduction in the penetration ability of the antibiotic. Such mutational changes in binding proteins are reported to occur in methicillin-resistant strains of *S. aureus*, pneumococci and gonococcus and in moxalactam treated gram-negative bacilli. Mutation generally occurs at a frequency of 1 in 10^5 - 10^{10} cell division. Resistance to streptomycin by enteric bacilli constitutes the example of spontaneous single step mutation while resistance to penicillin by gonococci exemplifies the development of slow step-wise resistance. Such resistance developed through genetic mechanisms are transformed from resistant cell to the sensitive cell in bacteria by transduction, transformation or conjugation process.

(c) The penetration of the antibiotic in the bacterial cell is governed by permeability of the cell-wall and energy supplied for the transportation. The transport of antibiotic may be hampered due to lack of energy. This may be induced by mutational or a plasmid coded product that interferes in the synthesis of ATP. Moreover alterations in the structural features of the antibiotic results into reduced transportation and decreased affinity of antibiotic to its binding sites. This specifically is reported to occur with aminoglycosides.

Nalidixic acid group and polymyxins are the only exceptional examples of antibacterial agents to which plasmid resistance is not reported to develop.

Table 5.2 : Bacteria where resistance develops through plasmid mediated mechanisms

Gram-positive bacteria	Gram-negative bacteria
(1) *Bacillus* species	*Citrobacter* species
(2) *Clostridium perfringens*	*Enterobacter* species
(3) *Staphylococcus aureus*	*Escherichia coli*
(4) *Staphylococcus epidermidis*	*Haemophilus influenzae*
(5) *Streptococcus faecalis*	*Neisseria gonorrhoeae*
(6) *Streptococcus pyogens*	*Pseudomonas* species
(7) *Streptococcus pneumoniae*	*Salmonella* species

(d) Sometimes the microorganisms may acquire resistance to the action of antibiotic by developing a totally separate pathway resistant to the attack of antibiotic. Thus, resistance develops due to bypassing the antibiotic-sensitive metabolic step. In these bypass mechanisms, a plasmid provides a cell with an enzyme that is refractory to the action of antibiotic. For example, *E. coli* when treated, with trimethoprim develops resistance due to designing of an altered dihydrofolate reductase enzyme.

In certain cases resistance may be acquired by reducing the demand of the metabolite which is influenced by the anti-bacterial agent. For example, sulphonamide-resistant strains of *Neisseria* requires less thymine than the sensitive strains.

(e) The antibiotic agent, instead of attacking the microorganism, may be utilised to antagonise a biochemical intermediate that is released by microorganism itself.

Table 5.3 : Pathogenic microorganisms causing infections in humans

Microorganism	Possible infection
(A) Gram-positive cocci	
1. *Staphylococcus aureus*	Abscesses, bacteremia, cellulitis, endocarditis, meningitis, osteomyelitis, pneumonia etc.
2. *Streptococcus bovis*	Bacteremia, endocarditis
3. *Streptococcus pyogenes*	Bacteremia, cellulitis, erysipelas, otitis media, pharyngitis, acute pneumonia, scarlet fever, sinusitis etc.
4. *Streptococcus agalactiae*	Bacteremia, meningitis, septicemia etc.
5. *Streptococcus faecalis* (Enterococcus)	Bacteremia, endocarditis and urinary tract infections
6. *Streptococcus viridans*	Bacteremia, endocarditis
7. *Streptococcus pneumoniae*	Arthritis, endocarditis, meningitis, otitis media, pneumonia, sinusitis etc.
8. *Streptococcus* (anaerobic)	Bacteremia, endocarditis, localized abscesses, sinusitis etc.
(B) Gram-negative cocci	
1. *Neisseria gonorrhoeae*	Gonorrhea and other infections of genitalia
2. *Neisseria meningitidis* (meningococcus)	Bacterimia, meningitis

contd...

(C)	**Gram-positive bacilli**	
1.	*Bacillus anthracis*	Anthrax, pneumonia
2.	*Clostridium botulinum*	Botulism
3.	*Clostridium perfringens* (welchii)	Gas gangrene
4.	*Clostridium tetani*	Tetanus
5.	*Corynebacterium diphtheriae*	Diphtheria
6.	*Listeria monocytogenes*	Bacteremia, endocarditis, meningitis
(D)	**Gram-negative bacilli**	
1.	*Aeromonas hydrophilia*	Osteomyelitis, septicemia, wound infections etc. Otitis media, sinusitis, oral infections etc.
2.	*Bacteroides* species	Bacteremia, endocarditis and tissue abscesses mainly in brain, intra-abdominal region and lung
3.	*Bacteroides fragillis*	
		Whooping cough
4.	*Bordetella pertussis*	Brucellosis
5.	*Brucella abortus*	Bacteremia, enteritis
6.	Campylobacter *fetus*	Infections of respiratory and urinary tracts
7.	*Citrobacter* species	Urinary tract infections
8.	*Enterobacter* aerogenes	Bacteremia, urinary tract infections
9.	*Escherichia coli*	Meningitis
10.	*Flavobacterium meningosepticum*	
11.	*Fusobacteriae*	Empyema, genital infections, lung abscess, ulcerative pharyngitis etc.
12.	*Haemophilus ducreyi*	Chancroid
13.	*Haemophilus influenzae*	Bronchitis, meningitis, otitis media, pneumonia, sinusitis, respiratory tract infections etc.
14.	*Haemophilus vaginalis*	Vaginitis, urethritis
15.	*Klebsiella pneumonia*	Pneumonia, urinary tract infections.
16.	*Pasteurella multocida*	Bacteremia, abscesses, meningitis etc.
17.	*Proteus mirabilis*	Urinary tract infections
18.	*Providencia*	Infections of urinary and respiratory tracts
19.	*Pseudomonas aeruginosa*	Bacteremia and infections of urinary and respiratory tracts
20.	*Salmonella typhi*	Typhoid fever
21.	*Salmonella* species	Bacteremia, gastroenteritis, paratyphoid fever, typhoid fever etc.
22.	*Shigella* species	Gastroenteritis
23.	*Vibrio cholerae*	Cholera
24.	*Yersinia pestis*	Plague
25.	*Treponema pallidum*	Syphilis

contd...

(E) Acid - fast bacilli	
1. *Mycobacterium leprae*	Leprosy
2. *Mycobacterium tuberculoseae*	Renal, meningeal, miliary and pulmonary tuberculous infections.
(F) Miscellaneous organisms	
1. *Borrelia recurrentis*	Relapsing fever
2. *Actinomyces israelii*	Abdominal, cervicofacial and thoracic lesions
3. *Chalamydia trachomatis*	Inclusion conjunctivitis, pneumonia, trachoma and urethritis
4. *Mycoplasma pneumoniae*	Atypical pneumonia
5. Urea plasma urealyticum	Urethritis

5.4 PATHOGENIC MICROORGANISMS

In 1877, **Pasteur** and **Joubert** reported for the first time the pathogenic potential of microorganisms. Thereafter the era of chemotherapy began. The term chemotherapy, first coined by **Paul Ehrlich**, can be defined as *"treatment of infection caused by pathogenic microorganisms leaving the host unaffected."* Microorganisms may gain entry to the tissues of the body; may release poisonous substances (toxins); may establish themselves in the organ and may alarm fatal reactions in the host. The whole process can be described as an infection. From the sites of initial infections, organisms may pass into the circulating blood and accommodate themselves at suitable places to release their next generations. The anti-bacterial agents were thus desired to be selectively toxic against microorganisms but with much reduced toxicity towards the host. People tried to find out the biochemical differences between the infective organism and the host. Selective toxicity of the chemotherapeutic agents against pathogenic organism could be achieved by just then exploiting these differences.

5.5 CLASSIFICATION OF ANTIBIOTICS

There are various ways by which antibiotics can be classified. The probable points of differences regarding chemical and pharmacological properties, antibacterial spectra and mechanism of action serve as the basis of classification.

(i) Depending upon clinical effectiveness, spectrum of activity and degree of selectivity, the antibiotics that inhibit only certain groups of microorganisms are called as 'narrow spectrum antibiotics'. Examples includes nystatin and bacitracin. These antibiotics exhibit a high degree of selectivity. Many antibiotics inhibit both gram-positive and gram-negative bacteria and/or other intracellular organisms, such antibiotics are referred to as 'broad spectrum antibiotics'. Examples include chloramphenicol and tetracyclines.

(ii) Depending upon the sources from which antibiotics are derived, they can be categorised as follows :

(a) Natural : These antibiotics are naturally obtained from the large scale fermentation of microorganisms. For example, bacitracin and polymixin are obtained from some bacilli while streptomycin is obtained from *Streptomyces griseus*.

(b) Semisynthetic : The observation that 6-aminopenicillanic acid can be obtained from the cultures of *P. chrysogenum*, leds to the development of this class. For example, during the commercial production of benzyl penicillin, the phenylacetic acid is added as the side-chain precursor to the medium in order to achieve predominance of the product.

(c) Synthetic : This class includes antibiotics which are of purely synthetic origin. Chloramphenicol, for example, initially was isolated from a fermented media in 1947 and later was produced synthetically on the commercial basis.

(iii) The general scheme of classification includes following different categories of antibiotics :

  (a) β-lactam antibiotics
  (b) Aminoglycoside antibiotics
  (c) Tetracycline antibiotics
  (d) Peptide antibiotics
  (e) Macrolide antibiotics
  (f) Lincomycins, and
  (g) Unclassified antibiotics

(iv) The fourth basis of classification of antibiotics is their mechanisms of action. Accordingly these agents can be categorised as :

(a) Drugs that interferes with the biosynthesis of bacterial cell-wall. Examples includes penicillins, cephalosporins, cycloserine, bacitracin and vancomycin.

(b) Drugs that interferes with the functioning of cytoplasmic membrane of bacteria or fungi. Examples includes polymyxins, amphotericin β, colistin and nystatin.

(c) Drugs that interferes with the protein biosynthesis in microorganisms. Examples includes erythromycin, lincomycins, tetracyclines and chloramphenicol.

(d) Drugs that interferes with the nucleic acid biosynthesis in microorganisms. Examples includes actinomycin, griseofulvin and rifampin, and

(e) Drugs that antagonises the essential metabolic processes in microorganisms. Examples includes sulphonamides, trimethoprim and most of anticancer drugs.

5.6 MECHANISMS OF ACTION OF ANTIBIOTICS

Today hundreds of antibiotics are clinically available and future prospects about new additions are also bright. The new additions can easily be accommodated in the present frame of classification because antibiotics follow certain common tracks to exert their antibacterial activity. All presently available antibiotics can be classified according to the target sites they prefer to exert their action. Following are major routes through which antimicrobial activity is exerted.

  (a) Inhibition of cell-wall synthesis,
  (b) Inhibition of protein biosynthesis,
  (c) Disorganisation of cytoplasmic membrane,
  (d) Interference in nucleic acid biosynthesis, and
  (e) Inhibition of biosynthesis of tetrahydrofolate.

(a) Inhibition of Bacterial Cell-wall Synthesis :

(i) UDP-acetylmuramyl – pentapeptide - UDP - N-acetylmuramic acid - (amino acid)$_5$ is called as 'Park nucleotide'.

The benzyl penicillin induced accumulation of Park nucleotides in the growth medium of *Staphylococcus* alongwith the presence of shorter peptide chain indicated that penicillin affects state IV (i.e. cross-linking) of bacterial cell-wall synthesis. This results due to the inhibition of transpeptidation reactions. The cell-wall network loses its rigidity and the cell ruptures by osmotic lysis.

The cell-wall is essential for the growth and survival of bacteria. Rigid stability of cell-wall is provided by a highly cross-linked lattice like structure, composed of peptidoglycans. There is a close structural similarity between penicillins or other β - lactam antibiotics and the D - alanyl - D - alanine end of the polypeptide side-chain of peptidoglycan.

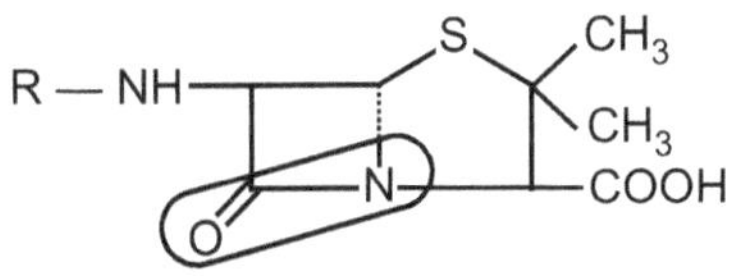

Penicillins

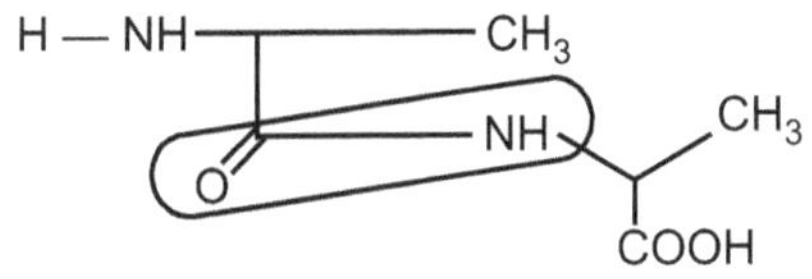

D-alanyl-D-alanine

The labile CO-N bond in the β-lactam ring of penicillin lies in the same position of peptide bond involved in transpeptidation. Due to this similarity, penicillin binds to the transpeptidase enzyme through covalent bonding instead of D - alanyl - D alanine end of polypeptide. Thus, the enzymes necessary for transpeptidation reaction (or for cross-linking of polypeptides) are occupied by the antibiotic. This irreversible inactivation of enzymes by penicillin results into the formation of faulty and weak cell-wall. Bacteria fail to divide. They may swell and then rupture with exudation of the cell-contents.

The reversible enzyme - penicillin complex undergoes an irreversible change resulting into the opening of the β-lactam bond. Thereafter the enzyme is released at a very slow rate from the inactive penicilloyl complex, and can not carry out its assigned functions.

(ii) The peptidoglycan hydrolase (autolysins) enzymes plays a key role in the lysis of bacteria. Penicillins are reported to decrease the availability of the inhibitors of autolysins. The uninhibited enzyme then performs its duty without any hesitation. However, autolysins are not necessarily present in all bacteria. For example, *Staphylococcus aureus* and *Streptococcus pneumoniae* lack these enzymes.

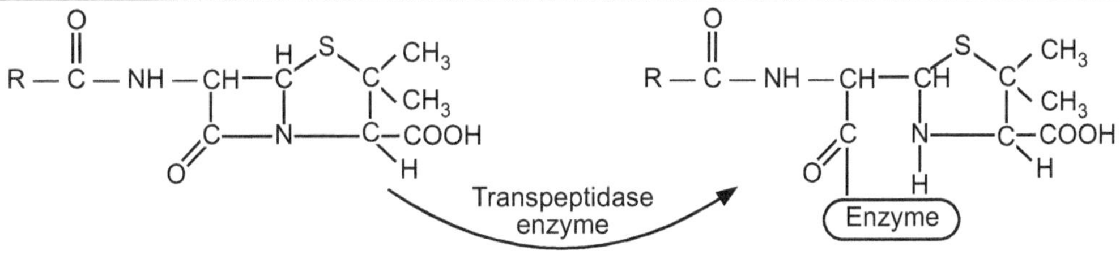

Penicillin → Penicilloyl - transpeptidase complex (irreversible nature)

Fig. 5.2 : Inactivation of transpeptidase enzymes

(iii) In bacterial cell, the cell-membrane is generally present inside the cell-wall. Some antibiotics may change or alter the permeability of the cell membrane, leaving the cell-wall undisturbed. For example, novobiocin, nystatin and polymyxins interfere with the integrity and functioning of cell membranes of microorganisms.

(iv) Unlike penicillins, vancomycin and ristocetin forms the stable 1: 1 complexes with D-alanyl – D-alanine end of polypeptide and interferes in the peptidoglycan synthesis. Bacitracin complexes with membrane lipid pyrophosphate protein of peptidoglycan and interferes in cell-wall synthesis.

(v) L-alanine is converted to D-alanine by the action of alanine racemase. Such two molecules get condensed to form D-alanyl-D-alanine by the action of D-alanyl-D-alanine synthetase enzymes. The substances which are unique to cell-wall of bacteria and other microorganisms include diaminopimelic acid, muramic acid, teichoic acid, amino sugars, amino acids, carbohydrates and lipids. Amino acids that are important for the cell-wall synthesis includes L-alanine, D-alanine, D-glutamic acid, L-lysine, meso-diaminopimelic acid, glycine, L-serine, L-threonine and D-aspartic acid. Due to the close structural similarity with D-alanine, D-cycloserine competitively inhibits both, alanine racemase and D-alanyl-D-alanine synthetase enzymes. This results into impairment in the synthesis of cell-wall.

(b) Inhibition of Bacterial Protein Synthesis :

Protein biosynthesis is perhaps one of the important processes that provide peptides. These may be assembled as per the needs of the organism in the proper sequence, to biosynthesis various enzymes and/or nucleic acids.

The important events in the protein biosynthesis can be outlined as -

(i) amino acid activation

(ii) formation of aminoacyl - t - RNA

(iii) peptide bond formation

(iv) translocation.

The antibacterial activity results due to the attack of the drug on one or more of the above events occurring on the ribosomal (r-RNA) surface.

The bacterial ribosomes differ from mammalian ribosomes. The difference has been figured out by their sedimentation coefficients. For example, bacterial ribosomes have the sedimentation coefficient of 70 (70 S) with two subunits 30 S and 50 S. While the mammalian cytoplasmic ribosomes are 80 S and give rise to 40 S and 60 S subunits. Mitochondria contain similar (but not identical) ribosomes to that of the bacterial ribosomes. Hence the degree of selectivity of an antibiotic will define its clinical effectiveness. For example, erythromycin does not bind to the mammalian ribosomes. It selectively inhibits bacterial protein synthesis by binding to the 50 S ribosomal subunits of sensitive strains of microorganisms. Protein synthesis in microorganisms is affected by many antimicrobial as well as anticancer agents. Chloramphenicol, macrolides and lincomycin bind to 50 S ribosomes while tetracyclines block the reaction between amino acid - t-RNA and ribosome on m-RNA. All these antibiotics destabilize ribosomes by inhibiting transpeptidation on polyribosomes by inducing conformational changes in ribosomes. They also interfere with translocation reactions.

It seems that the antibiotic bound ribosomal subunit still can offer the space and activity sufficient to produce small chain peptides. Thus, the ribosome cycle continues but polypeptide elongation is prevented. Similarly tetracyclines and streptomycin also bind to and inhibit the attachment of the 30 S subunits to the m-RNA.

(c) Disorganisation of the Cytoplasmic Membrane :

Cytoplasmic membrane lies next to the cell-wall and serves the purpose of protecting the vital bacterial cell constituents from damage. If this membrane is disorganised due to any reason, it results into rapid killing of that microorganism. In contrast to bacteria, the fungal membrane contains sterol as the membrane constituent, which is mainly ergosterol.

Antibiotics like polymyxins, may damage the integrity of the cytoplasmic membrane by disorienting the lipophilic groups present in the membrane. This leads to the leakage of intracellular components. Amphotericin B and nystatin have a high affinity for sterols present in fungal membrane. Hence, these antibiotics possess a potent antifungal activity. They combine with the membrane sterols and thus create pores or channels in the fungal membranes. They are ineffective against bacteria since bacteria do not have sterols as their membrane constituents.

Unfortunately mammalian cell membranes also consists of sterols. This is the reason why the margin of safety of antifungal antibiotics is quite narrow.

(d) Interference in the Bacterial Nucleic Acid Synthesis :

Nucleic acid synthesis is affected mainly by anticancer agents. Nucleic acids (i.e. DNA and RNA) are the vital ingredients of the microbial cell. DNA governs both the quality and quantity of RNA synthesis, while RNA is a key instructor that reads out the message on which the synthesis of various proteins and enzymes, necessary for overall growth of microorganism depends.

RNA molecules are synthesized by the polymerization of ribonucleoside triphosphates under the influence of DNA-dependent RNA polymerase enzyme. DNA template serves as a platform upon which the transcription occurs. Thus, the sequence of peptides in RNA being synthesized, is nothing but the copy of the sequence in that particular DNA - template on which, RNA has been synthesized. Antibiotics may affect the nucleic acid biosynthesis in two different ways :

(i) By interacting specifically with the enzyme (i.e. DNA dependent RNA - polymerase) which catalyses the polymerization of ribonucleoside triphosphates. OR

(ii) By interacting with the DNA template and thus disturbing the whole process.

Rifampicin represents an example of drugs acting through first mechanism. If it is added to the culture medium where the enzymes are synthesizing RNA chains, the enzyme process is not immediately inhibited. The bio-synthesis of new chains stops but partly formed RNA chains continue the process till completion.

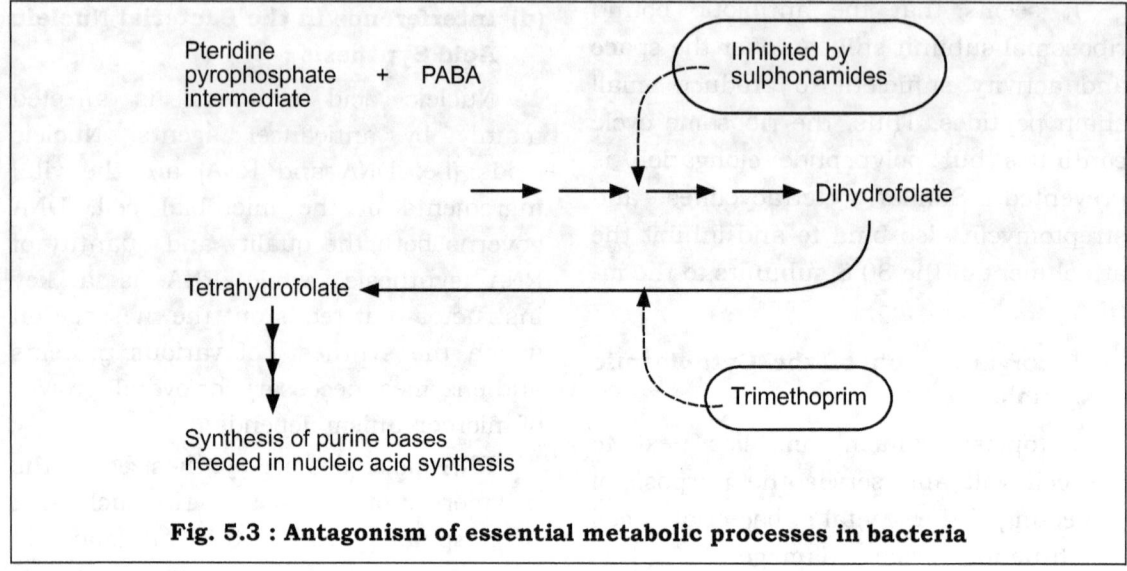

Fig. 5.3 : Antagonism of essential metabolic processes in bacteria

In brief, rifampicin does not interfere in chain elongation and termination but inhibits the chain initiation processes. Such sense of selectivity of action is not uniformly observed in the antibiotics which act through second mechanism. For example, rifampicin does not affect mammalian cell but actinomycin (which interferes with DNA template) is unselective in action, affecting both the host cells and bacteria. It binds specifically to helical double-stranded DNA and does not interacts at all with RNA synthesis.

(e) Inhibition of the Tetrahydrofolate Biosynthesis :

Sulphonamides are structural analogs of para-amino benzoic acid which is an essential metabolite in the bacterial cell and acts as a precursor of folic acid. Both in the host cells and microorganisms, the tetrahydrofolate serves as an essential co-factor in the transfer and reduction of 1-carbon fragment and for the production of nucleic acid via synthesis of methionine, thymine and other purine bases.

Due to the structural similarity with PABA, the sulphonamides interferes with the reaction between pteridine pyrophosphate intermediate and PABA. While trimethoprim selectively attacks and inhibits dihydrofolate reductase enzyme that catalyzes the reduction of dihydrofolate to tetrahydrofolate product.

The dietary folic acid is sufficient to meet the metabolic demands for tetrahydrofolate in the case of mammalian cells. Micro-organisms, however, are unable to utilize preformed folic acid and have to rely upon their own machinery to biosynthesize it from pteridine pyrophosphate intermediate and para aminobenzoate.

5.7 NEPHROTOXIC REACTIONS OF ANTI-MICROBIAL AGENTS

In the earlier paragraphs, we have discussed some important mechanisms of action by which antimicrobial agents bring about their therapeutic effectiveness. In many drugs, the adverse effects associated with the clinical use can be explained by considering them as the extension of their therapeutic effects. Nephrotoxicity is the main adverse effect associated with the use of most of antimicrobial agents. It occurs mainly due to the mechanism of action of these drugs and due to the fact that the urinary excretion serves as the dominating route for the elimination of major fraction of administered dose. The prominant nephrotoxic reactions of antimicrobial agents includes :

(a) **Hypersensitivity induced glomerular damage :**

It has been reported to occur with penicillins, sulphonamides, amphotericin etc.

(b) **Tubular necrosis at proximal tubule :**

It is caused by cephalosporins, polymyxins, aminoglycosides etc.

(c) **Distal tubular damage :**

It is characterised either by distal tubular acidosis (e.g. amphotericin) or hypokalemic alkalosis (e.g. penicillins, carbenicillin, ticarcillin).

(d) **Renal blood vessel damage :**

It is characterised either by decreased renal blood flow (e.g. amphotericin) or due to anaphylaxis reaction caused by penicillins, cephalosporins or sulphonamides.

(e) **Interstitial nephritis :**

It is reported to occur with penicillin or cephalosporin administration.

(f) **Obstruction in collecting duct :**

It is induced by sulphonamides while demethyl chlortetracycline causes nephrogenic diabetes insipidus.

5.8 NOVEL β-LACTAM ANTIBIOTICS

With the introduction of penicillins in the early 1940s, various microbial infections caused due to strains of *Staphylococci, Streptococci, H. influenzae* and *Neisseria gonorrhoeae* were soon brought under control. However, in the past several decades resistance to β-lactam has become an increasingly serious problem of concern. To deal with the problem of β-lactamase enzymes, attempts were made to synthesize new β-lactam antibiotics with increased stability to this enzymatic hydrolysis. The classic β-lactam antibiotics include two prominant classes like penicillins and cephalosporins. The non-classic β-lactam antibiotics are mostly derived after 1970. The prominant members of this category are reported in the table 5.4. Carbapenems possess a potent broad spectrum antibacterial activity in addition to β-lactamase inhibitory activity. They exhibit a high degree of activity against Gram-positive and Gram-negative bacteria but lacks significant activity against *Pseudomonas aeruginosa*.

Oxacephems are developed due to substitution of sulphur atom in dihydrothiazine nucleus by an oxygen atom while carbacephems are developed by replacing sulphur atom in dihydro-thiazine nucleus by a carbon atom.

5.9 β-LACTAMASE INHIBITORS

The emergence of antibiotic-resistance strains of microorganisms proved to be a major limitation to the clinical utility of antibiotics. β-lactamases can hydrolyze the β-lactam ring of different β-lactam antibiotics including penicillins, cephalosporins, carbapenems and monolactams. Various measures were then undertaken to develop such inhibitors that will bind or inactivate β-lactamases present in the microorganisms.

Table 5.4 : Non-classical β-lactam antibiotics

Examples	Year of introduction
1. 7 α-methoxy cephalosporins (cephamycins)	1971
2. Amidinopenicillins	1972
3. Nocardicins	1976
4. Clavulanic acid	1976
5. Carbapenems	
(a) Olivanic acids	1976
(b) Thienamycins	1978
(c) Epithienamycins	1977
(d) Asparenomycins	1982
(e) Pluracidomycins	1982
(f) Carpetimycins	1981
6. Oxacephems	1978
7. Carbacephems	1984
8. Monobactams	1981

In a microorganism, β-lactamases may be present at extracellular as well as intracellular sites. These enzymes when released into external environment, will prevent the access of antibiotic towards the microorganisms by rapidly inactivating the drug. The membrane bound intracellular β-lactamase will protect the organism from the residual antibiotic that escapes from the attack of extracellular enzyme.

Inactivation of β-lactam antibiotics is brought about by these enzymes through the cleavage of CO-N bond present in the β-lactam ring. Enzymes form a sort of irreversible complex with the carbonyl group. Studies with several different β-lactamases have implicated a serine residue as acylation site. Regeneration of the active enzyme from this complex then occurs through hydrolysis of the acyl linkage.

By providing false substrates having very high affinity for β-lactamase enzyme with long term occupying capacity (i.e. very slow rate of deacylation), we can effectively increase potency of β-lactamase sensitive antibiotics. Such substrates are known as β-lactamase inhibitors. However, such agents must be able to inhibit not only extracellular β-lactamases but should also be able to penetrate the bacterial cell-wall at adequate concentration to inhibit intracellular β-lactamases. They should also have the broad spectrum of activity covering β-lactamases present in both, gram-positive and gram-negative bacteria.

Examples of clinically used β-lactamase inhibitors includes clavulanic acid, sulbactam, olivanic acid and halogenated sulfone derivatives. These inhibitors in general possess weak antibacterial activity of their own.

5.10 SYNERGISTIC ANTIBIOTIC COMBINATIONS

Many antibiotics are effective only against gram-positive microorganism. Some agents show antibacterial activity only against gram-negative pathogens. Such a narrow spectrum of activity exhibited by these agents imposes limitation to their clinical utility. Moreover the emergence of antibiotic resistant strains of microorganisms has had a marked influence on chemotherapy. In certain cases, relatively high concentrations are required when a single antibiotic is used. Such high concentrations of the drug exposes the patient to the high risk of serious adverse effects. All the above circumstances emphasizes the need of using the combination therapy of such antibiotics having synergistic anti-bacterial activity. When used concurrently, antimicrobial drugs may exhibit additives, antagonistic or synergistic effects.

The combination antibacterial therapy not only broadens the antibacterial spectra but also reduces the probability of emergence of antibiotic - resistant strains of microorganisms. The combination therapy provides such a useful approach for both - to enhance the clinical efficacy of the antibiotics and to lower down the risk of serious adverse effects of the drugs at the same time.

Many newer β-lactam antibiotics are commonly used in combination with monoglycoside to provide a broader spectrum of antibacterial activity. In this, β-lactam antibiotics probably facilitates the penetration of monoglycosides in the bacteria.

Other examples of effective antibiotic combinations includes gentamicin and cephalosporin in the treatment of gram-negative bacteremic shock and carbenicillin with gentamicin to delay the emergence of resistant strains in tuberculosis and in severe *Pseudomonas aeruginosa* infection.

Such antibiotic combinations comprised of

(i) drugs having similar mode of action, and

(ii) bactericidal drug and bacteriostatic drug should never be used.

Several classes of agents are available for the treatment of bacterial infections (Table 5.4). These includes the β-lactams and the glycopeptides which target the peptidoglycan cell-wall, the tetracyclines and macrolides, which target bacterial protein synthesis and the quinolines whose mode of action is to bind with the complex formed between DNA gyrase and DNA, thereby forming a bactericidal ternary complex.

5.11 SUPRAINFECTION (SUPERINFECTION)

It is the emergence of a new strain or a new species of pathogenic microorganisms or fungi (usually *Candida albicans*) in the patient receiving antimicrobial treatment, especially of broad-spectrum antibiotic.

A normal non-pathogenic bacterial flora present in the human body includes more than 300 different species of organisms. Antibiotic therapy (especially with broad spectrum antibiotic), depresses this normal bacterial flora that leads to emergence of drug-resistant pathogenic microorganisms in the body. Suprainfection usually affects gastrointestinal and genital tracts.

The common symptoms of suprainfections include oral burning, xerostomia, black hairy tongue, stomatitis, glossitis, cheilosis, enteritis, colitis, diarrhoea and pruritus ani. Some members of normal bacterial flora of the human body are infective in nature but they remain silent because of strong cellular immune and phagocytic system of the normal adult. Suprainfection due to such members may also occur in patients with impaired cellular immune and phagocytic defence mechanisms.

β-LACTAM ANTIBIOTICS

6.1 INTRODUCTION

Sir Alexander Fleming in 1928, inoculated a petridish with *staphylococci* at St. Mary's Hospital, London. By accident, the petridish got contaminated with a mould, *Penicillium notatum*. After some time, Fleming noted a zone of inhibition of bacterial growth around the mould. He named the antimicrobial component present in the culture filtrate of the mould as penicillin after the species of the mould.

An extensive work was undertaken on penicillin by **Prof. Howard W. Florey** and **Dr. Ernst B. Chain** in 1939 at Sir William Dunn school of Pathology, Oxford University, England. They subsequently isolated and purified the active antimicrobial component and characterised the basic structure of penicillin. This work was supplemented by the efforts of the chemists Dr. Abraham and Dr. Heatley. Nobel prize was awarded to **Fleming**, **Florey** and **Chain** for their work on penicillin. The clinical effectiveness of penicillin was first tested on 12th February, 1941 in the form of a sodium salt. With the promising results obtained with penicillin, extensive work was carried out resulting into introduction of other penicillins. They are represented by the following general structure.

Site of attack of β-lactamase enzyme
A = β-lactam ring
B = thiazolidine ring

Fig. 6.1 : General formula for penicillins

Penicillins thus can be considered as the amido derivatives of 6-aminopenicillanic (6-APA) acid. In the basic skeleton, a thiazolidine ring (B) is fused with a β-lactam ring (A) which is a 4-membered cyclic amide. The cyclic amide bond is sensitive to the attack of lactamase enzymes produced by bacteria.

Biosynthesis of penicillins upto 1958–59 was dependent on the growth of *Penicillium notatum* and *Penicillium chrysogenum* in deep vat cultures. In 1959, Batchelor and his coworkers reported the isolation of 6-aminopenicillanic acid with the help of amidase from *P. chrysogenum*. This initiated the development of new semisynthetic penicillins by adding various chemicals to the fermentation process, the first being methicillin. These penicillins differ from each other in their antibacterial and pharmacological characteristics due to change in the structure of the acid moiety of the amide side-chain at C_6. For example, penicillin G (where R = $C_6H_5CH_2-$) after about 50 years of clinical use, still remained as an extremely effective and the only natural penicillin used clinically. Acylation of 6-aminopencillanic acid with appropriate carboxylic acids resulted in new penicillins, some of which are broad-spectrum antibiotics.

All clinically used penicillins are dextrorotatory in nature and are usually given in the salt form of sodium or potassium. They all differ in their antibacterial activity spectra, acid stability, oral effectiveness and sensitivity to the attack of β-lactamase enzymes. Except amidinocillin, all penicillins contain 6 – APA as a basic skeleton. In amidinocillin, 6-β-amidinopencillanic acid is a basic nucleus.

6.2 DEGRADATION PRODUCTS OF PENICILLINS

Natural penicillins are unstable in acidic and basic conditions. Instability in acid medium logically precludes their oral administration due to the highly acidic pH in stomach. At acidic pH, a sort of molecular rearrangement results. The compound is known as penillic acid and has no activity. Similarly at basic pH, penicillin molecule gets converted to penicilloic acid which is again an inactive form. Certain strains of microorganisms can destroy β-lactam antibiotics enzymatically. The enzymes more popularly known as penicillinases or β-lactamases can open the β-lactam bond. The difference in the susceptibility to the β-lactamase enzymes depends upon the nature of the amide side-chain at C_6. It also depends upon the bacterial strain involved.

Since penicillin was proved to be a wonder drug during second world war in healing the wounds and preventing the infections, extensive chemical studies were undertaken either individually or through co-operation of both, industry as well as government laboratories. Soon later, the scientists were disappointed due to relative instability of natural penicillins in acidic or basic medium. For example, benzyl penicillin was found to be relatively narrow spectrum antibiotic. It is susceptible to the degradation under acidic or basic conditions resulting into its oral ineffectiveness. It is readily inactivated by β-lactamase enzymes and many patients may develop allergic reactions to it. Many analogues had been synthesized in order to overcome these clinical deficiencies prevailing in natural penicillins. The main principle behind this drug design was the manipulation of polar amide side-chain. Variations in this moiety resulted in differences in antibiotic potency and in physiochemical properties including stability. This is usually done by introducing chemical inducers in the culture medium by varying the nutritional composition of the growth medium.

Benzyl penicillin (penicillin G) is considered as the prototype agent from the penicillin category. It is the most active of penicillins on w/w basis. Even after 50 years of its introduction, it is still used as primary agent in the treatment of *S. pyogenes* infections of upper and lower respiratory tract, *S. pneumoniae* infections, otitis media, pneumonia, meningitis, arthritis, *Neisseria infections*, trepanemal infections and syphilis. Procaine penicillin and benzathine penicillin are the repository forms of benzyl penicillin which when injected intramuscularly release benzyl penicillin slowly over a long period of time. Procaine penicillin contains equal molar parts of procaine and benzyl penicillin while benzathine penicillin is a mixture of 2 moles of benzyl penicillin and 1 mole of dibenzyl ethylene diamine.

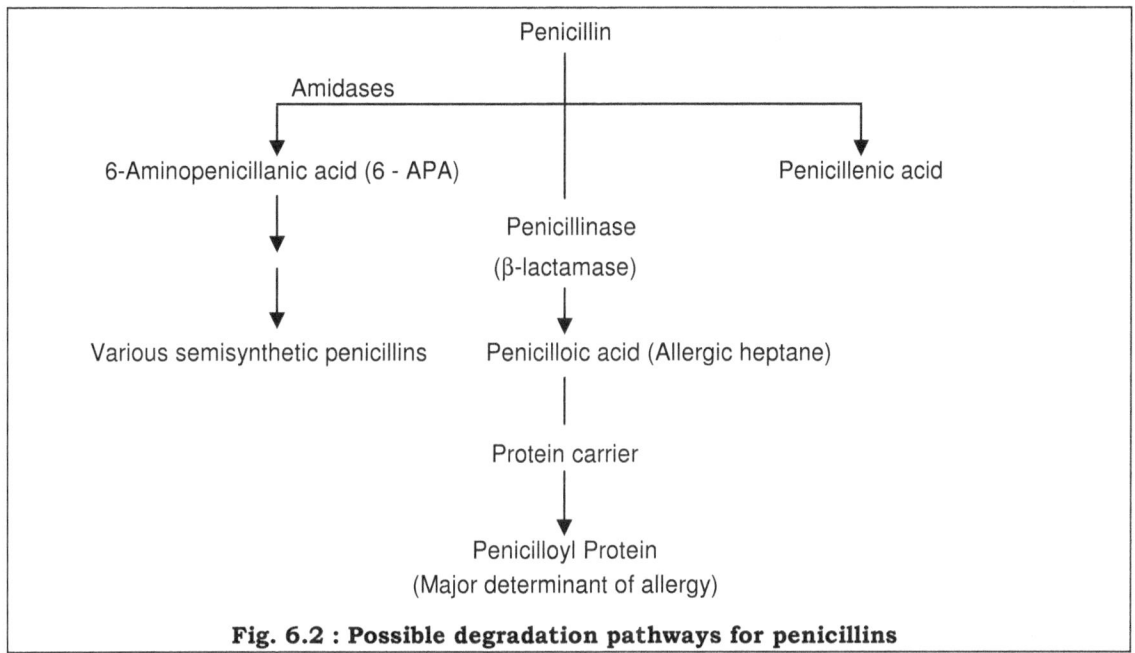

Fig. 6.2 : Possible degradation pathways for penicillins

Unfortunately benzyl penicillin is ineffective against gram-negative bacilli. The incorporation of an ionized or polar group or an acidic substituent at the benzyl carbon atom of benzyl penicillin imparted clinical effectiveness against gram negative bacilli.

Carbenicillin was found to be effective against both β-lactamase producing and non-β-lactamase producing strains of gram-negative bacilli.

6.3 CLASSIFICATION

Depending upon the spectrum of activity and the source of commercial production, penicillins can be classified as follows :

(A) Natural penicillins : Examples include penicillin G, penicillin V and - phenethicillin. All these antibiotics are having narrow antimicrobial activity, spectra and are effective only against gram-positive cocci, rods and gram-negative cocci.

(B) Penicillinase resistant penicillins : Examples include, methicillin, nafcillin, amdinocillin and isoxazolyl penicillins (e.g. oxacillin, cloxacillin, dicloxacillin, flucloxacillin). They are effective mainly against – gram-positive cocci and *Staphylococcus aureus*.

(C) Broad spectrum antibiotics : Examples include ampicillin, amoxicillin, carbenicillin, mezocillin, piperacillin etc. They are effective against both gram-positive and gram-negative bacteria.

(D) Miscellaneous antibiotics : All β-lactam antibiotics contain a four membered β-lactam ring which is fused with a second heterocyclic ring' through the nitrogen and a tetrahydral carbon. Difference in the structure of this second heterocyclic ring leads to the further sub classification. For example,

(i) Penicillins consist of β-lactam ring fused with thiazolidine.

(ii) Cephalosporins consist of β-lactam ring fused with a six membered dihydrothiazine ring.

(iii) Thienamycins consist of β-lactam ring fused with pyrroline ring, and

(iv) Clavulanic acid and its analogs consist of β-lactam ring fused with oxazolidine ring.

While in amdinocillin, 6-β-amino group is replaced by a 6-β-amidino group. It is extremely effective against gram negative bacteria but relatively less effective against gram positive cocci.

The antimicrobial activity of β-lactam antibiotics is measured in terms of international units. Since benzyl penicillin is the prototype of the series, it is taken as a reference standard to define the international unit (I.U.). Thus, 1 mg of crystalline sodium benzyl penicillin is equal to 1667 international units.

The β-lactam antibiotics are cell-wall inhibitors towards susceptible bacteria. It means that they can not kill or inhibit all bacteria. For example, benzyl penicillin has a fairly narrow antibacterial spectra. Particular fungi and many gram-negative bacteria are relatively insensitive to this agent. It is readily hydrolyzed by the enzyme, penicillinase. The pronounced hydrolytic susceptibility of the β-lactam bond to penicillinases, hindered the early progress in penicillin development.

Table 6.1 : Clinically used β-lactam antibiotics

Name	Oral absorption %	Biological half-life (hours)	Protein binding %	Acid stability	Penicillinase resistance	Spectrum of activity
(A) Penicillinase – susceptible penicillins (Natural penicillins) :						
(i) Benzyl penicillin (Penicillin G)	15 – 30	0.7	60	No	No	Narrow
(ii) Phenoxymethyl penicillin (Pencillin V)	60	0.8	80	Yes	No	Narrow
(iii) Phenethicillin	60	0.8	55 – 60	No	No	Narrow
(B) Penicillinase – resistant penicillins (semisynthetic penicillin)						
(i) Methicillin	Minimal	0.45	40	No	Yes	Narrow
(ii) Nafcillin	10 – 15	0.5 – 1.0	90	Yes	Yes	Narrow
(iii) Oxacillin	33	0.4 – 0.7	94	Yes	Yes	Narrow
(iv) Cloxacillin	49	0.5	95	Yes	Yes	Narrow
(v) Dicloxacillin	37	0.8	98	Yes	Yes	Narrow
(vi) Flucloxacillin	55 – 60	0.8 – 1.0	60 – 80	Yes	Yes	Narrow
(vii) Amdinocillin (Mecillinam)	Nil	0.9	10	No	Yes	Narrow

contd...

(C) Broad spectrum antibiotics :						
(i) Ampicillin	30 -50	1 – 1.2	20	Yes	No	Broad-spectrum
(ii) Amoxicillin	80	1 – 1.13	20	Yes	No	Broad-spectrum
(iii) Carbenicillin	10 – 15	1.1	50	No	No	Broad-spectrum
(iv) Indanyl carbenicillin	30	1.0	50	Yes	No	Broad-spectrum
(v) Ticarcillin	None	1.2	45	No	No	Broad-spectrum
(vi) Mezlocillin	10	0.8	20 – 40	No	No	Broad-spectrum
(vii) Azlocillin	10 – 12	1.0	25 – 45	No	No	Broad-spectrum
(viii) Piperacillin	None	1.0	16	No	No	Broad-spectrum

Following the realisation that the presence of phenylacetic acid in the fermentation leads to the predominance of the product benzyl penicillin, a wide variety of other organic acids was added to the growing culture. Thus, the second generation known as semisynthetic penicillins was born. The proper design of the side-chain has served not only to overcome many of the drawbacks of the early natural penicillins but also helped to develop broad-spectrum antibiotic. The involvement of acyl carbon in the hydrolytic cleavage of β-lactam bond was recognized. Improvement in the clinical qualities was then achieved by creating steric hindrances to this acyl carbon, thus making it less reactive. The fact was attested by attachment of an aromatic or heterocyclic ring directly to the amide carbonyl atom resulting into antibiotics with increased penicillinase resistance. Examples include, methicillin, oxacillin, dicloxacillin, nafcillin etc. An additional chlorine atom present in dicloxacillin promotes better oral absorption and an extended plasma half-life. One of the most successful penicillin candidates is ampicillin which is prototype of third generation β-lactam antibiotics. The third generation is characterized by increased oral activity. The early observation that 'drugs acylated by amino acids had somewhat greater oral activity' turned to be an inspiration behind its development. Thus addition of an amino group to benzyl penicillin also resulted into broadening of spectrum of activity along with increased oral activity. Ampicillin was the first of semi-synthetic penicillins to show significant activity against gram-negative bacilli. The next congener is amoxicillin. These aminopenicillins still suffer from the major drawback of undergoing hydrolytic cleavage by β-lactamase enzymes and thus are ineffective for most *staphylococcal* infections. In an attempt to improve further pharmacokinetic characteristics, prodrug development program for ampicillin was undertaken. As a result, bacampicillin, hetacillin and talampicillin appeared on the screen.

Carboxylic acid group if introduced at the primary amino moiety of ampicillin and other allied skeletons, significantly improves the activity spectrum of the lead. This resulted in the development of carboxypenicillins. Examples include carbenicillin, indanyl carbenicillin and ticarcillin. These compounds extended the spectrum of ampicillin to include *Pseudomonas auroginosa*. A parallel observation was also registered stating that acylation of the amino group of ampicillin broadened the antimicrobial spectrum of ampicillin. Azlocillin is the prototype drug in this series which is grouped under ureidopenicillins. In this series, the spectrum is still extended further to include strains of *Klebsiella* and *Proteus*. The 6 α-formamido penicillin, is a relatively new development in this field. This compound is extremely effective against gram-negative bacteria while showing little or no activity against gram-positive organisms. Recently new impetus has been added to the chemotherapy by the discovery of new ring systems in fermentation liquors. These include clavulanic acid, thienamycins and nocardicins.

Despite the enormous efforts expended during the past four decades, the β-lactam antibiotics field remains still a field of severe competition within itself. All these agents differ from one another in the following aspects :

    (i)   Acid stability
    (ii) Penicillinase resistance
    (iii) Antimicrobial potency, and
    (iv) Antimicrobial activity spectrum.

When the acid stability of penicillin is increased, the drug would not be destroyed by gastric acid and thus can be orally administered. In general, acid stable penicillins are less potent on w/w basis than benzyl penicillin. The penicillinase resistant penicillins are not hydrolysed by the enzymes produced by *Staphylococcus aureus* and hence they are effectively used to treat the infections caused by resistant strains of microorganisms.

6.4 MECHANISM OF ACTION

The β-lactam antibiotics include penicillins, cephalosporine, thienamycins, nocardicins and clavulanic acid derivatives. All of them are bactericidal and act only upon bacteria that are growing. They all act by producing damage to the bacterial cell-wall. Polymyxin antibiotics (e.g. bacitracin), cycloserine and vancomycin also act by same mode of action, but the mechanism is different. They mainly induce changes in the semipermeable properties of the membrane by acting as cationic detergents. This leads to leakage of cell constituents from the cell resulting into death of bacterial cell. **Park et al** in 1957 observed that the presence of penicillins in the growth medium of *staphylococcus* resulted in the accumulation of certain peptide complexes (later identified as uridine diphosphate – acetylmuramyl pentapeptide) and its breakdown products i.e. uridine - 5' - pyrophosphate and N-acetylmuramic acid. Park nucleotides, as they are known, were already shown to be an integral part of the bacterial cell-wall structure. This key observation by Park, led to the foundation of the concept that penicillins interfere in the biosynthesis of the bacterial cell-wall.

Accumulation of Park nucleotides in the growth media along with other related products with shorter peptide side-chain suggested that penicillin attack the state IV of the cell-wall biosynthesis (i.e. cross-linking) by the inhibition of transpeptidase reaction. Penicillins and cephalosporins are similar in stereochemical structure to D-alanyl-D--alanine end of the polypeptide side-chain of peptidoglycan. Because of this structural similarity and higher affinity to the β-lactam antibiotics, transpeptidase enzymes bind preferably to penicillin rather than to D-alanyl-D-alanine end of polypeptide. This results into formation of irreversible complex between antibiotic and transpeptidase enzyme.

Beside transpeptidases, other bacterial enzymes like, transglycosylases and D-alanine carboxykinases also get acetylated. This results into different effects on bacterial cells leading to cell lysis, production of spherical or elongated cells etc.

Due to the acylation of these bacterial enzymes, they can not participate to their full strength in the formation of bacterial cell-wall. This results into the formation of structurally weakened cell-wall and ultimately cell lysis.

6.5 PHARMACOKINETIC PROPERTIES

Most of β-lactam antibiotics are not adequately absorbed by the oral route. This occurs either due to their acid liability or due to their ionic characteristics. The presence of food impairs oral absorption of most of the penicillins. Exceptions include amoxicillin and penicillin V. The free penicillins are not suitable for oral or parenteral administration. They are usually administered in the form of their sodium or potassium salts.

In order to enhance oral effectiveness, a prodrug concept was applied to ampicillin. Bacampicillin and hetacillin were thus developed through the esterification of ampicillin. These esters remain stable in gastric fluids and are rapidly absorbed. In tissues and in circulation, these esters undergo hydrolysis by non-specific esterases to release ampicillin. The same approach was also applied to carbenicillin, a poor orally absorbed drug. Indanyl carbenicillin is an inactive ester form having good oral absorption. This form releases carbenicillin in the circulation through hydrolysis.

The third approach to increase duration of stay of these antibiotics in the body is to develop repository forms. These repository forms, when given intramuscularly, release the active drug slowly over a long period of time. For example, procain penicillin and benzathine penicillin release penicillin - G for 24 hours and four weeks respectively.

Due to the relative polar nature, most of penicillins penetrate cells and blood brain barrier insignificantly. They can also cross the placental barrier. Penicillins gets easily distributed into various body fluids like, interstitial fluids, synovial fluids, bone and serosal cavities. The extent of protein-binding of penicillins ranges from 20% to 95%. For example, aminopenicillins (ampicillin) bind to plasma-proteins to the extent of 15 - 20% while oxacillin analogs bind to plasma-proteins to greater than 90% extent. The plasma half-life of all clinically used penicillins ranges between 0.4 - 1.3 hour.

Most of the penicillins are insignificantly metabolized. They are rapidly excreted in urine mostly in active form. The major portion is eliminated by tubular secretion. Since probenecid can inhibit tubular secretion process, it may be used to decrease urinary excretion of penicillins and to increase their blood levels for longer period of time. Thus, probenecid prolongs the serum half-life of most of penicillins. Some penicillins may also be excreted into bile in significant amounts.

6.6 ADVERSE EFFECTS

The major adverse effects of penicillins can be categorised as follows :

(i) Allergic reactions : These reactions are characterized by pruritus, fever, apprehension, paresthesia, wheezing, choking, generalized urticaria, edema, angioedema, rhinitis, flushing, hypotension, shock and loss of consciousness. These hypersensitivity reactions may be immediate, accelerated or of late nature. Other hypersensitivity reactions include serum sickness, myalgia, bronchospasm and lymphadenopathy.

(ii) Gastrointestinal effects : These effects include, nausea, vomiting, diarrhoea, stomatitis, glossitis, enterocolitis, occasional bleeding and superinfection by *Candida albicans*.

(iii) Hematological reaction : These reactions include hemolytic anaemia, neutropenia, hematuria, thrombocytopenia and bleeding disorders. For example, ureidopenicillins inhibit platelet aggregation and induce bleeding, disorders by binding to adenosine diphosphate present in platelets.

(iv) Neurogenic effects : These effects are dose dependent and include myoclonic seizures and bizarre reactions.

(v) Renal effects : These effects include albuminurea, pyuria, renal casts, renal fever, renal tubular necrosis and interstitial nephritis.

(vi) Hepatic effects : These effects include alkaline phosphatase, elevated SGOT (i.e. serum glutamic oxalacetic transaminase) and SGPT, lactic acid dehydrogenase and sulfobromoplithalein retention.

(vii) Electrolyte disturbances : Since most of penicillins are administered - either in the form of sodium and potassium salts, electrolyte disturbances are found to occur in the form of hypokalemia and sodium overload.

(viii) Miscellaneous effects : These effects include phlebitis, Jarisch-Herxheimer reaction (characterized by fever, chills, muscle aches, headache, arthralgia and syphilitic skin lesions), disulfiram like effects, cheilosis, buccal ulceration and black hairy tongue.

6.7 HYPERSENSITIVITY REACTIONS

Hypersensitivity reactions may occur with any dosage form of penicillin. In some cases, the reaction is mild and disappears even when the use of drug is continued. While in others, reactions may persist for one to two weeks or longer after the therapy has been stopped. These reactions include immediate or delayed type skin allergies, fever, bronchospasm, serum sickness and other reactions.

Penicillin is degraded *in-vivo* to produce a number of antigenic breakdown products. The toxic manifestations may be due to the following reasons :

(a) A breakdown product, penicilloyl moiety results due to the opening of β-lactam ring. This fraction is considered to be the most important antigenic hapten of penicillins. This hapten then combines with the endogenous protein carrier to act as major determinant of penicillin allergy. Accelerated and late urticarial reactions are found to be mediated by antibodies formed in response to this major determinant.

(b) The degradation products, penicillenic acid and/or sodium benzylpenicilloate may react with sulfhydryl or amino groups present in the vital tissue proteins. The resulting complexes may serve themselves as the minor determinant of penicillin allergy. Immediate allergic reactions including anaphylaxis were found to be mediated by antibodies formed in response to these minor determinants.

(c) Certain other contaminants (mycelial residues) of high molecular weight originating from fermentation process may serve as a cause of allergic manifestations, and

(d) A non-protein polymer of unknown origin was found to be involved in certain cases of penicillin allergy.

These hypersensitivity reactions due to penicillins can be controlled by prompt administration of antihistaminics, adrenaline, volume expanders or vasopressor (to control hypotension) agents. Tracheostomy may be advised in few cases in order to correct airway obstruction resulting due to laryngeal edema.

6.8 THERAPEUTIC USES

Below mentioned are some important theraieutic uses :

(i) Penicillins are effective in the treatment of pneumococcal pneumonia, pneumococcal meningitis, otitis media, chronic bronchitis, acute tonsillitis (due to *Streptococcus pyogenes*) and bacterial endocarditis (*streptococcal* infection). However when endocarditis is caused by *Enterococci*, a combination of ampicillin with gentamycin is usually advised in order to obtain a synergistic antimicrobial activity.

(ii) Penicillins are also effective in the treatment of bacteremia, cellulitis, osteomyelitis and pneumonia.

(iii) If used in higher dosage, penicillins can effectively control gonococcal arthritis, disseminated gonococcal infections and other complicated gonococcal infections. They are also preferred to treat early forms of syphilis. However some patients may develop Jarisch, Herxheimer reaction when they receive penicillin in the treatment of syphilis.

(iv) Penicillins are highly effective against Haemophilus influenzae infections. For example, ampicillin is the drug of choice in the treatment of meningitis, osteomyelitis, epiglotitis, pneumonia, septic arthritis, otitis media and sinusitis caused by susceptible strains of *H. influenzae*.

(v) Penicillin G is indicated in the treatment of clostridial infections (e.g. tetanus and gas gangrene), actinomycosis, anaerobic brain and lung abscesses and other anaerobic infections.

(vi) Penicillins are also effective in the treatment of urinary tract infections caused by *E. coli*, *P. mirabilis*, *P. aeruginosa*, indole positive *Proteus* species and *Enterococci*.

(vii) In the treatment of typhoid fever *(Salmonella typhi)*, chloramphenicol may be substituted by ampicillin or amoxacillin.

(viii) Broad spectrum penicillins (e.g. mezlocillin) may be effectively used in the treatment of serious infections of urinary, bronchial and biliary tracts caused by gram-negative enteric bacteria.

(ix) Penicillin-G is indicated in the treatment of leptospirosis and infections due to *Pasteurella multocida*.

(x) Serious *Pseudomonas* infections like sepsis, endocarditis, pneumonitis or malignant otitis are usually treated with a combination of carbenicillin with an aminoglycoside.

(xi) Prophylactically penicillins may be used either alone or in combination to prevent bacterial endocarditis, congenital heart disease, idiopathic hypertrophic subaortic stenosis and recurrence of rheumatic fever. If major surgery is to be carried out, they may be given to the patient just before, during and in immediate postoperative period to avoid the possible infections with *streptococci* and gram-negative bacteria.

6.9 BACTERIAL RESISTANCE TO β-LACTAM ANTIBIOTICS

Following are some of the possible mechanisms which can be used to explain bacterial resistance to β-lactam antibiotics :

(i) The cleavage of β-lactam ring due to the attack of either penicillinases or cephalosporinases (collectively known as β-lactamases) is the major drawback of many penicillins. This makes them ineffective for most *Staphylococcal* infection. β-lactamases are present to some extent in almost all bacteria. Some bacterial species acquire resistance to the action of these antibiotics by the production of β-lactamase enzymes which terminate their antimicrobial activity by destructing the β-lactam nucleus. Production of β-lactamases may be plasmid-mediated or chromosomally mediated. Some microorganisms may produce more than one type of β-lactamases.

(ii) The protein channels are present in the complex outer layer of gram-negative bacteria through which antibiotic may penetrate in and then binds to binding sites. These bacteria develop resistance to the attack of antibiotics by reducing the cellular permeability to the antibiotic. This results into permeability block and inability of the antibiotic to penetrate and to bind with its binding proteins.

(iii) The sensitive strain may undergo mutational change and therefore acquires resistance to the antibiotics.

(iv) The antibiotic, instead of attacking the micro-organism, may be utilised to antagonise some specific biochemical intermediates released by microorganisms.

Thus, penicillin resistance develops into sensitive strains of microorganisms due to a single or sometimes overlapping of one or more mechanisms mentioned above.

Table 6.2 : General mechanisms of bacterial resistance

Antibiotics	Major mechanism of bacterial resistance
(1) Penicillins, cephalosporins chloramphenicol	Inactivation of antibiotic by β-lactamase and other enzymes.
(2) Aminoglycosides, sulphonamides, tetracyclines, polymixin B, chloramphenicol	Alteration in the cellular permeability to the antibiotic.
(3) Clindamycin and lincomycin, rifampin, fusidic acid and aminoglycosides	Alterations in the antibiotic-binding sites through mutation.
(4) Cycloserine, sulphonamides, trimethoprim	Bypassing the biochemical reaction sensitive to antibiotic.

6.10 PROBENECID

Most of the penicillins are excreted in urine mostly in an active form. They are mainly eliminated through tubular secretion. Probenecid has an ability to inhibit tubular secretion process. Hence, it may be effectively used to increase serum half-life and blood levels of penicillins by reducing the rate of their urine clearance. Beside penicillins, it also elevates blood levels of other organic acids. It is also valuable in the treatment of gout.

$$\begin{array}{c} C_3H_7 \\ \diagdown \\ N-SO_2-\!\!\left\langle\right\rangle\!\!-COOH \\ \diagup \\ C_3H_7 \end{array}$$

Probenecid

It is orally active. About 80 – 90% of absorbed dose is bound to the plasma proteins. It has a plasma half-life of 6 – 12 hours. Adverse effects are mild and include nausea, vomiting, epigastric discomfort and acidity. It should be used with caution in patients with peptic ulcer.

It may be administered along with pencillins in the oral dose of 0.5 g every 6 hours.

6.11 CEPHALOSPORINS

The concept that certain antibiotic producing fungi may be present in soil and other environment rich in bacteria led to a worldwide examination of soils, sewage, sludges and related materials for the presence of new series of antibiotics. The concept crystallized out with some success. A species of *cephalosporium* was isolated in July 1945 by **Prof. Giuseppi Brotzu** near a sewage outfall of the Sardinian coast. This mould produced three antibiotics which were named as :

(i) Cephalosporin N : It is a penicillin like structure, being a derivative of 6-aminopenicillanic acid.

(ii) Cephalosporin P : It is an acidic antibiotic which is steroidal in nature. A compound structurally similar to cephalosporin P is fusidic acid, an antibiotic produced by the mould Fusidium coccineum.

(iii) Cephalosporin C : It is a true cephalosporin. It is a derivative of 7-amino cephalosporanic acid. It serves as a lead nucleus for the development of totally new series of compounds, known as 'cephalosporins'.

The basic skeleton, 7-amino cephalosporanic acid was readily isolated by dilute acid hydrolysis of cephalosporin C. An extensive work was carried out on this basic skeleton at Glaxo (England), Eli Lilly (U.S.A.) and by Prof. Abraham at Oxford to develop clinically useful analogs of cephalosporin C. This work resulted into the development of cephalothin and cephaloridine which were subsequently followed by others. In 1972, cefamycin series was discovered.

Over 20 cephalosporins have become available for clinical use since cephalothin was first introduced in 1965. The 7-aminocephalosporanic acid is composed of a dihydrothiazine ring and a β-lactam ring.

The low potency of cephalosporin C soon made it clear that the natural product itself was unsuitable for the clinical use. The structure has to be modified in the laboratory to design more potent semisynthetic analogs. These semisynthetic cephalosporins are obtained by attaching different side-chains to 7-aminocephalosporanic acid just as penicillins. All these cephalosporins show variations in their potency and pharmacokinetic properties.

6.12 CLASSIFICATION

Cephalosporins can be classified on the basis of their chemical structure, antimicrobial spectrum, resistance to cephalosporinases and on their clinical features.

Classification method suggested by O' Callaghan in 1979 is based upon the pharmacokinetic features of cephalosporins. On this basis they can be categorised as follows :

(i) Orally administered cephalosporins : These include cephalexine, cephradine and cefactor.

(ii) Parenterally administered cephalosporins : These include cephalothin, cephapirin, cephacetrile, cephaloridine and cefazedone. These agents are sensitive to β-lactamase enzymes.

(iii) Cephalosporins that are resistant to β-lactamases but could be administered parenterally : Examples include cefuroxime, cefamandole, cefoxitin etc.

(iv) Unstable cephalosporins : Examples include, cephalothin and cephapirin.

The second scheme of classification of cephalosporins is based upon the potency sensitivity to β-lactamase enzymes and spectrum of antimicrobial activity.

The classification is given below :

(i) First generation cephalosporins : These antibiotics possess narrow spectrum of antimicrobial activity. They remain ineffective against *Bacteroides* species, *Citrobacter* species, enterococci, indole positive *Proteus* species and *Serratia morcescens*. Examples include cephaloridine, cephalothin, cephalexin, cephradine and cefadroxil. They display good activity against gram-positive bacteria and are refractory to staphylococcal β-lactamase.

(ii) Second generation cephalosporins : These are broad spectrum antibiotics effective against all such microorganisms which are resistant to first generation category. These agents also present resistance to β-lactamase attack. They may be used clinically against anaerobic pathogens. Examples include cefamandole, cefoxitin, cefuroxime and cefactor. They all have increased antimicrobial activity and more β-lactamase stability.

(iii) Third generation cephalosporins : This class appeared in the late 1970s. These agents are superior than previous two classes with respect to potency, spectrum of activity and stability to β-lactamase enzymes. They exhibit high activity against *Neisseria*, *H. influenzae* and many other common gram-negative enteric bacteria. However, they are ineffective against enterococci. Examples include cefotaxime, cefmenoxime, ceftizoxime, ceftriaxone, ceftazidime, cefoperazone and moxalactam. All of them contain an aminothiazole oxime moiety in the acyl side-chain. This shows marginal activity against *Staphylococci* and *Streptococci*, despite being stable to gram-positive β-lactamase.

Cephalosporins are significantly less sensitive to the attack of β-lactamase enzymes. This may be due to the presence of bicyclic cephem ring system present in them. Drug design in cephalosporins followed the similar prominent features involved in penicillins development. For example cefadroxyl was designed on the similar principles to that of amoxicillin. Like penicillins, attachment of phenylglycine moiety at 7 - amino cephalosporanic acid resulted in the compounds with increased oral activity e.g. cephaloglycin. As seen in azlocillin or mezlocillin, acylation of amino group present in phenylglycine moiety imparts anti-pseudomonal activity to the compound e.g. cefoperazone.

In general, substituents at C_7 - amino group in cephalosporins govern the potency while the substituents of C_3 position influence the pharmacokinetic features of the antibiotic. Placement of OCH_3 group at C_7 position may increase the compounds stability to β-lactamase enzyme. The replacement of sulphur by oxygen in the dihydrothiazine nucleus (as it is in moxalactam) enhances bacterial penetration ability of the drug. Presence of p-hydroxy phenyl ring in the substituent at C_7-amino group results into increased blood levels for the antibiotics.

A sulfonic acid moiety if present in acyl side-chain conveys antipseudomonal activity to certain penicillins. The analogy worked well with cephalosporins resulting into introduction of cefsulodin.

6.13 PHARMACO KINETIC PROPERTIES

Many members of first generation (e.g. cephalexin, cefadroxil) are orally well absorbed due to their acid stability. Most of the members of second and third generation cephalosporins are usually, administered parenterally.

Cephalosporins are polar compounds and less readily penetrate cells and CNS. However, moxalactam shows exceptionally good ability to penetrate CNS. However a good concentration of these antibiotics is attained in various body fluids (e.g. pleural, pericardial and joint fluids) and in liver, spleen, muscle, heart and kidney. The extent of protein-binding of various cephalosporins ranges from 40 – 80%. Cephadine, cephalexin, cefatazidime and cefadroxil have protein binding between the range of 10 – 20%. Ceftazidime has lowest degree of protein binding. The plasma half-life of clinically used cephalosporins ranges between 0.5 – 2.0 hours. However, ceftriaxone has the highest plasma half-life of 7 – 8 hours.

Table 6.3 : Clinically used cephalosporins

Name	Plasma half life (hr)	Protein binding %	% metabolism	β lactamase susceptibility
(A) First generation cephalosporins :				
(i) Cephaloridine	1 – 1.5	10 – 30	5 – 10	Yes
(ii) Cephalothin	0.5 – 0.7	65	30 – 35	Yes
(iii) Cephapirin	0.5 – 0.7	45 – 50	40	Yes
(iv) Cephalexin	1.0	10 – 15	5 – 10	No
(v) Cephaloglycine	1.5	15 – 25	90	No
(vi) Cefadroxil	1.2 – 2.0	20	5 – 10	No
(vii) Cephradine	0.8	6 – 20	5 – 10	No
(viii) Cefazolin	1.8 – 2.0	80	5 – 10	Yes
(B) Second generation cephalosporins :				
(i) Cafamandole	0.6 – 0.8	70	5 – 10	No
(ii) Cefoxitin	0.8	70 – 75	5 – 10	No
(iii) Cefuroxime	1 – 2	50	5 – 10	No
(iv) Cefaclor	0.6 – 0.9	25	30	No
(C) Third generation cephalosporins :				
(i) Ceftizoxime	17	30	5 – 10	No
(ii) Cefotaxime	1.0	40	50	No
(iii) Ceftazidime	1.8	17	5 – 10	No
(iv) Ceftriaxone	7 – 8	85 – 90	5 – 10	No
(v) Cefmenoxime	1 – 1.5	75	35	No
Moxalactam :	2.3	50	–	No

Many members of this class (e.g. cephalothin, cephapirin, cefoperazone etc.) are metabolised through desacetylation process. The resulting desacetylated metabolites are usually less active than the parent compounds. Major portion of most of cephalosporins are excreted in the urine in active form. They are eliminated mainly through tubular secretion. Hence like in penicillins, if concomitantly administered, probenecid will prolong the plasma half-life of cephalosporins. Probenecid also elevates the serum levels of cephalosporins. However unlike other cephalosporins, cefoperazone is eliminated primarily by biliary route.

6.14 ADVERSE EFFECTS

Most of the adverse effects produced by cephalosporins are similar to those produced by penicillins.

These effects can be categorised as follows :

(i) Allergic reactions : The nature of side-chain substituents plays an important role in inducing allergic reactions. These reactions mostly belong to type I and type II of allergic manifestations. They include rash, urticaria, fever, serum sickness, eosinophilia and hemolytic anaemia. In penicillin sensitive patients, cross-sensitivity is reported to occur due to structural similarity between cephalosporins and penicillins.

(ii) Nephrotoxicity : These effects include albuminurea, pyuria, renal casts, renal fever, renal tubular necrosis and interstitial nephritis.

(iii) Hematological reactions : These reactions include hemolytic anaemia, neutropenia, hematuria, thrombocytopenia and inhibition of platelet aggregation. The prophylactic use of vitamin K is advised in patients receiving moxalactam. This is because moxalactam or its metabolite is suspected to interfere with the vitamin K-mediated γ-carboxylation of glutamic acid, a step necessary for prothrombin to bind calcium and exert its biological effect.

(iv) Local effects : Many cephalosporins when injected intramuscularly induce thrombophlebitis and severe pain at the site of injection. Cephalothin is the example of most painful cephalosporin in this regard.

(v) Miscellaneous effects :

(a) Superinfections with *Pseudomonas, Klebsiella-enterobacter, E. coli, Proteus, Serratia* and *Candida* species has been reported to occur with cephalosporin therapy.

(b) Certain cephalosporins (e.g. moxalactam and cefoperazone) were found to induce disulfiram-like effects in alcoholic patients due to methyltetrazolethiol like nature of the side-chain.

Bacterial resistance :

Just like penicillins, the major drawback of cephalosporins is the development of antibiotic resistant strains of bacteria. The mechanisms of bacterial resistance for cephalosporins are similar to those for penicillin and include -

(i) Failure of antibiotic to bind with bacterial binding proteins.

(ii) Failure of antibiotic to penetrate bacterial cell-wall.

(iii) Destruction of antibiotic by cephalosporinase enzymes produced by bacteria. These agents are not usually affected much by penicillinase enzymes.

6.15 THERAPEUTIC USES

Below mentioned are some important therapeutic uses of cephalosporin.

(i) Orally active cephalosporins are, commonly used in the treatment of gastrointestinal infections and for the infections of upper and lower respiratory tract.

(ii) Second generation cephalosporins are effective against many gram-negative bacilli, especially *H. influenzae* species. They are indicated in the treatment of infections of skin, biliary tract, urinary tract and respiratory tract caused by gram-negative bacilli.

(ii) Due to the broad spectrum of activity and higher antimicrobial potency, the third generation cephalosporins are used in the treatment of serious infections of lower respiratory tract, biliary tract and bile tract. They may be used alone or in combination with aminoglycosides or chloramphenicol, in the treatment of penicillin resistant gonorrhea and meningitis.

(iii) Cephalosporins may also be used prophylactically to prevent possible infections at the time of biliary surgery, orthopedic surgery, vaginal hysterectomy and during the placement of prosthetic heart valves or prosthetic joints.

6.16 MOXALACTAM

Moxalactam is an example of 1-oxacephems where the sulphur atom in the dihydrothiazine ring is replaced by oxygen atom. This change imparts it a good CNS penetration ability. It is highly effective against enterobacteriaceae, especially *E. coli*, indole positive *Proteus* species, *Citrobacter* spp, *Proteus mirabilis*, *Enterobacter* spp; *Serratia mercescens*, *Pseudomonas aeruginosa*, *Klebsiella* spp.; *Hemophilus influenzae* and *anaerobes* including *B.fragilis*, *Fusobacterium nucleatum* and *Clostridium perfingens*. However, it is relatively less effective against gram-positive cocci, specifically *staphylococci* and *streptococci*.

It is usually given either by i.v. or i.m. route. Significant concentration of moxalactam was found to attain in bile, eyes, cerebrospinal fluid and other body fluids. It has greater ability to induce hematopoetic abnormalities. Suprainfection with enterococci was found to be associated with moxalactam therapy. It is reported that moxalactam acts as a β-lactamase inactivator in some cases. Probenecid has no effect on the renal handling of moxalactam.

6.17 OTHER β-LACTAM ANALOGS

The story of β-lactam antibiotics began in 1929, had propogated through two distinct phases, one marked by penicillin analogs and the second phase was dominated by cephalosporins. The day to day research is still adding new entities to the antibiotic literature and exposing one or more clinical deficiencies perceived in existing drugs. Whether, new basic skeletons designed, will reach the market place or add to the volumes of dead stock in the antibiotic literature is yet uncertain. Recently many new classes of β-lactam antibiotics have come up. These include :

(a) Thienamycins : The research groups at Merck were the first to isolate and characterise thienamycin from *Streptomyces cattleya*. Like penicillins and cephalosporins, it contains a fused bicyclic ring system comprised of β-lactam and a 3-carboxylic group but instead of β-acylamido side-chain, it possesses α-1-hydroxyethyl group. Two distinct features of thienamycin includes its broad spectrum of activity, and its β-lactamase resistant property make it effective against many strains resistant to penicillins and cephalosporins.

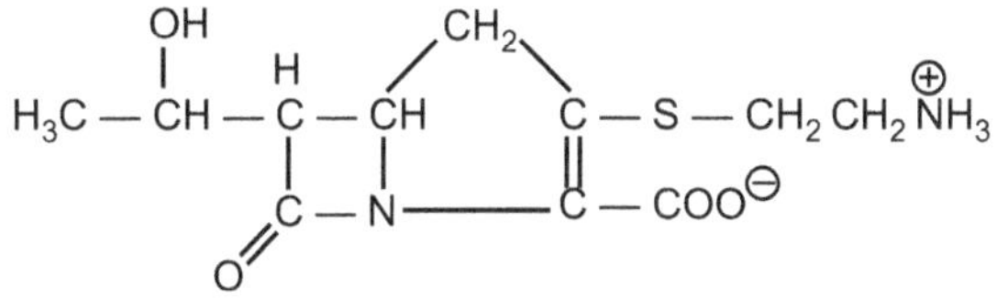

Thienamycin

Thienamycin itself is unstable, hence a n-formimidoyl derivative (i.e. impenem) was developed which is a stable synthetic compound with excellent antimicrobial potential. It has a plasma half-life of 1 hour. About 25% of administered dose is bound to the plasma-proteins. Extensive metabolism occurs by a dipeptide dehydropeptidase I, located on brush border of proximal tubular cells of kidneys. Coadministration of cilastatin (a dihydropeptidase inhibitor) causes prolonged inhibition of renal metabolism of impienem.

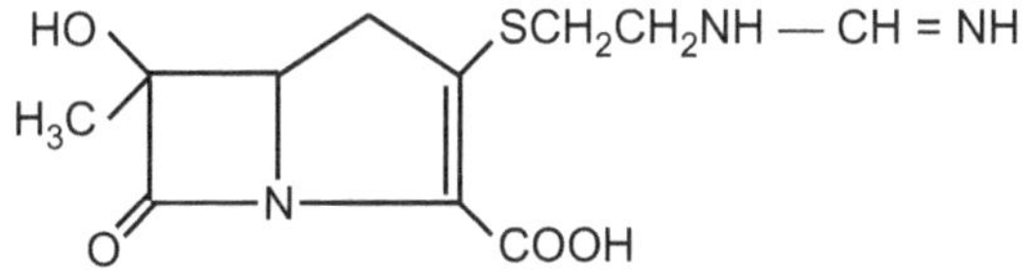

Imipenem

(b) Nocardicins : It is a group of about seven antibiotics isolated from various *Nocardia* species. Here we do not observe a fused bicyclic ring system which is the characteristic feature of β-lactam antibiotics. Nocardicin A is a narrow spectrum antibiotic. The status of nocardicins in the clinical utility still remained to be established.

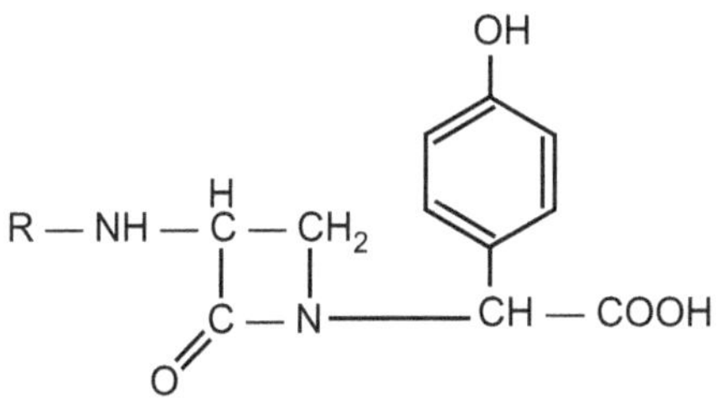

Nocardicins

(c) 1-Oxacephems : In these compounds, the sulphur atom from dihydrothiazine ring is replaced by oxygen atom and an additional α-methoxy group is present at C_7 position.

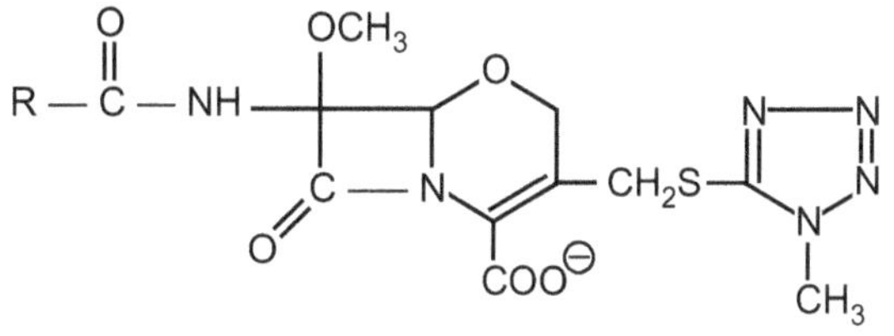

1-oxacephems

Moxalactam is an example of this class. It is a broad spectrum antibiotic having β-lactamase resistance property.

(d) 1-Carbapenems : These are structural analogs of penicillins where the sulphur atom is replaced by carbon. They differ from penicillins, in that the five membered ring is unsaturated. Olivanic acids stand example of this class. They are broad spectrum antibiotics isolated from *Streptomyces olivaceus*.

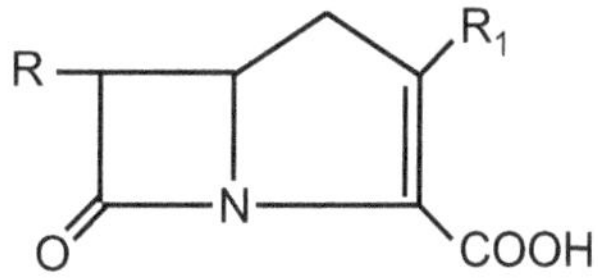

1 - carbapenems

Over 30 carbapenems have been isolated till date. Many are potent antibiotics with activity against a broad range of gram-positive and gram-negative bacteria.

(e) Monobactams : These are monocyclic β-lactam antibiotics isolated from *Chromobacterium violaceum*. The basic nucleus is 3-aminomono bactamic acid (3-AMA). They have little antimicrobial activity. They differ in the nature of acyl substituent and also in the presence or absence of a methoxy group at the 3 α-position of β-lactam ring. They show a high degree of stability to β-lactamases.

Azatreonam is an example of semisynthetic analog of monocyclic β-lactams. It is orally effective. About 56 - 60% of absorbed dose binds to the plasma-proteins. It has a plasma half-life of 1.7 hour. About 70% of the dose appears in the urine.

It has an excellent activity against most of gram-negative bacteria and is resistant to the β-lactamase enzymes. It however exhibits low activity against gram-positive bacteria and anaerobes.

(f) β-lactamase inhibitors : These agents exhibit weak antibacterial activity, and therefore are not entitled to be used as an effective antimicrobial agents. However they have an affinity for β-lactamase enzymes and they serve as the potent irreversible inhibitors of many β-lactamases produced by gram-positive and gram-negative bacteria. Due to these pharmacological features, they are not used as primary antibiotics but are usually combined with the conventional β-lactam antibiotics to prolong their serum half-life and serum concentration level. Thus, they protect the susceptible β-lactam antibiotics from enzymatic degradation. This results into potentiation of activity of β-lactam antibiotics. Example from this category includes Clavulanic acids.

Clavulanic acid consists of a β-lactam ring fused to an oxazolidine ring. It was isolated from *Streptomyces clavuligerus* (the same actinomycete which produced cephamycin). It has a plasma half-life of 1 hour. It can block both intracellular and extracellular β-lactamase enzymes through irreversible complex. The destruction of clavulanic acid occurs followed by the formation of a catalytically inactive stable clavulanate β-lacamase complex. Hence, it is also known as suicide inhibitor. It is presently marketed in combination with amoxicillin to inhibit enzymatic degradation of latter in amoxicillin resistant strains of *Staphylococcus aureus, E. coli, Klebsiella pneumoniae, Proteus mirabillis* and *B. fragilis*. This combination is effective against β-lactamase producing strains of microorganisms. It is usually combined with amoxicillin in 2 : 1 or 4 : 1 ratio in oral form and in 2 : 1 ratio for parenteral use.

Another effective β-lactamase inhibitor is sulbactam which has similar structure to clavulanic acid. Chemically it is an example of 6-desaminopenicillanic acid sulfone and it was produced by Pfizer.

Sulbactam has plasma half-life of 0.97 hour when injected intravenously. Along with its metabolites, it is mainly excreted through urine. The olivanic acids are natural products of *Streptomyces olivaceus* which were isolated by workers at Beecham pharmaceuticals in 1979. β-lactamases of plasmid and chromosomal origin are inhibited by olivanic acids.

(g) Cephamycins and Oxacephems : The clinically used examples of cephamycins include cefoxitin, cefmetazole and cefotetan. Substitution of oxygen for sulphur in the dihydrothiazine ring of the cephamycins led to the development of oxacephems. Moxalactam was the first oxacephem antibiotic introduced in 1978 as a broad spectrum agent. The cephamycins do not have antipseudomonal activity while oxacephems possess antipseudomonal activity. Both these classes are remarkably stable to hydrolysis by a wide range of β-lactamases.

6.18 PEPTIDE ANTIBIOTICS

The polypeptide antibiotics comprise of a rather diverse group of compounds that differ in

(a) their structural features, and

(b) antimicrobial activity spectra.

As the name indicates, chemically they are peptides that contain both, lipid moiety (fatty acids) and amino acids. Imino and N-methylamino acids occur frequently. They usually have D-amino acids and sometimes L-forms of same amino acids. Due to their amphoteric nature, they are categorised into three main types, i.e.

(i) Neutral peptide antibiotics

(ii) Acidic peptide antibiotics, and

(iii) Basic peptide antibiotics.

Except gramicidin D, most of these peptides are cyclic in nature. Their activity spectra is also widespread. For example, polymixins are effective specifically against gram-negative bacteria and are relatively ineffective against gram-positive organisms. While capreomycin and viomycin are used as antitubercular agents. A drawback common to all these agents is their undesirable side-effects particularly renal toxicity. They are highly toxic and have low therapeutic index. Their systemic use hence is rarely advised. Individual agents are described here.

(a) Amphomycin :

The typical peptidal nature of this antibiotic was first reported by **Bodanszky et al**. It exhibits activity mainly against gram-positive bacteria and it may occassionally be combined with anti-inflammatory agents for topical use.

(b) Bacitracin :

The antibiotic was discovered in 1943 by **Johnson, Anker** and **Melency** from *Bacillus lichen informis*, a strain of *Bacillus subtilis* at Columbia University. It was found to be a complex mixture of at least 10 polypeptides (A, A', B, C, D, E, F_1, F_2, F_3 and G) of which Bacitracin A fraction is believed to be most abundant and potent. Zinc, a divalent ion is reported to enhance its activity. Like penicillins, a thiazolidine nucleus is present in bacitracin but a β-lactam ring is absent. This thiazolidine nucleus is linked to a peptide through L-leucine.

Mechanism of action : Bacitracin inhibits bacterial cell-wall synthesis. A lipid pyrophosphate carrier C_{55} - isoprenyl pyrophosphate, is involved in the transportation of cell-wall precursors to the site of cell-wall synthesis. Bacitracin inhibits its dephosphorylation resulting into inhibition of reutilisation of this carrier.

Antibacterial spectrum : Bacitracin is mainly effective against gram-positive bacteria. Its zinc salt exerts bactericidal action against gram-positive cocci and bacilli, *Neisseria, H. influenzae, Actinomyces* and *Fusobacterium* species.

Pharmacokinetic properties : It is not orally absorbed. Because of the risk of serious nephrotoxicity, its parenteral use is not adviced. It is mainly used in the form of topical preparations (like creams, ointments and aerosols) frequently in combination with polymyxin β neomycin or hydrocortisone in the treatment of impetigo and other superficial skin infections. It is a common ingredient of many ophthalmic preparations which are used to treat external ocular infections caused by gram-positive organisms. It was orally evaluated for the treatment of diarrhoea caused by *Clostridium difficile*.

One unit of the drug equals to 26 mg of bacitracin, USP standard.

(c) Vancomycin hydrochloride :

It is an actinomycete antibiotic isolated from *Streptomyces orientalis* in 1956 by **Mc Cormick et al** at Lilly Research Laboratories. It is a tricyclic glycopeptide antibiotic that consists of a dissacharide (vancosamine and glucose), 3-substituted phenylglycines, 2 - β - hydroxyl chlorotyrosines, N - methylleucine and an aspartic acid residue. It has a molecular weight of 1450.

Mechanism of action : Vancomycin is a bactericidal agent that acts by inhibiting bacterial cell-wall synthesis. It binds to the terminal carboxyl group on the D-alanyl-D-alanine terminus of the peptidoglycan and prevents the polymerization of linear peptidoglycan by interferring with the formation of lipid phosphodisaccharide - pentapeptide complex.

Antimicrobial spectra : It is highly effective against gram-positive bacteria (e.g. *S. epidermitis, S. pneumoniae, S. viridans* and some strains of *S. faecalis*). However, gram-negative bacteria are resistant to its action.

Pharmacokinetic properties : Vancomycin is poorly absorbed when given by oral route. It can be used intravenously for the treatment of systemic infections. It is widely distributed in all body fluids (pleural, ascitic, synovial and pericardial) except cerebrospinal fluid. About 60% of administered dose is bound to the plasma-proteins. It has a plasma half-life of 5.6 – 7.0 hours. It appears almost unchanged in the urine and is excreted through the glomerular filtration.

Adverse effects include nausea, mascular skin rashes, chills, fever, urticaria, eosinophilia, anaphylaxis, thrombophlebitis, ototoxicity, nephrotoxicity and pain at the site of injection.

Vancomycin is used in the treatment of Staphylococcal pneumonia, endocarditis, empyema, osteomyelitis, septicemia and soft tissue abscesses. It may also be used to control severe staphylococcal infections in patients who are allergic to β-lactam antibiotics. It is a primary drug in the treatment of pseudomembranous colitis and diarrhoea caused by toxin producing bacteria such as *Clostridium difficile* and *Staph. aureus* where it is used orally in the adult dose of 125 mg every 6 hours. It exhibits synergistic effect when combined with either streptomycin or gentamicin.

Avoparcin and restocetin are the other glycopeptide antibiotics of vancomycin family. Avoparcin finds a role of animal growth promotant while restocetin could not be assigned to any clinical use.

(d) Tyrothricin :

It is a mixture of polypeptides obtained by extraction of cultures of gram-positive, aerobic, spore forming soil microorganism, *Bacillus brevis* in 1939 by Dubos. Gramicidin and tyrocidine are the active ingredients. Tyrothricin now is referred to as a partially purified antibiotic that contains 1 part of gramicidin and 4 parts of tyrocidine. Its antibacterial activity is due to its surfactant like feature. Chemically it is a cyclic decapeptide having activity against both, gram-positive and gram-negative organisms.

Tyrothricin is not a drug of choice because of its limited clinical utility. Since its systemic use may lead to lysis of erythrocytes, its use is restricted to topical applications.

(e) Gramicidin :

It is an open-chain bactericidal polypeptide that causes loss of intracellular cations by damaging the lipid components of gram-positive bacteria. Gramicidin is made up of atleast four components and measures 10 – 20% w/w of tyrothricin. Because of the severe toxicity, it should not be used systemically.

It is used topically in the form of drops, creams, and ointments to treat superficial eye and ear infections.

(f) Cycloserine :

It is one of the simplest antibiotic, isolated in 1955, from *Streptomyces orchidaceous, S. garyphalus* and *S. lavendulus*. Chemically, it is D-4-amino-3-isoxazolidone having broad spectrum of antimicrobial profile. It is effective against *E. coli, Nocardia* species, *Chalmydia, M. tuberculosis* and *Staphylococcus aureus*.

Mechanisms of action : Cycloserine bears structural similarity with D-alanine. Alanine racemase enzyme converts L-alanine to D-alanine. Under the influence of D-alanyl-D-alanine synthetase, a dipeptide (i.e., D-alanyl-D-alanine) is formed. Cycloserine inhibits all these early stages of bacterial cell-wall synthesis. It thus prevents the synthesis of cross-linking dipeptide that is necessary in the formation of bacterial cell-wall. Inhibition of dipeptide formation results in unability of bacterial cell to synthesize UDP-acetylmuramyl pentapeptide, a precursor for bacterial cell-wall synthesis.

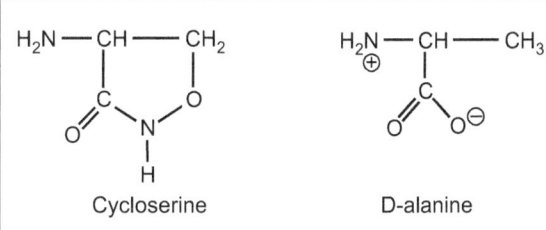

Fig. 6.3 : Structural similarity between cycloserine and D–alanine

Pharmacokinetic properties : It is orally well absorbed and gets widely distributed in the body fluids including cerebrospinal fluid. About 35% administered dose is metabolised to inactive compounds which are excreted in the urine alongwith 50% dose in unchanged form.

Adverse effects include headache, visual disturbances, nervousness, irritability, vertigo, confusion, seizures, twitching and psychotic reactions. It is contraindicated in patients suffering from epilepsy, mental illness or renal disfunctioning.

Today cycloserine is rarely used as an antibacterial agent. It is however effective in the treatment of urinary tract infections. It is used as a second-line antituberculosis agent and is also used to treat *Mycobacterium oviumintercellulare* infection in AIDS patients.

ANTIBIOTICS THAT AFFECT PROTEIN SYNTHESIS

7.1 AMINOGLYCOSIDE ANTIBIOTICS (Aminocyclitol antibiotics)

Aminoglycoside antibiotics includes streptomycin, gentamicin, kanamycin, tobramycin, neomycin, amikacin, netilmicin, spectinomycin and framycetin. They are all mixtures of water-soluble, basic carbohydrates that are closely related chemically. All these agents contain a six-membered 'aminocyclitol ring' either streptidine or 2-deoxystreptamine in their structures.

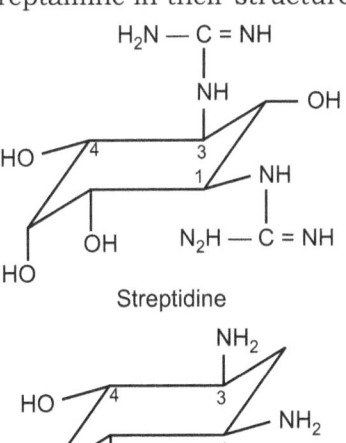

For example, streptomycin and dihydrostreptomycin contain streptidine while rest of the aminoglycosides contain 2-deoxystreptamine. To these basic skeletons, various aminosugars are linked glycosidically at positions 4 and 6. However in spectinomycin, no amino sugar is present. Except for gentamicins, all are the products of species of *Streptomyces*.

The aminoglycosides are used primarily to treat infections caused by gram-negative bacteria. They show poor oral absorption and due to this reason they are usually given by parenteral route. Due to high polar nature, they are insignificantly bound to the plasma-proteins. They are minimally metabolized in the body. Major portion of the administered dose appears in the urine. They are mainly eliminated through glomerular filtration. They possess very narrow therapeutic index. Their systemic use is also restricted due to severe oto- and nephrotoxicity. Development of bacterial resistance and increased awareness about their toxicities have initiated attempts to synthesize new analogs (e.g. sisomicin, 5-episisomicin, netilmicin, dibekacin etc.) in this series.

In summary, the aminoglycoside antibiotics contain two important structural features :

(i) amino sugar portion, and

(ii) centrally placed hexose ring either 2-deoxystreptamine or streptidine.

Thus, in kanamycin and gentamicin families, two aminosugars are attached to 2-deoxystreptamine. In streptomycin two aminosugars are attached to streptidine while in neomycin family, there are three aminosugars attached to 2-deoxystreptamine. The nomenclature of aminoglycosides depends upon the natural source of these antibiotics. For example, the name of antibiotic ends with "*mycin*" if it is obtained from *Streptomyces* species while the name ends with "*micin*" if the drug is obtained from *Micromonospora* species or semi-synthetically.

7.2 CLASSIFICATION

All aminoglycosides consist of two or more aminosugars, attached through glycosidic linkage to a highly substituted 1, 3-diaminocyclohexane (aminocyclitol) central ring. They can be categorised into :

(a) Streptomycin group : It includes streptomycin, dihydrostreptomycin, manni-sidostreptomycin and cycloheximide. All these agents are obtained from micro-organism *Streptomyces griseus*.

(b) Kanamycin group : It includes kanamycins (*Streptomyces kanamyceticus*), amikacin (semi-synthetically derived from kanamycin A). and tobramycin (*Streptomyces tenebrarius*).

Table 7.1: Currently used aminoglycoside antibiotics

Sr. No.	Antibiotic	Source	Year of introduction	Plasma half-life	Protein binding	Unchanged % excreted
1.	Streptomycin	*Streptomyces griseus*	1944; Waksman	2.5	30	50
2.	Neomycin*	*S. fradiae*	1949; Waksman	2.0	20	97
3.	Kanamycin	*S. kanamyceticus*	1957; Limezawa	4.0	15	100
4.	Gentamicin	*Micromonospora purpurea*	1963; Weinstein	4.0	40	100
5.	Netilmicin	*Micromonospora* species	1963; Weinstein	2.3 - 3.0	7 - 9	80 – 90
6.	Tobramycin (nebramycin)	*S. tenebrarius*	1968; Higgins	4.0	40	100
7.	Framycetin (soframycin)	*S. decaris*		–	–	–
8.	Paromomycin*	*S. rimosus formo-paramomycinus,*	1959	2.5	–	97
9.	Amikacin	Semisynthetic product from kanamycin	1972; kawaguchi	2 – 3	4 – 8	98
10.	Netilmicin (N-ethyl sisomicin)	Semisynthetic product from sisomicin	late 1970s	2 – 3	7 - 9	80 – 90
11.	Sisomicin		late 1970s	1.8	–	81
12.	Dibekacin		late 1970s	2.1	–	80

* About 3% administered dose is absorbed by oral route. Unabsorbed 97% dose appears unchanged in faeces.

(c) Gentamicin group : It includes gentamicins (*Micromonospora purpurea*), sisomicin and netilmicin. The latter two antibiotics are obtained through semisynthetic routes.

(d) Neomycin group : It includes neomycins (*Streptomyces fradiae*), paromomycin, lividomycin and ribostamycin.

All aminoglycosides have exposed hydroxyl and amino functional groups that are easily attacked by bacterial enzymes resulting into inactivation of the antibiotic. For example, the amino functions at C_2 and C_6 serve as the major target sites for bacterial inactivating enzymes. Inactivation occurs either due to acetylation of free amino group and adenylation or phosphorylation of free hydroxy groups by bacterial enzymes. Various modifications to protect these amino groups have been tried. The acylation (e.g. amikacin) and ethylation (e.g. 1 – N – ethylsisomicin) though not increase the antibacterial activity but help to protect the antibiotic from the attack of bacterial enzymes. Hence, amikacin has broad range of antimicrobial activity by virtue of its resistance to bacterial enzymes. Similarly in sisomicin series, 2 - hydroxylation and 5 - deoxygenation result in increased inhibition of bacterial inactivating enzyme systems.

7.3 MECHANISM OF ACTION

Aminoglycosides act by binding irreversibly to 30 S ribosomes resulting into interference in the bacterial protein synthesis. Antibacterial activity of all these agents markedly increase at alkaline pH, suggesting better penetration of these drugs inside the bacterial cell. Some of these agents may also alter the bacterial cell-membrane. Recent evidences suggest their inhibitory role at the pyruvate-oxalacetic acid step of Kreb's cycle resulting into reduction in energy production.

7.4 ANTIBACTERIAL ACTIVITY SPECTRA

Aminoglycoside antibiotics are highly effective against aerobic gram-negative microorganisms. They however remain ineffective against many gram-positive cocci and anaerobic bacteria. Streptomycin and kanamycin are also effective against atypical mycobacterial infections. Neomycin has antibacterial activity similar to streptomycin while kanamycin is preferred against serious infections with gram-negative organisms affecting urinary tract. Gentamicin and tobramycin are more active against *Pseudomonas aeruginosa*. The semisynthetic derivatives, like sisomicin and netilmicin are more effective against *E. coli*, *Enterobacter*, *Proteus* and *Klebsiella* species. The degree of their oto- and nephrotoxicities, determines their range of usefulness. Penicillins or vancomycin may be used in combination with aminoglycosides to exhibit synergistic activity against *S. faecalis*, *S. aureus* and viridans streptococci.

7.5 PHARMACOKINETIC PROPERTIES

Aminoglycosides are not usually given by oral route because of poor absorption. They may however be used for intestinal sterilization due to their local effect. They may be given either intravenously or intramuscularly to get systemic effects. Certain agents like neomycin and gentamicin may be applied topically.

Because of their cationic nature, they are widely distributed in extracellular fluids. They enter pleural, peritoneal and synovial fluids and can cross the placenta. They lack the ability to enter cerebrospinal fluid and eyes. The extent of binding to plasma-protein of these drugs varies from 0 – 20% and they show accumulation in red blood cells to the extent of 5 – 10%. They have the serum half-lives in the range of 2 – 4 hours. They are not metabolised *in vivo* and major dose appears unchanged in the urine.

7.6 ADVERSE EFFECTS

Below mentioned are some adverse effects of aminoglycosides :

(i) Prolonged use of aminoglycosides induces damage to both divisions of VIIIth cranial nerve. They have a long biological half-life (of several hours) in the inner ear. This leads to the destruction of vestibular sensory cells (vestibulotoxic) and/or of cochlear hair cells (cochleotoxic) depending upon the dose administered. Vestibulotoxicity is characterised by nausea, vomiting, vertigo, nystagmus and permanant deafness. Streptomycin and gentamicin possess vestibulotoxic nature. While cochleotoxicity is characterized by tinnitus, fullness in ears and gradual loss of hearing capacity. Kanamycin, neomycin, amikacin and tobramycin possess cochleotoxic potential.

(ii) Major fraction of administered dose appears unchanged in the urine, as a result aminoglycosides exhibit a high potential of nephrotoxicity. It is characterised by proteinurea, rising serum BUN, appearance of casts and inability to concentrate urine. The parenteral administration of neomycin is not advised because of high degree of nephrotoxicity potential associated with it. While streptomycin is virtually devoid of nephrotoxicity at therapeutic doses.

(iii) Aminoglycosides exhibit skeletal muscle relaxant effect by inhibiting the release of acetylcholine in the neuromuscular junctions. This effect can be partly neutralised by concomitant administration of either i.v. calcium salts or administration inhibitors. Loss of balance and a feeling of dizziness is usually reported to occur with streptomycin therapy.

(iv) Hypersensitivity reactions are quite common, with the use of aminoglycosides. They include drug fever, stomatitis, eosinophilia, exfoliative dermatitis, transient hypotension, angioedema and anaphylactic shock.

(v) Miscellaneous adverse effects include pain at the site of injection, gastrointestinal irritation and chances of suprainfection with staphylococci and fungi.

7.7 THERAPEUTIC USES

Aminoglycosides are effective against most of the aerobic gram-negative microorganisms, specifically *P. aeruginosa* and members of Enterobacteriaceae. They are preferred in the treatment of *Pseudomonas* infections in patients with cystic fibrosis. They may also be used to treat various subcutaneous, postoperative or traumatic wound infections caused by *Pseudomonas*, *Proteus* or *Klebsiella* species. Since they are ineffective against anaerobic organisms, they are combined with clindamycin or β-lactam antibiotics (which possess activity against anaerobic organisms) to treat sepsis or severe wound inections.

Many members of this class (e.g. neomycin, framycetin, gentamicin etc.) may also be used topically to treat infected wounds, burns and other skin infections.

Kanamycin and streptomycin show antimicrobial activity against *Mycobacterium tuberculosis*. Their role in the chemotherapy of tuberculosis is discussed in the relevant chapter.

(a) Streptomycin and dihydro-streptomycin :

The organism, *Streptomyces griseus* was isolated in 1943 by **Waksman et al** as a result of a well planned scientific search covering more than ten thousand organisms. Streptomycin was isolated from *S. griseus* in 1944. The three basic amino groups present in streptomycin structure can be used for salt formation. The antimicrobial activity of streptomycin is maximal at pH 7.8.

It is very poorly absorbed (< 1%) from oral route. Orally administered dose appears almost unchanged in the faeces. It is rapidly absorbed from s.c. and i.m. routes.

It is used alongwith tetracycline in the control of infection due to *Brucellasuis* or *Br. melitensis* in the dose of 1 – 2 g per day for 1 – 3 weeks. It may be used in the dose of 500 mg twice a day in the treatment of streptococcal endocarditis usually with penicillin G for about 4 – 6 weeks. It is highly effective in the treatment of all forms of plague (*Yersinia pestis*) in the dose of 1 – 4 g per day for 7 – 10 days. It may also be used i.m.ly in the therapy of tularemia (*Francisella tularensis*) in the dose of 1 – 2 g per day for 7 – 10 days. It is a bactericidal agent for tubercle bacillus. Hence, it may be used alongwith isoniazid and / or rifampin in the treatment of tuberculosis.

However antibiotic-resistant strains of bacteria gradually develop due to the acquired ability to synthesis inactivating enzymes (e.g. streptomycin phosphotransferase and streptomycin adenylyl synthetase) that break down the antibiotic. Instead of becoming sensitive, some strains of bacteria may actually become dependent on streptomycin and continue their multiplication until streptomycin is there.

(b) Neomycins :

It is a group of six antibiotics (A, B, C, D, E and F) which is produced by certain strains of *Streptomyces fradiae*. Neomycin A is a degradation product of neomycin B and C. Commercial preparations contain about 90% of neomycin B, remainder being neomycin C.

Qualitatively the antimicrobial activity and other properties of neomycin are similar with that of streptomycin. Susceptible organisms include *Enterobacter aerogenes, E. coli, Klebsiella pneumoniae, Proteus vulgaris, Staphylococcus aureus* and *Streptomyces faecalis*. It is orally unabsorbed. It should not be given parenterally because of greater risk of oto- and nephrotoxicities. Orally it is used for :

(a) preparation of the bowel for surgery to reduce the chances of postoperative wound, infections,

(b) therapy of hepatic coma, and

(c) treatment of diarrhoea, caused by enteropathogenic *E. coli.*

Topically (as a 0.5% solution) it can be used to reduce a number of resident bacteria on the skin and to control various infections affecting skin and mucous membrane. It also inhibits bacterial decomposition of perspiration.

Framycetin (soframycin) was isolated from *Streptomyces decaris*. It is found to be identical with neomycin B.

(c) Kanamycins :

They are produced by *Streptomyces kanamyceticus* and have properties and actions similar to streptomycin. Kanamycins A, B and C are closely related chemically. They do not possess D-ribose moiety that is present in neomycins. The use of kanamycin is restricted to treat serious infections of urinary tract caused due to gram-negative organisms. It may also be used orally for intestinal sterilization. Due to the toxicity and development of resistant strains of bacteria, kanamycin is largely replaced by newer agents from this class.

(d) Gentamicins :

It is a group of metabolic products of *Micromonospora purpurea* and consists of closely related broad-spectrum aminoglycosides (i.e. gentamicins C_1, C_2 and C_{1a}). Commercial preparations contain varying ratio of these three components. It is effective against many serious gram-negative bacillary infections. It is available in parenteral, topical and ophthalmic - otic preparations.

It is used to treat urinary tract infections, bacteremia, cerebral ventriculitis, infected burns, meningitis, pneumonia, osteomyelitis, peritonitis and otitis infections caused by *Pseudomonas aeruginosa*, *Enterobacter*, *Klebsiella* and *Serratia* species. Gentamicin impregnated polymethyl-methacrylate beads are used in the treatment of osteomyelitis. It is also used as a prophylactic antibiotic in surgical procedures. It may also be used in combination of penicillin to control enterococcal endocarditis.

(e) Paromomycins :

It is isolated from *Streptomyces rimosus*. It is inadequately absorbed from oral route. Major fraction of orally administered dose appears unchanged in the faeces. Paromomycin is chemically similar to neomycin except that it contains D-glucosamine instead of 6-amino-6-deoxy-D-glucosamine. It is a mixture of paromomycin I and paromomycin II. In addition to its effectiveness against gram-negative and *Mycobacterium* species, it is highly active against *Entamoeba histolytica*. The antibiotic has anthelmintic properties and may be used in the treatment of intestinal infestations of *Giardiasis*, *Taenia saginata* (beef tapeworm), *Hymenolepis nana* (dwarf tapeworm), *Diphyllobothrium latum* (fish tapeworm) and *Taenia sodium* (pork tapeworm). It is used alongwith metronidazole to control severe forms of intestinal amebiasis. It may also be beneficial in patients with hepatic coma where it alters the bowel flora, resulting into decreased ammonia production.

Semisynthetic Aminoglycosides :

These antibiotics were developed in late 1970s. They include tobramycin, sisomicin, netilmicin and amikacin. They were designed in order to acheive increased potency and more stability towards bacterial destructive enzymes. Their pharmacological activity spectra is similar to that of gentamicin.

(i) Tobramycin : It is an orally ineffective bactericidal aminoglycoside antibiotic isolated from a complex, nebramycin elaborated by *Streptomyces tenebrarius*. Chemically it is 3'-deoxykanamycin B. It is very effective against *Pseudomonas aeruginosa* and has a lower nephrotoxicity potential. Rest of the activities are similar with that of gentamicin.

Besides parenteral use, it is also available in the form of ophthalmic ointment or solution containing 3 mg /g or 3 mg / ml of the drug.

(ii) Sisomicin : It is chemically similar to gentamicin C_{1a}. The only difference is the presence of a double bond in one of the diaminosugar between the position 4' and 5' in sisomicin structure. It has similar activity spectra with gentamicin except its high effectiveness against *E. coli, Proteus* and *Klebsiella*.

(iii) Netilmicin : It is a broad spectrum N-ethyl derivative of sisomicin. Since it is poorly absorbed orally, it is usually given parenterally. It is used in the treatment of pneumonia, septicemia, bone infections, urinary tract infections, skin and soft tissue infections and intra-abdominal infections caused by susceptible gram-negative bacteria.

(iv) Amikacin : The free amino groups at C_2 and C_6 positions in kanamycin serve as the major target sites for bacterial inactivating enzymes. Attempts were made to design such antibiotics in which target sites or functional groups are either removed or sterically hindered. An example of such successful attempt is amikacin. It is a semisynthetic derivative of kanamycin A where L-amino group of 2-deoxystreptine is acylated with 2-hydroxyl-4-aminobutyric acid. In this case, the susceptible site in kanamycin is sterically hindered that results into resistance of amikacin to the attack of bacterial destructive enzymes. Though amikacin is less potent than gentamicin, it also has lower toxicity potential.

It is active against almost all strains of *Klebsiella, Enterobacter* and *E. coli* that are resistant to gentamicin and tobramycin. It is used in the treatment of

(i) Infections caused by nosocomial gram-negative bacilli.

(ii) Diseases caused by atypical Mycobacteria, and

(iii) Burns infected with gentamicin resistant strains of *Pseudomonas aeruginosa* or *Providencia stuartii*.

7.8 BACTERIAL RESISTANCE

(a) A new wave of hope propogated in medical profession with the introduction of aminoglycoside antibiotics. They have broad spectrum of activity. They are featured by projection of polar groups (i.e. free hydroxyl or amino groups) upon the basic carbohydrate skeleton. These polar groups unfortunately served as the platform for enzymatic deactivation of aminoglycosides resulting into development of antibiotic resistant strain of microorganisms.

The development of strains of *Enterobacteriaceae* resistant to aminoglycosides led to detailed study of mechanisms of bacterial resistance. At least 11 different antibiotic inactivating enzymes were identified. They include acetylases, adenylases and phosphorylases which are present in the periplasmic space of gram-negative bacteria. These enzymes induce molecular modifications of aminoglycosides by adenylating, phosphorylating or acetylating the free hydroxyl or amino groups present in the structure of these compounds. The free hydroxyl groups may get either adenylated or phosphorylated while amino group get acetylated by these enzymes. Due to such alterations in the structural features, aminoglycosides gradually loses their ability to penetrate the bacterial cell and to bind with ribosomes.

Unfortunately the resistance can be transmitted from one generation to another due to extrachromosomal R-factors which are self replicative and transferred by direct contact. The R-factor genetically controls the biosynthesis of microbial enzymes. Strains that carry R factor are resistant to streptomycin, kanamycin and other aminoglycoside antibiotics. Gentamicin and tobramycin frequently show cross-resistance.

(b) Antibiotic penetration and transportation in the bacteria is governed by presence of cation, oxygen tension, osmolality and pH of the media. It is an energy-dependent process. Permeability block is another possible mechanism to develop antibiotic-resistant strains of microorganisms where the energy-dependent step involved in the transport of antibiotic is missing. Permeability block can be transferred from one generation to another by R factors. Due to energy dependent transport, anaerobic bacteria are resistant to the action of aminoglycosides.

(c) The mechanism of minor importance includes less ability of bacterial ribosomes to bind with aminoglycosides due to ribosomal alterations brought about through mutation.

Table 7.2 : Aminoglycoside inactivating enzymes

Source	Inactivating enzymes	Inactivated antibiotic
1. *Proteus providencia*	2' - N - acetyltransferase	Gentamicin, Tobramycin
2. *Pseudomonas, Klebsiella, Enterobacter*	3' - N - acetyltransferase	Gentamicin, Tobramycin
3. *Pseudomonas, E. coli, Serratia*	6' - N - acetyltransferase	Gentamicin, Tobramycin Kamamycin
4. *Klebsiella*	2' - 0 - phosphotransferase	Gentamicin, Tobramycin Kanamycin
5. *Pseudomonas, Klebsiella, E.coli, S.aureus*	3' - 0 - phosphotransferase	Kanamycin, Neomycin
6. *S. aureus*	4' - 0 – adenyltransferase	Kanamycin, Tobramycin, Amikacin

7.9 TETRACYCLINE ANTIBIOTICS

A clear-cut division of work is observed amongst previous two classes of antibiotics. For example, β-lactam antibiotics are effective mainly against gram-positive organisms while aminoglycoside antibiotics are effective mainly against gram-negative organisms. Discovery of tetracyclines was the result of an attempt to develop such antibiotics which are effective against both gram-positive and gram-negative organisms of aerobic and anaerobic categories.

Table 7.3 : Clinically used tetracyclines

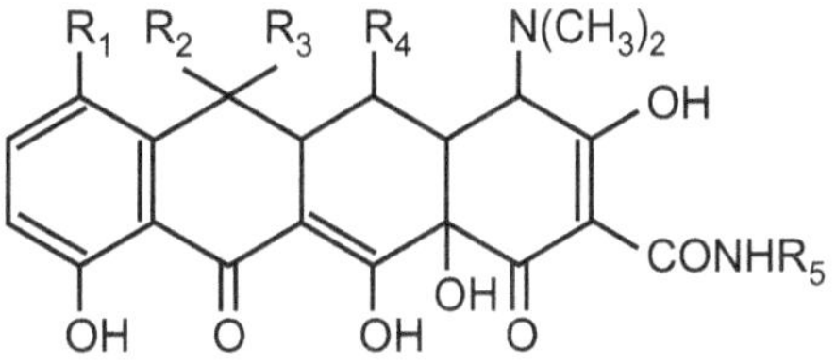

Tetracyclines

Sr. No.	Name	Source	Year of introduction	% binding plasma proteins	Serum half life (hr.)
1.	7-Chlortetracycline	S. aureofaciens	1948	40 – 70	4 – 6
2.	Oxytetracycline	S. rimosus	1950	20 – 35	8 – 10
3.	Tetracycline	Semisynthetically from chlortetracycline	1952	25 – 60	8 – 9
4.	Demeclocycline	Mutant strains of S. aureofaciens	1959	40 – 90	10 – 17
5.	Methacycline	Semisynthetically from oxytetracycline	1961	75 – 90	10 – 16
6.	Doxycycline	Semisynthetically from oxytetracycline	1966	25 – 90	12 – 20
7.	Minocycline	Semisynthetically from oxytetracycline	1972	70 – 75	12 – 19
8.	Rolitetracycline	Semisynthetically from tetracycline	–	–	–
9.	Lymecycline	Mannich base of tetracycline	–	–	–

Tetracyclines are obtained either as metabolic byproducts of various species of *Streptomyces* or as semisynthetic derivatives of the natural products. The series consists of about eight members. The first member of this series was 7-chlortetracycline that was discovered in 1948 by **Duggar**. They are all yellow amphoteric compounds forming salts either with acids or bases. They exist as zwitter ions at pH 7. They are poorly water soluble but readily form highly water-soluble sodium or hydrochloride salts. Except for rolitetracycline (which is given parenterally), tetracyclines are usually taken by oral route. Epimerization at C_4, is witnessed with tetracyclines in the solutions of intermediate pH range. These epitetracyclines exhibit much less activity than the neutral isomers.

They are broad-spectrum antibiotics. In the series, minocycline is most active against most of gram-positive and gram-negative organisms. Resistance to tetracyclines develops relatively slowly. Main examples of resistant strains of bacteria include *E. coli, Shigella* species, β-hemolytic streptococci, *D. pneumoniae, N. gonorrhoeae* and *Bacteroides*. Cross-resistance among the series is also reported except minocycline which is active against many bacterial strains that are resistant to other tetracyclines.

7.10 MECHANISM OF ACTION

Tetracyclines are reported to inhibit bacterial protein synthesis by preventing the formation of t-RNA - amino acid complexes. Their primary site of binding is 30S ribosomal units. Since this binding to ribosomes is not permanant, they are bacteriostatic. They also interfere with the functioning of bacterial cell-membrane by chelating essential divalent cations like calcium, magnesium, zinc, iron etc.

7.11 PHARMACOKINETIC PROPERTIES

Tetracyclines on administration by oral route, show incomplete and irregular absorption. The presence of foods and divalent cations further slow down their absorption. Tetracyclines are widely distributed in different body fluids and compartments. They are reported to be present in pleural, ascitic and synovial fluid. Besides this, they are also found in cerebrospinal fluid, biliary region and salivary and lacrimal secretions. Tetracycline and oxytetracycline are able to cross placental barrier. They have plasma half-lives mostly in the range of 6 – 12 hours. The extent of plasma protein binding affects the plasma half-life of the drug. For example, methacycline has a long plasma half-life because of its high binding capacity (75 - 90%) to plasma-proteins. Except chlortetracycline and doxycycline, all other tetracyclines are insignificantly metabolized in the body. Major portion of dose administered appears unchanged in the urine alongwith small portion in the form of inactive metabolites. They are eliminated in the urine mainly by glomerular filtration. Minor portion is also excreted in the bile and milk (in lactating women).

7.12 ANTIMICROBIAL ACTIVITY SPECTRA

Tetracyclines are bacteriostatic, broad-spectrum antibiotics. The basic nucleus common to all tetracyclines is a polycyclic naphthacene carboxyamide that is comprised of four fused, six-membered rings A, B, C and D. The group name, tetracycline thus describes the nature of backbone skeleton.

Tetracyclines have low solubility in water. This drawback may be overcome by aminoalkylation at carboxamido group using Mannish reaction. The clinically effective mannish derivatives include roliteracycline (i.e., pyrrolidino-methyltetracycline), lymecycline (tetracycline - L - methylenelysine) and clomocycline (N-methylol 7 - chlortetracycline). Semisynthetic analogs have also been designed in an attempt to enhance potency. Methacycline, doxycycline and minocycline are few such examples.

Tetracyclines are effective against most of gram-positive and gram-negative bacteria. They are used in treating many infections due to the *Rickettsiae, Chlamydia, Mycoplasma pneumoniae, Bacteriodes, Hemolytic streptococci* and *Staphylococci*, atypical *Mycobacteria* and amoebae. They are not much effective against fungi and share similar antimicrobial potency, pharmacological and therapeutic activities.

7.13 ADVERSE EFFECTS

Some commonly encountered adverse effects are as follows :

(a) GIT effects : These include nausea, vomiting, anorexia, diarrhaea and gastrointestinal irritation.

(b) Circulatory system : They induce blood coagulation probably due to their chelating effect on serum calcium. They also promote excretion of haemopoietic vitamins like, folic acid and vitamin B_{12}. Since the intestinal bacterial flora is destroyed by them, the chronic tetracycline therapy must be supplimented with a multivitamin preparation.

(c) Bone and calcification : Tetracyclines interfere in the development and calcification of bones by chelating calcium ions to form tetracycline - calcium orthophosphate complexes. The presence of these complexes is characterised by a yellow fluorescence on teeth which may turn up into brown discolouration over a period of time. This may result in the tooth staining, enamel hypoplasia and a reversible depression of linear bone growth if they are given to children below 8 years of age.

(d) Hypersensitivity reactions : Just like other antibiotics, tetracyclines also induce hypersensitivity reactions. These include skin rash, fever, eosinophilia, angioedema, burning of eyes, light headedness, photodermatitis and anaphylactic shock.

(e) Suprainfection : Tetracyclines depresses the natural bacterial flora present in gastrointestinal tract and genital tract. This leads to chances of developing suprainfections specifically with various strains of *Proteus* and *Pseudomonas, Candida albicans* and pencillinase-producing *staphylococci*.

(f) Protein synthesis : Tetracyclines also affect protein synthesis of host cells resulting into weight loss and negative nitrogen balance.

(g) Nephrotoxicity : Tetracycline may produce renal tubular necrosis while demeclocycline has been reported to induce nephrogenic diabetes insipidus.

Since they can easily cross placenta and due to their effect on development and calcification of bones they are contraindicated during pregnancy and in lactating women. They should not be used in patients with peptic ulcer and hepatic dysfunctioning. The increased demand for protein anabolism during pregnancy may make the liver more susceptible to the attack of tetracyclines to cause hepatotoxicity.

7.14 THERAPEUTIC USES

Tetracyclines are broad-spectrum antibiotics that can be used in the treatment of infections caused by both, gram-positive or gram-negative bacteria.

(i) They are drugs of choice in the treatment of cholera, relapsing fever, gonorrhea, syphilis, granuloma inguinale, chancroid, leptospirosis, actinomycosis and nocardiosis.

(ii) They are effectively used in the longterm treatment of sinusitis, chronic bronchitis, gas gangrene and cystic fibrosis.

(iii) They may be used to treat urinary tract infections caused by susceptible strains of gram-negative bacteria.

(iv) They are preferred in the treatment of infections caused by *H.influezae*, and pneumococcal and meningococcal meningitis, specially in patient having penicillin-allergy.

(v) They may be used in combination with aminoglycosides in the treatment of brucellosis, tularemia and plague.

(vi) They may be applied topically to control severe inflammation and corynebacterium acnes.

(vii) Some tetracyclines may be used as diagnostic agents to detect certain cancers (e.g. stomach, bladder, colon) because of their property to give yellow fluorescence in U.V. region.

7.15 CHLORAMPHENICOL

Originally isolated from *Streptomyces venezuelae* by **Ehrlich et al** in 1947, chloramphenicol (chloromycetin) shortly thereafter, was totally produced by a synthetic route at Parke-Davis laboratories. It contains chlorine atom and was obtained from an actinomycete. Hence, it was named as chloromycetin.

$$O_2N-C_6H_4-\overset{3}{C}H(OH)-\overset{2}{C}H(NHCOCHCl_2)-\overset{1}{C}H_2OH$$

Chloramphenicol

Chemically it consists of a p-nitrophenyl group, a propanediol skeleton and a dichloroacetamido side-chain. Out of the four stereoisomers, only L-form is biologically active. The para nitro group present on the phenyl ring is found to be responsible for the serious haematological abnormalities due to depression of bone-marrow. In thiamphenicol, this nitro group is replaced by a sulfo-methyl ($-CH_2SO_2$) moiety in order to reduce the toxicity. Similarly, the 3-hydroxyl group in the propanediol skeleton can be replaced by a fluorine atom to increase antimicrobial potency.

7.16 MECHANISM OF ACTION

Chloramphenicol binds with the 50 S subunit of the 70 S ribosome and blocks the formation of peptide bond. This results into inhibition of bacterial protein synthesis. Since the human mitochondrial ribosomes are quite similar to bacterial 70 S ribosomes bone-marrow supression and hematotoxic effects due to chloramphenicol are more pronounced because of inhibition of mitochondrial protein synthesis in bone-marrow.

Bacterial Resistance : It is developed by following mechanisms :

(i) The 3-hydroxyl group present in the propanediol side-chain gets acetylated by a plasmid-mediated enzyme known as chloramphenicol transacetylase,

(ii) Development of permeability block, and

(iii) Slow enzymatic reduction of nitro group.

7.17 ANTIMICROBIAL ACTIVITY SPECTRUM

Chloramphenicol has a broad spectrum of activity resembling to that of tetracyclines except it exhibits lesser activity against some gram-positive bacteria. It is specifically recommended for the treatment of serious infections caused by *Hemophilus influenzae, Salmonella typhi, Streptococcus pneumoniae, Neisseria meningities* and anaerobic infections, particularly due to *Bacteroides fragilis*. It possesses marked effectiveness against several gram-negative bacteria and also exhibits antirickettsial activity. Its ability to penetrate into CNS presents it as an alternative therapy for meningities.

7.18 PHARMACOKINETIC PROPERTIES

Chloramphenicol is available for oral, topical, intravenous and intramuscular administration. It is an orally effective drug. Orally it is used in the form of chloramphenicol palmitate while in the form of succinate, it may be used parenterally. It is well distributed in various body fluids including eye and cerebrospinal fluid. It also crosses the placental barrier. About 53% of administered dose is bound to the plasma-proteins. It has a plasma half-life of 4.0 hours. It is mainly metabolised in the liver by hepatic glucuronyl transferase enzymes to form glucuronyl metabolites. These inactive glucuronides are excreted in the urine alongwith minor amounts (5-10%) of unchanged drug.

7.19 ADVERSE EFFECTS

Some common adverse effects associated with chloramphenicol therapy are as follows :

(a) Haematopoietic toxicity : Chloramphenicol produces a dose-dependent, reversible depression of bone-marrow function. The p-nitro group present on the phenyl ring of chloramphenicol is found to be responsible for this effect. Haematopoietic toxicity is characterized by an elevated serum iron level, prolonged plasma iron clearance, vacuolation of both red and white blood cells, neutropenia, reticulocytopenia, thrombocytopenia and aplastic anaemia with pancytopenia. Since it can cross placenta it should be used with caution in late pregnancy. It is contraindicated in lactating women.

(b) Hypersensitivity reactions : These include various skin rashes, glossitis, stomatitis, cheilosis, angioedema, pruritus and blood dyscrasias.

(c) GIT effects : These include nausea, vomiting, gastric irritation, enterocolitis and diarrhoea.

(d) Suprainfection : Due to the broad-spectrum activity of chloramphenicol, suprainfection with *Staphylococcus aureus, Pseudomonas, aeruginosa, Proteus* species and *Candida* is likely to develop in patients receiving chloramphenicol.

(e) Other effects : These include headache, parethesias, myalgia, mood disturbances and renal damage.

7.20 THERAPEUTIC USES

Some important therapeutic uses of chloramphenicol are as follows :

(i) Chloramphenicol is used in the treatment of typhoid fever, meningitis, rickettsial disease, osteomyelitis, pneumonia, abdominal wound infections and drug resistant malarial parasites.

(ii) It is used to treat many anaerobic bacterial infections, specially due to *Bacteroides fragilis*, and

(iii) It may sometimes be used to treat urinary tract infections resistant to other antibiotics.

(iv) In *combination* with penicillins, it is used in the treatment of brain abscess.

7.21 MACROLIDE ANTIBIOTICS

The research glamour created by the discovery of penicillins still then continued its way resulting into identification of a totally new class known as macrolide antibiotics. Isolated from *Actinomycetes*, it is a group of chemically related compounds characterized by three common structural features that include :

(i) The presence of a large ring lactone (hence the name, macrolide),

(ii) Various ketonic and hydroxyl functions, and

(iii) Glycosidically linked 6-deoxy, sugars.

More often the lactone ring has 12, 14 or 16 atoms in it and it is partially unsaturated with the presence of a double bond in conjugation with a ketone function. At present, more than 70 such antibiotics have been reported. The presence of a dimethylamino group on the sugar moiety imparts basic properties to the macrolides.

These antibiotics are known as penicillin substitutes. They are employed to treat infections due to pencillin-resistant organisms or when patient is allergic to penicillin analogs. They are effective against gram-positive bacteria, both bacilli and cocci (like *staphylococci*, *streptococci*, *enterococci* and *pneumococci*). They are relatively ineffective against gram-negative organisms due to their inability to cross their cell-wall. At high concentration however, they may inhibit anaerobic gram-negative organisms, like *B. fragils*.

They are not influenced by penicillinase enzymes but organisms may develop resistance to macrolide antibiotics by other mechanisms. They may exert bacteriostatic or bactericidal effect depending upon the dose used and type of microorganism.

Table 7.4 : Macrolide antibiotics

Antibiotic	Source
1. Carbomycin A	*Streptomyces halstedii*
2. Chalcomycin	*Streptomyces bikiniensis*
3. Erythromycin	*Streptomyces erythreus*
4. Oleandomycin	*Streptomyces antibioticus*
5. Josamycin	*Streptomyces kitasatoensis*
6. Leucomycin A_1	*Streptomyces kitasatoensis*
7. Tylosin	*Streptomyces fradiae*
8. Spiramycin I	*Streptomyces ambofaciens*
9. Troleandomycin	Semisynthetic antibiotic

Erythromycin, oleandomycin, josamycin, spiramycin and troleandomycin are the current clinically used macrolide antibiotics.

7.22 MECHANISM OF ACTION

Macrolide antibiotics act by inhibiting bacterial protein synthesis by preventing peptide bond formation at 50 S ribosomal level.

7.23 ANTIMICROBIAL ACTIVITY SPECTRA

These agents are effective against gram-positive cocci, *Neisseriae listeriae, Corynebacterium diptheriae, Hemophilus influenzae, Bacteroides fragilis, Legionella pneumophila,* some rickettsiae, large viruses and amoeba. They are not effective against gram-negative bacteria, yeast and fungi.

Erythromycin : It is the most widely used agent amongst macrolides. Its isolation was reported by **McGuire et al** in 1952 from *Streptomyces erythreus*.

The large lactone structure is known as erythronolide. An aminosugar, desosamine is attached to C_5 while another sugar, cladinose is linked glycosidically to C_3. Other two structures closely related to erythromycin have been isolated from *S. erythreus*. They are known as erythromycins B and C. The B analog does not possess C_{12} - hydroxyl group and is more stable but less active than erythromycin A while C analog lacks cladinose methoxy group and is equipotent with erythromycin A. The commercial erythromycin contains 90% erythromycin A and about 10% erythromycin B with minute quantity of erythromycin C.

Erythromycin is acid labile. Hence it is presented in the capsules or as enteric coated tablets in order to protect it from gastric acid during its oral use. Number of its derivatives were designed to improve :

(i) its solubility characteristics,

(ii) its acid stability for better oral absorption, and

(iii) the acceptance by masking its bitter taste.

The basic nature of the dimethylamino group of desosamine moiety was utilized to prepare its acid salts, like lactobionate, glucoheptonate and stearate and esters of the 2'- hydroxyl group of the desosamine including the ethyl carbonate, ethyl-succinate and estolate. All these derivatives are tasteless and less acid-labile. The stearate or estolate form of erythromycin being more acid-stable are suitable for oral administration while lactobionate and glucohepto forms are used for parenteral administration because of their good water solubility. The 2'-esters are as such do not possess antibiotic activity and hence efficacy of particular ester depends upon the *in-vivo* rate of ester hydrolysis to release the free-base.

The free base, erythromycin possesses bitter taste. The presence of food in the stomach reduces its oral absorption. The unabsorbed drug exerts local antibacterial effect in the gut. About 80 – 85% of administered dose of erythromycin (and 95 – 98% of a administered dose of its derivatives) is bound to the plasma-proteins. It has a plasma half-life of 1.6 hours. In body, erythromycin is well distributed. It can enter cerebrospinal fluid only in the presence of inflammation. Small portion also crosses the placenta. About 12 – 15% dose appears unchanged in the urine and the rest is metabolized (through demethylation) or appears in the bile.

7.24 ADVERSE EFFECTS

Some commonly encountered adverse effects are as follows :

(a) General effects : These include nausea, vomiting, gastric irritation, diarrhea, anorexia, glossitis, stomatitis, cheilosis, suprainfection and thrombophlebitis with severe pain at the site of injection.

(b) Hypersensitivity reactions : These include headache, fever, eosinophilia, skin rashes and lymphocytosis.

7.25 THERAPEUTIC USES

(i) It is an effective agent used in the treatment of sinusitis, otitis media, acute bronchitis, pharyngitis and streptococcal tonsillitis.

(ii) It may also be used in the treatment of diphtheria, Mycoplasma pneumonia and amebiasis.

(iii) It may be indicated in the treatment of gonorrhea, syphillis and nongonococcal urethritis due to ureaplasma ureolyticum.

(iv) It may be prophylactically used in the treatment of rheumatic fever, and

(v) The pure base may be used topically alongwith benzoyl peroxide as adjunctive therapy to control mild to moderate inflammatory acne.

7.26 BACTERIAL RESISTANCE

(a) Bacterial resistance gradually develops to erythromycin. The drug may block the antibacterial actions of clindamycin and chloramphenicol. In resistant strains, the affinity of drugs to bacterial ribosomal binding sites is modified resulting into decreased binding of erythromycin with its binding sites.

(b) Oleandomycin : It was obtained from *Streptomyces antibioticus* by **Sobin et al**. It bears structural features similar to erythromycin and stands as an alternative to erythromycin in few cases. It is less preferred in the treatment of gram-positive bacterial infections due to less activity and a high incidence, of adverse-effects. It differs from erythromycin in having :

(i) L-oleandrose moiety instead of clandinose,

(ii) A 14-membered lactone ring possessing an exocyclic methylene epoxide at C_8, designated as oleandolide instead of erythronolide,

(iii) The position of linkage with both the sugars remained same, like desosamine at C_5 and L - oleandrose at C_3.

The triacetyl ester derivative of oleandomycin (Triacetyl-oleandomycin) is prepared by acetylating three hydroxyl groups, one in each of the sugars and one in the oleando-lide. It is preferred over oleandomycin because of :

(i) Its acid-stability which permits its oral use without enteric coating,

(ii) Retention of *in-vivo* antibacterial activity,

(iii) Superior pharmacokinetic properties, and

(iv) Its tasteless nature.

The adverse effects and therapeutic indications for oleandomycin and triacetyloleandomycin are similar to that of erythromycin. However both these drugs possess less antibacterial potency and hepatotoxicity in comparison to erythromycin.

(c) Spiramycin and Josamycin : These agents are well established clinically in Europe and Japan. They are mainly indicated for the treatment of gram-positive bacterial infections. Spiramycin is effective in prevention of sepsis seen after prostatectomy. Both have similar range of activity to that of erythromycin but are less effective. Compared to erythromycin, josamycin produces less gastric irritation and less likely to cause bacterial resistance. However cross-resistance among the members of macrolide series has been reported.

7.27 LINCOMYCINS

The antibiotic, lincomycin was obtained from *Actinomycete, Streptomyces lincolnensis* (so named because it was found in Lincoln, Nebraska). It is the example of sulfur-containing antibiotics. Released in 1963, this antibiotic was followed by its synthetic derivative, clindamycin (i.e. 7 - chloro - 7 - deoxylincomycin) in 1967. Clindamycin has improved antibacterial and pharmacokinetic profiles.

Lincomycins in general have similar antibacterial spectra, mechanism of action, pattern of bacterial resistance and cross-resistance to that of erythromycin. They exert bacteriostatic action on bacteria by inhibiting their protein synthesis. They interfere with the formation of peptide bond by binding with 50 S subunit of bacterial ribosomes. The susceptible strains of bacteria includes most of gram-positive cocci (e.g. *S. aureus, S. viridans, S. pyogenes, S. pneumoniae* and *S. epidermidis*), gram - positive bacilli (*B. subtilis* and *B. cereus*) and some anaerobes (e.g. *Clostridium perfringens*). Gram-negative bacteria are resistant to their action because of their inability to cross bacterial cell-wall.

Lincomycin is incompletely absorbed orally. The unabsorbed portion (about 40%) appears in the faeces. Presence of food further lowers the rate of absorption. About 50% dose is bound to the plasma-proteins. Adequate concentration of lincomycin is found to be present in pleural, peritoneal and synovial fluids. It has a plasma half-life of 4 – 5 hours. It is minimally metabolised in the body. About 10% dose appears unchanged in the urine. While clindamycin shows better oral absorption. About 92 – 95% administered dose is bound to the plasma-proteins. It has a plasma half-life of 2.7 hours. Principle metabolites include, N-demethylclindamycin and clindamycin sulphoxide that are excreted in the urine and the bile.

7.28 ADVERSE EFFECTS

Adverse effects include diarrhoea, abdominal pain, skin rashes, erythema, fever, anaphylactic shock, granulocytopenia and thrombocytopenia.

The use of lincomycins is associated with pseudomembranous enterocolitis which is due to suprainfection with *Clostridium difficile* in the intestine.

7.29 THERAPEUTIC USES

Below mentioned are some important therapeutic uses of lincomycins and clindamycin :

(i) Lincomycins are used in the treatment of streptococcal infections including endocarditis, pharyngitis and soft tissue infections.

(ii) Lincomycin is also used to treat osteomyelitis and *Bacteroides fragilis* septicemia.

(iii) Clindamycin is highly effective in the treatment of anaerobic pleuropulmonary diseases.

(iv) Clindamycin is also used orally or topically to treat acne vulgaris.

(v) Lincomycins may be used in combination with aminoglycosides to control serious anaerobic infections.

ANTIBIOTICS THAT INTERFERE WITH CYTOPLASMIC MEMBRANE FUNCTION

8.1 INTRODUCTION

Cytoplamic membrane is present next to the cell-wall, which serves the purpose of protecting the vital cell-constituents from the damage. It acts as an organ for selective intracellular transport as well as cell excretion. Antibiotics described in this chapter possess surfactant like properties that help them to damage the integrity of the cytoplasmic membrane by disorienting the lipophilic groups present in the membrane. The drug-induced alteration in the permeability of cytoplasmic membrane results into leakage of intracellular cations, amino acids and nucleotides and inhibition of vital cellular processes. This eventually results into the rapid killing of microorganisms.

Antibiotics interfearing with cytoplasmic membrane function are as follows :

(a) Polymyxin antibiotics, and

(b) Antifungal antibiotics (Polyene antibiotics).

8.2 POLYMYXIN ANTIBIOTICS

Polymyxin B and colistin are common clinically used agents from this category. They are relatively toxic and hence have restricted clinical utility. They are mainly effective against gram-negative infections and exert high activity against *Pseudomonas aeruginosa*. Nephrotoxicity is the main adverse effect that ranges from mild paresthesias and dizziness to the severe peripheral neuropathy and respiratory paralysis. Both these drugs are poorly absorbed when given by the oral route. Colistin has less antibacterial activity than polymyxin B. They are mainly used topically, frequently in combination with other antibiotics (e.g. bacitracin or neomycin) and with hydrocortisone.

The activity of polymyxin B is usually expressed in terms of units. About 10,000 units are considered to be equivalent with 1 mg of polymyxin B.

The polymyxins are strongly basic cyclic polypeptides holding a fatty acid side-chain. This is a group of relatively simple, basic cationic detergent peptides, first isolated in 1947 from various strains of *Bacillus polymyxa*. Atleast six polymyxins (A, B, C, D, E and M) are known that differ in the sequence of amino acids. Out of these, only polymyxin B and polymyxin E (i.e. colistin) are of clinical utility. Rest of the polymyxins are either more toxic or less potent. Polymyxins exhibit synergistic effect when combined with tetracyclines, chloramphenicol, carbenicillin or co-trimoxazole.

(i) Polymyxin B.:

It is a bactericidal antibiotic having a molecular weight of about 1000. It can readily form water soluble salts with mineral acids and has a pKa value of 8.9. Colistin differs from polymyxin B in the substitution of a D-leucine residue for D-phenylalanine.

Mechanism of action : Phospholipids constitute a major fraction of the cytoplasmic membranes. Polymyxin B and colistin get accumulated in this membrane because of their amphoteric nature. The fatty acid portion of the drug gets embedded into the hydrophobic portion of the membrane phospholipid while the polypeptide nucleus of the drug gets oriented towards the phosphate groups of the phospolipids. Such placement of antibiotic in the phospholipid fraction of cytoplasmic membrane impairs its function and damages its selective permeable nature. This results into the leakage of vital intracellular constituents of bacterial cell, followed by its death.

Antibacterial activity spectra : These antibiotics are effective against *Enterobacter, E.coli, Klebsiella, Salmonella, Pasteurella, Bordetella, Shingella* and *Pseudomonas aeruginosa*. However other organisms like *Proteus spp, Serratia marcescens* and *Providentia* are not susceptible to the action of these antibiotics and often produce suprainfection during their therapy.

Pharmacokinetic properties : Both, polymyxin B and colistin are poorly absorbed when given by oral route. Major dose is excreted unchanged through the faeces. Hence they may be used to treat some cases of bacterial diarrhoea. When given parenterally (rarely, for example, polymyxin B may be given intrathecally in the treatment of meningitis), it is inadequately distributed in various body compartments. Polymyxin B has a plasma half-life of 3 – 6 hours; while colistin has a plasma half-life of 4 – 5 hours. About 50% of administered dose of colistin is bound to the plasma-proteins. Little is known about their metabolism. They are excreted in the urine by glomerular filtration.

Adverse effects : These antibiotics are very safe almost devoid of adverse effects when used topically. However when used parenterally, show adverse effects that includes skin rashes, drug fever, malaise, vertigo, ataxia, numbness, muscle weakness, diplopia, headache, blurred vision, paresthesiae, facial flushing, slurred speech, mental disturbances and anaphylactic reactions.

The signs of nephrotoxicity include proteinurea, cylinduria, hematuria, presence of casts in the urine, an increased level of blood urea nitrogen (BUN) and renal tubular necrosis Polymyxin B is more nephrotoxic than colistin. They are contraindicated in patients with myasthenia gravis.

Preparations : Polymyxin B is marketed in the form of topical and ophthalmic preparations (0.25%) which may be used to treat the infections of skin, mucous membranes, eye and ear. While colistin is available as colistin sulphate for oral administration and sodium colistimethate, the methanesulfonate derivative for intramuscular administration. The latter is prodrug that slowly releases the drug through *in-vivo* hydrolysis. The prodrug is excreted faster than free base because of its less firm binding to the plasma proteins.

Therapeutic uses : Below mentioned are some important therapeutic uses :

(i) Polymyxin B is used topically in the treatment of infections of skin, mucous membrane, eye and ear.

(ii) Polymyxin B may be used orally to sterilize the intestine.

(iii) Colistin may be used topically to treat infections of skin, mucous membranes, eye and ear. Topical use is also indicated to treat external otitis due to *Pseudomonas aeruginosa*. Orally it is used to treat bacterial colitis in infants and children.

8.3 POLYENE ANTIBIOTICS

Polyene antibiotics are the compounds that contain unsaturated carbon rings or chains (i.e. –CH=CH–CH=CH–). About 60 polyene antibiotics, all produced by *Actinomycetes* have been reported till date from 1950. They are characterized by the presence of a large ring lactone (i.e. macrocyclic lactone) and a hydrophobic region coupled with a conjugated polyene system of four to seven double bonds. Many of them contain the glycosidically linked aminosugars, such as the aminodesoxyhexose (i.e. mycosamine) which is present in amphotericin B and nystatin. The polyenes are poorly soluble in water. Number of double bonds present in the skeleton serves as the basis of classification of these polyenes. For example, tetraene antibiotics (nystatin), pentaene antibiotics (filpin), hexaene antibiotics (endomycin) and heptaene antibiotics (amphotericin B, candicidin). The most important polyene antibiotics are amphotericin B and nystatin.

(a) Amphotericin B :

It is a mixture of two compounds A and B, isolated from (*Streptomyces nodosus*, a soil *actinomycete* in 1956). As the name suggests, amphotericis are amphoteric substances. Amphotericin B is a more potent antibiotic but with a narrow spectrum of activity.

Mechanism of action : In contrast to bacteria, the fungal membrane consists of sterols as the important constituent. The main sterol is ergosterol. Amphotericin B and nystatin have a high affinity for sterols present in the fungal membranes. They combine with these membrane sterols and thus create pores or channels in the membrane which results into the likage of intracellular constitutents and eventually the death of an organism. Since bacteria do not have sterols as their membrane constituents, amphotericin B and nystatin are ineffective against bacteria.

Unfortunately mammalian cell

membranes also consist of sterols. This is the reason why the margin of safety of these antibiotics is uncomfortably narrow.

Antimicrobial activity spectra : Amphotericin is used as either fungistatic or fungicidal in the treatment of histoplasmosis (*Histoplasma capsulatum*), blastomycosis (*Blastomyces dermatitidis*) and sporotrichosis (*Sporothrix schenckii*). The activity depends upon the dose of the drug and sensitivity of the fungi. The antibiotic also serves the purpose when injected directly into infected tissues such as the skin, eye or cerebrospinal fluid.

Adverse effects : These include nausea, vomiting, fever, headache, and thrombophlebitis.

Therapeutic uses :

(i) Amphotericin B is particularly effective against systemic infections caused by *C. albicans* and *Cryptococcus neoformans*. Nystatin and amphotericin B, both can effectively be used to control non-contaginous air-borne system fungal infections.

(ii) Amphotericin B can also be applied topically to treat oral and vaginal candidiasis. The methyl ester has equipotent, antifungal activity but has a better pharmacokinetic properties than amphotericin B.

(b) Nystatin :

It was isolated from *Streptomyces nourisei* by **Hazen** and **Brown** in 1951. The name of this antibiotic was derived from New York state from where it was discovered. It is slightly soluble in water and is unstable to moisture, heat, light and air.

Nystatin is both fungistatic and fungicidal. It has a specific action on *Candida albicans*. It is mainly used for the local treatment of oral, gastrointestinal and vaginal candidiasis and for the fungal infections of the cornea. It is ineffective against bacteria, protozoa or viruses. Amphotericin B has better results over nystatin in the treatment of systemic yeast infections. When used topically, nystatin is sometimes combined with iodochlorhydroxyquin.

Nystatin has similar chemical structure to that of amphotericin B. Mycosamine, an aminosugar present in amphotericin B, is also present in nystatin. The only difference between both these antibiotics is the nature of macrocyclic chromophore structure.

(c) Candicidin :

Other less popular members of polyene family are natamycin, hachimycin, candicidin and hamycin. Candicidin was isolated from Streptomyces griseus by **Lechevalier et al** in 1953, followed by the isolation of natamycin from *Streptomyces natalensis* in 1958. Candicidin is used topically in the treatment of vaginal candidiasis while natamycin follows the clinical foot-prints of nystatin.

ANTIBIOTICS AFFECTING NUCLEIC ACID SYNTHESIS AND MISCELLANEOUS ANTIBIOTICS

9.1 ANTIBIOTICS THAT ACT BY INHIBITING NUCLEIC ACID SYNTHESIS

Many drugs act by affecting various stages of nucleic acid (i.e. RNA and DNA) synthesis. These includes antibacterial agents (e.g. nalidixic acid, rifampin), antiviral agents (idoxuridine, vidarabine, acyclovir), and antineoplastic agents (bleomycin, cytarabine, methotrexate, mitomycin etc.). Some antibacterial agents like trimethoprim inhibit the early stages (nucleotide interconversion) of nucleic acid synthesis by blocking dihydrofolate reductase enzymes while some antineoplastic agents (e.g. 5-fluorouracil, 5-fluorodeoxyuridine) also attack on early stages by inhibiting thymidylate synthetase enzymes. Some of these agents are highly selective in their action and do not induce damage to the host-cells (e.g. rifampin) while the therapeutic use of some drugs is only due to their ability to attack on the host cells (e.g. antineoplastic drugs).

(a) Rifampin (Rafampicin) :

The rifamycins is a group of structurally similar, complex macrocyclic antibiotics that are isolated from *Streptomyces mediterrani* in Italy by Lepetit laboratories in 1957. They belong to a new class of antibiotics known as ansamycins. All the members (i.e. rifamycins A, B, C, D and E) are found to be active on the pharmacological screen. Out of hundreds of semi-synthetic derivatives prepared, rifamycin, rifamide (i.e. rifamycin B diethylamide) and rifamycin SV are found to be most effective and least toxic analogs.

Rifampin is a semi-synthetic derivative of rifamycin B. Chemically it is 3-(4-methylpiperazinyliminomethyl) rifamycin SV. It is a zwitter ion.

Antimicrobial activity spectra : Rifampin is a broad-spectrum bactericidal antibiotic released in 1971 in United States. It is highly effective against gram-positive organisms and many viruses. Some gram-negative bacteria (e.g. *E. coli*, *Pseudomonas aeruginosa*, *Proteus* species, *Klebsiella* etc.) are also susceptible to its action but bacterial resistance in gram-negative bacteria was found to develop rapidly. Rifampin is also highly effective against most strains of tuberculosis and many atypical mycobacteria.

Mechanism of action : Rifampin inhibits RNA-synthesis by binding with DNA dependent - RNA polymerase enzymes. It is the most potent inhibitor of these enzymes in the bacteria. Mammalian DNA - dependent - RNA polymerase does not bind rifampin significantly except when the drug is given at a very high concentration.

Pharmacokinetic properties : Rifampin is orally active drug. The presence of food reduces its oral absorption. About 90% administered dose is bound to the plasma-proteins. It is widely distributed in body tissues and fluids. It has a plasma half-life of 3.5 – 4.0 hours. A significant first-pass metabolism is reported to occur with rifampin. Principle metabolites include 25 - 0 - desacetylrifamycin (active) and 3-formylrifamycin (inactive). They are excreted in the urine alongwith 7 – 10% dose in unchanged form. Free rifampin undergoes an enterohepatic circulation. About 60 — 65% dose appears in the faeces through the bile circulation. Probenecid doubles rifampin serum level in humans by depressing hepatic uptake and by slowing deacetylation.

Adverse effects : Adverse effects includes nausea, vomiting, abdominal cramps, diarrhoea, headache, soreness of mouth and tongue, skin rash, urticaria, pruritus, fever, chills, eosinophilia, myalgias, jaundice, fatigue, drowsiness, dizziness, ataxia, confusion, muscular weakness, interstitial nephritis, hemolytic anaemia and thrombocytopenia.

Rifampin is a strong enzyme inducer and may interfere with the metabolism of a number of concomittantly administered drugs. It may also exert a partial or reversible immune suppressive effect in the patients.

Therapeutic uses :

(i) It is an effective antituberculosis agent. Since bacterial resistance develops rapidly, it should not be used alone for this purpose. Bacterial resistance develops because of the production of such DNA-dependent - RNA - polymerase that does not bind with rifampin. Isoniazidrifampin is the most effective combination in the treatment of tuberculosis.

(ii) Rifampin may also be included in the multi-drug therapy of leprosy.

(iii) It may also be used in the treatment of meningococcal infections and meningitis due to *H. influenzae*.

(iv) It is used alongwith β-lactam antibiotics or vancomycin in the treatment of some cases of staphylococcal endocarditis or osteomyelitis due to staphylococci, *S. aureus or S. epidermidis* that are resistant to other antibiotics.

(v) It may occasionally be used in the treatment of chronic furunculosis. It is also effective in the treatment of infections due to *Chlamydia trachomatis*.

(vi) Since it potentiates the antifungal activity of amphotericin B, it may be used with amphotericin B in the treatment of aspergillosis and the infections due to

Histoplasma or *Candida*.

(vii) Rifamide has no place in tuberculosis therapy. It rather finds its role in the treatment of cholecystitis.

Rifampin may be used in combination with clindamycin in the treatment of nocardiasis, leprosy, leishmaniasis and trypanosomiasis.

(b) Nalidixic acid :

It is an example of 4 - quinolone antibacterial agents. It was proposed to act by inhibiting DNA synthesis probably by interfering with specific enzymes. It is described in detail in chapter 4.

9.2 MISCELLANEOUS ANTIBIOTICS

This class of antibiotics includes such drugs which can not be specifically placed in the categories made on the basis of mechanism of action. They include spectinomycin, capreomycin, viomycin and fusidic acid. These antibiotics retain their reputation in the chemotherapy, though do not retain common structural features with any other antibiotic. Due to their high clinical utility, they deserve special attention.

(a) Spectinomycin :

It is an aminocyclitol bacteriostatic antibiotic produced by *Streptomyces spectabilis*. It is effective against a number of gram-negative bacterial species. It acts by inhibiting bacterial protein synthesis at the level of 30 S subunit of the ribosomes.

It is given by intramuscular injection. It is well distributed in different body fluids. About 15 – 20% administered dose is bound to the plasma-proteins. It has a plasma half-life of 2.0 hours. It does not undergo metabolism and appears almost unchanged in the urine.

Adverse effects include nausea, vomiting, chills, fever, urticaria, dizziness, insomnia and pain at the site of injection.

It is effective in the treatment of some gonococcal infections (i.e. acute gonorrheal urethritis and proctitis in the male and acute gonorrheal cervicitis and proctitis in the female) due to some susceptible strains of *Neisseria gonorrhoeae*. However it remains effective in the treatment of syphilis.

(b) Capreomycin :

It is an aminoglycoside antimycobacterial cylic peptide isolated from *Streptomyces capreolus*. It is a water-soluble bacteriostatic agent used as a 'second-line' antituberculous agent in the multidrug therapy against some streptomycin-resistant mycobacteria. Since it is poorly absorbed by oral route, it is given intramuscularly. About half the dose appears in the urine in unchanged form. Adverse effects includes skin rashes, fever, hearing loss, tinnitus, eosinophilia, leukopenia, transient proteinurea, renal and hepatotoxicities.

Besides its use as a second-line antituberculosis agent, it is also used to treat *Mycobacterium avium* - intracellulare infections in AIDS patients in the dose of 1 g i.m. daily.

(c) Viomycin :

It is a highly water-soluble, strongly basic cyclic polypeptide that was isolated from *Streptomyces puniceus*. It shares the similar chemical and pharmacological properties with capreomycin. It is used as a *'second-line'* drug in the treatment of tuberculosis.

Like capreomycin, viomycin is also a potentially toxic drug. Both these antibiotics are known for ototoxicity, blood dyscrasias and kidney damage. Viomycin is rarely indicated in children.

(d) Fusidic acid :

A compound structurally similar to cephalosporin P is fusidic acid which is isolated from the mould *Fusidium coccineum*. Fusidin is the sodium salt of fusidic acid. It is a steroidal bactericidal antibiotic specifically active against staphylococcal, infections, *Neisseria, Bacteroids, Clostridia, Corynebacterium diphtheria* and some mycobacteria species. It is however, essentially devoid of biological activities i.e. characteristic of steroids.

It is orally effective. It gets distributed to the most of body fluids except cerebrospinal fluid. About 90% administered dose is bound to the plasma-proteins. The drug is metabolised to various inactive glucuronide metabolites which are excreted through the bile and the faeces.

Fusidic acid acts by inhibiting the translocation in bacterial protein synthesis, by interfering with G factor and depressing GTPase activity. The drug is not effective against gram-negative organisms because of its poor penetration through their cell-walls.

Adverse effects include nausea, vomiting and diarrhoea. The intravenous administration of the drug may cause hypotension, hemolysis or thrombophlebitis. Bacterial resistance readily develops against fusidic acid. Development of cross-resistance between fusidic acid and cephalosporin P has been reported.

Fusidic acid is used in the treatment of infections caused by penicillinase producing *staphylococci*. Diethanolamine fusidate (580 mg) is equipotent with 500 mg of sodium fusidate. It is given slowly by i.v. infusion to treat osteomyelitis, bronthiectasis, endocarditis and deeply buried abscesses. Sodium fusidate is also available as a 2% ointment or gel form which is used topically to treat serious skin infections.

ANTIFUNGAL AGENTS

10.1 INTRODUCTION

Fungus is a parasite. The human fungi parasitic relationship results in mycotic illnesses, the majority of which involves superficial invasion of skin or the mucous membranes of body orifices. Fungi have different shapes and sizes. Some are large while others are minute parasitic and saprophytic cells. They differ from

- algae in the lack of photosynthetic ability.
- protozoa in the lack of motility, possession of chitinous cell-wall and ease of culture on simple media.
- bacteria in greater size and in the presence of certain intracellular structures like mitochondria and nuclear membrane.

Depending upon some basic differences, fungi may be classified as :

(a) Phycomycetes (algae like)

(b) Ascomycetes (sac like)

(c) Basidiomycetes (mushrooms), and

(d) Dueteromycetes.

In addition, the 'higher bacteria' like *Actinomyces* and *Nocardia* are sometimes grouped with the fungi.

Fungal diseases are generally referred as 'mycoses'. Fungal infections (or mycoses) fall into two well defined groups : the superficial and the deep seated mycoses. These mycotic infections may be categorised broadly as :

(i) Dermatophytoses (skin infections) of contagious in nature, caused by various *Trichophyton*, *Microsporum* and *Epidermophyton* species. These include superficial infections of keratinized tissues like, stratum corneum, hair, nails etc. Tinea capitis, Tinea corporis, Tinea cruris, Tinea unguium, Tinea versicolor, Tinea nigra and candidiasis are all grouped under superficial fungal infections. As a rule, these lesions are mild, superficial and restricted. The causative microbes are specialized saprophytes with the unusual ability to digest keratin. They have ultimate reservoir in the soil. Topical antifungal agents are effective here. However, to treat deeper infections systemic antifungal (e.g. griseofulvin) may also be given alongwith topical antifungal agents. Because of the keratolytic action of salicylate, it may often be used along with the topical antifungal agent to improve the drug penetration. Salicylic acid helps the drug to reach the site deep within the hyperkeratotic epidermis.

(ii) Candidiasis affects mainly the skin and mucous membrane. It is caused by *Candida albicans*. These infections mainly develop in the mouth, bowel or vagina and are called as local infections. They may sometimes become systemic and contagious.

Table 10.1 : Drugs of choice in the treatment of systemic fungal infections

Sr. No.	Disease	Fungus	Effective antifungal agents
1.	Actinomycosis	*Actinomyces israelii*	Penicillin G, cephalosporin, tetracycline
2.	Aspergillosis	*Aspergillus fumigatus* *Aspergillus niger*	Amphotericin B, rifampin
3.	Blastomycosis (North American type)	*Blastomyces dermatitidis*	Amphotericin B, rifampin and hydroxystibamidine, itraconazole
4.	Blastomycosis (South American type)	*Blastomyces brasiliensis*	Amphotericin B, miconazole
5.	Candidiasis	*Candida albicans*	Amphotericin B, nystatin, flueonazole
6.	Chromoblastomycosis	*Cladosporium*	Flucytosine, amphotericin B, potassium iodide
7.	Coccidioidomycosis	*Coccidioides immitis*	Amphotericin B, fluconazole miconazole, ketoconazole
8.	Cryptococcosis	*Cryptococcus neoformans*	Amphotericin B, flucytosine, fluconazole
9.	Histoplasmosis	*Histoplasma capsulatum*	Amphotericin B, hydroxystilbamidine, rifampin
10.	Phycomycosis (Mucormycosis)	*Mucor* species	Amphotericin B, hydroxystilbamidine
11.	Nocardiosis	*Nocardia* asteroides	Amoxicillin, cotrimoxazole, minocycline
12.	Paracoccidioidomycosis	-	Ketoconazole, amphotericin B
13.	Sporotrichosis	*Sporothrix schenckii*	Potassium iodide, amphotericin B, itraconazole
14.	Fusariosis	-	Amphotericin B
15.	Pseudoallescheriosis	-	Ketaconazole, itraconazole
16.	Zygomycosis	-	Amphotericin B

Itraconazole is a 1 : 1 : 1 : 1 racemic mixture of 04 diastereomers, each possessing three chiral centers.

Itraconazole
(Janseen, 1992)

(iii) Systemic fungal infection (see Table 10.1), is the third major category that involves fungal infections of bones, viscera, lungs and meninges. Many fungal infections occur either on skin (avascular region) or in poorly vascularized area (e.g. nails and hair). At such places, the drug cannot built up its therapeutic concentration necessary to exhibit antifungal activity. Besides this, clinical utility of many drugs is hampered mainly because of poor solubility and poor penetration ability. Currently there exist neither clinically available vaccines nor effective antisera for mycotic diseases. Due to various reasons (e.g. differences in solubility, diffusibility or inactivation by serum components), the agents showing excellent antifungal activity *in-vitro* studies, disappointed us when tested *in-vivo*. For example, miconazole and clotrimazole are inactivated by phospholipids and triglycerides. To cover such a broad range of systemic fungal infections, very few antifungal agents are available. These include polyene antibiotics (e.g. amphotericin B, nystatin), antimetabolites (e.g. flucytosine), griseofulvin and imidazoles (e.g. ketoconazole, miconazole and clotrimazole).

Regardless of the type of fungus that is causing an infection, treatment is extremely difficult because fungi, like mammalians, are eukaryotes. Many biochemical structures, especially the cell membranes, are nearly identical, as are many biochemical reactions.

In human cells, the sterol in the membrane is cholesterol. In fungi, the sterol is ergosterol. This difference is the only source of selectivity that we have in treating fungal infections.

Table 10.2 : Some clinically used antifungal agents

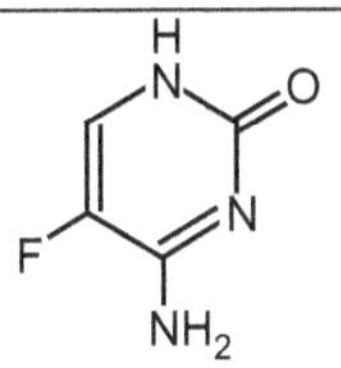

- 5-Fluorocytosine
- Tolnaftate 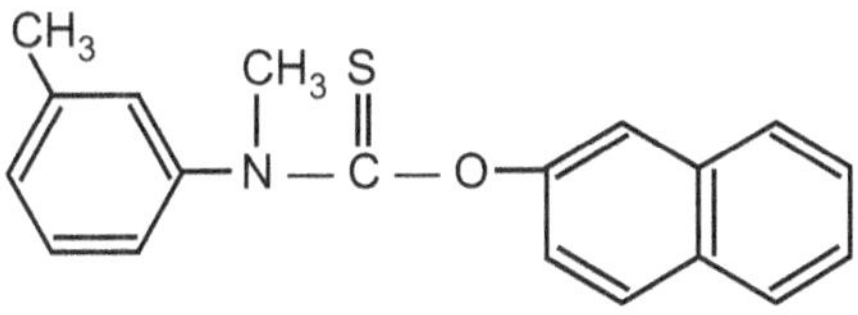
- Naftifine 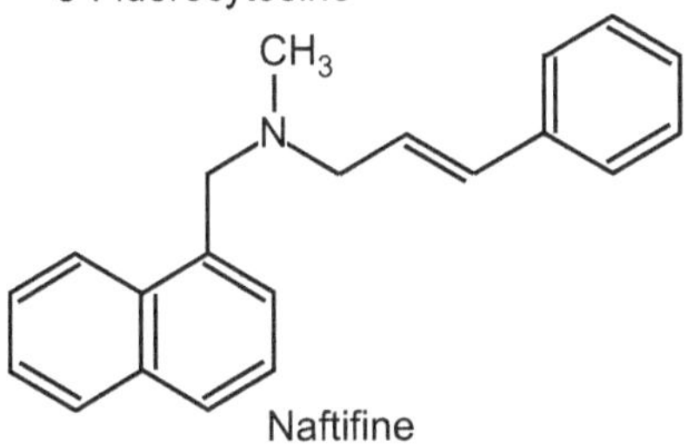
- Sulconazole 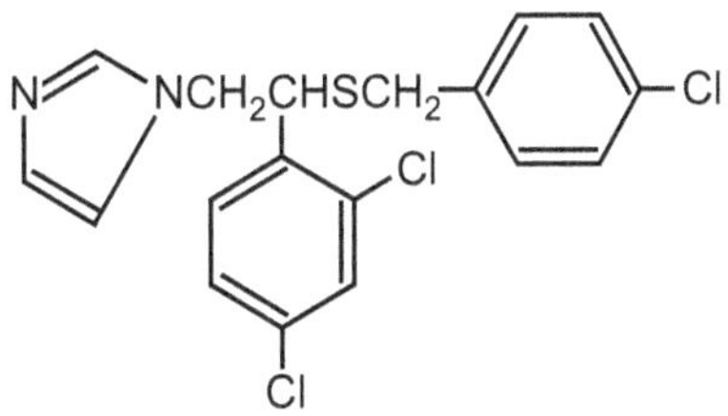
- Clotrimazole 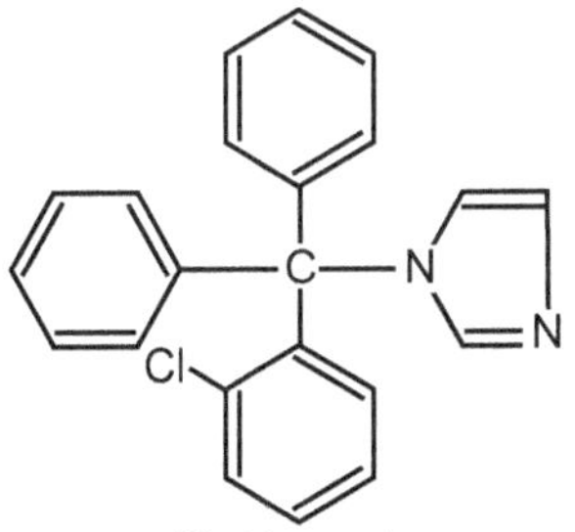
- Miconazole

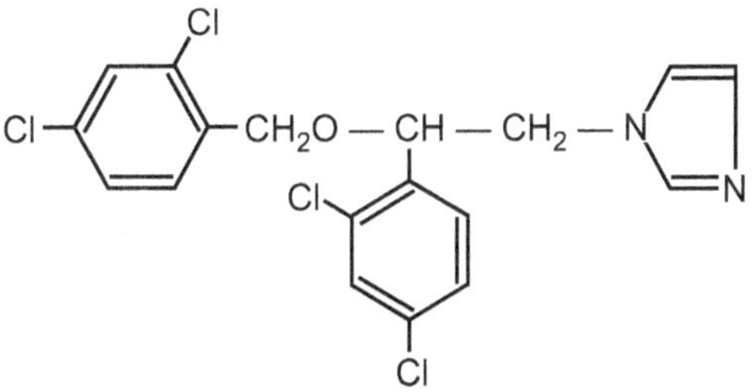

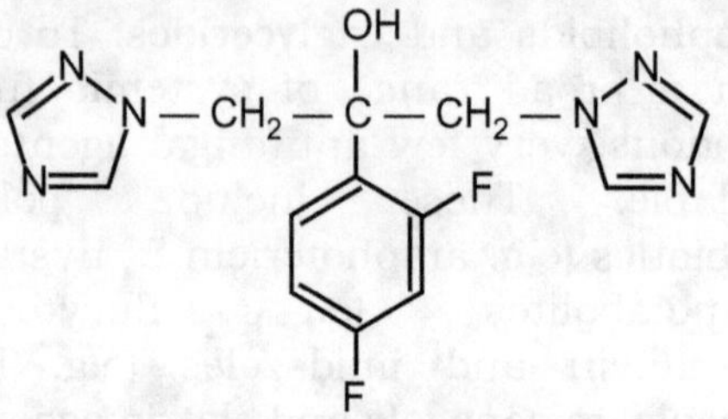

Fluconazole (1991, pfizer)

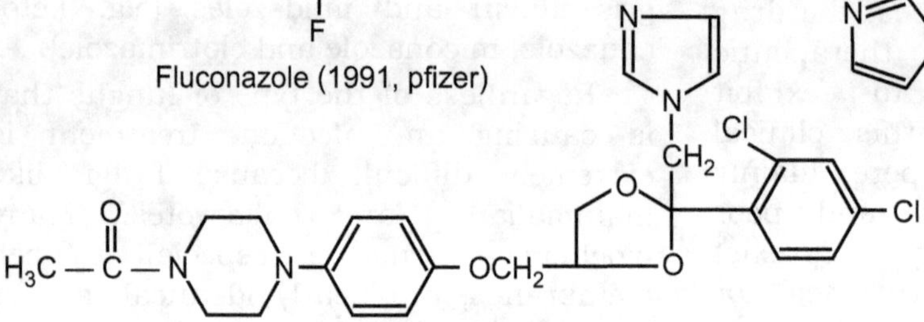

Ketoconazole (1981, Janssen)

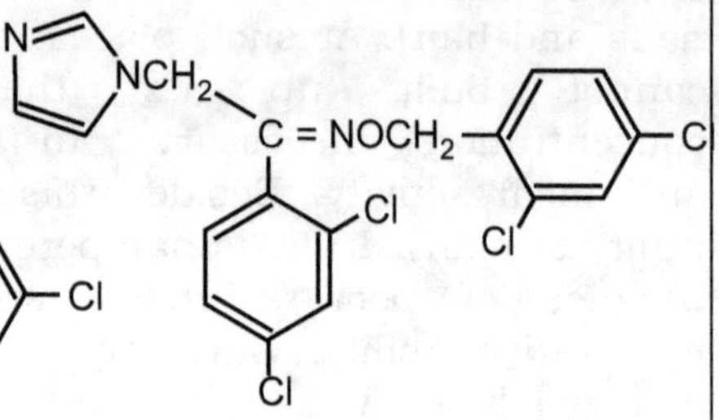

Oxiconazole

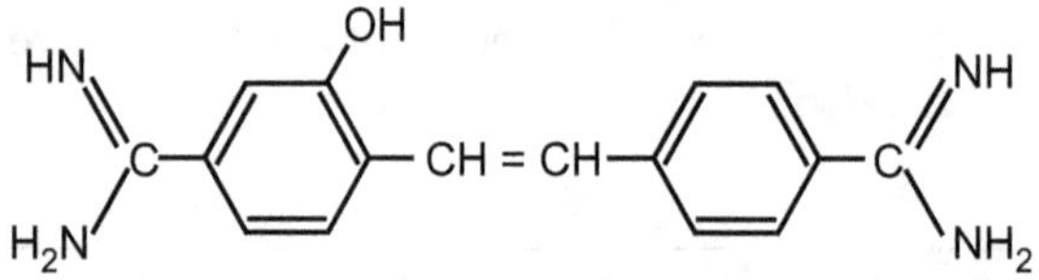

Hydroxystilbamidine

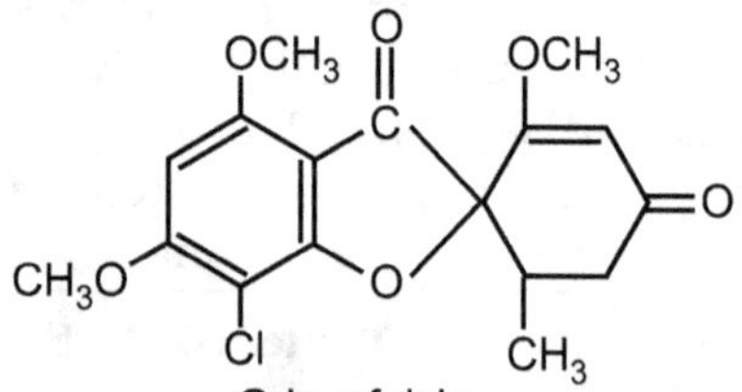

Griseofulvin

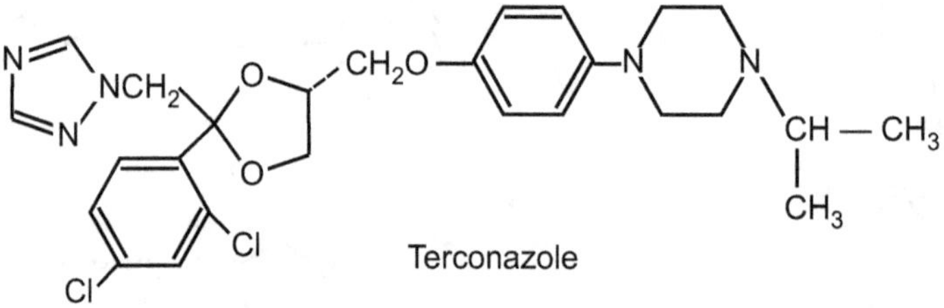

Terconazole

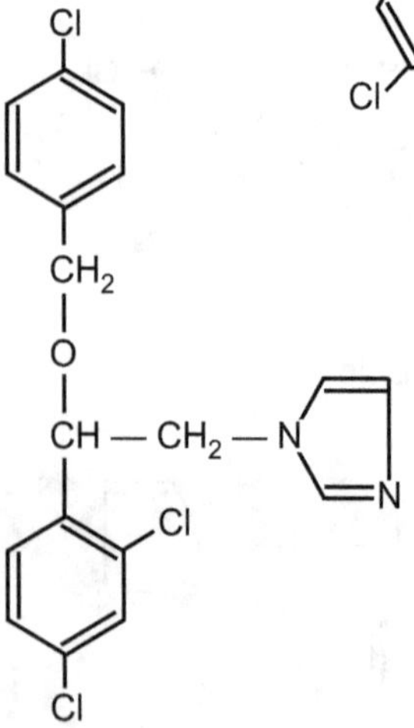

Econazole

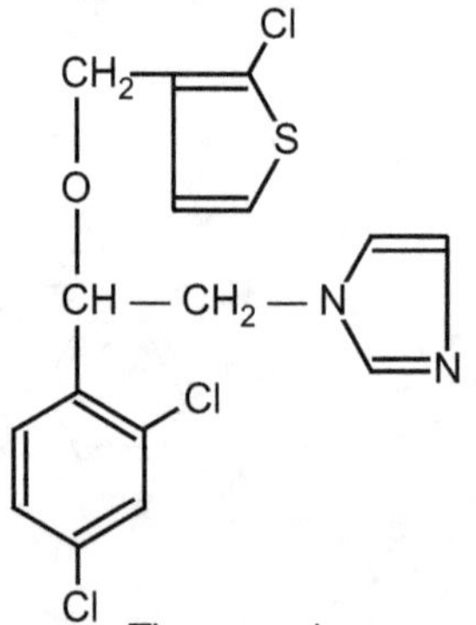

Tioconazole

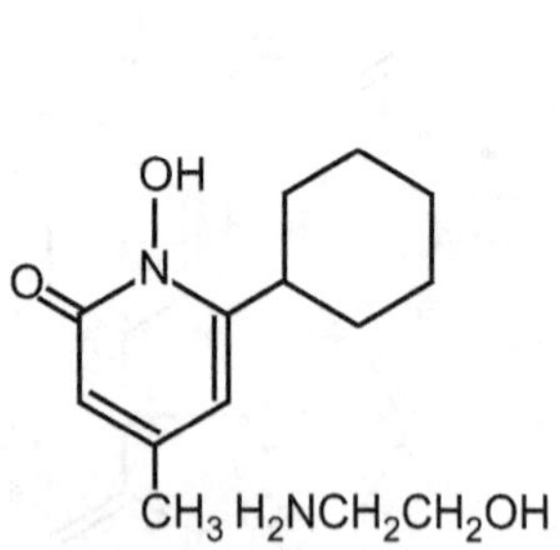

Ciclopirox olamine

10.2 CLASSIFICATION

On the chemical basis, currently used antifungal agents can be categorised as :

(a) Fatty acids
(b) Pyrimidine derivatives
(c) Imidazoles
(d) Allylamines
(e) Amidines
(f) Antifungal antibiotics
(g) Miscellaneous agents.

Due to diversified structures of various antifungal agents, attempts to define SAR also failed. In such cases, interpretation of the activity in terms of 'drug physicochemical parameters' projects better understanding of SAR studies.

(a) Fatty Acids :

In 1939, **Peck** reported that sweat has antifungal properties. The antifungal activity of ingredients of perspiration has nothing to do with the pH of the perspiration and the activity is attributed to the presence of fatty acids and their salts. Propionic acid, undecylenic acid and sodium caprylate are effective against infections due to *Trichophytons*, Microsporons and *Candida albicans*. The recognition of their antifungal activity led to their clinical use mainly in the form of sodium and zinc salts. For example, the mixture of sodium propionate and propionic acid may be used in the treatment of ringworm while undecylenic acid and zinc undecylenate, in the form of mixture, are effective against ringworm and monilial vaginitis. Effectiveness increases when zinc salts of these acids are used. They are applied in the form of an ointment, lotion or dusting powder. However, their application to eyes, ears, nose or other areas of mucous membrane should be avoided. Their antifungal activity is related to their ability to precipitate the fungal proteins. Heavy metal ions like Ag^+, Hg^{++}, Cu^{++} and Zn^{++} combine with the functional groups present on the surface of enzymes. Hence, when combined with an organic molecule, they potentiate the antifungal activity of the latter.

(b) Pyrimidine Derivatives :

5-Fluorocytosine is a fluorinated pyrimidine and is related in structure to fluorouracil and flouridine. First introduced in 1957, it failed to build up its career as an effective antineoplastic drug. Ten years thereafter when tested for antifungal activity, it proved its potential against *Candida* species and *Cryptococcus neoformans* infections.

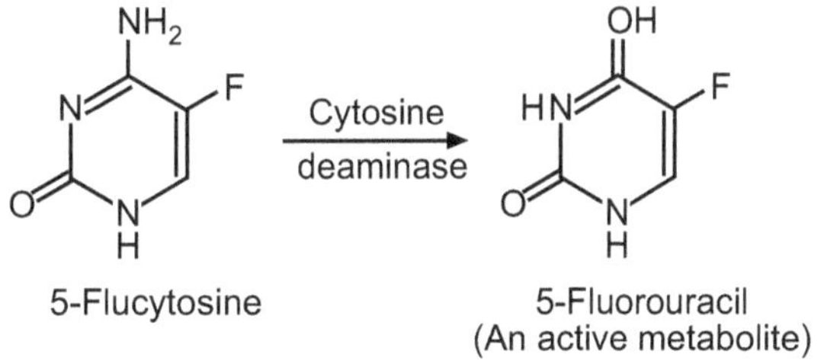

5-Flucytosine → (Cytosine deaminase) → 5-Fluorouracil (An active metabolite)

The antifungal activity of 5-fluorocytosine is attributed to the formation of 5-fluorouracil (an active metabolite) from the drug by fungal cytosine deaminases.

The active metabolite is further converted to 5 - fluro - 2' - deoxyuridylic acid which interrupts the fungal DNA synthesis by inhibiting thymidylate synthetase enzymes. Since mammalian cells do not contain cytosine deaminase, their function is not affected by flucytosine. Besides this, it is also suspected to interfere in protein synthesis.

It is not used topically. When used orally, about 4 % of administered dose is bound to the plasma proteins. It has a plasma half-life of 4.2 - 4.5 hours. It rapidly deaminates in fungal cells to the antimetabolite, 5-fluorouracil. About 80% of the dose appears in the urine in unchanged form.

Adverse effects include nausea, vomiting, diarrhoea, enterocolitis, headache, skin rashes, vertigo, anaemia, sedation, hepatomegaly, hepatic necrosis, leukopenia, agranulocytosis and thrombocytopenia.

Flucytosine is effective against infections caused by *C. neoformans, C. albicans, T. glabrata* and *S. schenckii*. It is also effective against chromomycosis caused by *Cladosporium* species and *Phialophora* species. It is used in combination with amphotericin B for the treatment of infections due to yeasts and yeast like fungi. Amphotericin renders the yeast cell-membrane more permeable to flucytosine. Hence, both drugs are used in the treatment of cryptococcal meningitis, Candida endocarditis, pulmonary and urinary tract infection. It may also be used in the treatment of chromoblastomycosis.

(c) Imidazoles :

Imidazole derivatives are associated with many therapeutic fields. Some have been employed as anthelmintics. Antibacterial and antiprotozoal activities also have been observed in some analogs.

The first azole to become available for clinical use (as a topical agent) was chlormidazole, introduced by **Chemie Gruenenthal** in 1958. It was followed by the introduction of miconazole by **Janssen** in 1969, clotrimazole by **Bayer's**. Later on in a new imidazole, econazole was launched by **Janssen** in 1974. Even today, the latter three agents remain the mainstay of topical therapy for many dermatophytoses.

Miconazole, clotrimazole, ketoconazole, econazole, itraconazole, fluconazole, tioconazole, bifonazole and terconazole are some currently used antifungal imidazole derivatives. They all have activity against a broad range of microorganisms including both fungi and bacteria. Clotrimazole, econazole and tioconazole are effective against superficial fungal infections while bifonazole and terconazole are effective in vulvovaginal candidiasis. Other imidazoles like, ketoconazole and miconazole are effective against both, superficial and systemic infections.

Imidazole derivatives act by damaging the fungal cell-membrane. They enhance the membrane permeability by inhibiting the synthesis of ergosterol which is the primary cellular sterol of fungi.

Clotrimazole shows poor oral absorption. Whatever amount absorbed, gets rapidly inactivated by cytochrome P-450 enzymes in the liver. It is a broad spectrum antifungal agent having fungistatic activity against dermatophytes, *C. albicans, C. neoformans, S. schenckii* and *B. dermatitidis*. It is used topically in

1-2 % concentration as cream, lotion and vaginal preparation to treat cutaneous candidiasis, vulvovaginal candidiasis and dermatophyte infections. It may sometimes be combined with an antibacterial agent in some treatment regimen. Miconazole is a potent antifungal imidazole derivative that may be used topically, intravenously or intrathecally. About 90% of administered dose is bound to the plasma proteins. It has a plasma half-life of 24 hours and is extensively metabolized in the liver.

The azole class of antifungals acts by damaging the fungal cell-membrane. These drugs selectively inhibit the biosynthesis of ergosterol by inhibiting fungal cytochrome P-450 sterol 14α-demethylase. Azoles thus inhibit demethylation at C_{14} of lanosterol thereby causing accumulation of 14α-methylated sterols that disrupt the various sterol functions in the cell. This mode of action, results into inhibition of fungal cell growth but does not bring about the death of fungal cell. Hence, the azoles are fungistatic.

Adverse effects include nausea, vomiting, headache, blurred vision, skin rash, burning, itching, irritation, weakness, arthralgia, seizures, confusion, anaemia and thrombocytopenia.

It is effectively used topically in the treatment of tinea pedis, tinea cruris, tinea versicolor, onychomycosis, cutaneous candidiasis, pruritus and other superficial dermatomycoses (2% cream, spray, powder or lotion may be applied topically twice a day for 1-2 weeks). To treat vulvovaginal candidiasis and vaginal infections caused by T. glabratus it may be used in the form of a 2% vaginal cream or 100 mg suppositories. The latter may be applied deep in vagina at bed time for 7 days and in the case of 200 mg vaginal suppositories, a three day treatment is usually advised.

Parenterally it may be used to control systemic fungal infections like, coccidioidomycosis, paracoccidioidomycosis, cryptococcosis, systemic candidiasis and mucocutaneous candidiasis. In patients with coccidioidal meningitis and urinary bladder infections, the i.v. route must be supplemented by intrathecal and intrabladder irrigation routes respectively. The free base may also be used topically to treat ophthalmic mycoses.

Ketoconazole is an orally active, broad spectrum antifungal agent that is chemically related to miconazole. About 99% of administered dose is bound to the plasma proteins. It has a plasma half-life of 2 - 4 hours. It is extensively metabolized in the liver primarily by oxidative o-dealkylation and aromatic hydroxylation to various inactive metabolites that are excreted (85 - 90%) in the bile. It serves as an effective antifungal agent in the treatment of mucocutaneous candidiasis, vaginitis, oral thrush, blastomycosis, coccidioidomycosis, non-meningeal cryptococcal disease, histoplasmosis and some dermatomycoses. It may also be concomittantly administered with flucytosine in the treatment of cryptococcal meningitis.

Econazole nitrate is used topically for the treatment of superficial fungal infections of the skin. While tioconazole is used in the treatment of dermatophyte infections and candidiasis.

From the many series of azoles that have been reported by diverse groups, several common structural features emerge : an imidazole or triazole heme-coordinating group, a halosubstituted aromatic ring separated from the azole moiety by two atoms, and a side chain. The latter represents the feature of greatest diversity across the family.

Variable length of the side chain explored by various groups suggests that this part of the pharmacophore may extend beyond the substrate binding site, perhaps into the substrate access channel.

(d) Allylamines :

The allylamines are the most prominent of a number of antifungal classes that exert their activity by inhibition of squalene epoxidase; the intracellular accumulation of squalene that results is thought to be the primary cause of the fungicidal consequences of exposure to the drug. The predominant example of this class of antifungal agents is terbinafine, which is one of the main drugs for the treatment of dermatophytosis.

The inhibition of squalene epoxidase by the allylamines is reversible and non-competitive with respect to squalene, NADPH and FAD and the agents have no effects on other enzymes in the ergosterol biosynthetic pathway.

The structural requirements for potent activity are represented in the broadest sense by two lipophilic domains linked to a central polar moiety by spacer of appropriate length; for good activity, the polar moiety is a tertiary amine, and one of the lipophilic domains consists of a bicyclic aromatic ring system such as naphthalene or benzo [b] thiophene.

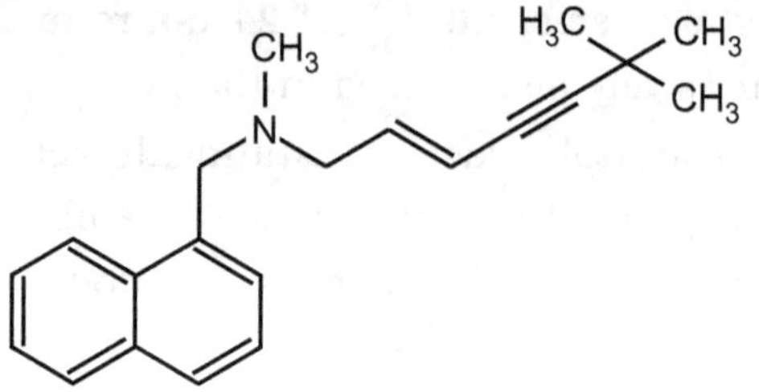

Terbinafine

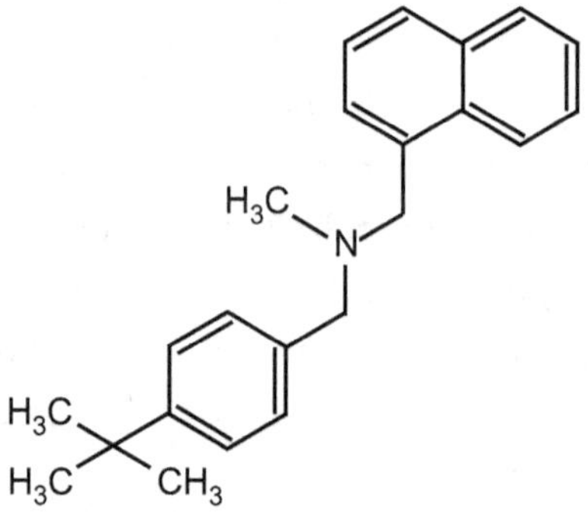

Butenafine

(e) Amidines :

In this category, hydroxystilbamidine and stilbamidine represent the examples of effective antifungal agents. These agents are active against fungi and protozoa. Generally they are used in the treatment of cutaneous blastomycosis, actinomycosis and cryptococcosis.

Hydroxystilbamidine disethionate is administered only by i.v. route. Nothing is known about its bio-transformation and excretion. Adverse effects include nausea, vomiting, diarrhoea, anorexia, rash, fever, chills, anaphylaxis, headache, malaise, fainting, hypotension, dizziness, pancreatitis, hypoglycemia and hepatotoxicity. It is used in the treatment of cutaneous and pulmonary blastomycosis and visceral leishmaniasis.

A solution of 225 mg in 200 ml of 5% dextrose water is freshly prepared and is given by i.v. infusion over a period of 2-3 hours every 24 hours.

(f) Antifungal Antibiotics :

(i) Griseofulvin : It is isolated in 1939 by Oxford, **Raistrick** and **Simonart**. Since it was ineffective against bacteria, its appearance on the clinical screen was delayed by almost about 20 years merely due to an ignorance about its antifungal activity. It is obtained from the yeast, *Penicillium griseofulvum*. Gentles in 1958, first reported its antifungal activity.

Griseofulvin affects only fungi with chitinous cell-wall. The drug is fungistatic rather than fungicidal. It is ineffective in the treatment of systemic mycoses. It may be used orally or topically in the treatment of superficial mycoses of skin, hair and nails caused by most strains of *Microsporum, Trichophyton* and *Epidermophyton*. It does not have effect on bacteria, yeasts or other fungi. Its antifungal activity is mainly due to its interaction with the polymerized microtubules. Microtubules are the protein structures found in eukaryotic cells that are responsible for the formation of mitotic spindles. The drug-induced disruption of mitotic spindles slows down the oxidative phosphorylation and nucleic acid synthesis in the fungal cells.

Griseofulvin is nil bound to the plasma proteins. However, it specifically binds to keratin and high concentrations are found in the stratum corneum. Significant concentration of drug is also retained by the nails. It has a plasma half-life of about 24 hours. Major metabolite is 6-methyl-griseofulvin that is excreted in the urine. Some fraction also appears unchanged in the faeces.

Adverse effects include nausea, vomiting, diarrhea, headache, blurred vision, dry mouth, fatigue, lethargy, peripheral neuritis, heartburn, erythema, albuminuria, leucopenia and hepatotoxicity. It is contraindicated during pregnancy and in patients with porphyria and liver failure.

Besides its effectiveness in mycotic infections, it also showed promising results in lichen planus, anginal attacks and Raynaud's syndrome.

(ii) Polyene antibiotics : In the early 1950s, polyene antibiotics were first identified. As the name implies, these compounds contain, unsaturated carbon rings or chains. About 60 polyene antibiotics (all produced by actinomycetes) have been reported in the literature.

All polyenes are characterized by the presence of a large ring containing a lactone group (i.e. macrocyclic lactone) and a hydrophobic region coupled with conjugated polyene system of four to seven double bonds. Many of them contain a glycosidically linked amino sugars. For example, an aminodesoxy hexose (i.e. mycosamine) is present in amphotericin B and nystatin. The polyene antibiotics are poorly soluble in water. The number of double bonds present in the skeleton serves as a basis of classification of polyenes. For example, they may be categorised as tetraenes (nystatin), pentaenes (filipin), hexaenes (endomycin) and heptaenes (amphotericin B). The most important polyenes are amphotericin B and nystatin. The former being an important therapeutic agent against most of the systemic antifungal diseases. Depending upon the concentration employed, polyene antibiotics exert either fungistatic or fungicidal effects.

These polyene macrolides preferentially bind ergosterol, the predominant fungal sterol, resulting in a permeable plasma membrane and rapid cell death. However, amphotericin also binds to cholesterol of mammalian cytoplasmic membrane. This results in alteration of mammalian cytoplasmic membrane and may explain the severe nephrotoxicity accompanying the use of amphotericin B.

(iii) Amphotericin B : Amphotericin is a mixture of two compounds A and B, obtained from *Streptomyces nodosus*, a soil actinomycete reported in 1956. As the name suggests, amphotericins are amphoteric in nature. Amphotericin B is more potent and it possesses a broad spectrum of activity. It is effective against *Aspergillus fumigatus; B. dermatitidis, Candida* species, *C. neoformans, H. capsulatum, Coccidioides immitis, M. audouinii, Paracoccidiodes brasiliensis, Rhizopus* species, *Rhodotorula* species, *Sporothrix schenckii, Torulopsis glabrata, Trichophyton* species *and Mycobacterium leprae*. It exerts maximum antifungal effect between the pH range of 6.0 - 7.5.

It is available in the form of mixture, lozenges and ointment. It has poor oral absorption pattern. It is effective against a number of fungal infections including aspergillosis, blastomycosis, *candida* infections, leishmaniasis, histoplasmosis, sporotrichosis and coccidioidomycosis. It is used topically to treat external ocular infections (i.e. mycotic conjunctivities). For topical use, amphotericin B is available in a 3% concentration as a cream, lotion and ointment. It may be used intravenously or subconjunctivally in the treatment of fungal corneal ulcers or endophthalmitis. In cryptococcal meningitis, it is usually combined with 5-fluorocytosine to get a synergistic action. It may also be given intra-articularly especially in sporotrichosis and coccidioidomycosis.

In many occasions, flucytosine, minocycline or rifampin in fact may be added to the regimen in order to reduce the minimum antifungal concentration of amphotericin B. Since the latter is one of the most toxic antimicrobial agent which is in use today, the reduction in the dose of amphotericin B, helps in improving the patient's comfort. Amphotericin B methyl ester has equipotent antifungal activity but has better pharmacokinetic features. However, it could not reach the market because of its ability to cause leukoencephalopathy.

(iv) Nystatin : Nystatin was first isolated from *Streptomyces noursei* in 1951 by **Hazen** and **Brown**. The name of this antibiotic was derived from New York state from where it was discovered. It is only slightly soluble in water and is unstable to moisture, heat, light and air. It exerts no effect on bacteria, protozoa or viruses. When used topically, nystatin may sometimes be combined with iodochlorhydroxyquin.

It is effective specifically against *Candida, Microsporum, Trichophyton, Leishmania, B. dermatitidis, C. neoformans, H. capsulatum, T. vaginalis* and dermatophytes. It is often combined with gention violet, procaine hydrochloride, antibiotics or hydrocortisone and is used topically in the treatment of candidiasis of skin, mouth, intestine, conjunctival sac, nails and vagina. It may be given as aerosol or instilled into conjunctival sac. However, it should not be used parenterally due to severe systemic toxicities.

Natamycin is yet another tetraene antifungal antibiotic obtained from *Streptomyces natalensis* in 1958. It is a broad spectrum antifungal agent specifically effective against occular infections caused by *Fusarium solani* and Myceliating fungi. It is used to treat fungal keratitis, fungal blepharitis and fungal conjunctivitis. It may also be inhaled into the respiratory tract to cure broncho-pulmonary aspergillosis and candidiasis.

Hamycin and candicidin are the examples of other antifungal polyene antibiotics. Candicidin was isolated in 1953 from *Streptomyces griseus* and is used topically in the treatment of vaginal candidiasis. Hamycin is isolated from *Streptomyces pimprima* and is effective against *Blastomyces dermatitidis, Histoplasma capsulatum, Aspergillus fumigatus, Cryptococcus neoformans* and *Candida albicans*. It may be used topically to control vaginal candidiasis.

(g) Miscellaneous Agents :

(i) Tolnaftate : Tolnaftate is a topical antifungal agent available as cream, solution, powder and aerosol in 1% concentration. It is a thiocarbamate derivative and is used in the treatment of cutaneous mycoses or ringworm infections. When used against other fungal or bacterial infections, it remains ineffective.

Like the allylamines, it is a non-competitive inhibitor of squalene epoxidase, with inherent selectivity for the fungal enzymes over mammalian. It is topically applied to the affected area twice a day. However, relapses may occur after cessation of therapy.

(ii) Cyclopirox olamine : It is a topically used broad spectrum fungicidal agent effective against dermatophytes. Its antifungal activity may be related to its ability to interfere in uptake of precursors needed for the synthesis of proteins and nucleic acid core. Adverse effects are few and include pruritis and burning at the site of application.

(iii) Potassium iodide : In the form of saturated solution of 1 g/ml, it may be used orally as an effective antifungal agent in the treatment of cutaneous and lymphatic forms of sporotrichosis, caused by *S. schenckii*. It is excreted in the urine. It probably acts by iodination of proteins in fungus cell membrane. Adverse effects include nausea, vomiting, diarrhoea, heart-burn, sneezing, shedding tears, metallic taste, acneiform skin lesions and swelling of parotid gland. Iodism is frequently encountered during the therapy.

Whitfield's Ointment :

It contains a mixture of benzoic acid (fungistatic agent) and salicylic acid (keratolytic agent). The keratolytic action of salicylic acid helps for desquamation of stratum corneum. This promotes the removal of offending fungus resulting into better penetration of antifungal agent.

Fungal Cell Wall :

The cell-wall is one of the most attractive targets in the fungal cell. It morphologically defines and protects the cell from lysis and its continued biosynthesis is essential for growth and survival. It is composed primarily of three polysaccharides; β-1, 3-glucan, chitin (β-1, 4-N-acetylglucosamine) and mannoprotein (largely α-1, 6-mannose). None of the major components of the cell-wall or enzymes involved in their biosynthesis occurs in mammalian cells.

Table 10.3 : Clinically used antifungal agents

	Drug	Uses	Possible mechanism of action
1.	Polyene antibiotics	Candidiasis, Histoplasmosis, Blastomycosis, Sporotrichosis	Interact with fungal membrane sterols and change the selective permeability of fungal membrane.
2.	Griseofulvin	T. capitis, T. circinata, T. pedis, Onochomycosis	Interacts with fungal micro-tubules and prevents cell division.
3.	Imidazole derivatives	Cryptococcosis, Histoplasmosis, Mucormycosis	Inhibits ergosterol synthesis in fungal cell membrane resulting into leakage of cell constituents.
4.	Flucytosine	Candidiasis Aspergillosis	Inhibits the formation of fungal nucleic acids.
5.	Tolnaftate	Cutaneous mycoses	Inhibits transport of precursors for proteins and nucleic acid in fungi.
6.	Ciclopirox	Cutaneous mycoses	Inhibits transport of precursors needed for the synthesis of proteins and nucleic acid in fungi.
7.	Potassium iodide	Sporotrichosis	Iodination of proteins in fungal cell-membrane.

Antibiotics :

Many antibiotics like, minocycline, tetracyclines, penicillines and rifampicin may be administered concomittantly with antifungal agents. Though they do not have antifungal potential, they can enhance the activity of antifungal agent (e.g. amphotericin B) when used in combination. Beside them, pyrrolnitrin, variotin and siccanin are other examples of antibiotics used in mycotic diseases.

Plant Products :

Many workers have described the plant products as effective antifungal agents in the treatment of skin disorders. However, the reports over antifungal properties of essential oils are quite meagre and fragmentary.

Other Organic Compounds :

Salicylic acid, aminacrine, acrisorcin, halopragin, p-chloro-metaxylenol, salicylamide, salicylanilide, iodochlorhydroxyquin, m-cresyl acetate, diamethazole, chlordantoin, gention violet, pecilocin, di-iodohydroxy quinoline, iodine, phenyl mercuric nitrate, thymol and zinc pyrithione possess significant antifungal activity. Most of them may be used in the treatment of ringworm infections of scalp, feet and groin. Haloprogin is a synthetic iodinated trichlorophenol available as a 1% cream. It is effective against various candidial and ringworm infections of the skin. Thymol in 1 - 2% concentration may be added to Whitfield's ointment to enhance its antifungal potential. Zinc pyrithione may be used as 1% solution to control infections due to the Pityrosporum ovale and Tinea versicolor. While salicylanilide may be used alongwith undecylenic acid in the form of 5 % ointment to exhibit antifungal activity.

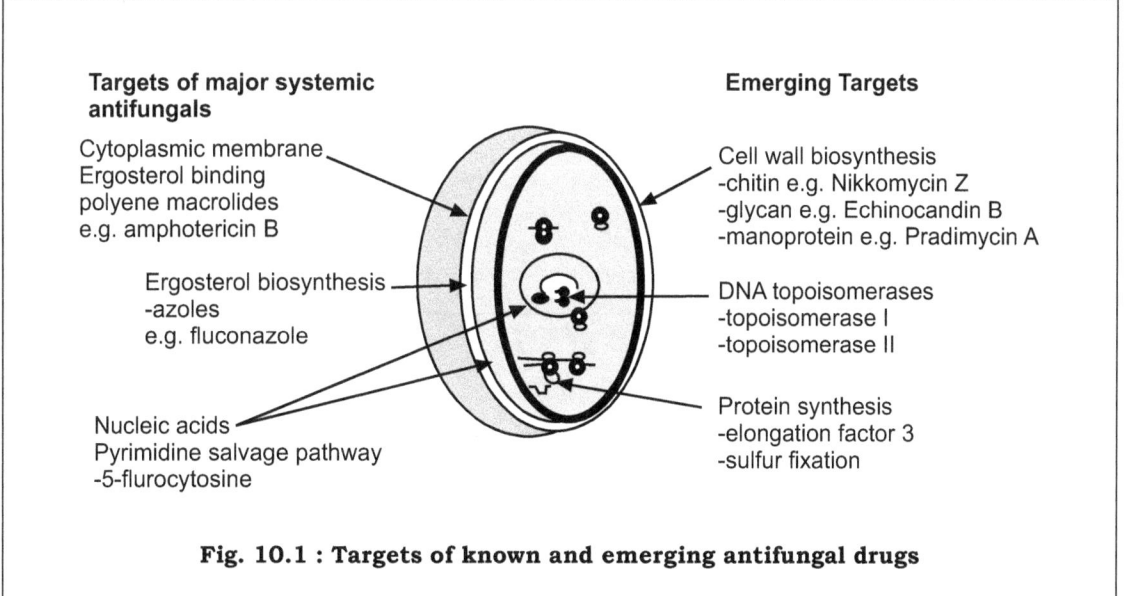

Fig. 10.1 : Targets of known and emerging antifungal drugs

10.3 NATURAL PRODUCTS

The various fungal organisms produce antibacterial substances along with such antifungal agents which do not exhibit significant antibacterial properties. Such types of anti-fungal antibiotics include pyrrolnitrin, variotin, siccanin and natamycin.

i) Pyrrolnitrin

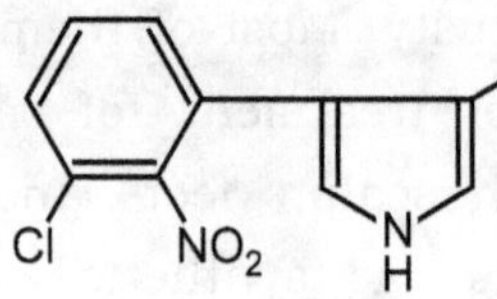

Source : *Pseudomonas fluoroscence*

ii) $CH_3 - CH_2 - CH_2 - CH_2 - \underset{OH}{\underset{|}{\overset{H}{\overset{|}{C}}}} - CH = \underset{}{\overset{CH_3}{\overset{|}{C}}} - CH = CH - CH = CH - \underset{O}{\overset{}{\overset{\|}{C}}} - N$

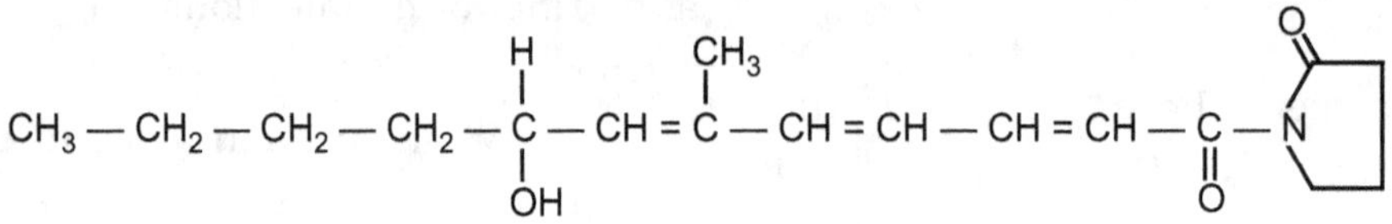

Variotin

Source : *Paecilomyces variotii*

iii) Siccanin

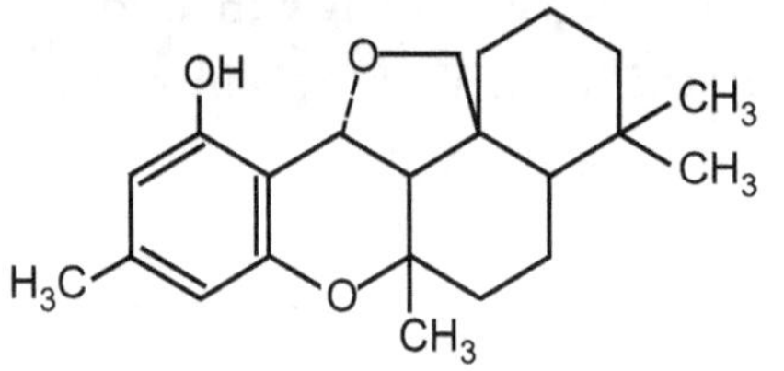

Source : Helminthosporium siccans

iv) $NH_2 - \underset{NH}{\overset{\|}{C}} - NH (CH_2)_8 - \underset{OH}{\overset{|}{CH}} - \underset{(CH_2)_3 NH_2}{\overset{|}{CH}} - NH - CO - (CH_2)_8 - NH - \underset{NH}{\overset{\|}{C}} - NH_2$

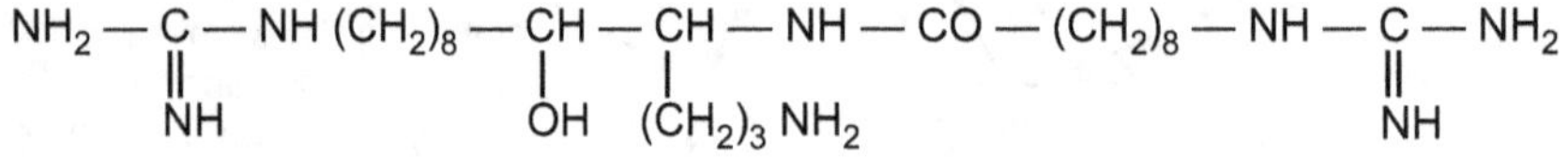

Eulicin

ANTIVIRAL AGENTS

11.1 INTRODUCTION

Viruses represent a separate and unique class of infectious agents, that can replicate only inside the living cells of organisms. Outside the host cell they are like any other non-living entity and are referred to as *virion* or *virus* particles. The smallest viruses possess a diameter of not more than 20 mm while in case of the large viruses, diameter may go upto 300 mm. The constitution of a virus is much more simple as compared to that of bacteria. According to **Lwoff**, an infectious agent that :

1. possesses simple chemical composition.
2. lacks the metabolic enzyme machinery.
3. lacks the protein-synthesizing system.
4. contains only one type of nucleic acid (i.e. either DNA or RNA), and
5. possesses a host-cell dependent machinery of multiplication can be named as virus.

Unlike bacteria, viruses do not possess cell-wall. Viruses consist of one or more strands of a linear or helical strands of either DNA or RNA enclosed in a shell of protein known as the 'capsid'. The capsid is composed of several sub-units known as capsomeres that decide the shape of the capsid. Though often be spherical, capsid may possess different shapes. In certain cases, capsid may be surrounded by an outer protein or lipoprotein envelope. This encircling membrane may be called as an 'envelope'.

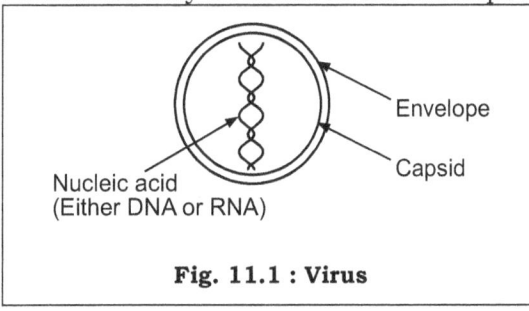

Fig. 11.1 : Virus

Since the biology of viral replication is dependent on the host cell metabolic machinery (e.g. protein synthesis, various enzyme systems), unlike bacteria, viruses can not be grown on the nutrient media. They can replicate only in the host cell which may be a bacteria, animal or plant cell. Hence, viruses are considered as obligatory intracellular parasites that utilize biochemical machinery and many products of host cell to sustain their viability.

Viral diseases includes influenza, smallpox, rabbies, poliomyelitis, yellow fever, ornithosis, psittacosis and lymphogranuloma venereum.

The viral replication may be outlined as under :

1. Adsorption :

The virion invades the host cell-membrane. The reactive sites on the capsid firmly bind with their complimentary sites on the hosts cell. The viral particle is encapsulated by hosts cell cytoplasm, forming a vacuole.

2. Uncoating :

The genetic material or viral genome (DNA or RNA) passes into the hosts cell, leaving the capsid covering outside the hosts cell. Sometimes uncovering of viral genome occurs within the hosts cell. This step is referred to as penetration into hosts cell. Only the viral genome is infectious to the hosts cell and the capsid of the protein coat determines the site of the attacks of virus within the hosts. The viral genome is different from the host's nucleic acids and hence it is infectious. Sometimes due to its proteineous nature, capsid contents may turn to be antigenic to the hosts cell and initiates a number of immunological reactions to the host.

3. Synthesis of viral components :

Viral genome enters the cytoplasm or nucleoplasm and directs or utilises the host's nucleic acid machinery for the synthesis of new viral protein and the production of more viral genome. Thus, it not only consumes the actual material for its own use from the hosts cell but also enjoys the services of the biochemical systems of the host to incorporate this material into the several proteinous subunits needed for its own replication.

4. Release of the virus :

Viral nucleic acid and capsid protein materials are synthesized in different parts of the hosts cell by the host-cell ribosomes. The m-RNA is synthesized from the viral genome. The host cell machinery, however, fails to differentiate between viral and cell directed orders. The large number of newly synthesized viral particles then have to be brought together for assembling new virions. The latter are released from the cell by budding process. They may acquire the lipoprotein envelope at the time of their release. The new virions then invade fresh host-cell and repeat the whole process. Since the host cell machinery is totally utilized for production of new virions, the normal cell functions cease at the time of replication. Some viruses induce the production of toxic intermediates that adds to their pathogenicity. Viruses are composed of one or more strands of a linear or helical nucleic acid core, consisting of either DNA or RNA, but not both. Viruses thus can be classified as per the type of nucleic acid present in them.

The types are :

(A) DNA viruses : This class includes pox viruses, papoviruses, adenoviruses and herpes viruses.

(B) RNA viruses : This class includes, arboviruses, myxoviruses, picornaviruses and rhinoviruses.

11.2 DESIGN OF ANTIVIRAL AGENTS

Viral chemotherapy is still in the phase of infancy. Although a great deal of work has been done, it has resulted in the development of only 3-4 clinically used agents. Presently immunization, public health measures and physical and chemical disinfection procedures play a vital role in the prevention of spread of viral diseases.

Viruses are essentially intracellular parasites. Unlike bacteria, the viral replication is totally dependent upon the energy, proteins and enzymatic machinery of the host cell. Bacteria have self contained biosynthetic machinery. Hence, the drug in chemotherapy enjoys the advantage of selective attack on bacteria due to many metabolic and molecular differences between the pathogen and the host cell. Since viruses literally take over the metabolic machinery of the infected human cell, a close relationship exists between the multiplying virus and the hosts cell. Virus replication is intimately dependent upon the hosts cell metabolism. This fact severely limits the usual opportunities to design antiviral agent having selective effect on the viral cell. Attempts to inhibit viral growth without damaging the host-cells became fruitless.

Viral infection or its presence in host cell is felt so late that it results into extensive viral multiplication and tissue damage. The late diagnosis and recognition of the disease state projects almost negligible chances for effective therapy. The drugs become useless, even if they are made available.

The important key events in the viral replication are diagrammatically shown in the figure 11.2.

It is apparent that various steps involved in the viral replication could be successfully utilized as the basis of designing antiviral agents. For example, the following sites in viral replication offered promising points for the attack of antiviral agents.

1. Adsorption of virus on the host cell,

2. Penetration of virus in host cell, and

3. Synthesis of viral genetic material.

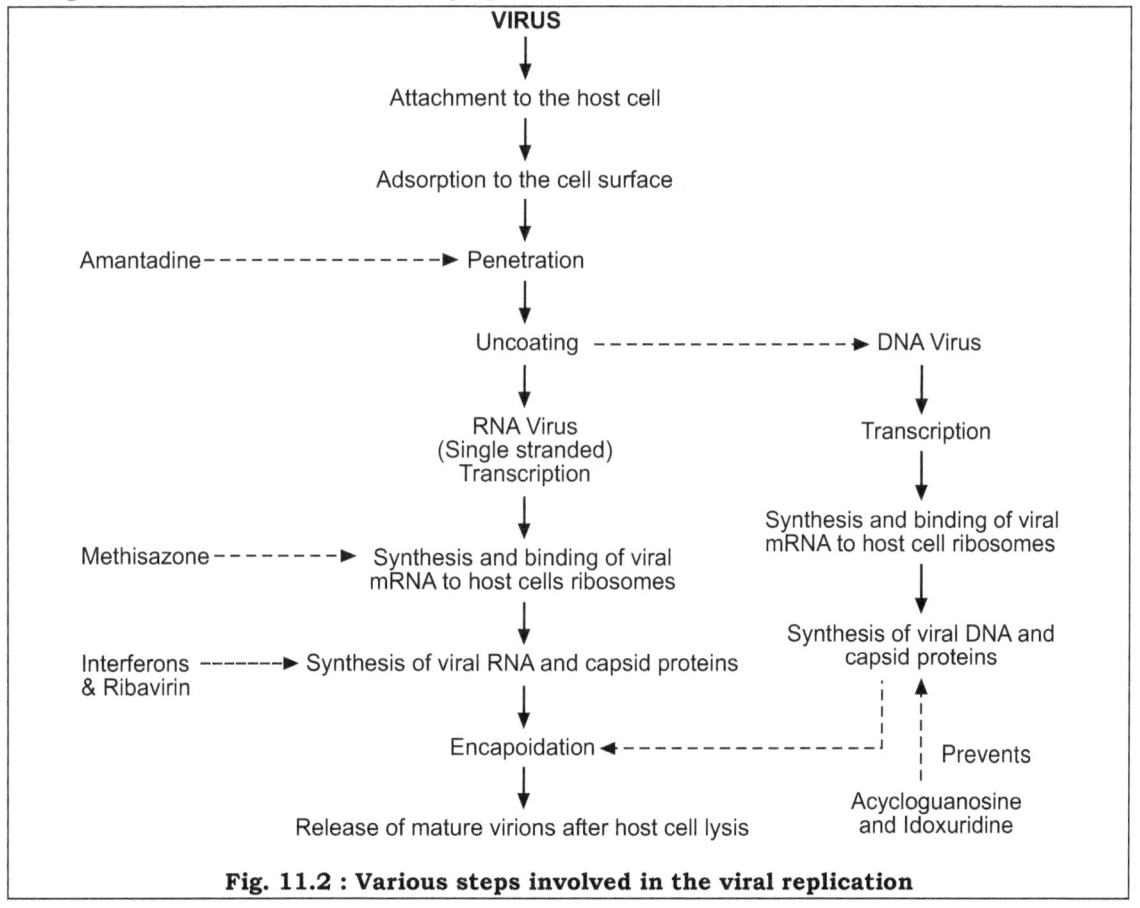

Fig. 11.2 : Various steps involved in the viral replication

Amantadine hydrochloride inhibits viral penetration and prevents influenza while methisazone and idoxuridine inhibit viral DNA synthesis. Due to one or more reasons (e.g. narrow activity spectra or toxicity) not a single drug in this area, enjoyed clinical popularity. The development of antiviral agent having selective toxicity to viral cells leaving host cells unaffected still remains a dream for the medicinal chemists.

Antiviral agents have often been proved to be disappointing due to the following problems in their development :

1. Lack of satisfactory experimental models.
2. Use of wrong virus in the laboratory.
3. Narrow spectrum of activity.
4. Limitations on uses due to their toxicity.
5. Difficulties in their clinical assessment.

These disappointing features of antiviral therapy force us to accept vaccines as the best prophylactic agents in the treatment of viral diseases. There are four forms of antigen used in vaccines. These include,

(a) Attenuated living,
(b) Killed by the chemicals, such as formalin,
(c) Toxoids (i.e. toxins which through the application of heat or formalin are converted to non-toxic form).
(d) Subunits prepared by purifying important antigens of microorganisms.

Vaccination can be effectively used to prevent measles, rubella, mumps, poliomyelitis, yellow fever, smallpox and hepatitis B. They have only prophylactic utility and remain ineffective once the infection has occured and spreaded within the host.

11.3 CLASSIFICATION OF ANTIVIRAL AGENTS

Various antiviral agents so far introduced, are found to possess very narrow spectrum of activity. For example, agents which are effective against DNA viruses are usually ineffective against RNA-viruses and drugs which show activity against RNA-viruses remain silent against DNA-viruses. During the course of antiviral therapy, the drug used receives very fast acknowledgement from the viruses, resulting into rapid development of drug resistant strains of viruses.

The currently available antiviral drugs can be chemically classified as :

(A) Purine nucleosides and nucleotides
(B) Pyrimidine nucleosides and nucleotides
(C) Thiosemicarbazones
(D) Benzimidazoles
(E) Adamantane amines
(F) Interferons
(G) Miscellaneous agents

(A) Purine Nucleosides and Nucleotides : Acyclovir triphosphate (Acycloguanosine) :

It is a synthetic purine nucleoside analog in which a linear side-chain (i.e. $-CH_2OCH_2CH_3$) is attached at 9th position instead of the cyclic sugar present in the guanosine molecule.

Acyclovir undergoes phosphorylation process with the help of viral thymidine kinase enzymes to form acyclovir triphosphate. The latter selectively inhibits herpes virus DNA polymerase. The faulty transcription in viral DNA leads to inhibition of virus replication process. The affinity of viral thymidine kinase enzymes for acyclovir is about 200 times greater than that of mammalian enzymes for the drug. This explains the selectivity of attack on the viruses.

It can be used orally, topically and intravenously. About 15% of administered dose is bound to the plasma proteins. It has plasma half-life of about 2.5 hours. It is excreted in urine mostly in unchanged form alongwith minor amount of inactive metabolite, 9-carboxy methoxy methylguanine.

Adverse effects include nausea, headache, amnesia, hypotension, tremors and coma. Local irritation, ulceration and burning may occur when it is applied to genital lesions.

It is effective against herpes virus infections, herpes zoster infections and infections caused by *varicella zoster* and *cytomegalovirus*. It may be used orally for the treatment of both initial and recurrent episodes of genital herpes. A 3% acyclovir ointment may be used for the treatment of ocular herpetic infection and herpes keratoconjunctivitis. It may also be used intravenously in the treatment of herpes simplex encephalitis. However, development of resistance to acyclovir may limit its clinical utility.

(B) Pyrimidine Nucleosides and Nucleotides :

(i) Idoxuridine : It was discovered in 1959 by **Prusoff**. It is a topically used antiviral agent chemically related to trifluridine and is effective against vaccinia and herpes simplex virus, pseudorabies, B. virus, myxoma virus, polyoma virus and some papovaviruses.

Idoxuridine is chemically very similar to thymidine, a compound which in the normal cell undergoes phosphorylation and then get incorporated into DNA molecule. Due to the structural similarity with thymidine, with the help of thymidine kinase and thymidine monophosphate kinase enzymes, it is converted to the active triphosphorylated derivative. The latter blocks DNA polymerase enzyme resulting into interference in nucleic acid and protein synthesis in DNA-viruses. It also prevents the assembling of viral components by inhibiting the synthesis of a protein required for their assembling. Since the host cell DNA synthesis is also affected, it produces host cytotoxicity. Hence, its systemic use is not recommended. It is thus usually given topically. Hence, serious side-effects rarely attend its use.

It is available in the form of ophthalmic ointment (0.5%) and ophthalmic solution (0.1%). It gets rapidly inactivated by deaminases or nucleotidases into 5-iodouracil and inorganic iodides. Adverse effects include pain, irritation, pruritus, inflammation or edema of conjunctiva and eyelids, corneal vascularization, lacrimation, stomatitis, neutropenia and thrombocytopenia. It is effective in the treatment of herpes simplex infections of eyelid, conjunctiva and cornea.

(ii) Trifluridine : It is a halogenated thymidine analog used as a topical antiviral agent. It is effective against herpes simplex virus, vaccinia and adenovirus. It is converted to the active 5-monophosphate form. Due to the structural similarity with thymidine, it gets incorporated, instead of thymidine phosphorylated form, into replicating viral DNA. This results into wrong expression of genetic information due to abnormal base pairing. It also blocks thymidylate synthetase and

Table 11.1 : Currently used antiviral agents

Acyclovir : R = — $CH_2OCH_2CH_2OH$
Ganciclovir : R = — $CH_2OCH(CH_2OH)_2$
Penciclovir : R = — $CH_2CH_2CH(CH_2OH)_2$
Famciclovir : R = — $CH_2CH_2CH(CH_2OCOCH_3)_2$

Zalcitabine : X = C
Lamivudine : X = S

Methisazone; R = CH_3
Isatin - β - thiosemicarbazone; R = H

Idoxuridine ; X = I
Trifluridine ; X = CF_3

(Zidovudine)

Vidarabine
($R_1 = R_2$ = H)
Fludarabine;
R_1 = F ; R_2 = $HOPO_2$

Cytosine arabinoside

Didanosine

Ribavirin

Foscarnet sodium

Amantadine; R = NH_2
Rimantadine; R = $-CH(CH_3)(NH_2)$
1-Adamantyl; guanidine R = $-C(NH_2)(=NH)$

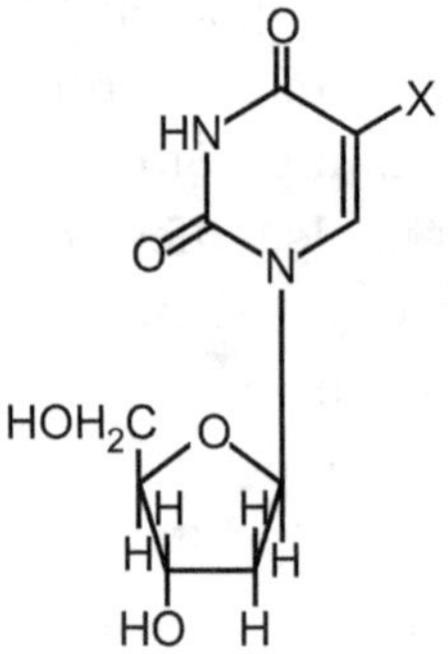

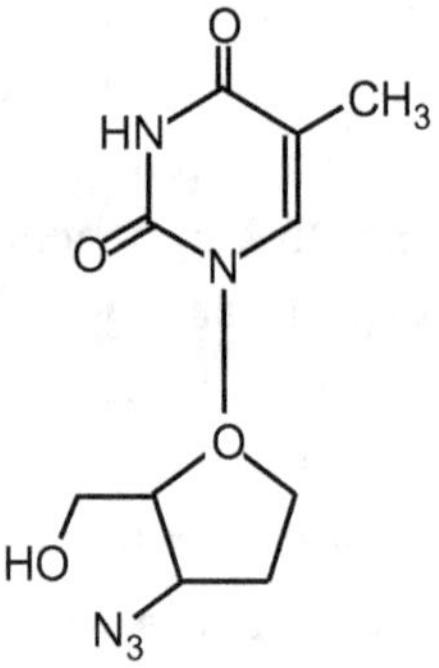

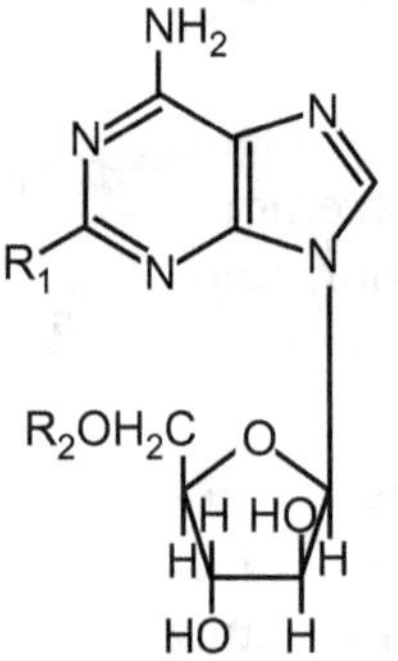

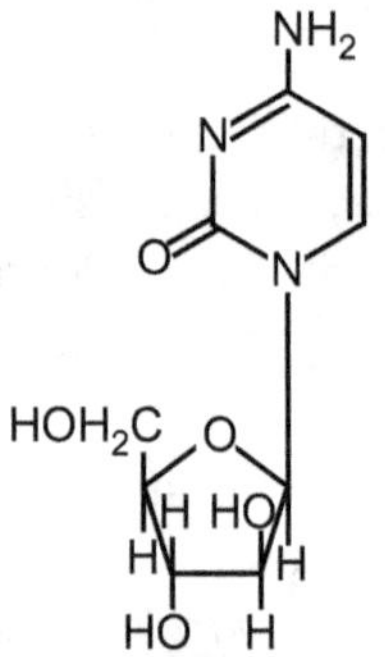

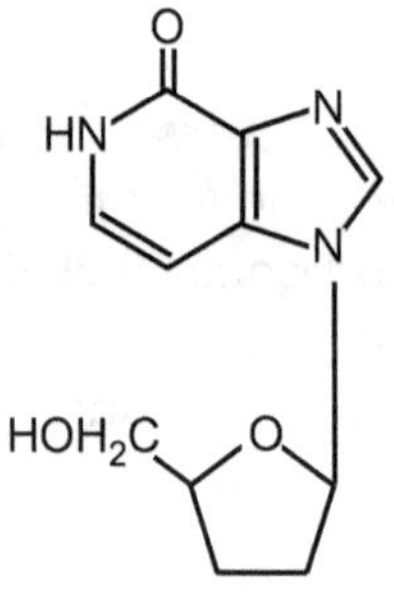

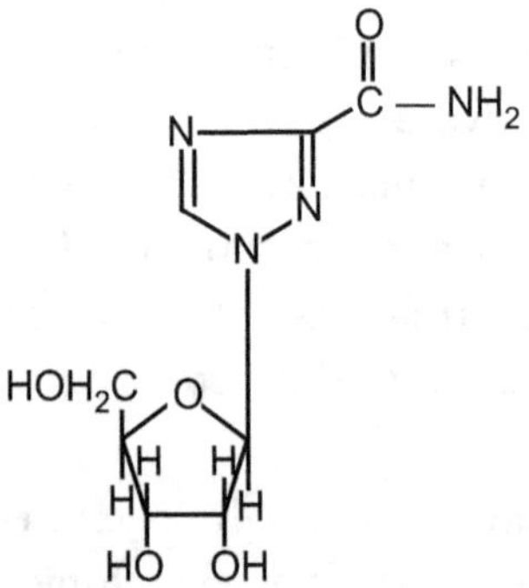

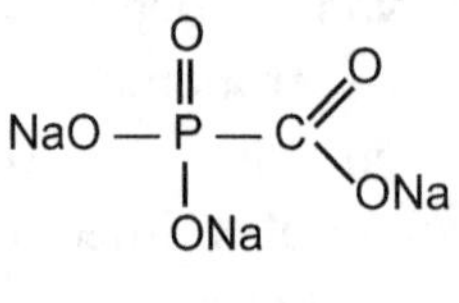

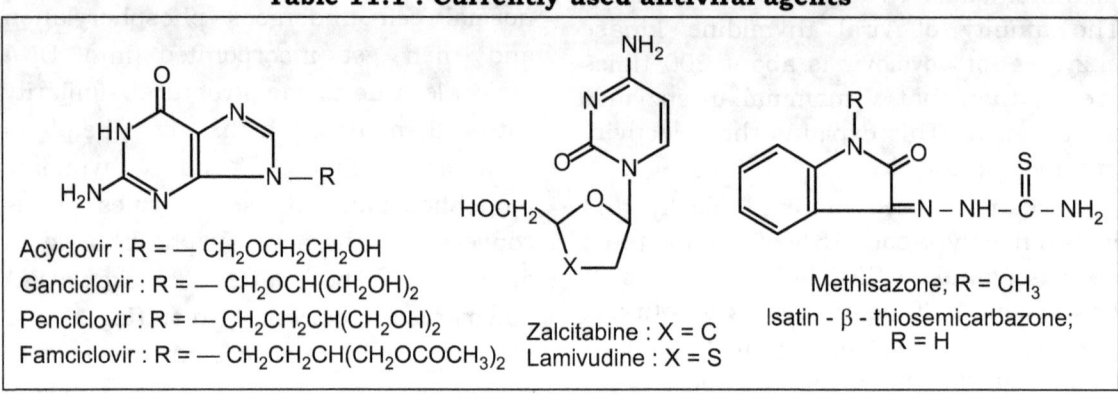

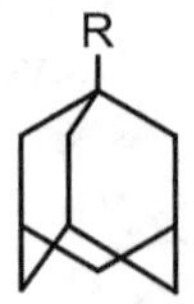

deoxythymidine kinase enzymes in the viruses. The overall biological effects may get reflected into :

(i) increased number of errors in viral protein synthesis,

(ii) increased rate of mutation, and

(iii) inhibition of viral replication process.

It has a plasma half-life of 12 – 18 minutes. Metabolism involves removal of deoxyribose by nucleoside phosphorylase with conversion to trifluorothymine. Urinary excretion of parent and metabolites is rapid. Adverse effects include stomatitis, reticulocytopenia, hypophosphatemia, anemia, neutropenia, megaloblastosis and hypocalcemia.

In the form of 1% ophthalmic solution, it is used to treat certain ocular infections (e.g. ocular kercititis and keratoconjunctivitis). It exhibits effectiveness in cases where idoxuridine treatment fails.

(iii) Vidarabine (Adenine arabinoside) (Area - A) : Vidarabine is a purine nucleoside. This antiviral agent is isolated from the bacteria, *Streptomyces antibioticus*. It is an analog of adenosine originally developed for the treatment of leukemia. It is converted *in-vivo* enzymatically to ara-ATP. The latter impairs early steps in viral DNA synthesis, presumably by inhibiting viral DNA polymerase. It exhibits considerable host toxicity due to part inhibition of cellular DNA polymerase enzymes.

It is effective against vaccinia, herpes simplex virus, cytomegalo virus, varicella zoster, pseudorabies and myxoma virus. It may be used topically as a 3% ophthalmic ointment or as i.v. infusion. About 20-30% administered dose is bound to the plasma-proteins. It has a plasma half-life of 1.5 hours. In the cornea and in the plasma, it metabolizes to ara-hypoxanthine (active; half-life is 3.3 hours) by xanthine oxidase enzyme through a process of deamination.

Adverse effects include nausea, diarrhoea, thrombophlebitis, hallucinations, tremors, dizziness and burning, itching and redness of the eyes. It should not be used to treat triviral infections.

It is used to treat herpes simplex infections in neonates. It is also used to treat herpes simplex encephalitis and herpes zoster infections in immuno compromised patients. It may have activity in cytomegalovirus infections and in type B virus hepatitis. In the form of 3% ophthalmic ointment, it may be used topically to control recurrent epithelial keratitis and kerato-conjunctivitis. However, it remains ineffective against bacterial, fungal and adenovirus infections. Its antineoplastic potential is under investigations.

Vidarabine-5'-monophosphate and vidarabine – hypoxanthine - 5' monophosphate are the vidarabine derivatives that are currently under investigation for their utility in antiviral therapy.

(iv) Ribavirin : It is a synthetic nucleoside chemically related to inosine, guanosine and xanthosine. It is a broad spectrum antiviral agent effective against nearly all major viruses. It has virustatic properties. It is *in-vivo* converted to ribavirin - 5' - monophosphate which acts as a competitive inhibitor of inosine 5' monophosphate dehydrogenase. This results into inhibition of guanine monophosphate synthesis, followed by inhibition of viral RNA synthesis.

It has a plasma half-life of 9 hours. It is extensively metabolized in the liver.

Principle metabolites include mono, di and triphosphate derivatives, tricarboxylic acid analog and 1, 2, 4-triazole carboxamide metabolite. Deribosylation and breakdown of triazole ring is also reported to occur.

Adverse effects include rash, conjunctivitis, blurred vision, reticulocytosis, dyspnea, chest discomfort, dizziness, anemia, and hypotension. It is contraindicated during pregnancy.

It is an investigational antiviral agent used in the treatment of infections due to respiratory viruses. It is used in the form of aerosol to treat severe lower respiratory tract infections due to respiratory syncytial virus (RSV). It is also undergoing evaluation in the treatment of human immunodeficiency virus (HIV) infections, like AIDS.

Adenine arabinoside and cytosine arabinoside are other examples from this category. Cytosine arabinoside (cytarabine) is effective against herpes viruses. It is presently used in cancer chemotherapy.

(C) Thiosemicarbazones :

In 1947, **Domagk** (sulfonamide fame) reported that some derivatives of benzaldehyde thiosemicarbazone protected laboratory animals against tuberculosis. This initiated an extensive investigation of the thiosemicarbazones during which the activity of methisazone (N-methylisatin - β thiosemicarbazone) was discovered. It is effective against a variety of poxviruses and some RNA viruses.

The antiviral action of thiosemicarbazone is perhaps due to the formation of metal chelate with various metal ions including Cu, Zn, Ni, ferrous and manganese. Methisazone thus acts by interacting with metalloenzymes that are necessary for the replication of certain viruses. The thiosemicarbazones may also react directly and specifically with viral nucleic acid.

Methisazone prevents replication of vaccinia viruses. It is poorly absorbed by oral route. Major metabolic pathways include demethylation, replacement of sulphur by oxygen in the side-chain and hydroxylation in the aromatic ring. Isatin - 3 - thiosemicarbazone is the active metabolite retaining half the activity of parent drug.

It is used as a prophylactic agent against small pox and for the prevention and treatment of generalised vaccinia or vaccinial encephalitis.

(D) Benzimidazoles :

Following two compounds of this family are found to show promising results in trials.

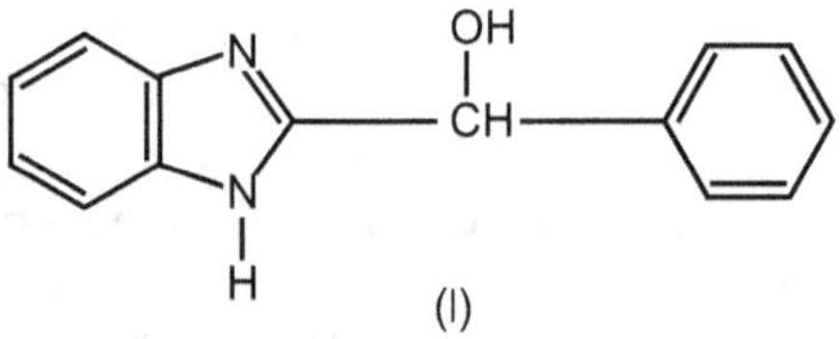

(I)

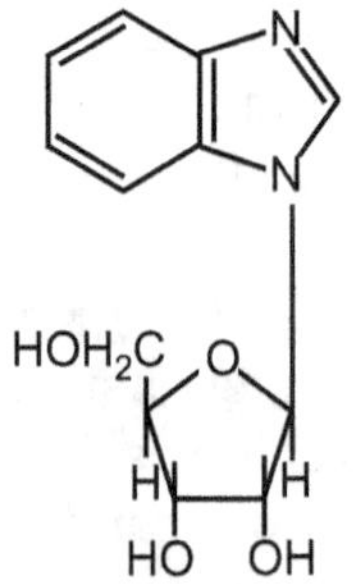

(II)

Both these agents do not interfere with the viral adsorption, penetration and uncoating. They appear to act by inhibition of viral RNA synthesis.

(E) Adamantane Amines :

Amantadine hydrochloride : It was first reported by **Davies et al** in 1964. It is a synthetic antiviral agent effective against infections caused by influenza A viruses including H3N2 and H1N1 subtypes. In higher concentrations, it is also effective against influenza B, rubella and other viruses.

Amantadine allows viral adsorption to the hosts cell but inhibits the uncoating of the influenza virus and prohibits penetration of viral genome into the hosts cell. Because the virion remains adsorbed to hosts cell surface, it becomes susceptible to attack by host's antibodies.

It is orally active and is completely absorbed from GIT. It has the plasma half-life of about 9 – 37 hours. It is not metabolized in the body and is excreted almost in unchanged form in the urine. The rate of urinary excretion depends on the urinary pH; acid urine facilitates rapid excretion.

Adverse effects include GI-upset, nervousness, insomnia, tremors, confusion, hallucination and coma. It is contraindicated during pregnancy and in patients with mental illness and epilepsy.

Besides its antiviral potential, it may also be employed in the therapy of parkinsonism.

Rimantadine is better tolerated and less toxic analog of amantadine which is currently undergoing clinical evaluation. It has similar actions and uses.

(F) Interferons (Antiviral Proteins) :

The presence of interferons was first reported in 1957 by scientists **Issaes** and **Lindermann** at the National Institute for Medical Research, U.K. The term is applied to a class of glycoproteins of molecular weights from about 20,000 to 50,000. Each contains approximately 150 amino acids. Interferons are produced from the hosts cell when it is infected or is exposed to an inactive virus. The endogenous synthesis of interferons is under the control of host cell RNA. There are three major types of human interferons that are designated as α, β and γ according to antigen specifications. The preferred abbreviation of interferon is IFN. Interferons can also be designated as per the source. For example, human (Hu IFN), bovine (Bov. IFN), murine (Mu IFN etc. Currently, major source of human interferons is white blood cells that have been cultured and then exposed to appropriate viruses. In body, after their release, they may attach to surface receptors of the adjacent cells and initiate the production of additional interferons.

Viruses differ in their ability to induce the synthesis and/or liberation of interferons. The adsorption of a virus to the hosts cell or the full infected condition of the hosts cell induces the formation and release of interferons. This is a sort of immunization process. The release of interferon imparts resistance to the person against the attack of viral infection. Generally, a person once infected with one virus, develops a resistance against other viral infections. This phenomenon is known as 'viral interference'. In non-infected cells, it can induce the formation of second inhibitory protein which has an ability to prevent the transcription of any viral m-RNA that might subsequently be produced in that cell.

Interferons are characterized by the following features :

1. They are non-toxic to the host cell.
2. They exhibit antiviral activity in extremely low concentrations, and
3. They do not possess antigenic activity.

Interferons appear very soon and sometimes within seconds after the viral attack. However, they lack specificity. Once released from the infected host cell, interferons induce the synthesis of translational inhibitory proteins in other non-infected cells. These proteins impair the translation of viral m-RNAs and thus interfere in the viral replication. The synthesis of viral RNA polymerase and viral thymidine kinase is inhibited. The transcription of viral genome is also found to be inhibited.

Interferon preparations may contain more than one type of interferon. These exhibit a unique broad spectrum of antiviral activity *in-vitro* and show promising effects when used in combination with vidarabine. Interferon preparations are effective against infections caused by varicella zoster, encephalomyocarditis virus, vesicular stomatitis virus, rabies, vaccinia, influenza B and cytomegalovirus.

Interferons are not orally absorbed. They are usually given by i.v. infusion and have plasma half-life of about 15 - 20 minutes. Metabolic pathways for interferons are not still known.

Adverse effects mainly include fever, reticulo-cytopenia, neutropenia and thrombocytopenia. They are clinically effective against chronic active hepatitis B viral infection, cytomegaloviral infection, congenital rubella infections and respiratory viral infections. Interferons are also showing promising results in the therapy of some cancers like, melanoma, multiple myeloma, osteogenic sarcoma, certain leukemias and breast cancer. Their use in organ transplantation is also being extensively studied.

Interferon synthesis and liberation in animals can be induced by :

1. **Biological inducers :**

These include human leukocytes, fibroblasts or lymphoblastoid cells, and

2. **Chemical inducers :**

These include :

(a) Polyriboinosinic polyribocytidilic acid which is a complex of polyinosinic and polycytidilic acids. Structurally this complex is a synthetic analog of a double stranded RNA,

(b) A new group of 6-phenylpyrimidine derivatives inducing the host cell to produce interferons, and

(c) Tilorone hydrochloride.

All these interferon inducers including viral infections produce diminished response upon re-exposure. It was proved difficult to make interferon in sufficient quantities for trials due to limitations of human tissue culture techniques. Recently, recombinant DNA technology has been employed as an alternative method of producing large quantities of interferon in prokaryotic (bacteria) cells. In this technique, genes for human interferon are inserted into *E. coli* genome. The interferon thus produced could be used to perform extensive clinical trials against a variety of human viral infections.

The major drawbacks of interferon therapy are :

(1) Interferons will have to be obtained from human subjects if it is to be used in the treatment of human viral disease.

(2) In human subjects, its serum half-life, is not more than 15 - 20 minutes. The brief survival of interferon in body may be attributed to its rapid distribution and excretion from the body.

(3) Numerous clinical trials of interferon utility suggested that it is not as useful in the therapy of viral infections as initially suspected.

(G) Miscellaneous Agents :

(i) Ureas and thioureas : Members of this class exhibit good antiviral activity but they could not be evaluated further because of their immunosuppresive side effects.

(ii) Guanidines and biguanidines : Guanidine hydrochloride shows selective inhibition of enteroviruses and more specifically polio viruses. But probably due to its rapid urinary excretion, the drug failed to achieve a clinical status. The mode of action involves the selective inhibition of viral RNA polymerases. An extensive investigation in this class is still going on.

(iii) Heterocyclic dyes : The members of this series having antiviral potential includes proflavin and neutral red. The herpetic lesions are painted with 0.1% solution of these dyes and then the painted area is exposed to 16 - 30 W fluorescent light for 15 minutes. This results in breakdown of viral DNA and death of the virus. The painted area may be re-exposed to the light at the interval of 6 - 8 hours.

(iv) Gamma globulin (Immuno globulin) : It is the antibody-rich fraction of the plasma which contains a variety of antiviral antibodies and is thought to act by preventing the penetration of virus into the hosts cell. It is orally ineffective. After a single injection, it offers protection against viral infection for about 2 - 3 weeks.

These immunoglobulins are derived from β lymphocytes and plasma cells in very low amounts. Usually only one class of immunoglobulins is initially synthesized by a given immunocyte and a clone of immunocytes synthesizes a specific type of immuno globulins.

Details about the fate of immunoglobulins are not available. Liver serves as a major site where they are degraded. Rarely immunoglobulines are eliminated through the urine.

(v) Antibiotics : A number of antibiotics of diversified structures have demonstrated antiviral activity to less or more extent. Extensive studies in this regard are yet to be made in this field. Examples of antibiotics possessing significant antiviral activity includes rifamycin, bleomycin, gliotoxins and clistamycin A. However, the doses for antiviral activity of these antibiotics are usually higher than the dose needed for antibacterial activity. Due to this reason the use of these drugs as antiviral agents is always accompanied by the high risk of adverse effects.

The antiviral activity of these antibiotics may be due to their ability to inhibit :

(i) assembling of particles into a mature virion, and

(ii) viral envelope formation.

Various polymerase enzymes involved in either RNA and DNA synthesis in viruses are the principle target sites of action of these antibiotics.

(vi) Idoxuridine : During the next decade, in 1959 Idoxuridine, another antiviral agent was discovered, by **Prusoff** and actively used against vaccinea herpes virus.

Idoxuridine (Herpid, Kerecid) competes with thymidine during synthesis of DNA. It interferes with the multiplication of herpes simplex virus which needs DNA, but, of course, it also interferes with mammalian cells, especially bone marrow.

In the form of solution in dimethyl sulphoxide, idoxuridine penetrates the skin and can be effective by topical application in cutaneous herpes zoster.

(vii) Other investigational antiviral agents : These include phosphonoformic acid, bromovinyldeoxyuridine, 2 - (3, 4 – dichlorophenoxy) - 5 - nitrobenzenitrile and 4, 6 - dichloroflavan. The former two agents are found to be effective against herpes virus infections while the latter two are effective against infections caused by enteroviruses or rhinoviruses.

ANTI-NEOPLASTIC AGENTS

12.1 INTRODUCTION

Tumour is a general term indicating proliferation of the cells which is no longer under the control of an organism. This unwanted proliferation of cells consumes a significant portion of the body's supply of food material and metabolic energy thereby leaving the patient progressively weaker. The advances that have occurred in the treatment of neoplastic disorders have placed clinical cures within reach. As knowledge has been accumulated in the areas of pharmacology, tumour biology, cytokinetics and drug-resistance, therapeutic strategies have been developed that maximize the tumour-cell kill, decrease the resistance and enhance the potential for cure by chemotherapy. Chemotherapy plays a significant role in the treatment of macrometastatis alongwith surgery or radiation.

12.2 CAUSES OF CANCER

Many factors are implicated in the induction of cancer. These factors may include :

(i) Exposure to the carcinogenic hydrocarbons or to excessive radiation.

(ii) 'A cancer family syndrome' has been described by **Lynch et al**. The hereditary factors involved in the causation of cancer include chromosomal abnormality, enzymes, immune defence system and hormonal imbalances. For example, the susceptibility to the lung cancer is associated with high inducible levels of the enzyme, aryl hydrocarbon hydroxylase.

(iii) Culture factors play a dominant role by causing about 70% of all cancers. Such important cultural factors include diet, smoking, drinking and sexual habits.

(iv) Occupational factors like, ionising radiations, chemicals and other carcinogenic substances play an important role. For example, coal tar, mustard gas, chromium, hematite, nickel and asbestos can trigger lung cancer in employees working in chemical, insulation and gas factories.

(v) Though it is known that viruses cause cancer in animals, their role in human cancers has not yet been proved.

12.3 CELL-CYCLE KINETICS

During cell cycle, each cell divides into two daughter cells having identical genetic material. Each of these cells may immediately re-enter a new cell-cycle or pass into a non-proliferative resting state. The growth and division of cells can be divided into four prominent phases of cell-cycle. These include :

(i) S - phase :

This phase is a phase of DNA synthesis. In human tumour, it is approximately of 10 to 20 hours.

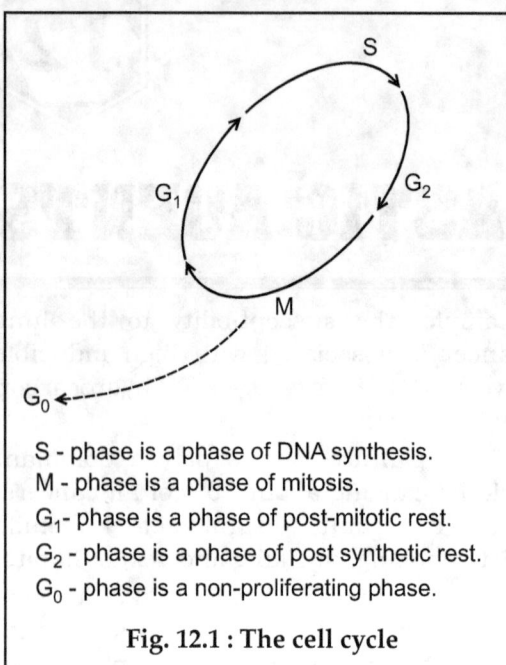

S - phase is a phase of DNA synthesis.
M - phase is a phase of mitosis.
G_1- phase is a phase of post-mitotic rest.
G_2 - phase is a phase of post synthetic rest.
G_0 - phase is a non-proliferating phase.

Fig. 12.1 : The cell cycle

(ii) G_2 - phase :

This period lasts for 1 to 3 hours during which the cell is made ready for mitosis. In this phase, the cells contain a tetraploid number of chromosomes. This phase is followed by mitosis.

(iii) M - phase :

It is a phase of mitosis that involves chromosomal condensation, spindle formation and cell division. It lasts for approximately one hour. The resulting two daughter cells may either immediately enter into G_1–phase (post mitotic rest) or pass into a non-proliferative resting phase (G_0 - phase).

Since proliferating cells are usually more sensitive to chemotherapy, the cells in G_0-phase are least affected by chemotherapeutic agent.

The cells readily pass into G_0-phase if they are far away from the blood vessels through which nutrients are supplied. The growth of a tumour usually follows exponential pattern, that is growth occurs initially at much higher rate which is then followed by a plateau region. The decrease in the growth rate with increasing tumour size may be co-related with an increase in the rate of cell loss due to hypoxic necrosis, immunological defence mechanism and poor nutrient supply. Since proliferating cells are generally more sensitive to chemotherapy, smaller tumours (i.e. tumours with high growth rate) will be more sensitive to chemotherapy than the large solid tumours (i.e. tumours with slow growth rate).

12.4 DIRECTIVE PRINCIPLES OF RATIONAL DRUG DESIGN IN CANCER CHEMOTHERAPY

(i) Cell parameters like morphology, immunogenicity, rate of multiplication, metastasis property significantly govern the responsiveness to anti-neoplastic agents, in case of individual heterogenic tumours which contain many sub-masses of different types of neoplastic cells.

(ii) In infections the invasion of microorganism is biologically foreign to the host and its distinct metabolic reaction can selectively be attacked by chemotherapeutic agents without disturbing the normal body metabolic processes. In addition, the immune mechanism and other host defence system offer major contribution to chemotherapy but since malignant cell is no way different than the normal cell, the host defence plays a negligible role in the therapy of neoplastic diseases. The addition of immuno stimulants to the therapeutic regimen helps the body's natural defence mechanisms to identify the cancer cells.

(iii) Neoplastic cells may develop resistance to drugs. Amplification of various genes usually occurs due to rapid proliferating rate in cancer cells. This serves as an important genetic mechanism for developing resistance to drugs. Hence, smaller tumours are more susceptible to the action of anti-neoplastic drugs than large tumours because of increased probability of drug resistant materials in large tumours.

(iv) Anti-neoplastic drugs kill a constant fraction of tumour cells rather than a fixed number of cells at a given dose. Such killing pattern is known as 'log-cell kill pattern'. Because of such first order cell kill kinetic, several dose schedules of therapy would be required to decrease the size of tumour to such an extent which would no longer be detectable clinically.

(v) Since many dose schedules of anti-neoplastic agents are to be repeated in order to get complete remission, the use of these agents is associated with high risk of adverse effects. These chemotherapeutic agents are more effective on the malignant cells with high proliferation rate. But since malignant cell is no way different than the normal cell, many normal tissues having high proliferating rate are also affected by anti-neoplastic agents. The toxicity of these agents hence, may be observed on rapidly proliferating normal tissues such as bone marrow, hair follicles, germinal tissues, lymphoidal tissues and intestinal epithelium. On the other hand, slow growing tumours and cells in the resting state are often unresponsive to these agents.

(vi) Most of the quantitative differences between normal and cancer cells relate to biochemical pathways, transport processes and DNA repair mechanism. Since differences between normal and malignant cells are merely quantitative rather than qualitative, it leads to certain degree of drug induced toxicity to normal tissues. Individual agent may produce its own distinctive adverse effects on heart, lungs, kidneys and other organs.

12.5 ADVERSE EFFECTS

The prominent adverse effects of anti-neoplastic drugs are exerted on rapidly proliferating normal tissues in addition to their chronic and cumulative toxicities.

(a) Bone marrow toxicity :

Bone marrow is an example of site where a rapid proliferation of hematopoietic precursor cells usually takes place. The toxicity is reflected in terms of myelosuppression which is characterised by leucopenia, thrombocytopenia and haemorrhage. Since white blood cells and platelet count are decreased in the presence of anti-neoplastic drugs, this results into an increased chances of life threatening infections and bleeding. However, few anti-neoplastic agents (e.g. bleomycin, L-asparginase and certain hormonal agents) have minimal myelosuppressive activity.

(b) Intestinal epithelium :

Anorexia, nausea, vomiting, stomatitis, dysphagia, esophagitis, peptic ulcer and diarrhoea are some of the few common adverse effects associated with the use of anti-neoplastic agents. Most of these effects appear as a result of damage to normally proliferating mucosa of GIT. However, nausea or vomiting occurs due to the stimulatory effects of these drugs on chemoreceptor trigger zones in the CNS.

(c) Hair follicle toxicity :

Alopecia or loss of hair is a common adverse effect specifically with methotrexate, vincristine, cyclophosphamide and doxorubicin. However, hair regrows if the therapy is discontinued.

(d) CNS toxicity :

These effects are of reversible nature which disappear after some days of therapy. They include headache, weakness, disorientation, somnolence, myalgias and parasthesias of hands and feet.

Orthostatic hypertension and chronic constipation are also reported to occur as a result of impairment of autonomic functions.

(e) Nephrotoxicity :

Uric acid production increases because of increased metabolism of nucleic acids released from destruction of tumour cells by anti-cancer drugs. This uric acid is a source of nephrotoxicity which can be minimised by either (1) adequate hydration of patient and alkalinisation of urine and/or (2) by prior administration of allopurinol. The nephrotoxicity is characterised by inappropriate anti-diuretic hormone secretion, hyponatremia, renal tubular damage, bladder fibriosis and electrolyte problems.

(f) Hepatotoxicity :

It is mainly caused by drugs like azathioprim, mercaptopurin, L - asparaginase etc. The extent of liver damage ranges from minimal elevation of transaminases, cirrhotic changes to even necrosis.

(g) Skin rashes :

Some of the anti-neoplastic agents (e.g. vinca alkaloids, nitrosourea, anthracyclins, mitomycin C etc.) are potent irritant. They must not be injected by s.c. or i.m. route, since they cause local tissue necrosis. Most of these agents may cause hyperpigmentation, flushing, hyperkeratosis, dermatitis or urticaria.

(h) Pulmonary toxicity :

Many drugs like bleomycin, methotrexate, busulfan etc. exert adverse effects on the lung function. These effects include allergic intestitial pneumonia and chronic pulmonary fibrosis.

(i) Cardiac toxicity :

Severe cardiac damage is reported to be induced by chronic administration of doxorubicin, daunorubicin and anthracyclins.

(j) Immuno suppression :

Most of the anti-neoplastic agents have an ability to suppress natural defence mechanism. These effects may be helpful in patients undergoing organ transplantation surgery. However, in normal patients the immuno suppressive effect of these drugs exposes the patient to the risk of various infections.

(k) Miscellaneous effects :

These effects include fever, anaphylaxis, cataracts, hemolytic anaemia, pancreatitis, pituitary insufficiency, adrenal insufficiency, coagulation problems, suppression of growth and carcinogenesity. Methotrexate is the potent teratogen.

(l) Germinal tissues :

Since germinal tissue is an example of rapidly proliferating tissues, its functioning is adversely affected by anti-neoplastic drug therapy. The prominent effects include impaired spermatogenesis and impaired oogenesis.

12.6 DRUG RESISTANCE

The cell-kill exhibited by anti-neoplastic agents follows first order kinetics. It means that a constant fraction of tumour cells rather than a fixed number of tumour cells are killed by anti-neoplastic agents at a given dose. Hence, in order to achieve complete clinical remission of the tumour, several cycles of therapy would be required. For example, most curable tumours require at least six to eight cycles of therapy. Development of resistance to the drug action is thus quite obvious that results into regrowth of tumour cells.

Tumour grows as a result of amplification of various genes. The increasing number of mutations that occur during the growth of a tumour results into development of sub-populations of heterogenous cells within the tumour. Hence, the tumours of same size and type will vary in their responsiveness to the drug therapy. The large tumours are usually less susceptible to the chemotherapeutic agents because of increased probability of drug resistant mutations. Various mechanisms used to explain the emergence of drug resistant tumour cells are discussed below :

(1) Pleiotropic resistance : This type of resistance develops due to decreased drug transportation or drug retention within the tumour cells. Due to the spontaneous mutations, overproduction of high molecular weight membrane glycoproteins, gp - 180 occurs resulting into alterations in the cell membrane permeability to the drug. This type of resistance is seen with the use of dactinomycin, vinca alkaloids and anthracyclins.

(2) Many anti-neoplastic agents should undergo metabolic activation in order to exhibit therapeutic effectiveness. They would be ineffective if they are not converted to their active metabolites. Some tumour cells develop resistance to the action of such anti-neoplastic agents by lowering down the concentration of enzymes which are involved in metabolic activation of such anti-tumour agents.

(3) In some tumours, resistance to the action of anti-neoplastic agents emerges because of their rapid inactivation.

(4) L-asparaginase acts by decreasing the concentration of aspargin in the concerned tumours. Resistance to its action can be developed due to drug related induction of enzyme aspargin synthetase. This enzyme increases the rate of formation of aspargin and compensate the loss made by L-asparaginase.

(5) Increased production of the target molecule is an important mechanism by which resistance can develop. For example, in the treatment with alkylating agents an increase in cell thiol content serves as an alternate target of alkylation.

12.7 COMBINATION THERAPY

The use of single chemotherapeutic agent is less effective and more toxic due to heterogenic nature of the tumour cells and the chronic nature of the therapy. The use of drug combination therapy would also be helpful to suppress the emergence of drug resistant tumour cells. The drugs which are included in combination therapy should have following characteristics :

(1) dissimilar modes of action,
(2) different spectra of adverse effects, and
(3) additive or synergistic anti-tumour activity.

Acute leukemia, carcinoma of breast, advanced ovarian carcinoma, soft tissue sarcoma, neuroblastoma, advanced small cell carcinoma of lungs and stage **III B** and **IV** of Hodgkins disease are few examples where combination therapy provides better results. For example, in the treatment of stage **III - IV** of epithelial ovarian cancer, **PAC** (i.e. cisplatin, adriamycin and cyclophosphamide) combination therapy is prescribed. In the treatment of ovarian cancer **CHAP** (i.e. cyclophosphamide, hexa methyl melanin, adriamycin and cisplatin) combination is commonly used while **PVB** (i.e. cisplatin, vinblastin and bleomycin) provides better results in the treatment of disseminated testicular cancer. While **CMF** (cyclophosphamide, methotrexate and 5-flouro uracil) combination therapy is commonly used in the treatment of breast cancer. A complete remission of acute lymphocytic leukemia can be achieved by using **VAMP** (vincristin, methotrexate, mercaptopurine and prednisone) combination.

12.8 CLASSIFICATION

Anti-neoplastic agents can be classified on the basis of their mechanism of action (i.e. particular phase of cell cycle).

Based upon their site of action, they can be categorised as :

(1) Phase specific agents : These drugs act at a particular phase of cell cycle. They are more effective on proliferating cells. For example, bleomycin attacks cells in G_2 - and early M-phase. Cytarabine kills cells only in the S-phase by inhibiting DNA synthesis. The effectiveness of phase specific anti-neoplastic agents is maintained by giving them through continuous infusion. Dactinomycin is more effective against cells in G_1-phase while doxorubicin kills cells in late S - phase. Many anti-metabolites are specifically effective against cells in G_1 and G_2 phases where they act by inhibiting RNA synthesis.

(2) Some anti-neoplastic agents exert their effect on both normal and malignant cells. Their activity is not influenced by the degree of proliferation. Even non-proliferating cells are also killed to the same extent. Carmustine and mechlorethamine, are common examples of antineoplastic drugs with above action.

(3) The members of this class are specifically effective against proliferating cells but they are not phase specific. Examples include flourouracil, cyclophosphamide, dactinomycin etc.

(i) S - phase specific agents :

These include alkylating agents like cisplatin, hydroxy urea, doxorubicin and daunorubicin.

(ii) G_2 - phase specific agents :

These include alkylating agents like bleomycin and doxorubicin.

(iii) M - phase specific agents :

These include vincristine, vinblastine and colchicine.

(iv) G_1 - phase specific agents :

These include prednisone, daunorubicin and L-asparaginase. Based upon their site of action, they can be categorised as :

(a) Anti-metabolites :

Anti-metabolites exert their anti-neoplastic action by acting as a false precursor for an enzyme or by acting as competitive antagonist for an enzyme. These drugs are usually structural analogs of normal body metabolites.

(b) Alkylating agents :

These drugs usually act by interferring in the synthesis, replication and transcription processes of genetic material. Because of their specific structural features, they can easily bind with either proteins or DNA molecules.

The anti-neoplastic agents can also be categorised in the following pattern :

(I) Alkylating agents :
  (A) Nitrogen mustards :
    e.g. cyclophosphamide, chlorambucil.
  (B) Alkyl sulfonates : Busulfan
  (C) Nitrosoureas : Carmustine, streptozocin
  (D) Ethylenimines : Thiotepa
  (E) Triazines : Dacarbazines

(II) Anti-metabolites :
  (A) Folate antagonists : Methotrexate
  (B) Purine analogues : 6-thioguanine.
  (C) Pyrimidine analogues : Cytarabine, flourouracil.

(III) Antibiotics :
  (A) Anthracyclines : Doxorubicin, daunorubicin
  (B) Bleomycins : Bleomycin
  (C) Mitomycin C
  (D) Dactinomycins (Actinomycin - D)
  (E) Plicamycins : Mithramycin, Mithracin

(IV) Vinca alkaloids :
  Vincristine, vinblastine

(V) Enzymes :
  L - asparaginase

(VI) Hormones :
  (A) Glucocorticoids
  (B) Estrogens / antiestrogens : Tanoxifen, estramustine
  (C) Androgens/antiandrogens : Cyproteron
  (D) Progestins
  (E) LH-RH antagonists : Buserelin, leuprolide.

(VII) Miscellaneous :
  1. Hydroxyurea
  2. Procarbazine
  3. Mitotane
  4. Hexamethyl melamine
  5. Cisplatin
  6. Etoposide.

(VIII) Monoclonal antibodies :

When the tumour size is small, the phase-specific agents are most effective because of the high growth rate. In such cases, the tumours can easily be cured even after a single agent chemotherapy. However, in larger tumours, more tumour-cells will be in non-proliferative stage. Hence, such tumours will respond better to a phase-non-specific anti-neoplastic agents. An alternative of treatment involves the use of surgery or radiation rays in order to decrease the size of the tumour followed by the use of phase-specific chemotherapeutic agent.

Most of the anti-neoplastic agents (e.g. methotrexate, cyclophosphamide, chlorambucil etc.) possess an ability to suppress both humoral and cellular immunities. Hence, besides their use in oncology, they may also be used in the field of organ-transplantation.

12.9 ALKYLATING AGENTS

With the discovery of clinical activity of selected nitrogen mustard during World War II, the era of modern cancer chemotherapy began. They are as such neutral compounds. However, under physiological conditions, alkylating agents form a cyclic, positively charged ions which then react with any negatively charged ions or with moieties having high electron density (i.e. nucleophiles). Alkylating agents act by the transfer of alkyl groups to biologically important cell constituents such as amino sulfhydryl or phosphate groups whose function is then impaired. Under physiological conditions, alkylating agents are positively charged and they react with any molecules that are negatively charged or have regions of high electron density (nucleophiles). Alkylating agents act by transfering alkyl groups to the biologically active cell constituents like, amine, carboxyl, sulfhydryl, phosphate, hydroxyl or imidazolyl groups. It is thought that DNA is the main target site for alkylating agents and protein or RNA synthesis is least affected by them at that dose levels.

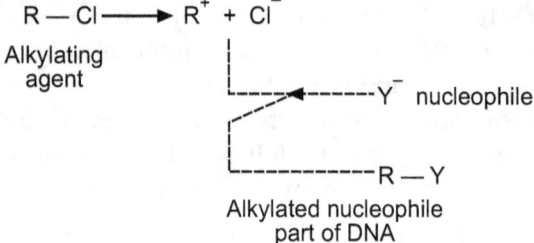

Alkylating agent / Alkylated nucleophile part of DNA

Most alkylating agents are bifunctional (i.e. have two alkylating arms). The cross-linking of DNA base-pairs resulting due to the bifunctional nature of alkylating agents may develop cytotoxicity. Alkylating agents may also interfere with the activity of ATP-NMN adenyl transferase, the enzyme required for the biosynthesis of NAD. As a result, there occurs inhibition of glycolysis.

The cross-linking of DNA base-pairs resulting due to the bifunctional nature of alkylating agents is also the basis of mutagenic and carcinogenic properties of the drug. Besides these agents, many members of other classes may act atleast in part by alkylation. Examples include estromustine, procarbazine, mitomycin C and dacarbazine.

(a) Nitrogen mustards :

These are toxic, vesicant and unstable compounds. At physiological pH, aliphatic mustard hydrochlorides are readily and unimolecularly converted via the free base to a relatively stable aziridinium ion, which once produced reacts biomolecularly with available nucleophilic centres. These agents act by alkylating N^7 and O^6 of guanine in DNA which leads to :

(1) Alteration of guanine so that it forms an abnormal base pair with thymidine (miscoding);

(2) Cleavage of the imidazole ring of guanine thus destroying guanine;

(3) Linking of guanine pairs, producing cross-linked DNA strands which cannot replicate; and

(4) Depurination of DNA causing actual breakage of the DNA strands.

The prototype of nitrogen mustards is mechlorethamine which was first synthesized in 1935 and still remains the alkylating agent of choice. It has very short-duration of action (plasma half-life is less than 10 minutes after injection) because of its rapid metabolism. Inactive metabolites are excreted in the urine alongwith traces of unchanged drug.

Adverse effects include nausea, vomiting, skin erruptions, anorexia, menstrual bleeding, hyperheparinemia, leukopenia, thrombocytopenia and thrombophlebitis. Its use is contraindicated in case of pregnant women.

It is effective in the treatment of testicular seminoma, multiple myeloma, leukemias, Hodgkin's disease and carcinomas of bronchus, ovary and breast alone or in combination with vincristine, procarbazine and prednisone. In the form of 0.01 – 0.04% ointment, it is also used topically in the treatment of mycosis fungoides.

Melphalan is a L-phenylalanine

Melphalan is a L-phenylalanine derivative of mechlorethamine which does not require metabolic activation and acts in similar fashion to mechlorethamine. It is an orally active antineoplastic agent having a plasma half-life of 90 minutes. About 50 – 60% administered dose is bound to the plasma-proteins. About 20 – 50% dose appears unchanged in the faeces while minor amounts in unchanged form are excreted in the urine. It is an effective antineoplastic agent used in the treatment of multiple myeloma, malignant melanoma, testicular seminoma, colon cancer and caricinoma of breast and ovary.

Cyclophosphamide is the most versatile nitrogen mustard having broad spectrum of antineoplastic and immunosuppressive activities. It is orally active and has a plasma half-life of 7.0 hours. It does not cross the blood brain barrier. Principal metabolites include 4-hydroxy cyclophosphamide, aldophosphamide, acrolein, phosphoramide mustard (all active), 4 – ketophosphamide, and carboxyphosphamide (both inactive). Considerable fraction also appears in the faeces in unchanged form.

The chloroethyl moieties of cyclophosphamide reacts with adjacent nucleotide bases resulting into the cross-linking of the DNA molecule.

It is used to treat Hodgkin's disease and acute lymphoblastic leukemia of childhood. It is employed to inhibit rejection in organ transplantation procedures because of its immunosuppressant activity. Along with methotrexate and fluorouracil, it may be used in the adjuvant therapy after surgery for carcinoma of breast. In high doses, it may be employed to cure Burkitt's lymphoma (a childhood malignancy with a very high growth rate).

Chlorambucil is an orally active phenylbutyric acid mustard having antineoplastic activity. It has a plasma half-life of 1.0 hour. It undergoes extensive metabolism in the liver. It shares the immunosuppressive, teratogenic and carcinogenic properties of alkylating agents.

It is effective against Hodgkin's disease, chronic lymphocytic leukemia, breast cancer, gastrointestinal cancer and prostate cancer. In some cases, it is used in the form of prednisolone ester of chlorambucil.

The *in-vivo* release of biologically active compound from a suitable derivative form is known as latentiation. Cyclophosphamide is an example of this concept. The phosphoramidase enzyme is more abundant in the neoplastic cells than in the normal cells. Hence, Cyclophosphamide was developed by phosphorylating the nitrogen mustard. The drug might be hydrolyzed in the tumour cells by the enzyme phosphoramidases.

The current view about mode of action of cyclophosphamide is that liver converts this drug to 4 - hydroxyl derivative which remains in equilibrium with aldophosphamide. The latter is cleaved to phosphoramide mustard and acrolein, both are cytotoxic compounds. The lower level of enzymes in tumour cells that prevents this cleavage may be the basis of selectivity of action of Cyclophosphamide on tumour cells.

(b) Alkyl sulfonates :

The members of this class are represented by the following general formula

$$CH_3SO_2-O-R$$

where R may be CH_3, C_2H_5, CH_2CH_2Cl or CH_2CH_2F.

Busulfan is the most potent member of this series. Chemically it is 1,4-butanediol - dimethane sulphonate. It is well absorbed orally with a plasma half-life of about 2 - 3 minutes. Methanesulfonic acid is the principal metabolite.

An electrophilic butyl intermediate is obtained through the cleavage of alkyl-oxygen bond which then causes the interstrand cross-linking of the DNA molecule. Adverse effects include nausea, vomiting, diarrhoea, skin pigmentation, amenorrhoea, sterility, hyperuricemia, impotence, granulocytopenia and thrombocytopenia.

It is a drug of choice in the treatment of chronic granulocytic leukemia. It is also used in other myeloproliferative diseases and essential thrombocytosis.

(c) Nitrosoureas :

They are represented by following general formula.

$$Cl-CH_2-CH_2-\underset{NO}{\underset{|}{N}}-\underset{O}{\overset{||}{C}}-NHR$$

(i) Carmustine (BCNU) :

    R = CH_2CH_2Cl

(ii) Lomustine (CCNU) : R = –⟨ ⟩

(iii) Semustine (methyl - CCNU) :

    R = ⟨ ⟩–CH_3

The fourth member of this series is streptozocin which is a natural product obtained from the fungus, *Streptomyces achromogenes*. They all are highly lipophilic drugs and can enter readily in cerebrospinal fluid. Their plasma half-lives vary from 5-15 minutes. They all possess similar pharmacological and toxicological prophiles.

The chloroethyl moiety present in their structure causes single - strand breaks, and interstrand cross-linkage of DNA molecules through alkylation. In addition, the isocyanate portion (R–N=CO) of the molecule causes, carbamylation of lysine residues of proteins. This results into an inhibition of DNA repair. Nitrosoureas may also inhibit several key enzymes involved in DNA synthesis and repair. Streptozocin produces rapid and severe depletion of NAD and NADH in liver and pancreatic cells. They are phase-nonspecific agents. Acute nausea, vomiting and delayed myelosuppression are characteristics of carmustine, lomustine and semustine, while renal toxicity has been noted with streptozocin.

Streptozocin is a natural broad-spectrum antineoplastic agent. Because of its poor oral absorption, it is given i.v. ly or intraarterially. Methylinitrosourea and other metabolites appear in the urine alongwith 10 – 20% dose in unchanged form. Significant respiratory excretion also occurs. About 1% dose also appears unchanged in the faeces.

Table 12.1 Clinically used antineoplastic nitrosoureas

Name	Plasma-protein binding (%)	Plasma half-life (hr.)	Prominent adverse effects	Important therapeutic uses
1. Carmustine	–	1.5	CNS toxicity flushing of skin. pulmonary fibrosis	Meningeal leukemias, brain tumors, breast tumors
2. Lomustine	40	0.25	Myelosuppression, nephrotoxicity	Primary brain tumors, small cell lung carcinomas, Hodgkin's disease
3. Semustine (methylated analog of lomustine)	–	36-72	Myelosuppression, nephrotoxicity, carcinogenicity	Adenocarcinomas of GIT, carcinoma of breast and Hodgkin's disease
4. Streptozocin (streptozotocin)	–	0.25	Myelosuppression, nephrotoxicity, hepatotoxicity	Malignant pancreatic insulinoma, Hodgkin's disease, malignant carcinoid tumors

Besides its use as an antineoplastic, agent, it may also be used to induce diabetic condition in experimental animals.

(d) Ethylenimines :

Just like to the phosphorylated nitrogen mustard derivatives, phosphorylated aziridines were also reported and were found clinically effective. For example, TEPA (Triethylene Phosphoramine).

When oxygen atom from TEPA is replaced by sulphur, the compound having greater stability results which was named as thio-TEPA. Ethylenimines act in the similar fashion as that of nitrogen mustard but are less potent. Thiotepa is an example of trifunctional alkylating agent. Orally it is absorbed in irregular manner. Its plasma half-life is 1.0 – 1.5 hours after i.v. administration. It is eliminated in the urine largely in the form of inactive metabolites.

Adverse effects include nausea, vomiting, anorexia, stomach pain, sore throat, difficult urination, skin rash, fever, chills, wheezing, mucositis, dizziness and myelosuppression.

It is used in the treatment of Hodgkin's lymphoma, early bladder cancer and carcinoma of ovary, breast and lungs.

(e) Triazines :

Capacity to generate reactive cation under physiological conditions is the most important requirement for an ideal antineoplastic agent. This fact was again revealed by triazine compounds. The *in-vivo* metabolic studies of 3, 3-dimethyl - 1 - phenyl triazene showed that extensive demethylation by liver microsomal enzymes is the source of generation of an active methyl cation. Other drugs of clinical utility include,

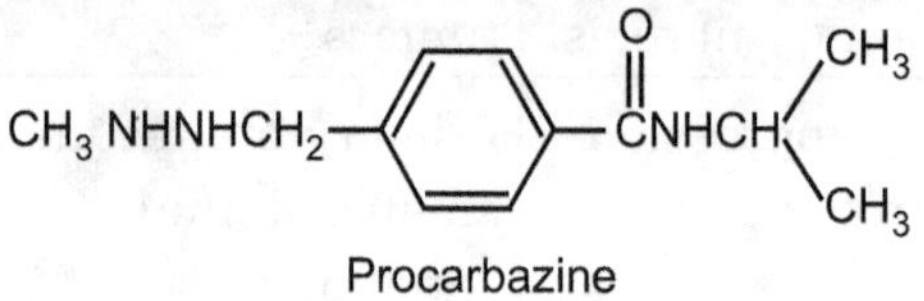

Procarbazine

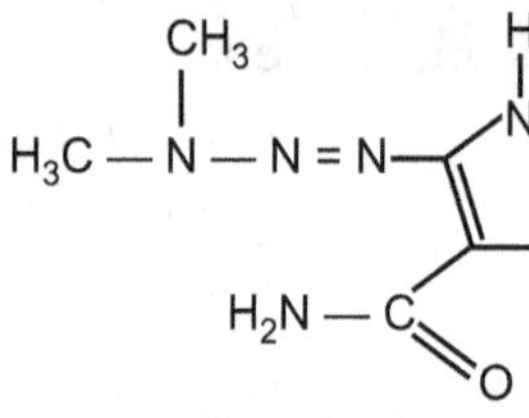

Dacarbazine

They act by inhibiting DNA, RNA and protein synthesis. Auto-oxidation of the agents generate hydroxyl radicals that lead effects similar to ionizing radiations, N-demethylation occurs *in-vivo*. Methylation of nucleic acids and selective transmethylation of purine bases, especially the 7th position of guanine and 1st position of adenine may occur due to generation of methly carbonium ions. Methylation of t-RNA contributes to the carcinogenic activity.

Dacarbazine was designed by shealy which has a structural similarity with an intermediate compound of purine biosynthesis known as 5 - aminoimidazole - 4 carboxamide ribonucleotide. While procarbazine was initially designed as a mono amino oxidase enzyme inhibitor. Procarbazine is orally active while dacarbazine is administered intravenously. Procarbazine has a plasma half-life of 7 minutes. Principal metabolite, N-isopropyl terephthalanic acid appears in the urine along with 2 – 5% dose in unchanged form. Other metabolic products like methane and carbon di-oxide are excreted through exhaled air.

Adverse effects include constipation, dry mouth, drowsiness, skin rash, myelosuppression and psychic disturbances.

It is used in the treatment of small-cell carcinoma of the lung, brain tumors, multiple myeloma and non-Hodgkin's lymphomas. It may also be used together with mechlorethamine, vincristine or prednisone in the treatment of Hodgkin's disease. It also possesses strong immunosuppressant activity.

Table 12.2 : Nucleic acid antimetabolites

Class	Natural substance	Antimetabolite
(A) Purine bases	Guanine	Thioguanine
	Hypoxanthine	6 - mercaptopurine
(B) Pyrimidine bases	Cytidine	Cytosine arabinoside
	Uridine	Azacytidine, azauridine
	Uracil	Fluorouracil

12.10 ANTI-METABOLITES

Chemical substances that take part in cellular metabolism are referred to as 'metabolites'. They are essential for normal cell function and replication. Antimetabolites are derived by incorporating one or two bioisosteric groups or other minor changes in the structure of the metabolites. They interfere with the utilization of natural metabolites by virtue of similarity of chemical structure. Presently they may be classified as :

(a) Amino acid inhibitors,
(b) Inhibitors of vitamins and coenzymes, and
(c) Antagonists of metabolites involved in nucleic acid synthesis
   (i) Glutamine antagonists
   (ii) Folic acid antagonists
   (iii) Purine antagonists, and
   (iv) Pyrimidine antagonists.

Antimetabolites act by competing for binding sites on enzymes or getting incorporated into DNA or RNA molecule leading to impaired cell growth and proliferation. For example, mammalian cells require preformed purines as essential components of DNA, RNA and various other coenzymes. Purine antimetabolites compete with purine bases and get incorporated into DNA or RNA molecules.

Most widely used antimetabolites include cytarabine, 5 - fluorouracil, 6 - mercaptopurine, methotrexate and 6 - thioguanine. Out of these, 5 - fluorouracil is a phase-non-specific agent while rest are cell-cycle phase specific agents.

(a) Purine base antagonists :

Mercaptopurine and thioguanine are the clinically used examples of this category. Both these drugs were developed by **Hitchings** in 1952.

Mercaptopurine is metabolized to 6 - thioinosine - 5 - monophosphate. This metabolite inhibits the conversion of inosinic acid to nucleotides, adenylate and guanylate. It also causes the blockadge of DNA biosynthesis through inhibition of *de novo* purine metabolism at several sites.

One of the methylated form of mercaptopurine is 6 - methyl - mercaptopurine - riboside (6 - MMPR) which may indirectly inhibit aminoimidazole carboxamide ribotide catalyze synthesis. Since xanthine oxidase catalyzes degradation of both mercaptopurine and 6 - MMPR, allopurinol (a potent xanthine oxidase inhibitor) potentiates its action.

Mercaptopurine is an orally active antipurine used as an antineoplastic and immunosuppressant drug. About 19% administered dose is bound to the plasma proteins. It has a plasma half-life of 0.19 – 1.25 hours. Principal metabolites include 6 - thiouric acid; mono, di and triphosphate nucleotides of 6-methylmercaptopurine ribonucleosides and inorganic sulphate which are excreted in the urine along with 22 – 30% dose in unchanged form.

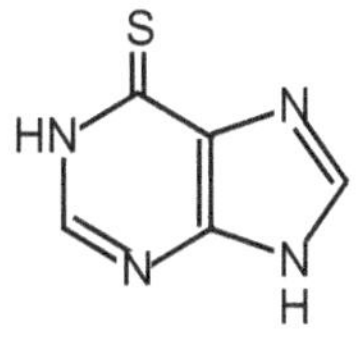

6-Mercaptopurine

Adverse effects include nausea, vomiting, anorexia, diarrhoea, stomatitis, jaundice, hepatic necrosis, hyperuricemia, thrombocytopenia, granulocytopenia and dermatological complications.

It is used to treat acute leukemia in children and lymphoblastic leukemias.

Thioguanine is yet another clinically used analog of natural purine base, guanine, in which the hydroxyl group at 6th position is replaced by the sulfhydryl group.

6 - thioguanine

Thioguanine competes with guanine for various enzymes. It partially inhibits guanine metabolizing enzymes, producing functionally altered nucleotides. Thioguanine is converted in body to, 6 - thioguanosine - 5 - monophosphate by the enzyme, hypoxanthine - guanine - phosphoribosyl transferase enzyme. This metabolite gets incorporated into DNA or RNA. Thioguanine, because of structural similarity with guanine, inhibits the synthesis of purine nucleotides through negative feedback mechanism.

Thioguanine is an orally effective antineoplastic agent. About 30% dose is absorbed upon oral administration. It has a plasma half-life of 80 minutes. Principal metobolites that appear in the urine include, inorganic sulfate, 6-thiouric acid and 2-amino-6-methyl thiopurine.

Adverse effects include nausea, vomiting, stomach pain, anorexia, diarrhoea, sore throat, joint pain, fever, jaundice, and bone-marrow depression. It is contraindicated during pregnancy.

Thioguanine is used in the treatment of acute granulocytic, acute lymphocytic and chronic agranulocytic leukemias usually along with cytarabine. It may also be used as an immunosuppressive agent specifically in patients with nephrosis and collagen -vascular disorders.

Another widely used agent from this category is azathioprine. It is an imidazolyl derivative of 6 - mercaptopurine. It has an antirrheumatic activity alongwith cytotoxic effect. It metabolizes in liver to 6-mercaptopurine. Its advantages over 6-mercaptopurine are related to ease of administration and pharmacological properties. It is orally effective drug having plasma half-life of about 0.16 hours. Azathioprine is used along with corticosteroids for prevention of rejection of renal transplant and for the treatment of severe rheumatoid arthritis.

(b) Pyrimidine base antagonists :

The clinically used examples from this category include, azacytidine, azauridine, 5 - fluorouracil and cytarabine.

(i) Azapyrimidines : Azacytidine and azauridine belong to this category. The former plays an important role in the treatment of acute myeloblastic leukemia while the latter blocks an enzyme, orotidylate decarboxylase and may have a specific role in the combination chemotherapy with other pyrimidine antimetabolites.

Azacytidine

5 - Azacytidine is an analog of cytidine and is rapidly phosphorylated and is then incorporated in both RNA and DNA. It inhibits protein synthesis and affects *de novo* pyrimidine synthesis by inhibiting orotidylic acid decarboxylase enzyme.

(ii) Fluoropyrimidines : This category includes fluorouracil, floxuridine and ftorafur. These are fluorinated pyrimidines having antineoplastic activity. Ftorafur is a tetrahydrofuryl conjugate of 5 - fluorouracil while floxuridine is a deoxyribonucleoside of 5-fluoruracil. Both these agents are *in-vivo*, vested to 5 - fluorouracil. They all have, similar pharmacological properties. Ftorafur has a higher incidence of neurotoxicity because of its increased lipophilicity.

Thymidylate synthetase enzyme catalyzes the conversion of uridylate to thymidylate. Fluoropyrimidines inhibit DNA synthesis by acting as an inhibitor of thymidylate synthetases. In the form of 5-fluorouridine triphosphate it also gets incorporated into RNA. Yet another mechanism of minor importance involves formation of 5-fluorouridylate which can inhibit RNA synthesis. The drug might be more effective in patients with liver metastases when given orally due to high drug concentrations in the portal system.

It is selectively toxic to proliferating cells. The precise mechanism probably differs from tissue to tissue, depending on the relative importance of fluorouracil effects on thymidine biosynthesis and on RNA metabolism. It also enhances the antineoplastic effect of irradiation in the treatment of bronchogenic carcinoma. Its combination with an anticoagulant (e.g. warfarin) leads to a synergestic reflection in its antitumor activity.

5 - fluorouracil

About 97% administered dose of fluorouracil is bound to the plasma-proteins. It has a plasma half-life of 74 – 100 hours. Its principal metabolites include 5'-fluoro-5, 6-dihydrouracil, α-fluoro-β-ureidopropionic acid and α-fluoro-β-alanine. The main metabolic end product is CO_2 which is expired by the lungs. About 11% of dose appears unchanged in the urine.

Adverse effects include nausea, diarrhoea, stomatitis, anorexia, dysphagia, dermatitis, loss of hairs, myelopathy, neurological manifestations, cardiac toxicities, leukopenia and thrombocytopenia.

It is the most active agent in the treatment of carcinoma of prostate, breast, ovary, pancreas, urinary bladder and gastrointestinal tract. It is also effective in the treatment of severe recalcitrant psoriasis. Topically fluorauracil may be used to treat premalignant keratoses of skin and multiple superfacil basal cell carcinomas. Topical fluorouracil is available as, 1 – 5% cream or 1 – 5% solution.

(iii) Cytarabine (cytosine arabinoside) : It is an analog of cytidine deoxycytidine. It requires activation through which it is converted to ara-cytosine triphosphate (an active form) by intracellular kinases. This activated triphosphate then competitively inhibits DNA-polymerases and kills the cells in the S - phase of the cell-cycle.

About 13% administered dose is bound to the plasma-proteins. It has a plasma half-life of 2.5 hours. Due to poor oral absorption, it is given by i.v. route. It is rapidly metabolised in the liver, kidney, intestinal mucosa and RBCs by the enzyme, cytidine deaminases. Arabinosyl uracil is the principal metabolite that appears in the urine along with 10% dose in unchanged form.

Adverse effects include stomatitis, fever, dermatitis, hepatic dysfunction, leukopenia, thrombocytopenia, anaemia and seizures.

(c) Folate antagonists :

Folic acid must be reduced to 1-tetrahydrofolic acid before it can serve the function of coenzyme. The reduction takes place step wise via dihydrofolic acid and both steps are generally thought to be carried out by the enzymes, folic reductase and dihydrofolic reductase. Folic acid coenzyme participates at three phases in nucleic acid biosynthesis. Probably the last phase is the most sensitive to the inhibitory action of folic acid antagonists.

Aminopterin and methotrexate are the examples of folic acid antagonists. These agents competitively inhibit the enzyme, dihydrofolate reductase, thus restricting the availability of tetrahydrofolic acid (THF) to the cells. Tetrahydrofolic acid is critically important to the metabolic transfer of one-carbon units in a variety of biochemical reactions. These include the biosynthesis of thymidylic acid (for DNA synthesis) and inosinic acid (needed for RNA synthesis). Protein synthesis is also affected. The enzymatic block produced by methotrexate can be bypassed by giving a reduced folate (i.e. *folinic* acid). This reversal of the action is commonly referred to as rescue.

Methotrexate is an orally active folic acid analog having anti neoplastic, antipsoriatic and mild immuno-suppressant activity. About 50 – 60% administered dose is bound to the plasma-proteins. It has a plasma half-life of 7.2 – 9.0 hours. It undergoes almost insignificant metabolism. About 85 – 95% dose appears in the urine in unchanged form. Small amount also appears in the stool in the form of polyglutamates. It is S-phase specific agent.

Adverse effects include anorexia, weight loss, bloody diarrhoea, ulcerative stomatitis, alopecia, interstitial pneumonitis, cirrhosis, nephrotoxicity, depression, aplastic anemia, leukopenia, thrombocytopenia, hemorrhagic enteritis, abortion and defective spermatogenesis.

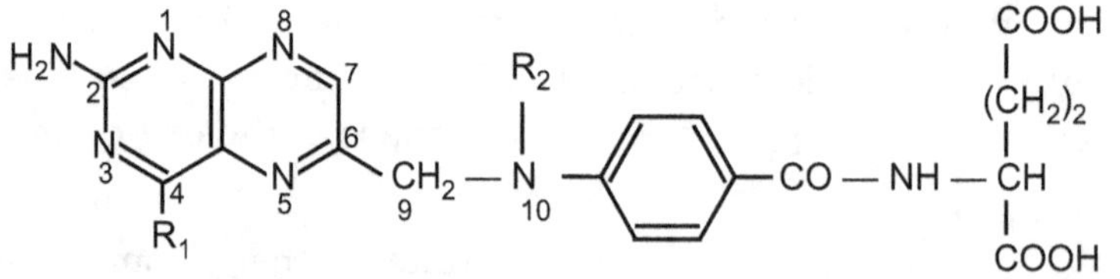

(i) Folic acid : R_1 = OH; R_2 = H
(ii) Aminopterin : R_1 = NH_2; R_2 = H
(iii) Methotrexate : R_1 = NH_2; R_2 = CH_3

It is an effective antineoplastic agent in the treatment of carcinomas of breast, tongue, pharynx, bladder and testes. It is usually used in conjuction with chlorambucil dactinomycin. It may be used in the treatment of choriocarcinoma and related trophoblastic tumours in women.

It is used to treat acute lymphoblastic leukemia in children. It may also be used to treat severe psoriasis, dermatomycositis rheumatoid arthritis. Being an immuno-suppressive agent, it may be used in organ transplantation procedures.

12.11 ANTIBIOTICS

This is a class of antibiotics which thought to be useful in cancer chemotherapy due to their cytotoxic properties. They differ from each other in individual capacity to interfere in protein, RNA and DNA synthesis at various stages. They may be given alone or in combination with other antineoplastic drugs.

(a) Actinomycin D (Dactinomycin) : It is an antitumor antibiotic isolated from genus *Streptomyces*. It is usually administered intravenously. It does not enter the CNS and is rapidly cleared from the plasma. About 15 – 20% administered dose is bound to plasma-proteins. It has a plasma half-life of 36 hours. It is mainly excreted in the bile and urine.

It intercalates between DNA base pairs and inhibits DNA-dependent RNA synthesis especially that of ribosomal RNA. It is a non-phase-specific agent more effective against proliferating cells. It is found to inhibit DNA - polymerase activity.

Adverse effects include nausea, vomiting, diarrhoea, and bone-marrow suppression. It is contraindicated in pregnancy. It is used mainly in the tumours, lymphomas, melanomas, sarcomas and gestational choriocarcinoma. It is also used to prevent organ rejection in transplantation.

(b) Mithramycin (plicamycin) : It is an antineoplastic antibiotic isolated from the cultures of *Streptomyces tanashiensis*. It is less effective by oral route. Inactive metabolites appear in the urine with significant fraction of unchanged drug.

It binds to DNA and acts by inhibiting the transcription. It is used in the treatment of disseminated testicular carcinoma. Since it lowers plasma calcium concentration in hypercalcemic patients, it may also be used in the treatment of hypercalcemia or hypercalciuria.

It forms complexes with DNA, probably with guanine, in the presence of divalent cations especially magnesium. It also inhibits DNA - dependent RNA synthesis without affecting DNA - synthesis.

(c) Bleomycins : These are relatively high molecular weight peptide antibiotics isolated from a Japanese soil actinomycete, *Streptomyces verticillus*. This mixture includes low molecular weight (1500 daltons) peptides, bleomycin A_2 and bleomycin B_2. Bleomycin A_2 is more potent than bleomycin B_2 as antitumor agent. All bleomycins (i.e. A_1, A_2, A_5, A_6, B_1 and B_2) contains a chromophore having sulphur. Bleomycin A_2 exhibits very low renal toxicity and may inhibit ATP-dependent DNA-ligase activity.

Bleomycin is effective against cells in late G_2-phase and early M-phase of cell-cycle. It inhibits DNA-synthesis, produces scission of single stranded DNA and also inhibits cell DNA repair by a marked inhibition of DNA-ligase. The process of DNA cleavage is facilitated in the presence of oxygen and ferrous ions.

It is administered either by i.m. or i.v. route. It does not bind to the plasma proteins and has a plasma half-life of about 1 hour. About 70% drug is excreted in the urine in unchanged form.

Adverse effects include hyperpigmentation, ulceration, keratitis, and vesiculation of the skin, pulmonary fibrosis, hypotension and anaphylactic reactions.

(d) Mitomycin C : It is an orally ineffective antineoplastic antibiotic, isolated from *Streptomyces caespitosus*. It inhibits DNA synthesis by alkylation of DNA and brings about interstrand cross-linking. It also induces single strand DNA cleavage.

Mitomycin C

It is given intravenously. It has a plasma half-life of 35 minutes. The half-reduced semiquinone free-radical is the active metabolite obtained through enzymatic reduction by NADPH - dependent reductase. Other inactive metabolites appear in the urine and bile along with 6 – 8% dose in unchanged form.

Adverse effects include nausea, vomiting, diarrhoea, stomatitis, chills, dermatitis, hypocalcemia, interstitial pneumonia, renal dysfunction, leukopenia and thrombocytopenia.

It may be used in the treatment of carcinomas of cervix, colon, rectum, bladder, pancreas, breast, testes, head, neck, lung and melanoma alone or in combination with other antineoplastic agent. It is also effective against lymphomas and chronic granulocytic leukemias.

(e) Anthracycline antibiotics : Doxorubicin and daunorubicin are structurally similar antitumor antibiotics belonging to the anthracycline group, They have been isolated from the cultures of the fungus, *Streptomyces peuceticus*. Doxorubicin is more potent and less toxic agent than daunorubicin. The structure consists of a planner anthracyclic ring system which is attached to a sugar moiety (i.e. daunosamine) by a glycosidic-linkage. The ability of these antibiotics to bind DNA is found to be associated with the structure of amino sugar. Both antibiotics possess immunosuppressive properties.

The maximal cytotoxic effects of both drugs were observed during the DNA - synthetic phase (S). The drugs are concentrated rapidly in the cell nuclei and are believed to intercalate (insert between the double helical strands of DNA) into DNA base pairs with inhibition of DNA-dependent RNA synthesis as well as DNA-dependent DNA synthesis by steric hindrance. This results into a single strand breaks in DNA. Free radicals are also reported to generate by anthracyclic ring that cause tissue macromolecule damage.

Daunorubicin is the most useful anticancer antibiotic. It is given by i.v. route. It has a plasma half-life of about 10 - 30 hours. It undergoes metabolism to form (active) daunorubicinol and inactive aglycones. The aglycones after conjugation, are excreted in the bile along with some unchanged drug. About 10 - 15% dose also appears in the urine in unchanged form that imparts red colour to the urine.

Adverse effects include nausea, vomiting, diarrhoea, skin rashes, fever, pruritus, stomatitis, hypotension, tachycardia, arrhythmia and bone-marrow suppression.

Daunorubicin is used in the treatment of acute leukemias, carcinomas of breast, endometrium, ovary, testicles, thyroid, lungs and many sarcomas and Hodgkin's disease.

12.12 VINCA ALKALOIDS

These are orally ineffective alkaloids obtained from leaves of *Vinca rosea* (*Cathranthus roseus*). Initially screened out for hypoglycemic activity, these alkaloids were found to possess antitumor activity. Clinically used examples of vinca alkaloids include, vinblastine and vincristine. They inhibit the cell-division (M-phase specific) by binding to tubulin, a class of proteins that form the mitotic spindle.

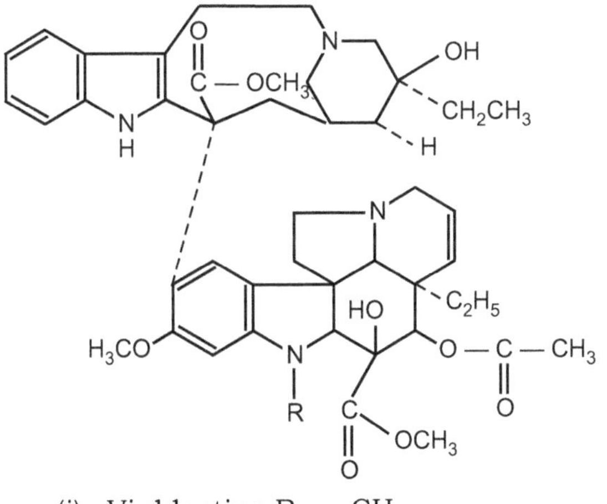

(i) Vinblastine R= —CH$_3$

(ii) Vincristine R= —CHO

Vincristine differs from vinblastine only in having an aldehyde moiety. About 80% administered dose of vincristine is bound to the plasma-proteins. It has a triphasic plasma half-life. Terminal half-life is 2.5 hours. It is extensively metabolized in the liver to various inactive metabolites, which are excreted mainly in the bile (67%) and in the urine (12%).

Adverse effects include nausea, vomiting, abdominal pain, constipation, alopecia, polyurea, ischemia, leukopenia, anemia and thrombocytopenia.

It is used in the treatment of Hodgkin's disease, solid tumours in the children, tumours of lungs, breast and cervix in adults and in acute lymphocytic leukemias. It may be used along with cyclophosphamide, bleomycin, doxorubicin and prednisone in the treatment of non-Hodgkin's lymphomas. In combination with prednisone, it may be used for inducing remission in childhood leukemia. While vindesine (desacetyl vinblastine carboxamide), a semisynthetic *vinca* alkaloid is effective against chronic granulocytic leukemia, lymphomas, systemic mastocytosis and non-small cell lung cancer.

12.13 ENZYMES

(a) **L – Asparaginase :** The asparaginase enzyme used clinically is extracted from bacterial cultures of *Escherichia coli* and *Erwinia carotovora*. The *E. coli* enzyme has a molecular weight of 130,000 dalton. It was observed that the enzyme hydrolyzes aspargine into aspartic acid and ammonia. Thus, the tumour cells are deprived of this essential nutrient. The enzyme also shows glutaminase activity causing a decrease in plasma glutamine and an increase in glutaminic acid. The lower aspargine and glutamine levels result into immediate inhibition of protein synthesis and a delayed inhibition of DNA and RNA synthesis.

The enzyme preparation is usually given either intravenously or intramuscularly. It has a plasma half-life of 11 — 23 hours. Adverse effects include hepatitis, pancreatitis, anorexia, hypoglycemia, allergy and coagulation disorders.

It is a drug of choice in the treatment of acute lymphoblastic leukemia. When combined together with methotrexate, it lowers down adverse effects and intensifies therapeutic efficacy of methotrexate.

12.14 HORMONAL AGENTS

Cancer state of organs whose functioning is mainly controlled by hormones may respond favourably to the hormonal therapy. Alterations of the hormonal levels cause remission of some cases of cancer of breast (e.g. androgens, glucocorticoids), prostate gland (e.g. estrogens, antiandrogens) and endometrium (e.g. progestins). Glucocorticoids may be used in the treatment of lymphocytic leukemias because of their lymphocytes-destruction ability. Hormonal therapy to tumours of other organs (e.g. kidney) may also produce favourable results.

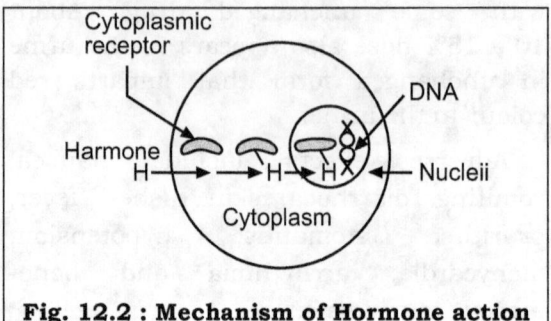

Fig. 12.2 : Mechanism of Hormone action

All hormone-sensitive tissues contain either cytoplasmic or cell-surface receptors. Steroidal hormones bind these cytoplasmic receptors and get transported into the cell-nucleus where they interact with genetic material. The hormone is thus, able to modulate the gene function and may alter cellular growth control. While the polypeptide hormones (e.g. insulin, prolactin; adrenocorticotrophic hormone) do not have affinity for cytoplasmic receptor but they bind to the cell-surface receptors and mediate their response via a second messenger (i.e. cyclic AMP). Some tumour cells also contain estrogenic receptors in their nuclei.

(a) Estrogenic derivatives : Estrogens may be used in the treatment of breast cancer in post menopausal women and prostate cancer. Estrogens are potent inhibitors of gonadotropic secretion and it is believed that they exert their major effect in prostate cancer by suppressing LH (leutenizing hormone) released from pituitary gland, thereby inhibiting testicular testosterone production.

Antiestrogens act competitively and antagonise the estrogen-induced responses of one or more target organs (e.g. uterus, vagina, breast or pituitary gland). Examples of antiestrogens include tamoxifen and clomifen.

On the similar lines, a number of drugs which interferes with the normal synthesis of hormones in the adrenal gland or pituitary gland, have been synthesized. For example, o, p–DDD and aminoglutethimide block adrenal steroidal biosynthesis and produce a state similar to adrenalectomy.

(i) Tamoxifen : It is an orally active non-steroidal antiestrogenic agent containing a triphenylethylene moiety. It exhibits a biphasic plasma half-life. Initial plasma half-life is 7 – 14 hours while the terminal half-life is greater than 7 days. It is extensively metabolized by hydroxylation that is followed by conjugation. N-demethyltamoxifen is the principal metabolite. All are mainly excreted in the faeces. Urinary excretion is the route of secondary importance.

Adverse effects includes anorexia, headache, pruritus, peripheral edema, dizziness, depression, pulmonary edema, hypercalcemia, leukopenia, thrombocytopenia vaginal bleeding and menstrual irregularities. It is contraindicated during pregnancy.

Tamoxifen is used in the palliative treatment of advanced carcinoma of the breast in postmenopausal women.

Just similar to antiestrogens, antiandrogens interfere with the action of androgens at the target organs. The antiandrogen, cyproterone acetate has elicited symptomatic improvement in advanced prostratic carcinoma.

(ii) Leuprolide (Gn-RH) acetate : It is a synthetic peptide analog of gonadotroping releasing hormone. It is about 80 – 100 times more potent than naturally occuring LH – RH. It has a plasma half-life of 3 hours.

Adverse effects include nausea, vomiting, constipation, headache, blurred vision, bone pain, edema, dizziness, impotence, gynecomastia, thromboembolism and swelling at the site of injection.

The chronic exposure of pituitary to leuprolide abolishes gonadotropic release and results in marked decrease in estrogen and testosterone production by gonads. Because of its ability to decrease the circulating concentrations of testosterone and gonadotropins, it is used as antineoplastic agent in the palliative treatment of breast and prostatic carcinomas.

(iii) Estramustine : The action of harmones seems to be related to receptors present in the cancer cells. So, the hormones if are linked to chemotherapeutic agents might be useful in directing the cytotoxic drug to the cancer cell. For example, in breast cancer, the combination of prednisolone to cyclophosphamide, methotrexate or 5-flurouracil results in an increase in the potency. Similarly a hybrid of estradiol and a nitrogen mustard has been synthesized and is used clinically in the treatment of estrogen-resistant prostatic cancer.

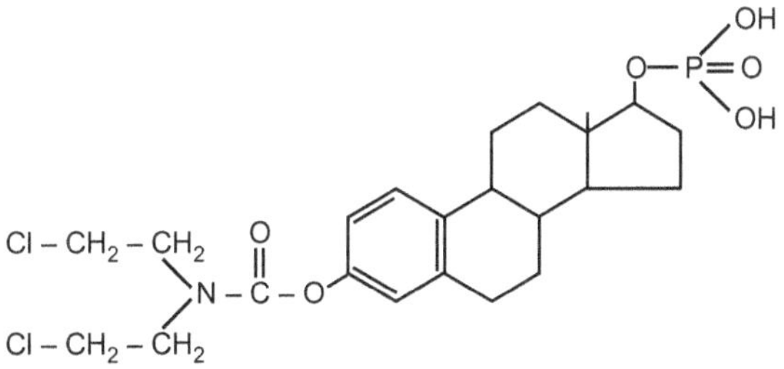

Estramustine phosphate

It is orally effective and has a plasma half-life of 1.3 hours. It is dephosphorylated in the body to release free estramustine which is then oxidized to an active metabolite, estromustine.

Adverse effects include nausea, vomiting, anorexia, diarrhoea, abdominal pain, peripheral eczema, tachycardia, arrhythmia, angina thrombosis and bone-marrow toxicity.

12.15 MISCELLANEOUS AGENTS

(a) Hydroxyurea : It is an orally effective antineoplastic agent that rapidly reduces high circulating granulocyte counts in chronic myelocytic leukemia. It is a S-phase specific agent.

It is nil bound in plasma. It has a plasma half-life of 2 hours. About 80% dose appears in the urine in unchanged form and rest is metabolized in the liver to carbon-dioxide which is eliminated through the lungs.

It impairs the DNA synthesis by inhibiting the enzyme, ribonucleotide reductase enzyme. Adverse effects include nausea, vomiting, diarrhoea, anorexia, stomatitis, chills, sore throat, alopecia, leukopenia, megaloblastic anaemia and thrombocytopenia.

It is used to treat chronic granulocytic leukemia, polycythemia versa, essential thrombocytosis and solid tumours such as lung or breast. In combination with radiotherapy, it may be used in the treatment of carcinomas of cervix, head and neck. It is also effective in malignant melanoma and hypereosinophilic syndrome.

(b) Cis-platin (Cis-diamine dichloroplatinum II) : It is an orally ineffective inorganic water-soluble platinum containing complex. It also has a bactericidal activity against *E. coli*.

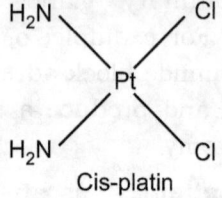
Cis-platin

It is a non-phase specific agent. It inhibits DNA synthesis by cross-linking complementary strands of DNA and therefore acts like a bifunctional alkylating agents. It may undergo sequential transformation with the loss of chloride and the resultant platinum species may act bifunctionally to cross-link adjacent nucleophilic centres of DNA through covalent binding. It binds to DNA at nucleophilic sites, such as N_7 and O_6 of guanine. It also exhibits extensive binding capacity to proteins.

It is usually given by i.v. infusion. About 92 – 95% administered dose is bound to the plasma-proteins. It has a plasma half-life of about 58 – 73 hours. About 40 – 45% dose appears unchanged in the urine.

Adverse effects include nausea, vomiting, ototoxicity, hypocalcemia, transient leukopenia, thrombocytopenia, impaired renal function, seizures, hypotension, tachycardia and anaphylaxis. Carboplatin and iproplatin are less toxic analogs of cis-platin.

Cis-platin is used in the combination chemotherapy of metastatic testicular and ovarian carcinomas and tumours of lung, cervix, bladder, neck and head.

(c) Etoposide and Teniposide : These

are semisynthetic glycosides of podophyllotoxin which are extracted from *Podophylum peltatum*. They are effective intravenously.

Etoposide has a plasma half-life of 3 – 12 hours. Its inactive metabolites appear in the urine along with 30% dose in unchanged form. About 15% dose is excreted unchanged in the faeces.

Adverse effects include nausea, vomiting, diarrhoea, stomatitis, dermatitis, anaphylaxis, bronchospasm, leukopenia, thrombocytopenia and hypotension.

Etoposide is S-phase and G_2-phase specific agent. It acts by complexing an enzyme, topoisomerase II. This leads to a single-strand breakage in the DNA.

Etoposide is used along with cis-platin, bleomycin or doxorubicin in the treatment of testicular tumours, breast tumours, diffuse histiocytic lymphomas, acute granulocytic leukemia, Hodgkin's disease and against small-cell carcinomas of lung.

(d) Monoclonal antibodies : These are obtained by an immunizing mice with an antigen from human cancer cells. Their efficacy is being evaluated in the treatment of lymphomas, leukemias, melanoma and colorectal carcinomas. They may also be used as target-oriented delivery system for radioisotopes.

(e) Hexamethylmelamine : It is an orally active antitumor prodrug that upon metabolic activation releases formaldehyde and ethylenimonium ion. The latter displays cytotoxic activity by inhibiting RNA and DNA synthesis. It has activity against carcinoma of breast, ovary, lung (small cell) and certain lymphomas. It is also useful in the treatment of colorectal gastrointestinal cancers.

Hexamethylmelamine

(f) Colchicine : It is an alkaloid obtained from the plant *Colchicum autumnale*. The colchicine analog, demecolcine is somewhat effective in chronimyclocytic leukemia but it shows its antitumor activity at (toxic) dose which can cause bone-marrow depression.

(g) Carboplatin : It is a second generation platinum analog having less toxicity while maintaining the antitumor effects of cis platin. It acts by causing inter and intra strand cross-linking of DNA.

It is given intravenously. About 80 - 84% dose administered, was found to bind with plasma-proteins. The plasma half-life ranges from 1.5 - 6.0 hours. The drug is mainly excreted through the urine.

The side-effects of carboplatin are mild in comparison to cis-platin. The dose-limiting toxicity of carboplatin is myelosuppression.

It is effective in the treatment of ovarian cancer, head and neck cancer, small cell lung cancer, cervical cancer and testicular cancer.

(h) Mitoxantrone : It is a novel thracycline derivative effective against Leukemia, lymphoma and breast cancer.

It is a phase-non-specific agent and acts by inhibiting DNA-synthesis.

Its reported terminal half-life values range from 1 - 215 hours. It is metabolized mainly in the liver and is excreted in the bile. Minor amount (< 10%) is also excreted through the urine.

Adverse effects include nausea, vomiting, mucositis, alopecia, cardiotoxicity, and leukopenia.

Mitoxantrone is effective in the treatment acute non-lymphocytic leukemia, lymphomas, breast cancer and other solid tumours.

(i) Alpha interferons : These are naturally, occuring proteins that have antiviral, anti proliferative and immunomodulatory activities. It is the first of series of biological products clinically used as antineoplastic agent. It was first approved for the treatment of hairy cell leukemia in 1986. It acts by inhibition of oncogene expression.

It may be given either intramuscularly (elimination half-life of 0.9 – 3.1 hours) or subcutaneously (elimination half-life of 1.8 - 3 6 hours).

Adverse effects include fever, chills, myalgias, headache, nausea, vomiting, fatigue and alopecia. They are all dose related and usually reversible.

Alpha interferons were found to be effective in hairy cell leukemia, lymphoma, multiple myeloma, renal cell carcinoma, melanoma and advanced breast cancer.

ANTI-TUBERCULOSIS AND ANTI-LEPROTIC AGENTS

13.1 INTRODUCTION

Tuberculosis and leprosy are the diseases caused by *Mycobacteria* species. Tuberculosis is caused by either *Mycobacterium tuberculosis* (in man) or by *Mycobacterium bovis* (in animals) while leprosy is caused by *Mycobacterium leprae*.

Tuberculosis is a disease of respiratory transmission. A person gets infected when he comes in contact with the environment contaminated with viable tubercle bacilli. These bacilli are expelled by coughing, sneezing, shouting and singing of a patient with active tuberculosis. When these bacilli are inhaled by a person, they are inoculated into his respiratory bronchioles and alveoli usually towards the apex of the lung. When these microorganisms are multiplied to the sufficient extent, an antigen-antibody interaction is evoked by the cell-mediated T-lymphocytes. Tubercles (Ghon foci) are then formed due to accumulation of macrophages at the site of infection. This may lead to either permanent suppression of the infection or some microbes may survive in the foci and may become the source of postprimary infection when these foci break down under the conditions of weak host defence mechanisms. This may occur immediately or months or years later. The hilar lymph nodes may get easily infected due to spreading of some macrophages containing active bacilli. The released microorganisms from the foci are circulated through lymph and blood to different parts of the body and infect (i) reticuloendothelial system (e.g. liver, spleen and lymph nodes), (ii) serosal surfaces and (iii) sites with high oxygen pressure (e.g. apices of lungs, renal cortex and epiphyses of growing bones). Due to the multiplication of microorganisms at these sites, numerous small foci develop throughout the body. This type of wide-spread infection is known as 'miliary tuberculosis'.

In some patients, the formation of Ghon foci leads to temporary suppression of the infection. Microorganisms may still be present in the foci. During coughing, the caseous material containing live microorganisms is expelled out leaving cavities in the lungs. These active bacilli may then either be :

(i) Swallowed by the same patient resulting into infection of his alimentary tract, or

(ii) Inhaled by a healthy adult resulting in an infection of his trachea, larynx or bronchi. Such cases are more possible in the conditions of overcrowding and poor personal and public hygiene. Infections of oropharynx, larynx and tracheobronchial tree respond fairly well to anti-tuberculosis therapy while infections in gastrointestinal tract, urinary tract or lymph nodes respond partially to the drug-treatment.

Tubercles are formed in the infected organs during the course of the disease. Hence, the disease is known as 'tuberculosis'. The main symptoms are cough, tachycardia, cyanosis and respiratory failure. Depending upon the site of infection, the disease is known as :

(i) Pulmonary tuberculosis (respiratory tract),
(ii) Genitourinary tuberculosis (genitourinary tract),
(iii) Tuberculous meningitis (nervous system), and
(iv) Miliary tuberculosis (a wide-spread infection)

A wide variety of drugs are clinically available for the treatment of tuberculosis. Efforts began in 1938 when sulfanilamide and dapsone did not satisfy the clinical requirements of antituberculosis therapy. The major breakthrough was given by **Waksman** and his co-workers by the introduction of streptomycin in 1944. This was followed by the introduction of p-amino salicylic acid, isoniazid, ethambutol and rifampin.

Chemotherapy of tuberculosis faced some special problems because of slow growth rate of mycobacteria and their intracellular location. Since the disease is chronic by its nature, the therapy needs to be continued for atleast about 1 - 2 years in most of the cases. In such a chronic treatment, if only single drug is used, the risk of development of drug-resistant strains of *Mycobacteria* is always high. This is coupled with the risk of drug toxicity due to high doses of a single drug needed. The obvious solution to this problem is to use combination therapy. When two or more effective drugs are used in combination, resistance will not develop. However, drugs with similar toxicological profiles should not be used together.

The drugs used in the combination therapy are usually selected from ethambutol, isoniazid and rifampin. The choice is dependent upon the type of disease and some patient-related factors.

For the sake of clinical convenience, these drugs are categorised into :

(i) First-line agents :

These are the drugs having high activity and reduced or minimal toxicities. Examples include, streptomycin, isoniazid, ethambutol and rifampin.

(ii) Second-line agents :

These are the drugs having less efficiency and significant toxicity. Examples include, pyrazinamide, ethionamide, amino salicylic acid, kanamycin, capreomycin, viomycin, amikacin and cycloserine. These drugs are relatively toxic. Hence, they should be used only when the organism develops resistance to the first-line agents.

The above scheme of classification of antituberculosis agents is made by taking into account efficacy, organism susceptibility and spectrum of adverse reactions of the drug.

Table 13.1 : Clinically used anti-tuberculosis agents

Drug	Route of administration	Plasma protein bound (%)	Plasma half-life (hour)	Principal metabolites	Prominant adverse effects
(I) First-line agents :					
1. Isoniazid	orally parenterally	Nil	1 - 1.5	Acetylisoniazid, isonicotinic acid and its glycine conjugate, isonicotinyl hydrazones, and N-methylisoniazid	Hepatitis, peripheral neuropathy and hypersensitivity
2. Streptomycin	intramuscularly intrathecally	50 - 60	5 - 7	Nil metabolism	Ototoxicity and nephrotoxicity
3. Ethambutol	orally	20 - 30	3 - 4	An aldehyde and dicarboxylic acid derivative	Optic neuritis and hypersensitivity
4. Rifampin	orally	90	3.5 - 4.0	25 - 0 - desacetyl - rifamycin and 3 - formyl - rifamycin	Hepatitis, fever, thrombocytopenia
(II) Second-line agents :					
1. p-Amino salicylic acid	orally	60	1.0	N-Acetyl derivative	GI-intolerance, hepatotoxicity, hypersensitivity, fluid retention
2. Kanamycin	intramuscularly	1 - 3	2.5	Nil metabolism	Ototoxicity and nephrotoxicity
3. Ethionamide	orally	10	1 - 1.5	Carbomoyl, thiocarbomoyl and 5-oxocarbomoyl derivative	GI-intolerance, hepatotoxicity and hypersensitivity
4. Pyrazinamide	orally	50 - 60	9 - 10	Pyrazinoic acid and 5-hydroxy-pyrazinoic acid	Hepatotoxicity and hyperuricemia
5. Cycloserine	orally	–	–	Minor metabolism	Rash, seizures, and psychoses
6. Capreomycin	intramuscularly	–	–	Minor metabolism	Ototoxicity and nephrotoxicity
7. Viomycin	intramuscularly	–	–	Minor metabolism	Ototoxicity and nephrotoxicity

13.2 FIRST-LINE AGENTS

(a) Streptomycin :

Amikacin, kanamycin and streptomycin are aminoglycoside antibiotics with *in-vitro* bactericidal and *in-vivo* bacteriostatic activity against *Mycobacterium tuberculosis*. All these agents exhibit more or less similar pharmacological and toxicological properties. Streptomycin reported in 1944, was the first clinically effective anti-tuberculosis agent. Its introduction radically changed the handling and prognosis of patients with these diseases. It is administered by i.m. route and occasionally by intrathecal route. Initially it was given in large doses. The development of drug-resistant strains and incidences of severe adverse effects then aroused the awareness about its dose-calculations. Presently, it is given in the combination with other drugs. It is a more preferred agent in the treatment of tuberculous meningitis than that of pulmonary tuberculosis. It helps to suppress the disease but does not help to eradicate it. This preventive action may result due to its inventory action on the bacterial protein synthesis.

It may cause nephrotoxicity, ototoxicity and blood dyscrasias in patients. Its potential to cause these adverse effects is related to dose and duration of the treatment. Streptomycin resistant strains are usually treated with kanamycin. If resistance develops to kanamycin then viomycin may be tried.

(b) Isoniazid :

Introduced in 1952, isoniazid is an extremely effective and safe antimycobacterial agent. Chemically it is a hydrazide of isonicotinic acid. It exhibits bacteriostatic action on the resting bacilli. Though its single agent therapy is approved, rifampin-isoniazid combination is the most favoured anti-tuberculosis therapy.

$$O = C - NHNH_2$$

Isoniazid

It is an orally active agent and its oral absorption is reduced by the presence of food and antacids. It does not bind to plasma proteins. It has a plasma half-life of 1-1.5 hours. It is well distributed to different body tissues and fluids including cerebrospinal fluid. Because of its widespread distribution in the body, it is equally effective against all types of tuberculosis. It undergoes significant first pass hepatic metabolism. The principal metabolites include acetylisoniazid, isonicotinic acid and its glycine conjugate, isonicotinyl hydrazones and N-methyl-isoniazid. They are excreted in the urine alongwith 10 - 25% dose in unchanged form.

Mechanism of action : Isoniazid inhibits mycolase synthetase, an enzyme necessary for the biosynthesis of mycolic acids. The latter are the important constituents of mycobacterial cell-wall. Since mycolic acids are present only in mycobacteria, isoniazid exhibits such a high degree of anti-mycobacterial action.

Because of its ability to complex essential metals such as copper or iron present in mycobacterial enzyme, it interferes with various enzyme systems requiring pyridoxal phosphate as a cofactor. This results in changes in the metabolism of lipids, proteins and carbohydrates. Nucleic acid synthesis is also affected.

Adverse effects :

Most of the isoniazid undergoes metabolism by N-acetylation process in the liver. The latter depends on the transfer of acetyl group from coenzyme-A by N-acetyl-transferase. Since the rate of acetylation is under genetic control, patients may be categorised as slow acetylators and rapid acetylators. In slow acetylators, the rate of isoniazid metabolism is slow resulting into more prolonged plasma levels of isoniazid than in rapid acetylators. Hence, slow acetylators are more susceptible to the adverse effects than do rapid acetylators.

The most common adverse effects of isoniazid include dryness of mouth, epigastric distress, allergic reactions, peripheral neuritis, mental abnormalities, methaemoglobinemia, and hepatotoxicity.

The most significant adverse reaction is hepatotoxicity that may arise due to acetylhydrazine, a toxic metabolite of acetylisoniazid. It is characterized by fatigue, malaise, weakness, anorexia, fever, arthralgias and increased serum glutamic-oxaloacetic acid transaminase (SGOT) level.

The neurotoxicity specifically is seen in malnourished patients, chronic alcoholics or slow acetylators. It usually occurs in the form of peripheral neuritis which is characterized by numbness and tingling in lower extremities and paresthesias in the hands and fingers. A supplimentary dose of pyridoxal phosphate (vitamin B_6) of 10 mg daily (for 50-100 mg isoniazid dose) corrects the neurotoxic effects of isoniazid.

(c) Ethambutol :

It is an orally effective bacteriostatic agent active against most strains of *M. tuberculosis, M. kansas* and *M. marinum.* However, *M. avium* and *M. intracellulare* are usually resistant to its action.

$$C_2H_5-\overset{\overset{\displaystyle CH_2OH}{|}}{CH}-NH-CH_2-CH_2-NH-\overset{\overset{\displaystyle CH_2OH}{|}}{CH}-C_2H_5$$

Ethambutol

Chemically, it is ethylene diamino-di-1-butanol. Activity is stereospecific. Dextro isomer is having the maximum antimycobacterium activity. Upon oral administration, it is well distributed in most of the body tissues and fluids except cerebrospinal fluid. Because of drug-retention ability, erythrocytes may serve the function of slow drug releasing depots. About 20 - 30% administered dose is bound to the plasma-proteins. It has a plasma half-life of about 3 - 4 hours. Major metabolites include an aldehyde and a dicarboxylic acid derivative which are excreted in the urine alongwith about 70% dose in unchanged form. SAR studies indicated that the nature of branching, distance between two nitrogen and extent of N-alkylation are the activity governing factors. Little is known about its mechanism of action. It probably interferes in the synthesis of proteins and nucleic acids by acting as an antimetabolite. Its complex forming ability is also a contributing factor to its bacteriostatic activity.

Adverse effects include nausea, vomiting, abdominal pain, optic neuritis, headache, drug fever, malaise, diminished visual activity, dermatitis, pruritus, joint pain, dizziness, confusion, hallucination and peripheral neuritis. It is contra-indicated in pregnancy and in children below 13 years of age. Monthly eye-examination of patients is necessary.

It is the most favoured drug used in combination therapy with rifampin or isoniazid against streptomycin-resistant strains of tubercle bacilli.

(d) Rifampin :

It is an orally active bactericidal semi-synthetic derivative of rifamycin B, a macrocylic antibiotic produced by *Streptomyces mediterranei*. Its oral absorption is impaired in the presence of food and p-amino salicylic acid. It is well distributed to almost every body tissue and fluid including cerebrospinal fluid. About 90% administered dose is bound to the plasma-proteins. It has a plasma half-life of 3.5 - 4.0 hours. The principal metabolites include 25 desacetylrifamycin (active) and 3-formylrifamycin (inactive). They are excreted in the urine alongwith 7-10 % dose in unchanged form. About 60-65 % dose appears in the faeces through the bile circulation.

Mechanism of action : DNA - dependent - RNA polymerase is an enzyme necessary for RNA synthesis. Rifampin acts on β-subunit of this enzyme resulting into formation of stable complex. This in turn, causes inhibition of bacterial RNA synthesis. However, mammalian enzymes are not affected by this drug.

Adverse effects include nausea, vomiting, headache, erythema, nervousness, restlessness, emotional disturbances, tremors, pulmonary edema, hyperglycemia, hypokalemia, increased cardiac output and cardiac arrythmias.

Rifampin is a first-line agent. Since bacterial resistance develops rapidly if rifampin is taken alone, its combination with either isoniazid or ethambutol are preferably used. However, combined use of isoniazid and rifampin may increase the risk of hepatotoxicity.

13.3 SECOND-LINE AGENTS

A number of second-line agents are available that may be used specifically when bacterial resistance or severe drug toxicity develops with first-line agents.

(a) Ethionamide :

Prothionamide and ethionamide are the congeners of thioisonicotinamide having antimycobacterial activity.

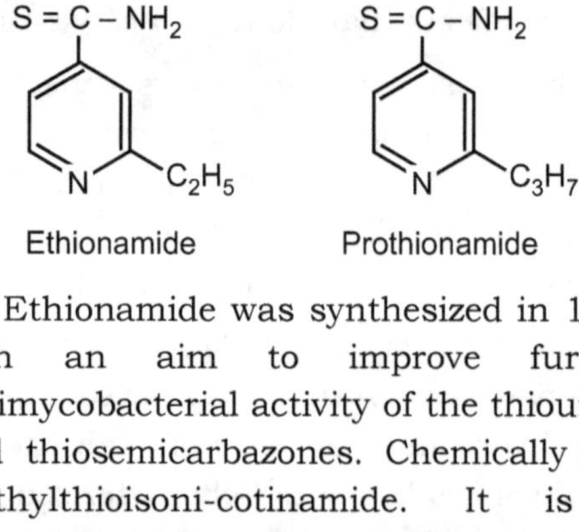

$S = C - NH_2$ $S = C - NH_2$

Ethionamide   Prothionamide

Ethionamide was synthesized in 1956 with an aim to improve further antimycobacterial activity of the thioureas and thiosemicarbazones. Chemically it is 2-ethylthioisoni-cotinamide. It is a thioamide analoge of isoniazid.

It is an orally effective agent. However to minimize mucosal irritation, it is usually given in the form of enteric-coated capsules. It is well distributed to various body tissues and fluids including cerebrospinal fluid. About 10% administered dose is bound to the plasma-proteins. It has a plasma half-life of 1 – 1.5 hours. Principal metabolites include carbomoyl, thiocarbomoyl and 5-

oxocarbomoyl analogs which are excreted in the urine alongwith < 1% dose in unchanged form.

Mechanism of action :

(i) It may interfere in peptide synthesis by acting as antimetabolite and inhibiting the incorporation of sulfur-containing amino acids.

(ii) It may inhibit mycobacterial mycolic acid synthesis.

(iii) It may affect dehydrogenase systems in tubercle bacilli, and

(iv) It may form a substituted isonicotinic acid derivative that may interfere with NAD-dependent systems.

Adverse effects include nausea, vomiting, anorexia, diarrhoea, headache, skin rashes, blurred vision, drowsiness, depression, asthenia, olfactory disturbances, restlessness, tremors, impotence and postural hypotension. Because of structural similarity, it blocks hepatic acetylation of isoniazid by acting as alternative substrate for acetylation.

It is used in combination with other antimycobacterial agents in the treatment of pulmonary tuberculosis resistant to isoniazid.

(b) p-Amino Salicylic Acid :

Because of its sour taste and irritant properties, this drug is mainly used in the form of its sodium, potassium or calcium salts. In the salt form, it is more water-soluble and less irritant to gastrointestinal mucosa. Moreover, aluminium hydroxide is usually included in its formulation to further reduce GIT-irritation caused by the drug. It is also available in the form of its phenyl and benzoyl esters.

It is an orally active drug and is widely distributed in various body tissues and fluids. About 60% administered dose is bound to the plasma-proteins. It has a plasma half-life of 1.0 hour. The principal metabolites include acetylated derivative, free and acetylated p-amino salicyluric acid and 2, 4-dihydroxy benzoic acid which are excreted in the urine alongwith about 40% dose in unchanged form. Probenecid prolongs its duration of action by inhibiting its tubular excretion.

Adverse effects include nausea, abdominal distress, diarrhoea, anorexia, eosinophilia, leukopenia, agranulocytosis, thrombocytopenia, hemolytic anemia and allergic reactions. Crystalluria may develop due to poor solubility of free drug and its metabolites in acidic urine. In children, it develops acidosis because of its strongly acidic nature.

Its structural similarity with PABA suggests its possible role in folate biosynthesis. It interferes with the transfer of one carbon units. It however is effective against only certain mycobacteria. Like ethionamide, it inhibits isoniazid metabolism by competing for hepatic enzymes involved in isoniazid acetylation. Hence, it elevates the serum isoniazid level when concomittantly administered. It also delays the development of bacterial resistance to streptomycin and isoniazid.

(c) Pyrazinamide :

It is a pyrazine analog of nicotinamide. It is a drug of low potency and constitutes part of short term (six months) multiple drug therapy alongwith streptomycin and isoniazid. Almost all structural modifications of pyrazinamide resulted in the decrease in the activity.

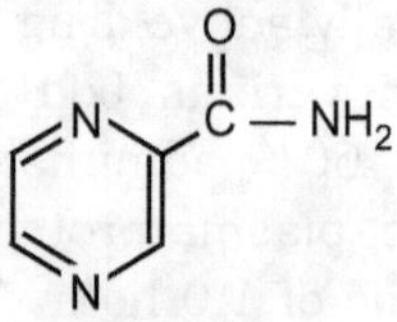

Pyrazinamide

It is an orally effective agent. About 50 - 60% administered dose is bound to the plasma-proteins. It has a plasma half-life of 9 - 10 hours. Principal metabolites include pyrazinoic acid and 5 hydroxypyrazinoic acid. They appear in the urine alongwith 4 - 14% dose in unchanged form.

Adverse effects include nausea, vomiting, urinary retention, anorexia, dysuria, drug rash, fever, malaise, arthralgias, jaundice, hepatic necrosis and decreased urate excretion. The pyrazinoic acid metabolites decrease the renal tubular excretion of urate and may induce hyperuricemia and acute gouty arthritis. The concomittant administration of p-amino salicylic acid was found to prevent or delay the appearance of hyperuricemia. The drug is contraindicated in patients with gouty conditions or hepatic dysfunction.

Its mechanism of action is still unclear. It acts probably by suppressing bacterial protein synthesis. Pyrazinamide is reserved mainly for the treatment of resistant strains of tubercle bacilli, where it is used alongwith isoniazid.

(d) Thioacetazone (Amithiozone) :

Based upon some encouraging results with sulphonamides and sulphones, **Domagk** and co-workers designed this drug in 1948. It was found to be effective in tuberculous laryngitis and enteritis but not in acute miliary or meningeal tuberculosis.

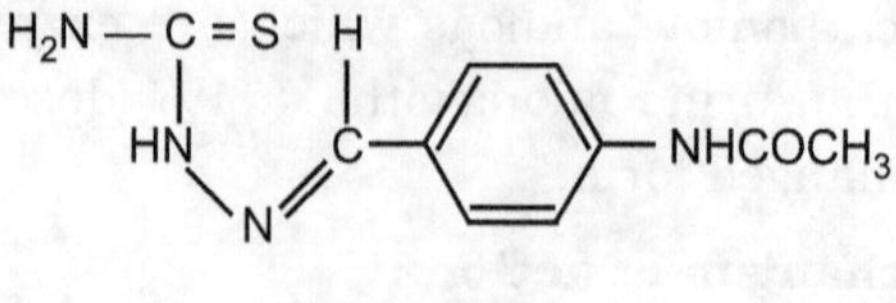

Thioacetazone

Chemically, it is a thiosemicarbazone. Due to its structural similarity with heterocyclic sulphonamides, it may have sulphonamide like action. It forms a copper complex that interferes with the biochemical carriers for copper in *Mycobacteria*.

It is orally effective and is excreted primarily in the urine. Adverse effects include nausea, vomiting, skin rashes, leukopenia, hemolytic anaemia, thrombocytopenia, hepatotoxicity and renal damage.

It is now rarely used to treat pulmonary tuberculosis and tuberculoid leprosy. It is however effective in delaying the emergence of isoniazid resistant tubercle bacilli. It may also be used in some combination regimens for leprosy. The drug is given in the daily dose of 50 mg which may then gradually be increased to 300 mg and then is continued for many months.

(e) Cycloserine :

It is an analog of D-alanine having broad spectrum antimicrobial profile. It inhibits the growth of some gram-positive and gram-negative bacteria.

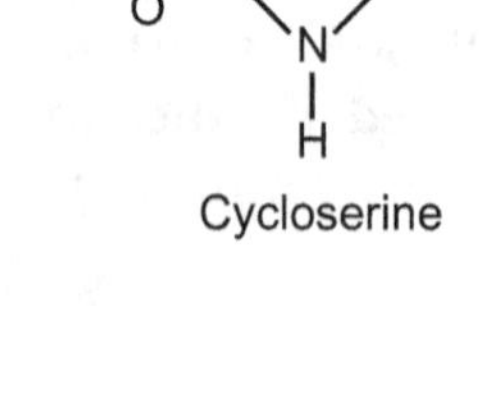

Cycloserine

It is obtained from *Streptomyces orchidaceus*. Chemically it is D - 4 - amino - 3 - isoxazolidone. It is orally effective drug. It is widely distributed in various body tissues and fluids, including cerebrospinal fluid. It is excreted in the form of its metabolites and 50% unchanged drug in the urine.

Adverse effects include headache, visual disturbances, nervousness, irritability, depression, confusion, tremors and psychoses. The concomittant administration of vitamin B_6 (100 mg three times a day) reduces its neurotoxicity.

Because of structural similarity with D-alanine, cycloserine prevents the synthesis of cross-linking dipeptide which is necessary in the formation of bacterial cell-wall.

Cycloserine is now rarely used in the treatment of tuberculosis. It is however used in the treatment and long-term suppression of urinary-tract infections.

(f) Capreomycin and Viomycin :

Both these antibiotics are strongly basic peptides having close structural resemblance. Capreomycin is produced by *Streptomyces capreolus* while viomycin is produced by *Streptomyces pumiceus*. Both share similar pharmacological and toxicological properties. Capreomycin is more potent but less toxic antimycobacterial agent than viomycin. The crude capreomycin is a mixture of four cyclic polypeptides, IA, IB, IIA and IIB. The clinically used drug consists mainly of IA and IB.

Like all other polypeptide antibiotics, these agents are given parenterally. Injections of these drugs are painful. Adverse effects include skin rashes, drug fever, blood dyscrasias, ototoxicity, nephrotoxicity and severe pain at the site of injection. Nephrotoxicity is characterized by pyuria, proteinurea, hematuria, nitrogen retention, and electrolyte disturbances. Viomycin is rarely indicated in children.

Both these agents act by binding to both 30 S and 50 S ribosomal subunits resulting into inhibition of bacterial protein synthesis.

Capreomycin is mainly used in combination with ethionamide or ethambutol against Streptomycin resistant strains of *M. tuberculosis*. Sometimes isoniazid or amino salicylic acid may also be used in the combination with capreomycin.

13.4 ANTI-LEPROTIC AGENTS

Leprosy or Hansen's disease is a chronic human disease caused due to an acid fast bacillus which produces nodules in the skin and loss of sensation in the affected region. Infection results into tissue loss, so fingers and toes became shortened and deformed as the cartilage is absorbed into the body. This dermatological infection is caused by *Mycobacterium leprae* and the disease develops very slowly over a period of years.

Once the bacilli are multiplied to the sufficient extent, antigen-antibody reactions are evoked by the cell-mediated immunity. These reactions may occur either suddenly in the absence of drug or during the anti-leprotic treatment. These hypersensitivity reactions are occurring not as a result of allergy to the drugs but they should be considered as allergic reactions to the metabolic products of the infecting organism. These reactions are called as 'lepra reactions'. In lepra reactions skin lesions appear which later on shows inflammation i.e. they become red, more prominent, swoller shiny and warm. Nerves also show inflammation and develop pain. Pain in nerves develops due to increased intraneural pressure because of oedema and cellular reaction of inflammatory process. To control these reactions, usually a glucocorticoid is added in the anti-leprotic drug regimen.

Based upon the area under infection and intensity of lepra reactions, leprosy can be categorised into following types :

(i) Tuberculoid Leprosy :

It is characterized by the presence of infection in restricted area and less pronounced lepra reaction. The latter indicates that very few number of microorganisms are present in the infected area of the skin. Hence dapsone alone may be effective.

(ii) Lepromatous Leprosy :

It is characterized by a widely disseminated disease with a high number of infecting microorganisms. Hence, this form needs more drastic (i.e. multidrug) and prolonged treatment.

(iii) Indeterminate Leprosy :

In very early stages of the disease, microorganisms are not multiplied to the extent to induce lepra reactions. This early form of the disease is known as indeterminate leprosy.

(iv) Borderline Leprosy :

Tuberculoid leprosy and lepromatous leprosy are the two extremities of the active form of the disease. All other forms that lie inbetween these two extremities are known as borderline forms of leprosy.

Treatment of Leprosy :

Relatively few drugs are available to treat this chronic dermatological disease. These drugs include dapsone, clofazimine, thiacetazone, ethionamide, prothionamide and rifampin. An ideal antileprotic agent should serve two important objectives. It should be able to control lepra reactions and it should eliminate viable bacilli from the blood and nasal secretions by stopping their multiplication. Because of the avascular nature of the lesions and slow growth of bacilli, a prolonged treatment of about 1 - 5 years is necessary to prevent relapse of the disease. Alongwith main drug, adjunct therapy with corticosteroids (to suppress the lepra reaction), aminoglycosides or antimalarial agents are useful.

(a) Sulfones :

The demonstration that tuberculosis induced in guinea pig could be controlled by sodium glucosulfone was a major advance in the chemotherapy of *Mycobacterium* infections. Chemically sulfones are the derivatives of 4, 4'-diaminophenylsulfone or dapsone. They are bacteriostatic in nature and are found to be effective in all forms of leprosy. They are cheap and easy to administer.

They are orally active and are well distributed in different body tissues and fluids. Many sulfones are *in-vivo* converted to dapsone. Acetylation and glucuronide conjugation are the main pathways for their metabolic inactivation. They are mainly excreted in the bile and reabsorbed from the intestine.

They all possess similar pharmacological properties. Due to structural similarity with sulphonamides, they share similar mechanism of action, metabolic pattern and range of adverse effects with sulphonamides. The most active antileprotic drug amongst sulfones is dapsone.

It is used in combination with rifampicin and clofazinine as multidrug therapy (MDT) for the treatment of leprosy.

Adverse effects of sulfones include nausea, vomiting, anorexia, insomnia, drug fever, hematuria, skin rashes, anaemia and methaemoglobinemia. The latter two effects are more pronounced in patients deficient in glucose-6-phosphate dehydrogenase enzyme. Burning sensation in hands and feet and hepatitis may also occur.

Besides their use in anti-leprotic therapy, some of them have shown good results in the treatment of malarial and rickettsial infections. Dapsone itself is used in treatment of both, lepromatous and tuberculoid types of leprosy.

(b) Rifampin :

Rifamycin B is a member of a group of structurally related, complex macro-cyclic antibiotics isolated from *Streptomyces mediteranei*. Rifampin is a semisynthetic derivative of rifamycin B. It is already discussed in antituberculotic agents. This drug has bactericidal action on the growth of *Mycobacterium leprae* in a dose of 600 mg per day. It is used in combination with other antileprotic agent in the treatment of sulfone-resistant leprotic disease.

(c) Clofazimine :

It is an orally active phenazine dye with bactericidal effect on *M. Leprae*. It was synthesized in 1954. It is widely distributed in different body tissues and fluids. It is accumulated specifically in liver, spleen and lymph nodes. It has a plasma half-life of about 2 months. It is insignificantly metabolized and is excreted mainly in unchanged form into urine and faeces. Minor amount is excreted in sweat, tears, saliva and milk.

Adverse effects include nausea, vomiting, eosinophilic enteritis, anorexia, diarrhoea, crampy abdominal pain, weight loss and red discolouration of the skin.

It acts mainly by interferring with the replication of bacterial DNA. Besides antibacterial activity, it also possesses anti-inflammatory activity that provides additional benefit to relieve the patient from leprae reactions. Because of its anti-inflammatory activity, the appearance of erythema nodosum leprosum is found to be delayed. It is often used in combination with other potent anti-leprotic agents to potentiate anti-leprotic activity. It may also be used to treat Buruli ulcer caused due to *Mycobacterium ulcerans*. Besides this, it is also used to treat pyoderma gangrenosum.

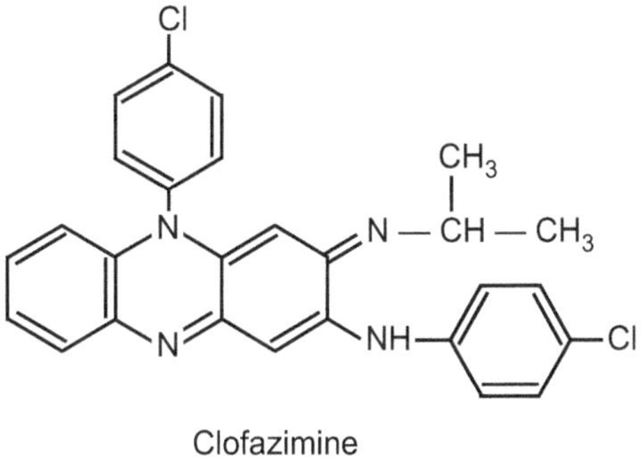

Clofazimine

Other drugs like ethionamide and prothionamide may also be used as second-line agents in the treatment of leprosy.

(d) Chaulmoogric acid :

The oil of chaulmoogra and hydnocarpus are used since from ancient time in the treatment of leprosy. These oils are extracted from the riped seeds of *Hydnocarpus anthelmintica*; *H. heterophylla* and other species of *Hydnocarpus*. It contains glycerides of chaulmoogric acid and hydnocarpic acid.

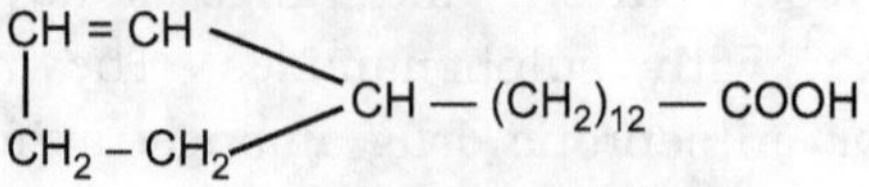

$$\begin{array}{c} CH=CH \\ | \\ CH_2-CH_2 \end{array} \!\!\!\! > CH-(CH_2)_{12}-COOH$$

Chaulmoogric acid

$$\begin{array}{c} CH=CH \\ | \\ CH_2-CH_2 \end{array} \!\!\!\! > CH-(CH_2)_{10}-COOH$$

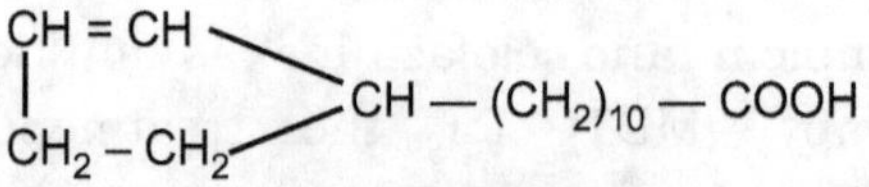

Hydnocarpic acid

Various derivatives of these acids have been prepared and may be topically employed in the therapy of leprosy, psoriasis, rheumatism and tuberculosis.

❖ ❖ ❖

ADENOHYPOPHYSEAL HORMONES

14.1 INTRODUCTION

In the multicellular organisms, different tissues are expected to perform specific functions in an orderly manner. A smooth co-ordination between these different functions is necessary for the adoptation of the organism in a constantly changing external and internal environment. In body, two major mechanisms operate to ensure this co-ordination between functions. These are explained below :

(a) Nervous system : This system, helps in co-ordaining functions with the help of neurohumoral transmission process, involved in receiving information (sensory input), processing of the information (integration) and transmitting the information (motor output). Besides this, the specific chemical agents i.e. neurotransmitters in nervous system are responsible for the transmission of nerve impulses across most synapses and neuroeffector junction.

(b) Endocrine system : This system includes a number of specialised glands (e.g. pituitary, adrenals, thyroid etc.) releasing chemical messengers which regulates variety of physiological and metabolic activities of adjacent or distant tissues either by influencing the activities of enzymes or by affecting the permeability of cellular membranes, thus monitoring passage of vital intermediates through the membranes of the cells. The chemical messengers are known as hormones and the glands which secrete them are known as endocrine glands or glands of internal secretion. The non-specific tissues like pancreas and intestinal mucosa also are responsible for secretion of certain hormones due to the presence of specialized cells in these tissues.

The active principles of the endocrine glands play a vital role in the body's economic system. The endocrine glands are mostly derived from epithelial cells. These glands secrete their hormones directly into the blood stream. Hence these are *'ductless glands'*. From the blood stream these secretions are conveyed to the various target tissues in the body to exert important functional effects.

The word *'Hormone'* was introduced by **Starling** in 1905, which was derived from the Greek word, *hormaein*, meaning *'to stir up'*. In a liberal sense, the term *'Hormone'* is not restricted to the secretions of the endocrine glands. For example, secretin, pancreozymin, noradrenaline, acetylcholine and even carbon dioxide come into this category. While prostaglandins and related compounds can be considered as local hormones because their effects are seen only on the cells of origin or on neighbouring cells.

Hormones are usually biosynthesized from lipids, amino acids and proteins. They are secreted in the blood stream either in an active form (e.g. estradiol) or in prohormone form. The prohormone form is then converted to the active form in the peripheral tissues through biotransformation. For example, pro-opio-melanocortin containing 285 amino acid residues is a prohormone form, from which ACTH, β-lipotropin, β-endorphin and MSH hormones are released. Similarly to exert physiological actions, testosterone has to be converted to the active form, dihydrotestosterone. Like various drugs, the hormone may get bound to the plasma proteins (inactive form) while the free form of hormone is the physiologically active form which exerts effects on a single target tissue or many target tissues. The hormonal action is usually brought about by very low concentration (i.e., $10^{-15} - 10^{-19}$ mol/l) of the free hormone in the extracellular fluid. This concentration is regulated by a variety of homeostatic mechanisms. Indeed the sole function of some hormones is to control secretion of other hormones through feedback mechanisms.

In glands like, adrenals, thyroid etc, usually the negative feedback inhibitory loops operate. However the positive feedback loops can also be seen at certain places. For example, the sudden rise in the secretion of lutenizing hormone at the 14th day of menstrual cycle is induced by high plasma concentrations of estrogens and FSH. Since hormones are known to control the line of demarcation between physiology and pathology, certain pathophysiological conditions, like pain, stress, shock, hypoglycemia and trauma also influence the secretion of hormones through higher brain centres. This is specifically true for the pituitary gland whose secretions are regulated by hypothalamic control. This control is exerted by the release of regulatory hypothalamic hormones. Hypothalmus receives signals from almost all possible sources in the nervous system. It is found that adrenergic, dopaminergic and tryptaminergic nerve tracts influence greatly the secretion of various hypothalamic regulatory hormones.

Most of the hormones were isolated in a pure form between 1920 to 1935. It was followed by identification and synthesis of these active principles. The knowledge about their chemistry was thus gradually built up. Hormones in general, possess very complex chemical structures. They may be steroids (e.g. sex hormones), proteins (e.g. insulin) or amino acids (e.g. thyroxine). Due to this wide structural diversity, hormones can be classified on the basis of the nature of physiological response (i.e. functionally) and on the basis of their mechanism of action.

14.2 CLASSIFICATION

Hormones can be classified in the following three manners :

[I] Hormones can be categorized on the

basis of their physiological responses :

(a) Hormones required to maintain (trophic) specific activities; examples include oxytocin, follicle-stimulating hormone etc.

(b) Hormones required for normal cellular metabolism and growth; examples include glucoskorticoids, growth hormone, insulin etc.

(c) Hormones required to maintain electrolyte and water balance; examples include aldosterone, vitamin D etc.

(d) Hormones required to maintain homeostatic mechanisms; examples include aldosterone, angiotensin etc.

[II] The hormonal action in many cases depends upon the adequate concentration of intracellular messengers like, calcium ions, c-AMP, inositol triphosphate, diacylglycerol and c-GMP. Hence **the hormones can also be classified on the basis of their mechanism of action** as follows :

(a) Hormones that act through intracellular receptors (i.e. nuclear receptors); examples include steroidal hormones, thyroid hormones, vitamin D, insulin, erythropoietin etc.

(b) Hormones that act by influencing c-AMP concentration; examples include growth hormone, oxytocin, thyroid stimulating hormone, follicle stimulating hormone etc.

(c) Hormones that act by influencing membrane inositol phospholipids; examples include angiotension II, gonadotropin releasing hormone, substance P, thyrotropin releasing hormone etc.

[III] **Hormones are classified generally in connection with the names of the glands that secrete them :**

(a) Anterior pituitary hormones, e.g. corticotropin, prolactin, growth hormone, follicle stimulating hormone etc.

(b) Posterior pituitary hormones, e.g. oxytocin and vasopressin.

(c) Thyroid hormones, e.g. thyroxine, calcitonin etc.

(d) Parathyroid hormones, e.g. parathormone

(e) Pancreatic hormones, e.g. insulin and glucagon.

(f) Adrenocortical hormones, e.g. cortisol, aldosterone etc.

(g) Ovarian hormones, e.g. estrogens and progesterone

(h) Testicular hormones, e.g. testosterone

(i) Placental hormones, e.g. chorionic gonadatropin and placental lactogen.

14.3 MECHANISM OF ACTION

The hormonal action in many cases depends upon the adequate concentration of intracellular messengers like, calcium ions, cyclic AMP, inositol triphosphate, diacylglycerol and c-GMP. The principal mechanisms of action for hormones include :

(a) Receptors for a number of hormones (e.g. glucagon, glycopeptide releasing hormones, parathyroid hormones, vasopressin etc.) function by regulating the concentration of the intracellular second messenger, cyclic adenosine – 3' 5' – monophosphate (c-AMP) through the activation of intracellular adenylate cyclase. This intracellular second messenger illucits a variety of effects, both at the cytoplasmic and nuclear level through protein phosphorylation - dephosphorylation processes. Thus effects upon cell permeability, synthesis of specific intracellular proteins, secretory phases and activation of enzymes are some of the effects propogated by c-AMP. It stimulates or activates a variety of protein kinases, such as insulin dependent - tyrosine kinase, phosphorylase kinase, pyruvate dehydro-genase kinase etc. The hormonal action is terminated by the phosphodiesterase enzymes which convert c-AMP into inactive 5'-AMP.

(b) Cyclic-GMP is yet another cyclic nucleotide that acts as intracellular second messenger. The hormone activates guanylate cyclase resulting into the formation of c-GMP. It functions in the way similar to c-AMP and brings about phosphorylation of a number of smooth muscle proteins. e.g. myosin light chain protein. Vasodilation and relaxation of smooth muscle are amongst the prominent effects of c-GMP.

(c) Intracellular receptors play a dominant role in the mechanism of actions of steroidal hormones, thyroid hormones, vitamin A and vitamin D. After entering into the cell, hormone forms a complex with specific cytoplasmic binding proteins. The hormone-receptor complex undergoes a conformational change and is thereby activated.

This activated complex then enters the nucleus and releases the free hormone. The hormone then binds to the acceptor sites on nuclear chromatin. This results in an increase or decrease in the production of certain RNA's and m-RNA's alongwith the corresponding enzymes and other proteins which leads to specific physiological response.

(d) Cytoplasmic calcium ion is another second messenger of hormone action. It is involved in a number of cellular activities like muscle contraction, enzyme activity and membrane excitability.

The action of a wide variety of hormones is operated through the Ca^{++} - signals that are generated by cytosolic Ca^{++} ion concentration. The signal generation leads to the rapid breakdown of membrane phosphatidylinositol - 4, 5 - biphosphate (inositol phospholipids) into myoinositol - 1, 4, 5 - triphosphate and 1, 2 -diacylglycerol through the action of phospholipase C. Inositol triphosphate mobilizes Ca^{++} ions from bound intracellular calcium stores. Thus, it acts as a messenger for the mobilization of intracellular calcium ions. While diacylglycerol activates a Ca^{++} - phospholipid dependent protein kinase C. The latter, independently initiates phosphorylation of different chains of target proteins. The products of hydrolysis of inositol phospholipids can thus be considered as second messengers while resulting increased cytosolic Ca^{++} - ion concentration can be considered as tertiary messenger which binds with intracellular Ca^{++} - dependent regulatory protein calmodulin. It is a protein having molecular weight of about 17,000 and is homologous to muscle protein troponin C in the structure and function. Generally each mole of calmodulin forms a complex with four moles of cytosolic Ca^{++} ions to initiate the phosphorylation of target proteins.

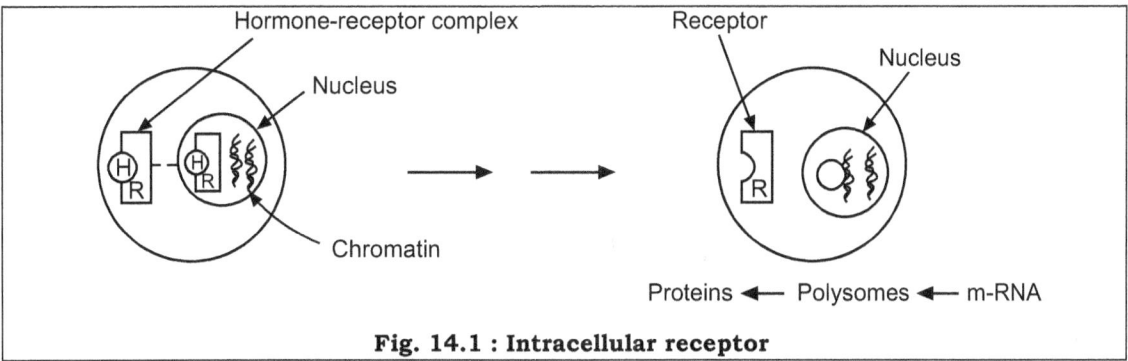

Fig. 14.1 : Intracellular receptor

14.4 THERAPEUTIC APPLICATIONS

Some of the natural hormones are orally ineffective (e.g. insulin) and most of them are biologically short-lived due to their rapid degradation in the body. This is specifically true for polypeptide hormones. These disadvantages were partly overcomed by their SAR studies, for example, diethylstilbestrol is a potent synthetic female sex hormone. Various synthetic hormonal agonists have been designed in order to prolong their biological half life and to increase the oral effectiveness.

The principle therapeutical applications of hormones are given below :

(a) As replacement therapy in order to treat the deficiency of that hormone due to dysfunctioning of concerned endocrine gland,

(b) As diagnostic tool to trace out functional defects in the endocrine system.

Today many synthetic peptide hormones are used therapeutically to regulate and to co-ordinate a variety of physiological and metabolic activities. For example synthetic analogs of vitamin D, parathyroid hormone, adrenocorticotropin hormone and thyrotropin releasing hormone are available. Many peptide hormone analogs and their antagonist are extensively used in medicine and they provide the centres for the development of future drugs. New methods for the synthesis of peptides and proteins are being evolved. Genetic engineering utilizing the principles of gene manipulation has delivered a recent advance technique known as *'recombinant DNA technology'*. With the help of 'SAR' studies it is now possible to suggest tricks to eliminate their side-effects and to increase their potency.

By using protein engineering, enzymic conversion and cell culture techniques, it is now possible to produce more pure polypeptide active molecules like human growth hormone, insulin, interferons, interleukin-2 erythropoietin, hepatitis B vaccine etc.

Basically, genetic engineering makes use of special enzymes, so called chemical scissors, to cut the carrier of the hereditary information (i.e. DNA) at certain points. The desired hereditary information is derived from other organisms and inserted into the DNA that has been cut open. This altered DNA molecule is channeled into the cell which may be a bacterial cell, a yeast cell or a mammalian cell. The reprogrammed cell then manufactures the desired product such as insulin etc.

14.5 PITUITARY HORMONES

The pituitary gland (hypophysis) is of prime importance from the point of view of hormonal activity in the body. Anatomically, it is situated in the lower region of the brain, known as sella turcica which is a bony-walled cavity. It is less than 1 cm in diameter and about 0.5 g in weight. It is joined to the hypothalamus through a narrow strip, known as median eminence. The gland is composed of :

(a) Adenohypophysis (i.e. anterior lobe of pituitary)

(b) Neurohypophysis (i.e. posterior lobe of pituitary)

(c) Infundibulum (i.e. neural stalk), and

(d) Pars intermedia.

Pars intermedia is present in most mammals except humans. The anterior lobe of pituitary is the main centre for the release of various hormones which are secreted by five distinct cell types. These are somatotroph, lactotroph, thyrotroph, gonadotroph and corticotrophilpotroph. Depending upon the structural (i.e. sequence of amino acids) and functional similarities, the hormones that are secreted from adenohypophysis are categorised into three broad groups.

Precursors of most of the above peptides (prohormones) are also found at other places like, brain, placenta and gastrointestinal tract.

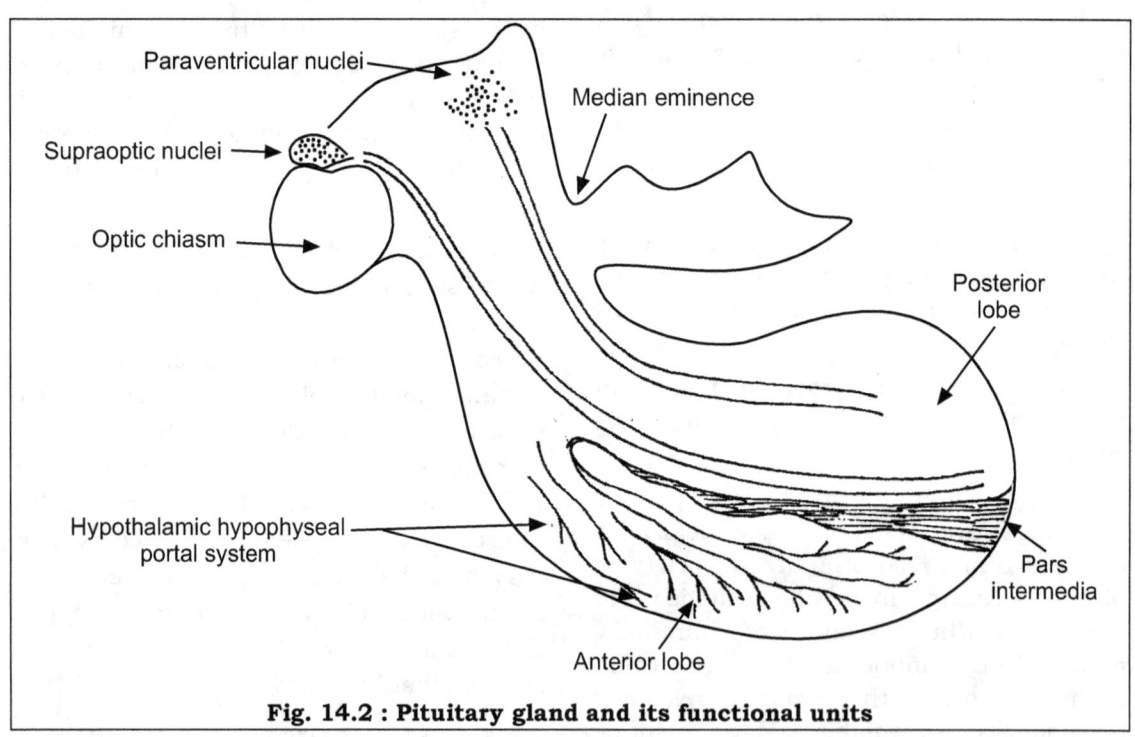

Fig. 14.2 : Pituitary gland and its functional units

14.6 HYPOTHALAMIC CONTROL OF ADENOHYPOPHYSIS

Hypothalamus is the controlling centre for the secretion of adenohypophyseal hormones. This control is exerted by the release of stimulatory and inhibitory hormones of hypothalamic origin in the adenohypophysis through a small artery known as median eminence. It surves as a communication link between adenohypophysis and lower most part of hypothalamus. Pituitary is highly vascular gland supplied with an extensive network of capillaries which circulates the blood coming from median eminence. Hence, it is known as hypothalamic - hypophyseal portal capillary network. Various stimulatory and inhibitory hypothalamic factors are synthesized by special neurons present in the hypothalamus which are released into median eminence through nerve fibres. On absorption into the circulation, they are carried to the pituitary gland through hypothalamicoadenohypophyseal portal system by antegrade (downward) blood flow. The control of hypothalamus functioning by adenohypophyseal hormones might also occur which was proposed to occur via retrograde (upward) blood flow.

Table 14.1: Hormones released from adenohypophysis

	Molecular weight	Amino acid residues
Group I		
Growth hormone	22,000	191
Prolactin	23,000	198
Placental lactogen	22,000	191
Group II		
Luteinizing hormone	30,000	α – 89 β – 115
Follicle stimulating hormone	32,000	α – 89 β – 115
Thyrotropin	28,000	α – 89 β – 112
Chorionic gonadotropin	38,000	α –92 β – 145
Group III		
Corticotropin (ACTH)	4,500	39
α - Melanocyte stimulating hormone	1,650	13
β - Melanocyte stimulating hormone	2,100	18
β - lipotropin	9,500	91
α - lipotropin	5,800	58

Hypothalamus receives signals from almost every possible source in the nervous system. Hence the rate of secretion of hypothalamic stimulatory and inhibitory factors is regularly influenced by various central neurotransmitters. Besides this, fluctuations in the nutritional status, electrolyte and water balance and other hormonal activities feed the relevant information to the hypothalamus so as to bring about compensatory changes in the rate of secretion of hypothalamic stimulatory and inhibitory factors. About nine such hypothalamic regulatory factors have been identified that control the hormonal secretion of pituitary gland. These are :

(a) Growth hormone releasing factor; GH–RF

(b) Growth hormone inhibiting factor; GH-RIH or somatostatin

(c) Prolactin releasing factor; PRF

(d) Prolactin release inhibiting hormone, PRIH

(e) Gonadotropin (FSH and LH) releasing hormone; Gn-RH

(f) Corticotropin releasing factor; CRF

(g) Thyrotropin releasing hormone; TRH

(h) Melanocyte stimulating hormone releasing factor; MRF

(i) Melanocyte stimulating hormone release – inhibiting factor; MIF

These hypothalamic regulating hormones secreted in almost very minute quantities are secretions of some of the adenohypophyseal factors (e.g., LH, FSH, etc.) and is governed by hypothalamic factors only in the stimulatory way while dual (stimulatory and inhibitory) feedback hypothalamic mechanisms operate to control the release of hormones like, prolactin, growth hormone etc.

The adenohypophyseal hormones undergo rapid hydrolysis to form smaller inactive fragments. Their short biological half-life promoted the interest in designing of their synthetic analogs. These synthetic peptide analogs of adenohypophyseal hormones were found to be more potent and have longer duration of action than naturally occuring hormones. For example, synthetic analogs of ACTH (cosyntropin), TRH, LH-RH have been prepared.

Oxytocin and vasopressin (antidiuretic hormone, ADH) are the hormones of posterior lobe (neurohypophysis) of pituitary gland. Both these hormones are identical in the amino acid sequence except at two positions. Due to this high degree of structural similarity, each hormone retains about $\frac{1}{6}^{th}$ activity of other hormone, besides its own activity. These hormones are secreted by the supraoptic and paraventricular nuclei of hypothalamus which are then transported to the posterior pituitary gland by large number of nerve fibres through hypophyseal stalk. Vasopressin is formed primarily in the supraoptic nuclei while oxytocin is formed primarily in paraventricular nuclei. The hormones are synthesized, transported and secreted in association with specific proteins known as neurophysins.

14.7 PATHOLOGICAL ENDOCRINE DISORDERS

Various hormones secreted from pituitary gland can be broadly divided into :

(a) Trophic (maintenance) hormones : These hormones govern the functioning of other endocrine glands; e.g. LH.

(b) Non-trophic hormones : This category of hormones directly influences the activities of the tissues; e.g. growth hormones.

Fluctuations in the rate of secretion and release of various hormones may occur during the pathological endocrine disorders. This results in the abnormalities in the physiological responses linked with these hormones. For example, elevated levels of growth hormone leads to giantism while dwarfism occurs due to low circulating levels of growth hormone. Abnormalities in the ACTH levels may result either in Cushing's syndrome or Addison's disease. In the pituitary gland, hyperpituitarism and hypopituitarism are well characterized endocrine disorders. They are defined in terms of collection of symptoms related with abnormal secretion of pituitary hormones.

(I) Hyperpituitarism : It results due to hypersecretion of pituitary hormones, especially that of growth hormone due to certain pathogenic conditions. Due to hypersecretion of tropic hormones, the functioning of related endocrine glands (e.g. adrenals, thyroid gland) may also be affected. Giantism is the usual common symptom. In men, impotency may occur while in females amenorrhea, galactorrhea and infertility are the main symptoms.

(II) Hypopituitarism : It is characterized by hyposecretion of pituitary hormones. Due to inadequate supply of trophic hormones, the functioning of adrenal gland is affected. Since adrenal gland is related with production of corticosteroid, adrenal deficiency makes the patient more sensitive to the physical stress and to infections. The impaired production of sex hormones is reflected into disturbances into menstrual cycle, growth of axillary and pubic hairs. Genital tract atrophies may also occur. Growth hormone deficiency results into hypopituitary dwarfism. The skin becomes thin, soft and wrinkled. The deficiency of trophic pituitary hormones suppresses the functioning of thyroid gland which results into -

(a) lack of sweating,

(b) low rate of metabolism,

(c) elevated plasma cholesterol level, and

(d) increased sensitivity to cold conditions.

The treatment usually consists of concomitant administration of growth hormone, glucocorticoids, sex hormones and thyroid hormone in proper doses. The replacement therapy with growth hormone and sex hormones in the treatment of hypopituitary dwarfism should be continued over the years in order to get expected rate of growth and sexual development. Disturbances in the thyroid functioning may however occur during this therapy resulting into hypothyroidism. Due to this reason periodic evaluation of the patient is necessary.

Table 14.2 : Hypothalamic regulatory hormones / factors

(a) (Pyro) Glu—His—Pro—NH$_2$

Thyrotropin releasing hormone

(b) HO—⟨benzene ring with OH⟩—CH$_2$CH$_2$NH$_2$

Prolactin release-inhibiting hormone

(c) H$_2$N—Ala—Gly—Cys—Lys—Asn—Phe—Phe—Trp—Lys—Thr—Phe—Thr
                        | |
                        | Ser
                        | |
                        └——— S ——— S ————————————————— Cys
                                                                                                                       |
                                                                                                                    COOH

Somatostatin
(Growth hormone release-inhibiting hormone)

(d) (Pyro) Glu—His—Trp—Ser—Tyr—Gly—Leu—Arg—Pro—Gly—NH$_2$,

Prolactin release-inhibiting hormone

(e) Tyr-Ala-Asp-Ala-Ile-Phe-Thr-Asn-Ser-Tyr-Arg-Lys-Val-Leu-Gly-Gln-Leu-Ser-Ala-Arg-Lys-Leu-Leu-Gln-Asp-Ile-Met-Ser-Arg-Gln-Gln-Gly-Glu-Ser-Asn-Gln-Glu-Arg-Gly-Ala-Arg-Ala-Arg-Leu-NH$_2$

Human growth hormone-releasing hormone

(f) (Pyro) Glu-His-Trp-Ser-Tyr-Gly-Leu-Arg-Pro-Gly-NH$_2$

Gonadotropin-releasing hormone

Table 14.3 : Some hormones of pituitary gland

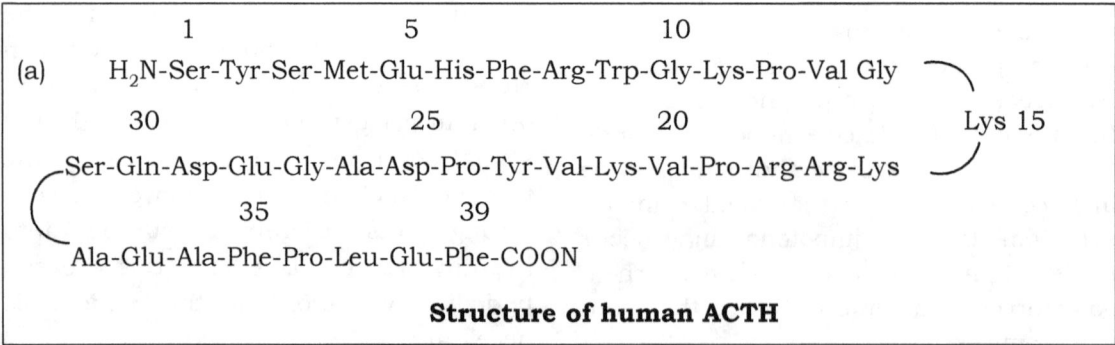

Structure of human ACTH

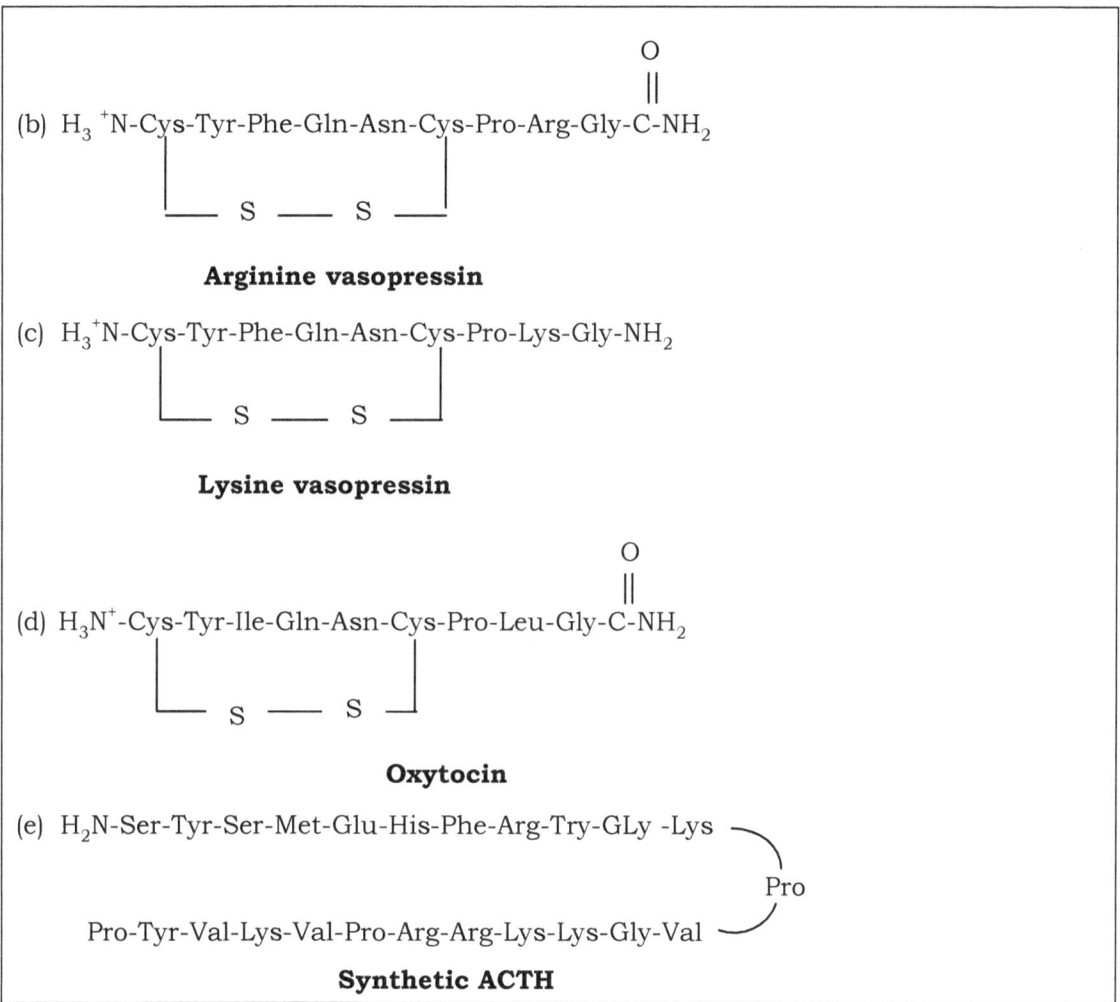

(III) Acromegaly : The condition results due to oversecretion of growth hormone after adolescence due to pituitary tumour. The bones do not grow in length. However bone thickness increases along with the growth of soft tissues. Thickness is more prominent in the small bones of the region especially that of hands, feet, cranium, nose, supraorbital ridges, lower jaw and the bosses of the forehead. The acromegaly person requires larger shoe as much as twice the normal size. Enlargement in the soft tissues (i.e. tongue, liver, kidney etc.) is also initiated. The treatment of acromegaly includes irradiation or surgical removal of tumour region. Dopaminergic agonist like bromocriptine may also be beneficial in certain cases of acromegaly.

14.8 ADENOHYPOPHYSEAL HORMONES

(A) Group I (Lactogenic hormones) :

This group consists of growth hormone, prolactin and placental lactogen. Both, growth hormone and prolactin are obtained from a single prolactin like precursor molecule.

(i) Growth hormone (somatotropin): It is the most abundant of all the active principles of anterior lobe of pituitary. It is a straight chain peptide of about 191 amino acid residues containing two intrachain disulfide bonds. It exerts prominent growth promoting effects on organs and tissues and influences the metabolism of carbohydrates, proteins and lipids. In the latter case, it is assisted by many other hormones like, insulin, glucagon, catecholamines and glucocorticoids. It has the generalized growth promoting effects which are assisted by several other specialized growth promoting factors circulating in the plasma. These include, epidermal growth factor, erythropoietin, insulin like growth factor, fibroblast growth factor and nerve growth factor.

(a) Growth of cartilages and bones : The growth of soft tissues and bones is promoted by growth hormones due to the accumulation of somatomedin like substances in the liver and the kidney. Somatomedin in turn induces the deposition of chondroitin sulphate and collagen. Enlargement in the organ size of adrenals, gonads, thyroid and liver is seen. An overall increase in the total body weight occurs. In general, the activity spectra of growth hormone can be evaluated by the growth of the thymus.

(b) Metabolism of carbohydrates and lipids : In the carbohydrate metabolism, growth hormone and insulin have effect, that depends on the state of the person. In unfasting condition, both hormones work together to give anabolic effects (i.e. use of the sugar and its conversion to lipids) while in fasting condition, growth hormone leads to moderate increase in the blood glucose concentration and exhibits diabetogenic effect. During fasting condition mobilization of fat and mild ketosis occurs under the influence of growth hormone.

(c) Metabolism of proteins : Growth hormone exerts anabolic effects by promoting protein synthesis and by suppressing breakdown of proteins. This is achieved by enhancing the rate of cellular uptake of amino acids and their incorporation into proteins. The ultimate result is retention of nitrogen and decreased plasma urea level.

(d) Lactogenic effect : Due to its close structural similarity with prolactin, growth hormone has considerable lactogenic activity. Upon synthesis, growth hormone is stored in the granules of specific acidophilic cells in the somatotroph region of adenohypophysis. Its secretion is governed by both growth hormone releasing factor and growth hormone release-inhibiting hormone from hypothalamus. Beside this, fasting, hypoglycemia, physical strain and emotional stress are the conditions that stimulate the release of growth hormone. Its biological half-life is only about 20 minutes, however its physiological effects are seen over much greater time. Serotonin antagonists (cyproheptadine), somatostatin and α-adrenoceptor blockers (phentolamine) can inhibit the secretion.

(ii) Prolactin : It is a straight chain peptide of about 198 amino acid residues synthesized and stored in pituitary lactotrophs. The first 40 amino acid residues of prolactin are identical to that of growth hormone. This high degree of structural similarity between prolactin and growth hormone explains similarity in the physiological responses of both the hormones. In females sucking serves as most potent stimulant of prolactin secretion. Beside this, various drugs like methyldopa and cimetidine also accelerate the prolactin secretion. Prolactin has prominent effects especially on the breast and the gonads. Proliferation and subsequent differentiation of mammary duct and alveolar epithelium is induced by increased concentration of prolactin during pregnancy. Besides this, enzymes necessary for lactose synthesis are induced and synthesis of milk proteins is also initiated. All these effects are brought out through intracellular receptor mechanisms. The breasts expand in size due to anabolic effects of insulin and growth hormone. Since prolactin plays important role in the overall growth and development of breast, it may be somewhere connected with mammary tumorigenesis.

During pregnancy, prolactin-concentration increases 20 – 40 fold. For example, the normal adult human plasma concentration of prolactin is about 5 – 10 ng/ml while during pregnancy it elevates upto 200 ng/ml. Prolactin helps to maintain the functioning of corpus luteum. This luteotropic effect is due to prolactin-induced increase in the luteal synthesis of cholesterol which acts as the precursor for the synthesis of sex hormones. The effects of gonadotropins on the gonads are also inhibited by prolactin. Both these above effects of prolactin maintain the stage of infertility during breast feeding which is known as natural mechanism contraception.

Prolactin secretion is under the dopaminergic control. It is suspected that prolactin release-inhibiting hormone (PRIH) is nothing but dopamine. Hence dopaminergic agonist (bromo-criptine) inhibits its release while dopaminergic antagonists (e.g phenothiazines) enhance prolactin secretion. Beside this, fasting, hypoglycemia, TRH, physical strain and emotional stress also stimulate the release of prolactin alongwith growth hormone. The plasma half-life of prolactin is nearly about 20 minutes.

(B) Group II

(i) **Thyrotropin (TSH)** : It is a peptide having two chains. The α-chain contains 89 amino acid residues while β-chain contains 115 amino acid residues. The biosynthesis of thyroid hormones is regulated by the plasma levels of thyroid stimulating hormone through a feedback mechanism. The inorganic iodide is taken up from the blood and is accumulated in the acinar cells of thyroid. The process is accelerated by TSH and is inhibited by perchlorate, thiocynate or cardiac glycosides. It thus helps in maintaining a constant amount of thyroid hormones in the circulation and in the tissues. Most of the physiological responses of TSH are mediated by the glandular c-AMP. It is devoid of any therapeutic applications. However it is frequently used as a diagnostic tool in the thyroid disorders.

(ii) Chorionic gonadotropin (CG) : The human chorionic gonadotropin is a glycoprotein having α-peptide chain (92 amino acid residues) and β-peptide chain (145 amino acid residues). Due to the similar pharmacological effects, it can be used as replacement therapy for leuteinizing hormone. In women, it may be used to treat infertility due to its ovulation stimulant LH-like effect. In such cases it is used in combination with other ovulation stimulants, like clomiphene or HMG. It exibits some thyrotropic activity. The plasma half-life of CG approximates to about 8 hours.

(iii) FSH (Follicle stimualating hormone) and LH (Lutenizing hormone) : These gonadotropins are secreted by adenohypophysis under the influence of FSH-RH and LH-RH hypothalamic regulatory hormones. In female, FSH provokes the maturity of one or more graphian follicles in the ovary while LH stimulates ovulation and luteinization of the follicles. While in males, FSH promotes sperm development or spermatogenesis by stimulating the seminiferous tubules and ICSH (LH) stimulates the interstitial leydig cells to secrete androgens. The plasma half life of FSH (30 minutes) and LH (1 hour) are comparatively shorter than that of CG.

Further details about their secretion, physiological actions, fate and excretion have been discussed in the chapter on 'Sex Hormones'.

(C) GROUP III

(i) Corticotropin (ACTH) : The adrenocorticoid secretion is under the influence of adrenocorticotropic hormone (ACTH) which is released by the anterior lobe of pituitary gland. The release of ACTH from adenohypophysis, in turn, is under the control of corticotropin releasing factor (CRF) that is secreted by hypothalamus. The release of CRF from hypothalamus can also be increased by the action of neurotransmitters like serotonin and dopamine. The plasma level of adrenocorticoids also controls the release of ACTH from adenohypophysis through the negative feedback inhibitory mechanism.

Though it is a peptide of 39 amino acid residues, the sequence of first 1 to 20 amino acids is sufficient to exert its physiological responses. The natural commercial ACTH is obtained from animal pituitaries. However synthetic ACTH analogs (e.g. cosyntropin) is also available in market. Further details about ACTH have been discussed in the chapter on 'Adrenocorticosteroids'.

(ii) Melanocyte stimulating hormone (MSH) : The colour of the skin is determined by the presence of melanin, the black pigment. It is present in the melanocyte cells that occur between dermis and epidermis regions of the skin. The skin colour is dependent upon the number of melanocytes, which in turn, are under the control of MSH. Changes in the skin pigmentation during menstrual cycle and pregnancy in lower animals is due to altered secretion of MSH.

Since ACTH, endorphins, lipotrophins and MSH are obtained from a single precursor i.e. pro-opiomelanocortin, all these peptides stimulate the secretion of each other. Depending upon minor changes in the amino acid sequences, three different MSH-peptides have yet been identified. They are designated as α-MSH, β-MSH and γ-MSH. Thirteen amino acids are present in α-MSH while eighteen amino acids are present in β-MSH. The sequence of first 13 amino acids in ACTH is identical to that of α-MSH. This similarity is suggestive of the fact that it is derived from ACTH. Due to this structural identity, ACTH retains about $1/40^{th}$ MSH like activity. While β-lipotropin serves as precursor for β-MSH and γ-MSH is directly obtained from amino terminal segment of pro-opiom elanocortin. In man, MSH does not seem to play any role.

(iii) Lipotropins (lipolytic factors) : The main precursor of ACTH, endorphins, lipotropins and MSH is a protein of molecular weight of about 30,000. This polypeptide on final cleavage produces two lipolytic factors, i.e. β - lipotropin (β-LPH) and γ-lipotropin (γ-LPH). β-LPH is the largest of all the cleavage products. These lipolytic factors induce lipolysis through a c-AMP dependent mechanism. Beside this, β-lipotropin also serves as the precursor for various hormonal peptides as shown in the Fig. 14.3.

(iv) Endorphins and enkephalins : These are endogenous opioid peptides obtained through cleavage of β-lipotropin molecule in the pituitary gland.

14.9 NEUROHYPOPHYSEAL HORMONES

(a) Vasopressin (antidiuretic hormone) :

It is a nonapeptide with the disulfide bridge. The antidiuretic action is exerted mainly at the distal tubules and collecting ducts of nephron. The hormone activates reabsorption of water at these sites. Fluctuations in the osmotic pressure of the blood activate hypothalamic osmoreceptors which in turn, govern the release of vasopressin. Beside antidiuretic effect, this hormone also stimulates

(i) vascular smooth muscle contraction, and

(ii) secretion of ACTH.

Therapeutically vasopressin may be used to treat disorders associated with renal water conservation e.g. diabetes insipidus.

(b) Oxytocin :

It is also a nonapeptide with the disulfide bridge. However it differs from vasopressin at positions 3 and 8. The principal effects of oxytocin are :

(i) contraction of uterine smooth muscles, and

(ii) milk-ejecting activity due to contraction of myoepithelial cells surrounding the alveoli of mammary glands.

The natural and synthetic oxytocins are mainly used as uterine stimulants in order to induce labour at the time of delivery or as abortifacients. Other agents having similar effects include, sparteine, ergot alkaloids (ergonovine) and prostaglandin $F_{2\alpha}$ (dinoprost tromethamine).

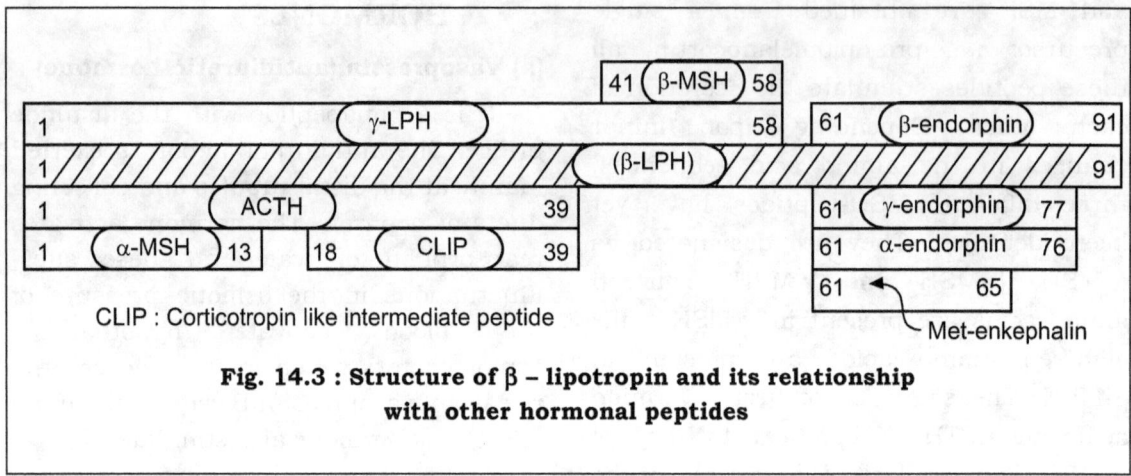

Fig. 14.3 : Structure of β – lipotropin and its relationship with other hormonal peptides

THYROID AND PARATHYROID HORMONES

15.1 INTRODUCTION

Wharton in 1656, first described about thyroid gland. All vertebrates have thyroid gland. It is not essential for life but it is necessary for proper growth and mental well-being of the person. In a healthy adult, it weight about 25 g and is composed of two lobes one on each side of the trachea, just below and anterior to the larynx. It is usually larger in women than in men. At the posterior surface of each thyroid lobe, parathyroid glands are situated. Thyroid gland consists of cells arranged in a close spherical fashion to create hollow spheres (follicles) which are the functional units of thyroid gland. They are approximately 300 µ in diameter. The follicles are filled with gelatinious, amber-coloured protein material, called as *'colloid'*. The colloid contains protein, thyroglobulin which is the storage form for the thyroid hormones. It is formed in the microsomes of the follicular cells. After synthesis, it is stored in the extracellular colloid present in the lumen. Thyroxine (T_4), triiodothyronine (T_3) and calcitonin are the hormonal products of thyroid gland.

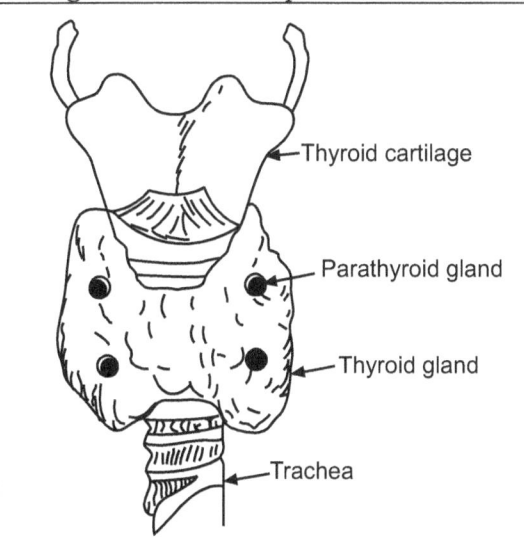

Fig. 15.1 : Thyroid and parathyroid glands

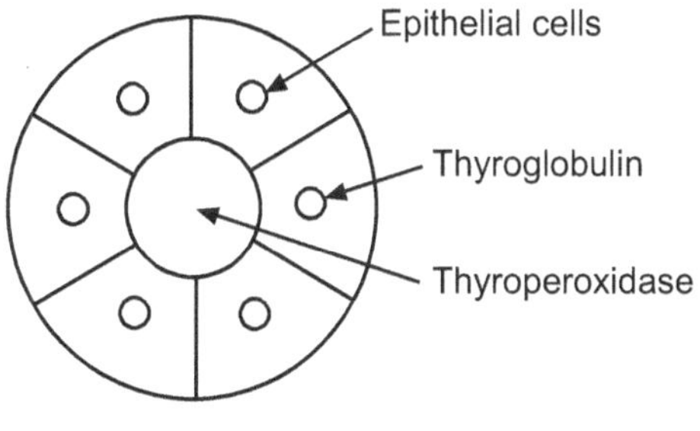

Fig. 15.2 : Functional unit of Thyroid gland

T_3 and T_4 hormones regulate the rate of metabolism and affect the growth and rate of functions of many other systems in the body. Both are synthesised by utilizing iodine and tyosine. Calcitonin, the third thyroid hormone plays important role in calcium homeostasis. Thyroid gland (or release of these hormones) is under control of thyroid stimulating hormone (TSH) produced by pituitary gland. The release of hormones from pituitary gland, in turn is under control of thyrotropin releasing hormone (TRH), which is produced by hypothalamus.

The normal iodine content in the human body is estimated to be near about 6 - 7 mg. On circulation, about 90% of this iodine is trapped by the thyroid gland while the rest of iodine remains in the circulation in the form of organic iodide (95%) (i.e. thyroid hormones, thyroxine and triiodothyronine) and free iodide (5%).

In thyroid gland, thyroglobulin is the storage form for thyroid hormones. On hydrolysis, thyroglobulin releases thyroid hormones along with several iodinated tyrosine residues. Thyroglobulin contains 115 tyrosine residues, each of which offers site for iodination. The major part of iodine present in the gland is consumed by thyroxine (35 %), 3, 5 - diiodotyrosine (34 %), and

Table 15.1 : Hydrolysis products of thyroglobulin

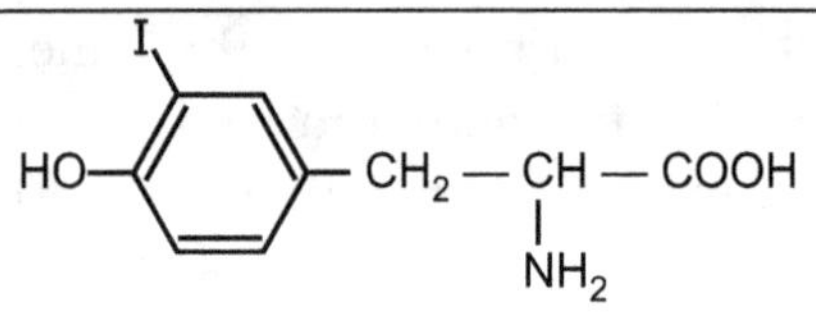

3-monoiodotyrosine (MIT)

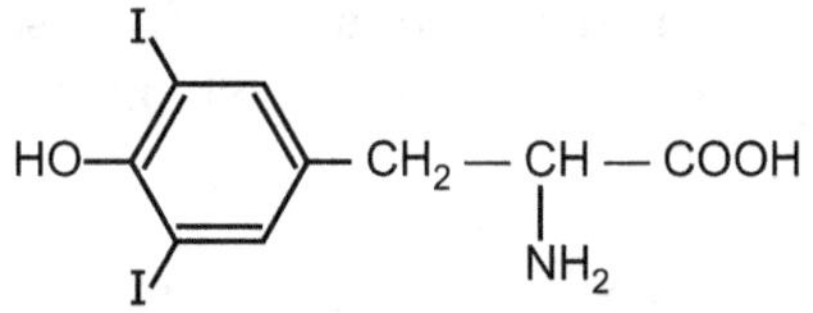

3,5-diiodotyrosine (DIT)

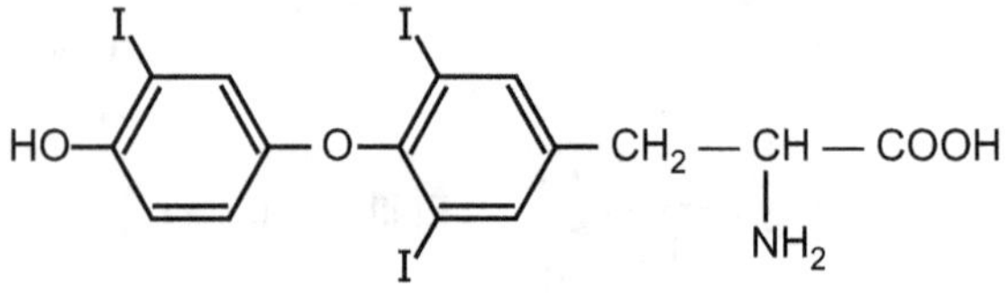

3, 5, 3' - Triiodothyronin (T_3)

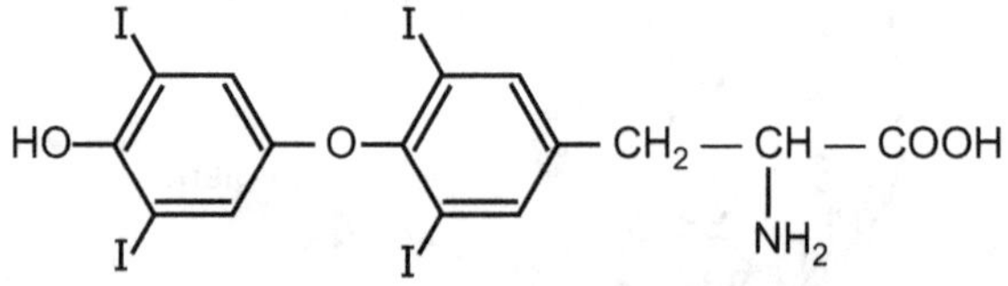

3, 5, 3', 5' - tetraiodothyronine (T_4) or thyroxine

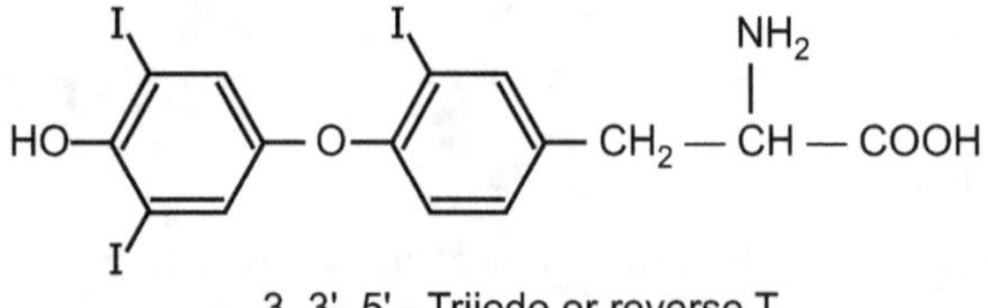

3, 3', 5' - Triiodo or reverse T_3 thyronine

3-monoiodotyrosin (24%) while triiodothyronine consumes only 5% of iodine available in thyroid gland.

Thyroglobulin is a complex glycoprotein composed of two identical subunits, each of which has a molecular weight of about 330,000. Its main products of hydrolysis include 3-mono iodotyrosin, 3, 5-diiodotyrosine, thyroxine, triiodothyronine and reversed triiodothyronine. The structural elucidation of thyroxine was done in 1926 by **Harington** while **Roche et al** reported the isolation of triiodothyronine in 1952. Thyroxine and 3, 5, 3' - triiodothyronine are the principal thyroid hormones. Chemically they are amino acids containing iodinated diphenyl ethers. The iodine atoms are necessary for binding of these hormones to thyroxine-binding globuline in the plasma. They also help in maintaining the active conformation' of the molecule. Triiodothyronine (T_2) is 4 times potent than thyroxine (T_4) in exerting the physiological response.

15.2 BIOSYNTHESIS, STORAGE AND METABOLISM OF THYROID HORMONES

The rate of biosynthesis of thyroid hormones is regulated through biphasic control. Thyroid stimulating hormone (TSH) released from anterior lobe of pituitary activates (positive stimulatory mechanism) the biosynthesis while the plasma level concentration of thyroid hormones control their own release through a negative feedback mechanism. The conversion of inorganic iodide to thyroid hormones takes place through following steps :

(a) iodine uptake by the thyroid gland,

(b) oxidation of iodine and iodination of tyrosyl residues,

(c) formation of thyroxine and triiodothyronine, and

(d) release of thyroid hormones.

These steps are explained in detail below :

(a) Iodine uptake by the thyroid gland : The iodine content of diet reaches the circulation in the form of iodide. Under normal circumstances, blood contains 0.5 µg of iodide per 100 ml while iodide content of thyroid gland is estimated to be 10 µg/100 gm. Thus, thyroid gland contains about 20 times more iodide than, it is present in the blood. Hence active transport must be present to pump the iodide ions from the blood to the thyroid gland against such a strong electrochemical gradient. This transport system is found to be present in the form of Na^+-K^+-ATPase pump. A very small quantity of iodide also enters the thyroid gland by diffusion process.

The functioning of thyroid iodide transport pump (i.e. Na^+-K^+-ATPase pump) is under the control of both thyrotropin (TSH) and the plasma levels of thyroid hormones. Besides thyroid gland, other body compartments such as salivary glands, gastric mucosa, skin mammary gland and placenta also show interest in the accumulation of iodides.

In thyroid gland, the iodide ions are taken up from the blood and are accumulated in the acinar cells of the thyroid gland. The process is inhibited by number of other ions through competition for same transport system. These include perchlorate (ClO_4^-), perrhenate (ReO_4^-), pertechnetate (TcO_4^-) and thiocyanate (SCN^-). Since it is basically a Na^+-K^+-ATPase pump, cardiac glycosides tend to inhibit the process.

(b) Oxidation of iodide and iodination of tyrosyl groups :

In order to bring about iodination of the tyrosyl groups, iodide be must be first undergoes oxidation to either a free radical state or to iodinium ion (I^+). This oxidation is brought about by thyroperoxidase enzyme in the presence of hydrogen peroxide which acts as oxidizing agent. Thyroperoxidase enzyme has a molecular weight of 60,000 and is found to be present in membranes at or near the apical surface of thyroid cell. The hydrogen peroxide is formed just near its site of utilization by an NADPH dependent enzyme that resembles with cytochrome C reductases. After oxidation, the iodide ions are incorporated into tyrosine residues to form monoiodo and diiodo tyrosines. The tyrosine acceptors are provided by the protein called as apothyroglobulin (ATG). Iodination (or organification) occurs within seconds and is inhibited by thiourea drugs which inhibit the oxidation and incorporation of iodide to form MIT and DIT Units.

(c) Oxidative coupling of iodotyrosyls to form thyroxine and triiodothyronine :

Depending upon the relative quantities of mono and diiodotyrosine residues available in thyroid gland, an even or cross combination of iodotyrosyl residues occurs. Thyroxine is formed when coupling occurs between two diiodotyrosyl residues while triiodothyronine results due to coupling of one monoiodo and one diiodo-tyrosyl residues. Since same thiourea drugs also inhibit the coupling reaction, it is proposed that the same thyroperoxidase enzyme system is involved in coupling reaction. The system catalyzes the reaction probably by enhancing the formation of free radicals of iodotyrosyls. Thyroxine formation usually occurs to slightly greater extent than triiodothyronine formation. Thyroxine part contains about ¼th of the iodine in the thyroid part.

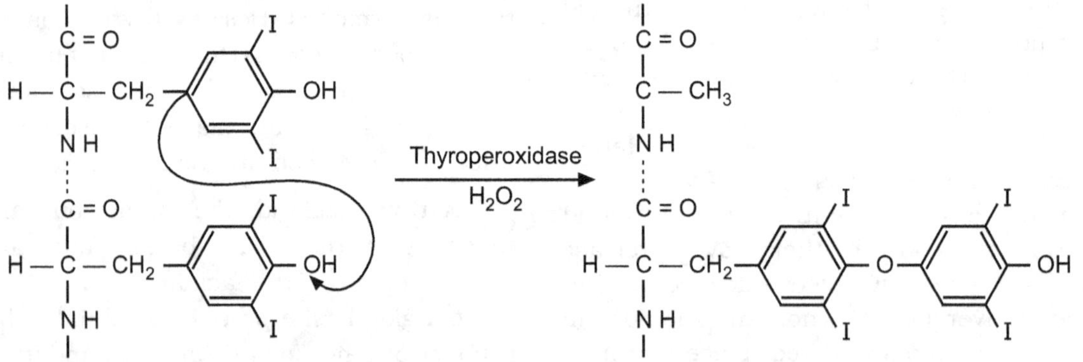

Fig. 15.3 : Coupling of two DIT units to form thyroxine

(d) Release of thyroid hormones :

Thyroxine and triiodothyronine are stored in the colloid through peptide linkages within the thyroglobulin molecule. Under the stimulation of thyrotropin (TSH), the thyroglobulin is removed from the colloid by endocytosis process. The endocytotic vacuoles then fuse with lysosomes containing several thiol endopeptidases (proteolytic) enzymes. When thyroglobulin is hydrolyzed within the phagolysosomes, the mono and diiodo tyrosines are also released along with thyroxine and triiodothyronine. Thyroxine and triiodothyronine are released into the circulation while the mono and diiodo tyrosines are retained in the gland where they are metabolized by deiodinase enzymes to release iodide and tyrosine residues. Both the iodide and tyrosines are recycled. The daily production of thyroxine and triiodo thyronine in thyroid gland is estimated to be about 70 mg and 25 mg respectively. However the major fraction (about 80%) of the total body triiodothyronine is obtained from deiodination of thyroxine in the peripheral tissues. The deiodinase enzymes were also found to be present in microsomal fraction of liver, kidney, muscle, heart and brain. The reaction may be assisted by NADPH. The 5'-deiodinases are blocked by propylthiouracil and a stable complex results. The triiodothyronine acts as a autoregulator of the synthesis of thyroid hormones. Besides this it also causes feedback inhibition of thyrotropin releasing hormone from hypothalamus.

15.3 PHARMACOKINETICS

After release from the thyroid gland, the thyroid hormones are circulated in the body by some carrier proteins. Thyroxine has higher affinity for thyroxine binding globulin which is a protein with molecular weight of about 63,000. It is synthesized in the liver. Its rate of synthesis is increased by estrogens (as in pregnancy) while it is decreased during androgen and glucocorticoidal therapy. Other carrier proteins include thyroxine-binding prealbumin and albumin. Due to their association with carrier proteins, bound form of thyroid hormones is not available for their physiological actions. Neither it can be metabolised nor it can be eliminated from the body. The bound form thus acts as the storage depot from which steady state supply of thyroid hormones occurs. This results in their longer biological half-life in the circulation. In the target organs, the dissociation of thyroid hormones from their carrier proteins usually occurs.

Thyroxine has the biological half-life of about 6 – 7 days. Due to the less affinity for carrier proteins, triiodothyronine has a shorter biological half-life of about 4 days. Liver is the principal site of metabolism for thyroid hormones. Most of the hormones are deiodinated. About 80% of the circulating thyroxine is deiodinated to triiodothyronine (T_3) or reversed triiodothyronine. The reversed T_3 is a very weak agonist.

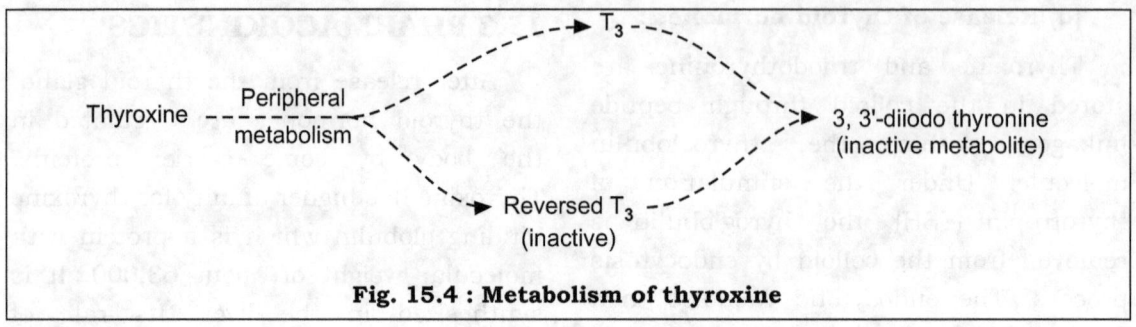

Fig. 15.4 : Metabolism of thyroxine

A small fraction undergoes deamination, decarboxylation or may remain even unchanged. During this metabolism, the diphenyl ether skeleton remains unaffected. They are excreted as glucuronides and as sulfates in the bile. This requires UDP-glucuronic acid and a microsomal glucuronyl transferases. Some fraction of hormone excreted in the bile is retained through enterohepatic reabsorption. In humans, about 30 — 40% of the thyroxine is excreted through the stool.

15.4 RELATIONSHIP BETWEEN THE GROWTH HORMONE AND THYROID HORMONES

Growth hormone induces the release of plasma insulin-like growth factor — I, which enhances the somatostatin release from hypothalamus. The increased somatostatin then cuts-off the release of thyroid stimulating hormone (TSH) from the adenohypophysis. Hence, the elevated plasma levels of growth hormone may induce hypothyroidism. The thyroid hormones T_3 and T_4 also are reported to activate the release of somatostatin which then suppress the release of TSH. This may be the mechanism through which thyroid gland exerts autoregulatory effect on the release of thyroid hormone from it.

15.5 PHYSIOLOGICAL ACTIONS OF THYROID HORMONES

Thyroxine and triiodothyronine are the principal thyroid hormones which are responsible for various physiological actions.

Below mentioned are some such physiological actions :

(a) Oxygen consumption, heat production and for the metabolism of carbohydrates, fats and proteins.

(b) Proper functioning of the gastrointestinal, cardiovascular, reproductive, skeletal and neuromuscular systems.

(c) Optimal functioning of catecholamines, antidiuretic hormone and glucocorticoids, and

(d) Normal growth and cell differentiation process.

(i) Growth and development : Proteins and enzymes play an important role in the growth and development of processes. Their synthesis is stimulated by the thyroid hormones which are capable of accelerating the synthesis of all forms of messenger, ribosomal and transfer RNAs. Thyroid hormones also participate in the synthesis of number of brain enzymes and in myelination of nerves. Hence, they are essential and plays very important role in normal mental functioning.

(ii) Calorigenic effects : Thyroid gland gets stimulated upon exposure to cold conditions. The released thyroid hormones then increase the basal metabolic rate of various organs including heart, liver, kidney and skeletal muscles. The metabolic rate of carbohydrates, fats and proteins also show marked increase. More rapid glycogenolysis occurs resulting into more oxygen consumption, heat production, mild hyperglycemia and sometimes glucosuria. The oxygen consumption further increases due to increased lipolysis and synthesis of triglycerides in adipose tissues. The patient often feels hot. Mental excitability and irritability have also been reported.

(iii) Cardiovascular effects : An increase in both the rate and force of heart contraction results in thyrotoxic patients. The cardiac stimulant effects of thyroid hormones are due to :

(a) an increase in the number of cardiac adrenoceptors, and

(b) hormone induced increase in the Ca^{++}-ATPase activity of myosin filament.

(iv) Miscellaneous effects :

Thyroid hormones, under certain conditions may enhance glycogenolysis, lipolysis and metabolism of cholesterol. Cholesterol is metabolized to bile acids.

15.6 MECHANISM OF ACTION

Most of the effects of thyroid hormones are brought about due to their nuclear binding in many cells. Thyroid hormones increase oxygen consumption, affects oxidative phosphorylation and results into swelling of mitochondria.

Thus, the increased oxygen consumption results primarily due to induction of mitochondrial α-glycerophosphate dehydrogenase. The role of thyroid hormones in the growth and development processes is due to their ability to induce more growth hormone production through transcription process. The protein synthesis is increased resulting into the positive nitrogen balance. However, hyperconcentration of thyroid hormones suppress protein synthesis and lead to the negative nitrogen balance.

15.7 THERAPEUTIC USES

Presently the marketed preparations of thyroid hormones usually contain either thyroglobulin or levothyroxine sodium. Levotriiodothyronine is also marketed as Liothyronine sodium. The 4 : 1 mixture of sodium salts of levothyroxine and liothyronine has been recently introduced. In the treatment of severe hypothyroidism, a synthetic TSH preparation may be given. These preparations are mainly used as hormone replacement therapy in the treatment of hypothyroidism, simple goiter, nodular goiter and cretinism. The success of therapy in cretinism is usually dependent upon the age at which treatment begins.

15.8 DISEASES OF THYROID GLAND

The functioning of thyroid gland is governed by the plasma concentrations of iodide, thyroid stimulating hormone (TSH) and the thyroid hormones. Vegetables, fruits, meat, fresh water fish, milk and eggs are good food sources of iodine. Under the influence of TSH, stimulation of all steps of thyroid hormone synthesis occurs resulting into increased vascularity of the gland. TSH induces an accumulation of glandular c-AMP through the activation of thyroid adenylate cyclase. Hypertrophy and hyperplasia of thyroid cells are also seen. These symptoms are mainly seen in thyrotoxicosis.

In thyroid hyperfunction, the elevated plasma levels of thyroid hormones suppress the release of TSH from adenohypophysis through the negative feedback mechanism. The rate of secretion of TSH is lowered down due to reduction in the number of TRH receptors in adenohypophyseal cells. Thyroid hyperfunctioning (i.e. hyperthyroidism) is characterised by thyrotoxicosis and sometimes by opthalmopathy (e.g. Graves' disease). The symptoms of thyrotoxicosis include excess heat production, increased motor activity, cardiovascular stimulation (i.e. sympathomimetic activation), loss of body weight, insomnia, anxiety, tension, increased peristaltic movements in GIT and osteoporosis due to Ca^{++} loss. Major forms of thyroid hyperfunction include Graves' disease and Plummer's disease. While hypothyroidism may result principally due to thyroid failure to release adequate quantities of free thyroid hormones. It may also arise secondary due to the suppression of pituitary or hypothalamic functioning. Major forms of hypothyroidism include myxedema, cretinism and juvenile myxedema.

(a) Simple goiter : The term *'goiter'* denotes any enlargement of thyroid gland. Normal secretion by thyroid gland needs an adequate intake of iodine. If the dietary supply of iodine does not meet the daily requirement, thyrotropin is released in higher concentration which results into the enlargement of thyroid gland. This enlarged thyroid gland is known as goiter (French word, goiter that means a neck). Depending upon the situations, goiter may be associated with over production, under secretion or with no alteration in the hormone secretion. Simple or non-toxic goiter results when an essentially normal thyroid gland secretes the hormones that do not meet the increased body demand during puberty, menstruation or pregnancy. The plasma level of TSH increases. This is either treated with exogenous thyroid hormones or by adding iodine to the diet, often in combination with salt.

(b) Myxedema : Thyroid hormone deficiency may result due to the spontaneous degeneration of glandular tissues, biosynthetic defects or impaired secretion of hormones. Myxedema is a case of severe hypothyroidism which causes the infiltration of the intercellular spaces of skin and muscle with mucopolysaccharide. The skin remains dry, the hair loose, the body colds, the pulse rate is low and the mental functions are impaired. The clinical manifestations of hypothyroidism attack virtually on every organ system. The metabolic rate falls and cholesterol starts acumulating in the blood. To face this situation, though higher amount of hormones are secreted, they are immediately inactivated by autoimmune reaction. When it happens specifically later in childhood, it is known as, juvenile myxedema which is characterized by failure of growth and development. Usual causes of myxedema are atrophy of thyroid gland, pituitary deficiency and overdoses with antithyroid drugs.

(c) Cretinism : It is the case of severe hypothyroidism in newborn that is unassociated with a goiter. The lack of proper growth and development in the newborn may be due to either inadequate iodine intake or the presence of goiterogenic factor in the mother. Cretins are abnormal dwarfs. It results in neurological, sexual, mental and physical retardations. The basal metabolic rate is depressed. It is characterized by multiple congenital defects. Myxedema and cretinism, both deficiencies are treated with thyroxine and triiodothyronine. The thyroid hormone replacement therapy is reliable and non-allergic.

(d) Graves' disease (diffuse toxic goiter) : Graves' disease, toxic adenoma, toxic multinodular goiter, thyroiditis are some of the diseases of thyroid gland where the gland secretes excessive quantities of hormones. A long acting thyroid stimulator has been isolated from the blood of some patients suffering from Graves' disease. This stimulator was found to be an antibody of immuno-globulin G type which acts through activating receptors for thyrotropin. This leads to a diffused enlargement of thyroid gland and excessive, uncontrolled production of T_3 and T_4. The thyrotoxicosis is also accompanied by ophthalmological changes which are brought about by the action of antibodies on retro-orbital tissues and eye muscles. The symptoms of thyrotoxicosis include, protrusion of the eyeballs with retraction of the upper lids, rise in metabolic rate but the body temperature is not usually raised (extra heat is lost by vasodilation and sweating). Metabolism of carbohydrates, fats and proteins increases, leading to an increase in the nitrogen excretion in the urine. This results in the general loss of body weight. Skeletal muscle weakness occurs along with tremors. Changes in the cardiovascular system (tachycardia, increase in the pulse rate and arrhythmia) have also been reported. The disease usually has been reported in young adults.

The patient should avoid the food having goitrogenic effect. These include cabbages, soyabeans, peanuts and mustard seeds. Hyperthyroidism may be treated by reducing the hyperactivity of the thyroid gland. This is achieved by partial thyroidectomy (surgical removal of some of the overactive part of thyroid gland) or by administration of radioactive iodine and / or antithyroid drugs. Since antithyroid drugs act by inhibiting the synthesis of thyroid hormones, greater quantity of TSH is released from pituitary gland in order to overcome the action of antithyroid drugs. This leads to thyroidal hypertrophy.

(e) Plummer's disease (toxic nodular goiter) : It is the case of hyperthyroidism in older patients. It gradually develops from long-untreated non-toxic goiter. It differs from Graves' disease in not having opthalmological changes in the patient.

15.9 DRUGS USED IN THE THERAPY OF HYPERTHYROIDISM

(a) Radioactive Iodine : Iodine treatment is probably the oldest method in the therapy of hyperthyroidism. In high concentrations, it exerts direct effect on the thyroid gland and reduces proteolysis and the release of thyroid hormone by inhibiting the stimulation of thyroid gland. It antagonizes both, thyrotropin (TSH) and glandular c-AMP actions on thyroid gland. This results into a decrease in glandular vascularity and reaccumulation of colloid in the follicles. It is usually administered in the combination with the table salt.

Out of several radioactive isotopes, ^{131}I isotope causes selective depression of thyroid activity by emitting β-rays which effectively destroy some of the secretory part of the gland. It has the biological half-life of about 8 days. This long biological half-life is due to its incorporation into the colloid of the follicles which acts as storage depot for it. Since thyroid gland absorbs most of the iodide supplied to the body, other organs remain unaffected. The effects of radiation are dose-dependent. Sodium iodide ^{131}I is a safe and effective compound which suppresses the thyroid function by radiation damage. It can also be used in the diagnostic tests to evaluate thyroid functioning.

(b) Antithyroid drugs : These drugs acts by inhibiting the synthesis of thyroid hormones. They exert immediate effect since they act at the first stage of iodine incorporation by the gland. They are categorised as :

    (i) Thioamides

    (ii) Aniline derivatives

    (iii) Polyhydric phenols.

    (iv) Ionic inhibitors

    (v) Miscellaneous agents.

(i) Thioamides : Thiourea and thiouracil derivatives are among the primary drugs to treat thyroid hyperactivity.

The methyl and propylthiouracil are effective drugs. They inactivate the peroxidase enzymes. Hence, the steps (i.e. iodination of tyrosine residues of thyroglobulin and coupling of iodotyrosines to form iodothyronines) catalysed by peroxidase are effectively inhibited by these drugs. Propylthiouracil also prevents the conversion of thyroxine to triiodothyronine in the peripheral tissues. However they do not influence the breakdown or release of thyroid hormones. Nausea, headache, loss or depigmentation of hairs, pain, skin rashes, agranulocytosis, and granulocytopenia are some of the adverse effects associated with these drugs. Other clinically used drugs from this category are methimazole and carbimazole. These drugs are useful in the treatment of hyperthyroidism, specifically in case of Graves' disease.

(ii) Aniline derivatives : These agents interfere some of the processes catalyzed by thyroid peroxidases, like iodide oxidation, organification and coupling of iodotyrosines. Examples include sulfathiazole, sulfadiazine, p-amino salicylic acid.

The carbutamide (an oral hypoglycemic agent) interferes in the uptake of iodine. It also interferes with the thyroid peroxidase activity.

(iii) Polyhydric phenols : The only clinical agent from this category is resorcinol. It possesses same mechanism of action like that of thioamides.

Resorcinol

(iv) Ionic inhibitors : These are all monovalent, hydrated anions and resemble in size with iodide ions.

They affect the power of thyroid gland to accumulate iodine by inhibiting the iodide transport mechanisms. Examples include, thiocyanate, perchlorate, fluoborate, fluosulfonate, difluophosphate etc. Potassium perchlorate sometimes may lead to fatal aplastic anaemia. This severely limits its therapeutic value.

(v) Miscellaneous agents :

(a) Lithium carbonate : Lithium appears to prevent the release of both hormonal and non-hormonal iodine from the thyroid gland. It is less preferred agent due to its adverse effects which include tremors with high risk of cardiac failure.

(b) Adrenergic blockers : Hyperthyroidism has some of the symptoms common with adrenergic overstimulation, due to this reason the adrenergic blockers are sometimes used in alleviating many of the signs and symptoms of hyperthyroidism, usually for short term treatment. Examples includes reserpine, guanethidine and propranolol. They may help in reducing tachycardia, tremor, anxiety, sweating and heat intolerance associated with hyperthyroidism.

15.10 PARATHYROID HORMONES (PARATHORMONES)

The four small parathyroid glands are attached to the surface of thyroid gland. These are yellow glandular bodies which weight from 0.05 to 0.3 gm. The normal function of parathyroid glands is to keep the blood calcium level constant. The normal blood calcium level is estimated to be 10 – 11 mg per 100 ml. Nearly half of it, is present in the plasma-protein bound form. The plasma calcium exists mainly as (i) ionized form (50%), (ii) protein bound form (45%) and (iii) organic bound form (5%). The unbound calcium elicits the physiological responses. Bone, kidney and intestine are the organs involved in the maintenance of blood calcium level with the help of three hormones :

(i) Calcitonin : It decreases plasma calcium level in hypercalcemia.

(ii) Parathyroid hormone and vitamin D : They increase plasma calcium level in hypocalcemia through their calcium mobilizing activity. This effect is exerted by the concerted action of parathyroid hormone and 1, 25-dihydroxy cholecalciferol. Parathormone also tends to increase the excretion of phosphate into urine (i.e. phosphaturic activity).

Above discussion shows clearly that homeostatic regulation of extracellular calcium and inorganic phosphate is principally governed by parathyroid hormone (PTH), calcitonin (CT) and various metabolites of vitamin D. The serum calcium level drops suddenly in parathyroidectomy, resulting into tetanic condition followed by convulsions.

Human PTH is a single-chain polypeptide composed of 84 amino acids, devoid of disulfide bonds and having a molecular weight of about 9,500. The biological activity was found to be associated with first 27 amino acid residues from N-terminal.

Synthesis and secretion of para hormones :

Preproparathyroid hormone is the precursor of 115 amino acids from which proparathyroid hormone (90 amino acids) is synthesised in the intracisternal space of endoplasmic reticulum through peptide cleavage. The parathyroid hormone is synthesized then in Golgi apparatus from proparathyroid hormone. The synthesized PTH is then trapped and stored in the secretory granules from where it is released into the circulation. However the prehormones of PTH are never released into the circulation.

The release of PTH is the c-AMP mediated effect. The negative inhibitory effect of plasma-calcium level on the release of PTH is because of lowering of c-AMP level in parathyroid cells by calcium. The circulating PTH has the biological half life of about 2 – 5 minutes. In circulation, it is partly carried out with the α-globin fraction of plasma proteins. It's metabolism to various peptide fragments occurs mainly in liver and major amount is excreted through the urine.

The parathyroid hormone acts mainly on kidney, bone and gastrointestinal tract and regulate the plasma calcium level by following ways :

(i) promoting absorption of calcium from gastrointestinal tract.

(ii) mobilising the calcium in the bones, and

(iii) decreasing calcium excretion in urine, faeces, sweat and milk.

The plasma calcium ion concentration in general and Ca^{++} ion concentration in parathyroid gland specifically appears to govern the rate of secretion of parathormone in the circulation. For example, in hypocalcemic condition, there is an increased release of parathormone resulting into hypertrophy and hyperplasia of parathyroid gland. Similarly in hypercalcemia, hypoplasia of the gland results due to decreased release of the hormone. The release of hormone is also slowed down under both hypermagnesemia and hypomagnesemia.

Physiological functions :

(1) Effect on bone : Osteolytic cells are responsible for the resorption of Ca^{++} and phosphate in the bone-forming osteoblasts, thus resulting into an increase in the resorption of Ca^{++} and phosphate.

(2) Effect on kidney : About 10,000 mg of calcium ions are reported to be filtered in the glomerular apparatus in a day. However only 100 mg of the amount is actually excreted through the urine. The rest of it is reabsorbed by the distal tubules of the kidneys back to the circulation. Both, PTH and active metabolite of the vitamin D (i.e. 1, 25 – dihydroxycholecalciferol) participate in this active reabsorption of Ca^{++}, probably by increasing the synthesis of carrier proteins for calcium ions. The renal excretion of magnesium and H^+ ions is also decreased by the hormone. While the renal excretion of phosphate, citrate, bicarbonate, sulphate and other amino acids is increased by parathormone. All these renal effects of the hormone are mediated through c-AMP present in the renal cortex.

(3) Effect on gastrointestinal tract : Parathyroid hormone tends to increase the rate of conversion of calcifediol to calcitriol in the kidney. This ultimately results in an increase in the intestinal absorption of calcium and phosphate ions from the diet.

15.11 HYPERPARATHYROIDISM

The condition is characterized by nausea, vomiting, anorexia, constipation (smooth muscle dysfunction), sketetal muscle weakness, muscle hypotonicity, anaemia, leukopenia and pychiatric manifestations. These symptoms may arise either due to hypersecretion of the hormone from the tumerous growth in the gland or to release of hormone like peptides from non-glandular sources. In such condition, it is known as primary hyperparathyroidism. However, when hypersecretion of parathormone occurs to correct low plasma calcium level under poor nutrition or renal diseases, the condition is known as secondary hyperparathyroidism.

In hyperparathyroidism, decalcification of bone leads to aching and pain. This is accompanied by skeletal abnormalities and deformation of bones. These symptoms become more evident in osteitis fibrosa generalisata.

The treatment of hyperparathyroidism involves the administration of low calcium diet and large volume of fluids. Sometimes surgical removal of adenomatous portion of the parathyroid gland can also be carried out.

15.12 HYPOPARATHYROIDISM

It is characterized by skeletal and smooth muscle spasm, tetany, convulsions, hypocalcemia, tachycardia, cataracts (due to increased concentration of Ca^{++} in the lens, since PTH reduces Ca^{++} concentration in lens) and psychiatric symptoms. This condition may arise either due to damage to parathyroid glands or due to some genetic default in the target tissues of calcium. (i.e. pseudohypoparathyroidism) The treatment consists of dietary supplementation of calcium ions and vitamin D.

15.13 THERAPEUTIC USES

Parathormone therapy is usually not used for any therapeutic purposes. However the hormone can be used to detect the cases of pseudohypoparathyroidism. It can also be used for the early control of tetany due to hypocalcemia.

15.14 CALCITONIN (THYROCALCITONIN)

Calcitonin, a hypocalcemic hormone, is a single-chain polypeptide composed of 32 amino acids. **Copp** in 1962, first reported its presence in the thyroid gland and he named it as Calcitonin. It has the molecular weight of about 3600. A cystine disulfide bridge is present between 1st and 7th amino acids. It is synthesized by the parafollicular "C" cells of the thyroid glands. These cells are also reported to be present in the parathyroid glands and thymus.

Calcitonin has opposite actions to that of parathyroid hormone. The decrease in the plasma calcium concentration occurs mainly due to hormone induced bone calcification along with inhibition of bone resorption process.

The plasma calcium level is thus maintained by the proper ratio of parathyroid hormone and calcitonin. Normally the blood contains < 100 pg of calcitonin per each ml. This concentration is governed by the plasma calcium level through the c-AMP system. In blood, the circulating calcitonin has the half-life of about 10 minutes. In comparison to men, the women usually have lower plasma level of calcitonin.

Mechanism of action :

(a) Calcitonin has opposite effects to that of parathyroid hormone, but it does not act as anti parathyroid hormone.

(b) Most of its effects are mediated through the accumulation of c-AMP in bone cells which are not attacked by PTH.

(c) The decreased bone resorption leads to an increase in the urinary excretion of phosphate while urinary excretion of Ca^{++}, Mg^{++} and hydroxyproline is decreased.

(d) It does not exert any effect on intestinal absorption of calcium ions.

For clinical uses, Salmon calcitonin is usually marketed in the strength of 200 MRC units/ml. Here one MRC unit is approximately equivalent to 4 µg of porcine calcitonin. Adverse effects include, nausea, swelling of hands and in some patients allergic reactions have also been reported due to formation of antibodies to calcitonin.

It is used clinically in various conditions (e.g. hyperparathyroidism, vitamin D intoxication etc.) characterized by hypercalcemia. It can also be used to increase bone resorption and bone formation in certain diseases.

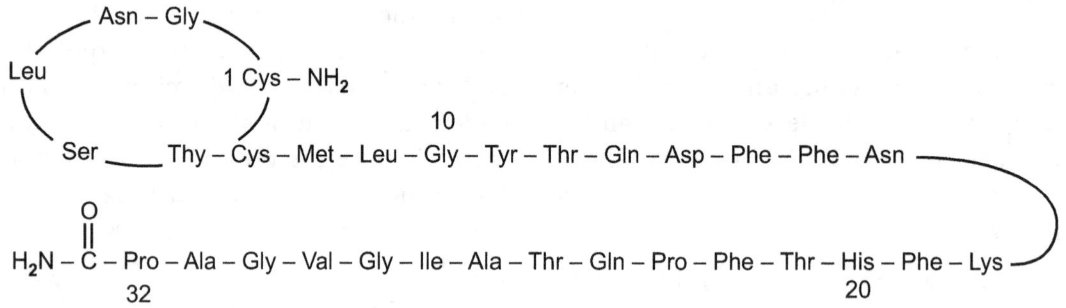

```
        ┌─ Asn – Gly ─┐
  Leu ─┤              │
        │   1 Cys – NH₂
        │              
  Ser ──┴── Thy – Cys – Met – Leu – Gly – Tyr – Thr – Gln – Asp – Phe – Phe – Asn ─┐
                                         10                                         │
   O                                                                                │
   ‖                                                                                │
  H₂N – C – Pro – Ala – Gly – Val – Gly – Ile – Ala – Thr – Gln – Pro – Phe – Thr – His – Phe – Lys ─┘
       32                                                                    20
```

Fig. 15.5 : Human calcitonin

SEX HORMONES

16.1 INTRODUCTION

The steroids form a group of structurally related compounds which are widely distributed in both, animals and plants. The structures of the steroids are based on the 1, 2-cyclopentenophenanthrene skeleton.

1, 2 - cyclopentenophenanthrene

A perhydrophenanthrene (rings A, B and C) is the completely saturated derivative of phenanthrene, while D is a five-membered cyclopentane ring.

The major therapeutic classes of steroids are :

(1) **Anti-inflammatory agents** : e.g. cortisone.
(2) **Sex hormones** : e.g. estrogen, progesterone and testosterone.
(3) **Oral contraceptives** : e.g. norethisterone.
(4) **Cardiac steroids** : e.g. digitoxigenin.
(5) **Diuretics** : e.g. spiranolactone.
(6) **Antibiotics** : e.g. fusidic acid.
(7) **Neuromuscular blockers** : e.g. pancuronium bromide.
(8) **Vitamin D precursor** : ergosterol.

Liver is the principal site for metabolism of almost every steroidal compound regardless of pharmacological activity associated with it. In liver, these compounds get inactivated mainly by oxido-reductive processes. The steroidal metabolites are mainly excreted through urine in the form of their glucuronide or sulfate conjugates. The extent or rate of their elimination in the urine can be studied in order to gain the information about endocrinological disturbances.

The principal metabolites for some of the steroidal hormones are enlisted in the Table 16.1.

The site of metabolic attack and the extent of metabolic transformation are governed by structural features of individual steroids. In the given skeleton, the more common metabolic transformations and their respective sites can be roughly represented in the Fig. 16.1.

16.2 SEX HORMONES

Estrogens, progesterone and testosterones the examples of human sex hormones. The sex hormones possess a steroidal nucleus and are produced in the gonads (i.e. testes in males and ovaries in the female). The main function of sex hormones is to regulate the ovulation in women and spermatogenesis in men. They are also responsible for the development of secondary sex characteristic, in both man and woman. The sex hormones are of three types :

(i) Estrogens (female sex hormones) e.g. 17-β-estradiol

(ii) Gestogens (corpus luteum hormone) e.g. progesterone, and

(iii) Androgens (male sex hormones) e.g. testosterone.

The biosynthetic pathways for androgens and estrogens utilize cholesterol as a starting material in the human body. The details about these biosynthetic pathways are represented in the Fig. 16.2.

Table 16.1 : Principal metabolites of some of the steroidal hormones in humans

Steroidal hormone	Site of attack	Principal metabolites
1. Cortisol	Oxidation of C-11 hydroxyl group Reduction of C-3 and C-20 ketone groups Reduction of Δ^4 - double bond	Pregnantriol – 11 – one
	Oxidation of C-11 hydroxyl group Oxidative cleavage of side chain at C-17	Andrenosterone
2. Estradiol	Oxidation of C-17 hydroxyl group Oxidation at C-16 atom	Estrone 16 – Ketoestradiol, 16 – Ketoestrone
3. Progesterone	Reduction of C-3 and C-20 ketone groups Reduction of Δ^4 double bond	Pregnandiol
4. Testosterone	Oxidation of C-17 hydroxyl group Reduction of Δ^4-double bond	Androstandione
	Oxidation of C-17 hydroxyl group Reduction of C-3 ketone group Reduction of Δ^4-double bond	Androsterone

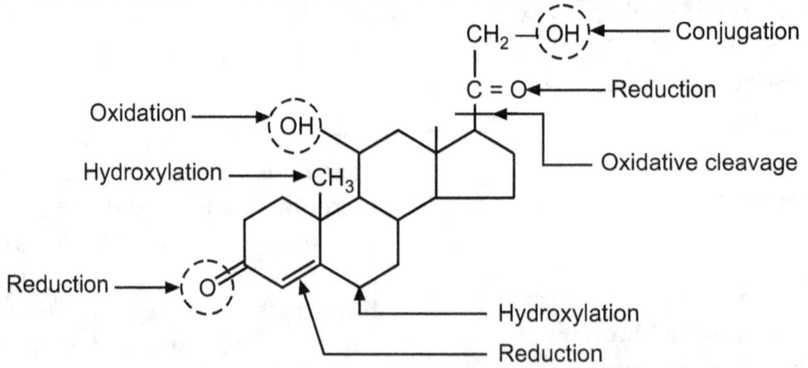

Fig. 16.1 : Probable sites and types of metabolic transformations in steroidal compounds

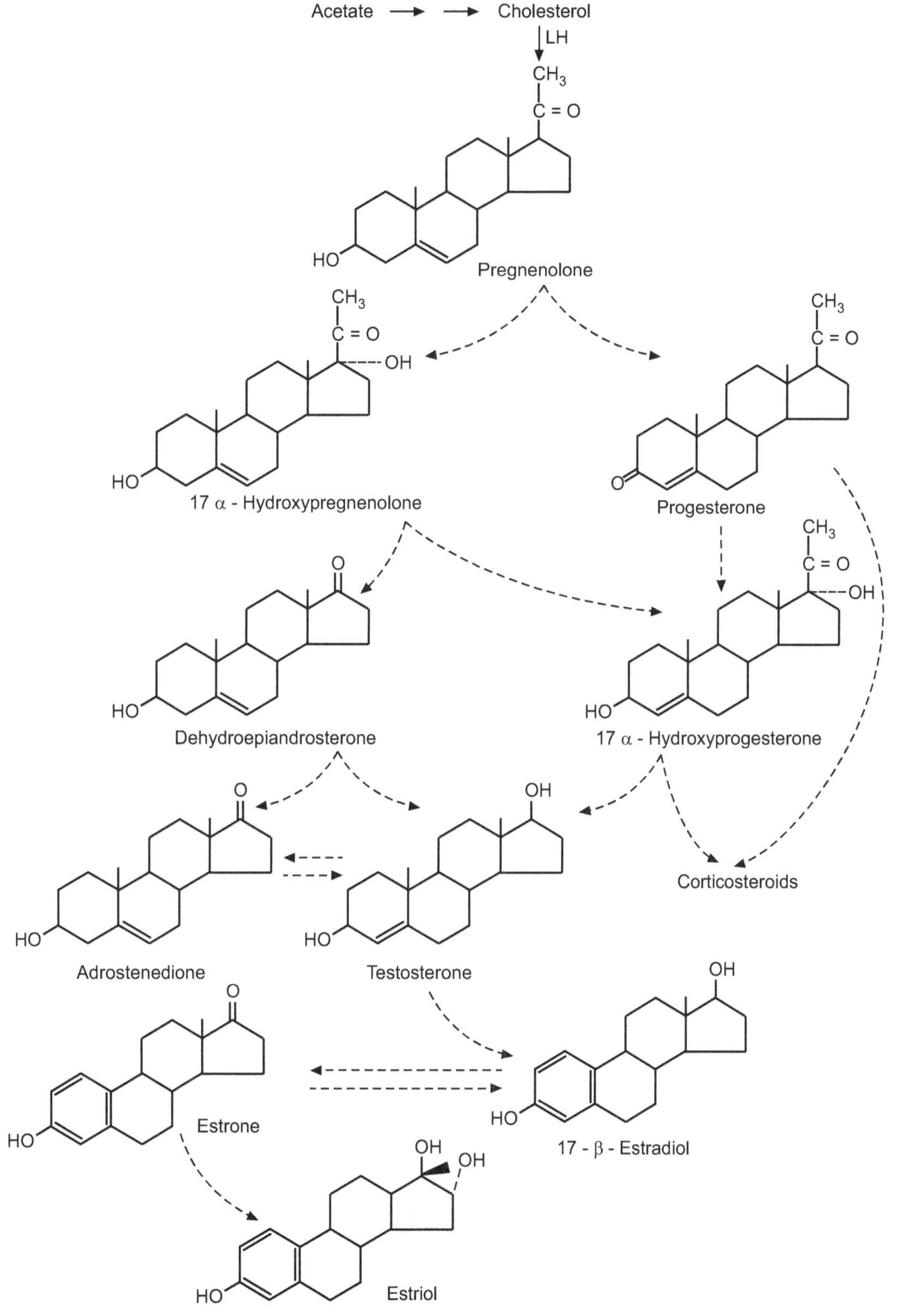

Fig. 16.2 : Biosynthetic pathways for sex hormones

Aminoglutethimide interferes in the biosynthesis of cholesterol. Hence the drug is used to treat breast cancer. The absence of enzyme systems necessary for the synthesis of other steroids (except progesterone) in the placenta and corpus luteum explains their inability to synthesize estrogens and androgens at required rate.

Though ovary is the main site of estrogen secretion in the female, other tissues like testes, adrenal cortex, liver, fat, skeletal muscles and hair follicles can also form significant quantities of estrogens from steroidal precursors. Estrogens are largely responsible for the development of secondary sex characteristics in women at puberty.

Progesterone is naturally secreted by corpus luteum and placenta. It is also synthesized by the adrenals and testes where it acts as a precursor for various steroidal hormones. The placental progesterone besides having its physiological effects on maternal organs, also acts as an important precursor for foetal corticosteroids and androgens.

Androgens or male sex hormones are synthesized from cholesterol in the testes and adrenal cortex. In the liver, androgens are formed from C-21 steroids. Small amounts are also secreted by the ovaries.

The plasma level concentration of all the sex hormones appears to be controlled through a negative feedback inhibitory mechanism by the following gonadotropic hormones : -

(i) Follicle stimulating hormone (FSH).

(ii) Luteinizing hormone (LH) or interstitial cell stimulating hormone (ICSH) and

(iii) Chorionic gonadotropin (CG; hormone of pregnancy).

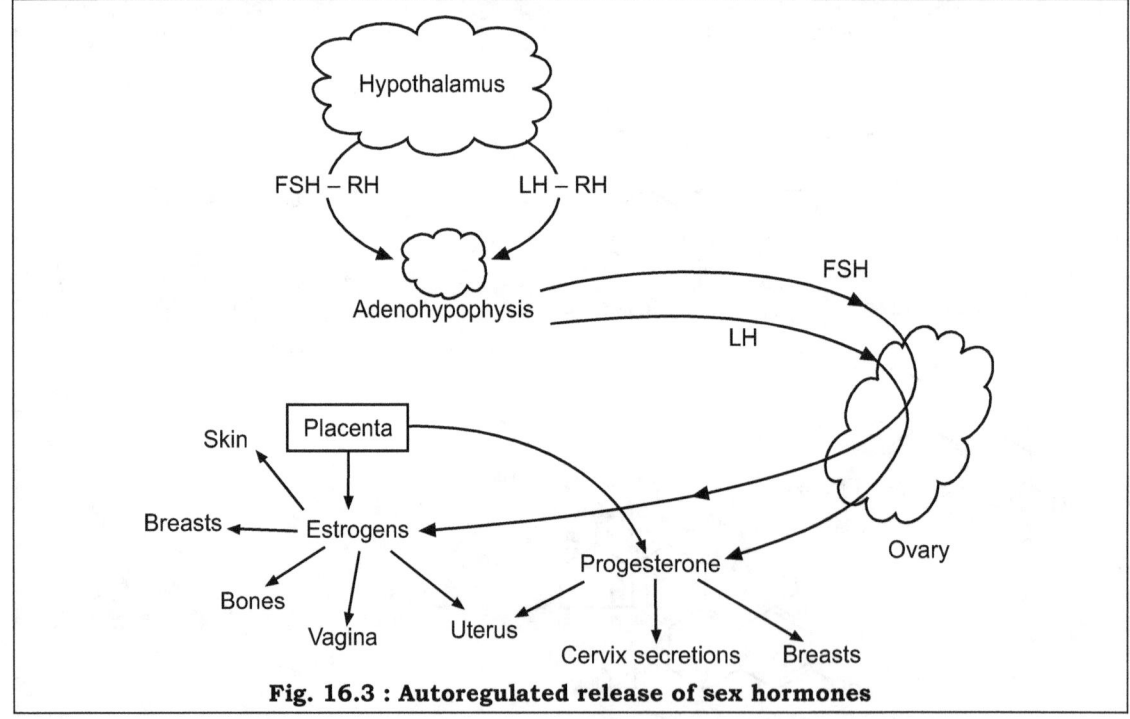

Fig. 16.3 : Autoregulated release of sex hormones

These hormones are secreted by adenohypophysis under the control of hypothalamus. For example, the release of FSH and LH from the adenohypophysis is governed by LH—RH (luteinizing hormone-releasing hormone) and FSH—RH secreted by hypothalamus.

In female, FSH provokes the maturity of one or more graphian follicles in the ovary while LH stimulates the ovulation and luteinization of the follicles. In male, FSH promotes sperm development or spermatogenesis by stimulating the seminiferous tubules while ICSH (LH) stimulates the interstitial leydig cells to secrete androgens. Autoregulation of the release of all these hormones occurs through feedback inhibitory mechanisms.

16.3 ESTROGENS

Estradiol, estrone and estriol are the examples of human estrogens. Their presence in the urine of a menstruating women was first reported by **Loewe** and **Lange** in 1926. This was followed by similar reports about their presence in the urine of pregnant women by Zondek in 1928.

These natural female sex hormones are not orally effective. Though they are well absorbed upon oral administration, they undergo extensive first pass hepatic metabolism. Hence synthetic estrogens like, ethinyl estradiol and diethylstilbestrol are usually orally used. In blood, the estrogens are circulated in the form of a complex with specific steroid binding globulins (SSBG). Liver is the principal site for their metabolism. Estriol (16 - α - hydroxylation), 2-hydroxyestrone and estrone sulfate are some of the principal metabolites of estrogens. The parent estrogens and their metabolites are excreted in the urine mainly in the form of glucuronide and sulfate conjugated products. The rate of formation and elimination of estrogens is specifically quite high during pregnancy. Hence urine of pregnant female is the rich source of estrogens.

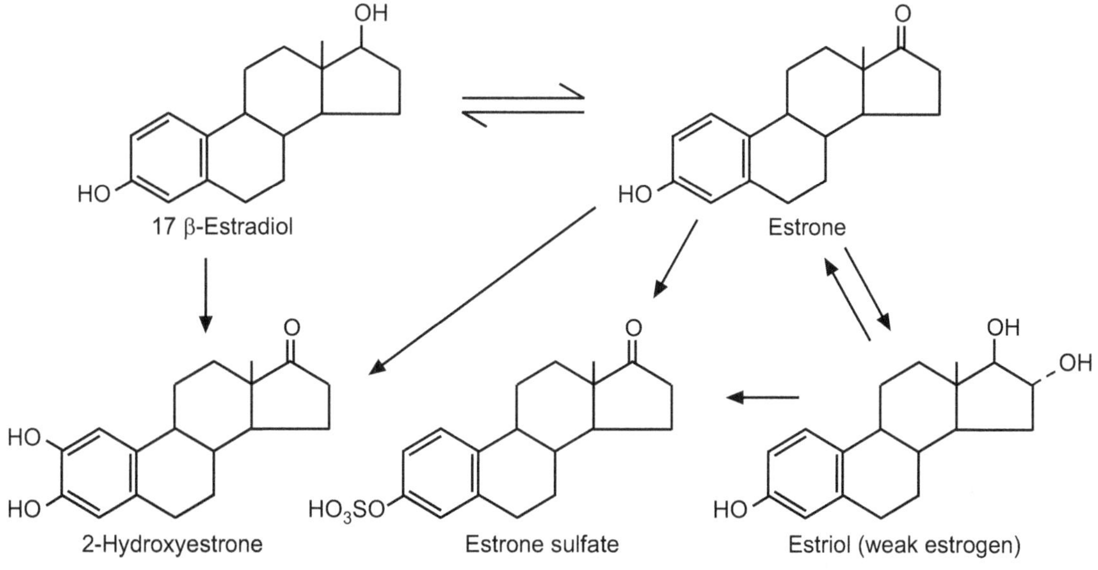

Fig. 16.4 : Metabolism of estrogens

Trans-diethyl stilbestrol ⇌ Trans-diethyl stilbestrol
(having resemblance with estradiol)

The 17-β-estradiol is the main human estrogen that exists in reversible equilibrium with the estrone and the estriol. The latter is a peripheral metabolite of estradiol and after getting converted to estrone sulfate, remains tightly bound to plasma albumin. Thus, estrone sulfate represents the most abundant form of estrogen circulating into the blood. Some part of the administered estrogen is also excreted through bile which is reabsorbed again by enterohepatic circulation.

17-β Estradiol is a potent estrogenic agent but it gets rapidly oxidized to estrone in the liver. Hence, it is orally less effective. Various modifications in the estradiol nucleus have been carried out in order to improve oral effectiveness and duration of action of the estrogens. For example, adding a 17 α-alkyl group (particularly 17 - α ethinyl derivative) to estradiol blocks the above mentioned oxidation and make the compound orally effective (ethinyl estradiol). Another estrogen synthesized by similar route is mestranol which is used in oral contraceptives.

The esterification of 17 β-hydroxy and 3 β-hydroxy functions also prolong the action where slow rate of absorption is due to low water solubility. 3-Benzoate; 3, 17-dipropionate; 17-valerate and 17-cyclopentyl propionate are the most commonly used ester forms. Slow hydrolysis of these esters releases the free estrogen over a prolonged period of time. Hence ester forms are termed as prodrugs.

According to **Schueler**, to have optimum, estrogenic activity a molecule should have a distance of about 8.55 A° between the groups that can form H-bonds (e.g. ketones, phenolic and alcoholic hydroxyl groups). The activity of non-steroidal estrogens can be explained on the basis of this hypothesis. For example, in diethylstilbestrol, this critical distance is 11.5°A and in estradiol, it is 10.9 A°. Many other potent steroidal and non-steroidal estrogens confirmed this hypothesis. The synthetic estrogens like, ethinyl estradiol and diethyl stilbestrol are relatively resistant to the metabolic biotransformations. Hence they are categorised as long acting estrogens.

Pharmacology :

(a) Estrogens are female sex hormones. They are responsible for the proper development of female reproductive system, specifically that of ovaries, fallopian tubes and uterine endometrium. They are essential for efficient ovulation and maintenance of uterine endometrium for the reception of sperm and for the fertilization process. The plasma estradiol concentration changes as per the need of each phase of menstrual cycle to bring about necessary modifications. For example, at the beginning of the cycle, concentration remains near about 50 pg/ml during ovulation phase; it ranges between 300 – 500 pg/ml while in the uteal phase, the level of estradiol is maintained (mainly by corpus luteum) near about 200 pg/ml. During menstrual cycle, estrogens bring about increased cervical watery secretions, and proliferation of the uterine and vaginal mucosa.

(b) Estrogens are responsible for the development of secondary sex characteristics in females at puberty. Some of the effects include breast development, pigmentation of the skin of the nipples, growth of axillary and pubic hairs and set up of femine behaviour. The fat deposition at appropriate places is the effect of estrogens that is assisted by pituitary hormones. Certain androgens (e.g. testosterone and androstenedione) are also secreted in ovaries which along with estrogens are responsible for rapid rate of growth of acne during puberty.

(c) Due to the negative feedback inhibitory mechanism exerted by estrogen on the release of FSH and LH, the secretion of FSH and LH will be lowered down by estrogens. In males, this may lead to a decrease in the gonadotropin-induced release of androgens. The consequences include inhibition of spermatogenesis and atrophic testicular tubules.

(d) Estrogens exhibit weak anabolic properties. Their administration is usually accompanied with retention of electrolytes (edema) and nitrogen (anabolic effect). They interfere in the fat metabolism resulting into a decrease in low density lipoprotein cholesterol and an increase in high-density lipoprotein. These metabolic effects are partly opposed by plasma progesterone.

(e) Several reports regarding carcinogenic effects of estrogens have appeared in the literature. The carcinogenic effects of estrogens are specifically reported on the organs like, uterus, testes, breast, bone and kidney. The risk of development of endometrial carcinomas is significant in both, premenopausal and postmenopausal women on estrogen therapy.

Mechanism of action :

Estrogens may act on the hypothalamic centre to inhibit the secretion of gonadotropin releasing factors thereby preventing pituitary gonadotropin secretion and the resultant ovulation. The transport of ova through the tubules is either accelerated or inhibited so that the ova enters the unprepared uterus where it is degenerated or expelled. Administered estrogens also alter the delicate balance of estrogen and progesterone required for implantation of the blastocyst in the endometrium. Estrogens also induce the formation of hormonal receptors necessary for the interaction of the different hormones. Most of the actions of estrogens are mediated by the activation of intracellular receptors. Intracellular receptors play a dominant role in the actions of the steroid hormones, thyroid hormones, vitamin A and vitamin D.

After entering the drug into the cell, it forms a complex with specific cytoplasmic binding proteins (receptors). The drug-receptor complex undergoes a conformational change and is thereby activated. This activated complex then enters the nucleus and releases the free drug. The drug molecule then binds to the acceptor sites on nuclear chromatin. Hence, some workers in the field consider chromatin as an actual or true receptor.

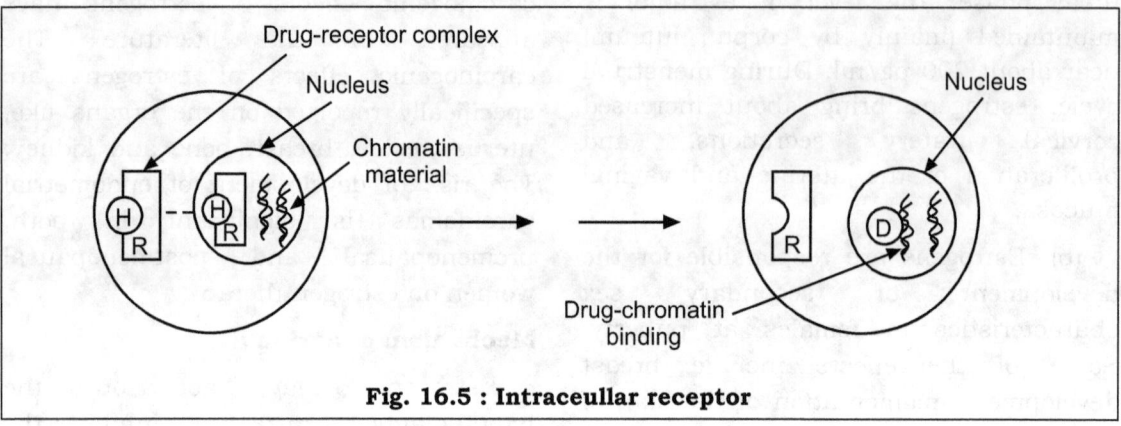

Fig. 16.5 : Intraceullar receptor

The drug binding to the chromatin material results into either an increase or decrease in the rate of production of certain types of RNAs that is reflected into alterations in the rate of synthesis of corresponding enzymes and other proteins. These alterations are thus ultimately projected into the biological response.

Adverse effects :

Mild adverse effects of estrogens include, nausea, vomiting, anorexia, mild diarrhoea, peripheral edema and thermogenic effect. These effects can be nullified by using low dose estrogens at the beginning of the therapy, that can be then gradually increased. At higher doses, estrogen induces anabolic effects by retention of nitrogen resulting into increase in the rate of synthesis of several proteins in the liver. These include, cortisol-binding protein, thyroxine-binding globulin, specific steroid binding globulin and renin substrate. This usually results into the disturbances in the plasma levels of cortisol, testosterone and thyroxine. A prolonged higher-dose estrogen therapy may lead to the hypertension along with vascular abnormalities and capillary fragility due to an increase renin substrate.

Therapeutic uses :

(i) In menopause, some of the symptoms are due to a decline in the secretion rate of estrogens by the ovaries. Estrogens thus can be used to replace the ovarian secretions during or after menopause.

(ii) Estrogens can also be used to prevent the process of bone resorption and loss of skeletal calcium ion in postmenopausal women. In the postmenopausal osteoporosis, the thinning and weakening of bones occur due to loss of both hydroxyapatite (i.e. calcium phosphate complexes) and protein matrix.

(iii) It is used as an ingredient for various oral contraceptive pills.

(iv) In larger doses, estrogens may be useful in women having metastatic breast cancer or in men having metastatic prostatic carcinoma. In prostatic carcinoma, the underlined cause is an increased androgen secretion. This cause can be suppressed by the administration of diethylstilbestrol.

(v) Estrogens are useful agents in the treatment of abnormal uterine bleeding.

16.4 ANTIESTROGENS OR OVULATION STIMULANTS

This is a group of drugs having diversified structures having an ability to inhibit various actions of estrogens. Their antiestrogenic activity (weak estrogenic activity) results into a direct effect on increasing FSH and LH production by the hypothalamus. This is mainly due to the blockadge of feedback inhibitory mechanism of ovary produced estrogens. As a result of the increased levels of FSH and LH, there occurs the stimulation of ovulation. These agents therefore are useful in the treatment of infertility in women. The excessive proliferation in ovaries induced by these drugs results into enlargement of the ovaries and formation of ovarian cysts. The increased levels of gonadotropins are thus responsible for ovulation and sustained function of corpus luteum. However these effects get terminated as soon as the therapy is discontinued.

Antiestrogens exert their effects mainly by competitively blocking estrogen receptor sites. Due to their higher affinity and less intrinsic activity, neither they evoke any pharmacological responses nor they allow endogenous estrogens to exert their effects. The clinically useful antiestrogens include clomiphene, ethamoxy-triphetol, danazol, tamoxifen etc.

Adverse effects of antiestrogens include, nausea, vomiting, depression, visual disturbances and enlargement of ovaries.

These agents are mainly used in the treatment of infertility and endometriosis in women. The dose fluctuations may result into hyperstimulation of ovaries; the multiple cyst formation increases the probability of multiple births. However, a long term treatment with clomiphene may cause inadequate cervical secretions (due to antiestrogenic effect) or sperm migration may become difficult.

Autoregulation of the hormonal secretion from hypothalamus, pituitary gland and ovaries is important for proper ovulation process. For example, the secretion of FSH and LH (which is necessary for ovulation) from pituitary gland is controlled by the release of a decapeptide, LH-RH from the hypothalamus. Thus ovulation can be stimulated by administration of LH and FSH. However animal preparations of these gonadotropins either have not been effective (due to species differences) or may cause antigen-antibody interactions. Therefore a limited amount of human LH and FSH extracts which is known as human menopausal gonadotropin (HMG) is tested and was found to stimulate ovulation effectively. HMG is usually administered with human chorionic gonadotropin (HCG) which has LH-like activity in women having functional ovaries to stimulate ovulation. While in men, they stimulate spermatogenesis. HMG should be used with caution because ovary enlargement is quite common. Abdominal pain has also been reported. Due to the stimulation of growth in many follicles, estrogen secretion from the follicles increases which is responsible for fever and arterial thrombosis.

Alternatively LH-RH and its stimulatory analogs can also be used to induce ovulation. However their administration leads to alterations in the ovum transport process through oviduct and may cause endometrium changes resulting into improper implantation of the blastocyst. The development of fertilized ovum is disturbed if they are administered during pregnancy, mainly due to the hyperstimulatory effects.

Analogues of LH-RH include :

(a) **Potent agonist of LH-RH**

D — [Ala]^6 — des — [Gly]^{10} — Pro^{19} — ethylamide — LH — RH

(b) **Potent antagonist of LH—RH**

(i) [D — Phe^2 — D — Leu^6] — LH — RH

(ii) [des — His^2 — D —Leu^6] — LH — RH and

(iii) [D — Phe^2 — D — Phe^6] — LH — RH

16.5 PROGESTERONE AND ITS ANALOGS (Progestins)

Progestins is a class of compounds having progestational activity. Examples include derivatives of progesterone and 19-nortestosterone. Though 19-nortestosterone may exhibit androgenic side-effects, its main activity remains progestational only.

Progesterone

19-nortestosterone

The 19-nortestosterone derivatives have marked ovulation inhibiting activity and thus can be used as oral contraceptive agents. Their weak androgenic property can be reduced by the suitable structural modifications.

At the beginning of this century, anti-ovulatory property associated with corpus luteum had been identified. The presence of active principle, progesterone was recognized and its isolation in the pure form from corpus luteum was reported in 1934. Its ability to inhibit ovulation was then confirmed by some experiments on rabbits.

The corpus luteum which is formed from the ruptured follicle after ovulation, starts secretion of progesterone. With development of corpus luteum, secretion rate of progesterone rises from 50 µg/day to about 1 – 2 mg/day. Progesterone is responsible for the maintenance of vascularity of uterine endometrium. The corpus luteum continues the secretion of progesterone to suppress the release of FSH and LH by feedback inhibitory mechanism and thus prevents further ovulation during pregnancy. It also inhibits the release of oxytocin which causes uterine contractions. Thus, progesterone prevents the spontaneous abortion of the implanted blastocyst. For this reason, it is often termed as the pregnancy hormone.

The natural hormone, progesterone has a very low potency when administered orally as it gets extensively metabolized during first pass hepatic circulation. Hence, various structural modifications have been done on progesterone nucleus in order to increase its oral effectiveness. These orally active progesterone derivatives (progestins) possess varying degrees of estrogenic, androgenic and progestational activities. While very few derivatives have purely progestational property. Some derivatives are metabolized to estrogens while some analogs may exhibit antiestrogenic activity. These synthetic progestins can generally be divided into two main classes :

(a) 17 α-hydroxy progesterone analogs and (b) 19-nortestosterone derivatives.

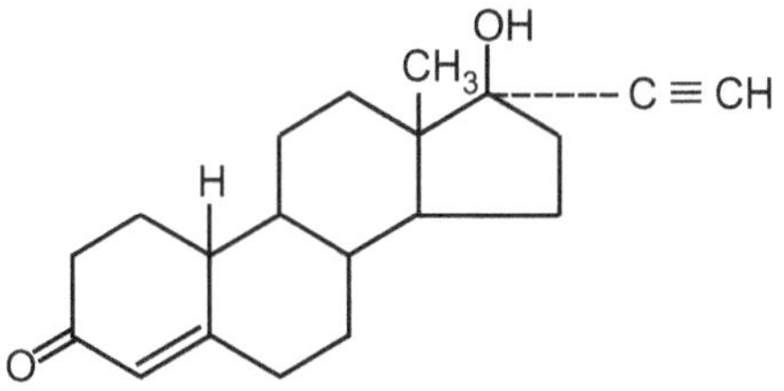

Norethisterone

However both the parent compounds, i.e. 17 α-hydroxy progesterone and 19-nortestosterone are orally inactive agents. Besides this, in the estrenol series (characterized by the absence of C-3 ketone function), the progestational activity (e.g. lynestrenol) is mainly influenced by the functional group present on C-17. Progestational activity may be further enhanced by introducing a double bond between carbons 6 and 7 in 6 - substituted - 17 α - hydroxy progesterone derivatives. Examples include, chlormadinone acetate which is a purely progestational agent of high potency.

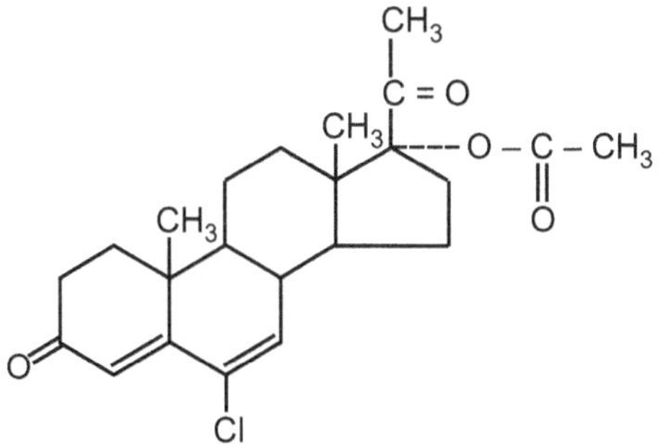

Chlormadinone acetate

Yet another compound, cyproterone acetate which is an antiandrogenic agent, exhibits potent progestational activity.

Most of the clinically used progestins (e.g. ethinodiol diacetate, norethynodrel, norgestrel) upon *in-vivo* metabolism get converted to norethisterone. Hence with some exceptions, it was concluded that the activity of many of the synthetic progestins is exhibited only after its *in-vivo* conversion to norethisterone. Some of these progestins exist in their recemic form, but the activity lies in most of the cases entirely with the levo form, e.g. norgestrel.

Pharmacokinetics :

Progestational activity appears to be restricted to molecules with a steroidal nucleus. Progesterone is not effective orally probably owing to its extensive degradation during its first pass hepatic circulation. Its half-life in plasma ranges from 3 to 90 minutes where it circulats by binding with sex steroid binding globulins. It is partially stored in body fats and may be utilized in various tissues as a precursor for biosynthesis of estrogens, androgens and corticosteroids. The metabolism of progesterone is extremely rapid and it can be biotransformed to many other steroidal hormones. In the liver, the side-chain at position 17 may be removed and it is mainly excreted as conjugates of 5 β-pregnanediol (i.e. pregnanediol glucosiduronidate) through urine. The measurement of urinary excretion of this metabolite can be used as an index of corpus luteum and placenta activity. Any premature drop in its urine level of a pregnant women may be considered as a warning signal of possible abortion.

Pharmacology :

(1) In menstrual cycle, progesterone is active if the endometrium is rich in the progesterone-receptors which are increased in number during the proliferate phase under the influence of estradiol. At the end of the secretory phase, the progesterone receptors are less numerous than those at the beginning of the proliferate phase. Both estrogens and progesterone act in a synergistic way for the development and maintenance of uterine endometrium in a condition favourable for implantation and growth of fertilized ovum. In this regard, progesterone has a biphasic feedback effect on ovulation. i.e. first it stimulates ovulation process and effects of estrogens. Following this initial phase, however, ovulation and estrogenic effects are inhibited by progesterone.

(2) The synthesis of progesterone from corpus luteum is governed by luteinizing hormone which exerts this regulatory effect through c-AMP. Progesterone acts on both, the endometrium (inner mucous lining of uterus) and the myometrium (muscle mass of uterus). It induces the secretory phase in endometrium during which the endometrial glands grow and secrete large amount of carbohydrates (glycogen) that will possibly be utilized by the fertilized ovum as a source of energy. The modification of endometrial stroma occurs. In case of myometrium, progesterone stops the spontaneous rhythmic contractions of the uterine muscles to prevent abortion. These effects are assisted by estrogens which help the progesterone to streamline uterine changes in the proper direction. Thus progesterone is necessary for maintenance of the uterus for implantation of a fertilized ovum and for the maintenance of pregnancy. The immunological rejection of foetus is also inhibited by progesterone.

(3) After fertilization of the ovum, the functioning of corpus luteum is maintained by the chorionic (placental) gonadotropin (CG) released by developing trophoblast into maternal circulation. The continued functioning of corpus luteum thus results into sustained release of progesterone which helps to maintain the growth and proliferation of uterine lining. Thereafter, placenta takes over the charge to release large amounts of estrogens and progesterone upto the time of delivery.

(4) Estrogens induce the release of thin and watery cervical secretions. While progesterone causes alteration in the nature of cervical secretions resulting into viscid and thick cervical mucous which is very resistant to sperm migration. Progesterone also alters fallopian tube secretions.

(5) The proliferation of acini of mammary glands occurs during pregnancy under the influence of progesterone and estrogens. After the delivery, the drop in the progesterone and estrogen level results into lactation.

(6) Progesterone has a thermogenic effect.

(7) It potentiates the synthesis of one specific oviduct protein, inhibin, having a molecular weight of approximately 20,000 dattons which is usually present in testes and ovarian follicular fluid. Inhibin suppresses the release of both FSH and LH.

To induce above effects, progesterone may require gene activation and transcription of chromosomal information through the stimulated m-RNA synthesis.

The intra cellular receptor activation by progesterone usually leads to an increase in the rate of synthesis of ovalbumin and inhibin.

Therapeutic uses :

Progesterone or progestins are commonly used for the treatment of variety of gynaecological conditions.

These include :

(i) Irregular uterine bleeding resulting due to endometrial hyperplasia.

(ii) Dysmenorrhea

(iii) Endometriosis

(iv) Endometrial carcinomas

(v) Habitual abortions

(vi) Premenstrual tension, and

(vii) Infertility in women.

Besides these uses, progestins are important constituents of oral contraceptive pills. The common adverse effects with progestin therapy are nausea, vomiting, drowsiness, edema etc.

16.6 ANDROGENS OR MALE SEX HORMONES

Androgens or male sex hormones are synthesized from cholesterol in the testes and adrenal cortex. Small amounts are also secreted by the ovary.

The growth and development procedures of male gonads are similar to those as seen in female. The hypothalamus controls the adenohypophysis through the same releasing factors as for the females, namely FSH-RF and LH-RF. These factors then bring about the release of FSH and LH (LH in male is called as interstitial cell stimulating hormone, ICSH) from the adenohypophysis.

FSH promotes sperm development or spermatogenesis by stimulating the seminiferous tubules. On the other hand, ICSH stimulates the interstitial leydig cells to secrete androgens. The released androgens have a feedback inhibitory effect on the hypothalamus-pituitary system that regulates gonadotropin secretion. This feedback inhibitory effect is exerted partly by activation of androgenic receptors and partly by activation of estrogenic receptors by estrogen that is synthesized peripherally from testosterone.

Testosterone

The active androgenic principle of testes is testosterone. An adult person secretes about 3 — 10 mg of testosterone per day which is utilized for the proper functioning of prostate and seminal vesicles. It has two main activities :

(a) Androgenic or male sex characteristics promoting activity :

It includes normal development, functioning and maintenance of male sex hormones and sexual characteristics. The thickening of vocal cords is induced. The pilosebaceous system is involved in the growth of hairs at ears, chest, axillary and pubic sites. The growth of mustache is also governed by the pilosebaceous system. Testosterone plays a vital role in the proper functioning of this system.

(b) Anabolic or muscle building activity :

It causes nitrogen retention (i.e. increase in protein synthesis) and thus promotes laying down of new tissue. It also stimulates the thickness, rise and linear growth of the bones. Hence it helps in the development of skeletal musculature and emotional get up of the male type. Depending upon the predominance of activity, these compounds can be categorised as :

(i) Compounds with prominent androgenic activity (i.e. androgens), and

(ii) Compounds with prominent anabolic activity (i.e. anabolic agents).

It would be highly desirable but may be impossible to separate these two activities totally. The only compound with purely anabolic but no androgenic activity is testolactone. It is used in the treatment of breast cancer.

Testolactone

Pharmacokinetics :

Testosterone is not effective orally because metabolic changes occur at 17-β-oxygen which is important for its attachment to the receptor site. An extensive first pass hepatic metabolism is reported with testosterone. Hence 17 α-alkyl groups are incorporated to prevent this metabolic attack which renders the compound orally active. Upon absorption into the circulation, testosterone gets firmly bound to sex steroid binding globulins, SSBG. The extent of this binding is increased by estrogens, thyroxine or in cirrhosis.

Testosterone metabolizes mainly to 17-ketosteroids (e.g. androsterone, etiocholanolone etc.) along with many other minor metabolites. In the target tissues of biological actions, testosterone exerts its physiological activity only after its reduction to dihydrotestosterone by cytosol 5 α-reductase enzyme which then activates the androgenic receptor sites to bring about its physiological actions. The various metabolites are then excreted through the urine mainly in the form of their sulfate or glucuronide conjugates.

Adverse effects :

(i) During long term treatment, musculinization in women occurs. This leads to the growth of facial hair, deepening of the voice and menstrual irregularities (if gonadotropin secretion is disturbed).

(ii) In both sexes, retention of water associated with electrolytes leads to gain in body weight in short term treatment but may cause edema if therapy is extended for long time. Edema becomes troublesome especially in the treatment of neoplastic diseases.

(iii) The 17 α - alkyl androgens may cause accumulation of bile in the biliary capillaries of the central portion of the hepatic lobules without any obstruction in the larger ducts. Hence if possible, their use should be avoided in patients with hepatic dysfunction.

(iv) On long term treatment, anabolic steroids can suppress endogenous production of testosterone and may lead to impotence after their withdrawal.

(v) They are incompatible with many drugs.

Therapeutic uses :

(a) They are given in the patients suffering from improper functioning of Leydig cells, faulty spermatogenesis and to restore and to maintain secondary sexual characteristic in boys with delayed puberty.

(b) They increase the rate of protein synthesis and promote laying down of the new tissues. Hence they can be used as anabolic or muscle building agents.

(c) In the treatment of dysmenorrhea and metastatic breast cancer.

(d) Since they stimulate erythropoietin synthesis, they can be used in relatively large doses to treat aplastic anaemia.

(e) Due to their effect on the growth of the bones, they can be used to increase the height of boys and girls.

16.7 ANTIANDROGENS

Compounds which are capable of antagonising the androgenic action are known as antiandrogens. They do so by the following mechanisms :

(a) They may compete with androgens for receptor sites in the tissues, e.g. cyproterone. It has potent progestational and antiandrogenic potential. It suppresses gonadotropin release.

However it is less favoured due to its carcinogenic property.

(b) They may inhibit the release of gonadotropins, e.g. oestrogens, progestins and testosterone itself.

(c) They may have pharmacological actions on the target tissues just opposite of those exerted by the androgens, e.g. estrogens.

The possible areas of clinical applications for antiandrogenic agents are:

(i) In the treatment of cancer of prostate, and

(ii) As male contraceptives.

Spiranolactone also has been found to have some antiandrogenic actions.

16.8 OVULATION

Today, the problem of severe concern is an ever increasing rate of population which is increasing in the exponential way. Every past second is associated with hundred of new arrivals in the word. On the other hand, due to several advancements in science and availability of so many life saving drugs, the death rate is comparatively negligible. The resulting population explosion severely damaged our economical, environmental and social aspects. The realization about possible consequences of population explosion was then reflected into the development of new field which can be called as *'antifertility research'*.

The need of birth control was first realized by **Margaret Sanger** who started working on this subject from 1910 to 1950, during which she tried to generate awareness about this problem in medical profession. She was later honoured for this work by the title *'Mother of Birth Control'*. The government started financing the research projects upon reproduction. As a result, intravaginal spermicidal agents were designed during 1950s. The next decade saw the development of oral contraceptive pills. At the same time, an independent work on antifertility agents resulted in the designing of a number of postcoital contraceptives and abortifacients. The introduction of safe and efficacious oral contraceptive agents was made during 1970s. This was then followed by designing of hormone-releasing intrauterine devices. The events of normal mammalian reproductive process serve as the basis for development of all these antifertility measures. These measures were found to be useful not only to avoid conception but also in the termination of unwanted pregnancies.

In order to understand the designing and mechanism of action of all these antifertility agents, the knowledge about the key events in the female reproductive process is necessary. Estrogens, progesterone and testosterone are the human sex hormones whose activities appear to be controlled by the following gonadotropic hormones.

(i) Follicle stimulating hormone (FSH), and

(ii) Luteinizing hormone (LH).

FSH and LH are secreted by the adenohypophysis under the control of FSH-RF and LH-RF hormones released from hypothalamus. The key event in the female reproductive process is ovulation.

There are about 500,000 primary follicles present in the both ovaries of the newborn. However about 400 ova are released during a woman's reproductive career. At the start of the menstrual cycle, plasma concentrations of estrogens and progesterone are low. Under the influence of LH-RH, FSH-RH or Gn-RH, the adenohypophyses releases FSH and LH. As a result, several graffian follicles each containing an oocyte, start enlarging and begin developing more rapidly than each others. Thus primary follicle may get converted to secondary and then to tertiary follicle during this follicular proliferative stage.

(a) Follicular phase :

However after few days, only one follicle continues the development process resulting into simultaneous suppression of growth of other follicles. The secretion of estrogen by the granulosa cells of major follicle may be responsible for suppression of FSH release and inhibition of growth of other follicles. The secretion of FSH is further suppressed by the release of inhibin from the major follicle. Inhibin was found to be peptide of molecular weight of about 20,000. Other follicles of retarded growth then undergo atresia. While further growth of the major tertiary follicle converts it into a mature graffian follicle. This follicle secretes progressively increasing concentrations of estrogens which are responsible for causing an increase in thickening and vascularity of the endometrium. This phase which is known as follicular phase or proliferative phase thus continues from day 1 to day 14 of the menstrual cycle. It is characterized by increased release of estrogen from the developing graffian follicle. Thus in summary, FSH induces the growth of primary follicles and initiates the formation of LH-receptor sites in the theca cells and the granulosa layer of the developing follicle. The estrogen secretion in the granulosa layer of the follicle is then initiated through the activation of these receptor sites by the circulating LH. The secreted estrogens then lead to

(a) suppression of the release of FSH.

(b) suppression of the growth of other follicles, and

(c) proliferation and vascularization of uterine endometrium and development of estrogen and progesterone receptor sites in it.

Estrogen besides suppressing FSH secretion also suppress the release of LH. However at high concentration, estrogen potentiates the release of LH.

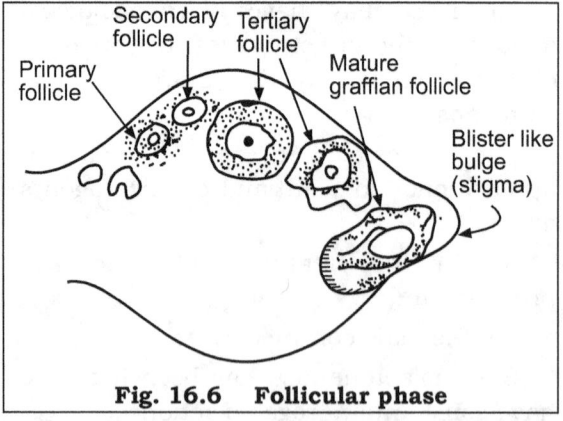

Fig. 16.6   Follicular phase

During follicular phase, the tertiary follicle steadily increases in its size. At one point of the ovary, blister like bulge appears. Under the influence of estrogens, thin and watery vaginal and cervical secretions increase which facilitate the sperm migration at the time of ovulation and total endometrial reconstruction begins. Estrogens induce a marked mitotic activity causing an increase in the number of cell-layers of the vaginal epithelium.

(b) Ovulatory phase :

Further thinning of the stigma wall occurs due to ever increasing size of the mature graffian follicle. On about 14th day of the cycle the increasing concentration of estrogens in the blood exerts action upon hypothalamus to cause a sudden but short-lived increase in plasma concentrations of LH and FSH. This is associated with an increase in follicular pressure due to increased contraction of smooth muscles in ovary causes graffian follicle to rupture. The released matured ovum then begins its journey along the oviduct to the uterus.

After the ovum is released, the ruptured follicle undergoes structural changes. The cyst collapses and the lining cells undergo lutenization. The cells get arranged in a compact way through which further enlargement of the cells is inhibited. Under the influence of LH, the empty follicle changes to corpus luteum which secretes progesterone and smaller amounts of estrogens. Life span of corpus luteum during non-pregnant cycle averages to about 11 days. If fertilization occurs, the developing placenta releases human chorionic gonadotropin (HCG) which helps to maintain the functioning of corpus luteum (i.e. secretion of progesterone) till placenta takes over the charge.

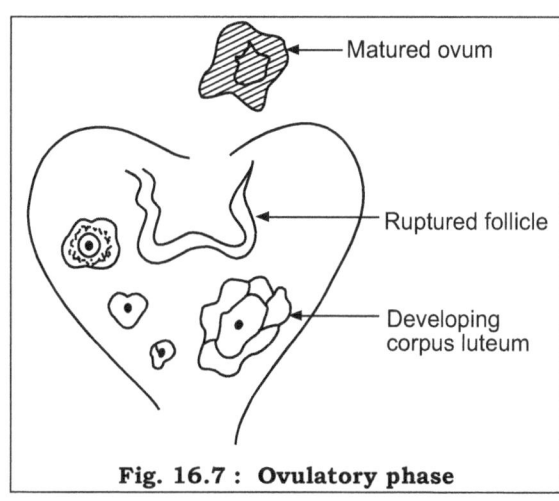

Fig. 16.7 : Ovulatory phase

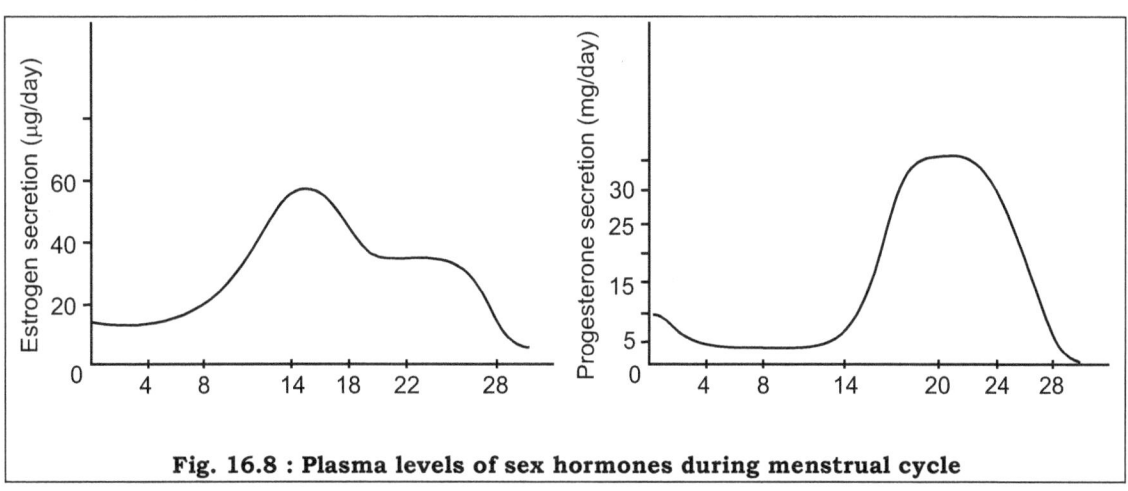

Fig. 16.8 : Plasma levels of sex hormones during menstrual cycle

(c) Luteal phase :

This phase is characterized by the formation of the corpus luteum which continues the secretion of progesterone. Under the combined influence of estrogens and progesterone, the uterine endometrium develops further. Glands become elongated tortous and full of mucous. Other cells of endometrium increase in size and number. The blood vessels become dilated and there is some exudation of fluid into the uterine cavity. At this time, the ovum reaches to the uterus. Thus, the phase prepares endometrium to receive and to imbed a fertilized ovum.

If fertilization of ovum does not take place upto about 26th day of the cycle, corpus luteum degenerates due to the action of prostaglandin $F_{2\alpha}$, which is secreted by the uterine endometrium. This results into decreased progesterone secretion which causes the superfacial layers of the endometrium to break down. Four to five days before menstruation, endometrial growth ceases. The blood flow decreases and dehydration of stroma occurs.

On about 28th day, the concentrations of estrogens and progesterone become to low to maintain the vascularisation of the endometrium. The necrotic endometrium gets fragmented and the surface epithelium breaks. The shed endometrium then leaves the body together with mucous and blood from the ruptured endometrial gland and blood vessels in the form of menstrual flow. Menstrual cycle varies from 19 days to 38 days in normal women. However in all the cases, a fairly constant interval of about 14 days can be seen between ovulation and menstruation. The menstrual volume usually ranges from 25 — 30 ml per cycle. However in some cases it may vary from 5 — 60 ml. Menstruation is usually accompanied by pain, headache, nausea, vomiting, abdominal pain and diarrhoea.

If fertilization occurs before the 26th day of the cycle, the corpus luteum persists, grows and continues to secrete progesterone which helps the endometrium to remain in favourable condition. The increased plasma level of progesterone suppresses the secretion of FSH and LH through feed-back inhibition and thus prevents further ovulation during pregnancy. The corpus luteum of pregnancy persists for about six months but its secretions reduce gradually as the placenta develops to its own capacity.

16.9 GYNAECOLOGICAL DISEASES

Various disorders affecting the functioning of normal female reproductive system have been identified. These are mainly due to either alterations in the hormonal levels during menstrual cycle or due to microbial colonization in the female genital tract.

(a) Menopause : The term is used to indicate a decline in the function of the ovaries usually during the age of early 50s of the woman. This is the end of female reproductive career. No ovulation takes place. Menstruation ceases. There after a gradual decline in the secretion of estrogen by the ovary occurs over a prolonged period of time.

(b) Dysmenorrhea : The term is used to describe painful menstrual periods. The main symptoms include nausea, vomiting, fatigue, diarrhoea, headache, and spasmodic pains in the lower abdomen and in the thighs. The prostaglandins (PGE_2 and $PGF_{2\alpha}$ released in the endometrium during menstrual cycle are responsible for most of these symptoms. Hence, most of the cases of dysmenorrhea can be relieved by the use of ibuprofen, naproxen-like non-steroidal antiinflammatory drugs. In few cases clonidine may become effective especially when etiology involves excessive stimulation of the uterus by adrenergic nerves.

(c) Hypomenorrhea (spotting) : The term refers to scanty flow during regular period. The bleeding may be so slight that it is called as spotting.

(d) Hypermenorrhea (menorrhagia) : It is just opposite to spotting. It describes abnormal perfused flow during regular periods.

(e) Oligomenorrhea : In normal cases the time gap between two successive menstrual flows is of about 28 days. If this time gap is increased to 35 days or more, it is known as oligomenorrhea. When the interval is larger than six months, the term amenorrhea is used.

(f) Polymenorrhea : When the interval between two successive menstrual flows is less than 21 days, it is known as polymenorrhea. The bleeding volume may or may not be normal. This situation mainly arises due to the failure of ovulation.

(g) Metrorrhagia : In this condition beside menstrual flow at stipulated time, abnormal bleeding occurs at any time during menstrual cycle. The bleeding may range from spotting to haemorrhagic flow. The common cause is uterine malignancy.

(h) Menometrorrhagia : The term refers to the uterine bleeding that is totally irregular in frequency and duration of episodes and excessive in amount. This abnormal uterine bleeding may also be described by the term, dysfunctional uterine bleeding.

(i) Endometriosis : The main symptoms include pelvic pain, dysmenorrhea, infertility and related menstrual problems. Some endometrial tissues migrate to ovary, bladder, uterus, appendix, gall bladder, lungs and other unusual places where they proliferate and give responses to sex hormones. Thus endometriosis is characterised by the growth of displaced endometrial tissues.

(j) Premenstrual syndrome (PMS) : It is characterized by anxiety, irritability, headache, abdominal distention, constipation, urination, insomnia, confusion and depression. The condition may be treated by drugs like spiranolactone, pyridoxine and progesterone. In refractory cases, clonidine, alprazolam or Gn-RH agonists can be used.

(k) Vaginitis : In normal woman, the vaginal pH ranges between 4.5 to 5.5 due to the presence of various aerobic and anaerobic microorganisms which catalyze the conversion of glycogen to the lactic acid. The thick vaginal epithelium consists of various species of bacteria including *Clostridia, Streptococci, Coliform* bacteria and *Lactobacillus*. Normally cervical muscus possesses antibacterial activity and contains lysozyme.

Under certain conditions (e.g. menopause), the thining of vaginal epithelium occurs along with change of pH from acid to alkaline range. The lactobacilli count decreases and the cervical mucus secretion declines. In usual cases, vaginitis is characterized by itching, burning, physical discomfort and changes in the vaginal discharges.

(l) Atrophic (senile) vaginitis : The alkaline vaginal pH along with decreased cervical secretions, lead to increased vaginal infections. In senile vaginitis, atrophic changes occurs due to chronic infection. Estrogen therapy proves to be useful in most of the cases to restore back the situation.

(m) Vaginal candidiosis : The condition is characterized by the presence of *Candida albicans* in the female genital tract and bowel. In few cases, *Candida glabrata* may also colonized. However no severe symptoms are usually associated with this condition.

(n) Trichomonas vaginitis : In this disease, usually vagina and lower urinary tract of both male and female get attacked. The symptoms include, itching, burning, postcoital bleeding etc. The vaginal discharge ranges in colour from mild yellow to green. The disease may get transmitted to male from female during sexual relationship.

16.10 ORAL CONTRACEPTIVES

Population has been growing with an ever increasing rate through an exponential way. As far as India is concerned, in the beginning of the 20th century, the country had a population of 23.8 crores. Now, it has more than 80 crores inspite of its division. This population explosion is needed to be controlled in order to avoid its adverse effects on the country's economical, social and environmental aspects. The awareness about the adverse effects of population explosion began to develop in the medical field that was reflected in the emergence of a new field *"antifertility research"*. The use of female sex hormones to prevent the development of the female egg was suggested as early as 1940. For example, it was known as far back as the beginning of this century that extracts of corpus luteum could be used to inhibit ovulation. In 1944, **Bickenbach** and **Paulikovics** showed that progesterone administration could inhibit ovulation. **Pincus** and his associates then at 'Puerto Rico family planning centre', started extensive field studies in 1955, on the use of steroidal hormones in oral contraceptive pills. Ten years i.e. from 1960 to 1970 had been of extreme importance for the field of fertility control as it marked the clinical introduction of oral contraceptive pills. Ethisterone was first orally active progestin. However its oral activity was still low that initiated further SAR studies. The first antifertility drug marketed was ENOVID, a combination of norethynodrel (a progestin) and mestranol (an estrogen) originally introduced in 1957 for the treatment of menstrual disorders.

The exact duration of survival of the sperms in the vagina is not known with certainty but it is believed to be about 1 – 2 hours. But immediately after the coitus, they can remain active for about 40 – 45 hours in the cervix and the uterine cavity.

Apart from the coitus interruptus, theoretically the fertility can be controlled by :

(i) controlling the central mechanisms.

(ii) preventing the union of sperm with ovum by using physical or chemical barriers, and

(iii) using drugs that modify the physiological mechanisms involved in reproduction.

Since hypothalamus plays a key role in controlling the gonadotropin secretions, emotional factors and drugs acting on hypothalamus can have an effect on ovulation. For example irregular menstrual bleeding is known in nurses on night duties and in air hostesses travelling over a long distance. Similarly traquillizers like chlorpromazine and reserpine are reported to modify the menstrual period in women.

Following are the proposed mechanisms through which fertility can be controlled when steroidal hormones are used :

(1) inhibiting ovulation
(2) modifying the cervical mucus
(3) slowing down the rate of ovum transport
(4) preventing the ovum maturation
(5) interferring with the implantation process, and
(6) by inhibiting spermatogenesis in males.

Most of the oral contraceptive preparations contain both, an estrogen and a progestin at varying dosage ratios. In estrogens, ethinyl estradiol, mestranol and diethyl stilbestrol are the most commonly used agents. Mestranol acts as a prodrug which upon *in-vivo* hepatic metabolism gets converted to ethinyl estradiol.

Diethylstilbestrol may be used as a postcoital contraceptive with certain caution. In progestin series, usually derivatives of 19 nor-testosterone are used as component of oral contraceptives. The series began with ethisterone, the first orally effective progestin. It was developed by **Inhoffen et al** from the male hormone testosterone through the addition of 17 α-ethinyl group. It resulted into a substantial decrease in the androgenic property with significant progestational activity. Other members of the series include, norethisterone, norgestrel, lynestrenol, norethynodrel, quingestanol acetate, ethinodiol diacetate etc.

Most of these orally active progestins act as the prodrug and get converted upon *in-vivo* metabolism to norethisterone.

Both the components (i.e. estrogen and progestin) brings about their contraceptive effect in the synergistic fashion.

Though oral contraceptive pills containing higher doses of progestin are more effective, estrogen is required for good cycle control. Reduction in its quantity may result in a greater incidence of breakthrough bleeding. The larger doses of progestin alone, may cause ovarian and endometrial atrophy and variations in the levels of FSH and LH may also occur. While if estrogens are used alone, that may lead to endometrial hyperplasia. Hence, progestin is required to inhibit the endometrial hyperplasia. It also helps in complete shedding of endometrium. Later it was found that most of the side-effects of oral contraceptives are mainly due to its estrogenic component. For example, the estrogen is responsible for nausea, headache, weight gain, hypertension, thromboembolic and related vascular diseases along with disturbances in carbohydrate and lipid metabolism. This leads to a gradual lowering of the dose of estrogens in the contraceptive pills. Current knowledge suggests the use of those contraceptive pills in which the estrogen content is less or equal to 50 µg. A step ahead to this, minipills (progestin only) were developed in order to eliminate estrogen completely. Minipills may be good choice in lactating women or patients who are sensitive to estrogenic adverse effects.

16.11 TYPES OF ORAL CONTRACEPTIVES

The following are the most commonly employed methods to effect contraception :

(i) Combination preparations
(ii) Sequential preparations
(iii) Minipills (or progestin alone)
(iv) Morning after or postcoital pills (or estrogen alone)
(v) Vaginal contraceptives or spermicidal agents
(vi) Interceptives or abortifacients
(vii) Progesterone blockers
(viii) Depot preparations
    (a) Once-a-month preparations
    (b) Intrauterine device
    (c) Biodegradable sustain release systems.
    (d) Non-biodegradable subdermal implants and vaginal rings
(ix) Condoms
(x) Chemical contraceptives for men or anti-androgens.

(i) Combination preparations :

The most common type of oral contraceptives is the combination preparation which contains a progestin and an estrogen. In this, ovulation is inhibited by the progesterone plus an estrogen.

The combination preparations are taken for 21 days, beginning from the 5th day of the menstrual cycle. These steroids initiate the development of endometrium into the form seen in the progestational phase of menstrual cycle. The fall in estrogen and progesterone levels at the end of treatment stimulates the shedding of the endometrium leading to regular bleeding. Bleeding usually follows after a 2-4 day latent period. The next course is started 7 days after the last dose or 5 days after the onset of menstrual cycle.

Thus *"three weeks on medication and one week off medication"* is the general rule. In some cases, a 28-days regimen is given which include 6 – 7 inert tablets or tablets for ferrous fumarate.

These preparations generally contain 0.02 to 0.15 mg of an oestrogen (commonly used estrogens are ethinyl estradiol or mestranol) and varying amounts of a progestin, e.g. norethinodrel, ethinodiol diacetate or norgestrel. Efficacy of the combination pills is due to the inhibition of ovulation by suppression of the mid-cycle burst of LH.

There is now an increasing tendency to reduce the amount of each steroid in the preparation without any loss of the contraceptive effectiveness. Most of the preparations contain 50 µg of estrogen but in a few preparations, even smaller amounts are present.

(ii) Sequential preparations :

In this method which is no longer used, the tablets to be taken for the first 15 days (starting on day 5 of the cycle) contain only estrogen while those supplied for the next five days are of combination type (i.e. contain estrogen and progestin). Estrogen acts by inhibiting ovulation mainly by blocking FSH release while progestin promotes maturation of the endometrium and facilitates withdrawal bleeding which generally begins 2-4 days after completing the regimen. The absence of progestin at mid-cycle in this preparation may account for higher rate of failure in comparison to the combination pills.

Because of increasing incidence of endometrial tumors and a lower efficacy associated with this type, sequential preparations are less reliable and less popular than combination preparations.

(iii) Mini-pills or Progestin only :

To reduce some of the risks associated with the use of higher doses of estrogens, mini-pills are developed which contains a small dose of progestins only and is taken daily without the drug free interval. Mini-pills are not as reliable as combination preparations and progestins alone are likely to permit 'breakthrough' bleeding. They are only currently used in women who exhibit intolerance towards estrogens. They are less effective and so pregnancy is possible during their administration.

(iv) Postcoital or Morning after pills :

These are used to prevent implantation of the ovum after some hours of the fertilization. They are intended only for emergency use. For example, for rape victims. Starting no later than 72 hours after the coitus, diethylstilbestrol 25 mg must be taken twice a day for continuous 5 days inspite of nausea and vomiting which commonly occur. Since estrogens do not interfere with fertilization these pills will be ineffective once implantation has occured. The chronic administration of diethylstilbestrol may be unpleasant and dangerous in some patients. These pills induce endometrial changes resulting into inhibition of implantation through hormonal imbalance and the estrogens also have luteolytic (break down of corpus luteum) action. They also alter the rate of ovum transportation. Ethinyl estradiol 5 mg daily to be taken for continuous five days can also serve the function. Withdrawal of large doses of estrogen induces bleeding. Extended period of therapy is necessary in certain cases. Since estrogens are used at relatively higher concentration, it may result into production of adverse effects like, edema, menstrual irregularities, thrombophlebitis etc.

(v) Vaginal contraceptives or spermicidal agents :

These agents fall into three categories

(1) **Surface active agents or sulfhydryl binding agents :**

e.g. nonoxynol-9, otoxynol etc.

(2) **Bactericides :** e.g. phenylmercuric acetate, benzethonium chloride, methylbenzethonium chloride etc.

(3) **Acids :** e.g. boric acid, tartaric acid and phenols.

They must be applied just before the intercourse deep into vagina. The contraceptive foam is marketed in the form of aerosol. Recently a disposable, polyurethane foam sponge impregnated with nonoxynol-9 has been marketed which can be easily removed from the vagina after the coitus, with the help of a ribbon loop attached to it.

(vi) Interceptives or abortifacients :

These substances are capable of preventing further development of the fertilized ovum even after the implantation has occured. Hence, they are also called as abortifacients. Examples include, ergot alkaloids, prostaglandins (PGE_2, $PGF_{2\alpha}$) and their analogs. Saline induced abortions have also been used in the past.

(vii) Contraception by using progesterone blockers :

The uterine endometrial is kept in the condition favourable for implantation and maintenance of pregnancy by various proteins whose synthesis is governed by progesterone induced activation of DNA-dependent m-RNA. Progesterone blockers may terminate the pregnancy through their interference with the binding of progesterone to its receptor sites on the chromatin material. The interference is caused through the competitive antagonism of progesterone by these agents. These agents are usually administered postcoitally or monthly to induce progesterone withdrawal bleeding and abortions.

(viii) Depot preparations :

(a) Once-a-month preparations : These contain a long acting estrogen combined with a short acting strong progestin. These are taken from the first time on day 22nd of a normal menstrual period and every 28th days thereafter. The short acting potent progestin induces normal bleeding shortly after the administration of the tablet. The estrogen however, by virtue of its slow release from fatty storage sites, inhibits the ovulation expected in the next cycle. An oil-filled capsule containing 2.0 mg of the long acting estrogen (e.g. 3-cyclopentyl ether of ethinyl estradiol, quinestrol etc.) and 2.5 mg of the progestin (e.g. quingestanol acetate) was given after every 4th week. Due to its lower efficacy, the pill was less popular amongst the users.

Even longer protection can be secured by giving larger intramuscular doses of progestin only. For example, medroxyprogesterone acetate in dose of 150 mg every three months, norethisterone oenanthate in dose of 200 mg every nine weeks and norethindrone enanthate in dose of 200 mg every 12 weeks. The long term use of these preparations however, is not recommended due to the associated risk of permanent infertility.

(b) Intrauterine device (IUD) : These are medicated devices intended to release a small quantity of drug into the uterus in a sustained manner over prolonged period time. These contain progestin. The progestasert – IUD contains a total of 38 mg of progesterone dispersed in the silicone oil within flexible T-shaped polymer that releases about 65 µg/day of progesterone into the uterine area for about 1 year to exhibit effective contraceptive effect without causing the systemic side-effects associated with other forms of hormonal contraception. Yet another IUD contains 52 mg progesterone and delivers about 65 mg progesterone daily for about two years.

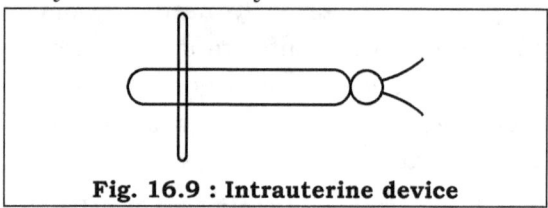

Fig. 16.9 : Intrauterine device

The silicone oil provides thermodynamic energy necessary for efficient diffusion of the drug from the reservior into the uterine cavity. Once the IUD is left in the uterus, it remains effective for as long as three years. An additional contraceptive effect is exerted by the release of copper from the IUD which interferes with the biochemical processes that regulate implantation.

Though IUDs are devoid of usual adverse effects associated with oral contraceptive pills due to their local and nonsystemic action, other side-effects like, bleeding and pelvic inflammatory conditions are usually associated with their use.

(c) Biodegradable sustain release systems : It includes the use of biodegradable polymers and microparticles to release the estrogen and progestin. Release of active drug occur by erosion, diffusion and cleavage of covalent bonds between the drug and the polymer. Polymer matrices includes caprolactone, glutamic acid, lactic acid and glycolic polymers.

(d) Non-biodegradable subdermal implants and vaginal rings : The contraceptive effect for more than five years was observed from non-biodegradable implants in which 200 mg of levonorgestrel was incorporated in 20.4 cm of polydimethyl siloxane tubing. The diffusion of the drug occurs through the silicon rubber tubing at the rate of 0.030 mg/day. However, the implant has to be removed by microsurgery after its use. Due to the cosmetic problem involved in the removal of implant, vaginal rings have been developed which consist of a polydimethyl siloxane core with a thin layer of levonorgestrel and estradiol (in 2 : 1 proportion). This in turn, is covered with a thin diffusion layer of polydimethyl siloxane to form a ring structure.

(ix) Condoms (male sheath) :

These are the latex rubber sheats having reservoir ends to collect the semen. They inhibit transmission of male semen by acting as mechanical barrier. They are usually marketed as lubricated or nonlubricated and are worn over an erect penis during the coitus. Thus, they can also be used to inhibit the transmission of veneral diseases.

(x) Chemical contraceptives for men or antiandrogens :

It is the most rarely used method. Antiandrogens can be used to suppress spermatogenesis. However the drug administration may also lead to impotency and loss of secondary sex characteristics in males. Hence the antiandrogen is usually administered along with a high dose of androgen to achieve synergistic suppression of gonadotropins and spermatogenesis. The examples of drugs from this category include cyproterone acetate, nitrofurazone and myleran. Androgen-estrogen combination (17 α-methyltestosterone, 10 mg and ethinyl estradiol, 20 mg) can be used to decrease the spermatogenesis. The sperm count returns to normal upon discontinuation of the therapy.

Upon chronic treatment, cholestasis, liver dysfunctioning and cardiovascular problems may be initiated by these preparations.

(xi) Miscellaneous contraceptive methods :

Besides oral contraceptive preparations, other ways to achieve fertility control include coitus interruptus, rhythm method, application of cap (the diaphragm and cervical caps) and loop etc. can be used. The sterilization methods are available for both, males (vasoctomy) and for females (tubetomy.)

The various assays and screening techniques used in antifertility studies are mainly categorised as :

(a) Tests involving centrally acting mechanisms :

(i) Inhibition of gonadotropin secretion and ovulation

(ii) Inhibition of releasing factors from the hypothalamus.

(b) Tests involving peripherally acting mechanisms :

(i) Regulation of uterine-cervical secretions,

(ii) Inhibition of implantation, and

(iii) Prevention of sperm capacitation.

16.12 PEARL INDEX

Results of antifertility studies about a particular drug in women can be evaluated in terms of Pearl Index which is defined as 'the pregnancy rate per 100 women versus years of exposure'. This term is thus an indication about the potency or efficacy of the contraceptive preparation.

$$\text{Pearl Index} = \frac{\text{Number of pregnancies} \times 1200}{\text{Total months of exposure}}$$

16.13 MECHANISM OF ACTION

Females do not ovulate during pregnancy — a time in which there are high levels of circulating blood progesterone. This observation served as a basis for development of oral contraceptives in general and combination preparation more specifically where an estrogen is usually combined with a progesterone in order to achieve full efficacy. Due to the painful nature of crystalline suspensions of progesterone (because of its low solubility), attempts were made to develop orally effective progesterone derivatives (progestins). The prominent effect of estrogen is to inhibit the release of FSH (i.e. inhibition of growth of follicles) while continued action of progesterone serves to inhibit the release of LH (i.e. inhibition of the release of matured ovum through ovulation process).

Following are some proposed mechanisms to explain the antifertility action of the oral contraceptive preparations :

(1) The primary mode of action of the oral contraceptives seems to involve blocking of ovulation of inhibiting the secretion of hypothalamus through feedback inhibition. In combination therapy, estrogen component owes its effectiveness mainly by inhibiting ovulation while progestin serves the major purpose of ensuring prompt withdrawal bleeding.

(2) The correct hormonal requirement which is essential for the execution of proper functions of cervix, uterus and fallopian tubes to promote fertilization is disturbed and cannot be maintained. For example, under the influence of progestin, atrophic endometrium often results. Implantation becomes difficult within such altered endometrium environment.

(3) At the time of ovulation, the cervical cell-lining is favourable for sperm migration towards uterus. Thin and watery nature of cervical secretions facilitate sperm penetration. However progestin causes the cervical mucous to become very thick and tenacious. Thus, provides a barrier for the passage of sperms through the cervix and reduces sperm survival.

(4) Progestin also alters motility rate of the ovum by altering fallopian tube secretions.

16.14 ADVERSE EFFECTS

Oral contraceptive preparations on administration may cause nausea, vomiting (mainly due to estrogen), headache (migraine like, due to estrogen induced increase in cerebrovascular pressure), corneal defects, photosensitivity, retinal thrombosis, optic peuritis (all due to progestin component) megaloblastic anaemia, breast tenderness, ischemic colitis, abnormal hair growth, acne, and chloasma (skin hyperpigmentation). Weight gain may also occur due to anabolic testosterone-like progesterone activity and partly due to water and salt retention in the body. Their administration leads to higher plasma levels of glucose and triglycerides. Upon chronic administration, oral contraceptive agents may induce hepatic lesions especially peliosis hepatica and hepatic adenomas. However the most serious side-effects of these agents include their effect on cardiovascular systems and their tumorigenic effect.

Oral contraceptive agents also exert some desirable side-effects. The incidences of occurrence of iron deficient anemia, benign breast disease, pelvic inflammatory disease, functional ovarian cyst, premenstrual tension and menstrual disorders are markedly lowered down. Hence, their administration may be beneficial under all these circumstances.

(a) Cardiovascular system : The adverse effects of oral contraceptive agents on CVS include, venous thromboembolism, thrombotic (cerebral and coronary) stroke, haemorrhagic stroke, hypertension, hyperlipidemia and myocardial infarction. Since the intensity and frequencies of these effects is quite low in the patients taking mini-pills (progestin only), these effects arise mainly due to estrogenic components of the pills that induces alternations in clotting factors (i.e. an increase in the release of factors VII, VIII, IX and X), lipoproteins, glucose tolerance and in various hemodynamic mechanisms (i.e. increased plasma concentrations of resin and angiotensin). The estrogenic component is also responsible for inducing structural vascular changes in veins and arteries which are then involved in occurance of thromboembolic diseases.

(b) Tumorigenic effects : This effect is mainly exerted on the organs like, vagina, uterus, breast and liver. These benign tumors may get ruptured early, due to their high vascularity resulting into haemorrhage. Both, estrogens and progetin are responsible for tumorigenic effects on long term administration. Focal nodular hyperplasia and liver cell adenomas are the usual forms of benign liver tumors seen associated with use of these agents. The tumors usually regress upon discontinuation of the therapy.

(c) Breakthrough bleeding : Spotting or irregular menstrual bleeding are the common effects of oral contraceptive pills. The estrogenic component should be raised if spotting occurs before midcycle while if it occurs after midcycle, the progestin part should be increased.

(d) Depression : This phase is characterized by alterations in the mood, easy fatigueness, inertness and lack of concentration. These depressant effects are mainly due to alterations in the metabolism of tryptophan to serotonin, vitamin B_6 may be given to relieve these symptoms.

(e) Other effects : The estrogenic component of the pills brings about a reduction in milk volume (i.e. lactation). If these pills are continuously used during pregnancy, they may lead to congenital limb deformation and musculinization in offspring.

Table 16.2 : Some marketed contraceptive preparations

Preparation	Oestrogen (mg)		Progestin (mg)	
[A] 1. Combination preparations (high dose oestrogens) :				
Envoid 5 mg	Mestranol	75	Norethynodrel	5.0
Envoid – B	Mestranol	100	Norethynodrel	2.5
Ovulen 1 mg	Mestranol	100	Ethynodiol diacetate	1.0
Lyndiol	Mestranol	75	Lynoestrenol	2.5
2. Combination preparations (medium dose oestrogen) :				
Norinyl 1	Mestranol	50	Norethisterone acetate	1.0
Anvlar 21	Ethinyl estradiol	50	Norethisterone acetate	4.0
Norlestrin	Ethinyl estradiol	50	Norethisterone acetate	2.5
Ovulen 50	Ethinyl estradiol	50	Norethisterone acetate	1.0
Ovran	Ethinyl estradiol	50	D-norgestrel	0.25
Minilyn	Ethinyl estradiol	50	Lynoestrenol	2.5
Demulen 50	Ethinyl estradiol	50	DL-norgestrel	0.5
3. Combination preparations (low dose oestrogen) :				
Microgynon 30	Ethinyl oestradiol	30	D-norgestrel	0.15
Eugynon 30	Ethinyl oestradiol	30	DL-norgestrel	0.5
Loestrin 20	Ethinyl oestradiol	20	Norethisterone acetate	1.0
[B] Sequential preparations :				
Ovanon	Metranol 80 (days 1 – 7)			
	Mestranol 75 (days 8-27)		Lynoestrenol (days 8-22)	2.5
[C] Progestin only (Mini-pills) :				
Micronor	—		Norethisterone	0.35
Femulen	—		Ethynodiol diacetate	0.50
Neogest	—		DL-norgestrel	0.75
Microlut	—		D-norgestrel	0.30
Turinal	—		Allylestrenol	0.50
Exluton	—		Lynoestrenol	0.50
[D] Postcoital	Diethyl Stilbestrol	25	twice daily for 5 days	
[E] Depot hormonal preparations :				
Depo-Provera	Medroxy progesterone acetate		400-1000 mg initially with a maintenance dose as low as 400 mg per month.	
Once-a-month	Quinestron (norethindrone acetate-3-cyclo-pentyl enol ether)		Quingestranol	
Hormone-releasing implants				
Progestasert	Progesterone releasing IUD	38 mg		

17 ADRENOCORTICOIDS

17.1 INTRODUCTION

The adrenal glands are flattened, cap like structures located on the top of the kidneys. The inner core of it, is known as medulla which secretes catecholamines (i.e. adrenaline). While the shell of the gland is known as cortex which surrounds the medulla.

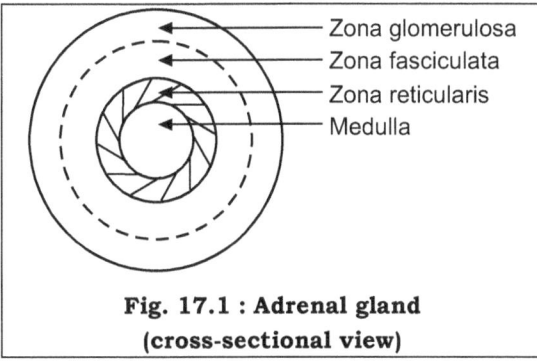

Fig. 17.1 : Adrenal gland (cross-sectional view)

The adrenal cortex is made up of three distinct zones. Zona glomerulosa is the outermost cellular area of the cortex which is involved in the production and the secretion of aldosterone under the control of reninangiotensin system. While zona fasciculata and zona reticularis are the inner zones of the cortex which are involved in the production and the secretion of corticosteroids and androgens under the control of pituitary gland.

The importance of adrenal cortex in the life-maintaining processes was first described by Addison in 1855 who has documented the symptoms of chronic deficiency of cortisol and aldosterone due to the progressive destruction or atrophy of adrenal cortex. The condition was thereafter, recognized by his name (Addison's disease). Just opposite to this, is the symptoms associated with chronic overproduction of cortisol (hypercorticism) which was first described by **Cushing** in 1932. The condition is known as 'Cushing syndrome'. These observations initiated the interest of scientists in the hormonal secretions of adrenal cortex. As a result, more than 30 steroidal compounds were isolated from the mammalian adrenal cortex in 1942. Depending upon their physiological functions, they were categorized as

(a) Glucocorticoids :

Cortisol and cortisone are the principal endogenous glucocorticoids. These steroids regulate the carbohydrate, protein and fat metabolism and are intimately involved in the operation of processes that enable the body to resist infections and stress. Their secretion is under the control of pituitary gland.

(b) Mineralocorticoids :

The principal endogenous mineralocorticoid is aldosterone which was discovered in 1954. These steroids mainly influence salt and water balance (and hence the control of blood volume and blood pressure) by maintaining proper electrolyte balance. Their secretion is under the control of reninangiotensin system.

Besides these steroids, small amounts of sex steroids such as, dehydroepiandrosterone, testosterone, progesterone and estradiol are also secreted by adrenal cortex.

The adrenocorticoid secretion is under the influence of adrenocorticotropic hormone (ACTH or adrenocorticotropin or corticotropin) which is released by the anterior lobe of pituitary gland (adenohypophysis). The release of ACTH from adenohypophysis in turn, is under the control of corticotropin releasing factor (CRF) that is secreted by the hypothalamus. The release of CRF from hypothalamus can also be increased by the action of neurotransmitters like serotonin and dopamine. Many drugs like, dextroamphetamine, methamphetamine, reserpine, phenothiazines, and 9-tetra-hydrocannabinol also stimulate CRF release. The plasma level of adrenocorticoids also controls the release of ACTH from adenohypophysis through the negative feedback inhibitory mechanism.

Based upon the work of **Bell** and his associates (1956), ACTH was proposed to be a peptide of 39 amino acids starting with serine (first amino acid) and ending with phenyl alanine (39th amino acid). Since the amino acid sequence from 1 to 13 in the structure of ACTH is almost identical with that of melanocyte stimulating hormone (MSH), it retains $\left(\frac{1}{100}\right)^{th}$ of the potency of MSH to stimulate melanocytes. Hence, chronically elevated ACTH levels may cause hyperpigmentation of the skin.

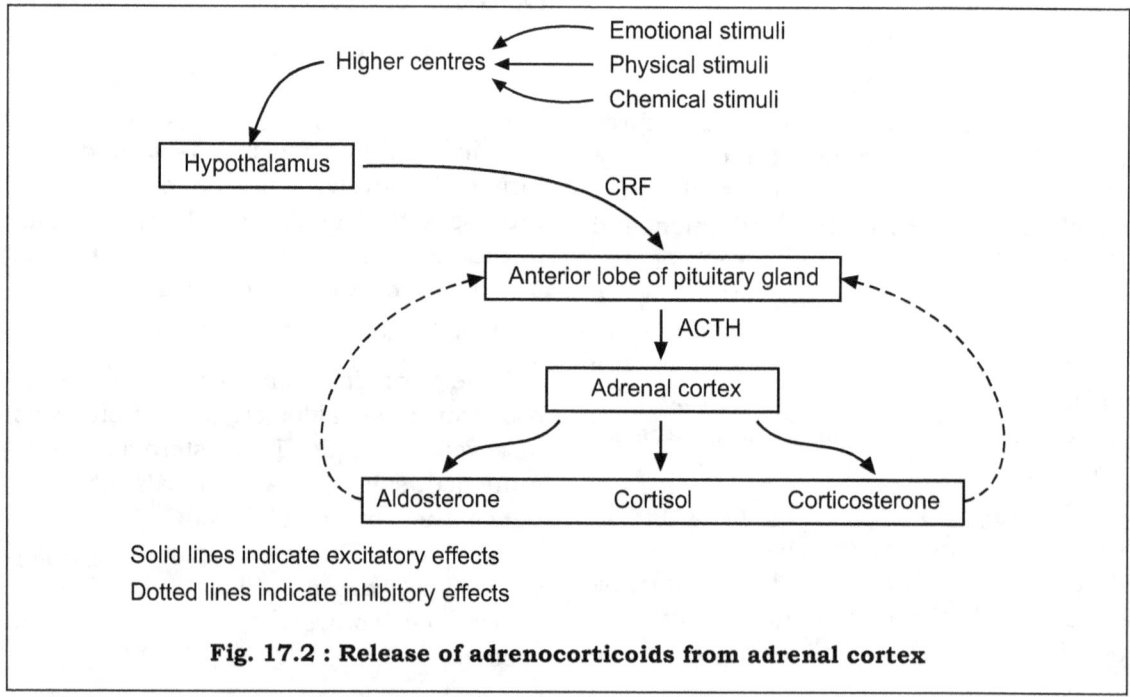

Solid lines indicate excitatory effects
Dotted lines indicate inhibitory effects

Fig. 17.2 : Release of adrenocorticoids from adrenal cortex

ACTH is essential for maintaining functional and structural integrity of the adrenal cortex. It controls the steroidogenesis in adrenal cortex by -

(i) Increasing the uptake of cholesterol from plasma lipoproteins into the adrenal cortex where cholesterol serves as the starting material for steroidogenesis and

(ii) Increasing the rate of conversion of cholesterol into pregnenolone through oxidative cleavage of its side chain in mitochondria.

Both these effects are mediated through ACTH - induced accumulation of c-AMP. Deficiency of ACTH may induce degenerative changes (atrophy) in adrenal cortex while higher plasma level of ACTH may cause hyperplasia of adrenal cortex resulting into increased steroidogenesis. Hyperpigmentation of the skin is yet another effect of chronically elevated ACTH levels.

In normal circumstances, the release of ACTH from the adenohypophysis is governed by a balanced system comprised of excitatory effects of CRF released from median eminence of hypothalamus and inhibitory effects of plasma corticosteroid concentration. The inhibitory effects of corticosteroids upon the release of ACTH are mainly exerted at the transcription level, resulting into decrease in the rate of synthesis of m-RNA for ACTH in the adenohypophysis. The basophilic cells of the adenohypophysis are the sites for ACTH secretion from a glycoprotein precursor of about 30,000 molecular weight. The molecule of ACTH is a peptide of 39 amino acids in which the sequence of amino acids from 1 to 13 resembles with MSH while the rest of the part has resemblance with lipotropins and the endorphins. Due to rapid enzymatic destruction, ACTH has a very short biological half life of about 15 minutes.

17.2 ADRENOCORTICAL STEROIDS

Various steroidal compounds isolated from adrenal cortex fall into following two categories :

(a) Corticosteroids :

(i) Glucocorticoids : e.g. Cortisol and cortisone are main endogenous glucorticoids secreted by adrenal cortex.

(ii) Mineralocorticoids : e.g. Aldosterone is the mineralocorticoid secreted by adrenal cortext.

(b) Sex steroids :

Estradiol, progesterone and testosterone are examples of adrenocortical sex steroids.

The biosynthetic process for these adrenocorticosteroids utilizes cholesterol as a starting material. Though adrenal cortex retains an ability to synthesize cholesterol from acetate, major part (60 – 75%) of cholesterol needed for adrenocorticosteroid biosynthesis is taken up from the low-density lipoproteins by uptake processes. In mitochondria, cholesterol is then converted into pregnenolone through oxidative cleavage of its side chain in the presence of ACTH. The resulting Δ^5-pregnenolone is then utilized in the production of corticosteroids and androgens through various enzymatic bioconversions in the presence of cytochrome P-450, NADPH and molecular oxygen. This scheme of biosynthesis of various adrenocortical steroid has been elaborately shown in Fig. 17.3. Various enzymes are involved to catalyze these biochemical reactions. The Δ^5-pregnenolone obtained from cholesterol is utilized as starting material for two different biochemical pathways resulting into production of C_{19}-androgens and C_{21}-corticosteroids respectively. Androstenedione is the principal product

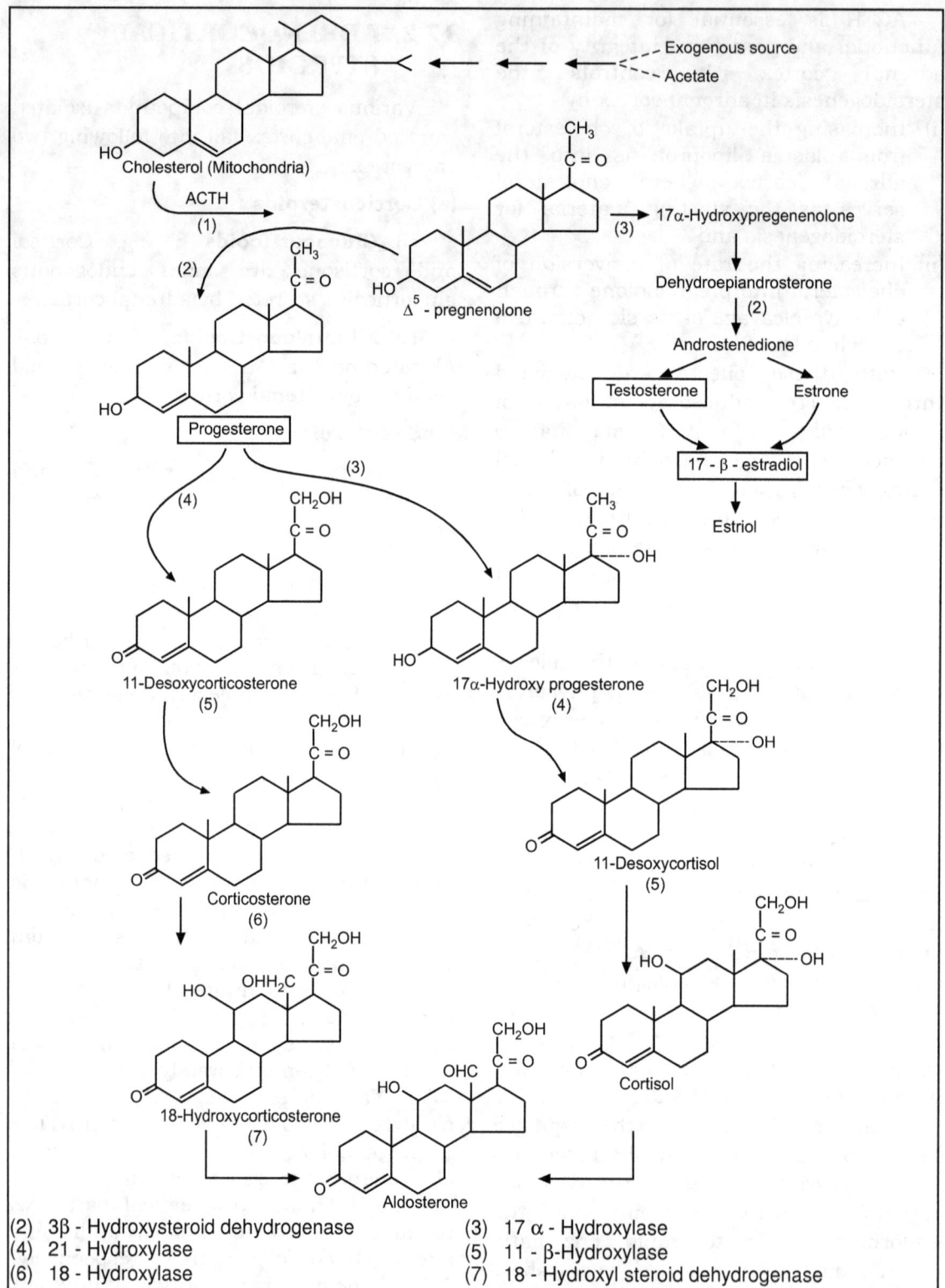

(2) 3β - Hydroxysteroid dehydrogenase
(4) 21 - Hydroxylase
(6) 18 - Hydroxylase
(3) 17 α - Hydroxylase
(5) 11 - β-Hydroxylase
(7) 18 - Hydroxyl steroid dehydrogenase

Fig. 17.3 : Biosynthesis of adrenocorticosteroids

of first pathway which is then converted into estrogens and testosterone. While in the second biosynthetic pathway, progesterone serves as a principal product which is then converted ultimately to cortisol and aldosterone through two distinct sub-pathways.

In an adult person, the daily production of cortisol ranges from 5.0 to 28.0 mg. Once synthesized, these adrenocorticosteroids are not retained into adrenal cortex. They are immediately released into the circulation. Hence under the conditions of strain, stress and inflammation, the body's demand for corticosteroids is met by increasing the rate of biosynthesis under the influence of ACTH.

Cortisone was the first corticosteroid to be used. Since glucocorticoidal activity runs parallel with anti-inflammatory effects, cortisone was introduced as anti-inflammatory agent in 1949. Glucocorticoids have the capacity to suppress the development of local heat, redness, swelling and tenderness by which inflammation is recognized at the gross level of observation. However a particularly difficult aspect of the synthesis of cortisol was the need to introduce the sterically hindered ketonic oxygen at C - 11 which requires the incorporation of number of intermediate chemical steps. This was reflected into an unusual rise in the price of the cortisol. (i.e. $ 200 per gm). In the early methods of chemical synthesis, desoxycholic acid obtained from ox bile was used as the starting material at Merck. A pioneer and more economic approach was made by Upjohn company which had used a strain of *Rhizopus arrhizus* to introduce hydroxyl group at 11-position in progesterone structure. This technique was then used to get cortisol at much cheaper rate (i.e. $ 3.50 per gm).

Though cortisol and cortisone are categorized as glucocorticoids, they possess too much salt-retaining (mineralocorticoidal) activity in the doses needed for therapeutic purposes. Considering above facts, efforts were made to develop new potent and low cost adrenocorticoids having minimum adverse effects. Table 17.1 shows the currently used synthetic steroidal antiinflammatory agents.

As it is revealed from the structures of clinically used steroidal antiinflammatory agents, the placement of double bond between C_1, and C_2, β-hydroxyl group at C_{11} and a hydroxyl group at C_{21} atom increase the glucocorticoidal and anti-inflammatory activity but these structural features also increase the ability of the molecule to induce peptic ulcer. Between 1953 to 1962, many derivatives of Δ^1-corticoids (especially fluorinated analogs) were synthesized and some became useful as clinical agents. Halogenation specifically at C_6 and C_9 positions markly increase both gluco corticoidal and mineralocorticoidal activities. However hydroxylation and methylation at C_{16} position markly lowered down the undesirable mineralocorticoidal activity associated with halogenated steroids.

Pharmacological actions :

Corticosteroids exhibit diversified functions in the body. The prominent amongst them include their effects on :

(a) Metabolism of carbohydrates, fats and proteins (i.e. glucocorticoidal activity).

(b) Electrolyte and water balance (i.e. mineralocorticoidal activity).

(c) Allergic and inflammatory responses, and

(d) The functioning of vital body systems including CNS and cardiovascular system.

Beside these effects, corticosteroids also influence the functioning of kidney, skeletal muscle and secretion of gastric juice. Thus, adrenal cortex is essential for the survival of human body under drastic changes in the surrounding atmosphere. Out of the endogenous corticosteroids, deoxycorticosterone is the prototype of mineralocorticoids while cortisol is the prototype of glucocorticoids. Aldosterone and corticosterone share considerable activities in both the sides.

(a) Carbohydrate, protein and fat metabolism :

Corticosteroid therapy leads to an increase in the liver glycogen deposition that results due to -

(i) an increase in glucose formation (i.e. gluconeogenesis),

(ii) reduction in glucose peripheral utilization, and

(iii) conversion of glucose to glycogen is promoted.

Proteins are also broken down to amino acids which, in liver serve as the substrates for enzymes involved in the production of glucose and glycogen. This results into an increase in the rate of excretion of nitrogen, released from excessive breakdown of proteins. During corticosteroid induced gluconeogenesis, amino acids from different tissues are mobilized to the liver that results into osteoporosis, atrophy of lymphatic tissues, reduction in muscle-mass and negative nitrogen balance.

During chronic hypercorticoidal stage (Cushing syndrome) there is an increase in the plasma insulin concentration. The lipogenic effects of insulin stimulate the mobilization of the fat from the peripheral fat depots to the back of the neck *("buffalo hump")*, supraclavicular area and to the face *("moon face")*.

(b) Electrolyte and water balance :

Mineralocorticoids enhance the reabsorption of sodium ions from the distal tubules of the kidney into the plasma. However, they speed up the excretion rate of both potassium and hydrogen atoms. Hence, during the chronic corticosteroid deficiency state (i.e. Addison's disease), circulatory collapse may occur due to excessive loss of Na^+ ions, swelling of erythrocytes, shrinkage of plasma volume and hyperkalemic condition.

Glucocorticoids antagonise the action of vitamin D on the gut and reduce the absorption of calcium and phosphate. The long term treatment thus may cause improper development of cartilage and linear growth in children. Thus, protein catabolism in the matrix of bone coupled with reduced Ca^{++} absorption inhibit the formation of new bony tissues and may result into osteoporosis.

(c) Cardiovascular system :

Overdoses of corticosteroids may cause hypertension due to elevated plasma Na^+ concentration. This increase in the blood pressure may lead to an increase in the glomerular filtration rate. Corticosteroids also induce, the hepatic angiotensinogen production and activate angiotensin aldosterone system. In the corticosteroid deficiency state, there is an increase in the capillary permeability, drastic fall in plasma Na^+ concentration, hypotension and reduction in cardiac output and heart size. Death may occur due to the circulatory collapse associated with renal failure.

Corticosteroids stimulate the erythropoiesis and production of polymorphonuclear leucocytes. In contrast, the production of eosinophils, monocytes, lymphocytes and basophils is decreased.

(d) Nervous system :

Due to their ability to control electrolyte balance, corticosteroids have prominent effects on mood, behaviour and excitability threshold of the brain tissues. Higher concentrations of corticosteroids may lead to CNS excitatory symptoms while in deficiency state, CNS depressant effects are usually observed.

(e) Skeletal muscle :

Due to the prominent effects of corticoids upon electrolyte balance, gluconeogenesis and circulatory system, the functioning of skeletal muscles is greatly influenced by alterations in plasma corticoid - concentrations. For example, in hypercorticoidal stage, antianabolic effects are seen due to increased protein breakdown, hypokalemia and negative nitrogen balance. This steroid induced myopathy results into weakness and fatigue of skeletal muscle. The latter symptoms are also seen in hypocorticoid state due to suppression of gluconeogenesis and inadequate blood circulation.

(f) Anti-inflammatory properties :

Edema, fibrin deposition, capillary dilation, migration of leucocytes into the affected area are the early signs of inflammation which are then associated with redness, swelling and increased pain sensation. The glucocorticoid activity runs parallel with anti-inflammatory effects of these steroids. The production of arachidonic acid metabolites (e.g. leukotrienes, endoperoxides, thromboxanes and various prostaglandins) is responsible for most of the inflammatory and immunosuppressive reactions. These steroids decrease the release of arachidonic acid by antagonizing phospholipase A_2 activity. The latter effect is exerted by formation of a peptide (i.e. macrocortin) whose synthesis is facilitated by glucocorticoids at transcription level. They also inhibit the migration of leukocytes by preventing the conversion of plasminogen to plasmin. The latter is responsible for migration of leukocytes due to its fibrinolytic effects. However the clinical utility of steroidal antiinflammatory agents fails to remove the underlying cause and the inflammatory manifestations are merely suppressed.

(g) Anti-allergic and immunosuppressive actions :

Besides their antiinflammatory activity, corticosteroids also have antiallergic activity and when given systemically, they alleviate the symptoms of asthma. They were equally effective in the treatment of hay-fever and in various disease conditions of the skin, such as eczema and psoriasis where they can be applied topically to reduce secondary (adverse) effects of systemic corticosteroid therapy. They modify the clinical course of a variety of diseases in which hypersensitivity is important. They effectively inhibit the formation of lymphokines which are usually produced from lymphocytes upon activation by antigen. The leukotriene formation is also inhibited due to the blockage of arachidonic acid release.

17.3 MECHANISM OF ACTION

(1) Corticosteroids react with the receptor proteins in the cytoplasm of the sensitive cells to form a steroid-receptor complex.
(2) This complex after a conformational change, moves into the nucleus and binds to nuclear chromatin material.
(3) The complex releases free corticosteroid which then interacts with the genetic apparatus resulting into an increase in the rate of synthesis of specific mRNAs.
(4) The m-RNAs so synthesised are responsible for an increase in the rate of synthesis of specific proteins or enzymes which are needed to evoke the biological response. Thus, steroid hormones act at transcription level. Many of the proteins whose production is so regulated by glucocorticoids have now been identified, together with their role in hormonal action.

17.4 PHARMACOKINETICS

Except desoxycorticosterone acetate, all the natural and synthetic corticosteroids are orally effective. They can also be administered parenterally in order to get rapid onset (i.v.) or prolonged duration (i.m.) of action. In the treatment of skin diseases, they can also be applied topically. The plasma half-life of cortisol in man is about 1.5 hours. Upon absorption, cortisol is bound primarily to α_2-globulin which is known as corticosteroid binding globulin (CBG) or transcortin and secondarily to albumin. About 90% of administered dose remains in the bound form while only 10% remains as the unbound or physiologically active form. Elevation in the CBG level occurs which is induced by estrogens or during pregnancy. Liver is the principal site for metabolism. Most of the cortico steroids are metabolized to tetrahydro derivatives by the reduction of (i) ketone group at C_3 to α-hydroxyl function and (ii) double bond present between C_4 and C_5. Since both functional groups essential for hormonal activity are reduced, tetrahydrometabolites are devoid of pharmacological effects.

In some cases corticosteroids may simultaneously undergo side-chain cleavage to give tetrahydro – 17 – ketosteroids. These metabolites are devoid of corticosteroidal activity but may exhibit weak androgenic activity.

In some biotransformations, reduction of C_{20} ketone function to $-CH_2OH$ may occur prior to the formation of tetrahydro derivatives. For example

Cortisol → → Cortol

Cortisone → → Cortolone

All the metabolites of corticosteroids are excreted through the urine in the form of their glucuronides. Minor amount of corticosteroid may appear unchanged in the urine. While biliary or faecal route of excretion is not of much importance. Drugs like phenylbutazone or phenobarbitone may speed up the metabolism of corticosteroids.

By incorporation of double bond between C_1 and C_2 or by fluorination, one can reduce the rate of metabolism of the corticosteroid.

17.5 ADVERSE EFFECTS

(1) Corticosteroids stimulate the secretion of several components of gastric juice. Hence, corticosteroid therapy is always associated with an increased risk of peptic ulcer.

(2) Due to their effects upon protein catabolism and Ca^{++} ion absorption, the prolonged administration of glucocorticoids in children may result into inhibition or arrest of the growth. Additionally, the DNA synthesis and cell division is also inhibited by corticosteroids.

(3) Myopathy may result due to chronic hyper corticoidism specifically in the proxima musculature of the extremities.

(4) CNS effects of corticosteroids mainly include nervousness, drowsiness hallucinations, restlessness, and insomnia.

(5) Upon chronic treatment of corticosteroid, the endogenous corticosteriod release gets gradually slowed down. Upon discontinuation of the therapy the endogenous adrenal function takes time to become normal. During this time a small dose of corticosteriod is needed to be given in order to protect the patient from any stressful events or from infections because his immune system is under suppressed condition.

(6) Besides these, other adverse effects include, glaucoma, glycosuria, hyperglycemia (anti-insulin effect), hypertension, dyspepsia and moon face (mobilization of fat).

17.6 THERAPEUTIC USES

(a) In chronic corticosteroid deficiency states (e.g. Addison's disease), the treatment with cortisol (glucocorticoid) and fludrocortisone (mineralocorticoid) constitute replacement therapy. Cortisol can also be administered in pituitary failure in order to maintain adrenocortical function.

(b) In various rheumatic conditions (e.g. rheumatic fever, rheumatoid arthritis, rheumatoid carditis etc.), prednisone can be effectively used.

(c) Prednisone is also effective in the treatment of collagen diseases, like sclerodema.

(d) In hypersensitivity reactions (hay fever, serum sickness, urticaria, bronchial asthma etc.), glucocorticoids are effectively used.

(e) Glucocorticoids can also be used in the treatment of infections and inflammatory conditions of eyes.

(f) Glucocorticoids are also effective in the treatment of severe burn, shocks and systemic infections.

(g) They can be topically applied to treat various forms of skin diseases.

17.7 TOPICAL ANTI-INFLAMMATORY STEROIDAL AGENTS

Glucocorticoids are highly effective in various forms of disease condition of the skin. In such situations, if they are used systemically, specifically in children, the secondary effects of systemic corticosteroid therapy (e.g. mobilization of fat, effect on protein catabolism, osteoporosis, suppression of immune system) become more severe. One way of minimizing these systemic adverse effects is to do topical application of the corticosteroids to the inflamed tissue. Numerous preparations containing either glucocorticoid alone or in combination with an antibacterial or antifungal agent are available for topical therapy.

Topical applications includes,

(i) Dermal ointments, creams, and lotions,

(ii) Ophthalmic ointments and solutions,

(iii) Respiratory aerosols and

(iv) Ear drops.

Maibach and **Stoughton** had identified about 20 dermatological disorders which respond to topical corticosteroids. Except cortisone and prednisone, most other glucocorticoids exhibit good topical activity. Some of these are, halcinonide, flumethasone, fluocinolone, fluorometholone, fluandrenolone, desonide, dichlorisone, fluclorolone, diflucortolone, clobetasone, clobetasol etc. All these drugs are potent topically acting agents.

Unfortunately steroid preparations are sometimes misused due to their drammatic relief effect in inflammatory conditions of the skin. However, corticosteroids may accelerate the fungal growth and spread and may cause local skin atrophy. Hence such potent steroids should not be applied to the facial skin.

Skin absorption of these agents is affected by a number of factors, such as, lipid solubility of the drug, extent of the skin damage, concentration of glucocorticoid, cream or ointment base used and factors concerned with patient.

Except for fludrocortisone, the topical corticosteroids do not cause adverse effects on absorption when applied on small areas of the intact skin. But systemic absorption may occur especially if the skin is damaged resulting in systemic problems.

Since these agents can mask the symptoms of infection, many physicians prefer not giving a topical anti-inflammatory steroid until the infection is controlled with topical antibiotics. The immunosuppressive activity of topical glucocorticoids can also prevent natural defence processes from curing the infection on their own ability. Like oral contraceptives, these steroidal agents should not be used during pregnancy.

17.8 MINERALOCORTICO-STEROIDS

Sodium retention, hepatic deposition of glycogen and anti-inflammatory effects are three basic properties of corticosteroids which are used to estimate their potencies. A corticoid having a predominant liver glycogen deposition (which parallels with anti-inflammatory effect) is known as glucocorticoid while a corticosteroid with predominant sodium retaining effects, is called as a mineralocorticoid. Examples include, aldosterone, 11 - desoxycorticosterone, fludrocortisol acetate.

Pharmacological actions :

(a) Electrolyte and water balance : They act on distal tubules of the kidney to enhance the reabsorption of sodium ions from the tubular fluid into the plasma. They increase the urinary excretion of both potassium and hydrogen ions.

In mineralocorticoid deficiency, proportionately more sodium than water is excreted through the kidney with resultant decrease in extracellular sodium ion concentration. The extracellular fluid becomes hypoosmatic and water moves from the extracellular space to the intracellular compartments. This dehydration of the extracellular spaces results into a marked reduction in the volume of extracellular fluids. Cells are hydrated and erythrocytes also swell.

The shrinkage of extracellular fluid volume, cellular hydration, hypotension and an impairment of renal function combine to cause circulatory collapse, e.g. Addison's disease. Hyperkalemia, acidosis and muscular weakness are some of the manifestations of aldosterone deficiency.

Aldosterone also exerts effects on other organs like, kidneys, salivary glands, sweat glands, exocrine pancrease, and the mucosa of GIT.

(b) Cardiovascular effects : Excess mineralocorticoid level may leads to excessive retention of sodium ions in plasma which results into hypertension.

Mechanism of action :

Aldosterone like other steroids, probably acts by influencing transcription level. The rate of formation is increased for such m-RNAs that serve as the templete for the synthesis of carrier proteins which subsequently facilitate the reabsorption of Na^+ ions in the distal renal tubules.

Progesterone, spiranolactone, actinomycin and puromycin block the aldosterone stimulated transport of Na^+ ions. However, they have no effects on the nonhormonal basal transport system of Na^+ ions.

17.9 DISEASES OF ADRENAL CORTEX

Corticosteroids participate in number of life-saving biochemical processes. They make it possible for humans to survive in highly fluctuating atmospheric conditions. In their absence, one would have to live the life in more rigid fashion. Under certain pathophysiological conditions, the functioning of adrenal cortex may get impaired, resulting into either oversecretion or deficiency of corticosteroids. The chronic overproduction of corticosteroids may give rise to the condition known as Cushing's syndrome while Addison's disease results due to chronic deficiency state of corticosteroids.

Cushing's syndrome :

The syndrome is characterized by deposition of fat over face, neck and trunk; hyperglycemia, decreased glucose tolerance, glycosuria, severe hypokalemic alkalosis, myopathy, osteoporosis, psychological changes, edema, hypertension, weakness and fatigability. The oversecretion of corticosteroids is usually accompanied with oversecretion of adrenal androgens (in the regions of zonae fasciculata and reticularis) which is responsible for other symptoms like, acne, hirsutism, amenorrhea and hypertrichosis in female patients.

The oversecretion of corticosteroids is responsible for all these symptoms. The fact was first-recognized by **Cushing** in 1932. Thereafter the disease state was recognized by his name Cushing's syndrome.

The overproduction of corticosteroids may result due to :

(a) Primary hyper cortisolism which arises mainly due to overproduction of corticosteroids from adrenal cortex independent of ACTH stimulation. It occurs due to adrenocortical tumours which releases corticosteroids in autonomic (unresponsive to plasma corticosteroid concentration) fashion. This hypersecretion of cortico steroids leads to suppression of normal pituitary functioning through the negative feed-back inhibitory mechanism. As a result, the secretion of ACTH decreases below normal level resulting into atrophy of the adrenal cortex.

(b) Secondary hypercortisolism which arises mainly due to overproduction of ACTH either from tumorous anterior pituitary lesions or from an overactive hypothalamus. The development of ectopic ACTH producing tumours at other sites (e.g. gall bladder, thymus, lung etc.) may be involved in some cases. In certain cases, secondary hypercortisolism also results due to secretion of ACTH-like substances. For example, increased CRF secretion also leads to secondary hypercortisolism.

During chronic alcoholism, the metabolic activity of liver gradually decreases resulting into decreased cortisol clearance from the body. The increased rate of release of ACTH and CRF induced by alcohol further contributes to development of pseudo-Cushing's syndrome.

17.10 INHIBITORS OF BIOSYNTHESIS OF ADRENOCORTICOSTEROIDS

Many drugs interfere in the biosynthetic pathway of adreno corticosteroids. These drugs can be effectively used in the treatment of Cushing's syndrome. Some may inhibit enzymes involved in the biosynthetic pathway while some drugs may be effective due to their adrenocorticolytic action. Clinically used agents from this category include :

(a) Mitotane (O, P' – DDD) : This compound was developed from the structures of insecticides like DDT and DDD. Due to its adrenocorticolytic action, it is useful in the palliative treatment of inoperative adrenocortical carcinoma. It is used to lower down the plasma levels of adreno-corticosteroids.

(b) Metyrapone : Chemically it is 2-methyl 1, 2 – di - 3 - pyridyl – 1 – propanone. It effectively inhibits the enzyme, 11 β - hydroxylase which is involved in the hydroxylation of steroidal nucleus at 11th-position. However, it is not favoured in the treatment of Cushing syndrome due to its severe toxicity reactions. Currently metyrapone is used as a diagnostic tool to evaluate the functioning of pituitary gland.

(c) Aminoglutethimide : Chemically, it is α-ethyl-p-aminophenyl - glutarimide. In early 1950s it was clinically introduced as anticonvulsant agent but it could not survive due to its severe toxicity reactions. In the biosynthesis of adrenocorticosteroids, aminoglutethimide effectively inhibits the conversion of cholesterol to 20 α-hydroxycholesterol which is essential for oxidative cleavage of the side chain of cholesterol. Thus, the production of all corticosteroids get hampered by aminoglutethimide administration. Besides this, the drug has destructive effects on zonae reticularis and fasciculata which additionally helps to potentiate the drugs effectiveness in the treatment of Cushing's syndrome. Prominent side-effects of aminoglutethimide include nausea, vomiting, anorexia, eye movements, sedation, dizziness, and lethargy.

17.11 ADDISON'S DISEASE

This condition is just opposite to that of Cushing's syndrome. It is characterized by chronic deficiency of corticosteroids which may arise due to destruction of the adrenal cortex region from infections and other pathophysiological condition. (e.g. tuberculosis, lupus erythematosus, Hodgkin's disease, AIDS etc.). The hypocortisolism results into development of weakness, anaemia, gastrointestinal irritability, loss of sodium ions, dehydration, hypotension etc. Urea and non-protein nitrogen accumulate in the blood due to renal impairment. Hyperpigmentation results due to elevated ACTH levels induced by hypocortisolism. Due to the subnormal plasma levels of corticosteroids, the patient must be protected from stressful and infectious conditions by the administration of exogenous corticosteroids.

Besides primary hypocortisolism, the risk of development of Addison's disease is elevated under certain disease conditions like, pernicious anaemia, diabetes mellitus, cerebral sclerosis and euthyroid goiter.

The treatment of Addison's disease usually consists of administration of both glucocorticoid and mineralocorticoid to the patient over a period of time.

INSULIN AND ORAL HYPOGLYCEMIC AGENTS

18.1 INTRODUCTION

The normal blood glucose level in humans ranges between 70 - 90 mg per 100 ml. Hyperglycemia is characterized by more than normal concentration of the blood sugar and hypoglycemia develops when the blood sugar level falls below the normal range. Diabetes mellitus is the condition arising due to abnormal metabolism of carbohydrates, fats and proteins. It is characterised mainly by an unusually high sugar level in the blood (hyperglycemia) and the presence of sugar in the urine (glucosuria). The ancient Greek and Roman physicians used the term *'Diabetes'* to mean large urine volume. The adjective 'melitus', a Latin word (meaning, honey), was added in 1674 by **Thomas Willis**. The large urine volume is due to the large amounts of glucose and urea in the urine (osmotic diuresis). Early references in Ayurveda to this disease had also been reported. Charaka referred to diabetes as a *'diseased flow of urine'* and mentioned that ants are attracted by urine of a person affected with this disease.

Because the biochemical basis of diabetes is still not clear, the disease is usually defined by its symptoms. These includes, hyperglycemia, hyperlipemia, glucosuria, polyuria (loss of water and salts), polydipsia (increase in thirst), polyphagia (excessive hunger), ketonemia (ketone bodies and fatty acids in the blood), ketonuria (ketone bodies in the urine), azoturia (increased production and excretion of urea and ammonia), poor wound healing and infection. Sometimes, the disease eventually causes serious complications like, kidney damage, retina degeneration, premature atherosclerosis, cataract, heart disease, neurological dysfunction and a predisposition to gangrene. A complex interplay of endocrinal, immunological, infectious and genetic factors is involved in the etiology of the disease. **Von Mering** and **Minkowski** were first to link the functioning of pancreas with the onset of this disease. In 1889, they induced similar diabetic symptoms in pancreatectomized dogs, implicating that the lack of a pancreatic hormone is the etiology of the disease.

It is now agreed that diabetes is characterized by a deficiency of effective insulin which is a pancreatic hormone. **Banting** and **Best** through a simple but intellectual experiment on pancreatic ductilgated dog demonstrated the role of insulin in diabetes. It was on the midnight of July 30, 1921 that they injected a pancreatic extract to a depancreatised diabetic dog on the verge of coma. Urine sugar abolished and blood sugar came down to normal after one hour. Insulin was thus born.

Diabetes could be caused not only by a deficiency of insulin but also by disturbances in the levels of certain other substances like, adrenaline, pituitary hormones, corticosteroids, aldosterone, oestrogen, thyroid hormones and glucagon. All these bioactive substances exert their own influence on blood-sugar level. Determination of glucose tolerance curve is the most useful pathological test for diabetes. In humans, pancreas (the organ lying behind the upper intestine) contains about a million islets of Langerhans, which constitute, about 1% - 2% of the pancreatic tissue. The cells from these islets can be categorised as :

(i) α - cells which are mainly present in the outer cortex and represent about 25% of the islet cells. They secrete glucagon.

(ii) β - cells which are concentrated mainly in the medulla and constitute about 60% of the islet population. Insulin is secreted by these cells.

(iii) D - cells or δ - cells which are involved in the secretion of somatostatin and inhibits the release of both, glucagon and insulin, and

(iv) PP or F cells which are responsible for the release of pancreatic polypeptide.

Thus, glucagon (α - cells), insulin (β - cells) and somatostatin along with gastrin (D - cells) are the principal hormones secreted and released by the islets. Proteolytic destruction of insulin by the digestive enzymes of pancreas during the course of extraction has been reported. Insulin may be regarded principally as a hormone of anabolism while glucagon as a hormone of catabolism. That is to say, insulin will pull out the excess of blood sugar under the glucostatic function of the liver where excess glucose is converted to glycogen. Similarly, when glucagon secretion is more (as in the fasting state), the body's energy needs are fulfilled by promoting conversion of glycogen to glucose in the liver and thus increasing the blood sugar concentration. Pancreatic somatostatin can inhibit the secretion of both insulin

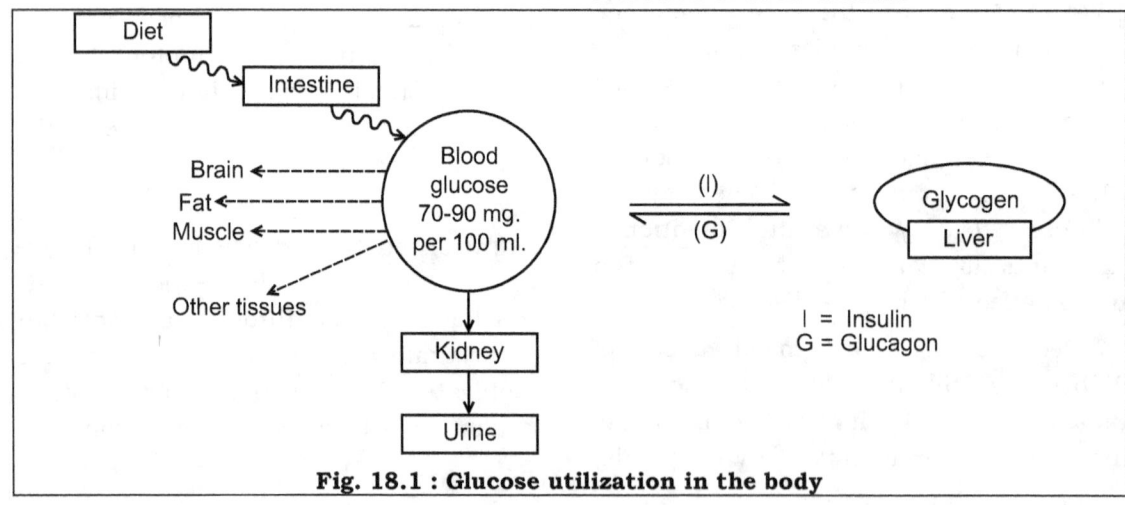

Fig. 18.1 : **Glucose utilization in the body**

and glucagon. It may be having its role in maintaining the proper ratio of insulin to glucagon. Thus, it is not the absolute blood level of insulin but, the insulin glucagon molar ratio (I/G) in the blood that determines the blood sugar level. It means in diabetes, the I/G molar ratio is disturbed instead of insulin secretion alone.

In insulin deficiency, following metabolic reactions get accelerated :

(i) Conversion of liver glycogen to glucose.

(ii) Conversion of fatty substances to glucose, and

(iii) Conversion of proteins to glucose.

As a result, the blood sugar concentration increases which leads to higher rate of excretion of glucose through the urine along with large amounts of water (osmosis diuresis). Due to the disturbed I/G ratio, the insulin dependent entry of glucose into the muscles and other peripheral tissues get paralyzed. Hence to meet the energy demands for their normal metabolic activities, these tissues utilise the deposited fat as a source of energy. The increased mobilization of fat (lipolysis) from the peripheral fat depots leads to increased formation of ketone bodies (ketosis). Proteineous material also undergoes metabolism, releasing nitrogenous waste products. Since some of the ketone bodies are organic acids, acidosis (ketoacidosis) develops partly due to the loss of Na^+ and K^+ ions with ketone bodies in the form of their salts in the urine. If the condition is not given proper attention, the chronic loss of water and electrolytes coupled with accumulation of H^+ ions can lead to diabetic acidosis and coma.

18.2 TYPES OF DIABETES

Under current clinical terms, diabetes mellitus can be categorised as under :

(i) Insulin - dependent, type I (IDDM or juvenile or brittle or unstable diabetes),

(ii) Non-insulin dependent type, type II (NIDDM or adult onset or maturity onset diabetes)

(iii) Other types :

(a) Insulin receptor abnormalities

(b) Hormonal etiology e.g., acromegaly

(c) Pancreatic disease

(d) Genetically related abnormalities

(e) Drug-induced conditions.

Another term 'diabetes insipidius' is sometimes used in which the urine of the patient remains tasteless. Now-a-days, the term 'diabetes insipidius' is reserved for the conditions produced by the disorders of the pituitary gland and the term 'diabetes mellitus' is used to describe the actual diabetes.

(i) Insulin Dependent Diabetes Mellitus (IDDM) :

This condition results when there is underproduction of insulin in childhood or adolescence. The principal derangement is the failure of β-cells to produce insulin in full capacity. The insignificant amount of insulin fails to properly utilise and metabolize carbohydrate as the available source of energy. To overcome the shortage in energy production, body attempts to find out other alternative pathways. To meet the energy demand, fat and protein metabolism gets accelerated. These metabolic alterations are symptomized by the presence of increased amounts of ketone bodies and nitrogenous waste material, both, in the blood and in the urine. In severe ketosis, coma follows. In less severe cases, poor wound healing, infections, nausea, vomiting, restlessness and drowsiness constitute as main symptoms. Evidences are gathering to suggest that juvenile diabetes may have a viral origin. Scattered reports support this proposal. The communicable nature of this type of diabetes adds to the evidence. The persons having genetic susceptibility to get affected by virus easily get diabetes. Recently 'encephalomyocarditis' virus was reported to produce diabetes when injected into mice. It is proposed that a viral attack may trigger an auto immune reaction which destroys some of the pancreatic β-cells and thus partially cuts-off the source of insulin. Though there is marked reduction in the number of β-cells, the number of α, D and PP cells appears to be unaffected. The number of β-cells may get decreased due to the patients exposure to certain chemicals. These chemicals selectively destroy pancreatic β-cells and thus reduce the secretion of insulin. Such agents include, alloxan, uric acid, dehydroascorbic acid, quinolones and streptozocin.

If viral etiology proves its correctness in near future, alone a suitable vaccine treatment would assure an easy and effective solution to this problem.

Table 18.1 : Insulin dependent versus non-insulin dependent forms of diabetes mellitus

IDDM	NIDDM
1. Lacks the ability to synthesize and release insulin due to destruction of some β- cells.	1. Can synthesize and release insulin but not enough to meet the requirement.
2. Occurs at an early age.	2. Occurs in the people usually over the age of forty.
3. Obesity is not the common factor.	3. Obesity is generally a contributing factor.
4. May be of viral origin.	4. May be of hereditary origin.
5. Equally affects male and female.	5. Females are more attacked than males.
6. The mass of α, D and PP cells remain unchanged.	6. The mass of β, D and PP cells remain unchanged.
7. Characterized by decreased secretion of insulin.	7. Characterized by increased secretion of glucagon.
8. Insulin therapy is the only answer.	8. Oral hypoglycemic agents can serve the purpose.

(ii) Non-insulin Dependent Diabetes Mellitus (NIDDM):

This type has more definite genetic and hereditary characteristics. This disease type announces its presence quite late. More often this is a disease of affluent and old aged people and is more common in women than in men. The patient retains a considerable number of functioning β-cells making insulin deficiency less severe. However the population of α-cells is increased without major changes in D or PP cells. Ketosis does not occur and wasting is not a common feature. This indicates that this type may not need any treatment except a strict dietary restriction.

Other types include latent diabetes where the symptoms arise only under the conditions of strain and stress. In some patients, biochemical tests confirm the presence of the disease but the persons enjoy the life like any normal person (i.e. mild non-obese diabetes). Similarly, due to complex hormonal and metabolic changes that occur during infection or pregnancy, gestational diabetes may develop.

Whichever may be the type, the principal cause behind each type of diabetes remains the same, i.e. deficient insulin production. All have acknowledged insulin as antidiabetic agent of great importance. Diabetes, if not treated with insulin or with any other oral hypoglycemic agent, may result in thickening of capillary basement membrane. Gangrene of the extremities and degenerative diseases of retina, nerve tissues and arterioles which accompany the disease can be explained on this basis. Cataracts and nerve lesions may be seen due to covalent interaction of glucose with tissue proteins in the lens and the nerve. Swelling occurs due to the accumulation of sugar in these lesions.

Mobilization of fat (lipolysis) is the process governed by insulin, glucagon and anterior pituitary hormone. Insulin has antilipolytic action. Hence in insulin deficiency, lipolysis is facilitated. The resulting fatty acid flow is directed to the liver where they are oxidised to acetyl CoA. The latter is converted into various ketone bodies. These include acetoacetic acid, β-hydroxy butyric acid and acetone. In ketosis, overproduction of ketone bodies occur. They enter the blood stream for distribution and oxidation in the kidneys, muscle, heart, brain and testis. Acetone is exhaled in the breath and the person has a characteristic acetone breath. It occurs in starvation, in severe diabetes, in the *'acidosis of childhood'* and during anaesthesia, where it serves as an important sign of the attack of coma. Insulin acts primarily by controlling and rectifying the disturbances in carbohydrate, fat and protein metabolism. It suppresses lipogenesis and prevents hyperlipemia and ketogenesis. The free fatty acids are again re-esterified to triglycerides in adipose tissues. Some of them are routinely utilized as a source of energy in tissues except brain, erythrocytes and adrenal medulla.

During insulin deficient state, glucose continues to get synthesized from amino acids and triglyceride, despite the high levels of circulating blood glucose. Insulin prevents this undesired protein and fat metabolism and promotes protein synthesis. Its anabolic effect is exerted through the catalysis of various enzymatic steps in glucogenolysis. During hyperglycemia, insulin promotes lipogenesis by -

(a) increasing the glucose transport in adipose tissues, and

(b) exerting antilipolytic effects.

Though all this is true, the clinical evaluation of insulin does not certify it as an ideal antidiabetic agent. Regardless of its ability to control certain symptoms and to prevent ketoacidosis and impending coma in diabetic patient, insulin has its own limitations which are listed below :

(i) Insulin must be injected, because if given orally it is destroyed by pepsin and trypsin. (It is not orally effective due to its proteinous nature. It gets easily destroyed in the gastric environment of stomach).

(ii) Clinical limitations are numerous. All marketed insulin preparations cause (a) allergic reactions, local or generalized, in sensitive individuals, and (b) antibody formation against insulin, requiring increasing doses or occasionally inducing insulin resistance. Available insulins are prepared with chemical structure which differ in one terminal amino acid where alanine is replaced by threonine; a preparation identical to human insulin is still sought. Desalanino pork insulin, recently synthesized and tested in animals, may have the same hypoglycemic properties and be less likely to induce antibody. The proteinous nature of the hormone triggers allergic reactions at the site of injection when given parenterally.

(iii) Insulin fails to give expected results if the restrictions of the diet and exercise are not strictly observed.

(iv) In diabetic patients, the disturbances in basic biochemical reactions leads to the alterations in the thickening of the basement membranes of many tissues, especially that of kidney and arterioles. Though insulin therapy rectifies the cause of the disease, already occurred consequences as mentioned above are left untouched. This gets reflected in long-term complications in cardiovascular, renal, neural and visual systems. Only when diabetic patient begins to develop cardiac and renal problems at a rate greater than the normal person, one realises that insulin therapy alone could not be the only answer to the treatment of diabetes. Disturbed carbohydrate metabolism alone does not constitute the etiology of the disease but remains only one of the segments of this complex disease. As time went by, the etiology of this disease was found to be many folded, ranging from purely endocrine nature to immunological, infectious and of genetic origin.

Diabetes may also accompany diseases of other organs, like that of liver, kidney, adrenal cortex, thyroid and pituitary gland. Glucocorticoidal therapy has been reported to aggreviate the disease conditions. Many drugs (e.g. thiazide diuretics) may also precipitate it in certain cases.

18.3 INSULIN AND ITS PREPARATION

Classically, diabetes mellitus has been characterized as the deficiency of insulin. Insulin is the first protein for which a complete amino acid sequence was established in 1956 by **Sanger**. Insulin is now regarded as the largest polypeptide hormone of known structure. The term 'insulin' was used first time to refer the hypoglycemic principle needed to control the diabetic symptoms by **De Meyer** in 1909. It is a typical globular protein which ranks as one of the first proteins obtained in crystalline form.

Insulin, with a molecular weight of about 6,000, is made up of two chains A (acidic) and B (basic), containing 21 and 30 amino acids respectively. Thus, total 51 amino acids are present in insulin molecule. The chains are bridged by two disulfide linkages and a third disulfide connection occurs within the shorter chain A.

Commercially insulin is obtained by extraction of the pancreas of animals like, cattle, pigs or fish. If compared with human insulin, the animal origined insulins are functionally similar but slightly differ structurally. Bovine insulin is contaminated with pancreatic polypeptide, somatostatin, glucagon and vasoactive intestinal polypeptide like substances. Beside this, commercial insulin preparations contain traces of proinsulin and C-peptides. These contaminations and minute structural differences are enough to induce weak antigen-antibody interactions when insulin from animal source is used therapeutically.

The chemical routes of insulin synthesis are quite expensive and time consuming. Reports describing synthesis of insulin by using recombinant DNA technology are being received. For example, **Ullrich et al** in 1977 have successfully incorporated the gene for rat insulin into bacterial plasmids. An achievement of high repute has been reported in 1983 by **Frank** and **Chance** who described the successful synthesis of human insulin by cloning of DNA in *Escherichia coli*. Commercial feasibility of such a project assures the supply of insulin at a cheaper rate.

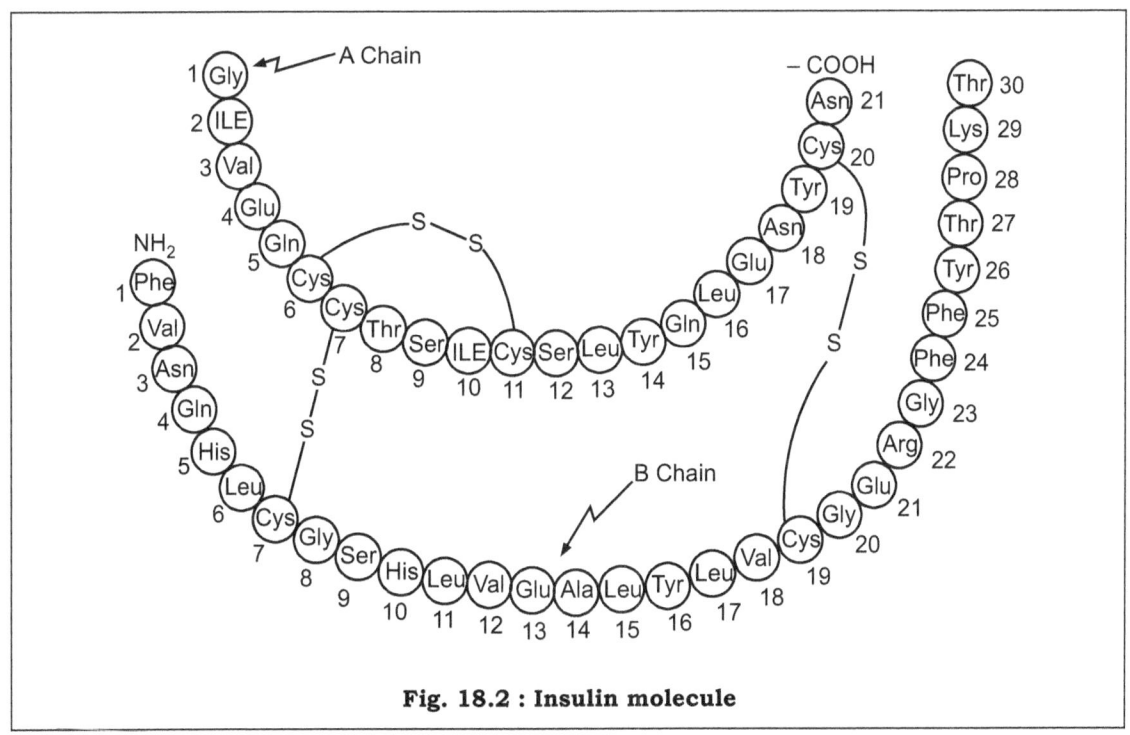

Fig. 18.2 : Insulin molecule

The term insulin also includes other substances like, insulin-like growth factors I and II. In aqueous solution, insulin has a tendency to get polymerized resulting into the formation of polymers (dimer or hexamer) of molecular weight ranging from 12000 to 36000. Two molecules of Zn^{++} are co-ordinated in the hexamer form which is then stored within the granules until it is discharged from the cell through exocytosis process. The biologically active form of insulin is found to be a monomer. The pH control of aqueous solution is therefore necessary to maintain the structure and activity of natural insulin. Differences also lie in the mammalian insulins. The most common positions at which differences cited are :

In chain A : positions 8, 9 and 10

In chain B : position 30.

Though physiologically active molecule of insulin was found to be present in its monomer form, it is stored as the hexamer in the storage granules of the β-cells. Insulin secretion is stimulated by amino acids, fatty acids, ketone bodies as well as by glucose.

18.4 BIOSYNTHESIS OF INSULIN

Rubenstein and **Steiner** in 1971 demonstrated that insulin is released in β-cells of pancreases through an enzymatic conversion of proinsulin. It is a single chain, high molecular weight-peptide and is devoid of any biological activity. A thiol-activated protease enzyme catalyzes this conversion. **Chance et al**, in 1976, going a step ahead, proposed the existence of precursor of even proinsulin, which he named as preproinsulin. The protease enzyme catalyses the cleavage of proinsulin molecule resulting into formation of insulin, four basic amino acids (arginine 31, arginine 32, lysine 64 and arginine 65) and one molecule of C-peptide (the connector containing amino acids from 33 to 63).

Preproinsulin (109 amino acids) is synthesized in the ribosomes of endoplasmic reticulum of the pancreatic β - cells. At this same site, the conversion of preproinsulin to proinsulin occurs. The latter is transferred through vesicles to the Golgi apparatus and stored in immature granules. The conversion of proinsulin to insulin is a slow and gradual process which continues along with maturation of the storage granules. As most of proinsulin gets converted to insulin (about 4 - 5 hours), the conversion products and starting material get crystallized with zinc. Thereafter, it may be released by exocytosis or may be stored further. The release is signalled by neuronal and/or hormonal factors.

18.5 SECRETION OF INSULIN

The capacity of pancreas to secrete insulin ranges from 1-2 mg per day. However, under fasting conditions, the insulin secretion may be increased to 20 µg per hour. The glucose concentration in the blood serves as a stimulus to the biochemical reactions needed to initiate insulin release. Other hypotheses stress the importance of glucose metabolites (e.g. ATP, glucose - 6 -phosphate, phosphoenolpyruvate etc.) and try to link the increase in the concentration of these metabolites with insulin release. Beside this, several hormones from GIT (e.g. secretin, gastrin, pancreozymin cholecystokinin vasoactive intestinal polypeptide etc.) also enhance the rate of insulin release.

The islets are richly innervated by adrenergic and cholinergic nerves. Within the pancreatic cells, glucagon and vagal nerve stimulate the secretion of insulin and somatostatin. Somatostatin inhibits the secretion of both, insulin and glucagon while insulin prevents the release of glucagon. This explains the interhormonal autoregulation of the insulin release. Under the conditions of strain and stress (i.e. increased catecholamine release), the insulin secretion is suppressed through the activation of α - adrenoceptors. Thus, depending upon quality and quantity of the food ingested, hypothalamus regulates the insulin secretion from β-cells through autonomic nervous system.

The breaking of storage granules of insulin requires the presence of intracellular calcium in an energy consuming process. The secretory granules contain about 10% of insulin of their total storage capacity. The secreted insulin is taken in the pancreatic vein that ultimately transports it to the portal vein. During its passage through the liver, a large fraction of released insulin (about 40 - 60%) from the portal blood is removed and metabolized by the action of metabolizing enzymes like,

(i) Glutathione - insulin - transhydrogenase which breaks the disulfide linkages through reductive cleavage and

(ii) Insulinase enzymes that further dearrange the chains A and B to smaller peptides and amino acids.

(iii) Some peptide bonds present in the insulin may be hydrolyzed by pepsin and chymotrypsin.

The remaining amount is made available to the systemic circulation. The insulin concentration in the plasma ranges from 6-26 µg/ml. It is mainly present in the free form while slight amount of the circulating insulin may be bound to α and β-globulins. The half-life of insulin in plasma ranges from 6.5 to 9.0 minutes.

18.6 CHEMISTRY OF INSULIN

In 1926, **Abel** isolated insulin in a crystalline form. By using X-ray crystallography techniques, **Dorothy Hodgkin** and her associates reported three-dimensional arrangement of atoms in insulin molecule. For such excellent work, she had been awarded Nobel prize. In the early 1960's **Sanger et al** established the exact sequence of amino acids in this polypeptide hormone. Utilizing the data of Sanger, the complete chemical synthesis of insulin was reported in 1963-64 by **Meienhofer et al** and **Kotsoyannis et al** but independently. To date, structural elucidations of insulins from atleast 25 species have been documented in the literature. The first total chemical synthesis of human insulin was claimed by **Rittel et al.** In human insulin, B-strand possesses a helical pattern in which A-strand appears to get entrapped.

The analogue, Lys (B 28), Pro (B 29) human insulin is prepared by reversing the sequence of two residues at positions B 28 and B 29. These changes result in an insulin molecule with a great reduced capacity for self association in solution. This makes it a rapidly absorbed analogue of human insulin.

18.7 PHYSIOLOGICAL FUNCTIONS OF INSULIN

(i) Insulin is an anabolic hormone. It catalyses the synthesis of various macromolecules and prevents undue breakdown of proteins, carbohydrates and fat. Thus, it promotes cell growth by deposition of carbohydrates, lipids and proteins.

(ii) It regulates the redox-potential gradient at the cell surface and by increasing the total number of hexose transporters, it facilitates the entry of glucose molecules to adipose tissues, cardiac tissues and skeletal muscles with minimum expenditure of energy. In the muscles and adipose tissues, glucose metabolises to acetyl CoA which is then utilised in the synthesis of fatty acids.

While in the liver, various enzymes (glucokinase, phosphofructokinase and pyruvase kinase) involved in the glucose metabolism are directed in such a way to favour glycogenesis and decreasing glycogenolysis. This explains the role of insulin in lowering down the blood glucose levels.

(iii) It lowers the plasma amino acid levels by increasing the transport of certain amino acids into the tissues. It enhances the incorporation of amino acids into protein. It inhibits protein degradation by acting at transcriptional and translational levels and establishes a positive nitrogen balance.

(iv) It promotes lipogenesis (fatty acid synthesis) and inhibits ketosis by

(a) deactivating the lipoprotein lipase enzyme, and

(b) enhancing the glucose transport to cell.

Ketosis disappears probably because insulin decreases the release of fatty acids from the adipose tissues by lowering the levels of c-AMP.

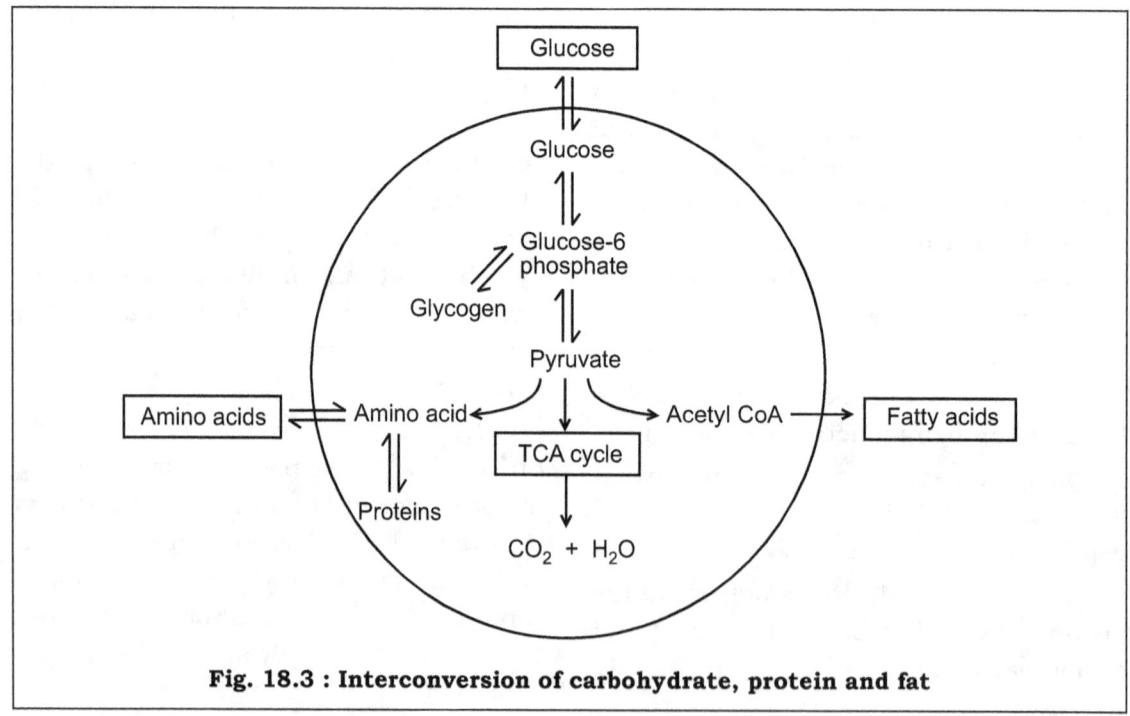

Fig. 18.3 : Interconversion of carbohydrate, protein and fat

18.8 MECHANISM OF ACTION

(i) Cyclic-AMP plays an important role in phosphorylation of various protein kinases involved in the metabolism of carbohydrate, proteins and fat. Various hormones affect the blood glucose level by influencing the concentration of c-AMP. For example, hormones like, epinephrine, glucagon and ACTH tend to increase intracellular c-AMP concentration. Similar effects are also exerted by secretin, thyroxine and TSH. While insulin, melatonin and PGF_2 tend to lower down intracellular c-AMP concentration. Thus, insulin promotes dephosphorylation of activated protein kinases.

(ii) Triglyceride lipase is involved in lipolysis process. It is activated by c-AMP through phosphorylation. Insulin exerts antilipolytic effect by catalysing dephosphorylation process. Similarly by dephosphorylation of pyruvate dehydrogenase, the conversion of pyruvate to glucose is inhibited by insulin. Hence, pyruvate has to get converted to fat.

(iii) Modern X-ray crystallography studies on insulin molecule indicated that the activity is exhibited only when insulin projects itself in a specific conformation. This requirement suggests the presence of receptor sites for insulin. According to *'insulin receptor theory'* insulin receptors exist in both, high affinity form and low affinity form. Insulin receptor is a membrane glycoprotein of an α_2, β_2 subunit structure. The α-units bind insulin and β-units function as tyrosine kinase. Insulin receptor contains two α-subunits (molecular weight 125,000) and two β-subunits (molecular weight 90,000) which are bridged by disulfide bonds. Insulin binds with the receptor surface. Amino acids, 1, 4, 5, 19 and 21 in chain-A and amino acids 12, 16, 24, 25 and 26 in chain B of insulin molecule participate in drug receptor interaction. The receptor activation then induces changes in the sensitivity of various protein kinases to c-AMP, beside lowering the intracellular concentration of c-AMP. The latter effect is brought about by desensitization of adenylate cyclase.

(iv) Beside the insulin receptor sites, the presence of distinct binding sites for insulin in different body organs has been proposed. These binding sites are mainly present in the nucleus, endoplasmic reticulum and Golgi apparatus, and participate in extending the duration of action of insulin specifically in the liver, adipose tissues and skeletal muscle.

18.9 INSULIN DEFICIENCY

The most prominent effects of insulin are exerted mainly on the liver, adipose tissues and skeletal muscle. These effects are anabolic in nature. Hence, the deficiency of insulin is mainly characterized by hyperglycemia, hyperlipemia, ketonemia, acidosis and azoturia.

During insulin deficiency, various routes of glucose utilization are suppressed. The rate of glucose transport across the cell membrane is also reduced (except brain, erythrocytes, leukocytes).

However, the rates of hepatic conversion of glycogen, fatty acids and proteins to glucose are accelerated. The overall result of such under-utilization and overproduction of glucose is hyperglycemia and elimination of excess glucose in the urine of the patient.

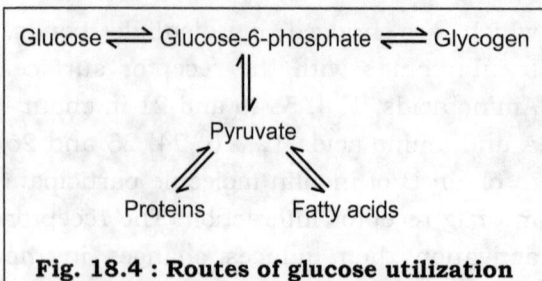

Fig. 18.4 : Routes of glucose utilization

Insulin exerts antilipolytic action. In its deficiency, mobilization of fat (lipolysis) proceeds uninhibited resulting into high plasma levels of free fatty acids. This leads to hyperlipemia. Lipogenesis from pyruvate - acetyl CoA system is also suppressed. Hence, acetyl CoA is utilized only in the production of ketone bodies, some of which are relatively strong acids. Ketonemia and acidosis thus develop due to higher rate of formation of ketone bodies.

In insulin deficiency, protein synthesis is suppressed. On the contrary, proteins are catabolised to glucose at relatively higher rate. As a result, production of urea and ammonia is enhanced. The increased excretion of urea and ammonia in urine (azoturia) is thus seen in the insulin deficient patients.

18.10 ADVERSE EFFECTS

Most of the adverse effects of insulin therapy are seen due to higher plasma insulin concentration. The hypoglycemic state in the brain may give rise to headache, blurred vision, mental confusion, coma and convulsions. Some of the early symptoms are due to secretion of epinephrine which promotes glycogenolysis and thus partly counteracts the hypoglycemia. The reflex release of catecholamines leads to sweating, weakness, and tachycardia. Peripheral edema also occurs due to the retention of sodium ions caused by insulin-induced activation of $Na^+ - K^+ -$ ATPase pump.

Mild to moderate allergic reactions (itching, swelling) may accompany the use of commercial insulin preparations due to proteinous contaminants and their antigenic nature. In certain cases, the use of antihistaminic agents can be advised. In more severe forms, however, insulin therapy has to be replaced by oral hypoglycemic agents.

18.11 INSULIN RESISTANT DIABETES

Patient is said to be insulin resistant when he does not respond to insulin therapy. In such cases, the insulin requirement may exceed 200 units per day. This may occur due to involvement of certain genetic or autoimmune factors, such as :

(i) Proinsulin may not be efficiently converted to insulin at the expected rate due to genetic defaults. Since proinsulin is weak hypoglycemic agent (only about 5% as active as insulin), diabetic condition may develop.

(ii) Even though insulin secretion is normal, the low intensity of biological effects of insulin may be due to decrease in both, the receptor sites and binding sites in the tissues.

(iii) Due to some autoimmune mechanisms, the anti-insulin antibodies may be generated and insulin-receptor interaction may be inhibited by these antibodies.

(iv) Oversecretion of physiological antagonists for insulin (e.g. glucagon, epinephrine) may be one of the reasons in insulin resistant diabetic patients.

18.12 INSULIN PREPARATIONS

(a) Short-acting Insulin Preparations :

As the plasma half-life of intravenously injected insulin is not enough to meet the requirements, one has to search for such insulin preparations, having quick onset and prolong duration of action. Presently, available insulin preparations differ only with respect to onset and duration of action. First clinically used form was amorphous insulin which was highly soluble in body fluids. This leads to its rapid excretion and hence it was to be replaced by other insulin preparations. In early 1940's came 'Regular insulin' which is a buffered solution of crystalline zinc insulin. Duration of action of this preparation still needs improvement. Chemically pure zinc insulin has physiologic action essentially identical to that of regular non-crystalline insulin as far as onset duration and rate of blood sugar reduction are concerned.

(b) Intermediate and Long-acting Insulin Preparations :

(i) Protamine-insulin preparations : The longer duration of action is due to protamine, a basic protein that leaves the site of injection more slowly.

(ii) Protamine zinc insulin preparations : Prolonged duration of action of insulin, a long time objective, was finally achieved by **Hagedorn** in 1935 with protamine zinc insulin. Developed in 1936, these suspensions were proved to be better than 'Protamine insuline' duration of action. This is prepared by complexing insulin with zinc and protamine. The products are available with 40 - 80 units/ml.

(iii) Globin zinc insulin preparation : Developed in 1939, its duration of action (12 - 18 hours) is less than protamine zinc insulin preparations (24 - 36 hours).

(iv) Isophane insulin suspensions : Developed in 1946, these suspensions contain protamine, zinc and insulin. It differs from 'protamine zinc insulin' in the method of preparation and contains less protamine than 'protamine zinc insulin'. This preparation has 'time activity' best adopted to the requirements of majority of diabetic patients. This has a blood-sugar lowering effect usually lasting over 24 hours.

(v) Lante insulins : The solubility pattern of insulin (and hence its absorption) is mainly governed by its physical state. For example, large crystals of insulin with high zinc content will be less soluble in body fluids and naturally produce long duration of action due to slow absorption. Such preparations are known as 'ultralante insulins'. This concept was utilized to develop such preparations which do not need a protein modifier (e.g. protamine or globin) to prolong their action. Stretching the same concept ahead, amorphous insulin exhibits rapid absorption and hence rapid onset of action. Such insulin zinc suspension is known as semilante insulin. A proper combination of ultralante insulin (7 parts) and 'semilante insulin' (3 parts) will naturally constitute a preparation having a rapid onset and intermediate duration of action; both the properties desirable for well clinical acceptance of the preparation.

(c) Very Long-acting Insulin Preparations :

Attempts to formulate insulin preparations with very long duration of action are made. The solubility of insulin at physiological pH 7.4 is mainly controlled by the amount of $ZnCl_2$ which is increased to 5 - 10 times than normally required to prepare *'soluble zinc insulin'*. The increased concentration of zinc ions form low solubility complexes with insulin molecules if the buffer is changed from phosphate to acetate. Such suspensions are reported in U.S.P.

18.13 LIMITATIONS OF INSULIN THERAPY

Present evidences regarding insulin therapy uncovered the limitations of insulin and do not agree to recognize insulin as an ideal hypoglycemic agent. Various problems encountered in insulin therapy are listed below :

(i) In the long term therapy, there is a risk of development of tumours at the site of injection.

(ii) Due to its proteinous nature, insulin triggers local allergic reactions in sensitive patients. Anaphylactic shock may occur in extreme cases.

(iii) Fluctuations in blood glucose levels may lead to visual disturbances which may extend to blindness. This is mainly due to disturbed osmotic equilibrium in the eyes.

(iv) If the dose schedule is not properly corrected according to the requirement, insulin therapy leads to hypoglycemic shock.

(v) Thickening of basement membrane of several tissues (due to poor control of blood glucose level), particularly of kidney and vasculature leads to renal and cardiovascular impairments.

(vi) Every exogenous protein is associated with antigenic properties to less or more extent. Naturally insulin administration in almost every patient leads to the production of insulin antibodies which bind insulin and decrease its effectiveness. This is known as 'insulin resistance'. This is the most severe problem of insulin therapy where the daily insulin requirement exceeds 200 units in comparison to the normal requirement of 50 units a day. This resistance thus, has an immunological basis and can be solved by shifting :

(a) from conventional to purified insulin therapy, or

(b) from one insulin type (e.g. bovine insulin) to another insulin type (e.g. porcine insulin).

Here the insulin from another origin will be new to the body and resistance to this insulin would not occur atleast for couple of months. This is due to the failure of the body mechanisms to recognize immediately the new insulin type (and therefore to generate antibodies for it).

18.14 ORAL HYPOGLYCEMIC AGENTS

Insulin, due to its proteinous nature, is destroyed in the gastric environment of the stomach. Some peptide bonds present in insulin structure are hydrolyzed by pepsin and chymotrypsin in GIT. Hence, it is orally ineffective. Therefore, it is usually given by subcutaneous injection.

The most attractive and direct approach to treat diabetes, however, will be administration of orally active hypoglycemic agents. Various limitations of insulin therapy along with its inactivation in GIT, encouraged medicinal chemists to find out potent and orally active hypoglycemic candidates which may stand firmly as alternative or substitute to insulin therapy in maturity onset type of diabetes. In juvenile type, strict dietary control along with exogenously administered insulin constitute the only treatment.

The presently available oral hypoglycemic drugs can be classified as :

(a) Guanidine derivatives,

(b) Sulfonylureas, and

(c) Miscellaneous agents.

(a) Guanidine Derivatives :

The parent lead compound of this series, guanidine was reported to lower blood glucose levels in animals in 1918. High toxicities associated with its use necessitated the search for better drug in this series. Subsequently, phenformin was reported which is comparatively more safe, non-toxic biguanide. It was soon followed by metformin, another biguanide. These biguanides are usually represented by following general formula.

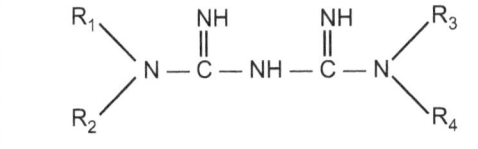

Fig. 18.5 : General formula for biguanides

Phenformin and metformin are similar in their actions. The normal therapeutic dose for both these biguanides ranges from 25 - 150 mg/day. They do not stimulate insulin release but remain ineffective in the absence of insulin. Because of lactic acidosis associated with the use of phenformin, it was withdrawn from the market.

The possible mechanisms of action of these hypoglycemic biguanides include :

(i) Inhibition of intestinal transport and absorption of sugars.

(ii) Potentiation of the action of insulin on glucose transfer processes into the cell.

(iii) Inhibition of hepatic gluconeogenesis, and

(iv) Enhancement of glucose utilisation processes and / or inhibition of oxidative phosphorylation in the peripheral tissues.

Biguanidines :

It dates back to 1920 when, two biguanidines i.e. synthaline A and B were reported to lower blood glucose level in diabetic patients. High toxicity, failure to offer advantages over insulin and a number of fatalities (renal and hepatic damages), associated with these drugs lead to their clinical termination.

$$H_2N - \overset{\overset{NH}{\|}}{C} - NH - (CH_2)_n - NH - \overset{\overset{NH}{\|}}{C} - NH_2$$

(i) Synthalin A; decamethylene; n = 10

(ii) Synthalin B; dodecamethylene; n = 12

Both the drugs are orally well absorbed. In liver, phenformin undergoes p-hydroxylation. Both, the drug and its p-hydroxy metabolite are then excreted through urine. Metformin is mainly concentrated in intestinal mucosa and salivary gland. It does not undergo metabolic degradations in body. Hence unlike phenformin, metformin can be given to the patient with liver or kidney dysfunction.

Severe side-effects of biguanide therapy include, nausea, vomiting, anorexia and fatigue. Biguanides also reduce the GIT absorption of amino acids and other ingredients of dietary-energy value. They also lowers down the plasma levels of triglycerides and cholesterol. In the treatment of maturity onset diabetes, biguanides thus offer two fold advantage. They induce weight loss and also reduce obesity along with their hypoglycemic action.

In patients with cardiac (myocardial infarction) or renal disease, phenformin treatment was found to increase blood lactic acid level. This lactic acidosis sometimes induces severe fatalities in patients. Lactic acidosis is characterized by dehydration, acidosis and a bicarbonate deficiency. This complication demands contraindication of phenformin in patients having liver, heart and kidney diseases. The increased incidences of lactic acidosis due to phenformin compelled FDA of U.S.A., to bring restrictions on the general marketing of the drug in July, 1977. Along with acidosis, prolonged use of phenformin is found to induce malabsorption of cyanocobalamin. On the creditable sides, biguanides sometime have been used in combination with insulin preparation for smoother control of brittle diabetes in some patients. They are also used in combination with sulfonylureas, in cases where treatment with either agent alone, fails.

At high doses, biguanides decrease cellular ATP/AMP ratio by inhibiting respiration. As a result of this, anaerobic glycolysis becomes the chief source of energy accompanied by a decrease in gluconeogenesis.

(b) Sulfonylureas :

The association of hypoglycemic activity with sulphonamide derivatives was first reported by **Janbon** in 1940s. This was soon followed by the introduction of carbutamide (antibacterial sulfonamide) by **Franke** and **Fuchs** in 1955. It was the first effective oral hypoglycemic agent from sulfonylurea class. Except carbutamide, other sulfonylureas lack antibacterial activity due to absence of amino group para to the $-SO_2NH$ on the benzene ring.

In all effective compounds, a substituted arylsulfonyl moiety is attached to N^1- of urea molecule.

These derivatives are structurally similar and bear essentially the similar properties. They differ in their duration of action and chemically in the nature of the substituent at para position (-X-) and R. The substitution of aliphatic side-chain present in the first generation hypoglycemic sulfonylureas by cyclopentyl or cyclohexyl group and addition of yet another ring structure to the aromatic nucleus resulted into development of more potent second generation series.

18.15 MECHANISM OF ACTION

Sulfonylureas affect various plasma factors that influence the insulin release.

(i) Sulfonylureas are found to be effective only in patients who retain functioning of islet β-cells or in non-insulin-dependent diabetic patients. Hence, the principal mechanism of action is to stimulate the production and secretion of insulin by the β-cells of pancrease. Glucose also stimulates insulin release but mechanism at molecular level differs from that of sulfonylureas.

(ii) These drugs may lower down the output of glucose from the liver by insulin independent mechanism.

(iii) Extrapancreatic effects : These effects could be linked to the hypoglycemic activity of sulfonylureas. These effects include in continuation,

- inhibition of lipolysis, inhibition of platelet aggregation, suppression of hepatic glucose output and enhancement of glucagon secretion by the α-cells.

These extrapancreatic effects of the sulphonylureas have been observed in various organs including, liver, fat and muscle.

(iv) Recently it was evidenced that chlorpropamide enhances the potency of available insulin by increasing the ability of insulin receptors to bind with the hormone (i.e. by increasing number of insulin binding sites).

(v) These drugs do not potentiate the action of exogenous insulin.

(vi) Sulfonylurea treatment leads to an increase in Ca^{++} influx into islet tissues, inhibition of catecholamine release and increase in c-AMP concentration in islet tissues.

18.16 PHARMACOKINETICS

These drugs are extensively bound to plasma proteins and mainly metabolized in liver. Except tolbutamide, whose chief metabolite (i.e. butyl-p-carboxyphenyl sulfonylurea) is in the form of carboxylic acid due to carboxylation of its methyl group, other sulfonylureas undergo metabolism rather slowly into more active and longer lasting metabolites. Acetohexamide undergoes reduction to give hydroxyhexamide. Much of its hypoglycemic activity can be assigned to this metabolite. Tolazamide metabolizes to number of weakly active metabolites. Glipizide and glyburide undergo slow metabolism to inactive hydroxylated derivatives which appear in the conjugate forms in the urine. Chlorpropamide appears in urine in unchanged form together with its metabolites.

18.17 ADVERSE EFFECTS OF SULFONYLUREAS

If overdoses of sulfonylureas are continued for prolonged period, it leads to degranulation of pancreatic β - cells. The common adverse reactions of this class can be categorized as :

(a) Cutaneous Reactions :

Skin rashes and photosensitivity.

(b) Gastrointestinal Reactions :

Nausea, vomiting, anorexia, mild toxic hepatitis with jaundice.

(c) Cardiovascular Reactions :

Increased risk of cardiac dysfunctioning, transient leukopenia, agranulocytosis, thrombocytopenia and fatal aplastic anaemia.

These reactions, except the cardiovascular effects are usually not severe and the incidences of these effects are also low. However, under the conditions of strain, stress, infection and dysfunctioning of renal, hepatic or cardiac origin, these drugs should not be used.

Sulfonylureas should be reserved only for the treatment of either non-insulin dependent diabetic patient or such patient where insulin therapy alone is inadequate or inconvenient. In certain cases, sulfonylurea therapy may be used to lower down the insulin-dose in insulin resistant patients.

18.18 GLUCAGON

Exactly after two years of the discovery of insulin, **Murlin** and co-workers reported another pancreatic hormone, glucagon in 1923 from the α-cells of islet of Langerhans. It is a single-chain polypeptide and has a molecular weight of about 3500. Besides having exactly opposite physiological role, it differs chemically from insulin in having no disulfide linkages. It is also found in cells of gastric foundus and bears structural similarity with the hormone secretion. Unlike human insulin, glucagon from human source is structurally identical to porcine and bovine glucagon.

Since glucagon is the physiological antagonist of insulin, its release is governed by dietary conditions, ANS and similar hormonal factors. It is biosynthesized from a precursor protein having a molecular weight of about 18,000.

Pharmacological Actions :

Since it is a physiological antagonist of insulin, its pharmacological actions and their consequences are just opposite to that of insulin. It promotes gluconeogenesis, ketogenesis and energy generation. Hence it is known as hormone of catabolism where it is assisted by epinephrine, growth hormone and adrenocorticotrophic hormone. Unlike insulin, it exerts positive inotropic effect on the heart and inhibits gastric acid secretion in stomach. Most of its actions are thought to mediate through the accumulation of c-AMP.

Its plasma half-life ranges from 3 - 6 minutes. It is inactivated mainly in liver, kidney and plasma through proteolytic enzymes resulting in the cleavage of the aminoterminal histidine moiety.

Therapeutically, it can be used in the treatment of acute hypoglycemic shock along with glucose and as diagnostic agent in detection of pheochromocytomas.

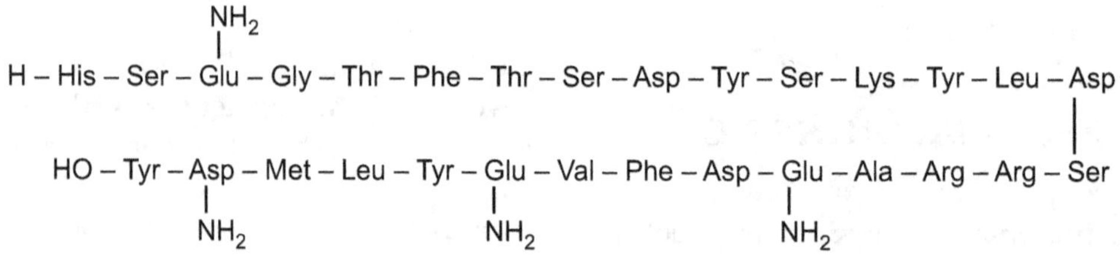

```
                    NH2
                     |
    H – His – Ser – Glu – Gly – Thr – Phe – Thr – Ser – Asp – Tyr – Ser – Lys – Tyr – Leu – Asp
                                                                                              |
    HO – Tyr – Asp – Met – Leu – Tyr – Glu – Val – Phe – Asp – Glu – Ala – Arg – Arg – Ser
                 |                     |                    |
                NH2                   NH2                  NH2
```

Fig. 18.6 : Structure of glucagon

DIURETIC AGENTS

19.1 INTRODUCTION

Depending upon the age and built, body water comprises of about 60 - 70 % of total body weight in the normal person. This body water is distributed in two main compartments - intracellular and extracellular. Potassium is the major ion present in the intracellular compartment while the volume of extracellular fluid is largely determined by the concentrations of sodium ions. The latter is valued to be about 15 % of normal body weight. The extracellular fluid is further subdivided into vascular and interstitial space. The porous capillary wall functions as a membrane of selective permeability and allows relatively free passage of water and low molecular weight agents. Large plasma-proteins, blood cells and lipid molecules can not cross the capillary wall. The inter-relationship between vascular and interstitial compartments was first described by **Starling** in 1909.

At the arterial end, there remains a net outward pressure of about 7 mm Hg and fluid passes into the tissue spaces. At the venous end, the net difference is of 10 mm Hg. Tissue fluid moves back into the capillary. This tissue fluid contains various ions, amino acids, glucose and foreign substances. These fluids bathe the organs and tissues of the body and thus create an internal environment. The composition and volume of these body fluids are to be maintained in order to make the internal environment compatible with life processes. This function is served by the kidneys. Kidney carries out this vital function related to the preservation of homeostasis. It is also a principal channel of excretion for many therapeutic agents and their metabolites.

Under resting conditions, in normal adult, about 650 ml of blood visits the kidneys every minute. Of this, about 125 ml/min protein free ultrafiltrate of plasma is formed through glomerulus filtration. Remaining plasma flows through element arterioles to bathe the peritubular surface of the nephron tubules. Out of 125 ml ultrafiltrate, about 80 to 90 % is reabsorbed by the epithelial cells of the proximal tubule. Remaining 10 to 20 % is reabsorbed from Henle's loop and distal tubule. Therefore, out of this 125 ml ultrafiltrate, on an average only 1 ml/min. is excreted as a urine.

Diuretic agent is usually employed to remove excess salts and water from the body. In fact, any substance that promotes urinary excretion of sodium and water can be called as a *diuretic*. However, the action of such agent should only be centered on the kidney. It is usually used acutely to maintain hemostatic and is not meant to induce a state of dehydration. Diuretic agents enhance the excretion of sodium and chloride ions at all plasma pH values. The potassium ions filtered at glomerulus are almost entirely reabsorbed in the proximal tubule and loop of Henle. Diuretic agents inhibit this reabsorption of potassium. Hypokalemia is therefore found to be associated with the chronic use of most of diuretic agents. Such cases should be dealt by the oral administration of potassium supplements.

The accumulation of excessive body fluid in the extracellular compartments of the body is due to retention of salts. It is generally referred to as edema. It may be due to hormonal imbalances, cardiac failure or abnormal functioning of that organ. Diuretic agent corrects this situation by mobilization of solute, principally sodium ions that results into fluid loss. It is also useful in the treatment of congestive cardiac failure, hepatic ascites (i.e. excessive amount of fluid in the abdomen associated with cirrhosis and other liver diseases), nephrotic syndrome (i.e. distal portions of nephron do not respond to antidiuretic hormone), hypertension, hypercalcemia, hypercalciuria, nephrogenic (i.e. decreased production of antidiuretic hormone), diabetic insipidus, proximal renal tubular acidosis, uric acid nephropathy and other conditions characterised by inadequate ADH secretions. Diuresis can be induced by either increasing glomerular filtration rate or by decreasing reabsorption of filtrate in proximal tubule, loop of Henle and the distal tubule. Most of the clinically used diuretic agents act by second mechanism.

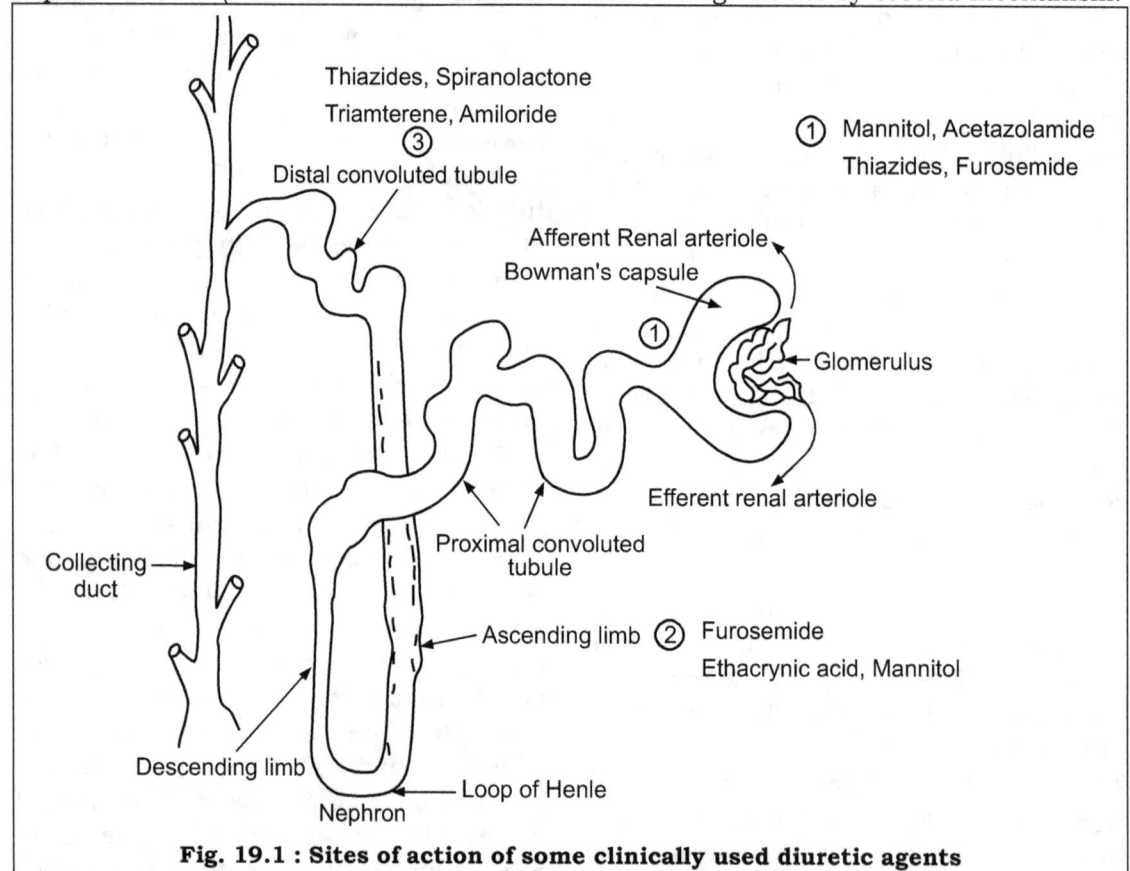

Fig. 19.1 : Sites of action of some clinically used diuretic agents

Nephron is a basic functional unit of kidney. Each kidney consists of about one million nephrons, which routinely filters water, electrolytes and non-electrolytes like glucose, urea, uric acid and creatinine. Each nephron has three functional parts.

1. **Bowman's Capsule :**

It encloses a microscopic ball of blood vessels, known as *glomerulus*. The blood enters the glomerulus through afferent arterioles under high capillary pressure. At the exit of glomerulus, the capillaries re-unite to form efferent arterioles. After the glomerular filtration, the filtered fraction is collected in the lumen of the capsule. Under normal circumstances, glomerular filtration is independent of arterial blood pressure.

2. **Renal Tubule :**

It is made up of three segments -
1. The proximal convoluted tubule,
2. The loop of Henle, and
3. The distal convoluted tubule.

The renal tubule has the ability, both actively and passively, to reabsorb large amounts of water and other substances (NaCl, glucose, amino acids etc.) that appear in the ultrafiltrate. Blood present in afferent arterioles has a pH of 7.4 while urine has an average pH of 6.00 due to acidification of fluid. This acidification of urine, potassium secretion and ammonia secretion occurs in the distal convoluted tubule.

3. **Collecting Tubule :**

Water reabsorption in the distal tubule and collecting ducts is regulated independently by antidiuretic hormone (ADH) which controls the water permeability of this part of the nephron. The collecting tubule finally joins a large collecting duct via the renal pelvis and ureter. The larger collecting duct releases its contents into urinary bladder where the urine is stored. The total volume of urine formed varies between 1 to 1.5 litres a day.

The process of diuresis helps in the mobilization of the edema fluid. In diuresis, the increased urine volume is due to the increased excretion of Na^+, H^+, Cl^-, HPO_4^{--}, Ca^{++}, Mg^{++} and HCO_3^- ions.

This may possibly results into hypokalemia, hyperglycemia and hyperuricemia. Hypokalemia is characterized by drowsiness, irritability, confusion, loss of sensation, dizziness, coma, muscular weakness, cardiac arrhythmias, tetany, respiratory arrest and increased sensitivity of myocardium to digitalis-like drugs.

19.2 CLASSIFICATION

Looking at dose response curve, a diuretic agent can be categorized as :

1. **Low-ceiling Diuretic :**

In this case, response increases proportionately with an increase in dose upto a threshold value. Thereafter, increase in dose, does not affect the response, or

2. **High-ceiling Diuretic :**

These are the major diuretics which are more commonly used clinically. It this case, the response runs linearly with the dose of the diuretic, even after the threshold dose.

Various diuretic agents can be conveniently studied under the following heads :

(i) Water and osmotic agents
(ii) Acidifying agents
(iii) Mercurials
(iv) Phenoxyacetic acids
(v) Xanthines
(vi) Inhibitors of carbonic anhydrase
(vii) Benzothiadiazines
(viii) Sulfamyl benzoic acid derivatives (high-ceiling agents)
(ix) Potassium sparing diuretics
(x) Uricosuric diuretics

(i) Water and Osmotic Agents :

Diuresis is generally desired to mobilize the edema fluid, resulting in the removal of excess extracellular fluid and electrolytes. Water does not fit in this definition. It is therefore used when it is intended to get increase in urine volume without altering the electrolytes or extracellular fluids. Ingested water rapidly dilutes the blood. This water induced fall in blood osmolarity, increases urinary excretion by inhibiting the secretion of antidiuretic hormone (ADH). Water is a diuretic agent which is of no value in the treatment of edema.

Osmotic agents prevent reabsorption of water. They are low molecular weight, non-metabolized, inert substances readily filtered in the glomerulus. They remain poorly reabsorbed in the renal tubule. The diuresis thus produced is proportional to the concentration of non-absorbable osmotic agent.

In the normal course, the solutes get reabsorbed as they pass from one segment to other in the renal tubule. Water also linearly diffuses into tubular cells to maintain the constant tonicity of tubular fluid. This linearity cannot be maintained in the presence of osmotic agent. The diffusion of water is reduced. This in turns, causes a reduction in the net reabsorption of sodium ions, producing a diuretic effect. They can cause a significant increase in the potassium ion excretion.

Commonly used osmotic agents are urea, glucose, sucrose, mannitol and isosorbide. Higher concentration of glucose present in the urine of patients with diabetes mellitus exerts an osmotic effect. This leads to polyuria of diabetes mellitus. The intestinal wall shares some structural features in common with the renal tubular cells. Naturally, the substances that fail to get reabsorbed in renal tubule, also remain unabsorbed in GIT, if given by oral route. Hence, osmotic agents must be administered parenterally to reach the circulation. Exception is urea. The 4 % solution of urea and 10 % invert sugar solution is generally used to cause diuresis. An extensively used agent is mannitol which after intravenous administration causes diuresis within 1 to 3 hours. It is a six carbon sugar with a molecular weight of 182. It has a plasma half-life of 100 minutes. About 80% dose administered appears in the urine in unchanged form. It should not be used during pregnancy. It is used to increase urine flow and it acts by inhibiting water reabsorption in kidney. It may also prevent a decreased renal blood flow observed with acute renal failure.

It is used to treat acute attack of congestive glaucoma (i.e. ocular hypertension). By increasing the osmolality of the plasma. It helps to withdraw intracellular water from the brain and cerebrospinal fluid. Hence, it may be used to reduce intracranial pressure and volume of cerebrospinal fluid. It is also used to treat oliguric phase of acute renal failure. It may be useful in the treatment of hemolytic transfusion reactions. It is also used in cardiovascular operations especially in the presence of severe jaundice.

(ii) Acidifying Agents :

Ammonium chloride, ammonium nitrate, calcium chloride and L-lysine monohydrochloride are some examples. These are inorganic salts which produces systemic acidosis and a transient diuresis.

In liver, the ammonium ion is converted into a neutral compound, urea. The excess of chloride ions left is excreted taking with an equivalent amount of sodium and appropriate amount of water. With this process the renal sodium reserve is exhausted resulting into the renal acidosis. Kidney develops compensatory mechanisms by producing ammonia which is exchanged in terms of sodium ions in the tubule. As a result, Na^+ ions are retained and ammonium ions are excreted in the form of ammonium chloride which quantitatively matches the amount ingested. Loss of sodium ions is thus prevented and acidifying agents thus lose their diuretic activity within first 1 - 2 days of treatment. If used alone, they are of no clinical value. They may be used in conjunction with the organomercurials because acidifying agents potentiate their action.

(iii) Organomercurial Compounds :

Though the first clinical use of mercurials (mercury chloride) dates back to sixteenth century, they had to wait till 1919 to get their potential recognized. Thereafter they dominated the diuretic field for more than 30 years. They are usually given by deep intramuscular injection and are still regarded as effective agents against severe edematous conditions. However they are least favoured because of their systemic and renal toxicities.

Oral administration of mercurials is unsatisfactory due to the irritation of gastrointestinal tract. They could not be administered intravenously because of cardiac toxicity. Most of them are mono or dicarboxylic acids or their amide derivatives possessing an alkoxymercuripropyl chain. The clinically useful organomercurials include mersalyl, mercurophyllin, mercaptomerin, chlomerodrin, merethoxyline, meralluride etc.

Theophylline attachment to the basic skeleton improves the absorption. Besides this, theophylline itself has a weak diuretic activity. It also lowers down the tissue irritation associated with the use of mercurials.

Mercurials mainly interferes in the functioning of enzyme systems responsible for reabsorption of chloride ions. Both, sodium and chloride ions are retained in the renal tubule along with appropriate amount of water. This results in diuresis. It is proposed that mercurials do not directly exhibit this activity. They undergo ionization to release divalent mercury ions which are the actual diuretic agent. Free mercury ions bind to the enzymes containing sulfhydryl (–SH) group. This inhibition occurs in both, the proximal renal tubule and loop of Henle. The most affected enzyme system is sodium-potassium activated ATP-ase pump system which governs renal reabsorption process. Due to this, a moderate increase in potassium loss also occurs. Dimercaprol or other vicinal dithiols have greater affinity for mercury ions. Hence if administered, they restore the activity of renal enzyme system and diuresis ceases.

Repeated use of organomercurials can lead to a systemic alkalosis. The production of alkaline urine prevents the formation of free mercury ions from the rupture of carbon-mercury bond in organomercurials. This leads to ceasation of diuretic activity of these agents. The response can be reestablished by the concomittent administration of acidifying salts, such as ammonium chloride. Side-effects of organomercurials includes nausea, vomiting, tissue irritation, allergic manifestation and systemic alkalosis. They may be used in the mobilization of edema fluid due to cardiac failure. They are also effective in the treatment of hepatic ascites due to liver cirrhosis and portal obstruction.

(iv) Phenoxyacetic Acid Derivatives :

Mechanism of action of mercurial diuretics outlined the importance of enzymes containing sulfhydryl groups in the renal transport mechanisms. Efforts were then made to develop effective sulfhydryl group blocking agents. Ethacrynic acid was the outcome of this research. It is an unsaturated ketone derivative of aryloxyacetic acid.

First used in 1963, the structure contains a highly reactive ethylene group which reacts with sulfhydryl group to form an adduct while the aryloxyacetic acid part favours the renal localization of the drug. It is an extremely powerful diuretic. On pharmacological basis (i.e. similar site of action), it is grouped together with furosemide and bumetanide into 'high-ceiling' or 'loop diuretic' category. All these three agents are organic anions. They are most effective agents available. They also possess some carbonic anhydrase inhibiting activity except ethacrynic acid. Diuresis is brought about by inhibition of active cloride reabsorption in the thick ascending limb of the loop of Henle. Hence, they are called as 'loop diuretics'.

Ethacrynic acid has the duration of action of 6 – 8 hours. It is orally effective and may be given intravenously. It is extensively bound to the plasma-proteins. It has a plasma half-life of 30 – 70 minutes. Its mtabolities are excreted in the urine in the form of sulfhydryl conjugates along with about 25% dose in unchanged form. The cysteine-adduct is the active metabolite which is more effective inhibitor of chloride transport than is the parent compound.

Adverse effects includes nausea, vomiting, vertigo, skin rashes, tinnitus, transient deafness, hyperuricemia, hypocalcemia, hypokalemia, hypoglycemia, transient granulocytopenia and thrombocytopenia.

It is used as antihypertensive agent in the treatment of mild to moderate hypertension. It may be used in the symptomatic treatment of hypercalcemia. It effectively controls edema of cardiac, pulmonary, hepatic or renal origin. Ethacrynic acid is a potent saluretic agent and is especially effective in the treatment of refractory edema where it may be used along with a potassium-sparing diuretic.

Ticrynafen (tienilic acid) is yet another derivative of this class. It is not a loop diuretic. Severe liver toxicity has been reported with its use.

Ticrynafen

Furosemide shares similar mechanism of action to that of ethacrynic acid. Both are the examples of loop diuretics. They may also increase the renal blood flow by causing renal vasodilatation.

Furosemide and bumetanide are sulfonamide derivatives, chemically unrelated with ethacrynic acid. They have an ability to inhibit Na^+–K^+ activated adenosine triphosphate system. They all may be used in the treatment of hypercalcemia because of their enhancing effect on the calcium ion excretion. Because of chemical similarity with thiazides, they also share thiazide adverse effects of serum uric acid elevation and diabetogenic potential. They also increase bicarbonate concentration in the plasma. Hence, their chronic use may lead to hypochloremic metabolic alkalosis. Ototoxicity also sometimes occurs which seems to be dose-related. It may be related with the disruption of electrolyte balance in the endolymph. Reversible and permanent deafness have been reported to occur with the parenteral use of ethacrynic acid in patients with uremia.

Furosemide is an orally active agent. Chemically it is a monosulphamylanthranillic acid derivative related to thiazide. About 99% administered dose is bound to the plasma proteins. It has a plasma half-life of 90 – 100 minutes. About 70% dose appears unchanged in the urine along with some fraction in the glucuronide form. About 30% dose appears unchanged in the faeces.

Furosemide is used to control refractory edema in hypertensive patients. It is also effective to treat edema of hepatic, renal or pulmonary origin. It may also be used for resistant edema of congestive cardiac failure. It is usually used alone or in combination with other antihypertensive agents in the treatment of hypertension and congestive heart failure. It may also be employed in the treatment of -

(i) Acute renal failure
(ii) Toxaemia of pregnancy, and
(iii) Life threatening hypercalcemia or hyperparathyroidism

(v) Xanthines :

They are mild diuretics and are rarely now employed as the primary diuretics. Theophylline, theobromine and caeffine are all methylated xanthines that occur in the nature. They are usually administered in the form of water soluble compounds. For example, theophylline is administered in the form of its ethylenediamine salt (i.e. aminophylline). Similarly xanturil, a mannich base of theophylline also possesses good diuretic activity.

Chemically xanthine is 2, 6-dihydroxypurine while theophylline, theobromine and caeffine are N-methylated xanthines. Mechanism of action of xanthine diuretics still remains unclear. Due to their cardiac actions, there is an increase in the renal blood flow and glomerular filtration rate. Xanthine derivatives also are expected to inhibit reabsorption of Na^+ and Cl^- ions in the proximal tubules without disturbing urinary pH or the activity of carbonic anhydrase enzymes.

Theophylline is the most potent orally active xanthine diuretic. It also has bronchodilatory, respiratory stimulant, cardiac stimulant and CNS-stimulant activities. It may also be administered by rectal or parenteral routes. Its derivative, aminophylline is effective as a diuretic only when it is given by the intravenous route. Aminophylline is a soluble theophylline salt prepared by complexation between one part of theophylline and one part of ethylene diamine. Latter compound is pharmacologically inert but helps to increase the amount of theophylline in the solution. It contains 85% anhydrous theophylline. It is available in the form of tablets, elixirs, rectal suppositories and injections. It has plasma half-life of about

5 – 8 hours. Principal metabolites include 1, 3-dimethyluric acid, 1-methyluric acid 3-methylxanthine and caeffine.

While oxtriphylline is a complex of choline and theophylline. It contains 50% anhydrous theophylline. Theophylline sodium glycinate contains 64% anhydrous theophylline. Theophylline monohydrate contains 91% of theophylline.

Aminophylline is mainly used in the management of asthma and chronic obstructive pulmonary disease.

(vi) Carbonic Anhydrase Inhibitors :

The enzyme carbonic anhydrase displays its activity at many sites including renal cortex, gastric mucosa, pancreas, eyes, erythrocytes and central nervous system. It is present in dense population particularly in erythrocytes and the renal cortex and plays an important role in the tubular reabsorption of bicarbonate and Na^+ ions.

It catalyses hydration of carbon dioxide to carbonic acid and also its dissociation, back to water and carbon dioxide. In next independant reaction, carbonic acid ionizes to hydrogen ion and a bicarbonate ion.

$$H_2O + CO_2 \underset{\text{Carbonic acid}}{\overset{\text{Carbonic anhydrase}}{\rightleftharpoons}} H_2CO_3 \rightarrow H^+ + HCO_3^-$$

These reactions occur in the cells of renal tubule. Through the sodium-hydrogen exchange programme, the Na^+ ions in the glomerular filtrate are reabsorbed in the tubules, primarily in the proximal tubule. The HCO_3^- ions are also reabsorbed from the glomerular filtrate.

Under the influence of carbonic anhydrase inhibitors, sodium-hydrogen exchange can not be operated. Sodium and bicarbonate ions are retained in the glomerular filtrate and can not be reabsorbed. This coupled with increased rate of excretion of potassium ions, and osmotic equivalent of water results in diuresis.

The use of carbonic anhydrase inhibitors is usually accompanied by systemic acidosis and alkaline urine. This is due to increased renal excretion of K^+, Na^+ and HCO_3^- ions (alkaline urine) and impairment of H^+ secretion (systemic acidosis).

Once acidosis develops, these agents are totally inactive as diuretics. Since the drug-enzyme complex is of reversible nature, the inhibitory activity of the drug ceases as soon as the depletion of bicarbonate store in the tubules occurs and they remain no longer effective as diuretic agents. This self-limiting action of these agents is a major drawback.

A large number of aromatic and heterocyclic sulfonamides exhibit carbonic anhydrase inhibitory activity. Acetazolamide is the prototype agent of this class. It is a non-competitive inhibitor of carbonic anhydrase enzyme. It also has antiepileptic activity. It is rarely used as the diuretic agent. However, it is preferred in the treatment of glaucoma and premenstrual tension. In glaucoma, it causes a partial depression of aqueous humor formation in the eyes by inhibiting carbonic anhydrase enzymes.

(vii) Benzothiadiazines :

They are also known as thiazide diuretics. They are the derivatives of 1, 2, 4 - benzothiadiazine -1, 1 dioxide. They all carry a 3 - sulfamyl - 4 - halogenated benzene ring and all exhibit identical properties, mode of action, site of action and same range of clinical applications. They mainly differ in their duration of action, where the drug having high lipophilicity displays a long duration of action.

Thiazide diuretics appeared on the clinical screen through the efforts to find out better inhibitors of carbonic anhydrase enzymes. Despite the free sulphonamide group, thiazides possess very weak carbonic anhydrase inhibition property. The heterocyclic benzothiadiazines are potent orally active diuretic agents. Quinazolinone derivatives closely resemble thiazides in their mode of action, therapeutic applications and spectra of side-effects. They differ chemically from thiazides in the nature of heterocyclic ring where the ring sulfone is replaced by the carbonyl group. They possess comparatively longer duration of action than thiazide diuretics.

Chlrothiazide, the first diuretic agent was introduced in 1958. Soon after, hydrochlorthiazide was introduced. In general, all hydrothiazides are more active than thiazide derivatives. Lipophilic substitution at position 3 of the heterocyclic ring enlarges the duration of action.

Thiazide diuretics are organic anions and are secreted in the proximal tubule. This secretion can be reduced by probenecid. These agents causes diuresis mainly by inhibiting active chloride reabsorption in the distal portion of the ascending limb or the very beginning part of the distal tubule. At therapeutic dose they exhibit mercurial like activity by impairing chloride transport mechanisms. Whereas at higher doses, their activity is partly due to carbonic anhydrase inhibition and partly by depressant action on distal tubular reabsorption. Thus, thiazides can share the mechanisms of action of both mercurials and carbonic anhydrase inhibitors. They also increase the excretion of potassium as a result of increased aldosterone levels. During the chronic administration, a state of metabolic alkalosis develops because of enhancement of H^+ ion secretion and HCO_3^- ions generation.

Due to their direct action on the renal vasculature, glomerular filtration rate may also be reduced. In long term treatment, there may be a gradual reduction in the diuretic response due to this depressant action on the glomerular filtration rate. This may be due to a slow emergence of the body's compensatory mechanisms (like increased aldosterone secretion). In patients having diabetes insipidus, diuretic action is not observed. In fact, thiazides may exhibit anti-diuretic activity in patients with nephrogenic diabetes insipidus. Such patients as such excrete large volume of urine even in absence of thiazide. When thiazide is used, urinary volume is further increased. This leads to emergence of renal adaptation mechanism because of drastic reduction in the plasma volume. Ultimately the urinary volume is decreased by increasing the reabsorption of sodium by proximal tubule.

The adverse effects of thiazide diuretics are usually rare. Gastrointestinal disturbances along with certain allergic reactions may occur. They should be used with caution in patients suffering from diabetes insipidus or renal failure. Hypokalemia usually occurs with thiazide therapy and is characterized by muscle weakness and cardiac irritability. It may be corrected by giving supplemental administration of potassium or using potassium sparing diuretic along with thiazides. The chronic use of thiazides may lead to hyperglycemia, glycosuria, hyperlipidemia, blood dyscrasias, hypersensitivity and pancreatitis. Through the competitive antagonism, thiazides decrease the secretion of uric acid into urine. The resulting hyperuricemia may leads to the acute attacks of gout.

The most commonly used examples of this category include chlorothiazide, metolazone and indapamide. They are all diuretics of choice in the treatment of edema associated with premenstrual tension, hormonal therapy and edema of cardiac, liver or renal origin. They also possess mild antihypertensive activity and may be used in the treatment of hypertension with or without edema. They may also be used in the chronic treatment of hypercalciuria to reduce the stone formation.

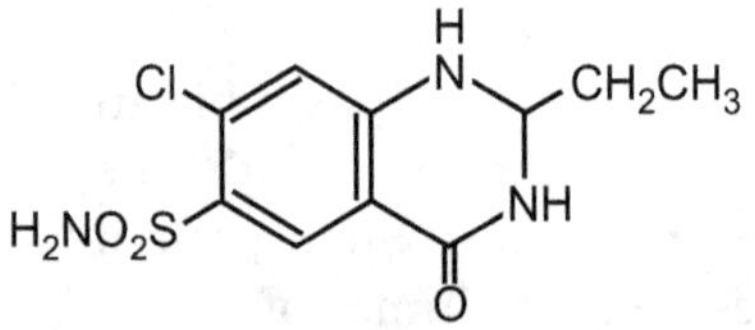

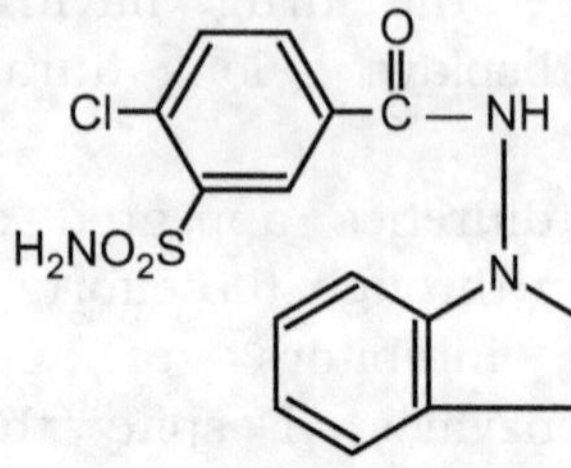

Indapamide
(Benzhydrazides)

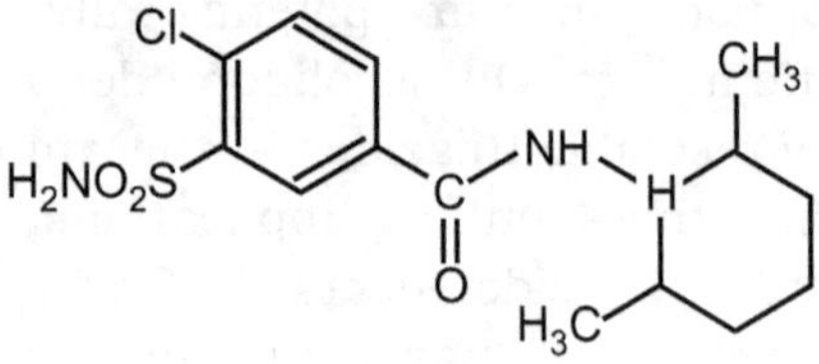

Clopamide
(Benzhydrazides)

Quinethazone (18 to 24 hours)
(Quinazolinones)

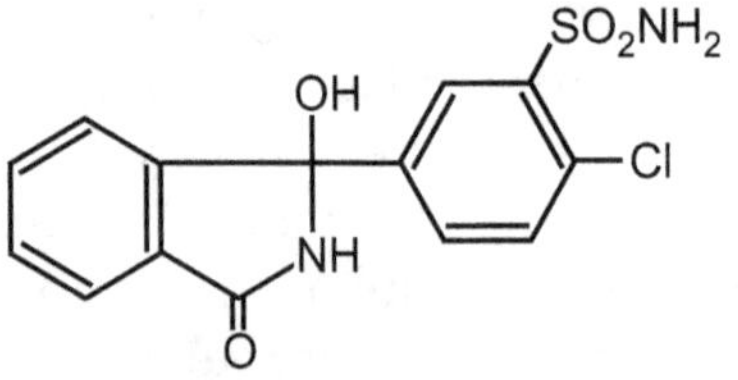

Chlorthalidone (48 to 72 hours)
(Pthalimidine)

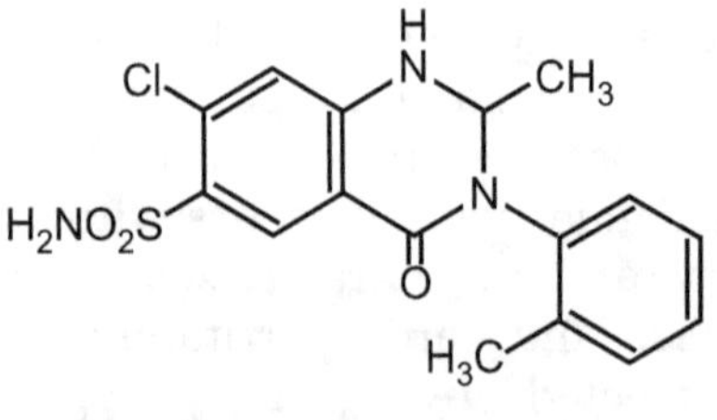

Metolazone (12 to 24 hours)
(Quinazolinones)

(viii) Sulfomyl Benzoic Acid Derivatives :

These analogs share many properties, mode of action, therapeutic applications and side-effects in common with ethacrynic acid. Furosemide, bumetanide and ethacrynic acid are more often grouped together and are called as loop diuretics or high ceiling diuretics. Unlike ethacrynic acid, both agents however induces loss of bicarbonate ions, probably due to the partial inhibition of carbonic anhydrase enzymes. Xipamide and clorexolone are the new agents of this class which are undergoing clinical trials.

Bumetanide is an orally effective diuretic agent. Chemically it is a 3-aminobenzoic acid derivative which is used to treat edema of cardiac, hepatic or renal origin. It exerts diuretic effect by inhibiting Na^+ transport in ascending limb of loop of Henle.

About 94 – 97% of administered dose of bumetanide is bound to the plasma-proteins. It has a plasma half-life of about

1 – 1.5 hours. It is minimally metabolized in the liver. About 50% of administered dose appears in the urine, in unchanged form and about 20% dose is excreted in the faeces.

Adverse effects includes gastrointestinal disturbances, headache, skin rash, dizziness hepatic dysfunction, electrolyte imbalance transient deafness, hypotension, hyperglycemia and hyperuricemia.

Bumetanide is used in the management of pulmonary edema. Since it promotes the urinary excretion of plasma calcium, it may also be used in the symptomatic treatment of hypercalcemia.

Furosemide

(ix) Potassium Sparing Agents :

These agents act at the distal segment of the nephron and decreases the excretion of potassium and hydrogen ions. Since only 5% of filtered Na^+ ions are normally reabsorbed in the distal tubule, they are not very potent diuretic agents. These agents are preferred in patients with low serum K^+ levels resulting from diuretic therapy with other agents.

Aldosterone plays a physiological role in regulating sodium and water balance by its action on the distal tubule. Renin (released by the juxtaglomerular cells of kidney) and angiotensin govern the secretion of aldosterone in the adrenal cortex. Aldosterone, deoxycorticosterone and hydrocortisone are potent antidiuretic mineralocorticoids. Under the influence of aldosterone, sodium is reabsorbed and is exchanged for potassium. Excretion of potassium is thus promoted. If this process is blocked, sodium and chloride ions alongwith equivalent of water will be retained in the renal tubule, resulting into diuresis. Similarly, potassium ions will not be excreted. Hence, drugs which blocks this process are known as potassium sparing diuretic agents. They are classified into :

(a) Agents that inhibit the production, release or physiological activity of aldosterone. They are called as 'aldosterone antagonists'.

(b) Agents that interfere with K^+ transport processes. They are known as pteridine derivatives.

(a) Aldosterone antagonists : The Na^+ - K^+ exchange is partially under mineralocorticoidal control. Aldosterone is the principal agent amongst them. Aldosterone receptors are located in several tissues, like salivary glands, colon and several segments of the nephron. In nephron, aldosterone receptors are more predominant in the cytoplasm of distal tubule cells and collecting system. Spiranolactone, an aldosterone antagonist is one of a series of steroidal derivatives having a lactone ring in the spiro arrangement at the 17th position. It is a synthetic steroid having structural similarity with aldosterone. It competitively inhibits the binding of aldosterone with its receptors. Spiranolactone thus effectively blocks the aldosterone induced Na^+ - K^+ exchange process, which otherwise occurs when aldosterone binds with its receptors.

Spiranolactone increases Na^+ and Cl^- ion excretion alongwith reduction in K^+ ion excretion. It also increases calcium excretion through a direct action on tubular transport. It does not prevent excretion of uric acid and is not diabetogenic in nature. It is effective only when mineralocorticoids are present.

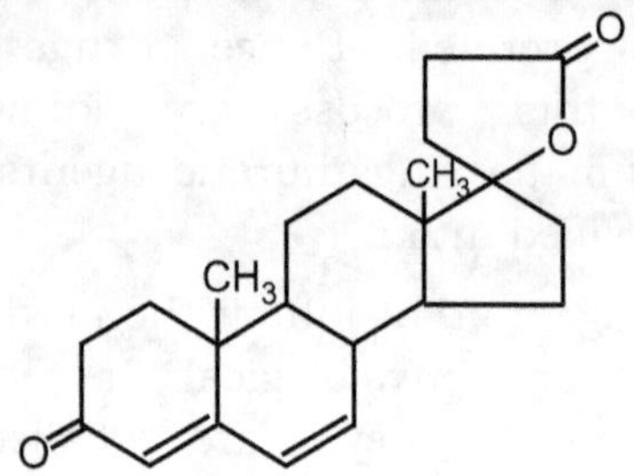

Canrenone

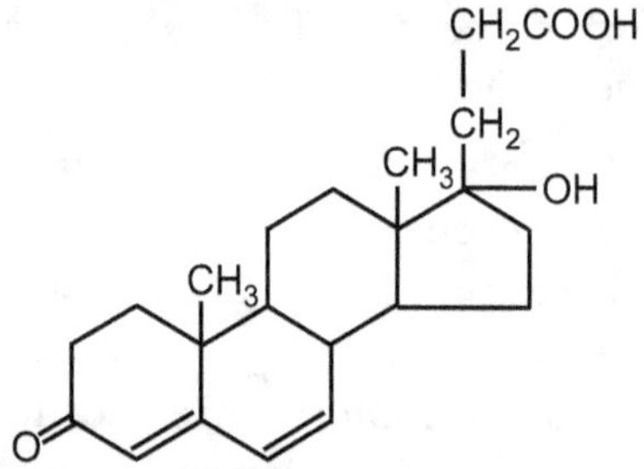

Canrenoate

Aldosterone antagonists are poorly absorbed orally and have delayed onset of action. Spiranolactone is a 17-spiro-lactosteroid with a 7-acetylthio group. It is an orally active aldosterone antagonist having mild diuretic activity. About 98 – 99% administered dose is bound to the plasma proteins. It has a plasma half-life of 10 minutes. It is extensively metabolized in the body. Principal metabolites include canrenone (active, plasma half-life is 13 – 24 hours) and canrenoate (inactive). Potassium canrenoate is also used clinically which gets converted *in vivo* to active canrenone in the body.

Adverse effects include nausea, vomiting, diarrhoea, headache, dizziness, lethargy, confusion, decreased sex drive, hirsutism, menstrual irregularity, gynecomastia, hyperkalemia and tumorigenicity. It is contraindicated in acute renal insufficiency or hyperkalemia.

It is used in the treatment of congestive heart failure and hypertension. It is also indicated in the management of refractory edema secondary to hyperaldosteronism.

It may also be used in the treatment of nephrotic syndrome and hepatic cirrhosis with ascites (i.e. excessive amounts of fluid in the abdomen. This leads to decreased appetite and respiratory difficulties). It may be used in the long term treatment of Conn's syndrome (i.e. primary aldosteronism). Since it inhibits adrenal androgen synthesis, it may also be used in the therapy of prostate cancer. For all above uses, it may either be used alone or in combination with thiazide diuretics.

Since spiranolactone induced antagonism is of reversible nature, spiranolactone is rather disappointing as a diuretic agent. After repeated doses, diuretic activity decreases presumely due to a compensatory change in the proximal tubule.

Amphenone B and metyrapone are the agents which interferes in the biosynthesis of aldosterone but do not qualify the standards for clinical utility.

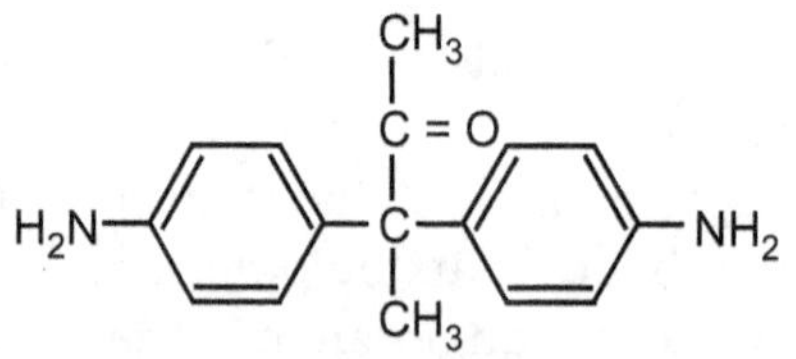

Amphenone B

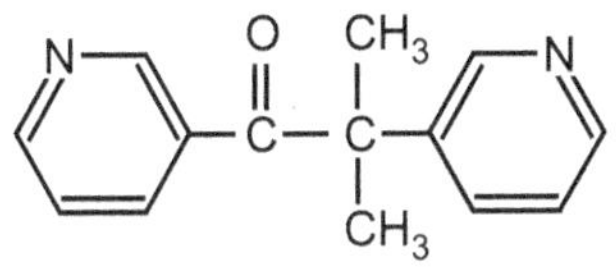

Metyrapone

All these aldosterone antagonists are useful only in those patients (patients suffering from liver cirrhosis or patients under digitalis treatment) for whom hypokalaemia would prove fatal.

(b) Pteridine derivatives : These drugs behave in a manner similar to that of spiranolactone. They increase the excretion of sodium and chloride ions, reduces potassium excretion but their mechanism of action is very much different than that of aldosterone antagonist. They cause diuresis even in the absence of mineralocorticoids. Triamterene and amiloride are clinically used agents of this class. They act by interferring with the Na^+ - K^+ exchange processes in the distal renal tubule by a mechanism other than antagonism of aldosterone. The site of action involves a mineralocorticoid independent portion of the distal tubule. They prevent the entry of Na^+ ions from the luminal side of the cells while inhibits distal tubular secretion of K^+ and H^+ ions by reducing the potential difference between the tubular cells and the lumen. The inhibition of H^+ — ions secretion in the distal tubule by these agents leads to alkalinization of the urine. They are only mildly effective when used alone. Triamterene is a synthetic pteridine analog having structural similarity with folic acid. Amiloride is an aminopyrazine derivative. They are often used as an adjunct to the long term thiazide therapy to reduce the loss of potassium. Triamterene is orally active. About 61 — 63% administered dose is bound to the plasma proteins. It has a plasma half-life of 4.2 — 5.0 hours. Both active and inactive metabolites appear in the urine along with 55 — 60% dose in unchanged form. While amiloride is poorly absorbed orally. It does not bind to plasma-proteins. It is excreted almost entirely in unchanged form in urine (50%) and in faeces (40%). It has a plasma half-life of about 6 — 9 hours.

Hyperkalemia is the most serious side-effect associated with all potassium sparing diuretic agents. This emphasizes the need of routine check up and monitoring of the serum electrolyte balance. Hyperkalemia may generate complications in patients with impaired renal function or who are taking potassium supplements in any form.

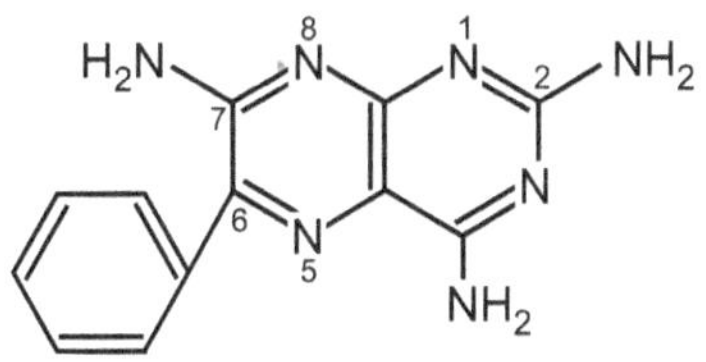

Triamterene

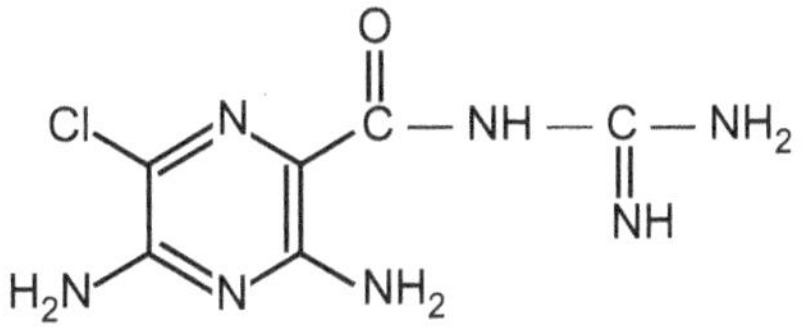

Amiloride

(x) Uricosuric Diuretics :

Uric acid is the principal end product of purine metabolism in man. The increased plasma urate level may be due to increased nucleic acid metabolism in neoplasms (cancers), excessive urate production from an inborn error of metabolism, defective excretion process by the kidney or may be induced by drugs like acetazolamide.

When plasma urate level crosses its solubility limits, it precipitates in the tissues in the form of crystals and may get deposited mainly as monosodium urate in the joints, subcutaneous areas and the kidneys. This leads to the acute attacks of gout. Many of the currently used diuretics usually lead to urate retention which favours and leaves a scope for cardiovascular disease, carbohydrate intolerance or nephropathy. Hence, attempts were made to develop diuretics which also possess uricosuric activity. Ticrynafen and indacrinone are the examples of diuretic-uricosuric category. Indacrinone is an orally active uricosuric diuretic having rapid onset and longer duration of action. It is currently undergoing clinical trials in the form of isomeric mixture containing 90% (+) and 10% (–) enantiomers. The (–) enantiomer is more potent natriuretic agent than the (+) enantiomer.

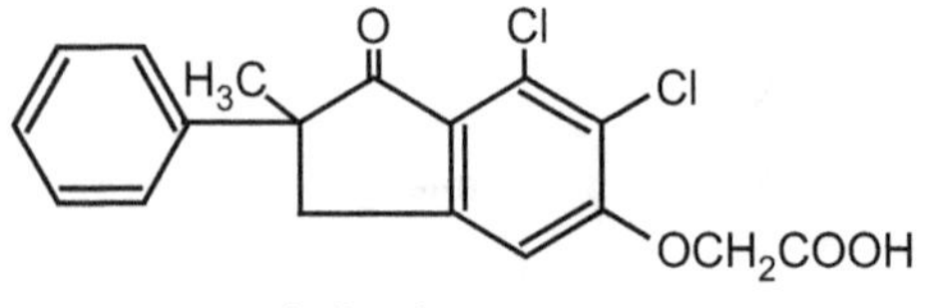

Indacrinone

19.3 ANTI-DIURETIC SUBSTANCES

Body possesses several compensatory mechanisms to get it suited with changing environmental conditions. As per the body's need, these mechanisms are switched ON or OFF. For example, the osmolality and ionic composition of the body's fluids are maintained by modification of blood flow or control of glomerular filtration rate (i.e. renal conservation of water). The only clinical condition where renal conservation of water is needed by anti-diuretics is diabetes insipidus.

This conservation is effected by many drugs, e.g. Posterior pituitary gland secretes anti-diuretic hormone which helps to maintain the body's water balance. Similarly, thiazide diuretics and ethacrynic acid exhibits anti-diuretic action in patients with diabetes insipidus. An oral hypoglycemic agent, chlorpropamide is also having anti-diuretic activity and may be used for this purpose in patients with diabetes insipidus.

❖ ❖ ❖

DRUGS ACTING ON GIT

20.1 INTRODUCTION

Gastrointestinal tract (GIT) is one of the vital organs present in the body. It possesses a battery of hormones and secretions which controls and carry out the processing to get the food in easily absorbable form. This is affected by the enzymatic breakdown of complex food molecules into monosaccharides, amino acids and glycerides. Dysfunctioning of any one of the GIT compartments may lead to human illness and discomfort. Most of the orally active drugs generally choose the signals of nausea and/or vomiting to inaugurate their side-effect session. Diarrhoea or constipation may sometimes mark their appearance. To be on the safer side, it is therefore needed to understand better the pharmacology of drugs acting on gastrointestinal tract.

Drugs acting on GIT may be broadly divided into gastric antacids, antiemetics, spasmolytic agents, laxatives-purgatives, antidiarrheals and anthelmintics.

20.2 GASTRIC ANTACIDS

As the name indicates, these agents are used to neutralize the excess of gastric acid secretion. In digestion of food, the important constituents of gastric juice are pepsin (a proteolytic enzyme) and hydrochloric acid. Pepsin is produced from pepsinogens which are located in mucous neck cells of oxyntic gland area, mucous neck cells of pyloric gland and in Brunner's gland. It has molecular weight of 35,000 and is most active at pH 2.0. Hydrochloric acid is secreted by the oxyntic (or parietal) cells of the stomach. This secretion is under the control of acetylcholine, histamine and gastrin. Gastrin, a heptadecapeptide was first reported in 1905 by **Edkins**. It contains seventeen amino acids out of which, only four at the acid end are concerned with its role in the stimulation of acid secretion. It is released from antrum of stomach while secretin and pancreozymin are released from duodenal wall in response to a fall in pH and stimulate the secretion of pancreatic juices. Pentagastrin, one of the gastrin analogs, is a powerful stimulant of acid secretion. All the three bases i.e., histamine, acetylcholine and gastrin, through an interlinked mechanism controls the turnover of gastric acid. Gastric antacids neutralise excess gastric acid secretion by mechanism which propagates through

(i) non-receptor mediated events or

(ii) receptor mediated events.

Examples includes H_2 - receptor blocking agents like cemetidine, ranitidine etc.

Gastric acid plays very important role in the formation of proteolytic enzyme, pepsin from an inactive precursor and pepsinogen. Gastric acid also provides lower pH to make the pepsin activated. Besides this, it also helps in inducing the release of secretin.

Gastric acid secretion is governed by histamine receptors, muscarinic receptors and gastrin receptors. Histamine, acetylcholine and gastrin promote the secretion of gastric acid by activating these respective receptor sites. Histamine is released by mast cells located in the lamina propria, acetylcholine is released by postganglionic vagal neurons and gastrin is released from the G cells located in the gastric mucosal antrum.

$H^+ - K^+$ - ATPase pump is involved in the secretion of gastric acid. It is located in the apical membrane of the parietal cell. The release of gastric acid (i.e. intracellular hydrogen ions) occurs through this pump by one to one exchange with luminal potassium ions. It is an energy dependent process. Cyclic AMP and calcium ions stimulate this proton pump resulting into the secretion of gastric acid, while prostaglandins, somatostatin, calcitonin, glucagon, dopamine and vasoactive intestinal peptide inhibit gastric acid secretion. Usually the basal acid secretion is high in the night hours with the low levels of acid secretion occurring during the daytime.

Mucus is the thick, viscous, physiological barrier which protects the gastric mucosa from the attack of pepsin and gastric acid. It is secreted from the surface epithelium columnar cells and the mucous neck cells of the cardiac, oxyntic and pyloric gland areas. It is secreted alongwith an alkaline fluid. It consists of glycoproteins and mucopolysaccharides. It increases the life span of gastric epithelial cells by providing a tenacious, slimy and alkaline coat over the inner surface of gastric mucosa.

One of the serious complications of hyperacidity is peptic ulcer which results due to the digestive action of pepsin and hydrochloric acid on the inner wall of stomach and duodenum. This results due to the failure of protective mechanisms of mucosa to prevent the autodigestion process. The feeling of gastric irritation is further potentiated due to increased spasms of GIT. The goals in peptic ulcer treatment are to reduce pain, accelerate healing rate, prevent complications and prevent ulcer recurrence. Peptic ulcer consists of a group of ulcerative disorders affecting the upper gastrointestinal tract. It is thought to occur from an imbalance between the effects of destructive factors (acid, pepsin, bile salts) and protective factor (mucus, bicarbonate, blood flow, epithelial cell regeneration and prostaglandin synthesis). Depending upon their location, ulcers can be classified as –

(i) Esophageal ulcers : They affect esophagus.

(ii) Gastric ulcers : They affect gastric mucosa.

(iii) Duodenal ulcers : They affect duodenum, and

(iv) Stress-induced or drug-induced ulcers.

When an ulcer is formed, the gastric acid present in the stomach causes pain and spasm. This in turn, inhibits healing process. The severity of hyperacidity ranges from gastritis (mucosal inflammation) to peptic ulcer. Most peptic ulcers are chronic in nature and visit the patient in the periodic fashion. Recurrence is associated with the development of complications, such as bleeding, perforation, penetration and obstruction. Depending upon the severity and location of an ulcer, one can start the treatment. The main objectives of treatment are :

(i) relaxation of the GIT smooth muscles (i.e. spasmolytic action). It is brought about by anticholinergic agents. However, they are now replaced by more potent and specific antisecretory agents which have fewer side-effects, and

(ii) reduction in the gastric acid secretion rate (i.e. antacids and H_2-blockers).

If drug treatment fails to achieve satisfactory results, bed rest and surgery may be needed to manage this chronic, relapsing condition. People with hyperacidity should avoid taking alcohol, coffee, cigarette smoking (stimulants of acid secretion) and mucosa irritating diet.

20.3 TREATMENT OF GASTRIC HYPERACIDITY

The stomach pH ranges from pH 1 when empty to 7 when food is present. In normal adult, about 22 mEq of acid is secreted per hour by about 1 billion parietal cells present in the gastric mucosa. In duodenal and gastric ulcers, the amount of acid secreted per hour reaches to 42 mEq and 18 mEq respectively. Emotional status of the person, smoking, alcohol and spicy food are known to be predisposing factors in peptic ulcer disease. To avoid this, mixture of antacids are often used. Antacids are weak bases and they raise the gastric pH above 4 (certain antacids like sodium bicarbonate may even elevate the pH to 7). It reduces the proteolytic action of pepsin. Antacids also helps in reducing spasms and provides symptomatic relief to pain. Absorption of antacids may disturb the acid-base balance of the body and cause alkalosis and local effects like, constipation or diarrhoea. Because the actual mechanism for relieving pain is not known, the evaluation of antacids is done quantitatively in terms of their acid-neutralising capacity (ANC value).

Gastric antacids are classified mainly into :

(a) Systemic Antacids (Alkalotic Agents) :

They get easily absorbed into systemic circulation and therefore are capable of changing pH of the blood. They may cause systemic alkalosis. Such alkalosis is enhanced by chloride loss (vomiting, gastric suction or diarrhoea) and by Na^+-ion absorption. Examples of antacids belonging to the category includes sodium bicarbonate and sodium citrate. Side-effects of these agents includes nausea, vomiting, diarrhoea, abdominal pain, irritability, headache, insomnia, myalgia and tetany.

(i) Sodium bicarbonate (baking soda) : It is a popular and widely used antacid. Due to its high water solubility, it neutralises gastric acid very quickly. Thus, it has a rapid onset but relatively very short duration of action. The pH may be significantly increased upto 7.

It is given orally. Major fraction appears in the urine while small amounts are decomposed to release carbon dioxide which is exhaled through the lungs.

$$NaHCO_3 + HCl \rightarrow NaCl + H_2O + CO_2 \uparrow$$

The carbon-di-oxide evolved during the reaction can cause belching and flatulence alongwith carminative action. In many antacid preparations, sodium bicarbonate is one of the ingredients. It is used in the dose of 1 - 5 g to give rapid relief from heartburn and dyspepsia. In general, the carbonate and bicarbonate antacids are preferably used when short-term antacid treatment is required. Adverse effects include nausea, vomiting, anorexia, stomach cramps, headache, frequent urination, weakness, nervousness, muscle cramps and irregular heartbeats. It is mainly used to treat metabolic acidosis (i.e. excessively high concentration of the acid in the urine like, cysteine in cystinuria or uric acid in hyperuricemia) due to a variety of conditions, including renal disease, diabetes, shock, dehydration or cardiac arrest. A 0.05 N solution may be used for continuous nasogastric irritation. Similarly a 5.0% solution is recommended for the treatment of dehydration.

(b) Non-systemic Antacids (Local Antacids) :

They are insoluble in water and are poorly absorbed due to their cationic nature. Since they do not have direct effect upon the acid-base equilibrium of the blood, systemic alkalosis does not result. Examples include aluminium hydroxide gel, magnesium trisilicate etc.

Systemic antacids are used to combat acidosis while local antacids are used in the treatment of peptic ulcer and hyperacidity. Most of the marketed antacid preparations contain aluminium and magnesium hydroxides. However, due to the toxicity reactions of sodium and calcium ions, their salts are not used for this purpose.

(i) Compounds of aluminium : These includes aluminium hydroxide, aluminium oxide hydrate, aluminium carbonate, dihydroxyaluminium aminoacetate, dihydroxyaluminium sodium carbonate and aluminium phosphate. All these aluminium compounds are used as antacids. These preparations possess both the neutralising activity and protective activity on the tender mucosal surface of the stomach and duodenum. They are used in the form of colloidal, viscous suspension and are found to possess a steady and prolonged action. The antacid activity is due to the liberation of aluminium cations. They also possess adsorbent activity for various gases and toxins. Independent of their buffering effect on gastric pH, they may also inhibit pepsin activity.

These preparations impede peristalsis and tend to induce constipation. But this drawback can be overcome by their combination with magnesium salts. For example, aluminium hydroxide is marketed mostly in combination with magnesium hydroxide. In prolonged use, aluminium salts produce phosphate deficiency. This is due to the reaction of aluminium chloride and dietary phosphate in the stomach to form insoluble aluminium phosphate. Due to the increased faecal phosphate excretion, additional dietary supplements of phosphate must be given.

The commercially available aluminium hydroxide gel is generally a mixture of the hydroxide, the hydrated oxide and a small amount of the basic carbonate. Various other preparations includes aluminium phosphate gel, aluminium carbonate, aluminium glycinate (i.e. dihydroxy-aluminium aminoacetate) and dihydroxyaluminium sodium carbonate.

In pharmacopoeia, aluminium hydroxide gel is described under suspension and anhydrous forms. In both dosage forms, aluminium hydroxide gel is popularly used. A loss of antacid property of the gels during the aging process is reported. Hence, the gel preparations are needed to be stabilised.

(ii) Magnesium containing antacids : A large number of official antacid preparations contain magnesium in the form of magnesium oxide (MgO) light magnesium carbonate (3 $MgCO_3$; $Mg(OH)_2$; $3H_2O$), heavy magnesium carbonate, magnesium hydroxide, magnesium phosphate and magnesium trisilicate.

Due to their insoluble nature, these compounds do not cause systemic alkalosis. Their antacid mechanism does not involve the liberation of CO_2 gas. The anion portion of magnesium salts seems to be important for their antacid property. They all function in the same manner, with magnesium trisilicate being the only exception.

$$MgO + 2\ HCl \rightarrow MgCl_2 + H_2O$$

The newly formed magnesium chloride undergoes further reaction with the bicarbonate (of the pancreatic juice) in the intestinal juice to form magnesium carbonate. The antacid action of magnesium trisilicate is slow, prolonged and powerful.

$$2\ MgO \cdot 3\ SiO_2 \cdot XH_2O + 4\ HCl$$
$$\rightarrow 2\ MgCl_2 + 3\ SiO_2 + (X+2)\ H_2O$$

The neutralising reaction yields hydrated silicon oxide which serves as an adsorbent and provides the protective coating over the mucosal layer and thus protects it from further attack of acid and pepsin. It may also absorb the pepsin. Thus, the activity of trisilicate may be considered as a protective and as an adsorbent.

This group of antacids is found to possess purgative action due to magnesium chloride and magnesium carbonate (formed in the GIT). For this reason, they are generally used with such antacids (e.g. aluminium or calcium salts) which cause constipation. For example, Gelusil is a preparation containing aluminium hydroxide gel and magnesium trisilicate combination. Similarly, Magaldrate is a chemical combination of aluminium hydroxide and magnesium hydroxide.

In patients with impaired renal function, magnesium ion retention may lead to magnesium poisoning. Hence, magnesium salts are contraindicated in such patients.

(iii) Calcium antacids : This category includes calcium carbonate and calcium hydroxide. They have quick onset of action. They raise gastric pH to nearly 7 and do not cause systemic alkalosis. Chalk is a natural calcium carbonate. It interacts with gastric acid in the stomach as per the following equation :

$$CaCO_3 + 2HCl \rightarrow CaCl_2 + CO_2 + H_2O$$
$$\downarrow$$
$$HCO_3\ \text{present in intestine}$$
$$\downarrow$$
$$CaCO_3$$

The carbonate present in the intestine leads to constipation similar to aluminium antacids. But unlike aluminium salts, their action is dependent upon their basic properties rather than on any amphoteric effect. To counteract constipating effect due to calcium, most of the calcium carbonate preparations are given in combination with magnesium antacids. Calcium antacids are contraindicated in patients having impaired renal function because they may increase the serum calcium level during prolonged use. The release of carbon-di-oxide in acid neutralization reaction adds to discomfort in some patients. Combination preparations of aluminium hydroxide gel, magnesium antacid and calcium carbonate are also available.

(iv) Bismuth containing compounds : These agents are commonly used for the treatment of mild diarrhoea. Bismuth carbonate and subnitrate also possess antacid property. This property is due to their ability to cover the gastrointestinal mucosa with a dry, inert and protective coating. Tripotassium dicitrato bismuthate is one of the agents from this category which is used in the treatment of ulcer. Along with the protective activity, this compound has antipepsin and spasmolytic activities. It actually promotes the healing of ulcers and also prevents their reoccurrence.

(v) Milk : It is regarded as a weak antacid having an additional protective action. Recently antacid formulations have come up with dried milk plus calcium carbonate and magnesium salts. The prolonged administration of such antacid formulations lead to the milk-alkali syndrome. This syndrome is characterized by hypercalcemia, hypoparathyroidism, acute alkalosis and renal damage. Usually the syndrome disappears as one discontinues the treatment.

Besides their use in peptic ulcer treatment, antacids may also be used in the treatment of Mendelson's syndrome, reflux esophagitis, dyspepsia, heartburn in pregnancy and in some cases of non-specific constipation or diarrhoea.

20.4 H_2-RECEPTOR ANTAGONISTS

Histamine is a powerful stimulant of hydrochloric acid secretion in gastric mucosa. In larger doses, histamine also augments the secretion of pepsin. These actions of histamine are mediated via H_2-receptors. Hence H_2-receptor antagonists are also termed as antisecretory drugs.

In 1972, **Black et al** first described selective H_2-receptor blockade for acid secretion. With the successful introduction of cimetidine in 1977, other analogs like ranitidine, famotidine and nizatidine are now available for the treatment of peptic ulcer.

Famotidine and nizatidine consist of a thiazole ring. In addition, nizatidine has the same ring side-chain of ranitidine. All these agents act as reversible, dose-dependent competitive antagonists at H_2-receptor sites resulting in inhibition of gastric acid secretion. They do not reduce gastric secretion of pepsin or pancreatic secretion of bicarbonate or enzymes. Famotidine has a potency 50 - 80 times more than that of cimetidine and 9 - 15 times more than that of ranitidine, while nizatidine is 6 - 10 times more potent than cimetidine.

Famotidine currently is indicated for the treatment of active duodenal ulcer and active benign gastric ulcer and for the treatment of pathological hypersecretory conditions (e.g. Zollinger - Ellison syndrome, multiple endocrine adenomas etc.)

Nizatidine is indicated for the treatment of active duodenal ulcer and maintenance therapy for duodenal ulcer patients. Both, famotidine and nizatidine may also be used in the treatment of gastroesophageal reflux disease, systemic mastocytosis and in the prophylaxis of stress ulceration.

20.5 ANTIMUSCARINIC AGENTS

Pirenzepine : It is an antimuscarinic agent having structural similarity with tricyclic antidepressant agents. However, it lacks antidepressant activity because of its poor penetration ability in the CNS. It selectively inhibits cholinergic receptors present in the gastrointestinal tract due to its greater affinity for the muscarinic receptors located in the gastric mucosa.

Adverse effects are few and includes dry mouth, blurred vision, constipation and urinary retention. It is used orally to heal gastric and duodenal ulcers in the dose of 100 - 150 mg per day.

20.6 TRICYCLIC ANTIDEPRESSANTS

These agents possess anticholinergic activity. The reduction in the gastric acid secretion is also brought about by their antagonistic action on both, H_1 and H_2-receptors. Doxepin and trimipramine are undergoing clinical investigations for their utility in the treatment of gastric and duodenal ulcers.

Adverse effects includes drowsiness and anticholinergic features. These agents may be used in patients unresponsive to conventional drug regimens.

20.7 H^+-K^+-ATPase INHIBITORS

Omeprazole : It is an orally effective benzimidazole derivative. It reversibly inhibits H^+-K^+-ATPase pump system in the parietal cell membranes resulting into decrease in the gastric acid secretion. It blocks the terminal phase of acid production by binding to an enzyme, hydrogen / potassium adenosine triphosphatase that is needed for extrusion of hydrogen ions into the gastric lumen. Suppression of gastric acid with omeprazole is long-lasting and may persist for three days or longer.

Adverse effects include nausea, diarrhoea and insomnia. It promotes rapid healing of peptic ulcers. It is used in the treatment of peptic and duodenal ulcers. In large oral dose, it is effective to control severe gastric acid hypersecretion seen in Zollinger - Ellison syndrome.

Adult oral dose is 30 - 80 mg per day prior to breakfast.

20.8 PROSTAGLANDINS

These are naturally occurring substances that mediate almost every biological function in the body. Chemically they are 20 - carbon oxygenated fatty acid derivatives of prostanoic acid. Prostaglandins inhibit gastric acid secretion stimulated by feeding, histamine or gastrin. Reduction in gastric acid secretion results in reductions in the gastric volume of secretions, acidity and pepsin content.

Prostaglandins, especially of the E class (e.g. 15, 15 - dimethyl PGE_2 and 16, 16-dimethyl PGE_2) possess antisecretory and cytoprotective (i.e. mucosal protective action) effects in the gastrointestinal tract. They appear to protect the mucosal layers by stimulating gastric mucus secretion and gastric and duodenal bicarbonate production. They reduce acid back diffusion. They also allow substantial movement of water and electrolytes in the intestinal lumen.

Misoprostol, a synthetic prostaglandin has been clinically used for the prevention of gastric ulcers caused by prolonged use of non-steroidal anti-inflammatory agents. Other synthetic prostaglandins which are under clinical trials include abraprostil, enprostil, riboprostil and trimoprostil.

20.9 MISCELLANEOUS AGENTS

(a) Carbenoxolone :

It is an orally well absorbed oleandane derivative of glycyrrhizinic acid which is a constituent of liquorice. Due to its ability to stimulate the production of 11-hydroxy corticosteroids, it possesses anti-inflammatory activity.

It is orally absorbed rapidly when pH is 2 or less. More than 99.9% of absorbed dose is bound to the plasma-proteins. Small amount undergoes metabolism to yield inactive glucuronide and sulphuric acid conjugates which are excreted in the bile. Minor amounts also appear in the urine.

It is used as an antiulcer agent to promote healing of gastric and duodenal ulcers. Its activity is due to its protective antipepsin and mucous secretion promoting properties. It also increases the volume of mucous secreted and increases its effectiveness. It reduces acid back diffusion and possibly augments secretin release.

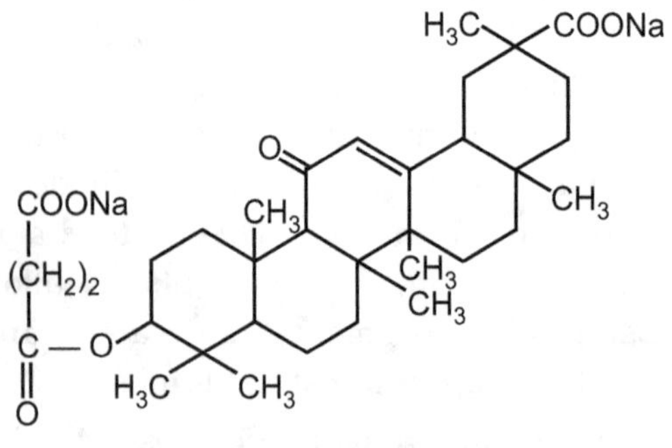

Carbenoxolone sodium

Adverse effects include alkalosis, oedema and hypokalemia, all are due to the mineralocorticoidal nature of the drug. It is contraindicated in cardiac failure and hypertensive patients. Adult oral dose is 100 mg two to three times a day for 4 - 8 weeks.

(b) Deglycyrrhizinated liquorice :

It contains about 1-3 % glycyrrhizinic acid. It possesses weak antispasmodic activity. It minimally depresses gastric acid secretion and does not affect mucous secretion.

(c) Metoclopramide :

Basically this drug is a good antiemetic because of its dopaminergic blocking action. It does not affect the secretion of either gastric acid or pepsin.

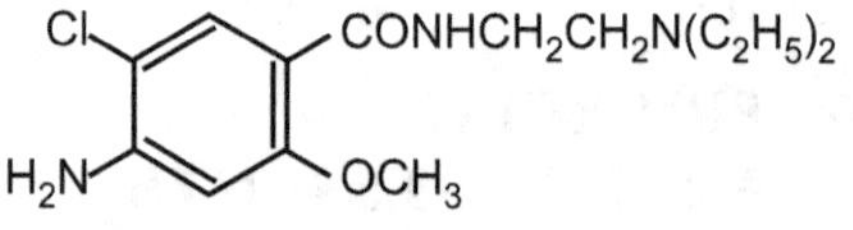

Metoclopramide

It promotes gastric emptying and relieves flatulence, dyspepsia and heartburn. Due to its indirect actions on peristalsis and ability to abolish the enterogastric reflux of bile, it is of value in the treatment of gastric ulcer.

Adverse effects include nausea, bowel disturbances, headache, facial grimacing, fatigue, drowsiness, lassitude, insomnia, restlessness, involuntary movement, dizziness and extrapyramidal effects.

It is used in the treatment of gastric and peptic ulcer. It is also employed in the management of reflux esophagitis and the control of gastroparesis in diabetes.

Adult oral dose is 10 mg about 30 minutes before each meal and at the bedtime.

(d) Sucralfate :

It is a complex of sulfated sucrose and polyaluminium hydroxide. It acts as a gastric mucosa protectant by adhering strongly with epithelial cells. It forms a protective barrier on the ulcer and prevents gastric acid, pepsin and bile salts from aggravating the ulceratic lesions. It also adsorbs pepsin, trypsin and bile acids. However, it does not have acid neutralising capacity.

About 3 - 5% dose is orally absorbed, rest of the fraction appears unchanged in the faeces. Systemically absorbed drug appears in the urine in the form of sulfate disaccharide. Adverse effects includes dry mouth, stomach discomfort, constipation, nausea, vomiting, xerostomia, dizziness and elevated plasma aluminium concentration. It is used to promote healing rate in duodenal and gastric ulcers. It is more effective in duodenal than in gastric ulcers. Antacids should not be taken for 30 minutes prior and after the dose of sucralfate.

Adult oral dose is 1 g about one hour before meal and at bedtime.

(e) Gefarnate :

It is a synthetic terpene that contains a number of isoprene units. Originally it was extracted from the white-headed cabbage. It has antipepsin activity. It is used in the treatment of gastric ulcer in the dose of 200 - 400 mg every 8 hours. However, it is not effective in the treatment of duodenal ulcer.

Maintenance Therapy :

Maintenance therapy is indicated in patients having a history of frequent relapses of hyperacidity. It reduces the rate of ulcer recurrences as long as the therapy is continued. It consists of continuous low-dose treatment with one of the H_2 - receptor antagonists cimetidine - 400 mg, famotidine - 20 mg or nizatidine - 150 mg at bed time. Other miscellaneous drugs includes urogastrone and sulglycotide. Urogastrone is a 52 amino acid polypeptide isolated from human urine. It is found to depress gastric acid secretion after parenteral administration, while sulglycotide is isolated from porcine duodenal mucosa. It was found to reduce peptic activity.

20.10 ULCERATIVE COLITIS

It is an inflammatory bowel disease characterized by inflammation of the mucosal layer of the colon and rectum.

(a) Sulfasalazine :

It is the drug of choice for the treatment of mild to moderate disease condition. It is a poor orally absorbed sulfonamide that does not have antibacterial activity. It splits into the gut to sulfapyridine and 5 - aminosalicylate moieties. The former is absorbed systemically and appears in the urine while the latter is excreted in the faeces and hence it is effective in inflammatory bowel disease. Adverse effects appear to be related to sulfapyridine while the therapeutic effects are related to 5-aminosalicylate.

Adverse effects include nausea, vomiting, anorexia, gastric distress, pancreatitis, headache, fever, arthralgia, malaise, dyspepsia, anaemia, agranulocytosis and thrombocytopenia.

Adult oral dose is 4 - 12 g in 4 - 8 divided doses per day. The effect is then maintained by a dose of 500 mg four times a day.

(b) Mesalamine :

It contains only 5-aminosalicylate. It is available in the form of oral preparations and as enemas. It acts locally on the lumen of the intestine and is thought to decrease inflammation in patients with ulcerative colitis by interference with arachidonic acid metabolism, resulting in a decreased production of leukotrienes.

Mesalamine enema is indicated for the treatment of mild to moderate distal ulcerative colitis, including ulcerative proctosigmoiditis and ulcerative proctitis.

Adverse effects includes anal irritation, headache and loss of hair. It is contraindicated in patients allergic to salicylates. It is available as a rectally administered suspension enema formulation which should be shaken prior to use. The usual dose is 60 ml enema once a day at bedtime to improve retention for mild to moderate ulcerative colitis.

20.11 ANTISPASMODICS
(Spasmolytic agents)

These are the agents that have an ability to relax smooth muscles of gastrointestinal tract. On the chemical basis, antispasmodic agents can be classified as -

(i) Atropine and its synthetic analogs
(ii) Synthetic aminoalcohol esters
(iii) Aminoalcohol ethers
(iv) Aminoalcohols
(v) Aminoamides, and
(vi) Papaverine and its synthetic analogs

Out of these, class (i) to (v) act by anticholinergic mechanism while class (vi) does not act by interfering with cholinergic nerve transmission. Anticholinergic compounds have some structural similarity with acetylcholine and contain some additional substituents that enhance their binding with cholinergic receptors. The acetylcholine molecule does not cover all the area of receptor. The area of a receptor which is not covered by acetylcholine molecule appears to be chiefly hydrophobic in nature. Hence, hydrophobic substituents increase the affinity of the antagonist for the receptor surface. The large hydrophobic group may not only increase the affinity of the blocking agent but through an 'umbrella effect' may also block the access of acetylcholine to the receptor site.

Papaverine and its analogs do not produce antispasmodic effect by interferring with cholinergic nerve transmission. It is believed to inhibit phosphodiesterase activity and adenosine uptake into the muscle cells. Since cholinergic nerve stimulation increases peristaltic movements of GIT (spasmodic), adrenergic nerve stimulation will produce antispasmodic effect through the stimulation of β-adrenergic receptor. Cyclic-AMP is the active factor which is a product of the response of β-adrenergic receptors. Papaverine and its analogs are inhibitors of phosphodiesterase, an enzyme that degrades cyclic - AMP.

20.12 EMETICS AND ANTIEMETICS

Nausea and vomiting are the most usual side-effects of many drugs. When a toxic or irritant substance is ingested, the body will try to expel it out and vomiting results. In sick condition, vomiting or nausea may often occur as a symptom of the disease.

Nausea, an unpleasant sensation is generally associated with vomiting. Severe nausea may sometimes occur in the absence of vomiting and severe vomiting can occur without the nauseating feeling. Vomiting (emesis) is a complex physiological process. Emetic centers present in the lateral reticular formation of medulla oblongata, regulate the process. These centers may get stimulated due to mechanical, chemical or peripheral stimuli. Sometimes, certain drugs may also activate these centers which results in vomiting. The chemoreceptor trigger zone (CTZ) plays an important role in stimulating the emetic process. It contains dopaminergic receptors. Since it lies outside the blood-brain-barrier, it can be easily activated by the attack of drugs. Certain drugs (e.g. apomorphine) activate CTZ and lead to vomiting. While some drugs depress the CTZ activity (e.g. chlorpromazine) and leads to antiemetic activity. In the medulla other important controlling centers of autonomic, cardiovascular and respiratory systems are also located in the viscinity of emetic centers. Hence, vomiting is usually preceeded by the signs of autonomic stimulation, sweating, salivation, pallor, bradycardia and other cardiovascular effects. Psychological factors play an important role in both, the emesis and antiemetic processes.

Emetics :

These drugs constitute a valuable part of treatment in poisoning cases. They are sometimes also used in low doses in cough preparations to stimulate flow or respiratory tract secretions. These drugs act either by local irritation (reflux) mechanisms or directly on the chemoreceptor trigger zone (i.e. central mechanism).

(a) Reflux or local emetics : These drugs cause vomiting by stimulating both, the vagus and the sympathetic nerve endings in the stomach and refluxly stimulate the emetic centers present in the medulla. The commonly used examples of this class includes sodium chloride, mustard, copper sulphate, zinc sulphate, ammonium bicarbonate and ipecacuanha. In case, if vomiting is not induced by copper sulphate, its absorption into the circulation may lead to serious toxic effect. Ipecacuanha tincture, in larger doses, has a strong emetic action and is very safe in use. It is prepared from the dried roots of Cephaelis ipecacuanha. It contains emetine, an alkaloid as an active constituent. It acts directly on CTZ as well as indirectly by irritating stomach. Action is enhanced if 200 - 300 ml water is ingested immediately after the administration of the syrup.

Adverse effects include stomach cramps, headache, itching, muscle stiffness, weakness, faintness, mild drowsiness, sweating and hypotension. It should not be given to semi- conscious or unconscious patients because of the risk of passing the vomitted material into the lungs.

Syrup of ipecacuanha is used to induce vomiting in cases of drug overdoses or poisoning due to other chemicals. Adult oral dose is 15 - 30 ml of syrup of Ipecac.

(b) Central emetics : These drugs activate the chemoreceptor trigger zone in medulla which then sends impulses to the vomiting centre itself. Examples include apomorphine, cardiac glycosides, morphine, veratrum alkaloids, nicotine, lobeline etc. Apomorphine is a morphine analog. It is a very short-acting central and peripheral dopaminergic agonist obtained by exposure of morphine to strong mineral acids. It is devoid of analgesic activity and exerts emetic effect by stimulating chemoreceptor zone in the brain stem which is connected with the vomiting centre. Like other opioids, it may cause respiratory depression alongwith circulatory collapse, if it is given in higher doses. Adverse effects include depression, euphoria, restlessness and tremors.

It is used in the management of poisoning due to oral ingestion of poisons or drug overdoses. When given subcutaneously or by intramuscularly in dosage upto 8 mg, it leads to vomiting within few minutes. Due to its short duration of action and adverse effects, it is not preferred in the treatment of Parkinson's disease.

Antiemetics :

These drugs are used to reduce or to prevent vomiting in conditions where it is common or may be expected. Vomiting occurs as :

(1) undesired side-effect of many drugs,
(2) in motion sickness or other disease conditions, and
(3) in pregnancy.

Most of the antiemetic agents possess atleast some degree of central depressant action. Many anticholinergics and antihistaminergic agents possess antiemetic property. The vomiting in pregnancy does not need the drug treatment, atleast for first trimester. Thereafter, apparently safer drugs are to be used to avoid the possibility of teratogenic effects of the drugs. The commonly used drugs in such cases are phenothiazines (e.g. chlorpromazine, prochlorperazine and promazine). Pyridoxine, one of B-complex vitamins is also used in various combinations. Drowsiness, dry mouth and related side-effects are due to the anticholinergic and antihistaminic nature of these drugs.

Classification of Antiemetics :

These agents are classified on the basis of their mechanism of action.

(i) CNS - depressants :

These agents depress the vomiting centres present in the medulla by non-specific mechanism. Examples include barbiturates, bromides, chloral hydrate etc.

(ii) Anticholinergic Agents :

These drugs relax the spasm of gastrointestinal muscles. They also act centrally to give antiemetic effect by inhibiting the cholinergic transmission. Examples include atropine and hyoscine. Side-effects associated with the use of these agents include dry mouth, blurred vision and giddiness which are mainly due to anticholinergic activity.

(iii) Antihistaminic Agents :

Histamine causes the contractions of smooth muscles of GIT. It also acts as a central neurotransmitter. Thus, antihistaminics act by both, relaxing the smooth muscles and also act centrally to depress vomiting centres. Examples include dimenhydrinate, buclizine, cyclizine, meclozine and promethazine. The selective activity of these drugs contributes further to their antiemetic activity. Some of these agents also possess anticholinergic action.

All agents from this class are H_1-receptor blockers. Dimenhydrinate is a combination of diphenhydramine and 8 - chlorotheophylline in equal molar proportions. It retains significant antimuscarinic and sedation properties. Adult oral dose is about 25 - 50 mg per day.

(iv) Drugs Forming a Protective Covering over the Gastric Mucosa :

Examples include bismuth compounds, kaolin etc. It has only a prophylactic use.

(v) Miscellaneous Agents :

Diazepam and diphenidol are vestibular depressants and can be used in the treatment of physiologically induced vomiting. Other miscellaneous agents include ipecacuanha preparation, pyridoxine, calomel and menthol.

(vi) Newer Antiemetic Agents :

(a) Trimethobenzamide : It is an orally active non-phenothiazine anti-emetic agent. Inactive metabolites appear in the urine alongwith 30 - 50% dose in unchanged form.

Adverse effects include diarrhoea, headache, blurred vision, skin rash, drowsiness, dizziness, convulsions, disorientation, coma, muscle cramps, jaundice and hypotension. Trimetho-benzamide suppositories contain benzocaine which may produce hypersensitivity reactions. Adult oral dose is 250 mg three to four times a day.

(b) Metoclopramide : Basically it is an antiemetic agent but it can also be used in the treatment of peptic ulcer. It is a cholinergic agonist which also has dopaminergic blocking action. It is used as an antiemetic agent in cancer chemotherapy (initially 2 mg/kg dose). It acts centrally to depress vomiting centres and also promotes emptying of the stomach.

Since metoclopramide also antagonises $5-HT_3$ receptor, similar antagonists like granisetron and ondansetron were developed as antiemetic drugs.

(c) Diphenidol : It is used as antiemetic agent. Adverse effects include nausea, indigestion, headache, nervous-ness, drowsiness and hypotension. In sensitive patients, anticholinergic symptoms may also develop.

(d) Benzaquinamide : It is a short acting drug used to prevent postoperative vomiting.

(e) Tetrahydrocannabinol : (l - Δ^9 - **THC**) : It is a psychoactive substance isolated from the flowering heads of hemp plant, *Cannabis sativa*. Though it is orally absorbed, it undergoes an extensive first pass metabolism. It has a biphasic plasma half-life. Initial half-life is 10 - 20 minutes while terminal half-life is 30 hours. Principal metabolites include 11 - hydroxy - Δ^9 - THC (active) and 11 - nor - Δ^9 THC - 9 - carboxylic acid (inactive). They are excreted in urine as well as in faeces.

Adverse effects include dry mouth, dizziness, somnolence, confusion, hallucination, dysphoria, euphoria, depersonalization, conjunctivitis, hypo-tension, tachycardia, tolerance and addiction.

It is used as an antiemetic agent to control nausea and vomiting induced by cancer chemotherapeutic agents. It may be given orally or by smoke.

20.13 LAXATIVES AND PURGATIVES

Constipation and illness have historically been associated with each other. Constipation is the infrequent or delayed evacuation of the faeces. It is a battle between the bowl and bowel. Regularity of the bowel movement is necessary to avoid a vague feeling of discomfort. Constipation is different from dyschesia (i.e. difficulty in a defaecation).

In a normal adult, approximately 9 litres of fluid and partly undigested food reach the cacum per day. Faecal fluid content of 200 - 300 ml usually results in some softening of stool. Large amounts of fluids can be retained in large intestine due to the hydrophilic properties of laxative. This increased pressure then facilitates the process of defecation. Faecal fluid values greater than 300 ml usually result in diarrhoea.

Cathartic (Greek term, katharsis = purification) is the general term used to describe all such agents which promote the passage of faeces. This category includes aperient, laxative, purgative and drastic agents. All have intensity of cathartic action in increasing order. Drastic agents include colocynth, croton oil, jalap and podophyllum. Since, they have potent cathartic action, they may induce severe mucosal irritation and gastroenteritis. Laxatives are the drugs which stimulate peristalsis and promote evacuation through the powerful contractions of the bowel. Defaecation results due to powerful peristalsis. Fluid and electrolyte changes develop in both, the large and small intestine with laxative use.

Classification of Laxatives :

These agents can be classified on the basis of their mode of action as follows :

(i) Stimulant or Irritant Laxatives :

These agents irritate the intestinal mucosa. This results into quick response to the distention. They also lead to the accumulation of fluids in the colon resulting into an increased pressure and stool softening effects. Examples include anthraquinone derivatives, castor oil, diphenylmethane derivatives (phenolphthalein and bisacodyl) and bile acids.

All the above agents produce laxative effect by stimulating peristalsis by irritation. They induce a reflux increase in the gut motility. They are inactive if given parenterally. Castor oil contains the triglyceride of ricinoleic acid which undergoes enzymatic hydrolysis in body to give glycerol and ricinoleate. The laxative action of castor oil is mainly due to ricinoleate. In addition, it has an emolient activity. It is obtained from the plant, *Ricinus communis*. Adult oral dose is 15 - 30 ml per day.

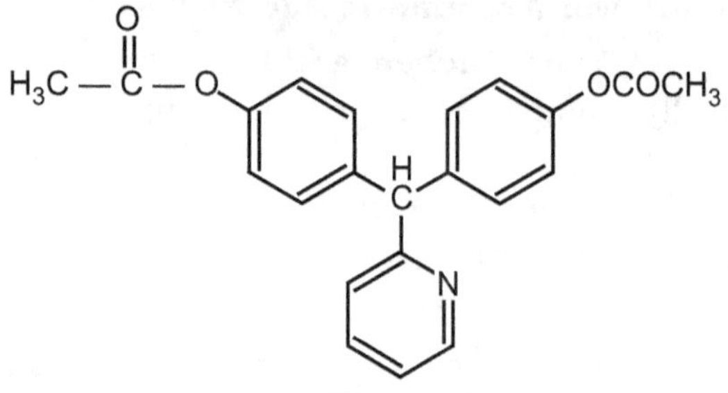

Bisacodyl

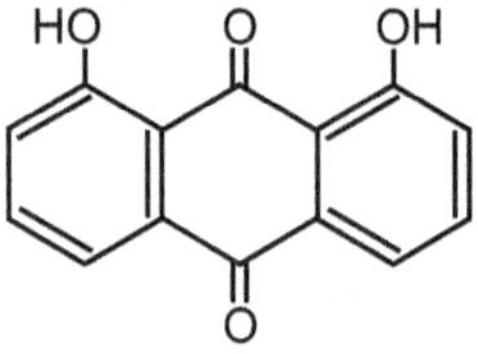

Danthron

(1, 8-dihydroxyanthraquinone)

Senna, rhubarb, aloe and cascara are the main sources of anthraquinone glycosides. These plants contain various oxymethyl quinones present, partly in free form and partly as inactive glycosides. These glycosides are released in the intestinal lumen under the influence of microbial flora. Emodin (trioxymethyl anthraquinone) and chrysophanic acid (dioxymethyl anthraquinone) are the active laxative constituents of anthraquinone glycosides. Emodin increases the retention of water and sodium ions in the lumen by inhibiting Na^+ - K^+ - ATPase pump present in the lumen mucosa.

Danthron is a synthetic derivative of anthraquinone glycoside. Anthraquinone glycosides can be obtained from :

(i) dried leaves of *Cassia acutifolia* and *Cassia angustifolia* (Senna leaves)

(ii) dried roots and rhyzomes of Rheum officinale (Rhubarb),

(iii) bark of *Rhamnus purshiana* (Cascara sagrada), and

(iv) juice of *Aloe perryi* (Aloe).

Adverse effects of stimulant laxatives include excessive purgative action. Sometimes larger doses of these agents may produce nephritis. They should not be used in pregnancy.

(ii) Bulk-forming Laxatives :

If the diet contains a bulk of non-absorbable residue, this part, by filling the intestine, exerts the pressure on the bowel wall. This pressure serves as a stimulus for normal defaecation. Since part of their activity can be attributed to their ability to absorb water (i.e. a hydrogel), patients should drink adequate amount of water to avoid dehydration. Examples of this category include methylcellulose, isapghula, agar, banana and psyllium seeds.

They act as the mechanical laxatives and are used when the faeces are dry and hard. Most of them are marketed in the form of granules which absorb water and swell up into the thick mucilage that is not digested but excreted unchanged. They indirectly stimulate peristalsis by their water content and their content of undigestible matter. The hydrogel which is formed, facilitates defaecation by lubrication of faecal mass because of its emolient property.

Bran is yet another example of bulk-forming laxatives. It comprises all undigestible fibre material derived from either fruits and vegetables or from cereals. It mainly contains carbohydrates in the form of cellulose, lignin and pectin. It is usually used in the treatment of diverticulitis.

(iii) Emolient Laxatives (Lubricants) :

These agents are also called as stool softeners. They act simply by lubricating intestinal mucosa. Softening of stool is assisted by reducing intestinal electrolyte and fluid transport. Examples include olive oil, glycerine, liquid paraffin etc.

Liquid paraffin is a mixture of liquid hydrocarbons, used as an emolient to lubricate and soften the faecal matter in constipation. It is available as oil or as a white emulsion. When given orally, it is not absorbed. Its continued use is contraindicated. It is a thick clear mineral oil which passes into the intestine in undigested form, softens the bowel contents, lubricates the intestinal channel resulting in smooth, painless movements. It is usually prescribed in the form of emulsion to which agar or phenolphthalein is sometimes added. Dose ranges from 8 ml to 30 ml.

Docusate sodium (dioctyl sodium sulphosuccinate) is yet another example of this category. It is an anionic type of surfactant having a wide variety of emulsifying, wetting and dispersing applications.

It is used as a faecal softner due to its emulsifying action. It increases the secretion of water and electrolytes into intestinal lumen. It apparently hydrates and softens the stool. It is incorporated into retention enemas. Because of detergent nature, it allows water to penetrate and soften the hard faecal matter. It is available in the form of docusate sodium, docusate calcium and docusate potassium. Adult oral dose is 50-300 mg per day while adult rectal dose is 50-100 mg as 0.10% solution. The polymers of polyoxyethylene and polyoxypropylene also possess the detergent properties and may find use as emolient laxatives.

(iv) Saline Laxatives (Osmotic Laxatives) :

They are salts of poorly absorbable anions and sometimes cations. Here the word, "saline" indicates certain compounds of sodium and magnesium. This class includes water soluble inorganic salts that contain multivalent cations or anions. Because of their ionic nature, these ions are slowly or incompletely absorbed from intestine. Consequently, water is retained in the intestinal lumen through osmotic effect exerted by these non-absorbed ions. Osmotic pressure depends upon molecular weight of the drug and concentration of such unabsorbed ions. The resulting semifluid faecal matter exerts a pressure on the luminal wall. Peristalsis is induced by the activation of stretch receptor present in the GIT mucosa resulting into a laxative effect. Magnesium salts, in addition, stimulate the secretion of cholecystokinin-pancreozymin, a hormone that stimulates the fluid secretion and motility and reduces absorption of sodium chloride. More commonly used saline purgatives include -

(a) Magnesium salts : e.g. magnesium sulphate and milk of magnesia (magnesium hydroxide).
(b) Sodium or potassium salts : e.g. tartarate, sulphate, phosphate and biphosphate.
(c) Potassium-sodium tartarate (Rochelle salt) and
(d) Lactulose.

Magnesium sulphate (epsom salt) is the most powerful saline laxative since both ions are least absorbed. It is used as a cathartic to provide complete evacuation of small and large intestine in patients with chronic liver disease. Adult oral dose is 5 - 20 g per day in divided doses. In patients with renal dysfunctioning, higher blood concentrations of magnesium are reported to occur due to inadequate removal of magnesium ions from blood. This may lead to CNS - depression or coma. Hence, its use is contraindicated in patients with renal dysfunctioning.

Lactulose is a semisynthetic disaccharide sugar. About 2 - 3% dose is orally absorbed. The unabsorbed dose is metabolized by intestinal bacterial (*Lactobacilli, Bacteroides* species, *E. coli* and *Clostridia* species) to lactic, acetic and formic acids and carbon-di-oxide. These low molecular weight acids initiate an osmotic drive. Systemically absorbed portion appears in urine in unchanged form. Each 15 ml contains 10 g of lactulose and minor amounts of other sugars like galactose and lactose. It is used orally (7 - 10 g) alongwith sufficient water to treat constipation.

Adverse effects of saline laxatives include anorexia, headache, hypogastric pain, bloating, flatulence, dehydration, weakness, myalgias, depression, and disturbance in water-electrolyte balance. Chronic treatment with saline laxatives may cause damage to colonic mucosa resulting into proctocolitis. In certain cases, systemic toxicity is reported to occur. Adequate fluid intake should be maintained to avoid dehydration due to hypertonic solution of the saline laxatives.

(v) Enemas :

These are the detergent containing preparations which are introduced through the rectum. Soapy water, saline, olive oil, cotton seed oil, glycerine, sodium phosphate or sodium biphosphate are the common ingredients of enema preparations. Hypertonic saline solution offers certain advantages over the detergent substances. They soften faeces and produce laxation either by fragmentation, liquefaction or lubrication. They increase the muscle tone of colon and rectum. Phosphate enemas lower the serum calcium level by inducing considerable loss of calcium.

(vi) Sulfur :

Chemically sulfur is very active element. It is therapeutically employed both internally as well as topically. Topically it acts as fungicide, parasiticide and keratolytic agent. If used internally, it exhibits a mild cathartic action which is due to its reduction to the sulphide anion in the intestine. This sulphide anion (S^-) neutralizes excess gastric acid to give hydrogen sulphide which is a mild intestinal irritant.

$$S + 2H_3O^+ \rightarrow H_2S + 2H_2O$$

(vii) Calomel :

Chemically it is mercurous chloride. Its cathartic action is due to the strong intestinal irritant property of mercuric cation (i.e., mercury albuminate) formed in the small intestine. The possibility of mercury poisoning has posed limitations on its use.

20.14 ANTIDIARRHOEALS

Diarrhoea means loose bowel movements resulting into the frequent passage of watery, uniformed stools with or without mucous and blood. This condition may arise due to the change in the nature of diet and routine or sometimes due to bacterial infection. The former type of diarrhoea is the mild form while the infective diarrhoea is more powerful and persistant. Organism escapes from gastric acid and other digestive processes and reaches the bowel. Its metabolic products irritate the nerve ending of intestinal wall leading to severe diarrhoea. In this condition, to compensate the loss of body fluids, a mixture of salt (sodium chloride or sodium bicarbonate) and water is to be given frequently. The simple type of diarrhoea may be controlled just by using intestinal adsorbents while infected diarrhoea needs the use of intestinal antiseptics.

(i) Adsorbents :

These substances have the power of adsorbing gases, bacteria or toxins without undergoing any chemical reaction. In addition to adsorbent action, they also possess the protective property. They form a coating over the intestinal mucosa to reduce its irritation. Examples include :

(a) Kaolin : It is a hydrated aluminium silicate used internally and externally in the form of very fine powder for its adsorbent properties. It adsorbs irritant toxins and bacterial toxins, reduces mucous secretion and binds water. It also provides a sort of protective coating over the inflamed mucosal walls. It is often used alongwith pectin (kaopectate is a mixture of 20% kaolin, pectin and hydrated aluminium silicate) for the symptomatic treatment of chronic diarrhoea. Adult oral dose is 45-90 ml after each loose bowel movement. Kaolin and morphine mixture is useful in the treatment of mild diarrhoea. Because of its constipatory effect, morphine increases effectiveness of this preparation.

(b) Calcium carbonate (chalk) : Its properties are quite similar to those of kaolin. Chalk and opium mixture is also available. It also helps to release flatulence and distension.

(c) Magnesium trisilicate and aluminium hydroxide : They have adsorbent property which is beneficial in the treatment of acidity and diarrhoea. They are also used in the treatment of flatulence and distension.

(d) Pectin : It is a purified carbohydrate product obtained from an acid extraction of the rind of citrus fruits or from apple pomace. It is mainly made up of polygalacturonic acid with some of the methylated hydroxyl functional groups.

It is used alongwith kaolin as an adsorbent and demulcent in the treatment of diarrhoea. Each 30 ml of this preparation contains 5.85 g of kaolin and 130 mg of pectin. Activated charcoal and bentonite are also used in the treatment of mild diarrhoea.

(e) Bismuth subsalicylate : Because of adsorbent property, it binds with intestinal toxins and provides protective coating to mucosal surfaces. Its administration leads to formation of grey-black discoloration of stools.

(f) Polycarbophil and various psyllium seed derivatives : It binds with water and bile salts. It is used to control diarrhoea that is associated with passing of excessively watery stools.

(ii) Diphenoxylate Hydrochloride :

It is a weak meperidine congener lacking analgesic activity. It has the plasma half-life of 2.5 hours. Upon metabolism, diphenoxylic acid (active metabolite) and hydroxy-diphenoxylic acid are excreted in the faeces.

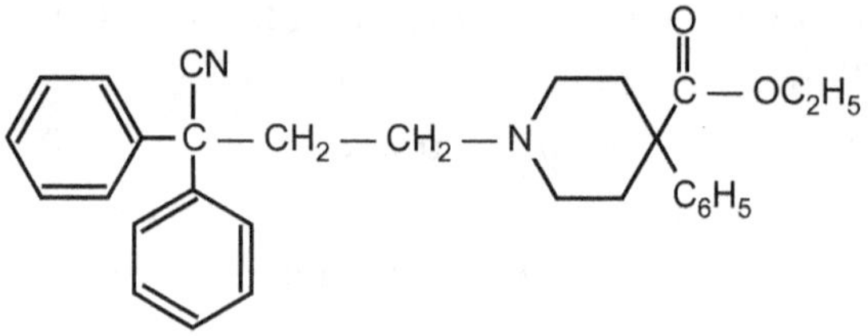

Diphenoxylate

Adverse effects include nausea, vomiting, abdominal discomfort, miosis, blurred vision, dry mouth, flushing, sedation and tachycardia. It is contraindicated in children under 2 years and in patients with obstructive jaundice.

Because of its constipating effect, it is used for the symptomatic relief of diarrhoea in patients with mild chronic inflammatory bowel disease and for infectious gastroenteritis. Atropine is added in subtherapeutic dose because of its spasmolytic activity. In lomotil, a mixture of diphenoxylate and atropine is present. Adult parenteral dose is 20 mg per day.

(iii) Loperamide :

It is a synthetic meperidine congener devoid of sedative or respiratory depressant actions. It is orally used as an antidiarrhoeal agent. About 97% administered dose is bound to the plasma-proteins. It has a plasma half-life of 7 - 14 hours.

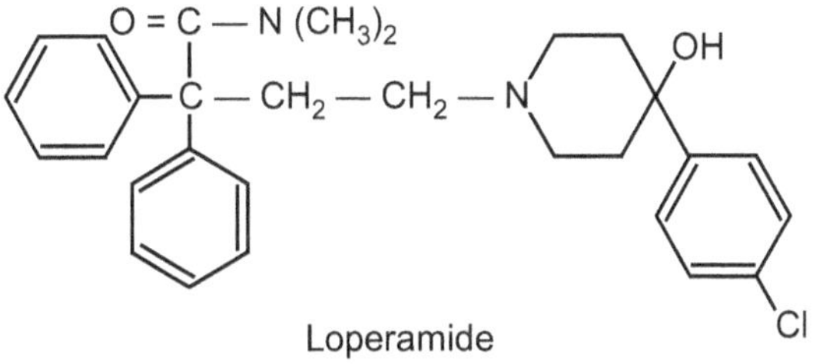

Loperamide

Major portion of administered dose appears unchanged in the faeces. Inactive metabolites are excreted in the urine alongwith 10% dose in unchanged form.

Loperamide exerts spasmolytic effect on GIT muscles by depressing slow cholinergic phase and rapid prostaglandin-mediated phase of smooth muscle contraction. It may act on intestinal nerve endings or ganglia.

Adverse effects include nausea, vomiting, anorexia, skin rashes, crampy abdominal pain, dry mouth and drowsiness. It is used in the symptomatic treatment of both acute non-specific diarrhoea and chronic diarrhoea. Adult oral dose is 4 - 8 mg per day.

(iv) Intestinal Antiseptics :

These agents are used to treat severe diarrhoeal forms which are due to microbial infection. They mainly comprise of certain members of the sulphonamides and antibiotics that are poorly absorbable in GIT and thus reach in high concentration to the small and large bowel. Examples include sulphasalazine, sulphaguanidine, phthalyl sulphathiazol, succinyl sulphathiazole etc.

Various combinations of sulphonamides and antibiotics alongwith kaolin are available either in the form of cream or suspension. Streptomycin, neomycin, chloramphenicol, tetracyclines, nystatin are the examples of such antibiotics used for this purpose.

A reduction in faecal volume contributes to the effectiveness of any antidiarrhoeal preparation. This is achieved by inclusion of a strong water absorbing agent (e.g. methyl cellulose) in the formulation.

20.15 SIALAGOGUES

Salivary secretion contains amylaseses (ptyalin) which initiate the process of digestion of food. Similarly, salivary secretion has a mouth clearing function. Drying of mouth is due to cessation of saliva secretion and indicates body's low water content.

Vasodilation and secretion are two associated phenomena occurring in salivary glands. These are under the influence of both, sympathetic and parasympathetic nervous systems. Vasodilation is under the control of parasympathetic nerves which when stimulated leads to the release of kallikrein (a proteolytic enzyme). The latter liberates the vasodilatory polypeptides (plasma kinins) from the plasma. Same channel operates in several other glands. Sialagogues are the drugs which increase the saliva secretion. These include,

(a) **Cholinergic drugs :** e.g. pilocarpine, physostigmine.

(b) **Adrenergic drugs :** e.g. ephedrine.

(c) **Bitters :** These are the substances which by virtue of their taste, stimulate reflexly efferent nerves supplied to the taste buds. They stimulate indirectly the appetite. To be effective, they are to be taken half-an-hour before the meals. Examples include strychnine, quinine, tincture of cinchona and nux vomica.

20.16 ANTISIALAGOGUES

These are the drugs which induce a reduction in the salivary secretions. These include,

(a) Anticholinergic Agents :

This class comprises of atropine sulphate. It is an alkaloid obtained from the plant, *Atropa belladona*. It is used as a preanaesthetic medication to inhibit salivary and bronchial secretions. Scopolamine is also a belladona alkaloid obtained from the shrub, *Hyoscyamus niger* and *Scopolia carniolica*. It may be used as a preanaesthetic agent due to its antisialogue and antiarrhythmic properties. Glycopyrrolate is a long-acting synthetic quaternary amine having antimuscarinic actions. It may also be used as antisialogogue.

20.17 APPETITE AFFECTING DRUGS

(a) Appetite Stimulants :

These include alkaloids having bitter taste. They stimulate appetite mainly by reflex vagal stimulation. They include strychnine, nux vomica and alcoholic beverages.

(b) Anorexiants :

These agents depress the appetite. They may be used as an adjunct in the management of obesity. They act mainly through the following mechanisms :

(i) by increasing the levels of plasma free fatty acids resulting in depression of appetite centres in lateral hypothalamus,

(ii) by inhibiting impulses reaching the appetite centers, or

(iii) by stimulating satiety center present in the medial hypothalamus.

Below mentioned are some common examples of anorexiants :

(i) Diethylpropion hydrochloride : It is a sympathomimetic agent having properties similar to amphetamine. Adverse effects include nausea, diarrhoea, constipation, dry mouth, mydriasis, restlessness, insomnia, tremors, increased blood pressure and tachycardia.

It is used as an anorexiant in the management of obesity.

(ii) Fenfluramine hydrochloride : Chemically it is a trifluoromethyl derivative of amphetamine and is a sympathomimetic appetite suppressant agent. It has a plasma half-life of 13 - 30 hours. Inactive metabolites are excreted in the urine alongwith 10 - 20 %

unchanged drug. Adverse effects include vomiting, diarrhoea, abdominal pain, dry mouth, alopecia, impotence and pulmonary hypertension.

It is used as a weight-reducing agent in obesity. Adult oral dose is 20 - 40 mg three times a day. Treatment may be continued upto 3 months and then the therapy can be gradually terminated.

(iii) Phendimetrazine tartrate : It is an orally active sympathomimetic agent having appetite suppressant activity. Upon hepatic inactivation, metabolites are excreted in the urine. Adult oral dose is 85 mg two to three times a day.

20.18 CARMINATIVES

These agents are mild mucosal irritants. They relieve gastric distension (e.g. flatulence, colic pain etc.) by expelling the gas from the gastro-intestinal tract. In addition to this, they also propagate the feeling of warmth in the stomach. Examples include sodium bicarbonate, tincture of ginger, dill water, soda water, oil of peppermint, aniseed, camphor, glycyrrhiza, cardamom and cinnamon.

Peppermint oil is a volatile oil obtained from the steam distillation of fresh aerial parts of *Mentha piperita*. It relaxes the colonic smooth muscles. Hence, it is beneficial in the irritable bowel syndrome. It is a weak antispasmodic.

Simethicone (Dimethylpolysiloxane) :

It is a surface active agent used as an antiflatulent usually in combination with antacids, antispasmodics, sedative or digestants. It is not absorbed orally and appears totally unchanged in the faeces. It does not exhibit any noticeable adverse effect.

It is used in the control of flatulence, gastric bloating and postoperative gaseous distention. It diminishes gastro-esophageal reflux and exhibits despeptic symptoms. It may also be used in the radiography of the bowel to reduce gas shadows and to improve visualization.

Adult oral dose is 40 - 80 mg after each meal and at bedtime.

20.19 DIGESTANTS

Gastrointestinal tract is one of the vital organs of the body. It possesses a battery of hormones and secretions which controls and carry out the processing to get the food in easily absorbable form. In digestion of food, the important constituents of gastric juice are pepsin and hydrochloric acid. Digestants are the substances which are used to compensate the deficiency of normal components of gastrointestinal secretion. They include,

(i) Betaine Hydrochloride :

It is a digestive preparation containing the equivalent amount of 1.0 ml of dilute hydrochloric acid, 32.4 mg pepsin and 110 mg of methyl cellulose. It induces a slow release of hydrochloric acid alongwith the release of gastric acid that occurs during digestion.

(ii) Pepsin :

It is a proteolytic enzyme which is an important constituent of gastric juice. The marketed preparation contains pepsin powder obtained from the oxyntic cells of the fresh stomach of the hog.

(iii) Dehydrocholic Acid and Sodium Dehydrocholate :

It is a semisynthetic cholate and is used as safe and effective oral laxative agent. It decreases the excretion of bilirubin and enhances the secretion of bile of low specific gravity (i.e. hydrocholeretic effect). Its administration may help to increase the absorption of fat and fat-soluble vitamins in conditions of partial biliary obstructive disease. Choline dehydrogen citrate may be effective as a lipotropic agent in patients with hepatic cirrhosis. Adult oral dose is 250-500 mg three times a day preferably after meals.

(iv) Pancreatic Extract :

It includes pancreatin and pancrelipase. Pancreatin is a cream coloured, amorphous powder obtained from fresh pancreas of hog or ox. It contains amylase, lipase and trypsin. While pancrelipase is obtained from porcine pancreas.

These enzymes may be used to treat conditions where pancreatic enzymes are either absent or deficient (e.g. chronic pancreatitis, pancreatectomy, cystic fibrosis, mucoviscidosis, gastrointestinal bypass surgery, ductal obstruction from neoplasm or steatorrhea). In postgastrectomy syndrome, these enzymes cause a reduction in steatorrhea and improves the nutritional state of a patient. Pancreatic extracts should be given with food, milk or alkali in an attempt to buffer the gastric contents. This is necessary to prevent inactivation of pancreatic enzymes.

(v) Chenodiol (Chenodeoxycholic Acid) :

It is the human bile acid mainly present in the form of glycine and taurine conjugates. When bile becomes supersaturated with cholesterol, it induces formation of cholesterol gall-stones. Chenodiol is used to decrease the cholesterol content of bile so that formation of cholesterolic gall-stones is inhibited. It acts by -

(a) reducing the rate of bile salt synthesis in the liver,

(b) inhibiting cholesterol absorption from intestine, and

(c) blocking HMG - Co reductase and cholesterol 7α - hydroxylase enzymes which play an important role in cholesterol synthesis.

Chenodiol is used to dissolve cholesterol gall-stones only in those patients in whom gall bladder function is in order and where gall stones do not exceed 2 cm in diameter. Usual adult dose is 14 - 16 mg /kg /day for 6 - 24 months.

20.20 ANTHELMINTIC AGENTS

Infestation with the parasitic worms is the most common disease in many tropical and subtropical countries. These parasitic worms firmly hold the intestinal mucosa and continue their reproduction by egg production. Worms parasitic to man can be categorised as cestodes (tapeworm), nematodes (round worms) and trematodes (flukes). Anthelmintics are the agents which are used to destroy or eliminate these parasitic worms from the gastro intestinal tract. They act by killing or paralyzing the worms so that such worms could be easily expelled out of gut.

Some anthelmintic agents also impairs the egg production process in worms. Depending upon the action, anthelmintic agents are categorised into :

(i) vermifuges or drugs that expel the worms from the body, and

(ii) vermicides or drugs that kill the worms in the body.

Classification :

Presently available anthelmintic agents are structurally diversified. On the chemical basis, they can be classified as

(a) Phenols
(b) Chlorinated hydrocarbons
(c) Antimonial compounds
(d) Dyes
(e) Piperazine analogs
(f) Heterocyclic compounds
(g) Alkaloids and plant extracts, and
(h) Miscellaneous agents

(a) Phenolic Anthelmintic Agents :

(i) Hexylresorcinol : It is an orally active broad spectrum anthelmintic agent, originally introduced as an urinary antiseptic. It is particularly effective in the treatment of trichuriasis. It causes tissue irritation and is not used in patients with peptic ulcer. Adult oral dose is 1000 mg once a day.

(ii) Dichlorophen : It is an anthelmintic agent effective in the treatment of tapeworm infections. It detaches worm from the bowel wall and promotes its digestion in the gut.

Adult oral dose is 75 mg / kg body weight, taken on an empty stomach in the morning. A saline cathartic should be given 2 - 4 hours after the drug to minimize the danger of cysticercosis.

Table 20.1 : Clinically used anthelmintic agents

Sr. No.	Worm infection	Drugs commonly used
1.	Ascariasis	Mebendazole, piperazine, pyrantel, bephenium
2.	Cestode infection	Paramomycin
3.	Cutaneous larva migrans	Thiabendazole
4.	Dracunculiasis	Niridazole
5.	Enterobiasis	Piperazine, pyrantel, pyrvinium
6.	Filariasis	Diethylcarbamazine
7.	Fascioliasis	Bithionol, hexylresorcinol
8.	Nematode (round worm) infection	Bephenium, mebendazole, pyrantel, hexyl resorcinol
9.	Onchocerciasis	Diethylcarbamazine, suramin
10.	Paragonimiasis	Bithionol

Contd...

11.	Schistosomiasis	
	S. haematobium	Lucanthone, niridazole, metrifonate, praziquantel
	S. mansoni	Hycanthone, niridazole, oxamniquine, praziquantel
	S. Japonicum	Praziquantel, niridazole, tartar emetic
12.	Strongyloidiasis	Pyrvinium, thiabendazole
13.	Trematode (fluke) infections	Bithionol
14.	Trichuriasis	Mebendazole
20.	Trichiniasis	Mebendazole, corticosteroids

(b) Chlorinated Hydrocarbons :

(i) Tetrachloroethylene : It is an unsaturated chlorinated hydrocarbon. It is not used as an anthelmintic agent presently and is now of historical importance only. Presently it is used only in veterinary practice and in the treatment of fluke infections in humans.

(c) Antimonial Compounds :

These agents are now less favoured as anthelmintics because of their high toxicity and difficulty of administration. They exert anthelmintic activity by selectively inhibiting schistosomal phosphofructokinase. This enzyme is necessary to catalyze the conversion of fructose - 6 - phosphate to fructose-1, 6-diphosphate. Examples include potassium and sodium antimony tartarate. Stibophen is a trivalent effective antimonial leishmanicidal agent with less intensity of adverse effects.

Adult intramuscular dose is 100 mg every second day for 1 - 3 weeks.

(d) Individual Anthelmintic Agents :

(i) Thiabendazole : It is an orally active, broad spectrum anthelmintic agent, effective against a wide range of nematodes. It exerts vermicidal activity specifically against *Strongyloides stercoralis*, *Trichinella spiralis* and *Trichiuris trichiura*. It acts by deforming the worm-eggs. However, the egg count returns to normal if therapy is discontinued. It has no effect on filariasis. It has a plasma half-life of 1.2 hours. It is excreted in urine mainly as 5 - hydroxy thiabendazole either in the form of glucuronide or sulfate. Adverse effects include nausea, vomiting, epigastric distress, anorexia, diarrhoea, numbness, skin rash, hyperglycemia, crystalluria and transient leukopenia.

Thiabendazole is effective in the treatment of *A. duodenal* (common hookworm), *E. vermicularis* (pin worm), *A. lumbricoides* (round worm) and

S. stercoralis infections. Adult oral dose is 3 g per day. In early trichinosis, treatment may be continued for 2-3 additional days while in disseminated Strongyloidiasis, treatment may be continued for atleast 5 days.

(ii) Diethylcarbamazine : It is an orally active agent belonging to piperazine category. It acts by sensitizing the microfilaria so that they become plagocytozed by fixed tissue macrophages. It is orally well absorbed and has a plasma half-life of 8 - 12 hours. Upon extensive metabolism, a variety of inactive metabolites are excreted in the urine alongwith 10% dose as unchanged drug.

It is used to treat infections caused by *W. bancrofti*, *W. malayi* and *O. volvulus*. It is a drug of choice for the treatment of filariasis due to *Tetrapetalonema perstans* or *Tetrapetalonema streptocerca*. It may also be used in tropical eosinophilia and Ascaris infections. Adult oral dose is 2 mg/kg body weight three times a day after meals for 1-3 weeks.

(iii) Lucanthone : It is an orally active antischistosomal agent derived from a yellow dye and is effective against *S. haematobium*. It acts by preventing helmintic ova production or its release. This results in the destruction of the parasite. It is less favoured clinically because of its adverse effects. Hycanthone is a hydroxymetabolite of lucanthone. It possesses marked schistosomicidal activity. Adult oral dose is 5 mg/kg two to three times a day for 5 - 10 days in the treatment of schistosomiasis.

(iv) Mebendazole : It is a benzimidazole derivative having broad spectrum anthelmintic activity. It shows poor oral absorption. About 78 - 80% administered dose is bound to the plasma-proteins. It has a plasma half-life of 2.5-5.5 hours. About 95% dose is excreted unchanged or as 2 - amino - 5 - benzoyl - benzimidazole (primary metabolite) in the faeces. Upto 2 - 5% dose appears in the urine unchanged or as primary metabolite.

It is effective in the treatment of ascariasis, trichuriasis, and hookworm infections in the oral dose of 100 mg twice a day for 3 days. In enterobiasis, a single oral dose of 100 mg is given. After 2 weeks, second dose of 100 mg may be given.

(v) Metrifonate : It is an organophosphorus compound which is an inhibitor of cholinesterase enzyme, and is used as anthelmintic and agricultural insecticide. It has a plasma half-life of 1.5 hours. It is extensively metabolized by plasma and schistosomal arylesterases. Principal metabolites include dichloro-(2, 2 - dichlorovinyl dimethyl phosphate) and various inactive products.

Adverse effects include nausea, vomiting, colic, abdominal pain, mild vertigo, lassitude, decreased sperm count and some intestinal nematodes.

It is used for the treatment of urinary schistosomiasis and of *S. haematobium* infections.

Adult oral dose is 5-15 mg/kg body weight 3 times after every 2 weeks.

(vi) Niridazole : It is an orally active nitrothiazole derivative having anthelmintic and antibacterial activities. It also exhibits amoebicidal and schistosomicidal activities. Besides this, it is also effective against guinea worm (*D. medinensis*) infestation.

It undergoes an extensive first pass hepatic metabolism. 1 - Thiocarbamoyl - 2 - imidazolidinone is the active metabolite. The metabolites appear both, in urine and faeces.

It is used in the treatment of *D. medinensis*. It may also be used for the therapy of schistosomiasis due to *S. japonicum*.

(vii) Niclosamide : It is a salicylanilide derivative having anthelmintic activity. It is effective only in the treatment of intestinal cestodes. Its oral absorption is poor. Major dose is excreted through the faeces.

It is used in the treatment of diphyllobothriasis (*Diphyllobothrium latum*), Hymenolepiasis (*H. nana*), Taeniasis (*T. saginata*) and Dipylidiasis (*Dipylidium conium*). *Enterobium vermicularis* is also susceptible. For destruction of tapeworm, niclosamide is the most effective and safe drug.

Adult oral dose is 500 mg usually in the fasting condition 3 - 4 times a day. Antiemetic may be given one hour before and purgative about 2 hours, after the treatment.

(viii) Oxamniquine : It is an orally active yellow dye having anthelmintic activity. Chemically it is 2 - amino methyl tetra-hydroquinoline derivative. It is especially effective against *Schistosoma mansoni* and has a plasma half-life of 1 - 2.5 hours. Principal metabolites include 6 - carboxyl and 2 - carboxylic acid derivatives which are excreted in the urine alongwith traces (0.4 - 1.9% dose) of parent drug.

It is an effective schistosomicidal agent used against *Schistosoma mansoni* and is also used in combination with metrifonate in the treatment of mixed mansoni and haematobium infections.

Adult oral dose is 15 - 60 mg/kg of body weight as a single dose given at bedtime.

(ix) Pyrvinium Pamoate : It is an organic dye used as anthelmintic agent. It is not orally absorbed. Major portion of administered dose appears unchanged in the faeces. Adverse effects are few and include gastric irritation, photosensitization, nausea, vomiting, diarrhoea, cramps and skin rash. It is used in the treatment of enterobiasis caused by pin worm (*E. vermicularis*).

Adult oral dose is 5 mg (base) / kg body weight per day.

(x) Suramin : It is a dye derivative having trypanocidal activity. Freshly prepared solution should always be used for i.v. administration. About 99% administered dose is bound to the plasma-proteins. It has a plasma half-life of 48 - 49 days. It does not undergo significant metabolism. About 60% dose appears unchanged in the urine.

It is used in the treatment of African trypanosomiasis and for onchocerciasis either alone or along with arsenical therapy. It is effective in the prophylaxis of Rhodesian and Gambian trypanosomiasis.

Adult i.v. dose is 1 g on days 1, 3, 7, 14 and 21 that is slowly injected in the form of 10% solution. The therapy may be continued for additional 5 weeks.

(xi) Piperazine citrate : It is an orally active anthelmintic agent available as citrate, phosphate or adipate salt form. It is effective against *Ascaris lumbricoides* and *Enterobium vermicularis* (oxyuriasis). Major dose fraction appears unchanged in the urine.

It is used in the treatment of oxyuriasis. A single daily dose of 65 mg/kg of body weight may be given for a week. The dose-schedule may be repeated after 15 days. It may also be used in the treatment of combined ascariasis and oxyuriasis.

(xii) Bephenium hydroxynaphthoate : It is a quaternary ammonium salt previously designed to treat hookworm infections. It is poorly absorbed from GIT. It is used to treat infections caused by *Ascaris lumbricoides*, *Trichostrongylus orientalis* and *ternideniasis*. It is excreted in urine only in trace amounts.

Adult oral dose is 5 g twice a day with empty stomach for 3 - 7 days.

(xiii) Bithionol : It is phenolic anthelmintic agent used for the treatment of paragonimiasis and fascioliasis. Adverse effects includes nausea, vomiting, diarrhoea, colic, urticaria and photodermatitis.

Adult oral dose is 50 mg/kg of body weight every second day for ten doses.

(xiv) Chloroquine : It is an orally effective 4-aminoquinoline antimalarial agent which may be used in the treatment of clonorchiasis. It acts by depressing ova output. It does not exert vermicidal effect.

(xv) Pyrantel pamoate : It is a poor orally absorbed broad-spectrum anthelmintic and neuromuscular blocking agent. It is effective against infections with hook-worm, pinworm, and round-worm. About 60 - 70% dose appear in the faeces in unchanged form. Inactive metabolites appears in the urine alongwith 10 - 20% dose in unchanged form. It is contraindicated during pregnancy and in children less than 2 years of age.

It is effective in the treatment of ascariasis, enterobiasis, ancylostoma, *Necator americanus* and Trichostrongylus. It may be used alongwith oxantel to treat mixed infections with *Trichuris trichiura*. Adult oral dose is 11 mg/kg to a maximum of 1 g per day. Treatment may be repeated, if necessary after an interval of two weeks.

In general, various anthelmintic agents exert their activity by producing toxic effects on both, gastrointestinal tract and the parasitic worms. They induce contraction of the worms which is followed by their tonic paralysis. Thereafter the worms are removed by the peristaltic movement of smooth muscles of GIT that helps to excrete out these parasites in the faeces. Metrifonate, an organophosphorus inhibitor of cholinesterase enzymes, produces rapid and almost complete inhibition of cholinesterases in the worms. Of course, the drug, to a certain extent, also affects the host due to its cholinesterase-inhibitory activity.

Depending upon the type of worm involved, anthelmintic agents are used alone or in combination with each other. For example, in tapeworm infections, niclosamide is a drug of choice. In nematode infections, piperazine, mebendazole and pyrantel palmitate are used because of their broad-spectrum of anthelmintic activity. For filaria, diethylcarbamazine is generally used, while in trematode infections, niridazole, bithionol and oxamniquine are effective agents.

❖ ❖ ❖

DIAGNOSTIC AGENTS

21.1 INTRODUCTION

The concept of nuclear pharmacy was first put forward by captain **William H. Briner** in 1960. The term 'radio activity' was first coined by **Curies** in 1898 to describe the radioactive decay of radium and polonium. Alpha, beta and gamma rays are the types of radiations obtained through radioactive decay. Some of the characteristic rays are known as x-rays.

In recent times, the role played by the radiation technology in various fields has assumed considerable significance. The applications of various types of radiation have been well established and have been successfully demonstrated in areas of great technical and economic effectiveness and of potential benefits to the public health and diagnostic field. They can also be used in the treatment of cancer and in radioimmunoassay. On the diagnostic side, they are used to trace the defective functioning of the body organs or to detect the abnormalities in the tissue structure. Hence, they are known as radiotracers or radioactive pharmaceuticals or radio-pharmaceuticals or diagnostic agents.

These agents are all X-ray opaque (i.e. X-rays do not pass through them). Naturally when such agent is injected into the body to fill up a specific organ which is to be examined, the organ would not allow X-rays to pass through. In such situation, if the X-ray film is placed behind the site concerned, the shape of the organ will be clearly outlined on the film. Thus, radiopaque substances help in delineation of body organs and tissues against their immediate environment during fluoroscopic or roentgenographic examination. The bio-distribution of these agents is known as 'scintiphotos' and is obtained with a radiation detective device known as 'scintillation camera'.

21.2 CLASSIFICATION

These agents are either radioactive forms (radioisotopes) of stable elements (like, iodine) or radioactive analogues of stable elements. They usually are devoid of any pharmacological effects. The structure of any radiopharmaceutical agent consists of :

(a) Radioactive Part :

It is the most essential part of radio-pharmaceutical. It gives off the radiations necessary for tracer activity.

(b) Non-radioactive Part :

This part has a very little effect upon the tracer activity of the agent. It is of complex nature and governs the tissue distribution or localization in a particular organ through its distinctive chemical or physical properties.

The various radioactive agents can be categorized as :

(a) Radioisotopes :

These agents may be used for kinetic studies (i.e. radioisotopes I) or for scanning studies (i.e. radioisotopes II) Kinetic studies include determination of total blood volume, plasma volume, and the excretion pattern of the drug and/or its metabolites through bile, faeces and urine. The scanning studies may be utilized to know the localization or uptake of particular ion into certain tissue or organ. Thus, examination of bone, brain, kidney, lungs, thyroid, spleen and liver can be done by the use of radioisotopes II.

Some commonly used radioisotopes include ^{22}Na (sodium chloride), ^{42}K (potassium chloride), ^{51}Cr (sodium chromate), ^{59}Co (cyanocobalamin), ^{125}I (various forms), ^{197}Hg (chloromerodin) etc.

(b) Radio-opaque Agents (Contrast Media) :

These agents have in common the property of opacity to X-ray radiations. Hence, they are used to facilitate X-ray diagnosis by visualizing specific body organs or systems. They may be further subdivided into :

(i) Positive contrast media : These agents have an ability to absorb X-rays. This leads to appearance of a darker shadow on the fluoroscopic screen and lighter shadow on X-ray film, of the organ to be visualized against its immediate environment e.g. radio-opaques.

(ii) Negative contrast media : These agents are transparent to X-rays. This leads to a lighter shadow on fluoroscopic screen and a darker shadow on the X-ray film. Examples include air, oxygen, nitrogen, carbon dioxide, nitrous oxide etc.

Radio-opaques or positive contrast media comprise of examples of diversified structures and pharmacological properties. The common feature of all these reagents is that they consist of elements of high molecular weight. These elements impart the property of opacity to these agents. Besides this, localization and concentration of contrast medium in the organ also influence the degree of opacity.

(c) Diagnostic Chemicals :

These agents are used to determine organ functioning.

(d) Diagostic Drugs :

By virtue of certain pharmacological properties, these agents are used to test specific disease states of the organs.

21.3 RADIO-OPAQUE AGENTS (Contrast Media)

Radio-opaque agents are drugs used to help in diagnosing certain medical problems. Most of the members of this class are organic compounds. Organic iodinated compounds are also employed as X-ray contrast media in the examination of many remote sites in the body. Iodine content upto 50% or more is necessary for proper radio-opacity. This iodine absorbs X-rays thus allowing the X-ray to make a 'picture' of the area. These agents can be classified further into :

(a) Water Soluble Contrast Media :

Most of these preparations contain either citrate or a phosphate buffer and a chelating agent. These agents are used mainly in urography and angiography. All the iodinated compounds are usually administered by systemic procedure or by retrograde method (i.e. by mechanical means). In all of these methods, toxicity or side-effects are mild if the patient is tested for his sensitivity prior to the administration of contrast media. Examples include Iodohippurate sodium, Diatrizoate meglumine, Metrizoic acid, Iothalamic acid, Ipodate sodium, Iodipamide, Sodium acetrizoate, Metrizamid.

(b) Water Insoluble Contrast Media :

These agents have a very slight solubility in water. Agents from this class are used mainly for cholecystography, bronchography and myelography. Examples include Iopanoic acid, Propyliodone, Iophendylate, Tyropanoate sodium, Iocetamic acid, Iodoxamate. To aid in diagnosing the disease, the patient should not eat or drink anything for at least six hours before the examination.

Table 21.1 : Commonly used terms in radiography

Sr. No.	Procedure	Organ visualized
1.	Radiography	X-ray examination
2.	Angiography	Blood vessels
3.	Arteriography	Arteries
4.	Aortography	Aorta
5.	Arthrography	Joints
6.	Bronchography	Lungs
7.	Cholangiography	Gall bladder and bile ducts
8.	Cholecystography	Gall bladder
9.	Esophagography	Esophagus
10.	Hepatography	Liver
11.	Hepatolienography	Liver and spleen
12.	Hysterosalpingography	Uterus and oviducts
13.	Lymphography	Lymph nodes and vessels
14.	Lymphadenography	Lymph nodes
15.	Myelography	Lumbar, thoracic and cervical regions of the brain and spinal cord
16.	Pelviagraphy	Pelvis
17.	Pyelography	Kidney and ureter
18.	Splenography	Spleen
19.	Splenohepatography	Liver and spleen
20.	Urography	Urinary tract
21.	Ventriculography	Ventricles of brain
22.	Salpingography	Follopian tubes

Based on chemical nature, the radiopaque agents may also be categorised as :

(i) Heavy Metals and their Salt :

Heavy metals with high atomic numbers may be used as radiopaque because of their high radiopacity. Tantalum dust is such an example of radiopaque agent used by insufflation in bronchography, esopha gography and gastrography. It has a particle size of 2.5 µm in diameter. It possesses the clearance half-life of 105-817 days. Ciliary activity and coughing helps in removing the metal particles from the bronchi.

The commonly used radiopaque heavy metal salts include barium sulphate, bismuth subnitrate, ferrites, tantalum oxide, thorium dioxide and some metal chelates.

Because of low systemic toxicity low water solubility and a lack of osmotic activity, barium sulfate is a preferred radiopaque used for X-ray studies of gastrointestinal tract. It was introduced by **Bachem** and **Gunter** in 1910 to replace toxic bismuth salts for GI roentgenography. Sodium citrate is added to stabilize colloidal preparation of barium sulphate while sorbitol is added to enhance the function. Some polybasic acids like tartaric acid may be added to obtain the preparation of specific gravity close to 3.

It is the most preferred agent for gastrointestinal roentgenographic examination and inhalation bronchography. It may be used in the form of a paste or a thick cream (esophageal studies) or as a suspension (in gastric or small intestine studies) or as a retention enema (in colon studies). The dose ranges from upto 300 g (orally) and upto 360 g (rectally). It is also used for bronchography in infants and in children.

Bismuth subnitrate was the first clinically used contrast medium for GI-roentgenographic examination. This agent and other bismuth salts are less favoured because of toxicity signs produced by bismuth.

Ferrites (Fe_2O_3) possesses about 80% opacity than that of barium sulfate. Four ferrites containing copper, zinc, nickel, mangnese and magnesium are used as radiopaques for roentgenographic studies of esophagus, bronchi, stomach and small intestine.

The significant toxicity associated with metal ions like, cobalt, nickel, lead and calcium can be lowered down through chelation process. Various chelating agents have been tried to sequester heavy metal ions for roentgenographic studies. These include edetic acid; 1, 2-diaminocyclohexane-N, N'-tetracetic acid; diethylenetriamine pentacetic acid; N, N' -(2-hydroxycyclohexyl) ethylene diaminediacetic acid, 2-hydroxycyclohexyl ethylene diamine triacetic acid; and β-hydroxyethylethylenediamine triacetic acid.

Thorium dioxide is used for angiography and cerebral arteriography. However, the long term radiation effects from thorium 232 induces fibrosis and neoplastic growth in liver and spleen. This results into fibrosis of their efferent lymph nodes. Because of these effects, it is less favoured.

Other metallic salts include tantalum oxide (in bronchography and esophagography), calcium tungstate, barium titanate and barium metatitanate. The latter barium salts are used for roentgenographic studies of hypopharynx, esophagus, stomach and small intestine.

(ii) Iodized Oils :

These preparations are formed by interaction of vegetable oils with hydroiodic acid. Chemically they are glyceryl esters and ethyl esters of iodinated fatty acid. Ususally they are yellow or amber coloured oils that decompose upon exposure to air or light to liberate iodine.

Upon administration, these oils liberate inorganic iodide in the body which appears in the urine. Pulmonary or systemic embolization is the only adverse effect of serious concern. Iodized oils may be used in lymphography, hepatography and hepatospleenography.

(iii) Organic Iodine Compounds :

Memebers of this series are the most widely used radiopaque agents in angiographic, cholegraphic, urographic and myelographic studies. Tetraiodophenolphthalein was the first clinically used agent from this series. It was used in 1926 by **Graham et al** in intravenous cholecystography.

In general, these agents contain either benzene or pyridine nucleus as iodine carrying moiety. Iodine content plays a governing role in determining the intensity of opacity. The non-ionic contrast media will be less toxic than ionic ones because of lower osmolarity.

Based on chemical features, organic iodine compounds can be subcategorized into:

(a) Triiodobenzoates : e.g. metrizoate

(b) Triiodoisophthalmates :
  e.g. iothalamic acid

(c) Triiodophenyl alkanoates :
  e.g. ipodate

(d) Triiodophenoxy alkanoates :
  e.g. iopronic acid

(e) Triiodobenzamides :
  e.g. metrizamide

(f) Triiodoanilides :
  e.g. iocetamic acid

(g) Dimeric triiodobenzoates :
  e.g. iodipamide

(h) Dimeric triiodoisophthalamates :
  e.g. iosefamic acid

(i) Other dimers and polymers :
  e.g. iozomic acid

(j) Diiodophenyl alkanoate :
  e.g. iodoalphionic acid

(k) Diiodopyridones :
  e.g. propyliodone

(l) Iodophthaleins :
  e.g. iodophthalein

(m) Miscellaneous :
  e.g. iodohippurate sodium

(I) Agents used in Urography :

The agents from this category should be readily soluble in water, less readily bind to plasma-proteins and should have minimal osmotic activity. They should have maximum tubular secretion and minimal tubular reabsorption. Examples of such agents include diatrizoate, iodamide, metrizoate, and iodohippurate sodium I 123.

Diatrizoate is an ionic, monomeric triiodinated benzoic acid derivative. It has poor oral absorption. It exhibits very low binding to plasma-proteins. It has a plasma half-life of 30-60 minutes. Major dose appears unchanged in the urine. Adverse effects includes chills, dizziness, headache, nausea, vomiting and sweating.

It is available as a salt of meglumine as well as of sodium. Combination of both these salts is preferred to lower down intensity of adverse hemodynamic, neurotoxic and cardiotoxic effects probably because of the sodium ions.

Diatrizoate is indicated for cholangiography, brain imaging, gastro-intestinal radiography, hysterosalpingography, urography and angiography.

Iodohippurate sodium I 123 is an agent of choice to assess renal function, effective renal blood flow and urinary tract obstruction. It has a plasma half-life of 20-30 minutes. It is excreted by both tubular secretion and glomerular filtration. Adverse effects are few and include nausea, vomiting, fainting and allergic reactions. Adult i. v. dose is 100-400 microcuries for renography and 1 millicurie for renal imaging.

(II) Agents used in Hepatography and Chole Cystography :

Liver is the main site for metabolic and detoxifying enzymes of the body. It is one of the largest playground for metabolic activities. This is the reason why liver damage cannot be recognised at its early stage. The decreased liver function cannot be identified until 70-90% of the liver cells get damaged. Agents whose excretion depends exclusively upon liver function, are used to detect the liver dysfunctioning. The rate of clearance of such agents from the plasma becomes a measure of the excretory capacity of the liver. These agents include iodipamide meglumine and cholecystographic agents. The latter class can be subcategorised as :

(i) Agents used to detect gall-bladder disorders : e.g. iocetamic acid, ipodate, iopanoic acid and tyropanoate, and

(ii) Agents used to detect biliary tract disorders : e.g. iopanoic acid and ipodate salts.

The agents used in cholecystography should pass slowly from blood to liver and then to the bile. Hence, these agents should bind strongly to plasma-proteins and should not be actively secreted in the urine. These agents or their glucuronide conjugates should be excreted largely through biliary secretory pathways. These agents are effective by both oral and intravenous routes.

All the above cholecystographic agents belong to the class of organic iodine compounds. They may be used for oral cholangiography to visualize biliary ducts. However i. v. cholangiography is a method of choice. All have high binding affinity to the plasma-proteins. On hepatic metabolism, these agents are converted to radiopaque glucuronides. They are mainly excreted through the urine and faecal routes. Adverse effects are few and includes nausea, vomiting, diarrhoea, skin rash, itching, dizziness and headache. Adult oral dose for cholecystographic agents ranges from 3.0 - 4.5 gm.

(III) Miscellaneous Radiopaque Agents :

(i) Metrizamide :

Metrizamide is a first generation non-ionic, contrast medium used as a diagnostic aid in cardiac, CNS, CSF and vascular disorders. It is a monomeric triiodinated benzoic acid derivative commonly used in myelography.

After intrathecal administration in sub-arachnoid space, metrizamide rapidly diffuses into cerebrospinal fluid. It rapidly penetrates into nerve root, sleeves, nerve rootlets and narrow areas of subarachnoid space and helps to visualize different regions of head and spinal cord. After i.v. injection, metrizamide helps to visualize vessels in its path of flow. Most of the dose administered appears in the urine. Adverse effects include nausea, vomiting, skin rash, wheezing, headache, restlessness, and irregular heartbeats.

Since metrizamide is isotonic with cerebrospinal fluid at an approximate concentration of 170 mg of iodine per ml of the solution, dosage of metrizamide is usually expressed in terms of iodine. For example, various commercial grades available include 2.5 g of metrizamide with 1.21 g of iodine, 6.75 g of metrizamide with 3.26 g of iodine and 13.5 g of metrizamide with 6.51 g of iodine per vial.

(ii) Iothalamate :

Iothalamate is available in the form of iothalamate meglumine and iothalamate sodium. It is an ionic, monomeric triiodinated benzoic acid derivative used in angiography and to trace out brain, pancreas, biliary tract and urinary tract disorders.

In the form of meglumine salt, it binds to plasma protein to the extent of 1-4% while about 8-27% administered dose of iothalamine sodium binds to the plasma proteins. Most of the administered dose appears unchanged in the urine.

Adverse effects include nausea, vomiting, unusual warmth and flushing of the skin, severe hypotension and redness, swelling or pain at the site of injection.

For peripheral arteriography about 20-40 ml of 60% solution may be administered in a single dose rapidly into bronchial artery in the arm or femoral artery in the leg. For brain imaging, about 2 ml of 60% solution per kg body weight (not above 150 ml) may be administered intravenously. For urography about 3 ml of 43% solution per kg body weight (not above 200 ml) may be given by i. v. infusion at a rate of 40-50 ml/min.

(iii) Iophendylate :

Iophendylate is a radiopaque agent used to trace out CNS and CSF disorders. After intrathecal administration into subarachnoid space, it gets rapidly distributed in different regions in head and in spinal canal. Hence, it is indicated for conventional lumbar, thoracic, cervical and total columnar myelography to determine the presence of abnormalities in CSF circulation or in CNS.

Adverse effects include nausea, vomiting, snuffy nose, headache, blurred vision, chest pain, wheezing, backache, fever and skin rash. In myelography, it may be injected intrathecally in the dose of 3.0 - 12.0 ml.

(iv) Iodipamide meglumine :

Iodipamide megiumine is an ionic, dimeric triiodinated benzoic acid derivative, used as a diagnostic agent in the disorders of gall bladder and biliary tract. It is extensively bound to the plasma proteins. Upon hepatic metabolism, it is mainly excreted through the hepato-biliary system. In the form of iodinated ion, it gets concentrated in the gall bladder bile and allows visualization of gall bladder and biliary ducts.

In cholangiography and cholecystography, it is given by i.v. infusion in the dose of 100 ml of 10.3 % solution slowly over a period of 30-45 minutes.

(v) Iohexol :

Iohexol is a second generation non-ionic contrast medium used for cardiac, vascular, CNS, CSF and urinary tract disorders. It is insignificantly bound to the plasma-proteins and has a plasma half-life of 2.0 hours. It is mainly excreted through urine. In myelography, it is injected intrathecally in the dose of 10-17 ml of solution containing equivalent of 180 mg of iodine per ml.

(vi) Iopamidol :

Iopamidal is a second generation non-ionic contrast medium used for cardiac, vascular, CNS and CSF disorders. It has a plasma half life of 2 hours. It is insignificantly bound to the plasma-proteins. It is mainly excreted through the urine.

In myelography, it is injected intrathecally in the dose of 10-15 ml of solution containing equivalent of 200 mg iodine per ml. While in arteriography, it may be injected into femoral artery or subclavian artery in the dose of 5.0-40.0 ml.

(vii) Ioxaglate meglumine :

Ioxaglate meglumine is also available in the form of its sodium salt. It has an elimination half-life of 61-140 minutes. It has very low binding affinity for plasma proteins. It is primarily excreted in the urine.

It is used mainly for diagnosis of cardiac and vascular diseases. In cerebral angiography, through percutaneous or via catheter, it is administered at a rate not exceeding normal flow in artery (i.e. about 5 ml/sec). In left coronary arteriography, it is administered via catheter in the dose of 2-14 ml. In right coronary arteriography, about 1-10 ml of the agent may be administered via catheter while in left ventriculography about 45 ml of the agent may be administered via catheter in a single dose.

(viii) Simethicone :

Simethicone is a surface active agent used as an antiflatulent. It may also be used as antifoaming agent during gastroscopy to enhance visualization and in radiography of the bowel to reduce gas shadows. Adult oral dose is 67 mg in 2.5 ml of water as a single dose.

21.4 ADVERSE EFFECTS ASSOCIATED WITH CONTRAST MEDIA

Ionic contrast media are usually more toxic than non-ionic contrast media. The high degree of toxicity of ionic contrast media may be attributed to cations as well as anions. The cations commonly present in ionic contrast media include sodium, calcium, magnesium and N-methyl-glucamine (i.e. meglumine). In order to reduce toxicities, usually a combination of sodium, magnesium and N-methylglucamine salts is preferred rather than any single agent. Beside this, toxicity may also be reduced by forming salt of acid form of the contrast medium with a basic amino acid.

The intensity and frequency of adverse effects of these contrast media are also influenced by the route of administration chosen. For example, the intensity of adverse effects is reported to increase in following order.

Intrathecal > Intravascular > Oral > Topical.

Nausea, vomiting, headache, mental confusion, cyclic changes in blood pressure, dizziness, blurred vision, flushing, wheezing, chest pain etc. are the common adverse effects reported to occur. Sometimes severe respiratory, neurological and CVS disturbances may accompany to increase the complexity of adverse effects.

21.5 DIAGNOSTIC CHEMICALS

Certain substances are retained or excreted almost exclusively only by a specific organ. Thus, depending upon the property of retention or excretion, the impairment in the organ function can be searched out. For example, phenol-tetrachlorophthalein when administered parenterally, is found to be excreted only in the bile. Hence, the failure to remove the dye through the bile is indicative of impaired functioning of the organ.

(a) Drugs Used to Test Kidney Function :

Examples from this category include p-aminohippurate, inulin and phenolsulphonaphthalein. To test kidney function, the bladder is completely emptied before the dye is administered. This is done under aseptic conditions by introducing a catheter into the bladder.

(i) p-Aminohippurate : It is administered intravenously in the form of its sodium salt and is not bound to the plasma-proteins. It distributes primarily in the extra-cellular space. It is exclusively excreted via the active secretory processes of proximal con-vuluted tubules in almost unchanged form. It has clearance rate of more than 600 ml/minute. Adverse effects include nausea and feeling of warmth.

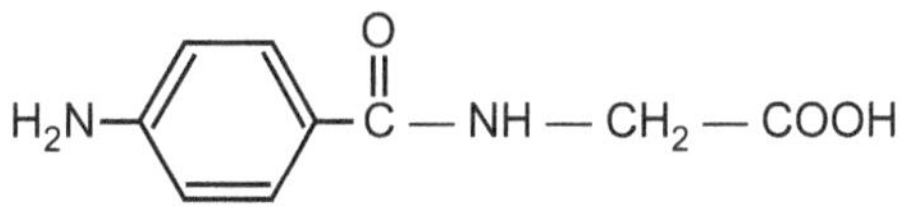

$$H_2N-\underset{}{\bigcirc}-\overset{O}{\underset{\|}{C}}-NH-CH_2-COOH$$

p-Aminohippuric aicd

It is mainly used to determine the functional capacity of the tubular excretory mechanism. The time period during which this agent is excreted in the urine, is used to determine renal function. It is available as a sterile solution containing 2 g per 10 ml. The adult dose is adjusted to get a plasma concentration of 10-20 mg/litre.

(ii) Inulin : It is a polyfructosan polysaccharide of plant origin having a molecular weight of 5000 and has a plasma half-life of 2-4 hours. It is rapidly distributed in extracellular spaces and does not undergo metabolism in the body. It is excreted almost entirely by glomerular filtration and its renal clearance rate is about 125 ml/min. It is also excreted in trace amount in the bile. It is devoid of any adverse effects. However, it may produce osmotic diuresis if used in larger doses. The loading dose (i.e. 100 ml at 10 ml/min rate) is administered by intravenous route, follwed by i.v. infusion at a rate enough to achieve a stable plasma concentration.

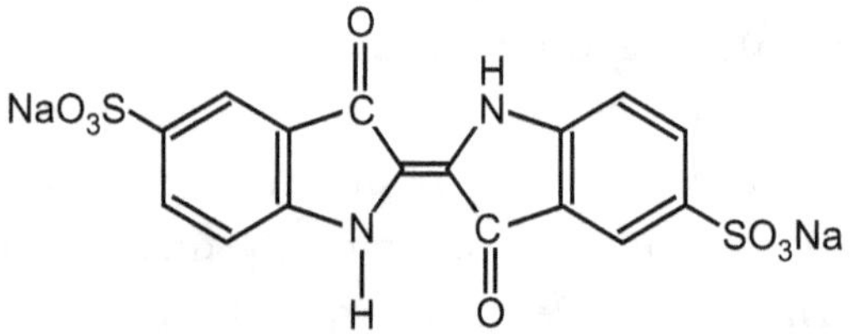

Liver is the main site for metabolic and detoxifying enzymes of the body. It is one of the largest playground for metabolic activities. This is the reason why liver damage cannot be recognized at its early stage. The decreased liver function cannot be identified until 70-90% of the liver cells get damaged. Agents whose excretion depends exclusively upon liver function, are used to detect the liver dysfunctioning. The rate of clearance of such agents from the plasma becomes a measure of the excretory capacity of the liver. These agents include indocyanine green, sulfobromopthalein sodium and rose bengal.

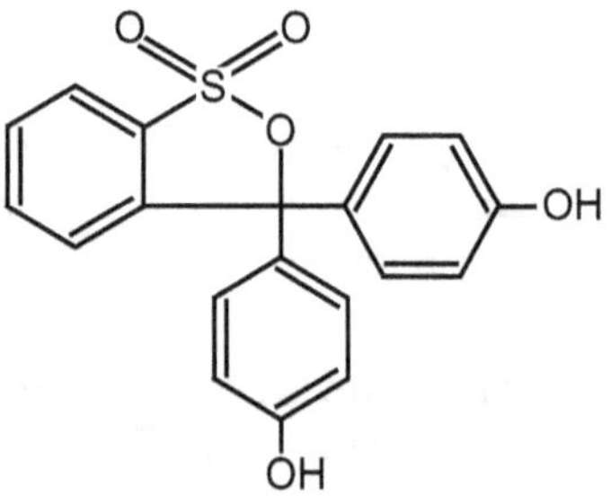

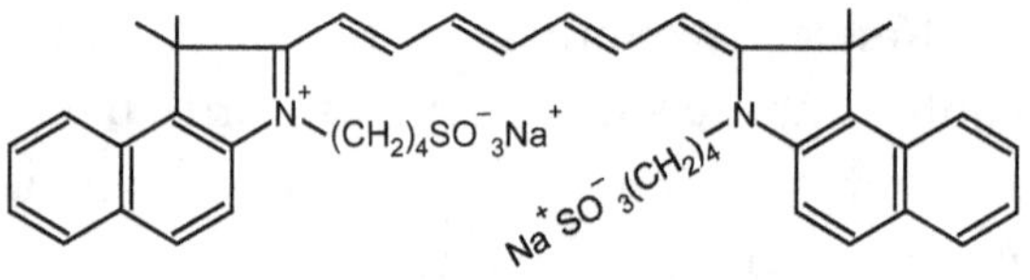

Indigotindisulfonate sodium

Indocyanine green

Phenolsulfonaphthalein

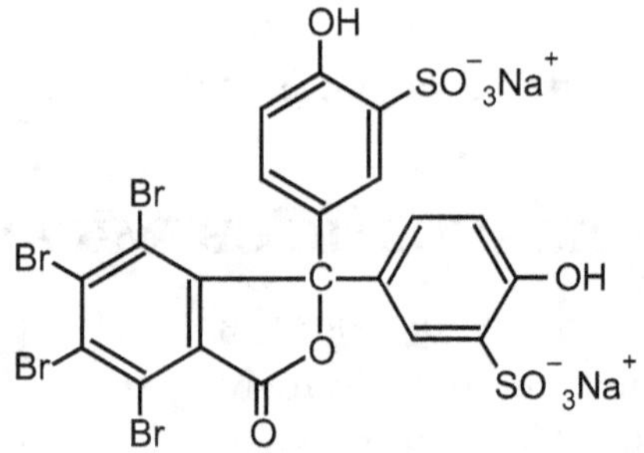

Sulfobromophthalein sodium

Other agents from this category include indigotindisulfonate sodium and phenolsulfonaphthalein. The latter agent is available as a sterile solution (6 mg/ml) in physiological saline. It is given intravenously in the dose of 6 mg.

(b) Drugs Used to Test Liver Function :

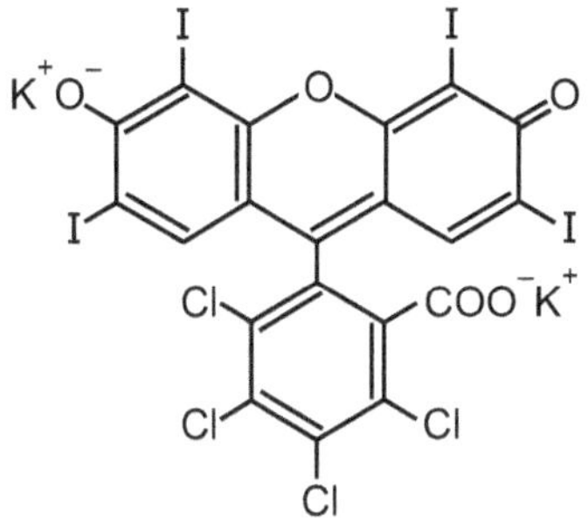

Rose bengal

Since these agents are almost exclusively taken up by liver and excreted unchanged in the bile, they are used to assess hepatic blood flow and hepatic (biliary) secretory function. The common adverse effects include localized acute thrombophlebitis and delayed hypersensitivity.

Indocyanine green is available as a sterile powder (25 mg and 50 mg vials) which is to be dissolved freshly at the time of use. It is given intravenously at a dose of 0.15 mg/kg body weight to test liver function. Sulfobromophthalein is available as a sterile ampoules (3.0, 7.5, 10.00 ml) of a concentration of 50 mg/ml. It is given intravenously in the dose of 0.5-2.0 mg per kg body weight.

(c) Agents Used to Test Gastric Function :

Many gastric stimulants are used to gather the evidence of hyper or hyposecretion of gastric acid. Proof about the absence of gastric acid in the stomach is necessary for the diagnosis of pernicious anaemia. While oversecretion of gastric acid confirms the case of peptic ulcer or peptic esophagitis. The gastric stimulants mainly used to test gastric function include, alcohol, caffeine, pentagastrin, histamine, phosphate, betazole hydrochloride etc.

$(CH_3)_3$ N–CO–CO–β–ala–Trp–Met–Asp–Phe–NH$_2$

Pentagastrin

Pentagastrin is a potent, short acting, synthetic carboxy terminal pentapeptide derivative of gastrin. It has a plasma half life of 10 minutes. It is used in the diagnosis of pernicious anaemia, atropic gastritis, gastric carcinoma or the cases of hypersecretion of gastric acid. Adult s.c. dose is 6 µg/kg body weight.

(d) Agents Used to Test Cardiac Function :

Examples from this category include evans blue and indocyanine green. They may be used to determine blood volume and cardiac output.

Evans blue is a water soluble dye with a molecular weight of 961. It is extensively bound to the plasma-proteins and has plasma half-life of more than 15 days.

It is relatively safe agent. In some patients, a blue-green tinge may be imparted to the skin. It is available as a single dose ampoule containing 25 mg (5.0 ml of 0.5% solution) for intravenous route. Indocyanine green may be given intravenously at a dose of 5 mg/kg body weight to determine cardiac output.

(e) Miscellaneous Diagnostic Chemicals :

These include fluorescein sodium, metyrapone, congo red and erythrosine sodium. Fluorescein sodium is mainly used for ophthalmological studies. Metyrapone is primarily used to determine residual pituitary function in patients with hypopituitarism, while erythrosine sodium is a dental diagnostic agent used to detect areas of plaque on the teeth.

Although an ideal diagnostic agent should have low toxicity and minimum pharmacological activities, no such diagnostic chemical is completely devoid of the risk. In all these preparations, mild side-effects are quite frequent. Hence, after intravascular administration of these agents, physician supervision and emergency facilities should be kept ready for atleast 30-60 minutes.

Table 21.2 : Currently used diagnostic drugs

Drugs	Diagnostic use
1. L-arginine	To test growth hormone secretion response
2. Dexamethasone	To test endocrine gland dysfunction
3. Epinephrine	To test denervation of postganglionic sympathetic pathways in the eyes
4. Histamine	To test gastric acid secretion
5. Mannitol	To test renal function
6. Metyrapone	To test pituitary function
7. Norepinephrine	To test denervation of sympathetic pathways
8. Pentagastrin	To test gastric acid secretion
9. Phentolamine	To test a state of pheochromocytoma
10. Tyramine	To test a state of pheochromocytoma

DRUGS ACTING ON BLOOD

22.1 INTRODUCTION

Blood is a transport system which carries oxygen from the lungs and dietary elements from the gastrointestinal tract to various body tissues and trains away carbon dioxide and waste metabolic products to their respective sites of excretion i.e. the lungs and kidneys. It also helps in maintaining proper electrolyte balance and pH. The main constituents of blood are :

(a) Solid elements (blood cells) : 45%

(b) Clear faint yellow fluid (plasma) : 55%

The blood cells or corpuscles are of three types :

(i) Red corpuscles or erythrocytes,

(ii) White corpuscles or leucocytes, and

(iii) Platelets or thrombocytes.

The leucocytes and the circulating antibodies serves as the defence mechanisms and guards against infections or provide protection. Red blood cells survive in the circulation for about 120 days. On an average a little less than 1% of the circulating red cells are being replaced daily. The circulation is controlled by hemostatic processes mediated by central nervous system and renal mechanisms.

Besides certain other factors, formation of red blood cells depends upon an adequate supply of iron and certain coenzymes, vitamin B_{12} and tetrahydrofolate. Drugs acting on blood are mainly studied under following heads :

(A) Coagulants and anticoagulants.

(B) Antithrombotic drugs.

(C) Haematinics, and

(D) Plasma expanders.

22.2 COAGULANTS AND ANTICOAGULANTS

Blood is retained as a fluid in the circulation by haemostatic mechanisms, which can be summarised under following heads :

(i) Vascular Mechanisms :

It involves the reactions and surface properties of the blood vessels. After the vascular injury, the precapillary vessels show vasoconstriction. Exposure of the subendothelial collagen after injury to thrombocytes or blood platelets results into platelet adhesion. This leads to formation of blood clot through the activation of intrinsic system.

(ii) Platelet Factors :

It involves the properties of platelet adhesion. The platelets adhere to the subendothelial collagen of the injured vasulature in the presence of the von

Willebrand binding factor. Platelets also stick to each other. The structural deformation of the platelets leads to loss of individual cell membranes and the release of the contents of platelet granules. The arrest of bleeding may be achieved through the formation of platelet plug.

(iii) Plasma Coagulation Factors :

Platelet adhesion and aggregation are stimulated by the release of ADP, thrombin and epinephrine. The platelet adhesion initiates the intrinsic system to cause clotting of blood via activation of Hageman factor XII to XII a. The production of thrombin also occurs. Each clotting factor initiates the activation of next clotting factor in the series until ultimately an insoluble fabrin clot is formed.

(iv) Fibrinolytic Mechanisms :

This mechanism helps to maintain the blood in fluid state and prevents the spread of effects of clotting elements in the body vasculature. During this process, the plasmin formation is initiated which then dissolves thrombi formed into the blood vessel. Plasmin causes the lysis of both fibrin clots and fibrin. Fibrinolysis thus can be viewed as a final stage of blood clotting. The first three mechanisms promote the blood clotting and prevent the blood loss. These four mechanisms operate with mutual understanding and in mutual benefit of each other with an aim to alter viscosity of blood as per the body needs.

22.3 PLASMA COAGULATION FACTORS

Injury initiates the blood coagulation process. The normal plasma clotting time is 12 seconds. The clot formation involves a series of complicated reactions characterised by vasoconstriction, adhesion and aggregation of platelets and formation of thick gel-like mass. The process involves a series of clotting factors which interact in the sequential manner that comprises many intermediate reactions. Except calcium, all these factors are proteins or lipoproteins and remain inactive in proenzymatic form under the resting conditions. They get readily activated by injury to the vascular endothelium.

In 1905, **Morawitz** first proposed the rational basis of blood coagulation, explaining the overall mechanism in the form of bioamplification system. According to him, blood platelets (thrombocytes) play a major role in initiating blood coagulation. The platelet contains thromboplastin which is a phospholipoprotein.

When blood sheds, the circulating platelets become sticky. They start adhering to each other and to the surface of injured subendothelial collagen. Structural deformation of platelets occurs resulting in the release of the contents of platelet and dense granules. This includes ADP (a powerful stimulant of platelet aggregation) and serotonin (a powerful vasoconstrictor) which are released along with calcium from the dense granules, while the contents of platelet include platelet growth factor, platelet factor IV, β-thromboglobulin, fibronectin, von Willebrand's protein and fibrinogen. All these factors facilitate the local conversion of plasma prothrombin into thrombin which acts as a potent bioamplifier during clotting process. Thrombin stimulates more ADP release from the platelets resulting into further platelet aggregation. Thrombin also activates formation of prostaglandins like thromboxane A_2 (TXA_2, synthesized by the aggregated platelets which acts as stimulator of platelet aggregation) and prostacyclin (PGI_2, synthesized by the vessel wall and inhibits thrombosis through increasing the c-AMP levels). Thus, thrombin participates to increase the size and strength of the platelet plug.

Thrombin is a peptidase. It splits off fibrinogen into fibrin monomers and two peptides - fibrinopeptides A and B. This is a sort of limited proteolysis.

The fibrin monomers then polymerize to produce a soft clot that gradually becomes firm and stable under the influence of Ca^{++} and fibrin stabilizing factor (factor XIII). This was, in brief, the theory of blood coagulation proposed by Morawitz in 1905. Meanwhile additional factors affecting coagulation have also been discovered (Table. 22.1).

Various factors need calcium ions for their activation. Some factors (e.g. factors II, VII, IX and X) require vitamin K for their activation. The present system of nomenclature denotes the activated form of clotting factor with a subscript a. Thus, thrombin became factor IIa. Some of these factors are present in the vascular system, either in the plasma or platelet. Hence, they are called as intravascular factors or intrinsic factors. Intrinsic factors catalyse blood coagulation process completely but at very slow speed.

Table 22.1 : Blood clotting factors

Factor	Synonyms	Molecular weight (in Daltons)
I	Fibrinogen	3,40,000
II	Prothrombin	68,700
III	Thromboplastin	–
IV	Calcium ions	–
V	Proaccelerin	4,00,000
VI	Not verified	–
VII	Proconvertin	45,000
VIII	Antihemophilia A - I factor	1,00,000
IX	Christmas factor	55,400
X	Stuart - Prower factor	55,000
XI	Plasma thromboplastin	1,60,000
XII	Hageman factor (contact factor)	74,000
XIII	Fibrinoligase (fibrin stabilizing factor)	3,20,000
HMW - K	High molecular weight kininogen	–
Ka	Kallikrein	–
PL	Platelet phospholipids	–

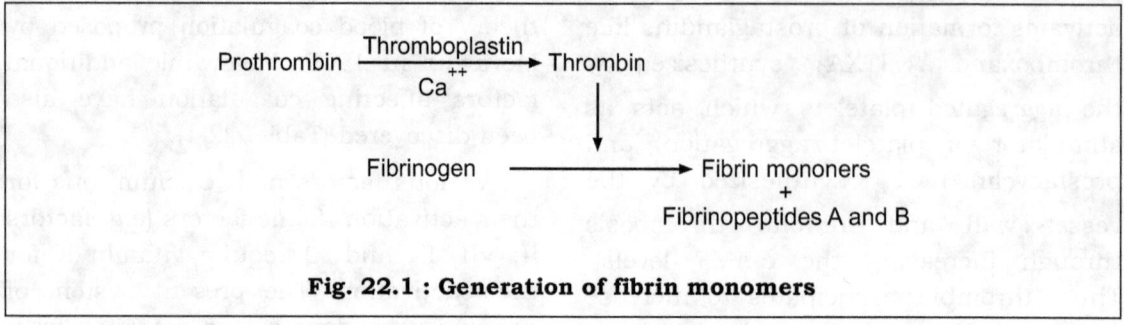

Fig. 22.1 : Generation of fibrin monomers

Their enzymatic actions need to be speed up by a second extrinsic pathway which consists of factor VII and tissue thromboplastin (factor III). Factor III is a lipoprotein comprising phospholipid, either phosphatidyl choline or phosphatidyl ethanolamine, complexed with a specific protein and is not present in circulating blood. It is widely distributed in the vascular endothelial membranes and in leukocytes. It is released after the damage to blood vessel walls. Both pathways are necessary for rapid and adequate hemostasis.

After vascular injury, Hageman factor (XII) attaches to the vascular endothelial surface and undergoes contact activation by kallikrein in the presence of high molecular weight kininogen. The activated form of Hageman factor (XII a) then initiates the activation of a series of clotting factor ultimately leading to blood clotting. Calcium ions, HMW-K and platelet phospholipid participates at various stages of the process along with activated form of clotting factor. Activation of factor X is the step after which the extrinsic system merges into the intrinsic system. Thus, it is the final stage in both the intra and extra vascular systems. The conversion of prothrombin to thrombin is then initiated by Xa in the presence of Ca^{++} and PL. Thrombin participates in the formation of fibrin monomers from fibrinogen. Fibrin then enmeshes erythrocytes and other blood elements resulting into a gelatinous mass that serves as the platelet plug at the site of vascular injury. Factor XIIIa helps to maintain the firmness and stability of the clot by catalysing the cross-linking peptide bonds between γ-amide of glutamine of one fibrin molecule with the ε-amino group of lysine moiety of another fibrin molecule. It is mainly present in the human platelets and in the plasma. Fibrinogen is synthesized in the liver along with many clotting factors. It has a plasma half-life of about 4 days.

Fibrinolysis is the last stage of blood clotting process. The process is initiated by conversion of plasminogen (profibrinolysin) into plasmin (fibrinolysin) under the influence of urokinase (fibrinokinase). Kidney is the site of production for plasminogen. The formation of plasmin dissolves the insoluble fibrin clot into soluble inert peptides. These fibrin degradation products also have an ability to inhibit fibrin polymerization.

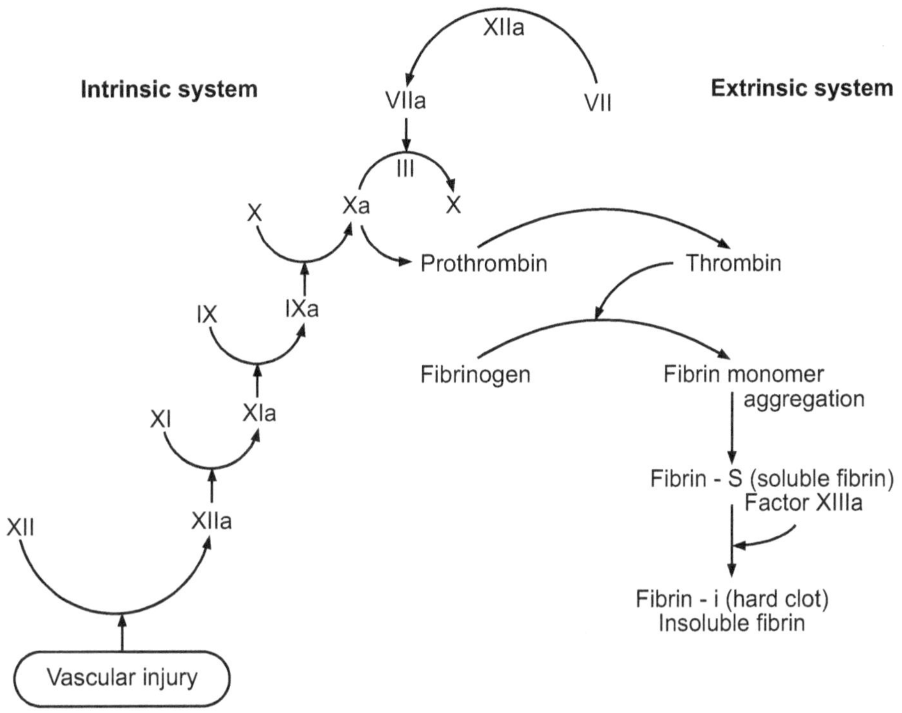

Fig. 22.2 : Participation of intrinsic and extrinsic systems in the blood coagulation

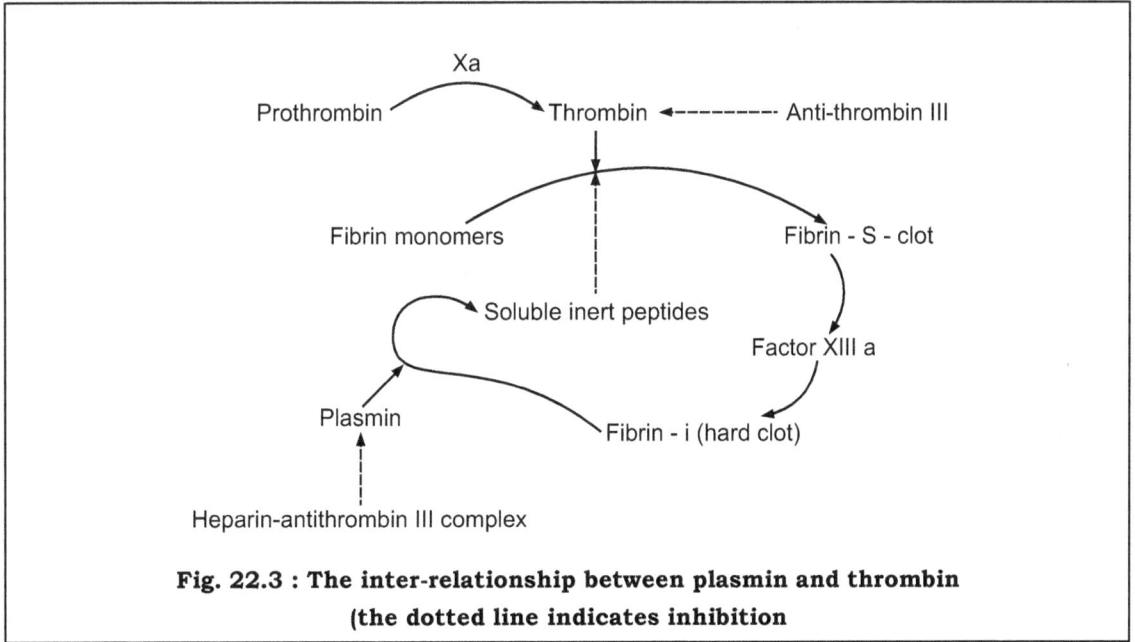

Fig. 22.3 : The inter-relationship between plasmin and thrombin (the dotted line indicates inhibition

Once the blood clotting process at the site of vascular endothelium is initiated, various coagulation factors may spread up into various body organs from the site of injury. Antithrombin III (heparin cofactor) is an important part of body's own natural anticoagulation machinery that localizes the fibrin clot at the site of injury and neutralizes the clotting factors at other sites of the body. Though liver is the principal site for its synthesis, antithrombin III is widely distributed in various tissues of the body. Its neutralizing effect is mainly exerted on factors IIa, IXa, Xa, XIa and XIIa. Its inhibitory action on blood clotting is due to its binding with thrombin (IIa). Similarly, the heparin antithrombin III complex also inhibits plasmin and thus may be a factor in regulating fibrinolysis process.

The fibrinolytic mechanisms maintain the blood in fluid state and dissolve any clot in the blood vessel formed due to fibrin monomers under pathogenic conditions. Plasmin is responsible for this clot dissolution. Thus, body possesses the finely balanced mechanisms that can both promote and prevent the coagulation process as per the demand of circumstances. It also illustrates the principle of enzymatic amplification during the whole process.

Many factors like fibrinogen, prothrombin, factors V, VII, IX and X have their sites of synthesis in liver. Hence, clotting abnormalities are likely to result during hepatic dysfunctioning and calcium and/or vitamin K deficiency. Similarly under certain conditions (e.g. an elevated platelet count, an increased platelet adhesiveness or increased plasma concentration of fibrinogen) arterial or venous thrombus may develop. In arterial thrombus, during the final stage of arterial occlusion, a red thrombus wraps the initial white thrombus. While the venous thrombus resulting from entrapment of red blood cells and platelets within the fibrin network may lead to pulmonary emboli. Due to their effectiveness in the prophylaxis of venous thrombosis or pulmonary emboli, anticoagulant drugs received much clinical attention. Besides this a number of drugs possess antithrombotic properties because of their ability to inhibit platelet aggregation. These antithrombotic agents are mainly useful in the treatment of myocardial ischemia and strokes arising due to the presence of arterial thrombi either in the heart or brain. Similarly, fibrinolytic agents, the third category of clinically useful drugs finds its application in the treatment of pulmonary emboli, proximal venous thrombi or coronary arterial thrombosis.

22.4 ANTICOAGULANTS

Two distinct pathways contribute to the formation of the blood clot. When the protein factors present in the circulation provide the whole cause and completion of the clotting process, the clot is said to be effected by the intrinsic system. While, when the blood coagulation is activated by the factors which are not originated from the circulating blood (e.g. tissue thromboplastin), the clot is said to be due to the extrinsic system. Agents used to modify the stages of clotting process may act by :

(i) potentiating the natural inhibitory elements of clotting process e.g. heparin,

(ii) reducing the rate of synthesis of vitamin-K dependent clotting factors e.g. warfarin, and

(iii) potentiating fibrinolytic mechanisms e.g. streptokinase, urokinase etc.

Various conditions contribute to bleeding disorders. These include thrombocytopenia (i.e. low platelet count), hemophilias (i.e. genetic defect in the synthesis of clotting factors. In some cases, certain clotting factors are totally missing from the plasma of the patient) etc. These bleeding disorders may lead to the clot formation (i.e. thrombus) in the artery or vein or even in the heart chamber. Thromboembolism is the next stage in which reduced blood flow occurs at sites quite distinct to the point of thrombus. Myocardial infarction, peripheral arterial emboli, deep venous thrombosis and pulmonary embolization are some conditions where anticoagulant therapy is generally needed. Many compounds prevent the availability of calcium ions during coagulation process. These include soluble salts of citrate, oxalate, fluoride or EDTA. All these compounds can be used as *in-vitro* anticoagulants. The clinically used anticoagulants fall under two categories :

(i) Heparin, and
(ii) Oral anticoagulants.

22.5 HEPARIN (Parenteral Anticoagulant)

Heparin occurs intracellularly especially concentrated in the basophil cells found in the circulating plasma. Its discovery was reported by **Howell** in 1922. It was first isolated from liver. Hence it was named as heparin. It is widely distributed in the tissues, particularly in the lungs and liver.

Jorpes in 1937 established its chemical composition and the first clinical use of heparin was also documented in the same year. Chemically it is a heterogenous group of highly electro-negative water soluble straight-chain mucopolysaccharides. It is a polymer consisting of alternate units of two disaccharides (i.e. D-glucosamine - L - iduronic acid and D-glucosamine - D - glucuronic acid) in addition to sulfuric acid. Besides this, 1 : 1 additional residues of glucuronic acid and fewer residues of N-sulfated glucosamine per heparin molecule are also reported in the structural analysis. Because of its acidic properties, heparin may also be called as 'heparinic acid'.

Commercially heparin is mainly obtained from bovine lung or porcine intestinal mucosa. In most of the samples, the number of repeating disaccharide units per molecule ranges from 6 to 15. Hence, its molecular weight also ranges from 8,000 to 50,000 dalton. The commercial samples of heparin may differ in their degree of polymerization and sulfation but biologically all heparins are almost equivalent. In clinical practice, heparin may be used during and after various types of surgery to reduce or to prevent intravascular clotting and thrombosis.

Pharmacological Properties :

(i) As an anticoagulant, heparin is effective both *in-vivo* and *in-vitro*. On administration, several clotting factors are neutralized by heparin and antithrombin III factor. Heparin neutralizes thromboplastin by forming an inactive complex with it, while in the absence of heparin, anti-thrombin III factor has an ability to neutralize thrombin but at quite slow speed. Heparin induces some conformational changes in the antithrombin III molecule, thus making it highly active.

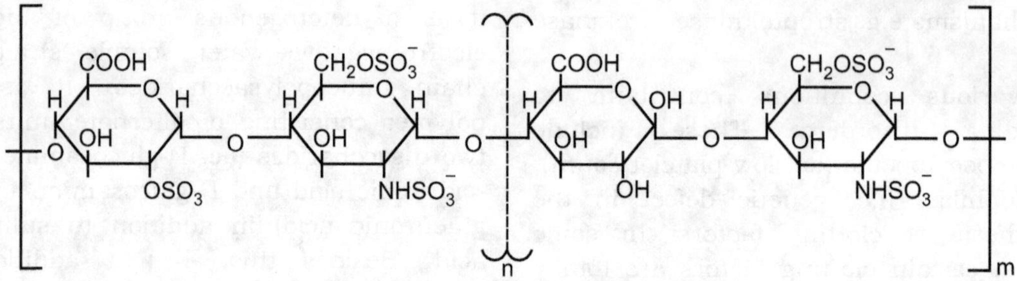

Fig. 22.4 : Polymeric nature of heparin structure

Hence, in the presence of heparin, the molecule of antithrombin III can neutralize thrombin and several other clotting factors (IXa, Xa, XIa, XIIa and kallikrein) at much faster rate by forming inactive complexes with these clotting factors. Thus, heparin may act as a catalyst in the neutralization of these clotting factors by antithrombin III factor.

(ii) During hyperlipemia, the plasma triglyceride level increases. The enzyme, lipoprotein lipase is responsible for the hydrolysis of these triglycerides into fatty acids and partial glycerides. These products are then metabolized by extrahepatic tissues. Heparin activates lipoprotein lipase. Thus, it helps to reduce hyperlipemia by lowering of plasma triglyceride level.

Pharmacokinetics :

Heparin is poorly absorbed (less than 15%) from GIT after oral administration mainly because of its polyanionic character (polarity), large molecular size and its instability in the gastric juice. Since its oral or sublingual administration is not effective, it is given parenterally. Because of its acidic properties, it induces local trauma followed by hemotonia formation, if it is administered intramuscularly. Hence, when low dose of heparin is required, it is usually administered subcutaneously or at intrafat sites. When large dose of heparin is required (as in pulmonary emboli), the intravenous route is favoured.

Heparin is significantly bound (95%) to plasma proteins. It is partially metabolized in the liver by the enzyme, heparinase. The metabolite, uroheparin has slight antithrombin like activity. The plasma half-life of heparin is estimated to be about one hour at a dose of 100 units/kg. However it is dose-dependent. For example, as the dose of administered heparin is increased to 400 units/kg, the plasma half-life also reaches to about 2 hours. In hepatic cirrhosis or renal dysfunctioning, the half-life of heparin becomes significantly longer. Heparin neither crosses the placental barrier nor it appears in the milk of lactating mothers.

Adverse Effects :

Heparin itself is of low toxicity and is an excellent anti-coagulant for short-term therapy. However, due to its commercial production from animal tissues, it may induce allergic reactions, specifically when given in high doses. Heparin also retains an inherent property to induce platelet aggregation. This may lead to thrombocytopenia in some patients. The major adverse reaction in heparin therapy is haemorrhage. The specific heparin antagonist, protamine (strongly basic low molecular weight proteins) may be used to neutralise heparin in cases of severe hemorrhage. Hence, heparin therapy is contraindicated in patients having intracranial hemorrhage, thrombocytopenia, severe hypertension, history of allergy or who consume large amount of ethanol.

Heparin is an excellent anti-coagulant for short-term therapy of 10-15 days. Oral anti-coagulants then can be used to extend the anti-coagulant effect for desired period.

Heparin Antagonists :

Severe hemorrhage may occur in patients receiving high dose of heparin. Protamine sulfate can be used in such cases to antagonise the effect of heparin. Protamines are strongly basic proteins of low moleculer weight. They were isolated from the sperm or mature testes of the fish belonging to the family Salmonidase. Protamine sulfate is usually administered intravenously to neutralise heparin by forming inactive complex with it. Dyspnea may develop, if the rate of infusion of protamine is rapid. An excess of protamine sulfate has anti-coagulant property.

Heparin may be used as an anticoagulant in surgical procedures and in the treatment of myocardial infarction and venous thrombi or thromboembolism.

22.6 ORAL ANTICOAGULANTS

The first orally effective anticoagulant was bishydroxy-coumarin. Isolated in 1939 by **Link**, its structure was established in 1940. In 1941, it was used clinically as the first orally effective anticoagulant (dicoumarol). Thereafter it has been used clinically for years in patients with a tendency of thrombus formation.

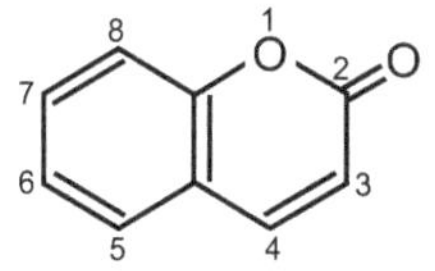

Coumarin nucleus

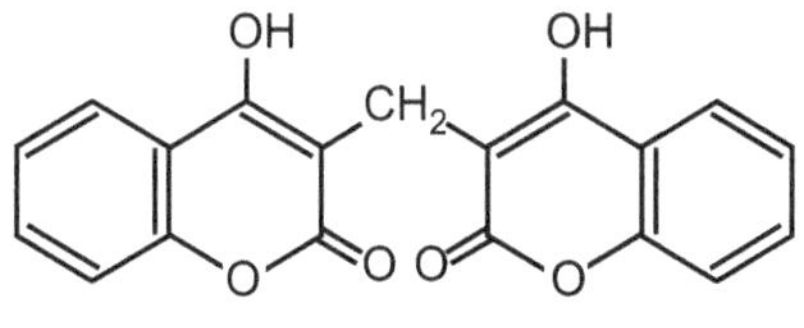

Dicoumarol

Dicoumarol itself has drawbacks as therapeutic agent mainly due to its poor and irregular absorption. Many analogs have been prepared. All these are water insoluble and possess either 4-hydroxycoumarin nucleus (coumarin derivatives) or indan - 1, 3 - dione nucleus (indandione derivatives). The latter are less preferred due to their greater toxicity. Some of these agents (e.g. phenprocoumon, warfarin) contain asymmetric carbon atom in their structure and commercially they are marketed as recemic mixtures. Usually the l - or S (–) - isomers are more potent anticoagulants than are the d - or R (+) isomers. All these agents differ from each other in onset and duration of their anticoagulant action. Coumarins do not have *in-vitro* activity. They exert *in-vivo* effect after a period of 1 - 2 days. Their effects last long. Coumarins suppress the synthesis of clotting factors (pro-thrombin, factors VII, VIII and IX) in the liver which results in the gradual decline in the concentration of clotting factors and hence a slow onset of action. Whereas the long duration of action may be due to the time taken by liver to accumulate again, enough concentration of clotting factors.

Mechanism of Action :

Vitamin K appears to be related to the important quinone coenzymes called as 'ubiquinones'. Since the oral anti-coagulants have close structural similarity with vitamin K, they exert anticoagulant activity by acting as non-competitive antagonists of vitamin K.

The activation of prothrombine involves formation of γ-carboxyglutamic acid residues which are important for entrapment of calcium ions. Calcium ions are needed at almost every stage to activate the clotting factors. The carboxylation process of prothrombine in hepatic microsomes is catalysed by vitamin K where the vitamin gets converted to its hydroquinone form. In normal circumstances, the inactive hydroquione form gets reconverted to the active vitamin K form by NADH-NAD^+ system.

The orally active anticoagulants inhibit the conversion of inactive vitamin K hydroquinone to the active vitamin K form. This leads to the accumulation of inactive vitamin K hydroquinone and depletion of the active vitamin K form in hepatic tissues. The oral anticoagulant agents thus prevent the hepatic synthesis of the biologically active forms of the vitamin K-dependent clotting factor, mainly prothrombin and factors VII, IX and X. The clotting time is prolonged due to the formation of structurally incomplete clotting factors. However, the onset of therapeutic efficacy can be seen only after existing plasma concentration of prothrombin and other vitamin K-dependent clotting factors have been declined. The vitamin K-dependent clotting factors have plasma half-life as follows : Factor II (60 hours), VII (6 hours), IX (24 hours) and X (40 hours). Hence, all these drugs show a long delay (about 3 - 5 days) in their onset of action. The rate of onset is independent of the size of the dose. The longer duration of their anticoagulant activity is mainly due to the long time required by the hepatic microsomal enzymes to convert coumarins into inactive hydroxylated metabolites. The mechanism of action and uses of indandione derivatives are similar to coumarins.

Pharmacokinetics :

Warfarin sodium is usually administered in the form of its racemic mixture. It is completely and rapidly absorbed from GIT. In the circulation, it is extensively bound (about 99%) to the plasma proteins. Unlike heparin, warfarin and phenindione do not have dose-dependent plasma half-life. Warfarin has the plasma half-life of about 35 days. The more potent levo-isomer of warfarin is metabolised (ring hydroxylation) in the liver to 7-hydroxy warfarin while the dextro-isomer is metabolized by side-chain reduction to a secondary alcohol. The formation of a 6-hydroxy warfarin from both isomers is also reported. All these hydroxylated metabolites are inactive and partly undergo glucuronidation. They are excreted through urine and stools.

Under many pathophysiological conditions, the response of a patient to oral anticoagulant therapy may be altered. For example, deficient bile secretion (decreased absorption of dietary vitamin K from GIT), oral antibiotic treatment (decreased vitamin K synthesis by the intestinal microflora), hepatic diseases (decreased rate of synthesis of clotting factors), all these conditions lead to increased response to oral anticoagulant therapy. However during pregnancy, the activity of some clotting factors (i.e. VII, VIII, IX and X) enhances, leading to decrease in the patient's response to oral anticoagulant therapy. Both, warfarin and dicumarol can cross placental barrier and can induce foetal and placental hemorrhage in therapeutic doses.

Due to their slow onset of action, usually heparin is administered first and the anticoagulant effect is then maintained by oral anticoagulant drugs.

Adverse Effects :

The safest and commonly used drugs are warfarin and bishydroxy coumarin. Side-effects of coumarin includes rash, nausea, vomiting, jaundice, leukopenia and thrombocytopenia. Minor hemorrhage during the therapy may be corrected by discontinuing the therapy. In the cases of overdoses, excessive bleeding and long prothrombin time may be treated by intravenous use of vitamin K or its synthetic derivatives such as menadiol diphosphate. Prothrombin itself may be given in the form of plasma or plasma concentrates if immediate treatment of overdoses is required.

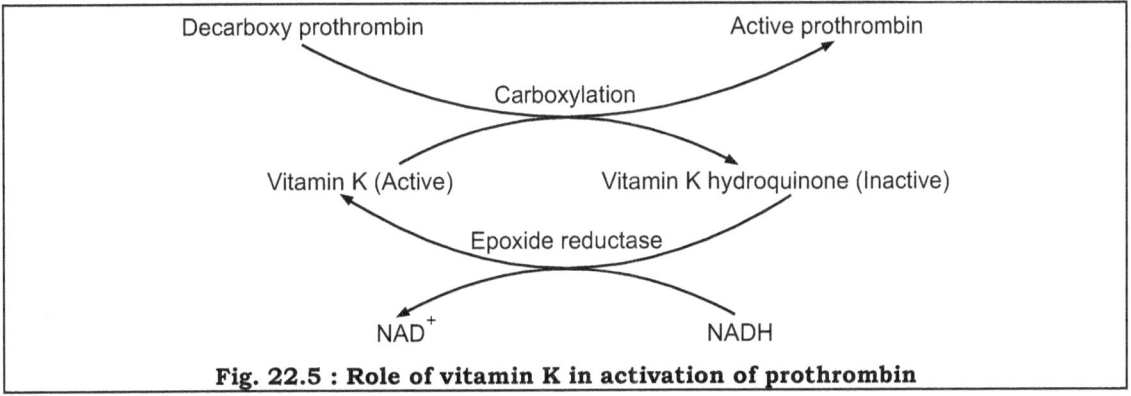

Fig. 22.5 : Role of vitamin K in activation of prothrombin

Untoward effects with indanedione anticoagulants include leukopenia, hepatitis, agranulocytosis and renal tubular necrosis. These drugs are less preferred than coumarins due to their greater toxicities. Their use is advocated only in patients who can not tolerate coumarins.

Oral anticoagulants are contraindicated in bleeding disorders, ulcers, local anaesthesia, hepatic or renal diseases.

22.7 ANTI-THROMBOTIC DRUGS

Thrombus and clot are not the terms bearing same meaning. Though both share some of the events in common, platelets have major role to play in thrombosis. Thrombus is a physical occlusion of blood vessel lumen due to formation of solid mass of fibrin and platelets. Platelets bind to the collagen in the vessel wall and promote other platelets to adhere. The process is stimulated by ADP released by already adhered platelets. Collagen, thrombin and arachidonic acid are the other inducers.

Thrombi can form in veins, arteries or in the heart chambers. But since the arterial blood flow is more rapid than the venous supply, the chances of arterial thrombi are relatively less. Thrombi produces plugging of the blood vessels that disturbs the uniform blood flow. In certain cases, it may cause the pulmonary or cerebral embolism resulting into an abrupt arrest of pulmonary or cerebral function. Though thrombus and clot are not identical terms, the hypercoagulability of the blood may potentiate the chances of thrombus formation. Atherosclerotic legions during thrombus formation may lead to cardiovascular complications, like myocardial infarction, rheumatic heart diseases etc. Antithrombotic drugs are generally used to prevent the growth or reoccurance of a thrombus. Examples includes aspirin, dipyridamole, clofibrate, hydroxy chloroquine, sulphinpyrazone, dazoxiben, tricyclic antidepressants and phenylbutazone. They all increase the platelet survival time and decrease the platelet aggregation by one of the following mechanisms.

(i) blocking the release of ADP and inhibiting the synthesis of prostaglandins, e.g. aspirin, sulphinpyrazole, dazoxiben.

(ii) increasing the concentration of c-AMP and potentiating the effect of prostacyclin e.g. dipyridamole.

(iii) alteration of platelet membrane in order to decrease platelet aggregation e.g. ticlopidine.

22.8 PLASMA EXPANDERS

The hemorrhagic shock may result from the loss of blood during burns, wounds or surgery. Mild shock results when there is a loss of 15% to 20% in total blood volume. Further loss of blood upto 40% of total blood volume may lead to severe shock, during which the cardiovascular functioning is severely affected. To restore this functioning, saline should be administered as an initial emergency measure. Plasma expanders then can be used to overcome the initial losses. They are of two types :

(i) Natural products
(ii) Synthetic products

(i) Natural Products :

These include transfusion of whole blood or the preparations of plasma proteins. Blood products containing plasma proteins are human albumin (albumisol) and plasma protein fraction (PPF). Both these preparations are usually given by intravenous infusion.

(ii) Synthetic Products :

Dextran, hetastarch, perfluorochemicals, polyvinyl-pyrrolidine and gelatin are some of the synthetic plasma expanders, out of which dextran has been used extensively. Dextran can be considered as almost close to an ideal plasma expander. Its chief defect being antigenicity. Dextrans are colloidal glucose polymers that are obtained from sucrose by the action of bacteria, *Leuconostoc mesenteroides*. The dextran molecule consists mainly of 1 : 6 glucosidic linkages with relatively few 1 : 4 linkages and has an average molecular weight of 40 millions. This form is not clinically suitable. Hence, it is partially hydrolyzed *in-vitro* to give dextrans with average molecular weight of 40,000; 70,000; 110000 and 150000 daltons. They are known as dextran-40, dextran-70, dextran-110 and dextran-150 respectively. Of these, dextran-40 and dextran-70 are of clinical importance.

Solution of dextran in isotonic sodium chloride is used to increase the circulating blood volume and to maintain the venous pressure, right atrial pressure, stroke volume and cardiac output. Only dextran solutions are used in the treatment of hypoproteinaemia, nephrosis, and toxaemia of late pregnancy. Dextran does not possess oxygen carrying capacity.

Dextran solutions are pharmacologically inactive and no significant deleterious effects on renal, hepatic or any other vital functions have been reported. Occasionally sensitization reactions may occur in some patients. The bleeding time, fibrin polymerization or platelet function may be impaired *in-vivo*. Dextrans are contraindicated in patients with anaemia, severe thrombocytopenia and low plasma fibrinogen level.

For clinical use, two forms of dextran are available. These are - dextran-40 injection which contains 10% dextran-40 in isotonic sodium chloride solution, while dextran-70 injection contains 6% dextran-70 in isotonic sodium chloride solution.

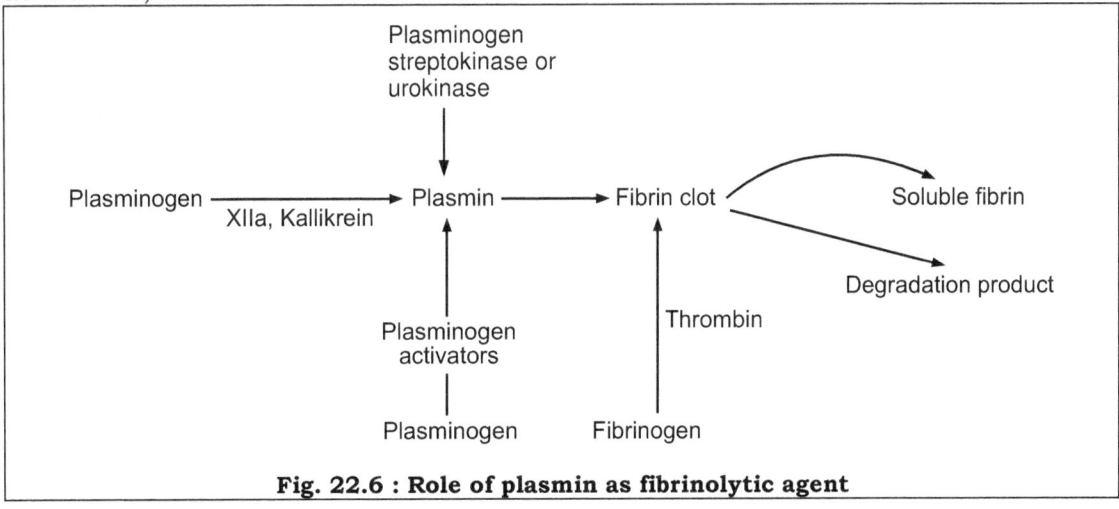

Fig. 22.6 : Role of plasmin as fibrinolytic agent

22.9 FIBRINOLYTIC AGENTS

The destruction or dissolution of a thrombus is caused by a proteolytic enzyme, known as plasmin which is released by its precursor protein, plasminogen. Plasminogen activators (e.g. streptokinase, urokinase) bring about this conversion.

Certain other compounds have been found to promote the synthesis of various plasminogen activators, e.g. anabolic steroids. They act indirectly as fibrinolytic agents. All these agents are useful in the treatment of pulmonary emboli and acute coronary thrombosis. Streptokinase and urokinase are the commonly used fibrinolytic agents in the treatment of such acute thromboemobolic diseases.

Streptokinase is obtained from group - C betahemolytic streptococci. It activates plasminogen by forming a complex with it, while urokinase is the natural body inducer of plasmin formation, first isolated from the human urine. It is now prepared from cultures of human renal cells. It catalyses the conversion of plasminogen to plasmin in human body. Heparin or oral anticoagulant should be administered after the treatment with these fibrinolytic agents has been completed.

Streptokinase is known to cause allergic reactions, fever and skin rashes. Hence urokinase is preferred in patients who are sensitive to streptokinase. However, urokinase is contraindicated in patients with severe wound, trauma, pregnancy or cerebrovascular injury.

Antidotes of Fibrinolytic Agents :

These agents are useful in the treatment of bleeding caused by hyperfibrinolysis. Such conditions include haemophilia, surgery of the prostate and gastrointestinal haemorrhage. Examples from this category include, ε-amino caproic acid and tranexamic acid. Both these agents prevent fibrinolysis by competitively inhibiting plasminogen. Tranexamic acid is a more potent agent. Both these agents effectively prevent fibrinolysis by both oral and intravenous administration.

$$H_2N - (CH_2)_5 - COOH$$
ε-aminocaproic acid

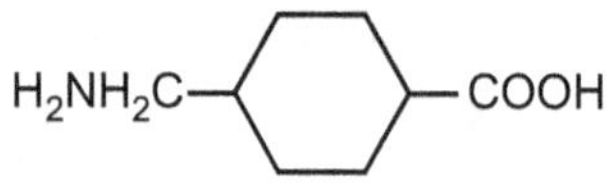

$$H_2NH_2C-\!\!\!\bigcirc\!\!\!-COOH$$
Tranexamic acid

The adverse effects include nausea, vomiting, dizziness, abdominal pain, hypotension and thrombosis.

Table 22.2 : Biological properties of plasminogen and its main activators

Agent	Source	Mol. Wt. (in Daltons)	Concentration ng/ml plasma	Half-life time
Plasminogen / plasmin	Liver	88,000 85,000	12×10^4	54 hrs. 0.1 – 10 sec
Tissue plasminogen activator	Vascular endothelial cells	72,000	6.6	5 – 10 min
Prourokinase / Urokinase	Kidney cells	54,700	7.5	5 - 10 min 15 min
Streptokinase	β-haemolytic streptococci	47,400	–	30 min.

22.10 HAEMATINICS

Human body is a complex living system comprising of many vital organs. A delicate system of co-ordination between the functioning of these vital organs in the human body exists in the form of blood, interstitial fluid and lymph. This system works to adjust the internal body environment according to the changes occurring into the surrounding environment of the person. The blood transports oxygen from the lungs, dietary constituents from the alimentary tract and the hormones from endocrine glands to the body organs. In organs, these constituents then diffuse to individual cells through interstitial fluid. The waste metabolic products including carbon dioxide released by tissue in the interstitial fluid are made free of micro-organisms, if any, by lymph vessels and then handed over to the blood. Blood trains away these waste products to their respective sites of excretion or detoxification viz., lungs, kidneys, liver or sweat glands. Beside this, blood also helps in maintaining proper electrolyte balance and plasma pH within the normal physiological limits.

The oxygen carrying capacity of the blood is due to the presence of erythrocytes or red blood cells that contain haemoglobin. Each erythrocyte, on an average contains 280 million molecules of haemoglobin. Thus, normal human blood contains about 15 g of haemoglobin per 100 ml of blood. It is synthesized in the erythrocyte precursor cells of bone marrow. Structurally, it is a conjugated protein consisting of the globin (protein fraction) and four non-protein iron-containing pigments known as 'heme'. In the lungs oxygen reacts with these pigments to give oxyhaemoglobin that exchanges free oxygen for carbon dioxide at the tissue level and get converted to carbaminohaemoglobin. It is the form in which, carbon di-oxide is transported to the lungs for excretion resulting in the regeneration of haemoglobin.

Red bone marrow of cranium, ribs, sternum, and proximal epiphyses of humerus and femur are the sites for production of RBCs. Red blood cells survive in the circulation for about 120 days after which they are catabolized by the reticuloendothelium. On an average a little less than 1% of the circulating red cells are replaced daily as the part of hemostatic processes mediated through central nervous system and renal mechanisms. The metabolic products of worn out RBCs include iron (which later associates with a protein to form hemosiderin), bilirubin pigment and globin. In bone marrow, the iron from hemosiderin is reutilised to produce new RBCs. Bilirubin is passed into the bile while globin is defragmented by the liver to yield amino acids which are then utilized into biochemical reactions.

One molecule of haemoglobin contains four atoms of iron. The total body content of iron is about 50 mg/kg for male and 37 mg/kg for female. Out of this, about 60% is utilized for haemoglobin formation, 20% is present in the iron stores (mainly in the form of ferritin, hemosiderin and transferrin. Ferritin is a complex of ferric ions with a protein, apoferritin found mostly in the liver, spleen and bone marrow) and remaining 20% is present in myoglobin, cytochrome, catalyase and other iron containing enzymes (i.e. haemenzymes).

Hence, iron deficiency may lead to -
(i) hypochromic (iron deficient) anaemia,
(ii) disturbances in muscle metabolism,
(iii) slow-down of the activities of haemenzymes, and
(iv) abnormalities in catecholamine metabolism and heat production.

The first evidence about the presence of iron in the blood was reported in 1713 by **Lemery**. Nearly 1.1 mg of iron is present per millimetre of the red blood cells. In the food, iron is mainly present in the form of organic ferrous or ferric complexes. Due to the digestive action of gastric acid and alkaline environment of small intestine, the dietary iron is then converted to ferrous hydroxide. A carrier intracellular protein known as apoferritin is present in the mucosal cells of small intestine that transports the dietary iron into the portal circulation. Certain factors like vitamin C, fats, and meals promote the absorption of iron. In the circulation, iron in the ferrous form gets converted to ferric form which is important for attachment with transferrin, a β_1 - glycoprotein plasma carrier for iron. **Laurell** in 1947 identified and named it as transferrin. It has a molecular weight of about 76,000. The serum iron is present only in the form of transferrin-iron complex which is then taken up to various intracellular sites by receptor mediated endocytosis. The iron then mobilizes into the cell while transferrin returns back to pick up other ferric ions.

The recommended daily intake of iron is estimated to be 12 mg. However, only 1 - 15 mg of iron is usually absorbed from dietary elements in humans. The major fraction of the absorbed iron is made available for the formation of haemoglobin in the marrow or extramedullary hemopoietic tissues. In normal man, iron is usually excreted out in the form of extravasated red cells, exfoliated iron containing mucosal cells of the skin and GIT, bile, loss of hair and nails. Women are more susceptible to iron deficiency than men due to extra iron loss during menstruation, pregnancy and lactation. Approximately 20 - 40 mg of iron is lost during each menstrual cycle in addition to other normal losses. In pregnancy and lactation, nearly 15 mg per day of iron may be needed.

Iron is an important constituent of haemoglobin and thus it is required for erythropoiesis (poiem = to make). Iron deficiency or iron loss may therefore result into a decrease in haemoglobin synthesis. Various conditions may give rise to iron-deficient erythropoiesis. These include nutritional iron deficiency, blood loss, inadequate absorption or its improper utilization. Beside this, nutritional deficiencies of copper, cobalt, folic acid, vitamin C and vitamin B_{12} also contribute for inferior erythropoiesis. This leads to the development of anaemic conditions. Anaemia occurs when the haemoglobin concentration of the blood is decreased below normal levels. Various forms of anaemia are recognized. For example, cell hypoproliferation leads to plastic anaemia; excessive destruction of red blood cells leads to haemolytic anaemia while iron-deficient anaemia and megaloblastic anaemia may result due to abnormalities in the maturation process of red blood cells.

Increased demands for haemoglobin are registered during growth, menstruation and pregnancy. If they are not fulfilled, anaemia is likely to result. In iron-deficient anaemia, symptoms include, fatigue, weakness, loss of appetite, breathlessness, difficulty in swallowing and inflammation of mouth. The only important use of iron in modern medicine today is in the treatment of iron-deficient anaemias. Beside anaemia, the deficiency of iron may also lead to decrease in the activity of iron containing enzymes, abnormalities in the biochemical processes (where iron serves as the cofactor) and disturbed nucleic acid synthesis.

Various iron salts are used in the treatment of anaemia. The most commonly used are, ferrous sulfate, ferrous fumarate, ferrous succinate, ferrous gluconate, ferrous lactate and ferric ammonium citrate. Ferrous salts are more rapidly absorbed than ferric salts if given orally. Ferrous sulfate is the most favoured iron salt due to its low cost. These iron salts are usually administered in the fasting state in order to enhance absorption. However, these preparations when given orally, usually induce gastrointestinal disturbances. The common adverse effects of oral therapy include nausea, vomiting, abdominal pain, diarrhea and heart-burn. Staining of teeth in young children and black stools may be observed.

If patient does not tolerate oral administration of iron, it may be given intramuscularly or intravenously. The intramuscular iron preparations include iron sorbitex injection, ferric ammonium citrate, ferrous gluconate, iron adenylate, iron polyisomaltose etc. The oral iron preparations take their own time in saturation of body's iron store. Beside this, maximally 40 - 60 mg of iron per day can be supplied to erythroid marrow by the oral therapy. These drawbacks are overcomed by the parenteral administration of iron.

Several forms of iron-dextran complexes are in use for intravenous administration. This route has an advantage over intramuscular route in that, it neither allows deposition of iron in muscle nor it induces local discolouration of the skin at the site of injection. Iron-dextran injection (Imferon) contains ferric hydroxide complexed with partially hydrolyzed dextran of low molecular weight ranging from 5000 to 7000 daltons in a colloidal solution form. Each ml contains the equivalent of 50 mg of element iron and may be given either by intramuscular or intravenous route. In circulation, iron gets dissociated from the sugar part of the dextran and is made available to the body tissues. Yet another iron-sorbitex injection (Jectofer) is available for intramuscular iron therapy. It is a solution of complex of iron, sorbitol and citric acid stabilized with dextrin and excess of sorbitol. It contains an equivalent of 50 mg iron per ml. The usual adverse effects of parenteral iron therapy include headache, fever, urticaria and rheumatoid arthritis. The systemic toxicities due to overdose include anaphylactic reaction, dizziness and tachycardia. In severe cases, cyanosis and circulatory collapse may occur which is followed by death.

The toxicities due to iron overdoses may be treated by gastric levage with sodium bicarbonate or phosphate solution. Milk and egg neutralise excess of iron by forming protein complexes with iron. Deferoxamine may be given if plasma iron concentration is quite high.

22.11 HAEMOPOIETIC VITAMINS

Besides iron, other elements are also necessary for normal haemopoiesis. These include copper, cobalt, folic acid, vitamin B_{12}, ascorbic acid, thiamine and tocopherol. Normal cellular maturation is governed by nuclear genetic (i.e. DNA, RNA) material whose synthesis is dependent upon vitamin B_{12} coenzymes and the folates.

Megaloblastic or macrocytic anaemia may result due to the dietary deficiency of cobalamins or folates. This results due to the abnormality in the erythrocyte maturation process. They are decreased in number but increased in the size resulting in overall deficiency of haemoglobin. Besides this polymorphonuclear leukocytes and giant platelets are also formed due to altered synthesis of genetic material. Morphological changes are also reported to occur in mucosal layer of mouth, stomach, intestine and vagina. Cobalamines are also necessary for proper functioning of the central nervous system.

Folic acid and cyanocobalamin (vitamin B_{12}) collectively are called as 'haemopoietic vitamins' because these vitamins are involved in the formation of red blood cells. Their deficiency may cut short the life-span of these cells and may lead to ineffective erythropoiesis. Other symptoms include constipation, anorexia, weight loss, atrophic glossitis and elevation of serum bilirubin.

Before folic acid can function, it must be reduced to 5, 6, 7, 8 - tetrahydrofolate. The reducing agent is NADPH and the enzyme dihydrofolate reductase catalyses this conversion. Vitamin B_{12} cofactors participate in the regeneration of tetrahydrofolate from methyl tetrahydrofolate. The folates are also involved in gluconeogenesis.

Table 22.3 : Haemopoietic vitamins

Folic acid (Pteroylglutamic acid)

Cobalamin

Well marked neurological symptoms (i.e. peripheral neuritis, atrophy of optic nerves, mental deterioration and degeneration of spinal cord) are often associated with pernicious anaemia. Both these vitamins are used to cure pernicious anaemia. Although vitamin B_{12} does not cure the anaemia caused by folic acid deficiency, folic acid does relieve some of the symptoms of anaemia caused by vitamin B_{12} deficiency. However, folic acid does not prevent the development of neurological changes seen in pernicious anaemia. A possible explanation may be that folic acid is the essential factor (required for the proper development of erythrocytes) and cobalamin is a cofactor which is needed to maintain normal nervous system.

Only cyanocobalamin (vitamin B_{12}) and hydroxycobalamin (vitamin B_{12b}) are used therapeutically. Other cobalamins of physiological importance are aquocobalamin, nitrocobalamin, methylcobalamin and 5'-deoxyadenosine coenzyme. Copper, pyridoxine and ascorbic acid are the drugs of secondary importance in the treatment of anaemia.

22.12 LIPID LOWERING AGENTS

Carbohydrates, proteins and fats are the body fuels which provide necessary energy for growth, maintenance and functioning of various organs in human body. Besides acting as the major form of energy storage, fatty acids are also involved in the formation of cell membranes. For example, phospholipids are the essential constituents of a variety of cell membranes. Plasma cholesterol can be freely utilized in the synthesis of various endogenous steroids and nerve cell membranes. Except plasma cholesterol, rest of the body lipids are catabolised to give carbon dioxide and water as end products, while bile acids are the ultimate end products of cholesterol catabolism. Only a small fraction of these bile acids is excreted through faeces while rest is reabsorbed by the enterohepatic circulation. The shedding of epithelial cells from the gut and skin offers the major route of cholesterol excretion. Atherosclerosis, thrombosis, myocardial infarction and pancreatitis are the clinical manifestations of elevated plasma lipid level. The term, hyperlipidemia denotes an elevated plasma cholesterol and / or plasma triglyceride level while the term, hyper-lipoproteinemias are the conditions in which there is elevated plasma concentration of cholesterol or triglyceride containing lipoproteins. The term lipoprotein was first coined in 1929 by **Macheboeuf** of Pasteur institute to denote lipoidal macromolecular complexes.

22.13 TYPES OF LIPOPROTEINS

There are separate mechanisms for the transport of lipids from exogenous (i.e. dietary origin) and endogenous (i.e. of hepatic origin) sources. The dietary triglycerides are hydrolysed to monoglycerides and free fatty acids by pancreatic lipase in the intestinal lumen. These dietary triglycerides and cholesterol are trapped by chylomicrons which are large lipoprotein particles having diameter ranging from 80 - 500 nm. Lipoproteins contain a hydrophobic lipid filled core surrounded by a monolayer of amphiphilic lipids and specific proteins i.e. apoproteins. The hydrophobic core acts as the storage package for triglyceride and cholesteryl esters. Apoproteins are categorised into 5 types, like A, B, C, D and E. Almost 6 classes of lipoproteins are identified in the human body which are involved in the transport of lipids from their sites of absorption and synthesis to the tissues where they are utilized. Size, density and the nature of apoprotein in the lipoprotein are the probable points utilized in the classification of lipoproteins. They are categorised as :

(a) Chylomicrons :

These are the largest species of triglyceride rich lipoproteins which are involved in the transportation of dietary fat from gut. These are secreted into the lymph and contain apoprotein A and B-48.

(b) Very Low Density Lipoproteins (VLDL) :

These are globular particles synthesized in the liver having diameter of 30-80 nm. They contain apoproteins B, C and E. They are involved in the transport of endogenous lipid from liver to the plasma.

(c) Intermediate Density Lipoproteins (IDL) :

These are the lipoproteins obtained when the triglyceride contents of VLDL are partially digested in capillaries by the action of extrahepatic lipoprotein lipase. They have a diameter of 20 - 35 nm.

(d) Low Density Lipoproteins (LDL) :

Due to further action of lipoprotein lipase on IDL in the circulation, most of the remaining triglyceride content of IDL is digested resulting into the loss of apoproteins C and E from their structure. The density of particle is increased and diameter is brought down to 18 - 28 nm. These particles are now termed as LDL which consist of cholesterol, phospholipid and apoprotein B - 100. LDL also contains B - 74 and B - 26. They have longest plasma half-life of about 1.5 days amongst the lipoproteins.

LDL particles are finally delivered to hepatic and certain extrahepatic tissues for further lysosomal degradation to release the cholesterol which can be utilized in cell membrane formation.

(e) High Density Lipoproteins (HDL) :

This is a group of heterogeneous lipoproteins having low lipid content. A further subclassification in HDL is based upon density value of these particles. HDL apparently enhances the removal of cholesterol from the arterial wall. Hence, chances of development of atherosclerotic lesions are more when HDL value falls below normal. While the elevated levels of VLDL, IDL and LDL are always correlated with increased risk of atherosclerosis.

22.14 LIPOPROTEIN TRANSPORT MACHINERY

Chylomicrons are the lipoproteins that trap the dietary triglycerides and cholesterol from the intestinal lumen and cross the intestinal mucosal cells to enter into circulation. In the adipose tissue and muscle, the chylomicrons are partly digested by lipoprotein lipase enzymes present in vascular endothelium resulting into fatty acids (i.e. hydrolysis products of triglycerides). These fatty acids then enter into underlying adipocytes or muscle cells where re-esterification to triglycerides occurs. The newly formed triglycerides are carried by the lymph and then by the blood to various body tissues for either storage or for utilization as a source of energy.

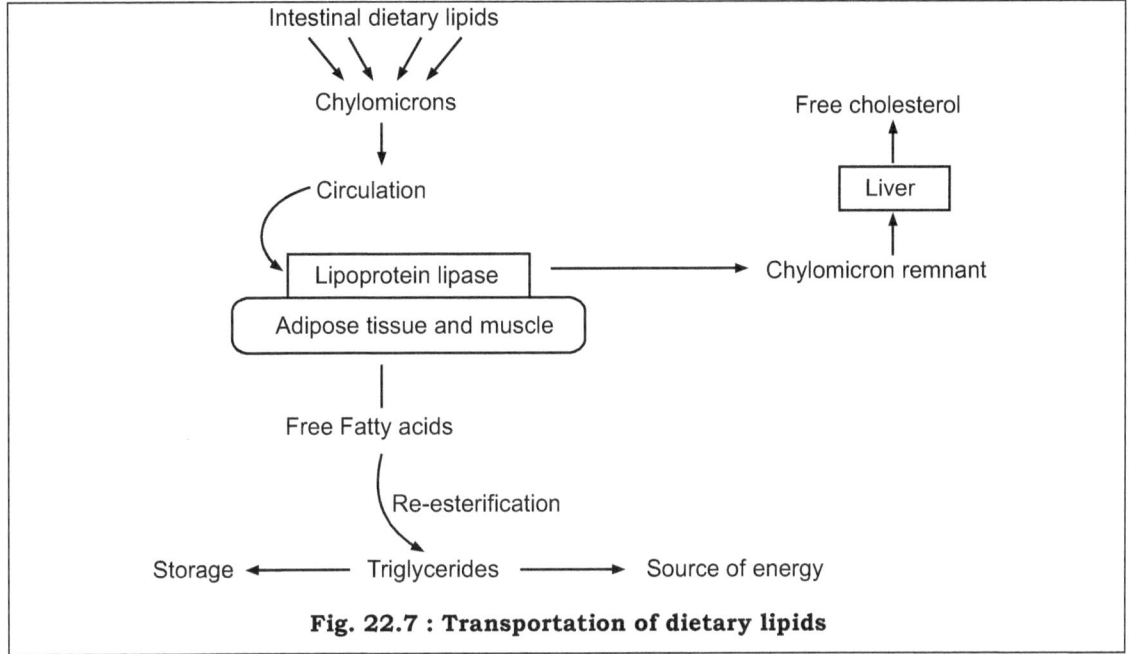

Fig. 22.7 : Transportation of dietary lipids

The remaining small fraction of triglyceride in the partly digested chylomicrons (now termed as chylomicron remnant, diameter 30 - 50 nm) is digested by hepatic lysosomal enzymes to generate free cholesterol. The transportation of endogenous (hepatic origin) lipids is quite similar to the transportation of exogenous (dietary) lipids. Liver releases triglycerides and cholesterol into circulation by packing them into the core of very low density lipoproteins (VLDL). Due to the partial digestion of VLDL by lipoprotein lipase enzymes present in the vascular endothelium, VLDL is then converted into intermediate density lipoprotein (IDL). Some of IDL particles are recycled through liver to get back VLDL while rest of them are further digested to give low density lipoproteins (LDL). These particles may be taken up by lysosomes present in the hepatic cells by the activation of LDL-receptors bound to the cell surfaces. The LDL particles thus taken up by receptor mediated endocytosis, are digested to liberate free cholesterol for cell use. Hence, an elevation in the level of circulating LDL particles may be seen in defective LDL-receptor mechanisms. Some LDL particles are also taken up in certain extrahepatic tissues by receptor mediated endocytosis process to release free cholesterol. Thus, LDL particles in the circulation act as the storage depot for major amount of body cholesterol.

The cholesterol released during the degeneration of cells in tissue damage is taken up by high density lipoproteins (HDL) where re-esterification with long chain fatty acid occur. The resulting cholesteryl esters are then handed over to VLDL or LDL particles by a cholesteryl ester transfer protein in plasma. These VLDL or LDL particles loaded with cholesteryl esters, then deliver their content into the liver. Thus, cholesterol conservation is maintained.

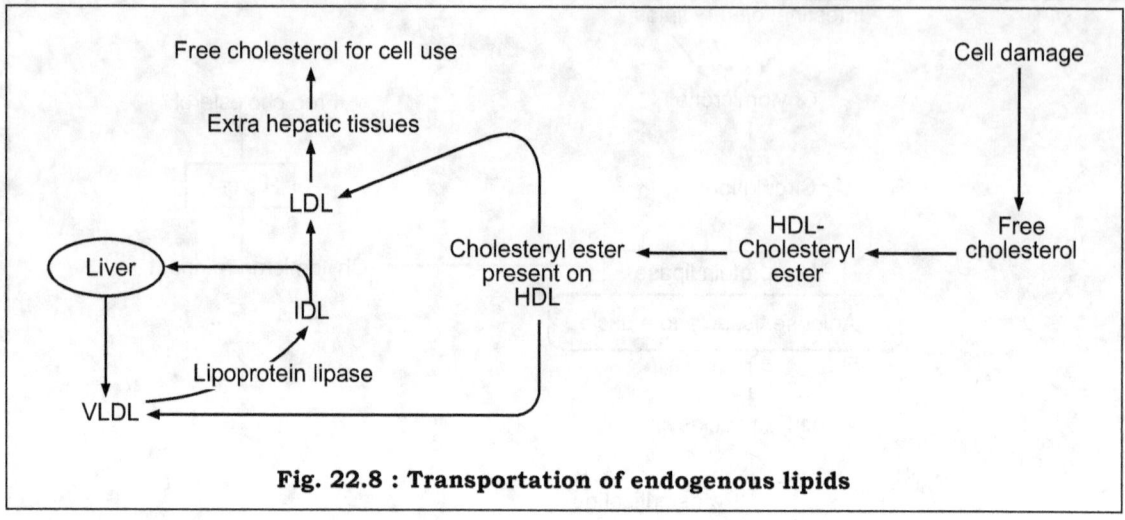

Fig. 22.8 : Transportation of endogenous lipids

22.15 HYPERLIPOPROTEINEMIA

Hyperlipoproteinemia is usually characterized by elevated plasma concentration of VLDL (mostly triglycerides) and / or of LDL (mostly cholesterol). The condition may arise mainly due to inherent genetic defect in the catabolism of various lipoproteins or due to presence of such diseases which induce generalised metabolic disturbances. Accordingly, hyperlipoproteinemia may be categorised as :

(a) Primary Hyperlipoproteinemia :

Here the genetic abnormalities in the person are usually responsible. If it arises due to single gene defect, it is known as 'monogenic hyperlipoproteinemia'. While if multiple gene defects along with non-genetic factors (i.e. obesity, high fat-riched diet) are involved, then it is known as multifactorial or polygenic hyperlipopro-teinemia. Examples of primary hyperlipoproteinemia include -

(i) Abetalipoproteinemia : It is an inherited genetic disorder characterised by the absence of chylomicrons, VLDL and LDL. The deficiency of all these apobetalipoproteins leads to deficiency of vitamin E and malabsorption of triglycerides.

(ii) Familial lipoprotein lipase deficiency disorder : As the name indicates, it is a familial (i.e. genetic) deficiency of lipoprotein lipase enzyme.

(iii) Familial type III hyperlipo-proteinemia (dysbeta-lipoproteinemia) :

The E-3 and E-4 isoforms of apolipoprotein E are absent resulting into an accumulation of remnant particles in the plasma.

(iv) Familial hypercholesterolemia : Due to deficiency of LDL - receptor sites on the cell membrane, hepatic catabolism of LDL-particles decreases. This leads to elevation in the plasma LDL levels.

(b) Secondary Hyperlipoproteinemia :

Elevated levels of VLDL, IDL and LDL particles are seen under certain diseased conditions. Diseases such as diabetes mellitus, uremia, corticosteroid excess, hypothyroidism, chronic alcoholism, nephrosis, glycogen storage abnormalities, acromegaly, obesity etc. induce metabolic abnormalities and increase the risk factor for atherosclerosis. The elevated levels of VLDL and / or LDL particles, hence can be brought to normal range by treating these underlying secondary causes along with the dietary control. Dietary therapy is always the beneficial step for all lipoprotein disorders which minimizes the concentration of lipids in the plasma and it should be strictly observed even if drug therapy has begun.

22.16 DRUG THERAPY OF HYPERLIPOPROTEINEMIA

Atherosclerosis, ischemia and acute pancreatitis are some of the clinical manifestations of hyperlipoproteinemia. During elevated levels of triglycerides (in the range of 300 - 800 mg/dl) and plasma cholesterol (about 150 - 200 mg/dl), the risk factor for above diseases is likely to increase. It is the elevated level of VLDL and/or LDL particles which is responsible for it. However, the elevated HDL particles (which participates into transport of excess plasma cholesterol into liver) offers safeguard against above conditions and leads to decrease in the risk of coronary atherosclerosis. Diet and weight control are the first line treatments of all patients with high cholesterol or triglyceride blood levels (hyperlipidaemia). However, there are patients who do not respond adequately to non-drug management.

Various drugs used in the treatment of hyperlipoproteinemia may act either by lowering the plasma level of VLDL or LDL particles. Persons with elevations of both VLDL and LDL levels may require combination therapy. These drugs show synergistic effect when used in combination. In some cases combination treatment with reduced doses of both drugs is more effective than a single agent with fewer adverse effects.

Various drugs used in the treatment of hyperlipoproteinemia may be categorised as,

(A) drugs that act by lowering the plasma LDL level,

(B) drugs that act by lowering the plasma VLDL level,

(C) drugs that act by lowering both, LDL and VLDL level, and

(D) miscellaneous lipid lowering agents.

Since LDL level is primarily related with cholesterol liberation, category A drugs mostly affect cholesterol. Similarly, category B drugs affect mostly triglycerides.

[A] Drugs that Act by Lowering the Plasma LDL Level :

(i) Probucol :

It is highly lipophilic sulphur containing bis-phenol compound. It lowers the plasma LDL level by increasing the rate of LDL removal from the plasma. It also causes lowering of HDL particle level by suppressing the synthesis of apoprotein A - 1 fraction of HDL particles. Major limitations of probucol is its high lipophilicity due to which it is retained in adipose tissues of the body. Hence, its lipid lowering effects are observed for months even after the discontinuation of drug therapy. Most of the drug is eliminated in the bile and faeces. The common adverse effects of probucol include nausea, flatulence, abdominal pain, diarrhoea, eosinophilia and angioneurotic edema. It is contraindicated in pregnancy and in cardiac dysfunction.

It is very poorly soluble in water and only about 1 to 10% of 1 g dose is absorbed from GIT. Since probucol is lipophilic it associates with lipids in the diet and is absorbed along with them and transported by chylomicrons and VLDL through lymphatics to the systemic circulation.

(ii) Dextrothyroxine :

There exists an inversely proportional relationship between plasma levels of cholesterol and thyroxine. This observation led to the clinical introduction of d-thyroxine as lipid lowering agent. It increases the hepatic catabolism of LDL and thus lowers the plasma concentration of LDL particles. In therapeutic doses, d-thyroxine still retains hypercalorigenic effect which is reflected in the increased cardiac function. This situation invites cardiac arrhythmias and anginal attacks.

(iii) Bile acid - binding resins :

Bile acids are the metabolic end-products of cholesterol which are released into the intestine. Major fraction (about 98%) of bile acids released into the gut is reabsorbed through the enterohepatic circulation and suppresses the microsomal hydroxylase enzyme involved in the conversion of cholesterol to the bile acids. Thus, due to enterohepatic reabsorption of the bile acids further catabolism of cholesterol is suppressed. Bile acids, through their emulsifying effect, also enhance the absorption of dietary lipids from the gut lumen. If the concentration of gut bile acid is lowered down by promoting their excretion in the faeces (and by inhibiting their enterohepatic reabsorption), naturally it will be reflected into :

(a) increased conversion of cholesterol to bile acids coupled with a compensatory increase in the rate of hepatic cholesterol synthesis. The latter needs an increased hepatic uptake and catabolism of circulating LDL particles. The overall result will be lowering of plasma LDL level and

(b) deficient absorption of dietary lipids into the circulation. This leads to decrease in plasma lipid concentration.

Cholestyramine and colestipol are the examples of bile acid-binding resins which form a sort of non-absorbable complex with bile acids due to the presence of quaternary nitrogen in their structure. Thus, these drugs promote their elimination from the gut and inhibit their reabsorption into the circulation. The fecal excretion of bile acids in fact, has been shown to increase 30 folds by these drugs.

Both cholestyramine and colestipol HCl are high molecular weight, water insoluble anion exchange resins. Since these resins carry a positive charge and bile salts carry a negative charge, both bind together to form relatively stable complexes in the intestinal lumen. This drain on the bile acid pool stimulates increased synthesis of bile acids in the liver from cholesterol, thus depleting the hepatic stores of cholesterol. These agents stimulate VLDL production in the liver and hence may increase triglyceride concentrations. In patients who have both raised plasma cholesterol levels and raised triglyceride levels it may be necessary to combine the use of resins with nicotinic acid or clofibrate.

Both these drugs are the examples of anion exchange resins and remain undigested and non-absorbable in the GIT. Hence, the drugs are considered safest antilipidemic agents due to the lack of systemic effects. They are used only in the patients who have elevated LDL levels. They are favoured in the treatment of type II hyperlipoproteinemia. In the treatment of familial hypercholesterolemia, usually a combination of cholestyramine and nicotinic acid gives better results. Besides bile acids, these resins also bind with other drugs due to their anionic nature. Thus, absorption of thyroxin, vitamin C, digitalis glycosides, iron, and warfarin is reported to be impaired by these resins.

The adverse effects include nausea, abdominal pain, flatulence, constipation, acidosis and hypoprothrombinemia. They are contraindicated during the pregnancy.

(iv) β - Sitosterol :

It is a plant sterol. Due to the structural similarity with cholesterol, this agent impedes the absorption of dietary cholesterol and produces a moderate reduction in cholesterol level. Its low efficacy and high cost decrease its popularity as lipid lowering agent.

[B] Drugs Acting by Lowering the Plasma VLDL Level :

(i) Clofibrate :

A series of esters of p-chlorophenoxy-isobutyric acid has been prepared, out of which clofibrate was found to lower the plasma lipid level more efficiently. Several derivatives of clofibrate are also in clinical use. They include bezafibrate, ciprofibrate, fenofibrate and etofibrate. Etofibrate is an ethylene glycol diester of nicotinic acid and clofibric acid.

Clofibrate is reserved for the treatment of type III hyperlipoproteinemia and hypertriglyceridemia which do not respond to other drugs.

The mechanism of action of clofibrate is not well defined. Various proposed mechanisms include :

(a) Stimulation of lipoprotein lipase enzyme activity.

(b) Increased cholesterol excretion.

(c) Inhibition of hepatic cholesterol synthesis.

(d) Increased intravascular catabolism of VLDL and IDL to LDL.

(e) Inhibition of hepatic VLDL synthesis.

(f) Increase in the plasma thyroxine concentration by clofibrate - induced displacement of thyroxine from albumin.

Due to displacement ability of clofibrate anion exerted on plasma albumin, potentiation of activities of many drugs (which are bound to albumin) can be seen during clofibrate therapy. Such drugs include sulfonylureas, coumarin and indandione anticoagulants.

Clofibrate is well absorbed from GIT. In the circulation, the ester linkage is hydrolysed to release p-chlorophenoxyisobutyric acid which then binds to plasma albumin. The acid metabolite is mainly excreted in the urine along with its glucuronide.

It hydrolyses to clofibric acid which is the active form. Following oral administration, maximum plasma concentration is usually attained with 3-6 hours. Clofibric acid is highly protein bound (93-98%) and has half-life of 13-17 hours. It is used in the management of a condition in which cholesterol rich VLDL and chylomicron remnant particles accumulate in the plasma (type III hyperlipidaemia).

Adverse effects include nausea, diarrhoea, skin rash, weakness, muscle cramps, impotency and myopathy. The drug is contraindicated during pregnancy and in patients with impaired renal or hepatic functioning.

(ii) Gemfibrozil :

It is a structural relative of clofibrate synthesized in 1968. It was introduced in 1971 in the treatment of hypertriglyceridemia. Besides lowering the plasma VLDL level, gemfibrozil also exerts additional beneficial effect by raising the plasma concentration of HDL upto 20% or greater.

It effectively lowers plasma triglycerides and apoprotein B production in the liver. It stimulates lipoprotein lipase activity, which results in increased clearance of triglyceride rich particles. It is sometimes used in combination with bile acid binding resins.

Its pharmacological actions, pharmacokinetics and mechanisms of action are similar to clofibrate. In addition to the adverse effects seen with clofibrate, this drug also induces musculoskeletal pain, anaemia, blurred vision and leucopenia upon chronic administration. Due to its enhancement effect on gallstone formation, gemfibrozil is contraindicated in patients with renal dysfunction or disease of gallbladder.

[C] Drugs that Lower the Plasma Level of both VLDL and LDL :

(i) Nicotinic acid :

Its use in the treatment of hyperlipoproteinemia was first introduced by **Altschul** in 1955. It brings about hypolipidemic action by decreasing lipolysis and by promoting hepatic storage of lipids. It also enhances the activity of lipoprotein lipase resulting into low circulating VLDL level. Since VLDL acts as the precursor for most of the circulating LDL, the low VLDL level results into low level of circulating LDL. Nicotinamide, however, lacks hypolipidemic activity. In many cases, nicotinic acid is coadministered along with bile acid binding resin to get better results.

In body, nicotinic acid undergoes extensive metabolism resulting into formation of various metabolites, such as nicotinamide, nicotinuric acid, methyl nicotinamide, N-methyl - 2-pyridone-3-carboxamide and N-methyl - 2-pyridone-5-carboxamide. These metabolites are mainly excreted in the urine along with some unchanged nicotinic acid.

Nicotinic acid has a long list of adverse effects. These include vomiting, diarrhoea, peptic ulcer, jaundice, hyperpigmentation, dry skin, postural hypotension, and cutaneous vasodilation (flushing) specifically in the upper part of the body. Gouty arthritis may develop due to the drug-induced elevation in the plasma uric acid level. It is contraindicated during pregnancy. Due to too many adverse effects of nicotinic acid, it is less frequently used alone in the treatment of hyperlipoproteinemia.

[D] Miscellaneous Lipid Lowering Agents :

(i) HMG CoA reductase inhibitors :

This category includes compactin and mevinolin which are basically fungal metabolites having structural resemblance with HMG CoA. These drugs competitively inhibit HMG CoA reductase enzyme by competing with the natural substrate, HMG CoA which is involved in the hepatic cholesterol biosynthesis.

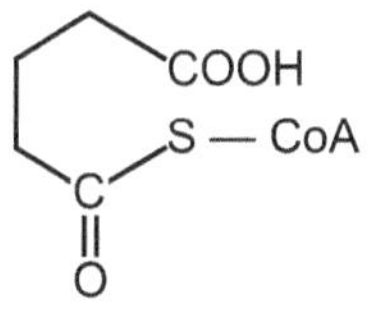

HMG CoA

HMG (Hydroxymethylglutaryl) CoA - reductase inhibitors, often referred to collectively as 'statins' a new class of lipid lowering agents.

Compactin was first isolated from the cultures of *Penicillium* species in 1976 by Endo while mevinolin (or monacolin K) was isolated from the cultures of *Aspergillus* and *Monascus* species. These drugs bring about specific, reversible and competitive blockage of HMG CoA reductase enzyme leading to decreased hepatic cholesterol synthesis. This induces an increased rate of hepatic uptake and catabolism of circulating LDL. Thus, the levels of total and LDL-cholesterol are significantly reduced.

The pharmacokinetic data is not available in man. In animals, however, these drugs are well absorbed and extensively metabolised, primarily in the liver.

Adverse effects are few and of mild nature. Like other hypolipidemic drugs, HMG – CoA reductase inhibitors are contraindicated during pregnancy.

(ii) Neomycin :

Neomycin is an aminoglycoside antibiotic. It exerts hypolipidemic activity only in oral administration while if given parenterally, neomycin does not reduce the plasma level of LDL. The poor absorption upon oral administration of neomycin indicates that its site of action is in GIT. The adverse effects (like, ototoxicity, nephrotoxicity) seen during parenteral administration of neomycin are not reported to occur with oral use of the drug.

(iii) Other agents :

Other agents having hypolipidemic activity include, sucrose polymers, eicosapentaenoic acid, propranolol and pindolol. Similarly estrogens also interfere in the fat metabolism resulting into a decrease in plasma LDL concentration and an increase in plasma HDL concentration. These metabolic effects of estrogens are partly opposed by progestin.

❖ ❖ ❖

MYOCARDIAL DISEASES

23.1 INTRODUCTION

One need not to stress upon the importance of cardiovascular system in the body. A major pharmacological action of a number of clinically used agents is merely due to their influence over cardiovascular system. Much advances have been witnessed in cardiovascular therapy over the past 20 years. For convenience of discussion, these drugs can be classified as below :

(a) *Positive inotropic agents* : e.g. dobutamine, digitalis glycosides, amrinone etc.

(b) *Vasodilators* : e.g. minoxidil, prazosin, hydralazine etc.

(c) *Drugs altering Renin-Angiotensin-Aldosterone system* : e.g. captopril, saralasin, enalapril etc.

(d) *Calcium antagonists* : e.g. nifedipine, verapamil, diltiazem etc.

(e) *Antiarrhythmic agents* : e.g. quinidine, lidocaine, bretylium etc.

(f) *Beta-adrenoceptor blocking agents* : propranolol, labetalol, oxprenolol etc.

(g) *Centrally acting antihypertensive agents* : e.g. clonidine, methyldopa, guanabenz etc.

To understand the effects of these drugs on the cardiovascular system, an understanding of normal heart functioning and propogation of cardiac impulse is essential. The above figure represents essential elements of cardiac impulse propogation.

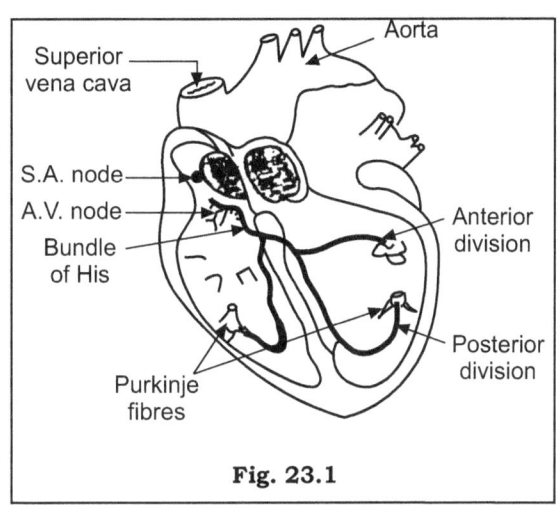

Fig. 23.1

The sino-atrial (S.A.) node cells possess an intrinsic ability of their own to generate and to propogate an impulse. The S.A. node is a specialised muscle which is self-excitatory. Hence, it is known as normal pacemaker. It sends out impulses rhythmically to the surrounding tissue in order to cause atrial contraction (atrial systole). The impulse thus generated by S.A. node, spreads through the atria and finally reaches atrioventricular node (A-V node).

A.V. node lies at the junction of atria and ventricles. The adjoining region of A.V. node is made up of non-conductive tissue while A.V. node possesses the capacity to conduct an impulse slowly and functions as a delay circuit. It thus acts as a "filter" of atrial impulses. The S.A. node is concerned with the rate of sinus rhythm while A.V. node acts as a controlling centre for ventricular contractions.

The signal generator (S.A. node) continuously initiates the impulses in a co-ordinated fashion which are received by A.V. node. The latter, after a short delay, sends an excitation wave (impulse) through the bundle of His and Purkinje system to the ventricular muscles, resulting into ventricular contraction (ventricular systole). Due to the large muscle mass, the ventricular conduction system is more elaborate where Purkinje fibres serve as final conducting components. The rate and force of ventricular systole is influenced by both, extrinsic factors, such as level of catecholamines and intrinsic factors like, the length of fibres, just before contraction.

The cardiac muscles are also innervated by both, sympathetic and parasympathetic nerves in order to control and cause the impulse generation to take place in a co-ordinated fashion. The tone of autonomic nervous system thus has prominent influence on ventricular rate. For example, adrenergic nerve stimulation (as under the conditions of strain or stress) causes increased heart rate (positive chronotropic effect) and increased force of contraction (positive inotropic effect). While vagal stimulation leads to increased filtration of atrial impulses through A.V. node resulting into suppression of both, rate and force of heart contraction. Following its release from the vagous nerve, acetylcholine first interacts with M_2 muscarinic receptors that slow heart rate, in part, by activating a cardiac potassium channel through a signal transduction mechanism involving G protein coupled receptors. This leads to cardiac pacemaker cell hyperpolarization, thus slowing the heart rate. An enhanced vagal activity at A.V. node appears to originate from several sites in nervous system such as - central vagal nuclei, nodose ganglion and autonomic ganglion.

23.2 MYOCARDIAL CELL

Sarcomere (myocardial cell) is the functional contractile unit of cardiac muscle. Each cell is characterized by the presence of one central nucleus, and a number of mitochondria and many myofibrils aligned along the cell's axis. The whole contractile process is supported by ATP. Mitochondria are the principal sites for energy generation where it is converted into creatine phosphate and ATP through the process of oxidative phosphorylation. Creatine phosphate functions as reserved depot of energy. The events necessary for the contraction of myofibrils are initiated by the operation of Na^+-K^+-ATPase pump. The energy needed for this process is released during hydrolysis of ATP by Mg^{++}-activated myofibrillar enzyme known as myosin ATPase. However, this enzyme cannot function in the absence of calcium ions.

The whole process of cardiac contraction involves active participation of :

(a) Na^+-K^+-ATPase pump,
(b) the release of calcium sequestered upon the sarcoplasmic reticulum, and
(c) activation of actin-myosin tension generating system.

23.3 ACTIN-MYOSIN TENSION GENERATING SYSTEM

Actin consists of twisted long strands, each of which is made up of actin monomers. These two strands are twisted around tropomyosin. While at regular intervals of about 400 A°, troponin is bound to these filaments as shown in the Fig. 23.2.

Troponin has three sub-centres :

1. Centre that prevents an interaction between actin and myosin is known as troponin I.
2. Centre that binds the troponin to the tropomyosin is known as troponin T.
3. While the third centre binds with calcium released from the endoplasmic reticulum.

The myosin filament possesses very high affinity for actin. The globular sub-unit of myosin have a site for ATPase activity. The troponin-tropomyosin system inhibits the interaction between actin and myosin, in the absence of calcium ions. The electrical impulse pushes out calcium ions sequestered in the nearby cisternae into the myofibrils. The calcium binds with troponin resulting into initiation of interaction between actin and myosin. Calcium ion also allows the combination of ATP with the ATPase site present on the globular part of myosin. It thus facilitates the energy release needed for contraction of the muscle.

Relaxation phase is characterized by disposal of calcium from vicinity of myofibrils back into cisternae through active transport. The energy needed is provided through the action of ATPase that can pump upto 4 ions of calcium per molecule of ATP consumed. Thus like contraction, relaxation phase also needs ATP. Removal of calcium from the myofibrils results into activation of troponin-tropomyosin inhibitory system which prevents actin-myosin interaction.

23.4 MOLECULAR BASIS OF MYOCARDIAL CONTRACTION

The cardiac cell is surrounded by a lipoprotein membrane, which behaves as if it has aqueous pores in it. Sodium ions are maintained at higher concentration in the extracellular fluid while potassium ions are at higher concentration inside the cell.

This unequal distribution (which is against the concentration gradient) of K^+ and Na^+ ions is maintained by the pump system in the sarcolemma of cardiac fibres. This ATP energized membrane pump system (Na^+-K^+-ATPase pump) actively pushes Na^+ ions out of the cell and K^+ ions into the cell and thus making the cell membrane electrically neutral (resting potential).

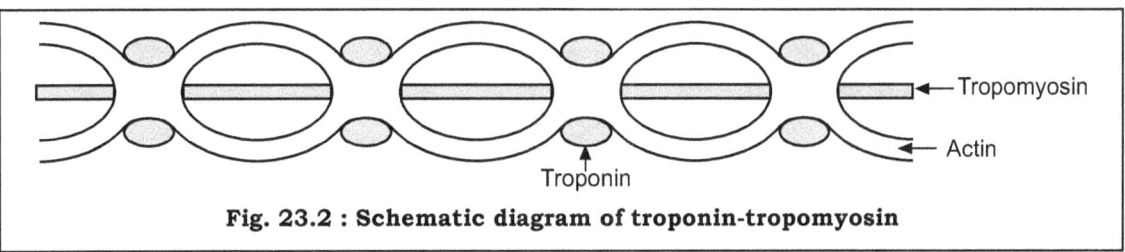

Fig. 23.2 : Schematic diagram of troponin-tropomyosin

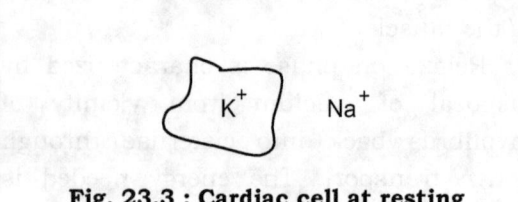

Fig. 23.3 : Cardiac cell at resting potential

When an impulse is initiated by S.A. node, electrical changes start occurring. More K^+ ions leave the cell than the Na^+ ions that enter in it, because of the differences in size of the ions and permeability of cell membrane to these ions. As a result, there is a net loss of positively charged ions from the cell. The inside of myocardial cell remains negative in comparison to its outside (– 90 mV) and the cell is said to be polarized. Since S.A. node has the most rapid intrinsic rate, the transmembrane potential in S.A. node remains – 70 mV during polarization state, while it remains – 90 mV in working muscle cells and non pace-making special conducting tissues (like, Purkinje fibres).

The polarized state of the cell serves as an electrical stimulus which causes conformational changes in the membrane to open ion channels (molecular gates) that selectively allows the permeation of Na^+ ions into the cell. This leads to reduction in intracellular negativity, by which depolarization commences (phase 4).

When this depolarization reaches a certain threshold level (– 70 mV), the permeability of the cell membrane (opening of fast ion channels) to Na^+ abruptly increases, allowing more rapid influx of Na^+ as well as Ca^{++} to produce spike action potential (phase 0), resulting into complete depolarization.

This upstroke causes the release of intracellular Ca^{++} ions from the sacs of sarcoplasmic reticulum into the cytoplasm. This rise in the level of free or "activator" calcium within the cell removes the inhibition of troponin-tropomyosin system over the contractile elements and initiates the contraction of cardiac muscle. Contraction of most mammalian hearts is thus initiated by and is proportional to the influx of extracellular Ca^{++} which in turn triggers the release of additional Ca^{++} from the sarcoplasmic reticulum.

Following depolarization, commences the phase of repolarization. It is characterized by removal of free Ca^{++} ions from the cytoplasm back into cisternae. It is an energy consuming process, that occurs in three sub-phases.

(i) A partial abrupt repolarization (phase 1) occurs as a result of closure of the fast sodium ion channels and an influx of chloride ions.

(ii) A prolonged repolarization i.e. plateau region (phase 2) occurs due to much slower K^+ efflux along with the slow influx of Na^+ and Ca^{++} ions.

(iii) Rapid but not abrupt repolarization (phase 3) occurs as a result of the closure of the slow inward channels for Na^+ and Ca^{++} ions and the opening of one or two fast outward channels for K^+.

The extracellular Ca^{++} ions that were influxed during depolarization are driven out (in fact exchanged for extracellular sodium ions) by a transport-system that is governed by concentration gradient and the transmembrane potential. Thus,

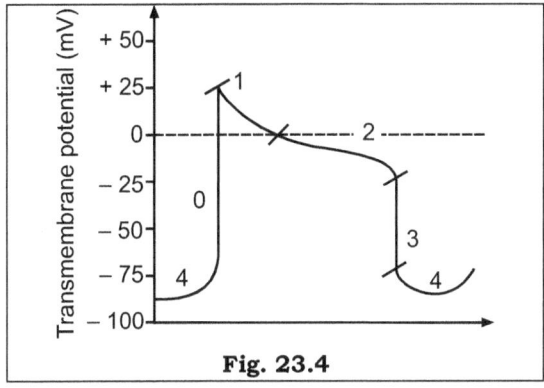

Fig. 23.4

at the end of repolarization (phase 3), the transmembrane potential is restored back again to –90 mV but now the intracellular fluid has lost K^+ and gained Na^+ ions.

Here Na^+-K^+-ATPase pump again plays a role. This pump utilizes ATP to actively transport Na^+ out of the cell and K^+ into the cell to restore normal levels of Na^+ and K^+. The pump transports Na^+ and maintains their respective gradients in a 3 Na^+ : 2 K^+ : ATP ratio. It uses energy from hydrolysis of the terminal phosphoryl group of one molecule of intracellular ATP to transport three Na^+ ions outwards and two K^+ ions inwards across the cell membrane against steep electrochemical gradients to restore normal levels of Na^+ and K^+. It is a dimeric protein with an α-subunit of 100 KD and a β-subunit of 55 KD. The α-subunit contains the ATP hydrolysis subsite, in which aspartate accepts the γ-phosphate of ATP. The function of glycoprotein β-subunit is not clear. The cardiac glycoside binding site, which is partially located on the outside of the α-subunit, inhibits the ATP-driven ion transport and the Na^+ dependent conformational change. The pump system present elsewhere in body has different α-subunits showing different steroid binding capabilities.

Thus, ATP, intracellular Na^+ ions and extracellular K^+ ions may be viewed as substrates and ADP, orthophosphate, extracellular Na^+ and intracellular K^+ ions as products of the enzymatic process. Many low molecular weight, non-steroidal inhibitors of different types have been studied. They are useful for analyzing various properties of Na^+ - K^+ - ATPase rather than being used as a prototype drug.

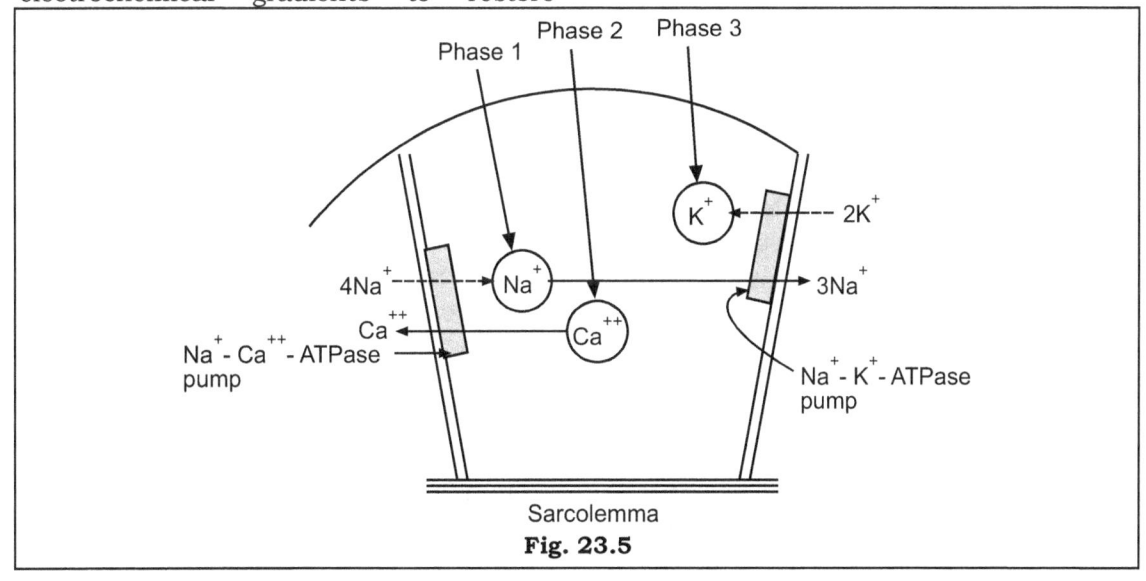

Fig. 23.5

The enzyme, Na^+-K^+-ATPase was discovered in 1957 by **Jens Skou** in the cell-membrane. It hydrolyses ATP molecule to release the energy necessary for functioning of this pump. The enzyme and the pump, both are tightly bound to the plasma membrane. The hydrolysis of ATP molecule needs the presence of Na^+, K^+ and Mg^{++} ions.

The myocardial muscle differs from skeletal muscle in having :

(a) Rhythmic automaticity (i.e. self-excitatory ability) of some specialised areas (like S.A. node).

(b) Greater sensitivity to direct action of neuro-transmitters.

(c) Longer refractory period due to the plateau region (phase 2) during relaxation.

23.5 CARDIOVASCULAR DISEASES

(a) Thromboembolic Diseases :

This group of diseases is characterized by adhesion of platelets to the inner vascular wall resulting into the interference in the functioning of extrinsic or intrinsic blood clotting system. The platelets adhere to the collagen exposed due to an injury to the vascular endothelium. The release of thromboxane A_2 results into vasoconstriction and enhances platelet aggregation. The permanent platelet fibrin clot initiates a series of events that may lead to myocardial infarction (a region with deficient oxygen supply) and to congestive heart failure.

The treatment of myocardial ischemia (deficient O_2 supply) may involve the therapies to improve coronary blood supply. This can be done either by means of drugs such as nitrates or by means of aortacoronary bypass grafts. The myocardial ischemia can also be treated by reducing the heart work-load so that the heart may work efficiently even under deficient O_2 supply. This can be done either by decreasing the pre-load (venous vasodilation) using drugs like nitrates, diuretics etc. or by decreasing myocardial contractility (using drugs like β_1-adrenoceptor blockers or Ca^{++}-channel blockers). However, the latter approach may result in a decrease in heart rate. Beneficial results may also be obtained by decreasing the after-load of the heart using drugs such as arterial vasodilators or Ca^{++} antagonists. However, any attempt to decrease heart work-load usually results in a decrease in the cardiac output. This limits the patient's capacity to carry out any work.

(b) Congestive Heart Failure :

The force of cardiac contraction is proportional to the degree to which cardiac muscle fibers are stretched. However, the contractile power declines if the muscle fibres are stretched beyond a critical length. This is known as 'Frank-Starling law' of the heart functioning. Under certain circumstances, the activation of neurohumoral system (e.g. increased release of catecholamines, elevation of plasma renin activity or plasma antidiuretic hormone level) may result into increased blood volume, venous return and end diastolic volume. The heart work-load increases resulting into stretching of muscle fibres beyond that critical length. If such situation remains for considerable period of time, this leads to a progressive decline in the force of heart contraction. Blood accumulates in the heart due to its inability to eject all the blood. So the heart work-load proportionate increases resulting into progressive increase in the stretching of muscle fibres and failure of the heart becomes gradually pronounced. The blood starts accumulating into large veins and in the tissues, highly perfused with blood. Thus congestion of both, pulmonary and systemic circulation results into peripheral edema (dropsy) and diminished exercise tolerance. This situation is known as congestive heart failure.

It is characterized by left ventricular dysfunction, reduced exercise tolerance and frequent ventricular arrhythmias.

Usually advanced age, hypertension, diabetes mellitus and ischemic heart diseases contribute to the development of congestive heart failure.

(c) Angina Pectoris :

It is characterized by a discomfort of cardiac origin resulting due to temporary ischemia of the myocardium. The myocardial ischemia results due to deficiency of oxygen during increased metabolic activities. The increased demand for oxygen can not be fulfilled due to coronary vessel constriction. The primary cause of angina is supposed to be atherosclerosis of large coronary arteries. This may lead to reflex vasospasm of coronary arteries that results into sudden, severe, substernal pain which often radiates to the left shoulder and along the flexor surface of the left arm. This occurs most commonly with exertion or emotional stress. Breathlessness sometimes occurs along with other discomforts. The duration of anginal episode may vary from 30 seconds to 30 minutes and may be relieved by rest or nitroglycerin. Hypertension and cigarette smoking are amongst the principal etiologies of angina pectoris.

(d) Arrhythmias :

The rhythmic contraction of the heart is possible due to the presence of intrinsic pace makers and conduction tissues in the heart. S.A. node is considered as normal pace maker due to its most-rapid intrinsic rate (60-100/ min). Hence, the rhythmic contractions of the heart are due to impulses generated by S.A. node. Therefore, if an impulse is generated from non-S.A. node region, that may interfere into S.A. node-organized contraction process, leading to arrhythmia.

For the heart to function as an efficient pump, the various contractile units must operate in a co-ordinated and rhythmic fashion. The generation of cardiac impulses in the normal heart is represented in Fig. 23.6. An impulse is generated by S.A. node and its conduction through A.V. node is shown by P wave while its conduction through bundle of His and Perkinje fibres is completed when the wave reaches to point Q.

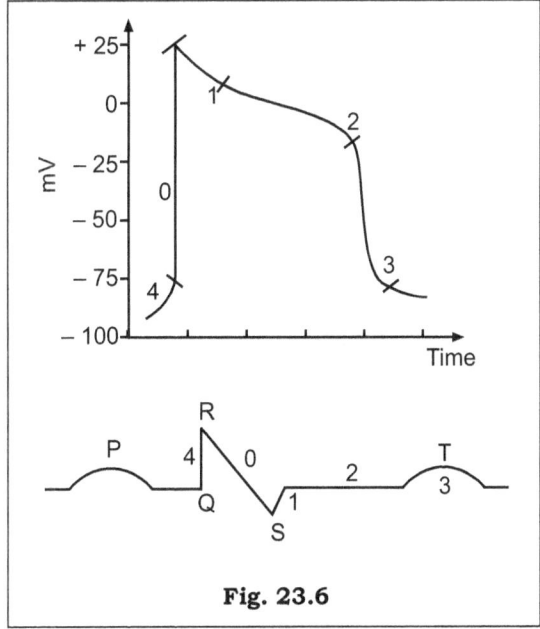

Fig. 23.6

The ventricular depolarization is indicated by QRS complex while ST segment represents repolarization of ventricles.

An arrhythmia may arise due to abnormality in –

(a) rate, regularity or site of origin of cardiac impulse, or

(b) conduction that causes an alteration in the normal sequence of the atria and ventricles.

It may be sub-classified as per the rate of beats and its anatomical location as follows :

(i) Sinus tachycardia : In this, an impulse is generated by S. A. node that spreads through atria and ventricles using normal conducting tissues. It is simply tachycardia (increase in the rate of impulse generation) due to increased S. A. nodal automaticity. Heart rate ranges between 100-180/min. It usually occurs even in normal individuals under the conditions of exercise, anxiety, stress or fright and ceases as soon as the underlying cause ends.

During myocardial infarction, increase in S.A. node discharge rate may be due to inhibition of vagal suppression or to sympathetic discharge. Efforts to suppress S.A. node rate by producing β-adrenergic blockade (propranolol) can lead to significant depression of myocardial contractility and is a potentially hazardous therapy which should be used with caution.

(ii) Atrial flutter and fibrillation : The severity of an increased automaticity enhances from tachycardia to flutter and then to fibrillation. Atrial flutter is characterized by rapid atrial firing at a rate of 150-300 beats/min of ectopic origin. Ventricular conduction and contraction remain unaffected due to filtering ability of A.V. node.

In atrial fibrillation, rapid and disorganized atrial rhythm at a rate of 350-600/min occurs due to random and changing firing (automaticity) of ectopic origin. A.V. node plays the role of filter to this rapid firing rate and censors majority of impulses, entering into the ventricular mass. This leads to random and irregular contractions of ventricular muscle fibres. Both, atrial flutter and fibrillation are more prone to occur in persons with advanced age. Atrial fibrillation is sometimes described as 'slow' or 'fast' depending on the ventricular rate. A patient with slow atrial fibrillation in which an effective A.V. node block permits only a small proportion of impulses to pass from the atria to the ventricles may not need treatment. In contrast, fast atrial fibrillation which occurs in patients with an ineffective A.V. node block, features rapid and irregular ventricular beats and consequent inefficient filling of the ventricles and inefficient circulation.

(iii) Sinus bradycardia : It is just opposite to sinus tachycardia and arises due to decreased automaticity (heart rate of less than 60 beats/min) of S.A. node with no conduction defects. Due to decreased heart rate, both, ventricular filling time and end-diastolic volume also increase. It usually occurs due to either increased vagal activity or decreased efficacy of S.A. node (because of myocardial ischemia).

Bradyarrhythmias are generally caused by tissue damage, a decrease in sympathetic autonomic tone or an increase in parasympathetic tone mediated by the vagus nerve. Increased vagal tone causes AV block of varying degree which reduces the rate of impulses reaching the ventricles. Immediate treatment is to decrease vagal tone with intravenous atropine which will decrease AV block and increase SA rate. If atropine is ineffective, intravenous adrenaline or isoprenaline may be used. The only oral treatment available for bradycardia is slow-release isoprenaline which is not generally satisfactory.

(iv) Sick sinus syndrome : It is a type of bradycardia (decreased automaticity) of no fixed etiology. Abnormalities in both, impulse generation and conduction system are witnessed. Electrolyte or endocrine imbalances may contribute to its development. The early symptoms such as, fatigue, dizziness and confusion may become severe upto congestive cardiac failure, if remains untreated.

(v) Atrioventricular block : It is characterized by reduced impaired A-V conduction. The bundle of His and Purkinje fibres may also come under affected area. Both cardiac (acute myocardial infarction or AV nodal disease) and non-cardiac (enhanced vagal tone) reasons may cause the development of A.V. block.

(vi) Premature Atrial Complexes (PAC) : PACs usually represents the re-entry of a stimulus, arising in S.A. node, which "echoes" back to the atrium, either at the A.V. junctional level or via intra-atrial conduction pathways. Less frequently, ectopic foci may become enhanced and compete with the sinus node pace maker.

(vii) Premature ventricular contractions : In this case S.A. nodal automaticity is not altered but additional impulses are generated from local tissues in the ventricular region. The development of ectopic foci in ventricular mass may be pronounced with the presence of cardiac disease. Certain drugs (e.g., catecholamines, methylxanthines) may also increase the frequency of its occurrence.

(viii) Paroxysmal (recurrent) supraventricular tachycardia (PSVT) : It is characterized by the appearance of narrow QRS complexes with a heart rate of 150-250 beats/min. The principal etiologies include re-entry and increased automaticity of atrial ectopic focus. Lidocaine is the preferred agent for the rapid control of ventricular tachycardai.

(ix) Re-entry : The electrical system of the heart consists of intrinsic pace makers and conduction tissues. An impulse is generated in S.A. node and it is conducted in bundle of His and Purkinje system through A. V. node in antegrade (towards ventricles) direction. Since the surrounding tissue is refractory in nature, an impulse terminates in Purkinje fibres. Thus, the conduction system is large enough so that the conduction pathways are repolarized before the next sinus impulse arrived at A.V. junction.

Due to the development of premature atrial impulse from any ectopic focus or due to partial or complete block in conduction, an impulse after causing ventricular contraction, travels in retrograde (towards atria) direction. Thus, the impulse may continue around the obstacle to establish re-entry circuit. The disturbances in conduction can be partial or complete (delay or complete block) or can be unidirectional or bidirectional and may occur with or without re-entry or circus movement.

(x) Ventricular flutter : It is characterized by the ventricular rate of 150-300 beats/min generated due to rapid and regular firing from ectopic foci of ventricular origin. If remains untreated, ventricular flutter may be converted into a more severe form, i.e. ventricular fibrillation.

(xi) Ventricular fibrillation : It is characterized by the ventricular rate of 150-500 beats/min generated in rapid and random fashion from ectopic foci present in ventricular mass. The co-ordination between the ventricular contractile elements is lost which results into disorganised and random ventricular contractions. This leads to irregular and ineffective pumping of blood from the heart.

CARDIAC GLYCOSIDES

24.1 INTRODUCTION

Cardiac glycosides are the example of positive inotropic agents (i.e. which increase the force of myocardial contraction). These positive inotropic agents are classified into :

(a) Cardiac glycosides

(b) β- adrenoceptor agonists, and

(c) Bipyridine derivatives.

All these agents act by increasing the amount of intracellular calcium ions resulting into more forceful contraction of cardiac muscles. However, they differ in the chemistry, mechanism of action and specific side-effects. All positive inotropic agents have the dose-dependent peripheral vascular effects, ranging from vasoconstriction (digitalis glycosides) to vasodilation (bipyridine derivatives). Except bipyridine derivatives, these agents also exhibit considerable arrhythmogenic potential.

Cardiac glycosides are naturally occurring drugs which are present in the glycoside forms, in a wide variety of plants and in a non-glycosidic form, in the poison of load. In plants, the leaves of *Digitalis purpurea* (purple foxglove) and *Digitalis lanata* (white foxglove) contains digoxin, digitoxin and deslanoside while seeds of various species of *Stropanthus* are the source of stropanthin (*S. kombe*) and ouabain (*S. lanata*). *Helleborus* species and squill (the freshly dried bulb of *Urginea maritima*) are botanical sources for other glycosides like Scillaren A.

Cardiac glycosides are the drugs that increase the force of contraction of heart muscles without increasing the oxygen consumption. Since they exert a positive inotropic effect without involving more expenditure of energy, they are called as cardiotonic agents. The first report regarding main indications and actions of an extract of digitalis leaves was first published by William Wilhering. Its selective action on the heart was first painted out in 1799 by John Ferriar. It was then in 1890 that Strophanthus was clinically used by Sir Thomas Fraser.

Chemistry :

Since the clinically used agents from this class (digoxin, digitoxin) are derived from the plants of the genus *Digitalis*, these cardiotonic glycosides are collectively termed as digitalis glycosides. These glycosides can also be obtained through synthetic routes, but the cost of production is very high. Hence, they are mainly obtained from plant source. In some plants, the cardiac glycosides occur in the form of their precursors. These precursors are themselves glycosidic in nature, that upon enzymatic hydrolysis releases cardiac glycosides along with a molecule of sugar. e.g. proscillaridin A. About 500 different cardiac glycosides from both, animals and plant sources are documented in literature. Cardiotonic glycosides are the conjugation products of a sugar and a non-sugar portion called as 'genin' or 'aglycone'. An aglycone is a steroidal nucleus having a 5- or 6- membered lactone ring attached at C-17 position. The lactone ring is usually unsaturated having $\Delta^{\alpha,\beta}$ structure. The saturation or loss of cyclic nature of the lactone ring results into decreased biological response. The aglycone portion may have structural resemblance to steroidal sex hormones and adreno-corticoids. However, it differs from endogenous steroidal hormones in having unusual cis-fusion of rings C and D. The glycosidic linkage occurs through C-3 hydroxyl group. This C-3 hydroxyl group of aglycone has been treated with many organic acids, xanthines and other reagents in order to get semisynthetic derivatives.

All aglycones exhibit similar set of pharmacological actions. It is the attached sugar moieties that play an important role in governing duration of action, partition coefficient, absolute potency and protein binding properties of glycosides. It also inhibits an enzyme induced metabolic change in the aglycone configuration.

At a time, the aglycone portion may combine with 1 to 4 molecules of sugar. The sugar attached through glycosidic linkage may be mono-, di-, tri- or tetrasaccharide.

24.2 PATHOPHYSIOLOGY OF HEART FAILURE

According to the **Frank Starling** mechanisms, the degree of force of heart muscle contraction is governed by the extent of ventricular muscle stretching. It does not apply to all degrees of muscle stretch. If the myocardial fibre is stretched beyond critical length, instead of an increase in force of contraction, a fall in contraction force results. A failing heart does not pump blood efficiently enough to meet the body's needs for oxygen and nutrients due to reduced power of contraction. Blood starts accumulating in the heart due to poor efficiency of the heart. The resulting progressive increase in end-diastolic volume leads to gradual increase in heart failure. The body's compensatory mechanisms get activated to cause increased sympathetic tone, elevation of plasma renin and plasma antidiuretic hormone activity. The manifestations of failing heart include :

(a) Stimulation of sympathetic nervous system, innervated to S. A. node resulting into vasoconstriction, tachycardia and sweating. These are largely the compensatory body mechanisms to counterbalance the effects of inefficient and poorly pumping heart.

(b) As a consequence, salt and water retention results into peripheral and pulmonary edema.

(c) Secondary symptoms include easy fatigability, breathlessness and hypertrophy of myocardium.

The main pharmacodynamic property of digitalis is its ability to increase the force of myocardial contraction. The first proof regarding cardiotonic activity of digitalis was given in 1938 by **Cattell** and **Gold**. The beneficial effects of the drug in patients with heart failure include increased cardiac output, decreased pre-load, decreased heart size and venous return, increased renal flow and diuresis; all these effects lead to relief of edema and normal heart rate.

The decreased heart size brings the heart under the range of operation of Frank-Starling mechanisms. Improved cardiac output cools down the compensatory sympathetic tone. The increased renal flow allows the drainage of retained edema fluid. The renal sodium ion excretion is increased due to competitive antagonism at mineralo-corticoidal receptor because of structural resemblance.

Chemistry of Aglycone Part :

(1) In digitalis glycosides the anellation of the A - B and C - D rings is cis (Z), the 3 - OH is axial (β), and all of these steroids carry a 14β-OH group. The C-17 side chain is an unsaturated lactone ring. The sugar part, binding to the 3-OH, is a tri or tetrasaccharide consisting mainly of digitoxose and glucose.

(ii) Strophanthin aglycone has a 5β-OH group in addition to other hydroxyls, upto a maximum of 6 in ouabain. The 19-CH_3 is replaced by an CHO or 1° alcohol and the sugars are the unusual rhamnose or cymarose.

(iii) The squill aglycones carry a six-membered lactone ring with two double bonds. None is used because of high toxicity.

(iv) The lactone ring is not essential. The coplanar side-chains instead of a ring have even higher activity.

(v) The activity of a compound depends to a great extent on the position of the 23rd-carbonyl oxygen, which is held quite rigidly by ring D and the double bond.

(vi) Removal of the sugar portion allows epimerization of the 3β-OH group, with a decrease in activity and an increase in toxicity due to changes in polarity.

Digitalis Agonists :

Compounds having digitalis activity fall into four categories, depending upon their mode of action.

(I) Inotropic and Na^+-K^+-ATPase inhibitors :

e.g. (a) Cardenolides

(b) Bufadienolides

(c) Cardenolide-3-bromo acetate.

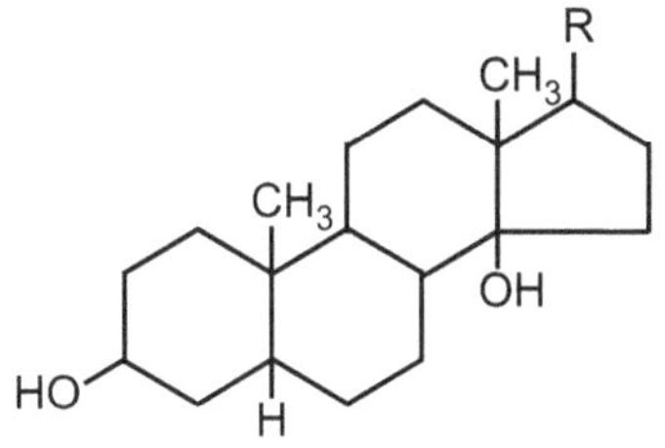

Active compounds : where

$R = $ COOCH$_3$, $R = $ C≡N , $R = $ CHO

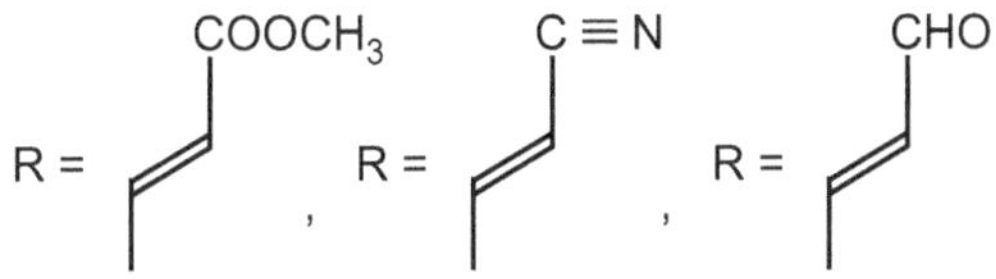

Compounds with moderate activity: where

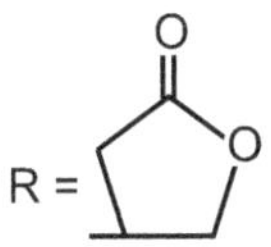

$R = $ (lactone ring)

Compounds with marginal activity: where

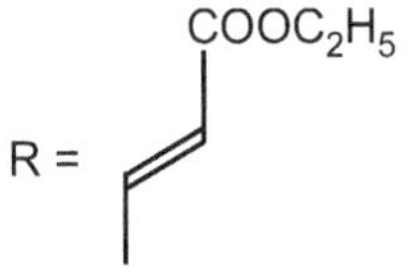

$R = $ COOC$_2$H$_5$

Inactive compounds : where

$R = $ COOCH$_3$

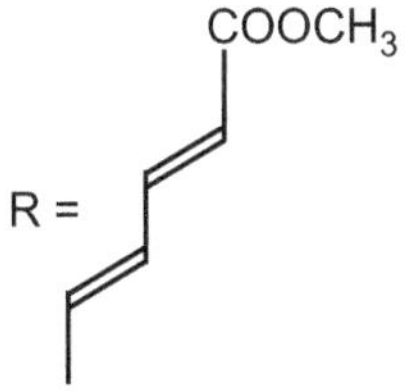

(II) Inotropic but not Na^+-K^+-ATPase inhibitors :

e.g. catecholamines, caffeine, veratrum alkaloids etc.

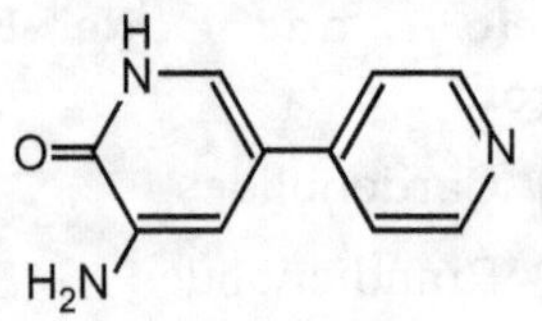

Amrinone

(III) Na^+-K^+-ATPase - inhibitors but not inotropic :

e.g. sodium azide, -SH blocking reagents, mersalyl, fatty acids, diisopropyl fluorophosphate and some steroidal alkylating agent, e.g.

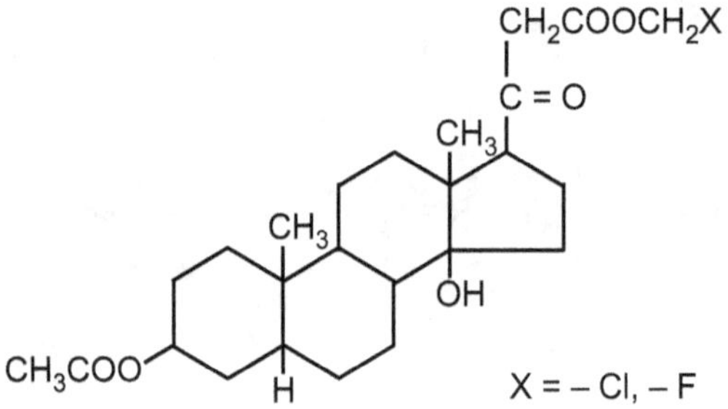

$X = -Cl, -F$

(IV) Na^+-K^+-ATPase inhibitors but inotropic activity is uncertain :

e.g. chlormadinone acetate.

Since H-bonding (which takes place between the side-chain and K^+-binding site of Na^+-K^+-ATPase enzyme) determines the degree of Na^+-K^+-ATPase inhibition, the molecule's dipole is an important parameter.

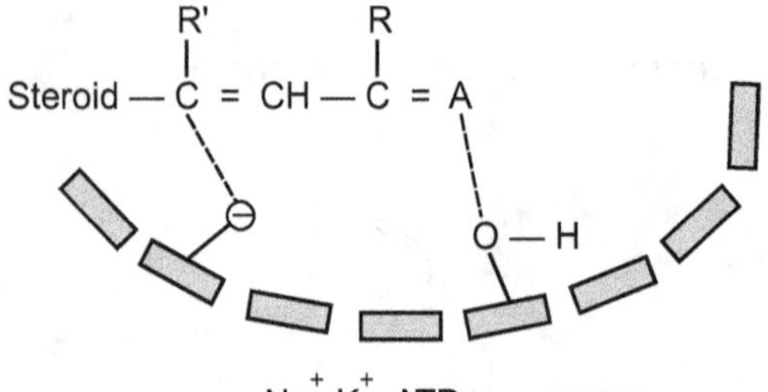

Steroid — $\overset{R'}{\underset{|}{C}}$ = CH — $\overset{R}{\underset{|}{C}}$ = A

Na^+-K^+- ATPase enzyme

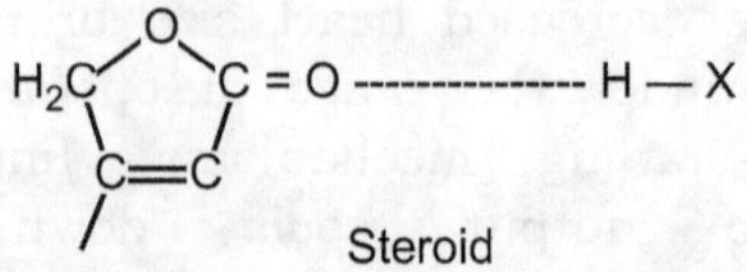

Steroid with $H_2C\diagup\overset{O}{\diagdown}C = O$ ---- $H - X$, $C = C$

Where, $X = K^+$ binding site on Na^+-K^+-ATPase enzyme.

With the help of PROPHET computer system from National Institute of Health, the most stable conformation of each of variety of genin was superimposed graphically with the digitoxigenin, a cardenolide prototype. It is found that the distance between the position of particular carbonyl oxygen (or nitrile nitrogen), relative to digitoxigenin serves a nearly perfect index of its activity.

Sugar Portion :

Though the sugars are not directly involved in cardiotonic activity, their attachment to the steroid (at C_3) contributes greatly to both, pharmacodynamic and pharmacokinetic parameters of the cardiac glycosides. Since the free genins are more rapidly absorbed and more widely distributed than the corresponding glycosides, this leads to their rapid metabolism to give less active 3-epimers, followed by rapid excretion via sulphates and glucuronides formation at free C-3 OH group. The free genins therefore are quite unstable as therapeutic agents. Pharmacodynamically, the genins are usually less potent than their glycosidic forms and show rapid onset and reversal of enzyme inhibitions. In contrast to this, the glycosides form very stable complexes with Na^+-K^+-ATPase enzyme. Replacement of the sugar moieties with nitrogen containing side chains gives potent analogs of digitalis e.g. N-(4'-

amino-n-butyl) 3-amino acetyl derivative of strophanthidine has about 60 times greater affinity towards Na^+-K^+-ATPase enzyme than the parent genin. H-bonding is the principal interaction involved between sugar and enzyme. Particularly 3-OH and 5-CH_3 groups seem to be binding groups in 2, 6-desoxy sugars.

24.3 MECHANISM OF ACTION

Digitalis glycosides are effective in cardiac failure, regardless of the etiological reason. The positive inotropic effect of digitalis is manifested in both, normal and failing hearts, although in the former, the increased output may be terminated by its direct vasoconstrictive effects.

Digitalis appears to have no indirect effect on mitochondria or on the uptake of any energy yielding substrates (i.e. either ATP or creatinine phosphate). Nor does it have any direct effects on the contractile elements within the sarcoplasm. It does not appear to reverse any biochemical defects associated with heart disease.

The intracellular concentration of Na^+ and K^+ are maintained by the activity of Na^+-K^+-ATPase pump. The hydrolysis of ATP by Na^+-K^+-ATPase system provides energy necessary for the operation of pump. The most probable explanation for the direct positive inotropic effect of cardiac glycosides is their ability to inhibit the membrane bound Na^+-K^+-ATPase pump. This inhibition results in impairment of active transport of Na^+ and K^+. The first well documented proof about the pump inhibitory activity of cardiac glycosides was provided by **Repke** and **Portius** in 1963.

The Na^+-K^+-ATPase is the prominent binding site for digitalis. It blocks membrane bound Na^+-K^+-ATPase in all tissues. But since it has a high affinity for heart muscles, it gets accumulated mainly in the left ventricles and conducting system. It binds with the external surface of the enzyme resulting into suppression of the active transport of Na^+ and K^+ ions. As a result, there is a gradual increase in intracellular Na^+ ions and extracellular K^+ ions. Cardiac fibres possess a mechanism for exchange of intracellular Na^+ ions with extracellular Ca^{++} ions. The increased intracellular Na^+ ion concentration activates this mechanism resulting into an increase in net influx of extracellular Ca^{++} ions, which in turn then causes the release of additional intracellular Ca^{++} ions from the stores in sarcoplasmic reticulum to activate contractile force. An elevation in the level of free intracellular Ca^{++} ions is also due to the drug's individual ability to interfere with Ca^{++} ion binding on sarcoplasmic reticulum. Thus, the positive inotropic effect of these glycosides is due to an increase in automaticity and excitability of myocardial muscle fibers.

The activity of Na^+-K^+-ATPase pump is regenerated due to the dissociative effect of increased extracellular K^+ ions on the drug - enzyme attachment. Even though the blockage of Na^+-K^+-ATPase pump seems to be the main mechanism through which digitalis glycosides exert their positive inotropic effect, many other ATPase inhibitors (such as actinomycin, quinidine, oligomycin, sodium azide, sulfhydryl blocking agents) fail to exhibit the expected positive inotropic effect on the heart. On the other hand, catecholamines (i.e. isoprenaline) have considerable cardiotonic actions but have very short biological half-life.

Besides this, acidosis, hypoxia, cardiac ischemia and decreased renal perfusion are some of the factors that bring down the efficacy of Na^+-K^+-ATPase pump.

24.4 OTHER EFFECTS OF DIGITALIS GLYCOSIDES

Besides their ability to inhibit the functioning of Na^+-K^+-ATPase pump, digitalis exerts some of its actions through its effect on autonomic nervous system and on vascular smooth muscles. For example, digitalis has a vasoconstrictor action on the vascular smooth muscle. The changes in the circulation brought about by digitalis are mainly reflection of reflex alterations in A.N.S. functioning. It also changes the heart sensitivity to the vagal and sympathetic neurotransmitters.

At low to moderate doses, digitalis exerts a negative chronotropic effect mainly due to the increased vagal activity and direct depressant action on the conducting tissue (A. V. node). Digitalis also increases refractory period of both, atrial and ventricular muscle. Thus, the depression of conducting tissue accompanied with increased refractory period may protect ventricles from excessive bombardment in atrial arrhythmias due to increased filtration through A.V. node. But this may lead to bradycardia and in toxic doses, even heart block. In addition, the presence of delayed after polarization due to low conduction velocity can slow down and impair impulse propogation giving rise to re-entrant rhythms.

In S.A. node, the rate of generation of impulse is decreased by mainly parasympathetic activation. The atrial myocardium however, remains almost unaffected at therapeutic concentrations of digitalis. A decrease in atrial action potential duration and effective refractory period is mainly due to the predominance of vagal tone. However high concentration of digitalis can decrease the excitability of all cardiac tissues. Digitalis-induced arrhythmias may result due to an enhanced sympathetic activity from the effect of digitalis on medulla oblongata. These arrhythmias can be treated by β-adrenergic blockers.

At the level of A.V. node, digitalis induces slow conduction and increased refractory period. Below this level, the effects on ventricular myocardial fibres are mainly exerted through Perkinje system. In all myocardial region, the only region which is strongly influenced by sympathetic tone is His-Purkinje system. It is least sensitive to the changes in vagal activity. In this region a decrease in refractoriness (i.e. shortening of action potential duration) is observed.

In summary, the most important hemodynamic effect of digitalis is its positive inotropic action which results in decrease in heart size leading to increased cardiac output with increased efficiency of the heart. Thus, it is an effective drug in congestive cardiac failure. It may also lead to cardiac arrhythmias due to increase in myocardial excitability and automaticity.

The vagal tone predominance usually results into :

(a) Decrease in atrial refractory period (increased atrial conduction velocity may convert flutter into fibrillation).

(b) Delay in conduction of impulses through A.V. node.

(c) Bradycardia.

The fluid in peripheral edema is drained out due to diuretic action of digitalis. This action is due to -

(i) Increased cardiac output with increased renal perfusion, and

(ii) Direct action upon the distal renal tubule by exerting competitive antagonism with aldosterone (due to structural similarity).

24.5 PHARMACOKINETIC PARAMETERS

Digoxin and digitoxin are the most commonly prescribed agents. Both are readily absorbed from GIT. However, to a considerable extent, digoxin is inactivated (to form 2 - hydroxydigoxin) by intestinal microflora while digitoxin is extensively (92-95%) absorbed. Certain drugs like, kaolin, antacids may interfere with the absorption. These glycosides possess relatively large volume of distribution (V_D). This accounts for their slow distribution in the body compartments. Digitoxin is extensively (> 95%) bound to plasma proteins while digoxin is also significantly (20-25%) bound to plasma proteins. Skeletal muscles, heart, kidneys and RBCs are the body tissues where most of the administered dose of cardiac glycosides get concentrated.

Digoxin has fairly rapid onset of action when administered intravenously while digitoxin is usually not given by i.v. route due to its slow onset of action. It has the longest duration of action, if used orally. Intramuscular route is not preferable for the administration of these drugs due to the induction of severe pain and muscle necrosis.

Other less commonly used cardiac glycosides include ouabain, lanatoside C and deslanoside. The latter acts as a precursor of digoxin in the body. All these drugs are poorly absorbed from GIT and are usually administered intravenously. Liver serves as the principal site of metabolism for all these glycosides. Digitoxin and digoxin are metabolized to relatively inactive dihydrodigoxin by hepatic microsomal enymes. Hence in case of toxicity, the rate of metabolism can be increased by giving metabolic enzyme inducers like, phenobarbital or phenylbutazone.

Other metabolic mechanisms involve cleavage of glycosidic linkage. The free genin portion is then excreted in the form of glucuronide. Part of the genin portion is also reported to undergo epoxidation.

The half-life of digoxin is estimated to be about 35-40 hours. It readily crosses placenta. Its metabolites (i.e. dihydrodigoxine, digoxigenin, dihydrodigoxigenin) are primarily eliminated in urine. The rate of elimination of cardiac glycosides is very slow which if not taken into consideration, may result into drug intoxication due to its accumulation. Hence, the cardiac glycosides are usually administered orally in two stages. The patient is treated with an initial dose of the drug to get therapeutic response. This dose administration is known as 'initial digitalization or loading dose'. The therapeutic response obtained through digitalization is further maintained by a low dose schedule which is known as 'maintenance dose'.

24.6 THERAPEUTIC USES

(A) Congestive Cardiac Failure :

The positive inotropic effect of these glycosides causes the heart to contract more strongly and efficiently. The beneficial effects of these drugs in patients with heart failure include : increased cardiac output, decreased heart size and venous pressure, diuresis and relief of edema. The reduction in myocardial oxygen demand decreases the intensity of compensatory sympathetic nervous system which results in a decrease in systemic arterial resistance and venous tone. However digitalis treatment is not effective when :

(i) heart failure is associated with very high preload or after load. In such cases the use of diuretics (which lower down blood volume and ventricular filling pressure) and/or vasodilators (which reduce preload, and after load) is given more weightage.

(ii) chronic treatment is required. This is due to a loss in therapeutic efficacy through development of significant tolerance to drug action. In such case vasodilators and/or inhibitors of angiotensin converting enzyme (saralasin, captopril) are the drugs of choice used along with digitalis or a diuretic.

(B) Atrial Arrhythmias :

At therapeutic doses, cardiac glycosides have a protective action upon the ventricles. This action is exerted by increasing the vagal tone and by a direct depressant action upon A.V. conduction. This results into an increased 'filtering' of the impulses which are generated at relatively higher rate during atrial arrhythmias. The reduction in conduction velocity and an increase in refractory period protect the ventricular muscles from excessive stimulation. Atrial arrhythmias where digitalis finds clinical use, include-atrial flutter, atrial fibrillation and paroxysmal atrial tachycardia.

However, the glycosides are contraindicated in patients having hypokalemia, hypercalcemia, impaired renal function or ventricular tachycardia. Quinidine or procainamide are better drugs to treat ventricular tachycardia.

24.7 ADVERSE EFFECTS

The cardiac glycosides have a low therapeutic safety margin. Consequently the adverse reactions are quite frequent and can be severe in toxic doses. These adverse reactions are mainly due to –

(i) An increased parasympathetic tone.

(ii) A loss of intracellular potassium (hypokalemia)

(iii) An increased intracellular Ca^{++} concentration.

These adverse reactions can be classified as :

(a) Gastrointestinal effects : Nausea and vomiting (due to direct action on chemoreceptor trigger zone in medulla), anorexia, abdominal pain, cramps, diarrhoea and increased secretion of urine.

(b) Visual effects : Photophobia, disturbed perception, blurred vision, objects appear green or yellow.

(c) CNS effects : Headache, giddiness, drowsiness, fatigue, delirium, confusion and convulsions.

(d) Cardiac effects : The cardiac effects of digitalis glycosides are much complicated due to unusual combination of -

(i) Decreased A.V. conduction and increased refractory period due to enhanced vagal activity, and

(ii) Increased abnormal or ectopic automaticity due to drug's direct effect.

Digitalis glycosides are used to treat a diseased heart. Due to the combination of above two effects, such a diseased heart easily get attacked by arrhythmias or A.V. block occurred due to an exaggeration of depressant action on conduction. Digitalis in high dose, is likely to induce the development of almost every known cardiac arrhythmia. The infarcted myocardium serves as a site to develop ectopic foci which is responsible for the occurrence of both atrial and ventricular tachycardia. It is better to discontinue drug therapy under such conditions.

24.8 DIGITALIS INTOXICATION

The large volume of distribution (V_D), low rate of elimination (longer duration of action), the concurrent effects of the glycosides on A.N.S. and on peripheral vascular smooth muscles (besides their action on Na^+-K^+-ATPase pump) and hypokalemia (in patients receiving diuretics along with digitalis) are the factors that provoke the sensitivity of the patient towards digitalis intoxication. The low therapeutic index of these drugs necessitates careful clinical observation of the patients during the period of initial digitalization. Hence, extreme caution is to be observed when they are given intravenously. Both hypokalemia and hypercalcemia sensitize myocardium to the glycoside action. In such a condition, a decline in resting membrane potential, brings the cell quite near to their threshold value for generating an impulse. This explains the basis of digitalis-induced extrasystoles during the therapy. An adequate potassium intake should always be maintained in the therapy when hypokalemia is reported. The hypokalemia, if remained uncorrected, may lead to the tachyarrhythmias in digitalis overdose (due to decline in resting membrane potential). Hence, if a diuretic is needed in patients receiving digitalis, then potassium sparing diuretics are to be used.

However, in toxicity signs due to conduction impairments (i.e. A.V. block), potassium intake may provoke the digitalis toxicity. Hence, it is contraindicated in cases of A.V. block. Under such conditions vagolytic agents are useful.

Digitalis exerts a blocking action on membrane buond Na^+-K^+-ATPase pump in all tissues. However, this inhibitory action is not pronounced in these tissue (except heart) to exert either other therapeutic or toxic effects.

An enhancement of automaticity by digitalis is the probable reason behind the drug induced atrial arrhythmias. Any antiarrhythmic drug can be used to suppress atrial arrhythmias due to digitalis toxicity.

A considerable fraction of orally administered digoxin is inactivated (to 2 - hydroxydigoxin) by intestinal microflora. Hence, in the patient receiving digoxin along with an antibiotic, the extent of absorption of active drug suddenly increases. This leads to appearance of toxic effects of digoxin in therapeutic dose level.

24.9 TREATMENT OF INTOXICATION

(1) Digitalis glycosides have very poor therapeutic index. In case of digitalis intoxication, the therapy should be immediately discontinued so as to lower down the plasma concentration of the drug.

(2) The patient should be evaluated to trace out hypokalemia if diuretics are concurrently administered. The plasma potassium level may be maintained in the upper normal level by giving potassium either orally or intravenously. The increasing extracellular K^+ ion concentration may produce the stimulatory effect on Na^+-K^+-ATPase pump, thereby decreasing the binding of digitalis with the pump system. The suppression of ectopic beats and abnormal rhythms (due to the drug induced automaticity) are other beneficial effects of potassium intake. However its administration is contraindicated in the presence of diminished cardiac conduction (e.g. sinus bradycardia, A.V. block). In such conditions atropine like drugs may improve the functioning of heart by suppressing the underlying cause (i.e. increased vagal tone).

(3) Digitalis increases the automaticity and excitability of myocardial fibres. In toxic doses digitalis may induce severe atrial arrhythmias. Many antiarrhythmic agents (e.g. propranolol, phenytoin, lidocaine) along with potassium salts can be used in suppressing digitalis induced atrial arrhythmias.

(4) In severe life-threatening digitalis intoxication (accidental or attempted suicides), above treatment may not be effective to get immediate response. In such cases, specific glycoside antibodies administration leads to rapid recovery of the heart functioning. Digitalis specific Fab antibody fragments were first evaluated for their effectiveness in humans in 1976. Like other antibodies, however their use is accompanied by emergence of allergic reactions in sensitive patients. This limits their use in patients with pre-allergic history.

24.10 ALTERNATIVES TO DIGITALIS THERAPY

The low margin of safety and inherent toxicities associated with the use of digitalis glycosides, led to the search for development of group of agents having positive inotropic effect. There was an increasing tendency to use vasodilators (hydralazine, prazosin, nitrates), diuretics or cardiac stimulants (β-adrenergic agonists) to reduce the preload and/or after load of the failing heart. However, adrenergic drugs have a shorter duration of action while vasodilators may not be the primary drugs of choice in all the cases. Out of available alternatives to digitalis, bipyridine derivatives are of special interest due to the combination of both positive inotropic property and vasodilatory effect in one compound. Examples from this class include, amrinone and milrinone.

Both these agents can be used orally as well as intravenously. Milrinone is considerably more potent but has relatively shorter duration of action than amrinone. Their use in congestive heart failure is mainly due to their positive inotropic and vasodilatory effects. The mechanism of the positive inotropic effect of amrinone differs from that of conventional positive inotropic agents. Since their efficacy is not decreased by the use of adrenergic blockers, the direct activation of adrenergic receptor is not their mechanism of action. Probably the mechanism may be related to an increase in intracellular concentration of c-AMP by inhibition of phosphodiesterase enzymes, (however, several agents that inhibit these enzymes, do not exert a positive inotropic effect). The increase in c-AMP then lowers the rate of influx of Ca^{++} ions resulting into vasodilation. The net effect is reduction in the afterload. The positive inotropic effect makes these agents useful in the treatment of congestive cardiac failure, where their inotropic effect is additive to that of cardiac glycosides.

Liver serves as the principal site for metabolism. About six metabolites of amrinone have been identified. Its use in the chronic treatment is not advisable due to serious adverse effects. Amrinone during long term use may induce immunologic abnormality. This along with long term inhibition of phosphodiesterase enzyme may contribute for the appearance of adverse effects. These effects includes nausea, vomiting, abdominal cramps, diarrhoea, fatigue and reversible thrombocytopenia, headache, fatigue and hepatotoxicity. Hence, its daily dose should not exceed 10 mg/kg.

Milrinone is quite a safe drug. Its use is not associated with most of the adverse effects seen in amrinone therapy. However efficacy of the drug appears to be age dependent.

Other drugs having positive inotropic effects include dopamine, dobutamine (β_1-agonist), ephedrine and pirbuterol. Pirbuterol is a β-adrenergic agonist having both, a positive inotropic and vasodilatory effect. The positive inotropic effect of catecholamines is due to a resultant increase in the intracellular Ca^{++} concentration that is brought about by the drug induced changes in c-AMP level. However in many cases, inotropic effect and c-AMP level may be dissociated.

Since the extracellular calcium is important in deciding the force of heart contraction, attempts were also made to design specific carrier molecules for Ca^{++} ions which will introduce more extracellular Ca^{++} ions into the cell. X 537-A is such an agent developed by **Holland et al** in 1975. Since the pacemaker activity is less dependent on Ca^{++} ion concentration and requires different ionic basis than the myocardial cell, this increased influx of Ca^{++} ions results in positive inotropic effect without associated tachycardia. However a decrease in apparent Ca^{++} ion sensitivity of the contractile proteins may occur in response to a fall in intracellular pH and to rise in cytoplasmic levels of inorganic phosphate and creatine phosphate.

24.11 ANTI-ARRHYTHMIC AGENTS

In order for the heart to function as an efficient pump, the various contractile units must operate in a co-ordinated or rhythmic fashion. As arrhythmia is an abnormality of,

(1) rate, regularity or site of origin of the cardiac impulse or

(2) the disturbance in conduction that leads to alteration in the normal sequence of activation of the atria and ventricles. Thus an arrhythmia may arise because of alteration in,

(i) Automaticity
(ii) Conduction, and
(iii) Refractory period of the myocardial cells.

Abnormalities of heart rate are included among the arrhythmias even though the actual rhythm of the beat is not necessarily disturbed in these conditions.

Origin of Arrhythmia :

The generation of cardiac impulses in the normal heart is usually confined to specialised tissues that spontaneously depolarize and initiate the action potential. These cells are located in the right atrium and are referred to as the sino atrial node (S.A. node) or pacemaker cells. When the impulse is released from the S.A. node, excitation of the heart tissue takes place in an orderly manner by a spread of the impulse throughout the specialised automatic fibres in the atria resulting in contraction of the atria. A.V. node functions as a delay circuit and conducts this impulse slowly to the bundle of His and finally, through the Purkinje fibre network in the ventricles, resulting into ventricular contraction. The P wave represents atrial depolarization and the QRS complex represents ventricular depolarization. The interval between the two (PR interval) is the time taken to conduct the beat through the AV node and is lengthened in AV block. The T wave denotes ventricular repolarization, and the QT interval denotes the time between depolarization and polarization of the ventricles. A prolonged QT predisposes to torsades de pointes (i.e. a fast ventricular rhythm with polymorphic QRS complexes). The events are represented in following figure.

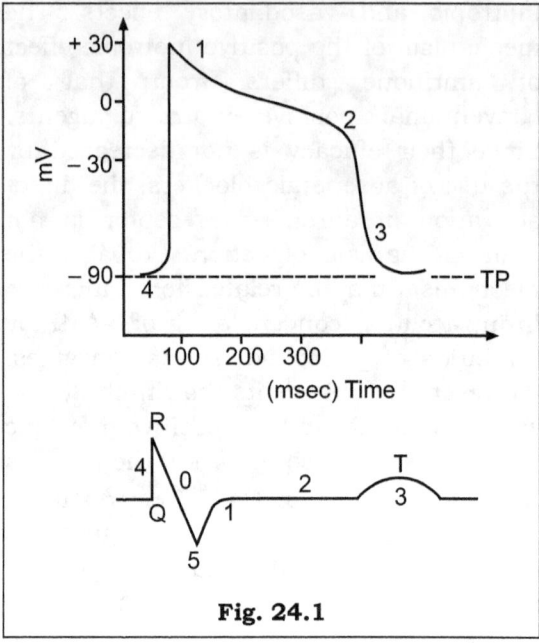

Fig. 24.1

Though the spontaneous electrical depolarization of the S.A. node (pacemaker) cells is independent of the nervous systems, these cells are innervated by both sympathetic and para-sympathetic nerves, which may cause an increase or decrease in the heart rate, respectively. Other special cells in the normal heart, which possess the property of automaticity (secondary pacemaker) may influence cardiac rhythm when the normal pacemaker is suppressed or when pathological changes occur in the myocardium to make these cells the dominant source of cardiac rhythm (ectopic pacemakers), especially when myocardial cell damage occurs because of localized myocardial disease (infarction) or from digitalis toxicity, excessive vagal tone, excessive catecholamine release from sympathomimetic nerves to the heart, or even high catecholamine plasma levels. If the S.A. node is prevented from operating normally, the A.V. node will usually take over as pacemaker or, if both are inactive, the ventricular conducting tissues will serve as pacemaker. Whenever the S.A. node is not the controlling pacemaker, the heart beat is less well co-ordinated and this may result in inefficient pumping with an increase in energy expenditure to maintain an adequate circulation or ineffective pumping with an inadequate circulation. The development of automaticity in these secondary pacemaker cells (e.g. special atrial cells, A.V. nodal cells, bundle of His or/and Purkinje fibres), may lead to cardiac arrhythmias.

In most cardiac cells, phase O is generated by the rapid inward movement of extracellular Na^+ ions through channels that selectively allow permeation of these ions. The phase 4 causes the so called 'm' gates (molecular gates) in the channels to open. The inward Na^+ current is very intense but of very brief duration. It is terminated by a process called as inactivation i.e. the closing of the gate in the Na^+ channel. The Na^+ channels can not be opened again until it is reactivated again on the propogation of second impulse, at threshold potential (T.P.).

In summary, the cardiac arrhythmias may arise from abnormalities in either impulse formation or impulse conduction or by both.

Abnormality in an impulse formation (automaticity) gives rise to changes in heart rate and to the development of ectopic (abnormal) beats, originating in secondary pacemaker cells. While disturbances in conduction can be partial or complete (delay or block), can be unidirectional or bi-directional and can occur with or without re-entry or circus movement.

Re-entry Phenomenon :

If pathway B is partially or completely blocked, the following events may occur :

(1) Due to very slow conduction through pathway B, if impulse arises at 'X' after the absolute refractory period of cells depolarized by A, the impulse may continue around the obstacle, as shown by the path b and/or follows A along path b'.

(2) If there is an unidirectional block in path B, impulse A may continue around the obstacle in the direction. If the obstacle is large enough so that the cells in the region of Y are repolarized before the return of a or b, then a circus movement may be established that may also propogate impulses in other directions (a" or b")

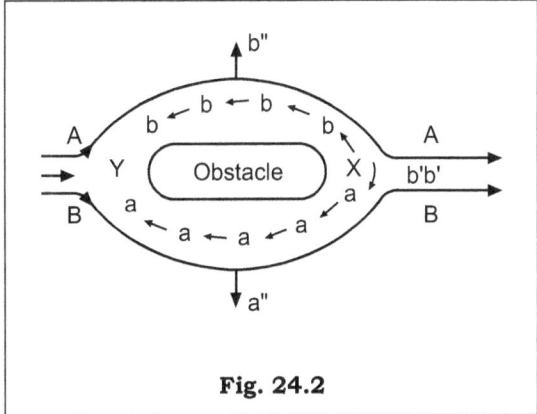

Fig. 24.2

Chemistry and Classification :

The major antiarrhythmic drugs were introduced into medicine as either antimalarials, anticonvulsants or local anaesthetics and it was only by chance that their antiarrhythmic properties were discovered.

These drugs may be divided into two broad categories :

(1) Those that act specifically by interacting with receptor (e.g. (β-adrenergic blockers) and

(2) Those that act non-specifically by accumulations in membranes (e.g. quinidine and local anaesthetics).

All these drugs basically decrease the membrane responsiveness to the transmembrane potential with decreased 'action potential' V_{max} during depolarization which results ultimately into prolong A.V. conduction, as shown below.

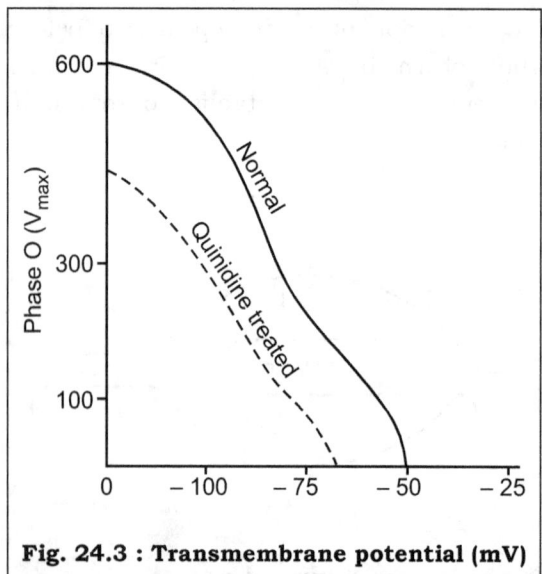

Fig. 24.3 : Transmembrane potential (mV)

Accordingly the various antiarrhythmic drugs are classified as :

(I) Membrane - depressant drugs (depressant of electrophysiological properties of myocardial cells).

e.g. Quinidine
Procainamide
Diisopyramide

(II) Drugs which facilitate impulse conduction and shorten refractory period while depressing automaticity.

e.g. Lidocaine
Phenytoin

(III) β-adrenergic blockers

e.g. Alprenolol   Atenolol
Sotalol   Metoprolol
Practolol   Propranolol
Pindolol

(IV) Selective Ca^{++} channel antagonists

e.g. Nifedipine
Verapamil

(V) Miscellaneous agents
Atropine   Edrophonium
Bretylium   Aprindine
Neostigmine

Mechanism of Action (for non-specific drugs) :

It is thought that these drugs act by accumulating in certain regions of the plasma membrane, where their action may be correlated with an increase in membrane surface pressure. The various biological functions of a cell are inhibited since the presence of these drugs affect the normal membrane components. Although this effect, is non-specific but it is selective i.e. not all but only certain membrane activities are inhibited, e.g. Na^+-K^+-ATPase activity is not affected by the therapeutic levels of antiarrhythmic agents. The drug decreases membrane permeability to the transport of certain ions by blocking certain ion channels or prevent the conformational changes in membrane proteins which are associated with the movement of "ion carriers" or the opening of "molecular gates (m gates)". This type of action is called as *Membrane Stabilisation*.

Mechanism of Action for Selective Ca^{++} Channel Antagonists :

Similar to other excitable tissues, action currents in cardiac muscle are carried by sodium and potassium ions but additional and important contribution to the inward flowing current (depolarization phase) is made by the movement of calcium ions. It is this continued inward calcium current that causes the delayed repolarization of cardiac muscle (pacemaker cells do not exhibit delayed repolarization). On the contrary, the three phases of repolarization are less sharply delineated from one another in pacemaker tissue). The ingress of calcium ions evokes the release of further supplies of free Ca^{++} ions from intracellular terminal sacs. The resulting increased concentration of free Ca^{++} ions then activates the contractile elements.

The energy for heart contraction is provided by the hydrolysis of ATP, catalysed by ATPase enzyme, which is present in the myosin fibrils. During diastole, this activation is inhibited by the troponin tropomyosin system, a protein complex closely associated with actin. This inhibitory action is blocked by combination of this protein complex with Ca^{++}, for which the complex exhibits higher affinity. Hence, higher intracellular Ca^{++} concentration will lead to culmination of systolic contraction. The antiarrhythmic action of Ca^{++} channel antagonists is due to their interfering action on the entry of Ca^{++} into the sarcofibrils either by obstructing the calcium channels or by depleting calcium stores at the membrane.

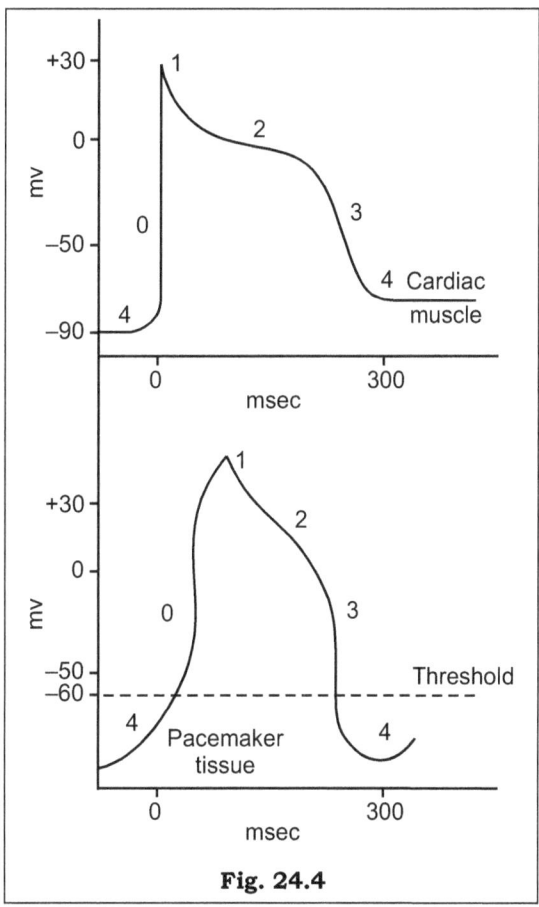

Fig. 24.4

24.12 ANTI-ANGINAL DRUGS

The word 'angina' (from the Greek verb meaning, 'to choke') is used to describe the pain or discomfort of cardiac origin which results due to temporary ischemia of the myocardium; that means the flow of blood is inadequate to maintain the metabolic demands of heart for oxygen and nutrients.

The heart normally extracts almost all the available oxygen from blood, hence the heart must therefore meet its increased metabolic demands for oxygen (in exercise or stress) by increasing the rate of coronary blood flow.

Angina is caused by the coronary vessel constriction which prevents this increase in blood flow. Reflex vasospasm of coronary arteries appears to be a primary cause of angina and it may be (but is not necessarily) superimposed on atherosclerotic coronary artery disease.

Angina is generally manifested by sudden, severe, pressing substernal pain, which often radiates to the left shoulder and along the flexor surface of the left arm. Breathlessness sometimes occurs along with other discomforts.

Numerous drugs have been used to treat angina, however, nitroglycerin has been known to be the most useful anti-anginal drug.

Classification of Antianginal Drugs :

(I) The Nitrites and Nitrates

(II) B-adrenergic antagonists e.g. Propranolol.

(III) Other drugs

(IV) Surgical procedures

(V) General measures

General Measures :

Certain general measures are indicated in the treatment of anginal patients to reduce the cardiac work load and to prevent further arterial degeneration.

The load on the heart can be reduced by,

(1) Correcting any obesity by avoiding heavy meals.

(2) Avoiding situations that lead to stress.

(3) Lowering of plasma levels of cholesterol and triglycerides.

(4) Avoiding excess of work and exercise.

Mechanism of Action of Antianginal Drugs :

These agents cause redistribution of coronary blood flow to the ischemic regions of the heart and also reduce myocardial oxygen demand. This latter effect is produced by a reduction in venous tone due to vasodilation effect and a pooling of blood in the peripheral veins that results in a reduction in ventricular volume, stroke volume and cardiac output. It also causes reduction in peripheral resistance during myocardial contractions. The combined vasodilatory effects cause a decrease in cardiac work load and reduction in oxygen consumption or demand.

24.13 ANTIHYPERTENSIVE AGENTS (HYPOTENSIVE AGENTS)

The normal systolic/diastolic blood pressures of a healthy adult person are supposed to be 120/75-85 mm Hg. The term hypertension, is generally defined as a pathologically elevated systemic arterial pressure. In this disorder, the small arteriole appears to be under excessive sympathetic nervous system stimulation which causes arteriole contraction and increased peripheral resistance to the transfer of blood from the arteries to the tissue capillaries and venous circulation resulting into increased blood pressure. Due to the variable nature of the systolic blood pressure, the term hypertension usually refers to an abnormal elevation in diastolic pressure. For practical guidance, usually the systolic/diastolic blood pressure above 160/95 is considered to be a state of hypertension. When the hypertension is due to the symptoms of definable causes, such as renal artery stenosis (pathological conditions of kidney which restrict the blood flow through the renal artery), a pheochromocytoma (a hypertensive condition caused by the release of large amount of catecholamines due to tumors in the adrenal medulla) or an endocrine disorder like aldenomas (excessive secretion of aldosterone by the adrenal cortex), it is referred to as secondary hypertension. While, when the cause of hypertension cannot be clearly defined, it is classified as essential hypertension.

Etiology of Hypertension :

The various factors which contribute to less or more extent to the state of hypertension can be classified as -

(a) Neural factors
(b) Hormonal factors
(c) Electrolyte factors
(d) Vessel wall factors, and
(e) Genetic factors.

(a) Neural factors : Stress or emotions causing excessive sympathetic outflow from the brain may result into an increased cardiac output and elevated peripheral resistance. The overproduction or incomplete destruction of sympathomimetic amines may further contribute to the elevated peripheral resistance. The abnormal levels of norepinephrine, epinephrine, adrenaline, dopamine and serotonin may play a peripheral as well as a central role in activation of vasomotor tone. Usually agents which block the effects of sympathomimetic amines are useful to treat hypertension caused by neural factors.

(b) Hormonal factors : Renin, a proteolytic enzyme found primarily in the kidney is released in response to lowered perfusion pressure and low sodium states of the circulating blood. It catalyses the conversion of Angiotensinogen to Angiotensin I (decapeptide). The latter is rapidly converted in the plasma by a chloride activated enzyme (primarily in the lungs) to Angiotensin II (octapeptide). Angiotensin II has three fold action.

(i) It constricts the arterial network to increase peripheral resistance.

(ii) It slowly triggers the release of aldosterone which in turn, increases sodium retention and plasma volume.

(iii) It causes an excessive release of catecholamines from adrenal medulla and from peripheral sympathetic nerves, resulting into an increase in cardiac output. The renin-angiotensin-aldosterone system thus affects all three primary factors which can cause hypertension, like

(a) Blood vessel constriction,
(b) Increased blood volume, and
(c) Increased cardiac output.

Though elevated renin-angiotensin levels appear to play a critical role in severe hypertension, other hormones and vasopressor substances may sometimes be important like arachidonic acid metabolites, prostaglandins, corticoids, kinins, vasopressin and some yet unidentified hormones. Prostaglandins (PGA, PGE) for example, cause a fall in blood pressure and renal dilation. They also initiate the release of renin by a central effect on the vagus.

(c) Electrolyte factors : The inability of the kidney to excrete an adequate daily amount of salt and water results into abnormal retention of salt and water in the blood which causes an increase in the blood volume. The net result is an increase in the workload on the heart. The blood potassium and blood selenium level may also play an etiological role in hypertension along with other dietary and environmental factors.

(d) Vessel wall factors : The vascular smooth muscles are highly sensitive to changes in the cardiac output. Hence, increased perfusion pressure due to increased cardiac output leads to structural changes (like wall thickening and hypertrophy of vasculature) in the blood vessels. The direct acting vasodilators, hence may be of value in this type of hypertension.

(e) Genetic factors : The increased sensitivity and susceptibility to various etiologic factors (which are mentioned above) by offsprings of hypertensives underlies the importance of hereditary factors in hypertension.

Classification :

All currently available antihypertensive drugs acts mainly by interfering with normal hemostatic mechanisms and this provides a useful basis for the classification of these drugs. They are classified as :

(1) Drugs that alter central sympathetic nervous system activity.

e.g. Methyldopa, Clonidine.

(2) Adrenergic receptor blockers

(a) β-adrenergic blockers

e.g. Propranolol, Metaprolol

(b) α-adrenergic blockers

e.g. Phentolamine

(3) Drugs that act at postganglionic sympathetic nerve endings.

e.g. Resperpine, MAO inhibitors.

(4) Drugs that interfere with the Renin Angiotensin system.

e.g. Captopril, Saralasin.

(5) Vasodilators :

(a) Arteriolar :

e.g. Hydralazine

(b) Arteriolar and Venular

e.g. Nitroprusside, Prazosin

(I) Drugs that Alter Central Sympathetic Nervous System Activity :

(a) Drugs affecting the norepinephrine pathway : These drugs produce their hypotensive action by affecting the biosynthesis, storage, metabolism and release of catecholamines (norepinephrine) at the postganglionic presynaptic nerve terminals.

α-Methyldopa : Its antihypertensive activity is attributed to its *in-vivo* metabolite, α-methylnorepinephrine which acts as a false transmitter (a weaker agonist of neurotransmitter, norepinephrine) centrally as well as peripherally.

It is used to treat moderate to severe essential hypertension. It does produce tolerance and its effects may be potentiated by thiazide diuretics.

Other compounds of interest from this category are :

Metaraminol : It is a metabolite of α-methyl-m-tyrosine. It causes a gradual lowering of blood pressure by replacing norepinephrine in sympathetic neurones.

Methyloctopamine : It is a para isomer of metaraminol.

(b) Dopamine - β - hydroxylase Inhibitors : Dopamine - β - hydroxylase enzyme catalyses the conversion of dopamine to norepinephrine. The agents from this class inhibit the enzyme, which results into decreased norepinephrine synthesis. e.g. Fusaric acid.

(c) Monoamine oxidase inhibitors : The intracellular norepinephrine is metabolised (N-deamination; oxidation to aldehyde) by MAO. Inhibition of MAO prolongs the level and action of intracellular norepinephrine which causes a negative feedback on norepinephrine synthesis or by accumulation of false transmitter amines peripherally. e.g. pargyline.

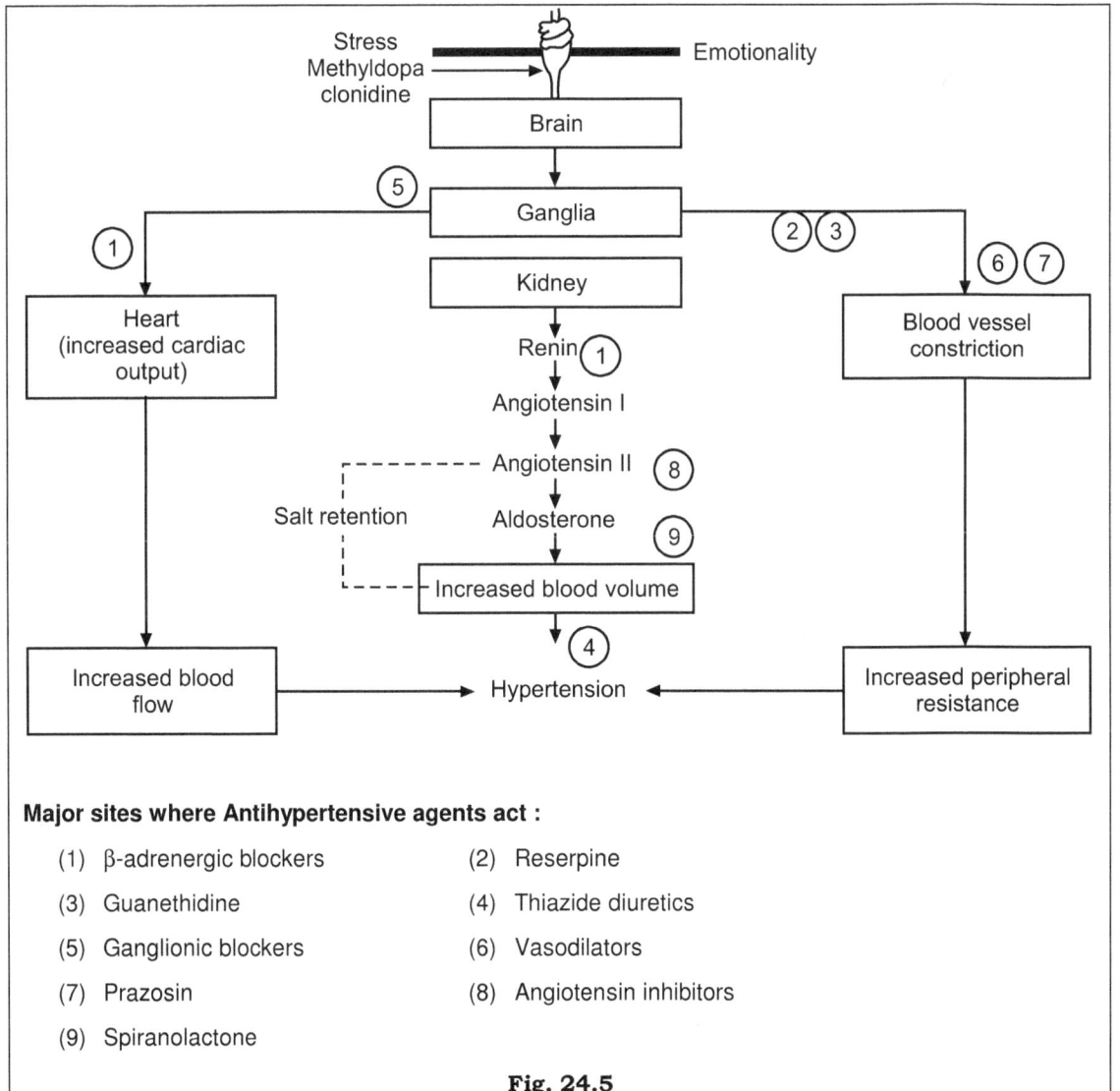

Major sites where Antihypertensive agents act :

(1) β-adrenergic blockers   (2) Reserpine
(3) Guanethidine   (4) Thiazide diuretics
(5) Ganglionic blockers   (6) Vasodilators
(7) Prazosin   (8) Angiotensin inhibitors
(9) Spiranolactone

Fig. 24.5

(d) Drugs acting centrally : These drugs act on the central control over sympathetic function e.g. Clonidine.

Clonidine acts directly on the α-adrenergic receptors in the midbrain and hypothalamus region which decreases the sympathetic outflow and causes vasomotor relaxation. As similar to other drugs which act centrally, clonidine and its analogs exert sedation and inhibition of salivation. Other analogs of clonidine are flutonidine, tolonidine, guanabenz and guanafacine.

(II) Drugs Which act Through Vascular Mechanisms :

The relaxation of peripheral arterioles may result into consequent reduction in the peripheral resistance and lowering of blood pressure. This can be achieved by,

(a) Adrenergic receptor blockers.

(b) Vasodilators

(a) Adrenergic receptor blockers :

(i) α–adrenergic receptor blockers : These drugs block the peripheral effects of norepinephrine, thereby reducing the vasoconstriction of vascular smooth muscles. Examples include phentolamine and tolazoline.

(ii) β-adrenergic receptor blockers The agents from this class are dealt in detail, elsewhere in this book (adrenergic drugs).

(b) Vasodilators : The elevated peripheral resistance is the main cause behind most of the hypertensives. These agents act by inducing vascular smooth muscle relaxation, thereby decreasing the peripheral resistance without having any action over sympathetic nervous system. Example, include sodium nitroprusside, diazoxide, hydralazine, hydrocarbazine, minoxidil, nifedipine, etc.

(III) Drugs that Act at Postganglionic Sympathetic Nerve Endings :

Among the various alkaloids from the different species of Rauwolfia, reserpine is the only one widely used antihypertensive agent today.

Reserpine produces autonomic suppression by depletion of norepinephrine and serotonin stores in central and peripheral sympathetic neurons.

The active transport of norepinephrine back to the tissue storage sites is inhibited by reserpine which results in its rapid inactivation by intraneuronal monoamine oxidases. Similar drug, deserpidine lacks the 11-OCH_3 group of reserpine but produces the same degree of hypotensive activity.

(IV) Drugs that Interfere with the Renin-Angiotensin System :

The renin-angiotensin system is involved in the action of nearly all major classes of antihypertensive drugs and its control is important to the success of any antihypertensive therapy. The drugs from this class can be divided as :

(a) Inhibitors of Angiotensin converting enzyme : e.g. captopril.

(b) Angiotensin II Antagonists : e.g. Saralasin (a peptide analog of angiotensin) is a specific and competitive antagonist of angiotesin II.

(c) Aldosterone Antagonist : Spiranolactone, prorenoate and canrenoate are clinically useful agents from this category.

ANTI-ANGINAL AGENTS

25.1 INTRODUCTION

Due to continuous activity, muscles regardless of their nature, require a constant supply of energy. Specifically the oxygen needs of cardiac muscles are relatively higher. Unlike skeletal muscles, the cardiac muscles normally extract almost all the available oxygen (approximately 75 – 80%) from the blood at rest. Hence there is no scope for extraction of more oxygen under the conditions of increased metabolic demand unless the coronary blood flow is increased. These conditions stimulate carotid sinus mechanisms to increase blood supply to the heart. The oxygen thus extracted, is utilized to generate high-energy phosphates. The rate of formation of such high-energy phosphates is increased to meet the demands of heart.

Under the conditions of strain or stress, the rate and force of heart contraction increase which results into an increase in arterial pressure and/or ventricular volume. This increase in the work-load of the heart requires the generation of more amount of energy. This can be fulfilled by increasing the coronary blood flow. This coronary vascular resistance is a limiting factor which is governed by autonomic activity, accumulation of metabolite products and mechanical obstruction in the large coronary arteries. The presence of coronary artery disease can severely limit such an increase in blood supply to the heart. Thus, an atherosclerotic coronary artery disease will result into

(a) an inadequate nutrient and oxygen supply to the cardiac muscles,

(b) decrease in the generation of high energy phosphates, and

(c) accumulation of local metabolites in the striated muscles.

Under these conditions the tone of smooth muscle in the large epicardial coronary arteries increases that results into irregular and nonlinear coronary blood flow coupled with coronary artery spasm. The discomfort becomes more evident under the conditions of exertion or emotional stress and can be relieved by rest or by drug therapy. However even in the absence of any therapy, these symptoms are partly relieved after some time due to autoregulatory dilation (of limited extent) of coronary arteries. This autoregulation is brought about by accumulated local metabolites resulting into curing of temporary ischemia of the myocardium. This leads to restoration of the blood flow through an increase in the arterial diameter.

If autoregulation fails to maintain adequate blood supply to the heart (probably because of atherosclerotic coronary artery disease), the symptoms persist and get manifested by sudden, severe substernal pain which often radiates to the left shoulder and along the flexor surface of the left arm. This temporary myocardial ischemia sometimes results into breathlessness and a sense of discomfort of cardiac origin. The word, angina pectoris (angina meaning to choke) is used to describe all above symptoms. It is not a disease but the characteristic pain due to ischemia resulting from the relative hypoxia of the myocardium. The reflex vasospasm of coronary arteries appears to be a primary cause which may be intensified by the presence of atherosclerotic coronary artery disease. The atherosclerosis, if remains untreated for longer time, may result into collateral vessel growth alongwith interruption of coronary blood flow.

The imbalance between the coronary blood flow and metabolic requirements of myocardium results in the temporary myocardial ischemia. This can be relieved by either :

(a) increasing the coronary blood flow, or
(b) decreasing the metabolic demands for oxygen.

Numerous drugs are available which act through either of the above mechanisms. However nitrites, vasodilators and β-adrenoceptor blocking agents are most useful antianginal drugs. Beside them, xanthines (aminophyllenes), papaverine, heparin and MAO-inhibitors can also be tried. Certain factors like cigarette smoking, excessive intake of caffeine containing beverages, obesity, increased serum cholesterol level, hypertension and diabetes mellitus are also known to potentiate the symptoms of angina pectoris. Beside these, exercise, strain, stress, cold or meals are reported to assist the anginal attacks. Hence precautions are to be taken to lower down the potency of these risk factors, and measures are also to be taken to reduce the cardiac work-load and to prevent arterial degeneration.

25.2 TYPES OF ANGINA PECTORIS

Three different types of anginal attacks have been recognized. This categorization is based upon the differences in the cause and symptoms. These types of angina include,

(a) Classical angina : This type of anginal attack occurs mainly due to physical exertion or mental stress and hence it is also known as angina of efforts. In most of the cases atherosclerotic coronary artery disease is also a contributing factor.

(b) Unstable angina : In this type, atherosclerotic coronary artery disease is the prominent cause. The characteristic feature however, is that the attack is accompanied by vasospasm.

(c) Prinzmetal's or varient angina : Both the above types of anginal attacks can be relieved by rest. However varient anginal attacks may be seen at rest, usually in the morning. This is an example of anginal attack seen in patients who are free from atherosclerotic coronary stenosis.

25.3 NITRITES AND NITRATES

These agents are esters of polyalcohols with nitric acid (nitrates) and nitrous acid (nitrites). Organic nitrates and a group of inorganic and organic nitrites are included under this category of antianginal drugs Nitro compounds however are devoid of antianginal activity. Nitroglycerin was the first member of the series clinically introduced in 1879 by **William Murrell** for the relief of anginal pain. It was used as an explosive in its pure form. The other members of this series have similar pharmacological properties and differ only in potency, rate of onset and duration of action.

Pharmacology :

These drugs markedly reduce the tone of smooth muscle contraction. Since the effect on vascular smooth muscles is more pronounced the bronchial and gastrointestinal system can be protected by adjusting the dose. At therapeutic doses, these agents do not interfere with the functioning of sympathetic or parasympathetic innervation of the smooth muscles.

Their cardiovascular effects are more pronounced. The dilation of both, arterial and venous smooth muscles is brought about resulting into decrease in blood pressure and decreased venous return. The reduction in the ventricular afterload results into decrease in myocardial oxygen consumption. Additionally the dilation of large coronary arteries further improves the myocardial blood supply to relieve ischemia. The decrease in systemic and pulmonary arteriolar resistance results into a fall in blood pressure which is reflected into weakness, dizziness and activation of reflex compensatory mechanisms. The activation of baroreceptor and other reflexes occurs leading to tachycardia and an increase in heart contraction.

Since capillaries do not have smooth muscles, they remain unaffected. However the capillary blood flow is increased indirectly by relaxation of precapillary sphincters.

These agents do not exert direct antianginal effects in patients with angina due to atherosclerosis. In such case they do not cause the coronary artery dilation. However the myocardial ischemia is relieved by redistribution of coronary blood supply to the ischemic regions of the heart.

The pressure of cerebrospinal fluid in brain is reported to increase by nitrites due to dilation of smaller vessels of menings which often results in an intense headache. Similarly intraocular pressure is also found to increase due to dilation of retinal and other intraocular vessels.

Mechanism of Action :

The mechanisms of action of nitrites and nitrates are similar. Infact nitrates have to converted *in-vivo* to nitrites to exert antianginal effects. In smooth muscle cell, these agents get denitrated to release nitrite ions (NO_2^-). This nitrite ion then interacts with receptor site having sulfhydryl prosthetic group. Yet another mechanism proposed for the action of nitrites involves the production of prostaglandins (e.g. prostacyclin as an intermediate step.

The widely accepted mechanism is based upon the generation of free nitric oxide (NO) radicals which activate guanylate cyclase enzyme resulting into an increase in the rate of formation of c-GMP. The accumulation of c-GMP then brings about relaxation of smooth muscles of all types of vessels through dephosprorylation of light chain of myosin in smooth muscles. The effect is more pronounced in vascular smooth muscles. In the case of rapidly acting amyl nitrite, the arterial dilation is so marked that reflex vasoconstriction usually results.

Pharmacokinetics :

The bioavailability of all orally administered nitrites and nitrates is very poor (about 10%) mainly due to extensive first pass metabolism in the liver. Hence to be effective orally, the drug has to be given in quite high doses. The sublingual route therefore, is the preferred route for most of these agents which are directly absorbed into the circulation, eliminating detoxification in liver. For example, nitroglycerin has a very rapid onset of action (3 — 5 minutes) by sublingual route. Isosorbide dinitrate is available in sublingual as well as chewable and oral tablets. Nitroglycerin can be absorbed through intact skin. It is also available in the ointment form. Other nitrites like, sodium nitrite and mannitol hexanitrate are partly absorbed through GI tract. Amyl nitrite and related nitrites are highly volatile liquids. Hence they are usually administered by inhalation route to provide very rapid absorption eliminating the first pass metabolism in liver. Isosorbide dinitrate, pentaerythritol tetranitrate and erythrityl tetranitrate are the examples of longer acting organic nitrates.

In the liver these agents are denitrated by glutathione-organic nitrate reductase enzyme. Nitroglycerine is completely broken in the body and mixtures of nitrites and nitrates are eliminated. The partially and fully denitrated metabolites are having much longer half lives but are less active vasodilators. About 70% of absorbed nitrite ions disappears from the body in the form of ammonia and rest is eliminated through urine. The denitrated metabolites are also excreted through urine in the form of glucuronides.

Amyl nitrate is administered by inhalation route. It is readily absorbed from lungs into the circulation. Liver partly destroys it and the drug is partly excreted in unchanged form.

Adverse Effects :

(a) **Headache :** It is the most common adverse effect to nitrites. A transient, throbbing sensation in the head appears to be due to dilation of meningeal vessels which leads to an increase in cerebrospinal pressure. It is more common with longer acting nitrites. Headache usually gets disappear with repeated administration or also can be controlled by aspirin.

(b) The increase in intraoccular pressure may cause glaucoma.

(c) Nitrite ion can oxidise ferrous ions (hemoglobin) to the ferric ion form (methemoglobin) which lacks the ability to carry oxygen. Hence when about 10% of this conversion takes place, a cynotic tinge to the skin (pseudocyanosis) may develop. Anaemia results due to less ability of blood to carry oxygen.

(d) The postural hypotension coupled with cerebral ischemic may result into dizziness fainting and weakness. Marked hypotension occurs if nitrites are given with antihypertensive agents.

(e) Nausea, vomiting, involuntary passage of urine and faeces are the symptoms seen due to activation of central vagal nuclei by hypoxia.

(f) The hypotension resulting from an exaggerated response to nitrites is usually accompanied by reflex tachycardia.

(g) Tolerance to various pharmacological actions (including adverse effects) of nitrites usually develops upon chronic administration due to alteration in the functioning of the guanylate cyclase-c-GMP system. This can be avoided either by using lowest effective dose possible or by shifting to other alternative drug therapy. However the nitrite should not be suddenly withdrawn which may otherwise leads to severe coronary vasospasm. This is so probably because the ischemic myocardial regions may get sensitized in the absence of the drug.

Beside having antianginal activity, nitrites can also be used to treat biliary spasm and that of urinary tract.

25.4 β-ADRENOCEPTOR BLOCKING AGENTS

During the conditions of physical exercise and mental strain, the sympathetic drive to the heart increases, thus resulting into an increase in cardiac work. The myocardial oxygen demand increases in response to an increase in the rate and force of heart contraction induced by noradrenaline. The β-adrenoceptor blocking agents act by reducing the cardiac work through antagonising sympathetic drive to heart. The myocardial oxygen demand sharply declines due to their ability to reduce rate and force of heart contraction. Thus, these agents do not act by increasing coronary blood flow; instead the myocardial oxygen demand is decreased. Hence they are useful in management of stable angina pectoris. But in vasospastic angina, their effectiveness is markly affected due to coronary vasoconstriction induced by unopposed α-adrenoceptor activation. However in such cases, the vasoconstrictor and bronchoconstrictory effects can be minimised by using cardioselective β_1 - adrenoceptor blocking agents (e.g. metaprolol, atenolol etc.) in low doses. Due to antagonising effects at both α-and β-receptors, labetalol is more effective antianginal agent but it has less effect on heart rate.

Beside β-adrenoceptor blocking action, in some cases beneficial effects are also brought about by these agents by causing redistribution of coronary blood flow to the ischemic regions of the heart. These agents when combined with nitrites will markly inhibit activation of reflex compensatory mechanism like, reflux tachycardia. The additive antianginal effect of both these categories of drugs helps to lower down the effective dose of nitrites.

Though propranolol is the most widely used agent from this category, other agents can also be used considering the details about their duration of action, selectivity of action and adverse effects associated. The details about these factors have been described elsewhere.

The commonly occuring adverse effects of β-adrenoceptor blocking agents include nausea, dizziness, fatigue, mental depression, light headedness, peripheral edema, A.V. block, bradycardia and orthostatic hypotension. The CNS adverse effects can be minimized by the use of less lipophilic agents like, atenolol or nadolol. While in patients with any cardiac dysfunction, partial agonists (i.e. blockers with considerable intrinsic activity) of adrenaline can be used. The treatment with β-adrenoceptor blocking agents should not be suddenly discontinued due to the risk of pronounced rebound effect.

25.5 CALCIUM CHANNEL BLOCKING AGENTS

Good vasodilatory agents may not necessarily act as good antianginal agents. Ischemia itself induces maximum coronary vasodilation through autoregulatory mechanisms. The directly acting (e.g. hydralazine) vasodilators do not dilate coronary artery, but exert antianginal action probably by causing redistribution of coronary blood flow to the myocardial ischemic regions. The directly acting vasodilators and α_1-adrenoceptor blocking agents are more specifically useful in the treatment of vascular insufficiency in the limbs.

Vasodilation induced by calcium-channel blocking agents however relieve the symptoms of anginal attack by acting at both,

(a) myocardial cell level through the interference in the contraction-relaxation process. The myocardial oxygen consumption is decreased due to reduction in myocardial contractility, and

(b) vascular smooth muscle level through the inhibition of intracellular transport of calcium resulting into vasodilation.

Papaverine is a vasodilator having smooth muscle relaxant property. Verapamil has been developed in order to obtain a more potent analogue of papaverine. The R (+) isomer of verapamil has much lower potency than the S (–) isomer. Nifedipine, verapamil and diltiazem are the most commonly used calcium-channel blocking agents. All these agents are no way structurally related to each other. They act principally by inhibiting the entry of calcium ions into the cells or preventing their mobilization from intracellular storage sacs resulting into decreased intracellular Ca^{++} - level.

Pharmacology :

They exert relaxant effects mainly on arterial smooth muscles while venous circulation (i.e. heart pre-load) remains unaffected. The relaxation of arterial smooth muscles results in decrease in systemic vascular resistance. All these agents can cause hypotension. The reflex sympathetic compensatory mechanisms get activated due to decrease in arterial blood pressure resulting into tachycardia which is more evident with nifedipine.

These agents increase coronary blood flow through dilation of coronary arteries. The coronary resistance decreases and myocardial oxygen supply increases. Nifedipine is the most potent coronary artery dilator in the series. It also produces a greater degree of systemic vasodilation.

The inhibition of influx of calcium ions into the cardiac cell results in interference in myocardial excitation-relaxation process. The myocardial oxygen consumption is lowered down due to a decrease in the rate and force of myocardial contractivity. Verapamil exerts greater decrease in myocardial constractility than nifedipine while diltiazem is the least potent in this regard.

Mechanism of Action :

The depolarization process, in myocardium and smooth muscle cells requires the influx of extracellular calcium ions through voltage sensitive calcium channels. This calcium after reaching into the cytoplasm induces the release of intracellular calcium from the storage sacs present on sarcoplasmic reticulum. In smooth muscles, the contractile process is initiated by phosphorylation of the light chain of myosin mediated by Ca^{++} calmodulin complex. While in myocardial cell, the Ca^{++} influx through slow channels results into development of spike-action potential needed for myocardial contraction. Hence a decrease in intracellular Ca^{++} concentration will bring about both, relaxation of smooth muscles and myocardial cells. The effect is more pronounced on vascular smooth muscles resulting into decrease in peripheral vascular resistance. However bronchial, gastrointestinal and uterine smooth muscles are also get relaxed. These agents do not affect the tone of skeletal muscle contraction since the extracellular calcium influx is not necessary for contraction of skeletal muscles.

These agents block the calcium channels in depolarized membranes through binding from inner side of the membrane. The vascular effects are more pronounced on arteries than veins. The calcium channel blockade by these agents is relieved either by increasing the concentration of calcium or by administration of drugs which increase the transmembrane transport of calcium ions. Due to decreased peripheral resistance, the blood pressure is reduced. However the therapy is not usually associated with orthostatic hypotension. They are useful specifically in the treatment of varient angina due to their ability to relieve focal coronary artery spasm.

The inhibition of transmembrane calcium flux by these agents also results in inhibition of secretory events in glands and nerve ending usually at higher doses, e.g. insulin release is hampered. In *in-vitro* studies their ability to interfere with platelet aggregation is also reported.

Verapamil and diltiazem produce less hypotension but markly depress S.A. node and A.V. nodal conduction. Hence these are drugs of choice in patients with arterial flutter or fibrillation. However due to their myocardial depressant effects, they should not be concomittently administered with β-blockers in patients with myocardial dysfunction. Nifedipine, on the contrary does not depress myocardial functioning *and can be* used in combination therapy with β-blockers.

Pharmacokinetics :

Like nitrites, these agents exhibit an extensive first pass metabolism in liver upon oral administration. Nifedipine usually is given sublingually where the absorption is quick and almost complete. The N– or O– dealkylation is the main metabolizing pathway which converts parent drugs into inactive products. The phenolic metabolites undergo glucuronidization and then get excreted through urine.

Adverse Effects :

The excessive vasodilation induced by these agents is responsible for occurance of adverse effects like, headache, dizziness, flushing, peripheral edema and hypotension. The effects are more pronounced with nifedipine due to its greater vasodilatory ability. The peripheral edema caused by these agents can be reduced by concomittent administration of a diuretic agent.

Due to its greater vasodilatory ability, nifedipine exerts intense hypotension which is usually accompanied by reflex tachycardia. However nifedipine does not depress myocardial functioning.

Verapamil and diltiazem cause bradycardia and depress A.V. conduction and ventricular functions. Hence their use is contraindicated in the patients on β-blocker therapy. If used in combination therapy, they augment the negative chronotropic effects of β-blockers and may prove dangerous in patients with cardiac dysfunction.

Besides their use in angina pectoris, calcium channel blocking agents can also be used in the therapy of hypertension, cardiac arrhythmias, migraine headache, and premature labour.

25.6 OTHER ANTIANGINAL AGENTS

(a) Papaverine : As we know, ischemic myocardium itself acts as a stimulus for the dilation of coronary arteries. This autoregulation is brought about by local release of adenosine by ischemic myocardium. However this adenosine concentration which is responsible for coronary artery dilation, is gradually lowered down due to its uptake by erythrocytes and other cells. Papaverine is found to inhibit phosphodiesterase activity and adenosine uptake process in the muscle cells. It is also used to dilate the blood vessel wall in the embolization in the limbs.

Dipyradamole is yet another drug acting similar to papaverine. It is also found to potentiate prostacyclin action.

(b) Aminophylline : It is a theophylline derivative having antispasmodic and diuretic actions. It stimulates respiration and partly relieves some of the symptoms of angina. Excitation of vagus may cause bradycardia.

(c) MAO - inhibitors : These drugs do not cure the basic cause in angina but exert analgesic effect to relieve anginal pain. Since pain sensation acts as an important signal to the patient about the limitation of his heart functioning, by using MAO-inhibitor the patient may lose this signal. Hence, some people have criticized the use of MAO-inhibitors in angina.

Other miscellaneous drugs which can be used in the treatment of angina include, isoxsuprine, nylidrin, cyclandelate, nicotinic - acid and nicotinyl alcohol.

25.7 COMBINATION THERAPY

Nitrites, β-adrenoceptor blocking agents and calcium channel blockers are the prominent categories of antianginal drugs. Each of them act by different mechanisms. For example, nitrites preferably reduce preload and calcium channel blockers reduce afterload of the heart. While β-blocking agents decrease the rate and force of heart contraction. Hence, if the drugs from two different categories are used concurrently, the effective minimum dose for each drug can be minimized. This will result into reduction in frequency and intensity of adverse effects of the drugs used. For example, if used individually,

(a) Nitrite therapy will induce reflex tachycardia and an increase in the force of heart contraction.

(b) β–blocking agents induce constriction of coronary arteries due to unopposed α-adrenoceptor activation. Similarly they depress myocardial contraction process resulting into a decrease in rate and force heart contraction, and

(c) In calcium channel blockers, except nifedipine, other members depress S.A. node, A.V. nodal conduction and ventricular functioning.

Thus, nitrites can be combined

together with β-blocking agents where mutual benefits are reflected in inhibition of :

(i) coronary vaso constriction by nitrites and

(ii) reflex tachycardia by β-blockers.

If β-blocker is to be combined with calcium channel blocking agent, nifedipine is a drug of choice because it lacks myocardial depressant activity.

25.8 GENERAL MEASURES

Longer acting organic nitrates may be used as prophylaxis. If tolerance develops to the drug action, other short acting agents are useful. When anginal attack appears to be due to mental strain, sedatives give better results. In severe cases, anticoagulant therapy or surgical procedures can be employed.

Besides the drug therapy, certain general measures are indicated in the treatment of angina patients to reduce the cardiac work load and to prevent further arterial degeneration. The load on the heart can be reduced by :

(i) Correcting any obesity by avoiding heavy meals.

(ii) Avoiding situations that leads to mental strain.

(iii) Lowering of plasma levels of cholesterol and triglycerides, and

(iv) Avoiding excess of exercise and excessive work.

ANTI-ARRHYTHMIC AGENTS

26.1 INTRODUCTION

In order for the heart to function as an efficient pump, the various contractile units must operate in a co-ordinated or rhythmic fashion. The generation of cardiac impulses in the normal heart is usually confined to specialized tissues that spontaneously depolarize and initiate an impulse. These cells are located in the right atrium and are referred to as S.A. node or normal pacemaker cells. It is a self excitatory in nature and sends out the impulses rhythmically which spread through the atria causing atrial contraction or atrial systole.

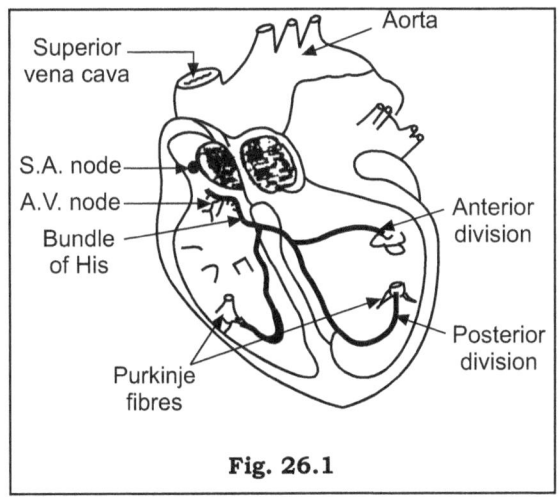

Fig. 26.1

Since the atria must contract and release their contents before the ventricles commence their contraction, the atria and ventricles must be separated from each other by a layer of non-conductive tissue, except for one small region that conducts an impulse slowly and functions as a delay circuit. This region is called as A.V. node (i.e. atrioventricular node).

The signal generator (S.A. node) continuously intiates the impulses in a co-ordinated fashion which are received by A.V. node that after a short delay sends, an excitation wave through the His – Purkinje system to the ventricular muscles resulting into ventricular contraction or ventricular systole. Here the A.V. node functions as a filtration unit for the impulses generated by S.A. node. It will allow the passage of only such number of impulses that would be needed for proper contraction of the ventricular muscles. The events are represented in the figure 26.2. In most of the cardiac cells, phase 0 is generated by the rapid inward movement of extracellular Na^+ ions through channels that selectively allow permeation of these ions. The phase 4, when reaches to threshold potential, results into the opening of 'm' gates for sodium ions. The inward sodium current is very intense but very brief and leads to the phase of depolarization (phase 0). It is terminated by the process called as inactivation, i.e. the closing of ion channels for sodium. The Na^+ channels can not be reopened until it is reactivated again when the propogation of second impulse touches the threshold potential.

Following depolarization, commences the phase of repolarization. It is characterised by

(a) Phase 1 : Closure of the fast inward Na^+ current and an influx of chloride ions.

(b) Phase 2 : The plateau of the action potential is due to a prolonged repolarisation. It is one of the most unusual characteristic of cardiac action potential. Here slow influx of Ca^{++} ions occurs.

(c) Phase 3 : This occurs as a result of the closing of slow inward channels for Na^+ and Ca^{++} ions and opening of one or two fast outward channels for K^+ ions. This time-dependent outward K^+ current causes the fibre to repolarize to normal diastolic value of V_m.

With the end of phase 3 of repolarisation, the transmembrane potential is restored again back to -80 mV (Phase 4) until again activated by a propogating impulse.

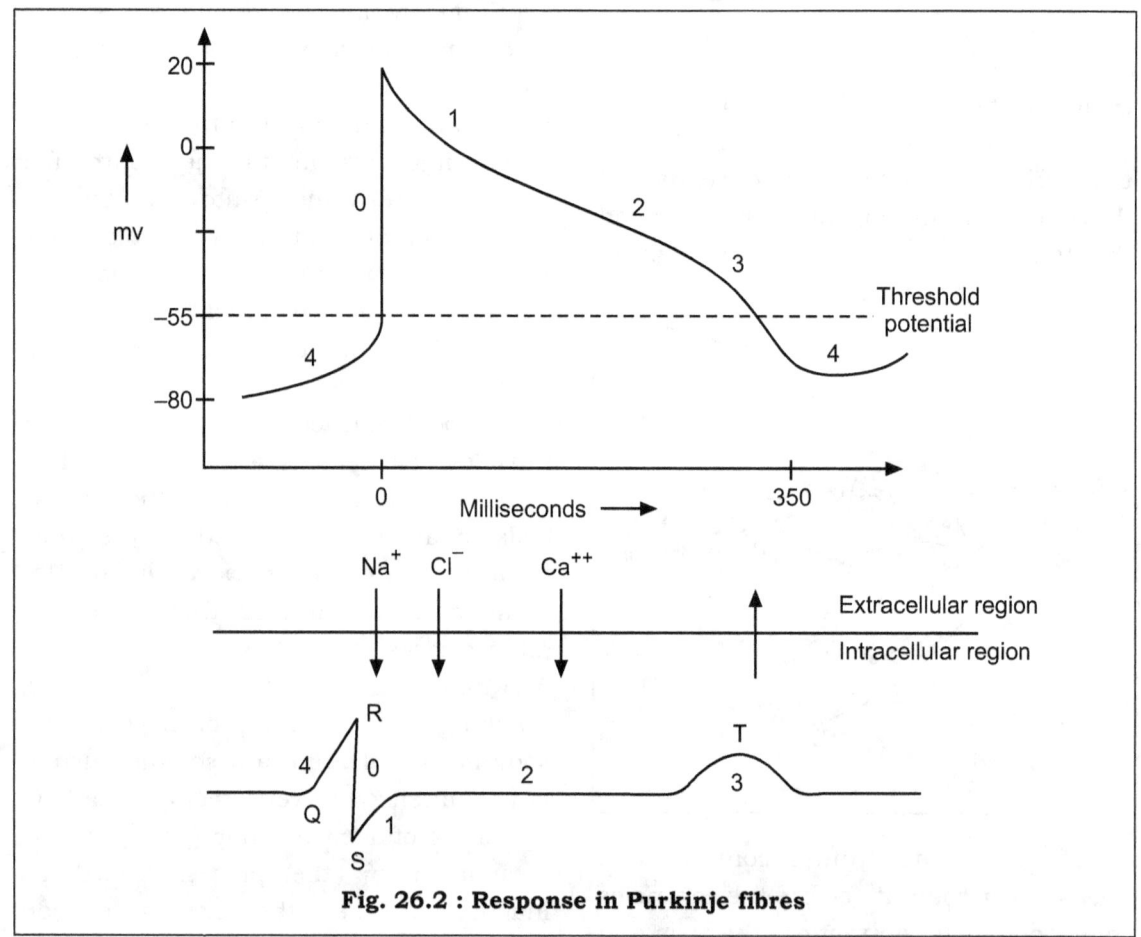

Fig. 26.2 : Response in Purkinje fibres

However many cardiac cells differ from Purkinje fibres in the pattern of development of action potential as shown in the Fig. 26.3. The phase of depolarization (Phase 0) is neither stiff nor intense and sub-phases of repolarisation are difficult to distinguish from each other. Such type of pattern can be seen in the cells of S.A. node and A.V. node region.

Except in S.A. node and in A.V. node, the interval between two successive impulses is considerable and it is known as effective refractory period. The excitability (intensity of an impulse to cause contraction) and automaticity (ability to generate impulse) are the important factors that govern the rhythmic contraction of the heart.

Though the spontaneous electrical depolarization of S.A. node cells is independent of the nervous system, these cells are innervated by both sympathetic and para sympathetic nerves, which may cause an increase or decrease of the heart rate, respectively. Other special cells in the normal heart which possess the property of automaticity (secondary pacemaker) may influence cardiac rhythm when the normal pacemaker is supressed or when pathological changes occur in the myocardium to make these cells the dominant source of cardiac rhythm. This is specifically true when myocardial cell damage occurs due to localized myocardial disease (infarction). Cardiac rhythm also changes under certain conditions such as digitalis toxicity, excessive vagal tone or high catecholamine plasma concentration.

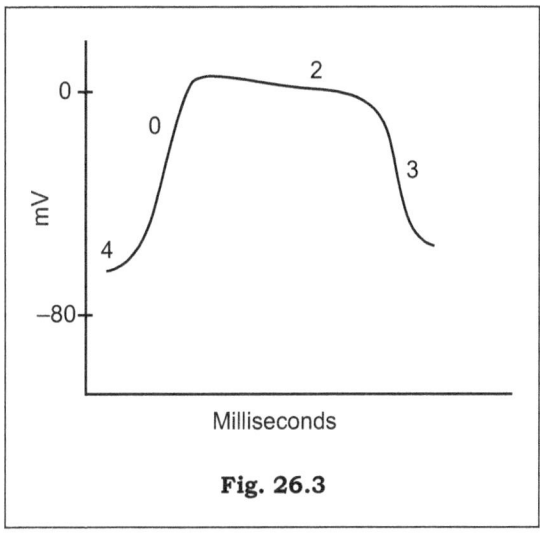

Fig. 26.3

The development of automaticity or increase in excitability in these secondary pacemaker cells (e.g. special artrial cells, certain A.V. nodal cells, His-Purkinje system) may lead to disturbances of rhythm. This is the origin of cardiac arrhythmia. For example, the rate of impulse generation (automaticity) increases under the conditions of anaemia, fever, hyperthyroidism or excessive catecholamine release from sympathetic nerves. Due to the catecholamine release, the rate of spontaneous firing substantially increases in the His Purkinje system leading to arrhythmias. These conditions contribute to the development of sinus tachycardia. While the administration of adrenergic β-blocking agents or excessive vagal tone may lead to sinus bradycardia. Increased vagal activity can decrease the intrinsic activity of sinus nodal pacemakers by increasing potassium conductance resulting into their hyperpolarization. The latter effect is more evident in trained athletes.

Thus, an arrhythmia may arise because of alterations in

(a) Automaticity, or
(b) Conduction, or
(c) Refractory period of the myocardial cells.

Alterations in impulse generation (automaticity) give rise to changes in heart rate and to the development of ectopic (abnormal) beats, originating in secondary pacemaker cells. They are classified as :

(a) Abnormal Automaticity :

For most cardiac cells, the resting transmembrane voltage is about – 80 to – 90 mV. When this potential is reduced to less negative values (e.g. – 55 to – 60 mV), spontaneous diastolic depolarization occurs leading to repetitive automatic firing from myocardial cells.

(b) Triggered Activity :

An increase in the excitability of myocardial cells may lead to an interruption by secondary depolarization peaks, in the process of repolarization. When the process of repolarization begins, the membrane potential is again lifted up to cause secondary depolarization. A new impulse is thus generated to excite the neighbouring myocardial cells. If secondary depolarization interrupts the repolarization phase during phase 2 (plateau region), it is known as 'early after depolarization' while if secondary depolarization occurs after repolarization is completed, it is termed as 'delayed after depolarization'. The frequency and intensity of both these types is governed by prior action potential.

In delayed after depolarization, an extra impulse (extrasystole) will be generated only if that secondary depolarization touches to threshold value. If it fails to cross threshold potential (as shown in figure 26.4), that premature depolarization will disappear without any consequences.

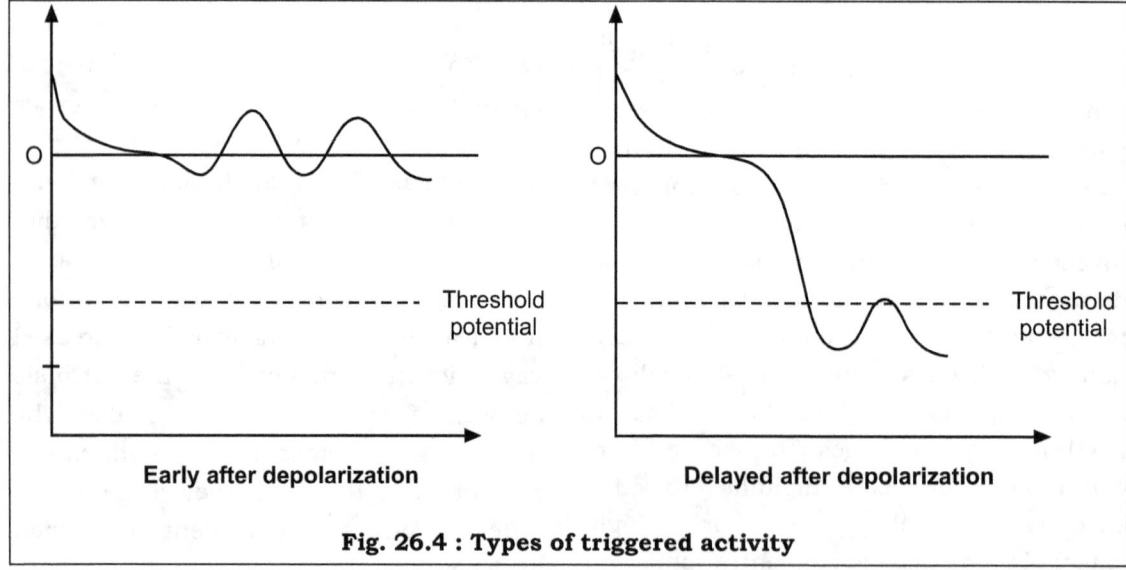

Fig. 26.4 : Types of triggered activity

Abnormalities or disturbances in the conduction of an impulse from atria to ventricles is also a prominent cause in arrhythmias. If it is delayed, a first degree block of conduction results. If it is partially blocked, it is known as a second degree block. While when it is totally arrested, it may result into complete heart block. The block in the conduction may be unidirectional or bidirectional and may lead to reentry or circus movement phenomena. Both reentry and trigger activity are not self-initiated but can be considered as self-sustained events. Any anatomical or functional barrier due to either premature impulse generation or due to any disease condition may induce circus movement. It is equally evident in the regions where conduction is normally very slow (sinus and A.V. node) and regions where conduction proceeds with very high rate (Purkinje fibres). For example atrial flutter is often the consequence of reentry movement. The ectopic focus takes over the function of pacemaker because of its high rate of discharge of impulses. The rate of discharge is rapid but regular while in atrial fibrillation, it is irregular and uncoordinated.

Arrhythmia thus develops due to the disturbances in rate of discharge and / or conduction that cause an alteration in the normal sequence of activation of the atria and ventricles. They are categorised according to the rate, regularity or site of origin of such disturbances. The major antiarrhythmic drugs were introduced into medicine as antimalarials, anticonvulsants or local anaesthetic agents and it was only by chance, that their antiarrhythmic properties were discovered.

26.2 CLASSIFICATION

Based upon mechanism of action, these drugs may be divided into two broad categories :

(a) Those that act specifically by interacting with receptor sites, e.g. adrenoceptor blocking agents, and

(b) Those that act nonspecifically by accumulation in membranes e.g. quinidine lidocaine etc.

The present classification is based upon the site of action and gives more stress upon the electrophysiological properties of these antiarrhythmic agents. Accordingly they are classified as :

Class 1: Membrane - stabilizing agents or sodium channel blocking agents : Quinidine, lidocaine, procainamide, phenytoin, disopyramide, mexiletine, tocainide, encainide, propafenone.

Class 2 : β-adrenergic blocking agents : Alprenolol, metoprolol, propranolol, pindolol etc.

Class 3 : Drugs causing prolonged repolarization and an increase in refractory period : Amiodarone, bretylium, sotalol, clofilium etc.

Class 4 : Calcium channel blockers Verapamil, diltiazem etc.

Just similar to other excitable tissues, action currents in the cardiac muscles are carried by the exchange of sodium and potassium ions but additional and important contribution to the inward flowing current depolarization phase) is made by the movement of

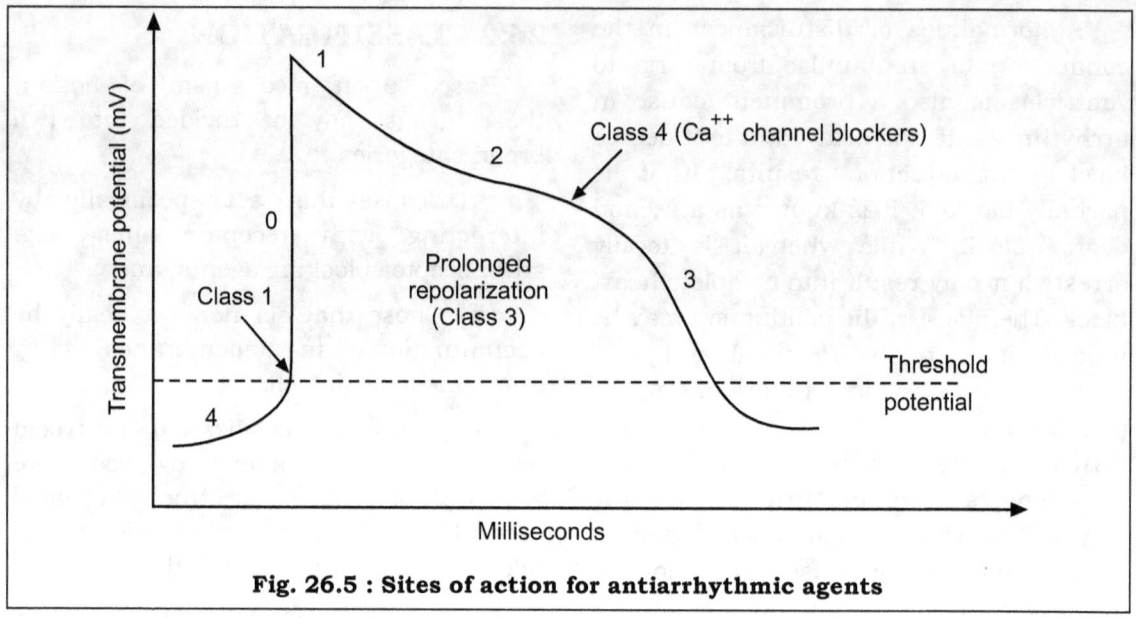

Fig. 26.5 : Sites of action for antiarrhythmic agents

calcium ions. The phase 0 is initiated by an intense but brief inward sodium current. The class 1 antiarrhythmic agents inhibit this sodium influx. This effect (local anaesthetic or quinidine – like effect) results in an increase in the excitability threshold and delayed conduction. This is known as membrane stabilizing effect. Automaticity is also depressed due to their effect on phase 4. However they do not influence the resting membrane potential.

Depending upon their effect on the membrane responsiveness (conduction velocity) and phase of repolarization (refractory period), the class 1 antiarrhythmic agents are further subclassified as :

(i) Class 1a agents : These agents increase the effective refractory period (ERP) resulting into prolongation of QT interval. They include quinidine, procainamide, diisopyramide etc.

(ii) Class 1b agents : These agents do not influence the effective refractory period. Repolarization occurs more quickly. Examples include lidocaine, phenytoin, mexiletine, tocainide etc, and

(iii) Class 1c agents : They act mainly by decreasing conduction velocity and are considered as most potent agents from this class e.g. propafenone, encainide, flecainide etc.

Since the conduction in A.V. node is mainly influenced by autonomic tone, class 1 antiarrhythmic agents are mainly prescribed in the treatment of arrhythmias where A.V. node is not involved. The return of sinus rhythm in atrial flutter or fibrillation is mainly brought about by the use of class 1a antiarrhythmic agents. While class 1 agents are mainly used in the treatment of arrhythmias where reentry is involved because of their effect on conduction velocity.

The resting membrane potential greatly influence the potency of these agents. For example, an antiarrhythmic effect of these drugs will not be seen in hyperpolarization phase (due to low level of extracellular potassium).

Class 2 agent act specifically by antagonising the cardiac effects of catecholamines. They are β-adrenoceptor blocking agents. Hence they will be effective only in the treatment of catecholamine induced arrhythmias, e.g. supraventricular tachyarrhythmias. Thus, they are considered to have narrow spectrum of antiarrhythmic activity. Though inhibition of catecholamine induced hyperactivity is their main mechanism of action, certain members of this class (e.g. propranolol) also exerts *"quinidine-like"* effect at relatively higher concentration.

Class 3 antiarrhythmic agents prolong the phase of repolarization resulting into an increase in effective refractory period. However the resting membrane potential and phase of depolarization remain unaffected. The energy for heart contraction is provided by the hydrolysis of ATP, catalysed by ATPase enzyme which is present in the globular fraction of myocin fibrils. During diastole, this activation is inhibited by the troponin-tropomyosin system. This inhibitory action is blocked by combination of this system with Ca^{++}, for which the system exhibits higher affinity. Hence higher intracellular Ca^{++} concentration will lead to culmination of systolic contraction. The antiarrhythmic effect of Ca^{++} channel blockers result due to their interference with the entry of Ca^{++} into the sarcofibrils through closing of Ca^{++} channels. However nifedipine, a Ca^{++} channel blocking agent does not possess antiarrhythmic property.

These agents block the slow channels of the membrane. The prolongation of conduction time and effective refractory period is more pronounced at A.V. node region. They do not affect the phase of depolarization. Many members of this class also possess antianginal activity, e.g. verapamil, prenylamine.

All these antiarrhythmic agents regardless of their site of action have effect on peripheral blood vessels. With few exceptions, they exert negative inotropic effect on heart and cause peripheral vasodilation. This effect may be short-lived due to reflex activation of sympathetic nervous system. The adverse effects are dependent upon dose, route and duration of administration and disappear upon discontinuation of the therapy.

26.3 QUINIDINE

Quinine and quinidine both are represented by the same structure but differ only in the steric configuration of the secondary alcoholic group present between a quinoline moiety and a quinuclidine ring. Due to the same structural features quinidine retains antimalarial and antipyretic properties of quinine.

Quinidine is the dextrosterioisomer of quinine having a prominent depressant effect on myocardial cells.

Pharmacological Properties :

(a) Cardiovascular effects : In heart, quinidine depresses myocardial automaticity, excitability and raises the value of threshold potential towards less negative side. Through its sodium channel blocking action, the initiation of phase 4 and phase 0 is also delayed resulting into a decrease in the conduction velocity. Thus a decrease in the excitability, membrane responsiveness and conduction velocity makes it an effective drug to control arrhythmia caused by overactivation of atrial, ventricular and Perkinje cells. Through direct and antivagal properties, it prolongs effective refractory period of myocardial cells which qualifies its use in the treatment of reentrant arrhythmias.

It causes a negative inotropic effect and peripheral vasodilation, mainly in venous bed (i.e. venodilation). In patients suffering from coronary artery disease, peripheral vasodilation effect of quinidine may prove to be helpful. This coupled with myocardial depression may result into decreased cardiac output and hypotension. These effects become more evident when quinidine is administered by intravenous route. These effects soon nullified by reflux activation of sympathetic nerves and results into an increase in myocardial contractility.

(b) A.N.S. effects : Like atropine, the myocardial effects of vagal stimulation are antagonized by quinidine. Similarly the peripheral vasodilatory effect is due to its α-adrenergic blocking activity. The overall effect on the A.N.S. results into an increase in the sinus rate and A.V. nodal conduction.

Pharmacokinetic Properties :

For oral administration quinidine is available in its sulphate and gluconate form. However it can be administered intravenously as well as intramuscularly. Its distribution is rapid to all important body compartments, with brain as an exception. The drug is extensively bound (90%) to the plasma proteins. Due to high affinity for hemoglobin, it is also deposited in erythrocytes.

It is extensively metabolized into the liver to different non-phenolic hydroxyl derivatives and their conjugates. Some of these metabolites still retain antiarrhythmic property. These include o-desmethyl quinoline, 3-hydroxyl quinoline and 2'-oxoquinidinone. A small fraction of the administered drug also appears unchanged in the urine. Since it is a weak base, its excretion is facilitated by making the urine acidic.

Adverse Effects :

Most of the antiarrhythmic agents exert adverse effects related to visual, gastrointestinal tract, central nervous system and cardiovascular system but differ in the frequency and intensity of occurrance of these effects. Quinidine is considered as an agent with low safety value. Hence a careful watch and control of a physician is needed during the therapy. Most of the side-effects are dose dependent and may disappear if the therapy is discontinued. They include :

(a) CVS effects : In the overdose or quinidine poisoning, a substantial suppression of conduction in myocardial cells occurs resulting esulting into A.V. block. Ventricular tachyarrhythmia may develop due to enhanced automaticity of Perkinje fibres. The drug and its metabolites can be removed either making the urine acidic or by dialysis.

It suppresses myocardial contractility. This coupled with peripheral vasodilatory effect may lead to hypotension and decrease in coronary blood supply. This effect becomes more pronounced when quinidine is given intravenously.

(b) Gastrointestinal effects : These effect are mild and may disappear after some days of the treatment. They include, nausea, vomiting, diarrhoea and abdominal pain.

(c) Cinchonism : During chronic treatment, the cinchona alkaloids may produce headache, blurred vision, photophobia, psychosis or confusion.

(d) During continued treatment, quinidine may produce hypersensitivity reactions which are characterized by fever, thrombocytopenia and anaphylactic shock.

Quinidine is 6-methoxycinchonine. Cupreidine (6-hydroxy cinchonine) possesses a less degree of adverse effects and has a higher therapeutic margin than quinidine.

Therapeutic Uses :

Quinidine decreases membrane responsiveness, excitability and conduction velocity. It also reduces myocardial contractility. These features entitle the use of quinidine as a broad spectrum antiarrhythmic agent. It is specifically indicated in the treatment of

(a) Paroxysmal supraventricular tachycardia

(b) Ventricular tachyarrhythmias

(c) Digitalis induced arrhythmias.

26.4 PROCAINAMIDE

This drug was developed from the structure of procaine which itself can act as antiarrhythmic agent. However the rapid rate of hydrolysis (short duration of action) and adverse CNS effects of procaine make it unsuitable drug for systemic administration. These drawbacks of procaine were partly overcomed by replacement of ester linkage (in procaine) by an amide linkage (procainamide). Procainamide was introduced in 1950 for the treatment of a variety of arrhythmias and can be administered by different routes. However its clinical utility is again paralyzed by its short duration of action and diversified CNS adverse effects. Hence its chronic administration is not advised on this ground.

Pharmacological Properties :

(a) Cardiac effects : Its effect on automaticity, excitability, membrane responsiveness and conduction velocity does not differ much from those of quinidine. An increase in extracellular K^+ ion concentration leads to pronounciation of cardiac effects of both, quinidine and procainamide. Its antiarrhythmic property is retained by N-acetylprocainamide which is one of the major metabolite of procainamide.

(b) A.N.S. effects : It does not have significant antivagal or α-adrenoceptor blocking activities. However impairment of cardiovascular reflexes occur mainly due to its ganglion blocking property.

Pharmacokinetic Properties :

It is mainly available in the form of its

hydrochloride salt and can be administered orally, intravenously or by intramuscular route. Upon oral administration, absorption is rapid and almost complete. It is weakly bound to plasma proteins. It has easy and rapid access to different body compartments except brain. Because of its quicker elimination from the body, frequent administration of drug is needed.

A larger fraction of administered dose is eliminated unchanged through urine. Liver is the principal site for its metabolism where considerable fraction is metabolized through N-acetylation to give N-acetylprocainamide. This metabolite still retains antiarrhythmic activity and eliminated mainly by renal route. Hence renal impairment may lead to accumulation of both, parent drug and its acetyl metabolite.

Adverse Effects :

The cardiac and extracardiac adverse effects of procainamide are similar to that of quinidine. However the drug may cause ventricular tachyarrhythmias in overdoses. Chronic administration of the drug is accompanied by hypersensitivity reactions due to the development of antinuclear (RNA, DNA) antibodies. An increase in an immunogenicity appears to be resulted due to combination of drug or its metabolite with a nuclear material. This combination acts as antinuclear antibodies and causes fever, agranulocytosis or skin rashes. Agranulocytosis appears to be due to the formation of antileukocyte antibodies or drug-exerted bone marrow toxicity.

However, the adverse effects disappear as the therapy is discontinued or if N-acetylprocainamide is used instead of procainamide. The appearance of low intensity of adverse effects during N-acetylprocainamide therapy seems to be due to regeneration of minute amount of procainamide through deacetylation process in the liver.

Therapeutic Uses :

Procainamide is used to treat a wide variety of arrhythmias. However its clinical utility is limited by its low therapeutic index. In therapeutic doses, it is not effective in the treatment of atrial arrhythmias and digitalis-induced arrhythmias. It is specifically effective and the drug of choice in the treatment of ventricular arrhythmias.

26.5 DISOPYRAMIDE

Introduced in 1978, the drug is used orally in the treatment of ventricular arrhythmias. It has pharmacological properties similar to that of quinidine. However, effects at certain points just vary in intensity, e.g. it substantially raises the refractoriness in atria and ventricular mass but less effective in His-Purkinje fibres. As far as effects on A.N.S. are concerned, it retains antivagal effect of quinidine but is devoid of adrenoceptor blocking activity. Unlike quinidine, this drug causes arteriolar constriction after i.v. administration, resulting into an increase in blood pressure.

Orally it is well absorbed. It is less significantly bound to plasma proteins. The major fraction of the dose administered, is excreted unchanged in urine while a part of the dose metabolises to mono-N-dealkylated derivative as a major metabolite. This metabolite retains antiarrhythmic activity of the parent drug.

Adverse effects are less intense and less frequent. They include, dry mouth, blurred vision, constipation, urinary retention (all due to anticholinergic property of the drug), nausea, vomiting and hypertension. The latter effect is more evident if the drug is administered intravenously.

26.6 LIDOCAINE

First synthesized by **Lofgren**, in 1943, lidocaine was introduced into clinical practice as a local anaesthetic agent. The first report on its cardiac effects was published in 1950. It then became the principal drug of choice in the treatment of ventricular arrhythmias due to high margin of safety and efficacy. Both, onset and termination of antiarrhythmic effect are rapid upon i.v. administration. This property of the drug assists the physician to judge the dose needed for that arrhythmia.

It suppresses automaticity, excitability and conduction velocity. It also prolongs the effective refractory period. In ventricular fibrillation, the drug acts mainly by lifting the threshold potential towards zero. The cardiac effects are more evident in ventricular mass. Since the cardiac effects of lidocaine are use-dependent, its efficacy is lowered down upon chronic administration.

Lidocaine exerts less effects in atria. Hence it is not much effective in the treatment of atrial flutter or atrial fibrillation. It also does not interfere in either sympathetic or vagal tone to the heart.

Lidocaine can not be given orally due to its extensive first pass metabolism in the liver. Nausea, vomiting and abdominal discomfort accompanied with oral administration also serve as the major limitation. Hence, it is available in the form of hydrochloride salt for i.v. route. Hence, even though the arrhythmia is controlled by i.v. administration of lidocaine, one has to dependent upon another orally effective antiarrhythmic agent for the continuation of long term treatment. This problem initiated a search for orally effective derivative of lidocaine which resulted into the introduction of tocainide - an orally effective antiarrhythmic agent of lidocaine family.

The drug binds to plasma proteins to the extent of 60 – 70%. It gets rapidly distributed to different body compartments. In liver, it is extensively metabolized mainly to monoethylcylxyli dine and then to monoethylgly-cinexylidide. The accumulation of latter may result into CNS adverse effects.

Adverse effects are mainly of CNS origin and include, drowsiness, disorientation, muscle twitching, convulsions or respiratory arrest.

26.7 PHENYTOIN

Phenytoin in the form of its sodium salt, is the more widely used drug for all types of epilepsy except petit mal. It was first synthesized by **Biltz** in 1908 and was introduced into clinical practice by Merrit and Putnam in 1938. For the treatment of arrhythmias, the drug can be given orally or by i.v. route. Due to a long elimination half-life of the drug, the therapy is usually initiated with a loading dose.

Its cardiac effects are almost similar to that of lidocaine and are 'more evident in ventricular mass. It shortens the effective refractory period of His-Purkinje system. Like lidocaine, it does not influence peripheral cholinergic or adrenergic nervous system. However centrally, it may decrease efferent sympathetic activity that probably contributes to certain arrhythmias.

On oral administration, absorption of the drug occurs in incomplete and erratic fashion. The drug is extensively bound to plasma proteins. In liver, drug undergoes metabolism to give inactive mono and di-hydroxylated derivatives which are excreted through urine in the form of glucuronides.

Adverse effects of drug therapy include, nausea, vomiting, epigastric pain, anorexia, megaloblastic anaemia, blurred vision, mydriasis, drowsiness, ataxia, hallucinations and behavioural changes.

Like lidocaine, phenytoin is least effective drug to control atrial arrhythmias and used mainly to treat ventricular arrhythmias and arrhythmias induced by digitalis.

26.8 MEXILETINE AND TOCAINIDE HYDROCHLORIDE

Lidocaine can not be orally administered. This drawback was overcomed by the introduction of mexiletine and tocainide. Since both these drugs are the structural relatives of lidocaine, they resemble with lidocaine in their pharmacological profile and therapeutic uses. Chemically mexiletine is 1 (2', 6' - dimethylphenoxy) - 2 - aminopropane while tocainide is the primary amino analog of lidocaine.

Compared to lidocaine, both these drugs have more ability to reduce conduction velocity and to prolong refractory period of the accessory pathways. The depression of conduction results into prevention of reentry or circus movement which is the cause of arrhythmic attacks. They are given either orally or intravenously for the treatment of ventricular arrhythmias that are not responding to other drugs. Unlike quinidine (but like disopyramide) tocainide causes peripheral vasoconstriction. It is also reported to possess antithrombotic effect.

Beside having a local anaesthetic action, mexiletine also inhibits the reuptake process for γ-amino butyric acid, (GABA) which acts as an inhibitory neurotransmitter into the CNS. This results into an accumulation of GABA, leading to CNS depression. However a temporary phase of CNS excitation seen after i.v. administration of the drug may be attributed to its MAO-inhibitory activity.

Both drugs are indicated for the long term oral treatment of ventricular arrhythmias. On oral administration both drugs are rapidly and almost completely absorbed. However there is a difference in the extent of metabolism in liver, e.g. mexiletine is extensively metabolised and only 10 – 15% of the dose administered appears unchanged in the urine while considerable fraction of tocainide escapes the metabolic attack and leaves the body through renal route.

Due to the structural similarity with lidocaine, both these drugs possess similar adverse effects and therapeutic uses to that of lidocaine. However a high frequency of adverse effects are exhibited in the induction phase of mexiletine.

26.9 ENCAINIDE

It is a new benzanilide derivative, structurally related with procainamide, introduced in 1973. Chemically it is 4-methoxy - 2' - [2 - (methyl - 2 - piperidyl) ethyl] benzanilide hydrochloride. Even in very low concentration, it suppresses the conduction, specifically in His-Purkinje system due to the blockade of fast Na^+ ion channels.

It suppresses automaticity and conduction resulting into prevention of reentry circuits. Hence it is effectively used orally to treat fetal ventricular tachycardiac and premature ventricular systoles.

Liver is the principal site for metabolism. Various active metabolites (e.g. 0 - desmethylencainide, 3 - methoxy - 0 - desmethylencainide, N - desmethylencainide and N-O-di-desmethyl encainide) have been identified upon chronic administration.

Flecainide is yet another orally effective fluorinated analogue of procainamide. It can also be administered intravenously. Chemically it is 2, 5 – bis - (2, 2, 2 - trifluoroethoxy) - N - (- 2 - piperidylmethyl) benzamide. It has similar pharmacological properties to those of encainide. However incorporation of terminal amino group into a lipophilic ring significantly increases lipophilicity of the drug resulting into an increase in antiarrhythmic activity.

Flecainide does not undergo extensive metabolism. Only meta - 0 - dealkylated flecainide metabolite has been reported to be excreted through urine.

Both, encainide and flecainide are highly potent antiarrhythmic agents, effective in nonogram quantity. This high potency of the drugs does not allow even minor fluctuation in the plasma concentration of drug. Hence these drugs have low therapeutic index. However flecainide does not produce frequent GIT adverse effect when used orally. Both are used in the long term treatment of premature ventricular contractions.

Lorcainide is yet another Na^+-channel blocking agent having similar pharmacological profile. It is an orally effective antiarrhythmic drug having similar therapeutic indication to that of encainide. It is metabolized in the body through aromatic hydroxylation and N-de-alkylation (norlorcainide) processes.

Besides its use in the treatment of premature ventricular contraction, lorcainide and encainide are also useful drugs to treat Wolff-Parkinson - White syndrome. This syndrome is seen in the patients having higher susceptibility to supraventricular paroxysmal tachycardia and is characterized by a short PR interval and a broad QRS complex. This specifically results from an unusually rapid conduction of impulses from atria to the ventricles. It is usually accompanied by fear, faintness, anginal pain or a fluttering sensation in the chest.

26.10 CLASS 2 β-ADRENERGIC BLOCKING AGENTS

It is found that β_1 – adrenoceptors are predominant in the heart (along with few β_2-adrenoceptors). Stimulation of β_1-adrenoceptor therefore, results in an increased heart rate and increased contractions of heart muscles. Therefore selective β_1-adrenoceptor blocking activity gained a high clinically importance as antiarrhythmic and antihypertensive agents.

Propranolol is the prototype member of aryloxypropanolol class of β_1 - adrenoceptor blocking agents. Other effective antiarrhythmic agents from the class include alprenolol, metoprolol and timolol. All these agents exhibit similar pharmacological profile, adverse effects and therapeutic uses. Hence only propranolol will be discussed in this section.

Cardiac Effects :

The antiarrhythmic effect of propranolol is mainly due to its β_1 - adrenoceptor blocking activity. Due to its high lipid solubility, the drug can penetrate nerve tissues and exerts cardiodepressant effects. This explains its high membrane stabilizing effect. In therapeutic doses, propranolol suppresses normal automaticity specifically in His--Purkinje system but does not affect the duration of action potential. An antiarrhythmic action is mainly due to prolongation of effective refractory period of A.V. node that results due to β_1-receptor blocking effect. This is prolongation of ERP results into suppression of reentry movements in paroxysmal supraventricular tachycardia. However very high concentration of the drug is needed to raise threshold potential in Purkinje fibres. In therapeutic doses, it slows down the conduction in atria and A.V. node and reduces sinus rate. In larger doses, it has quinidine like membrane stabilization effect on myocardium.

A.N.S. Effects :

Propranolol is considered as a non-selective β-adrenoceptor blocking agent. It does not influence the functioning of either α-adrenoceptor or vagal tone.

Pharmacokinetic Properties :

Propranolol is an orally effective agent. Due to extensive plasma protein binding (90 – 95%) of the drug, variations in plasma concentration of propranolol are quite usual after oral administration. It suffers an extensive first pass hepatic metabolism. To avoid this, the drug can also be given intravenously in emergency conditions.

A propranolol metabolite of particular interest is 4-hydroxy propranolol which still retains antiarrhythmic activity. Naphthoxylacetic acid, isopropylamine, propranolol glycol etc. are some of the major metabolite of propranolol, isolated from human urine along with some glucaonide conjugates.

Adverse Effects :

Adverse effects of propranolol are mainly associated with CNS, bronchial tract and metabolic processes. Most of them are due to the blockadge of β-adrenoceptors. These include nausea, vomiting, constipation, dizziness, hallucinations etc. Due to non-selective blocking action, bronchoconstriction results through the blockadge of β_2-adrenoceptors in bronchial muscle. It thus may become life threatening in patients suffering from asthma. In toxic doses, the conduction in atria and A.V. node is much suppressed which give rise to conditions like A.V. block or asystole. During chronic treatment, β-adrenoceptors become highly sensitive to catecholamines. Even minute amount of catecholamine will be sufficient to activate the receptors leading to cardiac arrhythmias. Hence the propranolol treatment should not be suddenly discontinued. Instead the withdrawal of the drug should be gradual.

Therapeutic Uses :

Since the antiarrhythmic action of propranolol is due to

(a) Depression of conduction in atria and A.V. node and

(b) β-adrenoceptor blocking effect.

The drug will be effective only in the treatment of arrhythmias caused due to

(i) Increased sinus automaticity (supraventricular tachyarrhythmias, e.g. atrial flutter, atrial fibrillation etc.).

(ii) And increased sympathetic discharge (under the conditions of emotional strain or stress).

Propranolol however, is not drug of choice in the treatment of most of ventricular arrhythmias due to requirement of quite high doses. More than 1000 mg/day may be needed to treat resistant arrhythmia.

Propranolol can also effectively suppress digitalis-induced arrhythmic attacks although phenytoin or lidocaine are more preferred drugs in this regard.

26.11 CLASS 3

This includes drugs causing prolonged repolarization and an increase in refractory period. Main examples from this category are amiodarone and bretylium.

Amiodarone :

It is a benzofuran derivative, originally developed as an antianginal agent but latter gained reputation as an orally effective antiarrhythmic agent. Though it possesses a hydrophilic cationic side-chain, it is devoid of local anaesthetic activity.

Its cardiac effects include :

(a) It decreases conduction velocity and prolongs refractory period.

(b) It increases threshold potential during ventricular fibrillation and

(c) It inhibits thyroxine – dependent metabolic pathways in the heart due to its structural similarity with thyroxine.

Orally it is well absorbed and concentrates mainly in body fat and fatty tissues like liver, muscle and spleen. It undergoes slow metabolism in liver resulting into long elimination half-life. During chronic treatment, its desethyl derivative accumulates in plasma.

Amiodarone has a low therapeutic index. It interferes in the functioning of thyroid specifically in long term therapy. It interefere in the metabolism of thyroid. Thyroid-stimulating hormone level may be increased resulting into insensitivity to thyroid hormone. It is effective drug in the treatment of recurrent ventricular tachycardia.

Bretylium :

Though originally introduced in 1950s as antihypertensive agent, bretylium is now not used for this purpose. Its use as antiarrhythmic agent was initiated in 1978 and it was then routinely used in the treatment of ventricular arrhythmias either by i.v. or i.m. route in the form of bretylium tosylate.

Pharmacological Properties :

(a) **Cardiac effect** : In therapeutic doses, bretylium does not exert any significant effect on automaticity, membrane responsiveness or conduction in the ventricular muscles. However it lifts threshold potential towards zero and prolongs the duration of action potential in both Perkinje's fibres and ventricular mass. A decrease in effective refractory period may be seen in A.V. node and ventricular region.

(b) **A.N.S. effects** : Bretylium does not influence vagal activity. However it greatly influences the sympathetic turnover. It utilises the same transport system which is involved in reuptake of norepinephrine into the nerve terminales. It is taken up by amine pump in the adrenergic neuron. It displaces norepinephrine and then blocks subsequent release of catecholamines. Its accumulation in adrenergic nerve fibres causes local anaesthetic effect at that site resulting into prevention of release of norepinephrine in response to nerve impulse. Bretylium induced blockade of uptake of catecholamines, potentiates the actions of circulating catecholamines. This may lead to repolarization and increased conductivity in the affected region.

Bretylium causes peripheral vasodilation which may be followed by transient vasoconstriction and hypertension due to the initial release of catecholamine. During chronic treatment, hypotension resulted due to its postganglionic sympathetic neuronal blocking action, can be corrected by concomitant administration of protryptiline, a tricyclic antidepressant agent.

Pharmacokinetic Properties :

Bretylium is administered intravenously in the form of bretylium tosylate for short term use. Bretylium is not effective orally due to its poor absorption resulting from marked polarity. However bethanidine sulfate, a structural relative of bretylium is now available for oral use which has similar properties.

Due to the polar nature, the drug does not need metabolic biotransformations and is excreted almost-entirely unchanged through the urine (about 72% of administered dose).

Adverse effects include nasal stiffness, breathlessness, diarrhoea, postural hypotension, muscular weakness and mental changes. In the case of severe hypotension, the drug should be immediately withdrawn. In many patients, tolerance to these adverse effects has been reported to occur.

Bretylium is not a drug of first choice to treat cardiac arrhythmias. It is reserved for the treatment of severe, refractory and nonresponding ventricular arrhythmias.

26.12 CLASS 4

Calcium Channel Blocking Agents :

Calcium ions play an important role in governing the functioning of essential events in myocardial cells. For example, it maintains

(a) force of myocardial contraction,

(b) tone of vascular smooth muscules,

(c) S.A. nodal activity, and

(d) A.V. nodal conduction.

The calcium channel blocking agents inhibit the transmembrane calcium ion flux through the voltage dependent slow ion channels in a dose-dependent manner. Examples include that of verapamil, diltiazm, nifedipine and beprildil. This inhibition of calcium ion channels results into (a) suppression of slow inward current of depolarisation and (b) negative inotropic effect, as far as heart is concerned.

Due to the inhibition of calcium channels, the force of contraction is reduced and hence reduces oxygen consumption. This effect coupled with their coronary vasodilatory activity has promoted their use as effective antianginal drugs.

They prolongs the effective refractory period resulting into slowing of A.V. nodal conduction. This imparts them an ability to interrupt the circus movement of the impulse. Hence, they can also be used in the treatment of arrhythmias arising due to circus movement e.g. supraventricular tachycardia. Now all calcium channel blocking agents are effective antiarrhythmic drugs, e.g. nifedipine lacks antiarrhythmic potency and is mainly used as antianginal agent. Verapamil is an effective antiarrhythmic drug in the treatment of paroxysmal supraventricular tachycardia due to A.V. nodal reentry. It is also effective when increased coronary artery spasm is the basic cause of ventricular fibrillation.

Verapamil :

Structurally it can be considered as a papaverine derivative. Due to its coronary vasodilatory activity, it is usually indicated in the treatment of angina pectoris and supraventricular arrhythmias.

Its antiarrhythmic activity is due to its ability to suppress automaticity of S.A. node, to decrease conduction velocity through A.V. node and prolongation of refractory period. In cardiac Perkinje fibres, the rate of phase 4 depolarization also decreases. The latter effect thus inhibits triggered activity. Due to its coronary vasodilatory effect, it protects ischemic cells and thus prevents the formation of ectopic foci, in myocardial cells.

It is devoid of any effect on cholinergic or β-adrenergic receptors. However α-adrenoceptors were found to be antagonised.

It can be administered orally as well as intravenously. However its oral effectiveness is hampered due to extensive first pass metabolism in liver. One of its metabolites, norverapamil retains vasodilatory activity.

Adverse effects include nausea, vomiting, constipation, hypotension, peripheral edema, A.V. block, bradycardia, dizziness and fatigue. Norepinephrine (to treat hypotension) and atropine sulphate (A.V. block) are usually given in severity of adverse reactions of verapamil.

Therapeutic Uses :

(1) It slows down A.V. nodal conduction. Hence it is useful to maintain ventricular tone in atrial flutter or fibrillation. It is also effective in the treatment of ventricular tachyarrhythmias arising due to coronary artery spasm.

(2) It is also effective in the treatment of atrial tachycardia with A.V. block induced by digitalis toxicity.

Contraindication :

Due to its diversified effects on cardiovascular system, its use is contraindicated in following conditions :

(a) Severe left ventricular dysfunction.

(b) Sick sinus syndrome

(c) Atrial flutter or atrial fibrillation

(d) Hypotension.

❖ ❖ ❖

ANTI-HYPERTENSIVE AGENTS

27.1 INTRODUCTION

Blood pressure is a biophysical parameter which is closely related to the mechanisms that control perfusion or irrigation of blood to various tissues. The normal systolic/diastolic blood pressure of a healthy adult person are supposed to be 120/75 - 85 mm Hg. A highly complex regulatory system operates for perfusion of blood into various tissues. The fluctuations in the vascular environment are nullified through the activation of baro and chemoreceptors which maintains the blood pressure at a constant value.

Many mechanisms operate in equilibrium with each other in order to maintain a constant blood pressure. These mechanisms include, central mechanism, peripheral adrenergic activation, baro and chemoreceptor, cardiac output, viscosity of blood, renin-angiotensin aldosterone system, vascular factors, blood volume etc. The mutual functioning of all these hemodynamic mechanisms in equilibrium with each other appears to be like a mosaic, as represented in the Fig. 27.2.

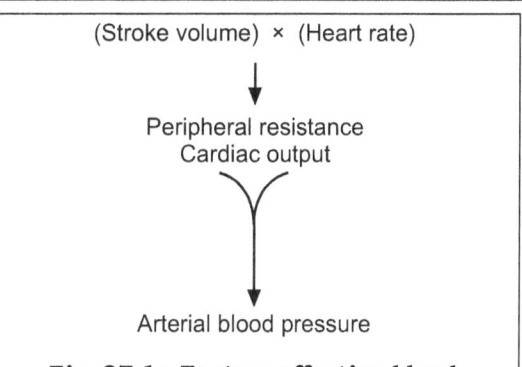

Fig. 27.1 : Factors affecting blood pressure

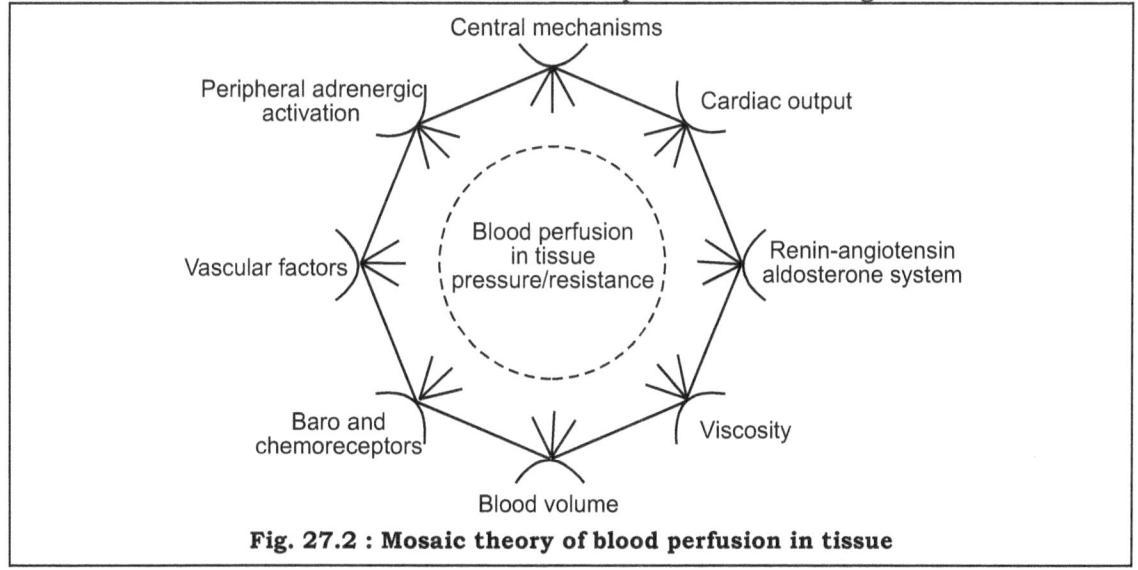

Fig. 27.2 : Mosaic theory of blood perfusion in tissue

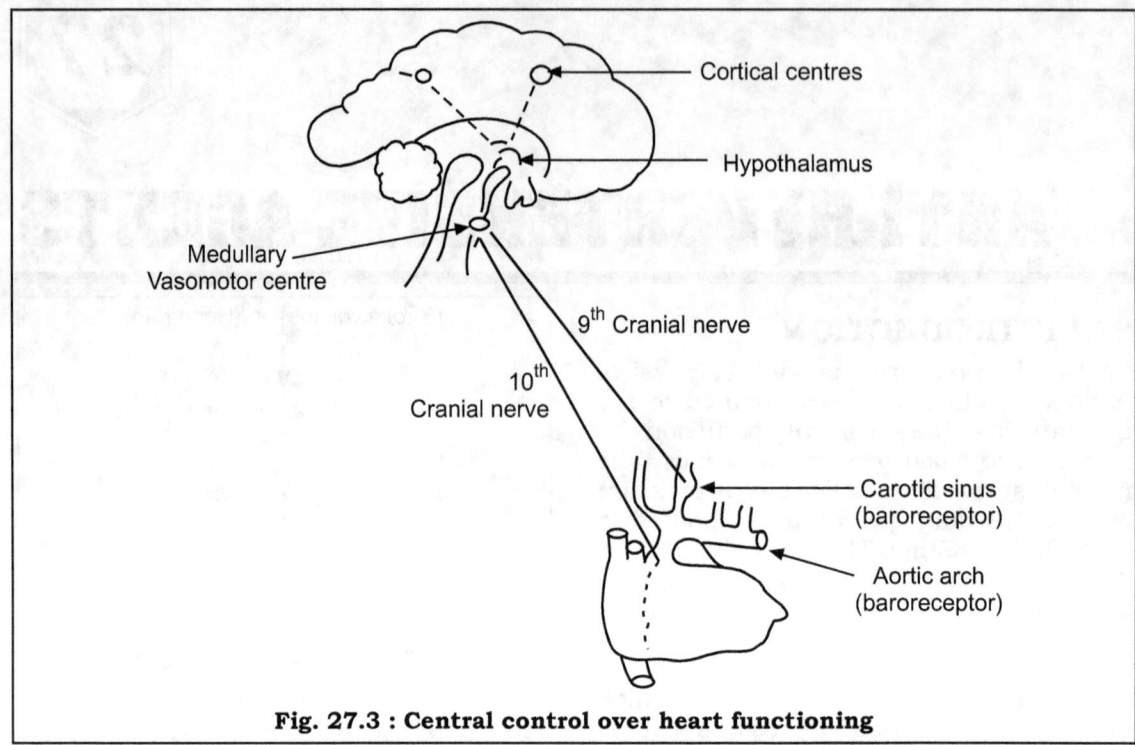

Fig. 27.3 : Central control over heart functioning

Hypertension results due to disturbances in these hemodynamic mechanisms which is reflected through increased peripheral vascular resistance and high diastolic blood pressure.

The vascular fluctuations in the circulation are communicated and controlled by baro and chemoreceptors. The baroreceptors are pressure sensitive receptors located in the walls of heart and blood vessels, e.g. carotid sinus and aortic arch receptors. When there is a fall in blood pressure in carotid sinus, it stimulates sympathetic nervous system resulting into vasoconstriction and an increase in blood pressure. On the other hand, an increase in blood pressure activates these baroreceptors resulting into arterial dilation thus opposing a tendency for permanent hypertension. The loss of this inhibitory activity of baroreceptors may lead to moderate hypertension. While chemoreceptors which are also located in vessel wall are sensitive to changes in oxygen content of the blood. They induce vasoconstriction in order to compensate any fall in oxygen concentration in blood. The effects of activation of the baro and chemoreceptors are mediated through the release of renin which then initiates the activation of angiotensin - aldosterone system. Renin (molecular weight 42,000) is a proteolytic enzyme that catalyses the formation of active pressure hormone, the angiotensin. Its presence in the kidney was first discovered in 1898. It was named 'renin' by Bergman due to its renal origin. Kidney is the rich source of renin where it is stored in the granular juxtaglomerular (JG) cells in the walls of the afferent arterioles, in the form of prorenin (a zymogen with a molecular weight of 63,000). The prorenin in turn, is obtained by intracellular proteolysis of an inactive precursor, preprorenin. Both prorenin and preprorenin are also present in plasma.

Renin - Angiotensin system is an important part of the homeostatic mechanisms in the body. It get activated by decreased blood volume, low renal pressure (baroreceptors in renal afferent arterioles) and low sodium ion concentration in the plasma (chemoreceptors in renal afferent arterioles). It regulates the electrolyte balance by controlling aldosterone secretion by adrenal cortex.

The components of renin-angiotensin system are present in many other tissues. Prostaglandins also are found to stimulate the release of renin in response to inflammatory stimuli. For example, PGI_2 (prostacyclin), through its vasodilating action, activates the baroreceptors and stimulates the renin release. Similarly the IG cells are directly innervated by central sympathetic nerves. Hence, under the conditions of strain and stress, the sympathetic stimulation may lead to the hypertension due to the activation of renin-angiotensin system. The renin-angiotensin system then regulates the blood pressure and plasma sodium at normal level by exerting generalized vasoconstriction and inducing aldosterone release. The effect of sympathetic nerve stimulation is revealed in the Fig. 27.4.

Hence, antihypertensive agents which act at adrenergic terminal, may act by various mechanisms like,

(i) Interfering with the synthesis of noradrenaline and forming false neurotransmitter, e.g. methyl dopa.

(ii) Increasing the metabolism of free noradrenaline.

(iii) Inhibiting the release of noradrenaline at post ganglionic adrenergic nerve terminal, e.g. bretylium.

(iv) Inhibiting reentry of noradrenaline into storage sites, e.g. reserpine.

(v) Antagonising noradrenaline at receptor sites, e.g. α- and β-adrenergic antagonist.

It is found that $β_1$-receptors are predominantly present in heart (along with few $β_2$-receptors). Stimulation of $β_1$-receptors therefore, results in an increase in rate and force of heart contractions. Therefore selective $β_1$-adrenoceptor blocking agents gained a high clinical importance as antihypertensive agents. At present, we have cardioselective $β_1$ - blockers, such as metoprolol, and atenolol, nonselective β-blockers like, propranolol. While labetalol can inhibit responses of both, α- and β-adrenoceptor activation.

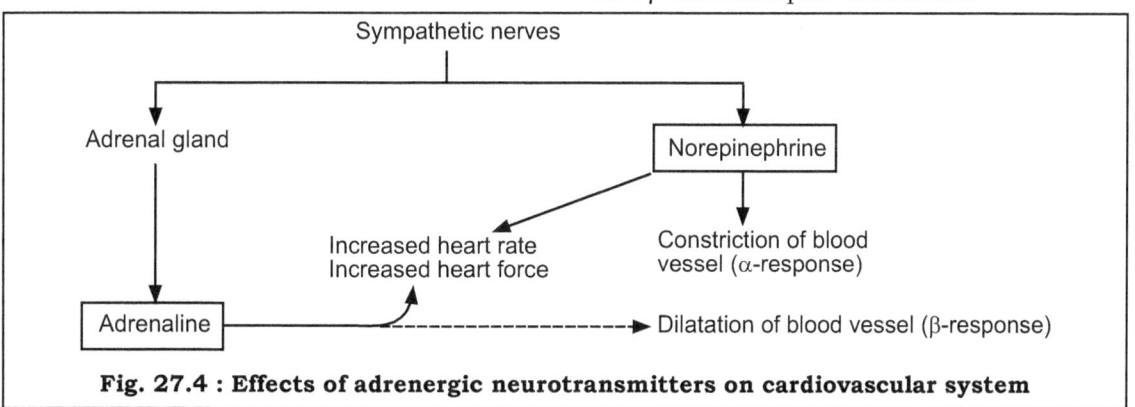

Fig. 27.4 : Effects of adrenergic neurotransmitters on cardiovascular system

An increased cardiac output and increased vascular resistance play an important role in elevation of blood pressure. They can be brought to the normal level by administration of drugs which act at peripheral vascular system, such as diuretics and vasodilators. In the treatment of hypertension, vasodilators act by lowering the elevated systemic vascular resistance while diuretics bring down the increased plasma volume and increased cardiac work-load.

The term hypertension is generally defined as a pathologically elevated systemic arterial pressure. In this disorder, the small arterioles appear to be under excessive sympathetic nervous system stimulation which causes arteriolar constriction and increased peripheral resistance to the transfer of blood from the arteries to the tissue capillaries and venous circulation resulting into increased blood pressure. Due to the variable nature of the systolic blood pressure, the term hypertension usually refers to an abnormal elevation in diastolic pressure. For practical guidance, usually the systolic/diastolic blood pressure above 160/95 is considered to be a state of hypertension.

When the hypertension is due to the symptoms of definable causes, such as renal artery stenosis (i.e. pathological condition of kidney which restrict the blood flow through the renal artery), pheochromocytoma (a hypertensive condition caused by the release of large amount of catecholamines due to tumors in the adrenal medulla) or an endocrine disorder like aldenomas (excessive secretion of aldosterone by the adrenal cortex), it is referred to as secondary hypertension. Secondary hypertension may be classified as neurogenic, renal, endocrine and cardiovascular. When the cause of hypertension cannot be clearly defined, it is classified as essential hypertension. In the presence of essential hypertension, the primary cause in most of the patients is increased vascular resistance.

Along with other factors like, hypercholesterolemia, diabetes and smoking, hypertension is an important contributory risk factor for the development of arteriosclerotic cardiovascular diseases. Usually in men, hypertension is more common before the age of 45-50 years. After this age, it is more common in women.

Sustained hypertension may seriously affect the functioning of vital systems like cardiovascular system, central nervous system and renal system. In heart, the increased systemic pressure leads to an increase in the cardiac workload. The resulting cardiac overwork then becomes a prominent cause of left ventricular hypertrophy.

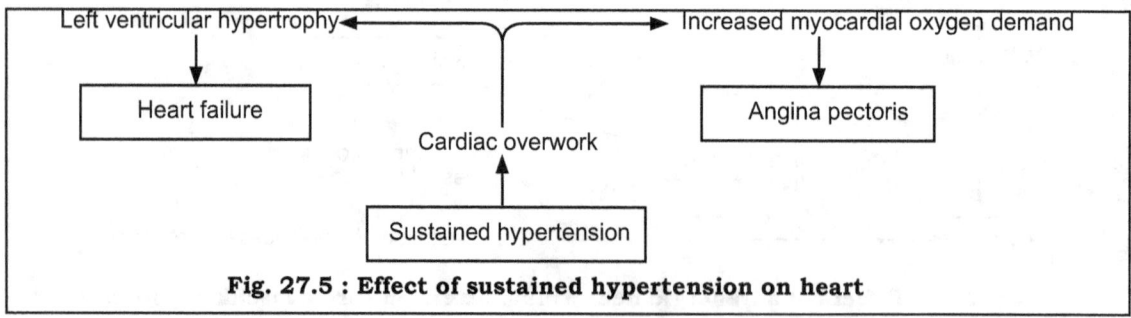

Fig. 27.5 : **Effect of sustained hypertension on heart**

The sustained hypertension may disturb the functioning of central nervous system resulting into vertigo, dizziness, occipital headaches, dimmed vision, vascular occlusion and hemorrhage while in kidneys, renal arteriosclerotic lesion of the afferent and efferent arterioles develop, resulting into renal failure.

27.2 ETIOLOGY OF HYPERTENSION

The various factors which contribute to less or more extent to the state of hypertension can be classified as -

(a) Neural factors
(b) Hormonal factors
(c) Electrolyte factors
(d) Vessel wall factors, and
(e) Genetic factors.

(a) Neural factors : Stress or emotions causing excessive sympathetic outflow from the brain may result into an increased cardiac output and elevated peripheral resistance. The overproduction or incomplete destruction of sympathomimetic amines may further contribute to the elevated peripheral resistance. The abnormal levels of noradrenaline, adrenaline, dopamine and serotonin may play a peripheral as well as a central role in activation of vasomotor tone. Usually agents which block the effects of sympathomimetic amines are useful to treat hypertension caused by neural factors.

(b) Hormonal factors : Renin, a proteolytic enzyme found primarily in the kidney, is released in response to lowered perfusion pressure and low sodium states of the circulating blood. It catalyses the conversion of angiotensinogen to angiotensin I (decapeptide). The latter is rapidly converted in the plasma by a chloride activated enzyme (primarily in the lungs) to angiotensin II (octapeptide). Angiotensin II has three fold action.

(i) It constricts the arterial network to increase peripheral resistance.

(ii) It slowly triggers the release of aldosterone which in turn, increases sodium retention and plasma volume.

(iii) It causes an excessive release of catecholamines from adrenal medulla and from peripheral sympathetic nerves, resulting into an increase in cardiac output. The renin-angiotensin-aldosterone system thus affects all three primary factors which can cause hypertension, like

(a) Blood vessel constriction,
(b) Increased blood volume, and
(c) Increased cardiac output.

Though elevated renin-angiotensin levels appear to play a critical role in severe hypertension, other hormones and vasopressor substances may sometimes be important like arachidonic acid metabolites, prostaglandins, corticoids, kinins, vasopressin and some yet unidentified hormones. Prostaglandins (PGA, PGE) for example, cause a fall in blood pressure and renal dilation. They also initiate the release of renin by a central effect on the vagus.

(c) Electrolyte factors : The inability of the kidney to excrete an adequate daily amount of salt and water results into abnormal retention of salt and water in the blood which causes an increase in the blood volume. The net result is an increase in the workload on the heart. The blood potassium and blood selenium level may also play an etiological role in hypertension along with other dietary and environmental factors.

(d) Vessel wall factors : The vascular smooth muscles are highly sensitive to changes in the cardiac output. Hence, increased perfusion pressure due to increased cardiac output leads to structural changes (like wall thickening and hypertrophy of vasculature) in the blood vessels. The direct acting vasodilators, hence may be of value in this type of hypertension.

(e) Genetic factors : The increased sensitivity and susceptibility to various etiologic factors (which are mentioned above) by offsprings of hypertensives underlies the importance of hereditary factors in hypertension.

27.3 CLASSIFICATION

All currently available antihypertensive drugs act mainly by interfering with normal hemostatic mechanisms and this provides a useful basis for the classification of these drugs. They are classified as :

[A] Drugs Affecting Sympathetic Tone :
   (i) Drugs that alter central sympathetic activity
       e.g. methyldopa, clonidine.
   (ii) Drugs that act as adrenergic neuron blockers,
       e.g. guanethidine, reserpine.
   (iii) Ganglionic blocking drugs
       e.g. trimethaphan.
   (iv) α-adrenoceptor blocking agents
       e.g. prazosin, phentolamine.
   (v) β-adrenoceptor blocking agents
       e.g. propranolol, atenolol.

[B] Vasodilators :
(a) Direct vasodilators :
   (i) Arterial dilators e.g. hydralazine
   (ii) Balanced vasodilators,
       e.g. minoxidil.

(b) Calcium channel blocking agents
    e.g., nifedipine

[C] Agents Acting on Renin-Angiotensin System :
   (i) Renin inhibitors
   (ii) Angiotensin antagonists e.g. saralasin.
   (iii) Angiotensin converting enzyme inhibitors. e.g. captopril, enalapril.

[D] Diuretics :
   (i) Thiazides
       e.g. hydrochlorothiazide
   (ii) Loop diuretics e.g. furosemide
   (iii) Potassium sparing diuretics
       e.g. triamterene.

27.4 GENERAL CONSIDERATIONS

These drugs produce their hypotensive action by affecting the biosynthesis, storage, uptake, release, metabolism and adrenoceptor activation by sympathomimetic amines. Agents acting at both, central sites (reserpine, guanethidine) and at peripheral sites (cardioselective β_1-antagonists) are included in this class. The adverse effects includes diarrhoea tachycardia, or thostatic hypotension, increased renin secretion and development of tolerance. Other effects includes sedation, dry mouth and depression.

The lowering of blood pressure by drugs like methyldopa and clonidine is brought about probably by stimulation of central presynaptic α_2-adrenoceptors, thereby reducing the release of efferent sympathetic traffic from CNS.

Guanethidine may be considered as a representative example of the drugs that depress the functioning at adrenergic neurons. Drugs in this class appear to act by more than one mechanism. These agents mainly act by causing a gradual depletion of catecholamine stores from central and peripheral adrenergic nerve endings resulting into reduced sympathetic tone. Unlike clonidine, the therapy with reserpine and methyldopa is usually associated with extrapyramidal side-effects.

Alpha adrenoceptors are subclassified as postsynaptic α_1-adrenoceptors and presynaptic α_2-adrenoceptor. The α_1-receptors are predominantly present in smooth muscle cells of arterial walls. While α_2- receptors are present on the presynaptic adrenergic neurons and exert inhibitory influence over the release of norepinephrine.

Activation of postsynaptic α_1-receptors leads to arterial vasoconstriction resulting into an increase in peripheral vascular resistance. Hence α_1-adrenoceptor blocking agents can be clinically used as antihypertensive agents. Examples include, prazosin, trimazosin and indoramin. They appear to exert vasodilatory effect through the blockade of α_1-adrenoceptors. Prazosin is the first member of this class, reported in 1974 followed by trimazosin. Both are quinazoline derivatives. They mainly affect the venous vascular bed but become more balanced during long term treatment. They affect to varying degree, the functioning of renin-angiotensin system resulting into sodium and fluid retention. They tend to produce tolerance if used chronically. They are mainly used in the treatment of hypertension and heart failure.

β-adrenoceptors are mainly present in heart, pulmonary vessels, vessels supplying blood to skeletal muscles and are also involved in glycogenolysis and lipolysis. The β-adrenoceptor blocking agents act by the competitive inhibition of the effect of catecholamines on β-adrenoceptors. Previously it was proposed that the antihypertensive effect of these drugs results due to a downward suppression of functioning of baroreceptors.

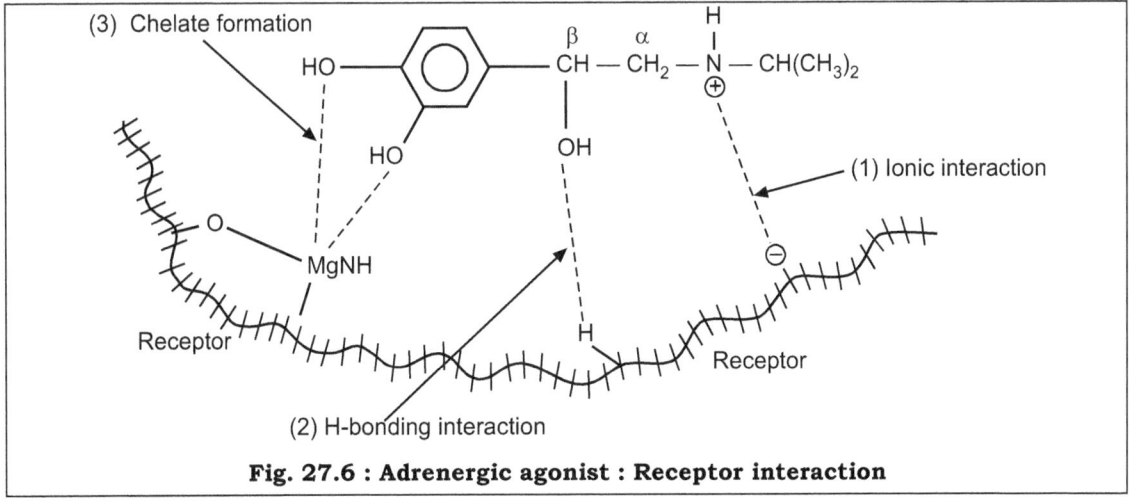

Fig. 27.6 : Adrenergic agonist : Receptor interaction

But now the antihypertensive effect of β-adrenoceptor blocking agents is explained on the following lines :

(a) Decreased renin release occurs due to inhibition of β_1-receptors while renal plasma flow and rate of glomerular filtration are reduced by blockade of β_2-receptors.

(b) Decreased norepinephrine release occurs from the postganglionic sympathetic nerves due to the blockade of presynaptic β-receptors.

(c) Central mechanism has been proposed for some lipophillic β-blockers, and

(d) The cardioselective β_1-blockers act by exerting a reduction in rate and force of heart contraction. However such cardioselectivity is of relative nature and is seen only at low doses.

Due to interference in glycogenesis, these drugs may cause hypoglycemia like symptoms during chronic treatment.

Dichloroisoproterenol was the first β-blocker introduced in 1960s. All β-adrenoceptor blockers are analogues of adrenoreceptor agonist, isoproterenol whose interaction with the receptor is shown in the Fig. 27.6.

The β-blockers compete with agonist molecules at three principal reactive sites. They are characterized by a substituted aromatic ring and a side-chain.

The nature of aromatic substituent affects receptor activation ability (i.e. intrinsic activity) while the side-chain appears to govern affinity of these antagonists for the β-adrenoceptors. Usually affinity is proportional to chain-length. The configuration of asymmetric β-carbon atom is crucial to define the pharmacological activity of the compound. The aromatic substituents also govern the lipophilicity of the compounds and thus their central effects.

Due to the presence of asymmetric β- carbon atom in the side-chain, these compounds usually exist as pairs of enantiomers. The laevoisomers are much more potent (50 – 100 times) β-blockers than their dextroisomers. Except timolol (laevoisomer), all other β-blockers are available commercially in the form of their recemic mixture.

Dichloroisoproterenol, due to its weak antagonistic property was soon replaced by pronethalol. But soon it was also withdrawn from clinical testing because of reports that it caused thymic tumours in mice. However soon after propranolol, a close structural relative of pronethalol, was developed. It is a non-selective β-blocker having almost negligible intrinsic sympathomimetic activity (ISA) and is considered now as a prototype of β-blocker series. It was then followed by atenolol, acebutotol, metoprolol, pindolol, oxprenolol, labetalol, sotalol, timolol, nodolol, practolol and tolamolol.

Practolol was found to induce mucocutaneous reactions while tolamolol was reported to initiate animal tumour development. For these reasons, both these drugs have been withdrawn from clinical use.

The relative lack of postural hypotension and sexual disfunctioning coupled with good therapeutic index are the added advantages of β-blockers over other antihypertensive agents. The membrane stabilizing or 'quinidine like" effect associated with certain β-blockers (e.g. propranolol) do not play any significant role at the doses needed for their antihypertensive action.

The β_2-receptors are predominantly present in lung, particularly in bronchial muscles. The β_1 to β_2 - receptor percentage in human lung is estimated to be nearly 30 : 70. Hence, β-blockers besides exerting their antihypertensive action, may antagonise lung β_2-receptors causing bronchial constriction, a case contraindicated in hypertensive patients suffering from bronchial asthma. The ratio of cardiac to lung activity has been evaluated for propranolol (2 : 1), practolol (15 : 1) and for atenolol (200 : 1). Atenolol and metoprolol are the examples of cardioselective β_1-antagonists that have much greater affinity for β_1-receptors in the heart than the β_2-receptors present in other tissues. While non-selective β-antagonists (e.g. propranolol) are mainly reserved for the treatment of migraine and tremor. The elevated peripheral resistance is the main cause behind most of the hypertensive cases. Vasodilators act by inducing vascular smooth muscle relaxation, thereby normalizing the elevated peripheral resistance which is the main hemodynamic abnormality in this condition.

The drawback of vasodilator therapy is the reflex activation of compensatory mechanisms such as sympathetic activation (resulting into an increase in the heart rate and cardiac output) and activation of renin-angiotensin-aldosterone system (resulting into increased extracellular fluid due to salt and water retention). The latter effect is much pronounced with hydralazine and diazoxide that cause mainly arterial dilation. This elevation of plasma renin activity and reflex tachycardia induced by vasodilators can be minimized by concurrent administration of a diuretic along with β-adrenoceptor blocking agent.

Vasodilation can be brought about by :

(a) Pure vasodilators e.g. hydralazine, minoxidil.

(b) Indirect vasodilators :
   (i) α_1-adrenoceptor blocking agents and
   (ii) Angiotensin converting enzyme inhibitors.

Renin is a proteolytic enyme involved in the synthesis of a decapeptide, angiotensin I. The latter is converted to an octapeptide, angiotensin II by a peptidyldipeptide hydrolase (converting enzyme) in the vascular endothelial cells and epithelial cells of the proximal tubule and small intestine. The converting enzyme is a metalloenzyme (Zn^{++}) and requires the presence of chloride ions. Its activity is suppressed by hypoxia. Angiotensin II is a potent vasoconstrictor and initiates the release of aldosterone. It also independently controls Na^+ transport by epithelial cells in the gut and kidney.

Thus, activation of renin - angiotensin aldosterone system leads to vasoconstriction and hypertension. Hence, drugs that antagonise the effect of renin, angiotensin or aldosterone can be used in the treatment of systemic hypertension, congestive cardiac failure and pulmonary hypertension. The drugs from this class can be subcategorized as -

(a) Renin antagonists
(b) Aldosterone antagonists,
(c) Angiotensin II antagonists, and
(d) Converting enzyme inhibitors.

At present, renin antagonists do not have therapeutic potential while aldosterone antagonists may principally be used as diuretic agents. Saralasin is an example of angiotensin II competitive antagonist while captopril (1977) is an example of orally effective converting enzyme inhibitor.

Sodium retention and consequent fluid retention usually serve as the initiating factor in hypertension. Certain antihypertensive drugs (e.g. adrenergic neuron blocking agents, vasodilators) are unable to retain their efficacy due to reflex activation of plasma renin. In such cases diuretics can bring about impressive results by suppressing renal tubular reabsorption of sodium, thus reducing the blood volume and the cardiac output. They exert antihypertensive action by promoting the loss of salt and water through the kidneys. However they too, are not free from adverse effects and may induce reflex renin activation and metabolic changes like, hypokalemia, alkalosis, hyperglycemia and hyper uricaemia. Sexual dysfunction is also reported due to long term treatment with diuretics.

From the forgoing discussion, it becomes clear that none of the above categories qualifies the test for ideal antihypertensive agent. Their efficiency is largely paralyzed due to emergence of compensatory reflex mechanisms in the body. For example, vasodilators lead to reflex tachycardia and elevation of plasma renin activity while sympatholytics gradually lose their effectiveness due to fluid retention. The sympatholytics can abolish reflex tachycardia associated with vasodilator therapy while the fluid retention caused due to sympatholytics and vasodilators can be effectively neutralized by the use of diuretics. Such a combination of a sympatholytic, vaso-dilator and a diuretic agent presents most effective antihypertensive treatment where very low incidences of side-effects result due to comparatively low doses of each of the three components.

27.5 DRUGS AFFECTING SYMPATHETIC TONE (SYMPATHOLYTICS)

(i) Drugs that Alter Central Sympathetic Activity :

(a) α-methyldopa : Tyrosine and DOPA are the principal intermediates in the biosynthesis of catecholamines in the body. Drugs having structural resemblance with these intermediates will then, naturally compete with the enzymes which convert these intermediates into norepinephrine. α-methyltyrosine and α-methyl dopa are the examples of drugs developed through this concept. Both get acted upon by enzymes instead of tyrosine and dopa resulting into false neurotransmitters instead of norepinephrine, which have less potency than norepinephrine.

Since the rate of decarboxylation of α-methyl dopa is considerably slower than that of dopa, it ties up the enzyme, dopa decarboxylase for longer period of time and is effective inhibitor of the biosynthesis of norepinephrine. Instead of norepinephrine, α-methyl norepinephrine is formed which has weak central as well as peripheral actions. Thus, pressor response to adrenergic stimuli is reduced.

α-methyldopa

Since it is a potent agonist at presynaptic α_2-receptors in the CNS, it causes an inhibition of further release of central sympathetic outflow. This central mechanism is now recognized as the main site of action of methyldopa and the concept of 'false neurotransmitter' responsible for peripheral effects is considered as a secondary mechanism of action. Methyldopa is one of the oldest and commonly used antihypertensive agents. Its antihypertensive effect results from a decrease in peripheral vascular resistance without affecting cardiac output. Its use is also suggested in the treatment of malignant carcinoid and pheochromocytomas. It is an antihypertensive agent of choice in pregnant women and children. The plasma level of the drug can not be correlated with its antihypertensive effect since the action is due to its metabolite (α-methyl norepinephrine) and not due to the drug. The drug gradually loses its efficacy due to weight gain and fluid retention.

The drug absorbs orally in an erratic fashion. It is principally eliminated via kidney. For parenteral use, methyl dopate hydrochloride preparation is available which is methyl ester of methyl dopa.

The side-effects associated with its therapy include, nasal stuffiness, gastrointestinal upset, liver damage (e.g. obstructive jaundice, hepatitis), agranulocytosis, edema, weight gain, postural hypotension, impotence and allergic reactions. It enters the CNS quite readily. The CNS-effects include, sedation, vertigo, extrapyramidal signs and psychic depression. A sudden increase in blood pressure may be observed if the drug is withdrawn abruptly.

Due to such a long list of adverse effects, methyl dopa is usually administered along with a diuretic agent (i.e. thiazide) to lower the incidence of adverse effects.

(b) Clonidine : Primarily designed as nasal decongestant, its antihypertensive potential was screened out latter. Clonidine is an imidazoline compound, structurally quite similar to tolazoline.

Clonidine

Cardiovascular activity and blood pressure are centrally governed mainly by hypothalamus, the nucleus tractus solitarii and the nucleus of vagus nerve. Catecholamines are the principal neurotransmitters in this region except at vagus nerve. Clonidine is a potent agonist of presynaptic inhibitory α_2-adrenoceptors. By activating these receptors, it reduces the sympathetic traffic from the CNS.

The inhibition of sympathetic function results in corresponding dominance of parasympathetic tone resulting into bradycardia. Clonidine is α_2-agonist. It stimulates both, central and peripheral α_2-receptors resulting into reduced norepinephrine release. It lowers down mild to moderate hypertension by reducing vasomotor tone. It has a number of chlorpromazine like actions which indicates the presence of multireceptor sites for its action.

After oral administration Clonidine lowers heart rate, stroke volume and peripheral resistance. It is a drug of choice in hypertensive patients with renal failure. At higher oral doses or during intravenous administration, an initial increase in blood pressure can be explained on the basis of stimulation of peripheral postsynaptic α_1-adrenoceptors resulting into vasoconstriction.

It has a good oral absorption. Liver is the principal site of metabolism to yield inactive metabolites. These metabolites along with unchanged fraction of the drug are excreted through urine.

Side-effects include, dry mouth, nausea, impotence, postural hypotension and rebound hypertension after sudden withdrawal. Due to lipid solubility, the CNS side-effects are also prominent and include, insomnia, restlessness, depression and sedation. The drug's ability to activate postsynaptic α_1-adrenoceptors and to exert chlorpromazine - like effects further increases the range of its side effects. Hence it is usually administered along with a vasodilator or β-blocking agent.

It is an effective antihypertensive agent when used along with thiazide diuretics.

Other examples of drugs belonging to this class include guanabenz and guanfacine. Like clonidine, they also act by stimulation of central presynaptic α_2-adrenoceptors and have similar pharmacological and toxicity profile to that of clonidine. Guanabenz also acts peripherally by inhibiting the release of neurotransmitter from adrenergic nerve - ending resulting into relaxation of vascular smooth muscles. Guanabenz is administered orally in its acetate form. Both the drugs, guanabenz and guanafacine undergo significant metabolism. The hydroxylated metabolites along with fraction of unchanged drug are mainly excreted through the urine. Both these drugs are having relatively longer half-life. Hence sudden withdrawal of these agents rarely cause rebound hypertension.

(ii) Drugs that Act as Adrenergic Neuron Blockers :

(a) Guanethidine : A number of antihypertensive agents exert their activity by affecting the storage and release of norepinephrine. This is achieved by inhibition of Ca^{++} - influx into the nerve terminal. Examples include, bretylium, guanethidine and xylocholine. Guanethidine may be considered as representative of drugs that depress the function of postganglionic adrenergic nerves. It utilizes the same transport system which is involved in re-uptake of norepinephrine into the nerve terminals and reaches in the nerve. Upon accumulation in adrenergic nerve fibres, it induces a gradual depletion of catecholamine intraneuronal storage sites and itself acts as a false neurotransmitter and released by nerve stimulation resulting into a decreased pressor response. The effects of guanethidine are cumulative over long-term treatment.

Guanethidine sulphate

Guanethidine does extensively bind to plasma proteins, resulting into a delayed onset of action and long duration of action. It does not cross blood-brain-barrier and does not disturb CNS catecholamine flux. It depresses heart functioning due to its hypertensive effect. It decreases myocardial competence. During chronic treatment, blood volume increases due to the retention of sodium ions and generalised weakness develops. Cumulative effects may give rise to complications when the dose of the drug is increased.

Side-effects include postural hypotension, edema, generalised weakness and diarrhoea. Postural hypotension is considerably intense shortly after arising from the sleep and is due to fluctuation in the peripheral vascular resistance. Edema appears to be due to the expansion of blood volume in the capillary bed having suppressed norepinephrine mediated vasoconstriction. Diarrhoea is probably due to guanethidine induced release of serotonin in intestine. A sudden withdrawal of the drug during chronic administration produces a super-sensitivity of effector cells for norepinephrine. The drug neither cause impotence nor it develops tolerance to the patient.

(b) Reserpine : It is an example of *Rauwolfia* alkaloids obtained from the roots of *Rauwolfia serpentina* from Apocynaceae family. Once, reserpine was one of the most favoured antihypertensive agents. Due to its moderate potency and a high incidence of adverse effects, it is rarely used today as an antihypertensive agent. Its parenteral administration in the emergency treatment of severe hypertension brings down the blood pressure in a smooth and gradual fashion.

It acts centrally and peripherally to deplete stores of catecholamines and 5-hydroxy tryptamine. It paralyzes the functioning of storage vesicles, which thereafter loose interest to store newly synthesized norepinephrine. This neurotransmitter then escapes into cytoplasm, where most of it is deaminated by intraneuronal MAO enzymes. Probably by blocking ATP - Mg^{++} - dependent mechanism, it also lowers down the uptake of norepinephrine in chromaffin granules. At all these sites of action, reserpine exhibits cumulative effect upon repeated administration. Upon chronic administration, tissues become hypersensitive to catecholamines due to adaptive changes in the adrenoceptors. In some patients extrapyramidal effects can also be seen.

Reserpine exhibits an initial sympathomimetic activity before it induces hypotensive effect. (The cardiac output is reduced and the fall in the blood pressure is usually associated with bradycardia. It is also reported to cause arteriolar dilation). The mild sedative and tranquillizing effect of reserpine may contribute to its antihypertensive action.

Reserpine has prominent action on GIT. It increases motility and tone accompanied with abdominal cramps and diarrhoea. It promotes gastric acid secretion and the cases of ulceration and hemorrhages are reported due to chronic administration of the drug. It may induce sodium and water retention that can progress to frank congestive cardiac failure.

(iii) Sympathetic Ganglion Blocking Drugs :

In sympathetic ganglia, the release of norepinephrine from the interneuron activates the postganglionic α-adrenergic receptors resulting into characteristic catecholamine response. The ganglionic stimulation may lead to the release of adrenaline and noradrenaline from adrenal medulla and sympathetic nerve terminals. The ganglionic blocking agents can reduce the level of sympathetic activity. Hence, they were once widely used in the treatment of hypertensive cardiovascular disease. Since mechanisms governing transmission in all autonomic ganglia remains same, their non-selectivity of action leads to numerous side-effects. Hence, they are now totally replaced by more selective and less toxic β_1-adrenoceptor blocking agents.

The report about the effectivity of triethylsulfonium salts as ganglionic blockers, led to the development of trimethaphan. It has a very short duration of action; hence it is available only for parenteral administration. The hypotensive action can easily be reversed within few minutes of stopping the drug administration. Trimethaphan, in high doses, can stimulate the release of histamine resulting into a direct vasodilation. Hence it should be used with caution in patients with asthma or allergy.

During prolonged administration, tolerance may develop while some patients may show hypersensitivitiy responses when they are treated with ganglionic blockers. Examples of clinically useful agents from this category include, trimethaphan, mecamylamine, pentolinium, hexamethonium etc. Their absorption is poor and unpredictable. Due to ionic nature, they are not attacked much by metabolising enzymes and get excreted through urine in almost unchanged form.

The side-effects associated with their use are mainly due to their unselective blocking action and include, nausea, vomiting, dry mouth, anorexia, decreased tone and motility of GIT, xerostomia, anhydrosis, cycloplegia and postural hypotension. These side-effects sufficiently disturb the patient and limit their chronic use.

(iv) α-adrenoceptor Blocking Agents :

The α-adrenoceptors are categorized as postsynaptic α_1-adrenoceptors and α_2-adrenoceptors. α_1-receptors are present on smooth muscles of blood vessels and gland cells while α_2-receptors are present on pre and post-synaptic sites on the nerves and are also present in the CNS. The activation of postsynaptic α_1-receptors leads to vasoconstriction while the activation of presynaptic α_2-receptors present on the nerve terminals leads to inhibition of neurotransmitter release. Thus, α_1-adrenoceptor blockers (i.e. vasodilation results, hence also called as indirect vasodilators) or α_2-adrenoceptor agonists will have a potential of antihypertensive action. For example, prazosin and methoxamine act on α_1-receptors while the antihypertensive action of clonidine and α-methyl-norepinephrine is due to their α_2-agonistic property.

The α-receptor blockers in most cases, do not show selectivity of action and also inhibit presynaptic α_2-receptors. This causes an increase in norepinephrine release due to withdrawal of inhibitory action of receptor. This results into an intensification of the effects of reflex sympathetic stimulation on the heart (e.g. reflex tachycardia and augmented contractile force).

(a) Quinazoline derivatives : Examples from this class include prazosin and trimazosin. Prazosin (1974) exerts its antihypertensive action by blocking postsynaptic α_1-adrenoceptor resulting into vasodilation of the arterioles. In therapeutic doses it does not affect the cardiac output and heart rate. No other pharmacological action is reported. The decreased arterial vascular resistance and reduction in arterial and venous tone are the effects mainly due to vasodilation caused by blockage of vascular α_1-blockers are also termed as 'indirect vasodilators'. Its use is accompanied by modest tachycardia (blockade of inhibitory presynaptic α_2-receptors) and low level of plasma renin (α_1-blocking effect).

The prazosin hydrochloride is orally active and gets extensively metabolized in liver through o-dealkylation and glucuronide conjugation. Due to the active metabolites the duration of hypotensive effect is prolonged than expected.

Adverse effects include nausea, nasal stuffiness, peripheral edema, tachycardia, drowsiness, palpitation and fluid retention. In sodium deficient individuals, hypotension with sudden loss of consciousness may occur after initial dose.

Prazosin is mainly used in patients with severe congestive cardiac failure or with hypertension.

Like prazosin, trimazosin is a quinazoline derivative. Chemically it is 2-hydroxy-2-methylpropyl 4 - (4 - amino - 6, 7, 8 - trimethoxy - 2 quinazolinyl) - 1 piperazine carboxylate monohydrochloride. It is a less potent α_1-blocker than prazosin, otherwise pharmacologically similar to prazosin. Indoramin is yet another example of vascular α_1-receptor blocking agent. Chemically it is 1 [2 - (3 - indolyl) ethyl] derivative of 4 - benzamido piperidine and resembles with the structure of procainamide.

(b) Phentolamine : The pharmacology of a large series of 2 substituted imidazolines was first studied by **Hartmann** and **Isler** in 1939. In addition to α_1-receptor blocking activity, these agents enjoy to varying degrees, sympathomimetic, parasympathomimetic, histamine like, antihistaminergic, MAO and cholinesterase inhibitory activities. The dominance of any of the above properties can be effected by the structural changes in the basic skeleton. Phentolamine and tolazoline are the examples of clinically employed agents from this class, in the management of hypertension.

Phentolamine

Tolazoline

The blockade of α-receptors produced by these drugs has a quick onset and is of short duration. Due to their structural resemblance with histamine and α_1-receptor blockers, they act as powerful vasodilators. The peripheral vasodilation is counter balanced by reflex increase in the cardiac rate and contractile force. An increased release of norepinephrine due to presynaptic α_2-receptor blockade results in tachycardia and an increased cardiac stroke volume. In higher doses, phentolamine releases histamine and can block 5-HT receptors.

These drugs can be administered orally as well as parenterally. Imidazolines do not undergo major metabolism *in vivo* and get excreted largely in an unchanged form through the urine.

Side-effects arise mainly due to their stimulatory action at cardiac and GIT sites. They include, nausea, vomitting, diarrhoea, abdominal pain, headache, flushing, shivering, tachycardia, anginal pain and cardiac arrhythmias. Hence, these drugs should not be used in patients with peptic ulcer or having coronary arterial disease.

(v) β-adrenoceptor Blocking Agents :

Unlike α-adrenoceptor blocking agents, β-adrenoceptor blockers exhibit structural similarity with isoprenaline or norepinephrine. Hence structural requirements of these agents have been fairly well defined. This structural similarity of β-adrenoceptor blockers with isoprenaline (agonist) imparts :

(i) A greater specificity of action. These agents act more selectively on β-receptors and do not interfere with cholinergic, histaminergic or serotonergic responses and

(ii) Some degree of sympathomimetic intrinsic activity. These agents, with some exceptions, still retain sympathomimetic properties and can be termed as partial adrenergic agonists. Due to their partial agonist nature, they have less ability to induce bradycardia, pulmonary obstruction and rebound hypertension, in comparison to other antihypertensive agents.

It is important to note that the β-blocking effect and intrinsic sympathetic activity do not run opposite to each other. A potent β-blocking agent (e.g. pindolol) may still retain a high intrinsic sympathetic activity. This is probably because the functional groups involved in receptor blockade may in certain cases be quite different from the functional groups involved in receptor activation.

Similarly their structural resemblance with local anesthetics, enable these agents to exert a membrane stabilizing effect or a quinidine-like action, e.g. propranolol. This property justifies their use to treat cardiac arrhythmias.

β-receptor responses are largely of relaxant nature. The major exception to this generalization is the cardiac $β_1$-receptors, stimulation of which, increases the rate and force of heart contraction. Therefore, selective $β_1$-adrenoceptor blocking agents gained a high clinical importance as antihypertensive - drugs. The cardioselective $β_1$-blockers act through the following postulated mechanism :

1. Inhibition of renin release.
2. Reduction of cardiac output.
3. Inhibition of synaptic norepinephrine release and
4. Restoration of vascular relaxation responses.

On the basis of their relative affinity for β-receptor sub-types, these agents can be categorised into three classes.

(a) Non-selective β - blockers :

e.g. propranolol, pindolol, alprenolol, nadolol, bunolol, sotalol, timolol, oxprenolol, penbutolol etc.

(b) Selective $β_1$-blockers

e.g. Acebutolol, atenolol, metoprolol, practolol, tolamolol, pafenolol etc.

(c) Selective $β_2$ - blockers :

These agents do not find any clinical utility. Butoxamine is a somewhat selective $β_2$ antagonist.

The non-selective β-blockers bring about a blockade of both, $β_1$ and $β_2$ -

adrenoceptors. β_2-receptors are predominantly present in lung, particularly in bronchial muscles. The non-selective β-blockers will also block β_2-receptors in the lungs, resulting into bronchial constriction, a case contraindicated in patients suffering from bronchial asthma. Hence, a patient suffering from obstructive airway disease should not be treated with a non-selective β-blocker because of the possibility of aggravating bronchospasm. In such patients, cardioselective blockers should be used. These agents also inhibit glycogenolysis mediated by β - receptors in liver and skeletal muscles, thus reducing blood glucose level. Hence, they should be used with great caution in patients undergoing the therapy with insulin or oral hypoglycemic agents.

A non-selective β-blocker, propranolol is considered as a prototype of this series. Due to its lipophilic nature (log P value of 3.65 in octanol : water system) it exerts a wide range of CNS side-effects. Sotalol (1964) and practolol were the antihypertensive β-blockers with mild CNS effects due to incorporation of hydrophilic moieties in their structures. Practolol was the first cardioselective β_1-blocker launched in 1970. In the severe mucocutaneous toxicity induced by practolol the patient may suffer from blindness deafness, intestinal obstruction and a lupus like skin rash. This lead to a decrease in its popularity as antihypertensive agent and it was withdrawn from the market. Atenolol was the next compound prepared by **Hull** and co-workers through an incorporation of methylene group between the amide function and the aromatic ring. It was found to possess a longer biological half-life in comparison to the previous drugs. It was first marked in 1981 as cardioselective β_1-blocking agent. Acebutolol is yet another β_1-blocker. Its non-selectivity of action is attributed to the generation of an active but non-selective metabolite. Tolamolol was recently developed selective β_1-blocker. Like pronethalol, it was withdrawn from the clinical use because of its ability to induce tumor in animal testings. Nadolol is yet another example of long-acting β-blockers. Like atenolol, it is excreted largely in unchanged form through urine.

Structurally all these cardioselective β_1-blocking agents appear to be more hydrophilic in nature than the lipophilic propranolol, a non-selective β-blocker.

Some scientist hence considered - β_1-receptor structure more hydrophilic than β_2-receptor. According to them, the hydrophilic para substituent on the aromatic ring interacts with the hydrophilic site of β_1-receptors through hydrogen bonding to exert selectivity β_1-receptor blockade.

Pharmacology :

(1) By its tonic activity, sympathetic nervous system exerts an important control over the rate and force of heart beats. β-blockers hence cause reduction in the rate and force of heart contraction.

(2) β-blockers cause a fall in stroke volume, systolic blood pressure, cardiac work capacity and coronary blood flow.

(3) β - blockers inhibit the renin release from the juxtaglomerular cells of the kidney which is thought to be mediated through β-receptors.

(4) The cardiac effects of β-blockers are often reflected in an increased total body sodium and extracellular fluid volume. Postural hypotension is not prominent feature of β-blocker therapy.

(5) Some of the β-blockers have quinidine-like or membrane stabilizing activity due to the decreased inward sodium current.

All β-blockers are orally effective. In emergency conditions, intravenous administration is favoured. Lipophilic β-blockers (e.g. propranolol, metoprolol) get extensively metabolized while hydrophilic β-blockers (e.g. atenolol, nadolol) are almost excreted in unchanged form. The hydrophilic drugs are found to have longer half life values than lipophilic drugs. Many β-blockers like propranolol, metoprolol and oxyprenolol are metabolised mainly by hepatic microsomal enzymes. At least eight metabolites of propranolol have been isolated from the urine. Some of the metabolites of propranolol and alprenolol retain significant pharmacological activity and help to prolong their effects. Long duration of action and central effects associated with propranolol and alprenolol can be partly attributed to their high lipophilicity.

Adverse Effects :

(1) Mild adverse reactions include nausea, vomiting, mild diarrhoea, insomnia hallucination and muscle weakness.

(2) Heart failure may develop suddenly or slowly in patients with myocardia insufficiency.

(3) These agents cause impairment of conduction through A – V bundle but the inotropic action of digitalis is not inhibited.

(4) Non-selective β-blockers may lead to the attacks of bronchospasm due to an increase in airway resistance in asthmatic patient or in patients having a history of allergy.

(5) These agents depress the carbohydrate metabolism and potentiate the action of hypoglycemic agents in diabetic patients. They also mask tachycardia which is an important sign of developing hypoglycemia.

(6) Some of these agents causes withdrawal symptoms if abruptly withdrawn during longterm treatment. This is due to the super sensitivity of β-receptors induced by chronic blockage. The incidence and intensity of such withdrawal symptoms are lower with agents having longer biological half-life, e.g. atenolol, nadolol.

These agents are used in the management of hypertension, usually alongwith diuretics. They can also be used as an adjunct with vasodilators to reduce the reflex tachycardia. All these therapeutic applications of β-blockers are based upon their ability to reduce the effects of catecholamines on the heart.

27.6 VASODILATORS

The elevated peripheral vascular resistance is the main cause behind most of the hypertensive conditions. Vasodilators act by dilating the arterioles by which there is a fall in blood pressure without interfering with the functioning of sympathetic nervous system. The α_1-adrenoceptor blocking agents (indirect vasodilators) bring about vasodilation by interfering with sympathetic functioning. The vasodilators are sub-classified as :

(a) Direct Vasodilators :

(i) Arterial vasodilators e.g. hydralazine, and

(ii) Arterial and venous vasodilators : e.g. sodium nitroprusside.

(b) Indirect Vasodilators :

e.g. α_1-adrenoreceptor blocking agents.

(c) Calcium Channel Blockers :

Verapanil, nifedipine, diltiazam are some examples of calcium channel blockers. The calcium channel blockers, unlike direct vasodilator cause dilation of coronary arteries, and markly affect the automaticity, conduction velocity and refractory period in myocardial cells. While direct vasodilators have little direct effect on the heart functioning in therapeutic doses. Like antispasmodic agents they principally act through direct musculotropic effect resulting into the relaxation of peripheral vascular smooth muscles.

(a) Direct vasodilators :

(I) Arterial vasodilators :

(i) Hydralazine : Hydralazine induces peripheral vasodilation and thus lowers the peripheral vascular resistance. It causes an accumulation of c-GMP through the activation of guanylate cyclase. The accumulated c-GMP then brings about relaxation of arteriolar vascular smooth muscles. The occurance of postural hypotension is rare due to the preferential dilation of arterioles than veins. However the drug effect is partly nullified by the occurance of compensatory reactions, like, increase in heart rate and cardiac output (reflex increase in sympathetic outputs) and increase in plasma renin activity. These compensatory reactions limit the use of hydralazine especially in patients with coronary artery disease.

The oral absorption of hydralazine hydrochloride is rapid and almost complete. The drug binds extensively (80 – 85%) with the albumin fraction of plasma protein. Besides N-acetylation, the drug is metabolised by ring hydroxylation. It is eliminated mainly in the form of glucuronide salts.

Adverse effects include nausea, vomiting, headache, weakness, dizziness, fatigue, palpitation, tachycardia, anxiety, angina and nasal congestion. In severe cases, production of a lupus erythematous like syndrome is reported. The drug has a wide range of adverse-effects. Hence, usually it is not given alone as an anti-hypertensive agent. It is concurrently administered with a diuretic and a β-blocker to lower down the incidence of adverse effects. The occurance of compensatory reactions (increase in heart rate and cardiac output) makes its use troublesome in patients with angina or myocardial ischemia. Its use is advocated during pregnancy. The drug is also available in parenteral form to treat severe hypertension during emergency.

(ii) Minoxidil : It is yet another potent orally active direct vasodilator having actions quite similar to hydralazine. It was introduced in 1980 and lowers down peripheral vascular resistance by accumulation of c-GMP. Its use is accompanied by the reflex activation of sympathetic activity resulting into increase in

(a) heart rate and cardiac output and
(b) plasma rennin and plasma aldosterone activities.

Its effectiveness gradually decreases due to sodium ions and water retention, and the occurance of compensatory reflex reactions. It is quickly and almost completely absorbed when orally administered. Prolonged antihypertensive action results due to its slow rate of metabolism. Liver is the principal site of its metabolism. The metabolites are excreted through urine mainly in the form of glucuronides. A minor fraction of the drug administered may be excreted in unchanged form.

Adverse effects include palpitation, tachycardia (reflex activation), weight gain, fluid retention and hypertrichosis (hair growth). Hence it is usually concurrently administered with diuretics in order to reduce Na^+-reabsorption. Its use in women is less favoured due to hypertrichosis. The increased hair growth is supposed to be due to increase in cutaneous blood flow.

Minoxidil is a potent vasodilator usually recommended in the treatment of severe hypertension.

(iii) Diazoxide : It is an example of orally active vasodilator having structural relationship with thiazide diuretics. However it has no diuretic action. On the contrary it causes Na^+-retention resulting into pronounced fluid retention. But like diuretics, it reduces carbohydrate tolerance resulting into a marked diabetogenic effect. This makes it unfit for long term use in hypertensive patients. It has similar properties to that of hydralazine. Its hypotensive effect declines due to pronounced fluid retention and occurance of reflex compensatory mechanisms. Like minoxidil, its effectiveness can be maintained by concomitant administration of a diuretic and a β - blocking agent.

It is extensively bound to plasma. It is principally metabolised in liver to inactive metabolites. A significant fraction of administered dose is excreted through urine in unchanged form.

Adverse effects include tachycardia. hyperglycemia, hyperuricemia, Na^+-ion retention and allergic reactions. It is recommended in the treatment of severe hypertension, usually along with a diuretic.

[II] Arterial and Venous Vasodilators :

(i) Sodium Nitroprusside : It is potent vasodilator released into the market in 1974. It is an example of balanced vasodilator causing the relaxation of both, arteriolar and venous vascular muscles. Its hypotensive effect is brought about by decreased peripheral vascular resistance, decreased preload and after load on the heart. Due to its potent action it is administered only by intravenous infusion. Rapid onset and termination of action are the added advantages of its therapy. However it induces an increase in plasma renin activity.

Like all nitrites and nitrates, sodium nitroprusside causes an activation of guanylate cyclase by generation of free nitric oxide (NO) radicals. The resulting accumulation of c-AMP then brings about vasodilation through dephosphorylation of light chain of myosin in vascular smooth muscles. The molecule in its structure, contains five cyanide ions which are converted into non-toxic thiocyanates in liver. These thiocyanates are then excreted through urine. However in some patients the signs of cyanide poisoning may appear. In such cases, the patients are treated with hydroxy cobalamin.

Adverse effects of sodium nitroprusside include, nausea, vomiting, sweating, restlessness, weakness, apprehension, and muscle twitching. The impairment of thyroid function may be seen due to accumulation of thiocyanate ions in the body.

Sodium nitroprusside is a drug reserved in the treatment of severe hypertension and in the management of severe refractory congestive cardiac failure.

(b) Calcium Channel Blocking Agents :

The action of a wide variety of hormones and drugs is operated through the calcium ion signals, generated by cytosolic Ca^{++} ion concentration. The binding of cytosolic Ca^{++} with the intracellular Ca^{++} - dependent regulatory protein, calmodulin causes initiation of phosphorylation of target proteins that results into contraction of smooth muscle. The important cardiovascular functions governed by calcium ions include :

(i) Pacemaker activity in the S.A. node and A.V. nodal conduction.
(ii) The force of heart contraction, and
(iii) Coronary and peripheral arterial smooth muscle tone.

Hence calcium channel blocking agents will be useful clinically in

(i) Atrial flutter and fibrillation (suppress the pacemaker activity and A.V. nodal conduction).
(ii) Hypertension (exerts negative inotropic effect).
(iii) Ischemic heart diseases (coronary vasodilation).
(iv) Hypertension and congestive heart failure (peripheral vasodilation), and
(v) Pulmonary hypertension (pulmonary vasodilation).

The negative inotropic effect exerted by these agents suppresses the reflex sympathetic activation of heart. The above range of cardiovascular effects (alongwith non-cardiac effects) differentiates calcium channel blocking agents from direct vasodilators. The latter do not dilate the coronary artery.

Verapamil, nifedipine, diltiazam, nicardipine, are some of the prominant examples of calcium channel blockers. They principally act by the inhibition of transmembrane calcium ion flux through the voltage dependent slow ion channels. However the possibility of the presence of additional intracellular sites of action can not be excluded. Structurally calcium-channel blockers are no way related with each others. However they retain a perfect degree of lipophilicity necessary to penetrate the cell membrane. These agents interact with at least three binding sites on the calcium channel in an allosteric fashion. Most of these drugs possess a tertiary nitrogen atom in their structure. Once they reach at their site of action, this tertiary nitrogen gets quaternerised and forms a stable complex with the prosthetic group of the ion channel or may bind with calcium co-ordination site which is very near to the calcium channel. Thus, the operation of channel is hampered. Thus, calcium channel blockers bear similarity of mechanism of action with local anaesthetics (i.e. sodium ion channel blockers).

All these calcium channel blocking agents bear the same set of adverse effects which include,

(i) GIT : Nausea, diarrhoea, cramps, etc.

(ii) Due to vasodilation : Headache, flushing, peripheral edema.

(iii) Cardiovascular effects : Transient hypotension, bradycardia, palpitation, A.V. block etc.

(iv) Central effects : Depression, dizziness, fatigue insomnia, light headedness etc.

(v) Other effects : Nasal and chest congestion, chills, sweating, fever, allergic reactions etc. Due to high degree of fluid retention, concomitant use of a diuretic is usually required. They have wide range of clinical utility. They are used in the treatment of -

(i) Cardiac arrhythmias, e.g. atrial fibrillation, supraventricular tachycardia

(ii) Angina pectoris,

(iii) Hypertension,

(iv) Congestive cardiac failure, and

(v) Migraine.

27.7 AGENTS ACTING ON RENIN-ANGIO TENSIN SYSTEM

Renin (molecular weight $\cong 42,000$) is a proteolytic enzyme, which is produced and stored in the granules of the juxtaglomerular cells in the walls of the afferent arterioles of the kidney. On release into the renal arterial blood stream, renin catalyses the conversion of angiotensinogen (inactive precursor) into angiotensin - I. Angiotensinogen is a circulating α_2 - globulin with 14 - amino-acids. It is synthesized in liver and is circulated in the plasma.

Some renin inhibitors have reached clinical trials, but further development has been limited by poor bioavailability.

Angiotensin - I (decapeptide), which has less intrinsic activity is converted to more active form, angiotensin - II (octapeptide) by angiotensin converting enzyme. Angiotensin - II is one of the most potent vasoconstrictor agent. The renin angiotensin system is an important part of homeostatic mechanisms in the body. It works to maintain the blood pressure at the normal level. It also regulates the electrolyte balance by controlling aldosterone biosynthesis and release from adrenal cortex. Similarly, the juxtaglomerular cells are directly innervated by central sympathetic nerves. Hence, under the conditions of strain and stress, the sympathetic stimulation may lead to hypertension due to the activation of renin angiotensin system.

The potential benefit of angiotensin - II antagonists has been demonstrated using the peptide saralasin, which is a specific angiotensin-II inhibitor. However the poor bioavailability of this agent has driven a search for orally active non-peptide compounds. In consequence, losartan was recently marketed for the treatment of hypertension.

Angiotensins are the potent vasoconstrictors. They tend to increase the peripheral vascular resistance. The angiotensin-induced release of aldosterone increases the sodium ion retention in plasma, resulting into an increase in plasma volume. The overall result of all these effects is hypertension. Hence, one can expect that angiotensin antagonists would be effective antihypertensive agents. This expectation was proved to be correct by the development of Saralasin (1971) and Captopril (1977), each being the member of two distinct classes. Saralasin, losartan, valsartan, eprosartan and saprisartan are the examples of competitive antagonist of angiotensin - II, while captopril is inhibitor of angiotensin converting enzyme (ACE) which leads to decrease rate of angiotensin - II synthesis.

(a) Saralasin :

It is a substituted analog of angiotensin - II, designed by **Pals et al** in 1971, which acts by competitively blocking the angiotensin receptor sites.

Sar - Arg- Val - Tyr - Val - His - Pro- Ala
Saralasin

In the structure of angiotensin – II, the phenylalanine at position 8, is replaced by alanine (results into decreased intrinsic activity) and sarcosyl is substituted at NH_2 - terminal (in order to increase the resistance to enzymatic hydrolysis by aminopeptidases) to yield saralasin molecule. It does not cross blood-brain-barrier and is retained in the vascular and extracellular fluid compartments to block angiotensin receptor sites. This results into decreased peripheral vascular resistance and blood pressure. An increase in blood pressure at initial stage of therapy may be due to the partial agonistic nature of the drug. In some cases a rebound hypertension after drug withdrawal may be seen which is due to sudden increase in plasma renin activity.

The plasma half life of saralasin (3 – 4 minutes) is very short. It is immediately get converted to inactive fragments by peptidases present in plasma and tissues. The adverse effects of saralasin include, severe hypotension, rebound hypertension and acute hypertension.

The drug is used in the form of its acetate to lower down the blood pressure in certain renin dependent hypertensive patients. The antihypertensive action of saralasin is potentiated by the concurrent administration of directly acting vasodilators.

(b) Captopril :

The less potent vasoconstrictor agent, angiotensin-I is converted to angiotensin -II, potent vasoconstrictor by a peptidyl dipeptidase (or dipeptidyl carboxypeptidase) enzyme which is also known as angiotensin converting enzyme (ACE) is known to be inhibited by a non-apeptide BPF_{9a} (bradykinin potentiating factors) present in the venom of pit viperus. This non-apeptide is termed as teprotide and has quick onset of action but lacks oral effectiveness. This lack of oral effectiveness was overcomed by introduction of captopril at the Squibb laboratories by **Cushman**, **Ondetti** and co-workers in 1977 which is structural relative of teprotide. It was marketed as antihypertensive agent in 1980 in the treatment of severe hypertension.

$$HS-CH_2-\underset{\underset{}{|}}{\overset{\overset{CH_3}{|}}{CH}}-CO-N\underset{H}{\diagup}-COOH$$

(mer) captopril

Chemically, captopril is D – 3 –

mercapto - methyl - propanoyl – L – proline. It inhibits ACE in highly specific fashion. It thus lowers down the synthesis and release of angiotensin – II. The actions exhibited by angiotensin – II (vasoconstriction and aldosterone release) are also inhibited. This results into the arteriolar dilation, decreased cardiac force of contraction and less fluid retention (diuresis). Though angiotensin mediated aldosterone release is inhibited, an adequate aldosterone level is maintained by other mediators like ACTH and plasma potassium ion concentration. The ACE - inhibition leads to elevated levels of circulating renin and angiotensin – I which may in part, be responsible for terminating the action of captopril.

Captopril is orally effective agent. The parent drug and its metabolites (disulfide dimer and cysteine disulfide) are mainly excreted through urine.

The adverse effects may be due to the presence of –SH group in the structure and its ability to inhibit angiotensin converting enzyme (kinase – II). The same enzyme also catalyzes the degradation of bradykinin, a potent vasodilator. Hence captopril potentiates the action of endogenous bradykinin. Frequent adverse effects include headache, fever, loss of taste, vertigo, minor gastrointestinal disturbances and severe hypotension. These effects are dose-dependent and may disappear upon the continuation of drug therapy.

Captopril is mainly used in the treatment of -

(i) mild to moderate essential hypertension, and

(ii) chronic congestive heart failure.

Its effectiveness in the therapy may be increased by the concurrent administration of either a diuretic agent or β-adrenergic blocking agent.

(c) Enalaprilic Acid (enalapril) :

It has similar pharmacological effects, mechanism of action and therapeutic uses to that of captopril. Like captopril, it does contain a "proline surrogate".

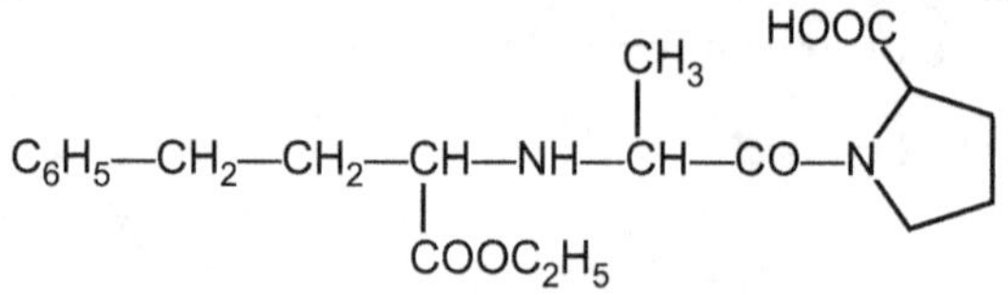

$$C_6H_5-CH_2-CH_2-\underset{\underset{COOC_2H_5}{|}}{CH}-NH-\underset{\underset{}{|}CH_3}{CH}-CO-N\begin{pmatrix}\\ \\COOH\end{pmatrix}$$

Enalapril (monoethyl ester of enalaprilic acid)

Due to poor oral absorption, enalaprilic acid is administered in the form of its monoethyl ester, enalapril. Enalapril acts as a prodrug and releases enalaprilic acid *in-vivo*. In comparison to captopril, it has higher potency, slower onset of action (due to the release of enalaprilic acid from its prodrug) and longer duration of action.

(d) Aldosterone Antagonists :

Antagonists of renin and aldosterone have also been developed to cause deactivation of renin-angiotensin system. However renin antagonists possess poor therapeutic applicability while aldosterone antagonists are clinically used as diuretic agents.

Aldosterone, deoxycorticosterone and hydrocortisone are potent antidiuretic mineralocorticoids. Spiranolactone, an aldosterone antagonist is a steroidal derivative having a lactone ring in the spiro arrangement at 17th position. Due to the structural similarity, it competitively inhibits the binding of aldosterone with its receptors.

Spiranolactone

Spiranolactone increases Na^+ and Cl^- ion excretion alongwith reduction in K^+ ion excretion. It also increases calcium excretion through a direct action on tubular transport. However after repeated doses, diuretic activity decreases presumably due to compensatory changes in the proximal tubule. Canrenone and canrenoate are the metabolites of spiranolactone and they still retain antialdosterone activity. Amphenone B and metyrapone are the agents that interefere with the biosynthesis of aldosterone but did not qualify the standards of clinical utility.

27.8 DIURETICS

Diuretic agents are usually effective in the treatment of edemas of cardiac, hepatic, renal or pulmonary origin. Some of these agents also possess mild antihypertensive activity and may be used in the treatment of hypertension with or without edema. The mean arterial pressure falls due to reduction in plasma volume and cardiac output. While a modest rise in plasma renin activity and renal vascular resistance occurs through reflex activation. Out of several classes of diuretics, agents from

(a) thiazide diuretics
(b) loop diuretics, and
(c) potassium sparing diuretics

classes are usually used to increase effectiveness of primary antihypertensive agents. Thiazides are more effective antihypertensive agents than loop diuretics, while potassium sparing agents are often used as an adjunct to long term thiazide therapy where they potentiate the diuresis and reduce the loss of potassium. The loop diuretics (e.g. furosemide, ethacrynic acid) are reserved when thiazides fail to give expected results.

Hypokalemia is the most serious side-effect of the diuretic therapy, specifically in patients with dysfunctioning of heart, liver or carbohydrate metabolism. Hence in such patients, potassium chloride administration is necessary to compensate the loss of potassium due to diuresis.

Thiazides are derivatives of 1, 2, 4 - benzothiadiazine, 1, 1 - dioxide. They all exhibit identical properties, mode of action, site of action and same range of clinical applications. Principal drugs include, chlorothiazide, hydrochlorothiazide, polythiazide, methylclothiazide etc. Except chlorothiazide, these agents have the great advantage of being effective in oral form. Due to weak carbonic anhydrase binding affinity, these agents get accumulated in erythrocytes.

The adverse effects of thiazide diuretics are usually rare. Gastrointestinal disturbances, alongwith certain allergic reactions may occur. Hypokalemia usually occurs with thiazide therapy which may be corrected by giving supplemental administration of potassium or using potassium sparing diuretic agent alongwith thiazide. Hyperglycemia and glucosuria may occur which precipitate the onset of diabetes mellitus. The drug induced elevation of serum uric acid level may cause gout. Impotence may also occur in rare cases during prolong treatment.

Ethacrynic acid, furosemide and bumetanide are the examples of loop diuretics. Nausea, vomiting, diarrhoea, headache, dizziness, hypotension, hypokalemia and hypochloremia are side-effects associated with loop diuretics. Ototoxicity also sometimes occurs which seems to be dose related. While spiranolactone, triamterene and amiloride are the examples of potassium sparing diuretics. Side-effects of these agents include nausea, mental confusion and hyperkalemia.

FAT-SOLUBLE VITAMINS

28.1 INTRODUCTION

The term 'vitamin' was first introduced by **Funk** in 1911 when he had isolated an unknown factor from the extract of the husks, which he later used in the treatment of beriberi. The work was initiated due to a number of earlier reports on conditions like beriberi, pellagra, rickets, and night blindness which were thought to be due to lack of some unknown factors in food. Many such unknown factors subsequently were identified.

The name *'vitamine'* was originally given to these accessory food factors because they were known to be vital for life and they were all believed to be amines. When it became clear that they have diversified structures and some of them do not contain even nitrogen, **Drummond** suggested the modification that led to the term, *vitamin.*

Most enzymes are proteins but the active sites often contain groups other than amino acids. These are metalloenzymes in which zinc, iron, cobalt, manganese or other transition metals are the catalytic centres. Many enzymes require cofactors - small molecules bound to the enzyme – in order to become effective catalysts. For example, all the vitamins from B-complex family are all cofactors.

The diet is the basic source of nutrients. It mainly contains essential trace minerals, inorganic nutrients, essential amino acids and vitamins. Together with certain amino acids, the vitamins constitute a total of twenty four organic compounds that have been characterized as dietary essentials. These are non-energy-producing organic substances that, along with carbohydrates, proteins and fats, are required in the diet but in small quantities for normal health and growth of the human-beings. The essential amino acids are organic substances but due to their requirement in larger quantities, they do not fit into this definition.

Vitamins are essential because man can not synthesize these compounds which are necessary for normal growth and healthy well-being of human life. With the possible exceptions of vitamins D, K and biotin, the rest of the vitamins must be supplied in the diet. The requirement of these vitamins in minute quality is indicative of their catalytic role in the cell. Besides this, it is also suggestive of their role as coenzymes or a part of coenzyme systems necessary for various metabolic reactions. Vitamins A and D instead of acting like coenzymes, behave more similar to that of hormones and bring about their actions by acting on intracellular receptor sites. However many vitamins need biological activation to carry out this function. For example, phosphorylation followed by coupling with purine or pyrimidine bases is required for the activation of vitamins like riboflavin or niacin.

Though the daily requirements of vitamins vary with age, sex and physical condition, in general, normal individual ingesting a well balanced diet gets adequate supply of these vitamins and needs no supplement. Vitamins K and biotin are synthesized by microorganisms in intestinal tract. Hence, a prolong dietary deficiency of these vitamins does not evoke any deficiency symptom. However, if the person is under the treatment with oral antimicrobial agents, the intestinal microbial flora get disturbed. This results into deficiency of these vitamins. Similarly the water soluble vitamins are easily washed out in cooking water and are destroyed at elevated temperature. While fat soluble vitamins are relatively stable at usual cooking temperatures.

Under the deficiency of vitamins (avitaminosis), additional amounts of vitamins are required. Avitaminosis usually arises from :

(i) Poor dietary intake.
(ii) Inadequate absorption in GIT due to prolonged diarrhoea or drug treatment.
(iii) Diseases of liver (chronic alcoholism) and biliary tract.
(iv) Other conditions like, anorexia, malabsorption, allergies and poor teeth.

Though the diet is well balanced, increased demand for vitamins are seen during - growth, pregnancy, lactation, under stress, in fever etc.

28.2 CLASSIFICATION

The present classification of vitamins is based upon their solubility in oil and water. This differentiation was first made by **Mc Collum** and **Davis** in 1915 where the fraction of dietary essential present in fats was termed as fat-soluble fraction A, while fat-immiscible fraction was named as water-soluble fraction B. The latter was subcategorized further as vitamin B_1, vitamin B_2 etc. when the fraction was further qualitatively scanned.

The fat-soluble fraction A, now termed as fat-soluble vitamins includes vitamins A, D, E and K. They are usually associated with the lipids of the food and are absorbed from the intestine with these dietary lipids. Usually the presence of bile is necessary for their proper absorption from the intestine. They are stored in liver. Hence, the diseases of liver or biliary tract impair their absorption and storage. Due to their lipophilic nature, they are eliminated from the body at relatively low rate which accounts for low degree of tolerance of a person towards overdosages of these vitamins. Structurally fat-soluble vitamins resemble closely with partially cyclized isoprenoid polymers. Water-soluble vitamins are, in general derivatives of endogenous polar substances like, sugars, amino acids, pyridines, purins or pyrimidine bases. They include vitamin B-complex and vitamin C.

The term, B-complex vitamins is a collective designation for a group containing thiamine, riboflavine, pyridoxine, nicotinic acid, pantothenic acid, biotin, folic acid and cyanocobalamin. These vitamins form a part of various coenzyme systems which either become linked with one another or with specific metabolic systems. For example, thiamine, biotin and pyridoxine are involved in decarboxylation of keto acids and reverse reactions while vitamins like, pantothenic acid and folic acid form a part of coenzymes involved in condensation and carrier functions.

Many of the water soluble vitamins have one feature in common and that is their ability to take part in reversible oxidation-reduction processes. They constitute vital redox systems. For example, riboflavine and porphyrines exist in both, oxidized and reduced states. They tend to occur together and some of them regulate different stages of the same metabolism. Similarly dietary deficiencies of any one of the B-complex vitamins are commonly complicated by deficiencies of more than one member of the group. Hence treatment with B-complex preparation, as a whole, is usually indicated.

Table 28.1 : Classification of vitamins

Name	Deficiency Symptom
(A) Fat-soluble vitamins :	
(I) Vitamin A	Night blindness
(II) Vitamin D	Rickets
(III) Vitamin E	Sterility in male, Abortion in female
(IV) Vitamin K	Clotting defects
(B) Water soluble vitamins :	
(I) B-complex vitamins	
(i) Thiamine	Beriberi
(ii) Riboflavine	Photophobia
(iii) Pantothenic acid	Dermatitis
(iv) Nicotinamide	Pellaegra
(v) Pyridoxine	Anaemia
(vi) Biotin	Dermatitis
(vii) Folic acid	Pernicious anaemia
(viii) Cobalamin	Pernicious anaemia
(II) Ascorbic acid or Vitamin C	Scurvy

28.3 VITAMIN A

Vitamin A was first recognized as a vitamin by **Mc Colum** and **Davies** during 1913-1915 which was later found to prevent and cure eye conditions characterized by xerophthalmia (i.e. drying and thickening of conjunctiva). It has the empirical formula $C_{20}H_{29}OH$ where the terminal hydroxyl group is usually present in the form of its ester. In 1931, it was first isolated from natural source while its synthesis was first reported in 1946.

Dietary Sources :

Fish liver oils, milk, butter, cheese, egg yolk and green vegetables.

Vitamin A is biosynthesized in animals from the plant pigments called as 'carotenoids' (provitamins) which are composed of isoprenoid units. The provitamins (i.e. carotenoids α, β and γ) are most abundantly present in carrots and other yellow vegetables. The absorption of these provitamins in intestine is accelerated by lipids and bile salts.

β-carotene is the rich source of retinol (vitamin A_1). An oxygenase enzyme located in the intestinal mucosa cleaves the β-carotene, yielding 2 moles of vitamin A_1 aldehyde or retinal which is then reduced to vitamin A_1 (retinol) by alcohol dehydrogenase enzyme.

The rate of conversion of inactive provitamin form into retinol is lowered down in certain diseases like diabetes mellitus. In the liver of freshwater fish, yet another closely related 3-dehydroretinol has been found. It was named as vitamin A_2.

(i) Retinol;   R = – CH$_2$OH
(ii) Retinal;   R = – CHO
(iii) Retinoic Acid; R = – COOH

Due to the structural features, retinol can exist in eight stereoisomeric forms. The synthetic retinol is all-transisomer having a straight side-chain while all other cis-trans isomers are bent at one, two or three double bonds. Retinoic acid is a partially active form of retinol and shares only few of its biological activities. The β-ionone ring present in the above structure and conjugated double bond system present in the side-chain is necessary for the activity.

Physiological Functions :

(i) There is an evidence that vitamin A is actively involved in growth and differentiation of epithelial tissues. It maintains the integrity of mucous membranes throughout the body. It stimulates basal epithelial cells to produce mucous. It is required in the formation of mucous to lubricate the membranes of the eyes, mouth, skin, GIT and urino-genital tract. This effect is evidenced to a greater extent in the eyes than in any other part of the body.

(ii) Vitamin A also plays a role in maintaining cell membrane, protein synthesis and skeletal muscle formation. Retinoic acid (vitamin A$_1$ acid) plays an active role in it.

(iii) It is required in dental development and influences the shape of the bone in growing organisms and thus controls health and growth. This is suggestive of close relationship between the functions of vitamins A and D with regard to cartilage, bones and teeth.

(iv) Its presence is essential in reproduction and embryonic development.

(v) However, the most important function of vitamin A is in the maintenance of visual process. Retina is the photosensitive part in the eye which is composed of cone shaped and rod shaped nerve cells. The rod shaped nerves are sensitive to dim light or to the light of low intensity while the cone shaped nerve cells are sensitive to light of high intensity and colour vision. Rhodopsin is the photosensitive pigment present in these nerve cells which is synthesized by a combination of opsin (protein) and the cis-isomer of vitamin A aldehyde. Light rays cause activation of rhodopsin resulting into initiation of a chain of events that ultimately leads to propogation of nerve impulses to optic nerves.

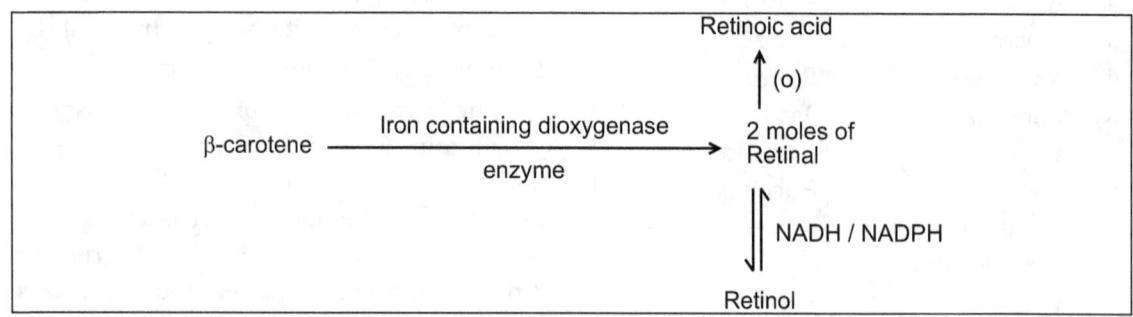

(vi) It is believed that vitamin A also plays an important role in the synthesis of endogenous hydrocortisone in the body.

Role of Vitamin A in Vision :

Retina is the innermost layer of the wall of the eye. In retina, the layer which is highly sensitive to the light is known as the layer of rods and cones. They act as light receptors of the eye. The photosensitive pigment of these receptors is rhodopsin which is formed by the combination of opsin with cis-isomer of retinal. Retinal is the functional vitamin in the vision process.

Vitamin A is stored in the liver as retinol which is then transported to the retina by some carrier proteins such as retinol-binding proteins (RBP). This transportation is stabilized by prealbumin. In retina, the RBP-retinol complex breaks and retinol is released which is deposited in the pigmented epithelial cells in the outer segments of the rods and cones.

In retina with the help of retinol dehydrogenase enzyme, the retinol from retinol-ester is oxidized to all-trans retinal. The latter gets converted to 11-cis-retinal by the enzyme retinal isomerase.

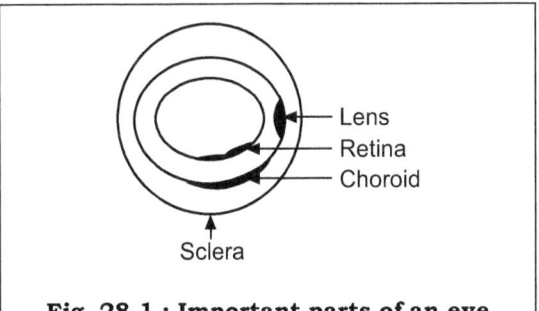

Fig. 28.1 : Important parts of an eye

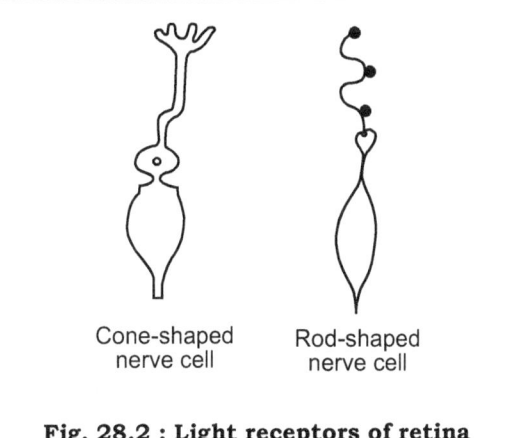

Fig. 28.2 : Light receptors of retina

In dark, 11-cis-retinal interacts with ε-amino group of lysine residues in opsin through a Schiff base linkage to form rhodopsin, a colourless protein. Rhodopsin is the real photosensitive pigment of the eye having a molecular weight of about 30,000 daltons. Porphyropsin, iodopsin and cyanopsin are the pigments present in cone cells but are responsible for colour vision. They too contain 11-cis-retinal but differ from rhodopsin in having protein moiety other than opsin.

On exposure to light, photodecomposition of rhodopsin occurs resulting into,

(a) activation of another protein, transducin, and

(b) degradation of rhodopsin back to opsin and all trans-retinal through different intermediates.

The activation of transducin then produces a photoexcited rhodopsin which causes a phosphodiesterase to be activated. This enzyme hydrolyzes hundreds of guanosine 3'-5' cyclic phosphate molecules. Cyclic GMP keeps sodium channels open across membranes, but when the GMP is

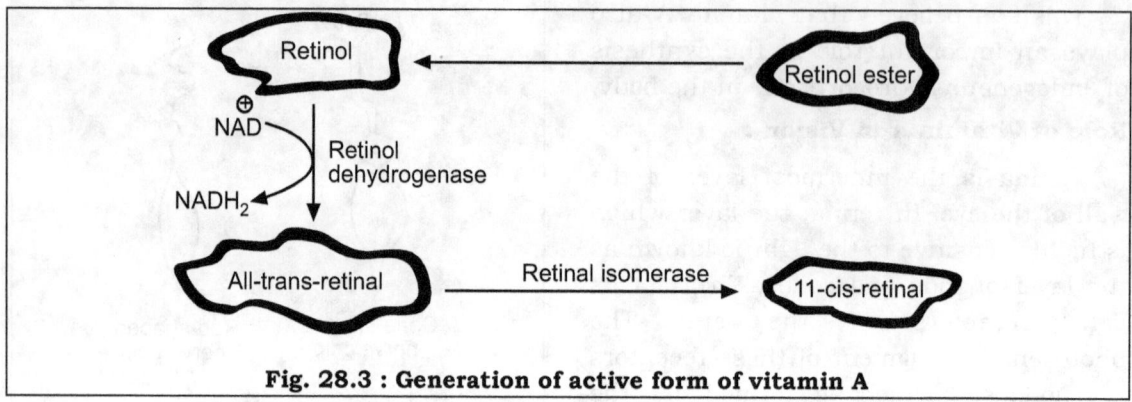

Fig. 28.3 : Generation of active form of vitamin A

hydrolysed, the sodium channels close and the passage of millions of sodium ions is blocked. Thus, the absorption of each proton is amplified many times to produce a nerve impulse. The nerve impulse transmission takes place through optic nerves. The all trans- retinal then gets converted again to 11-cis-retinal and the whole process is repeated.

Thus, rhodopsin in the eyes is degenerated by light and is regenerated in the dark to an enormous number of times. In deficiency of vitamin A, concentrations of retinal and of rhodopsin in the retina fall. The incomplete regeneration of rhodopsin results into night blindness (nyctalopia). Under the prolonged deficiency of retinal, opsin does not remain stable and undergoes degradation resulting into disorientation in the rods and cones. Permanent blindness thus may result if these changes become irreversible.

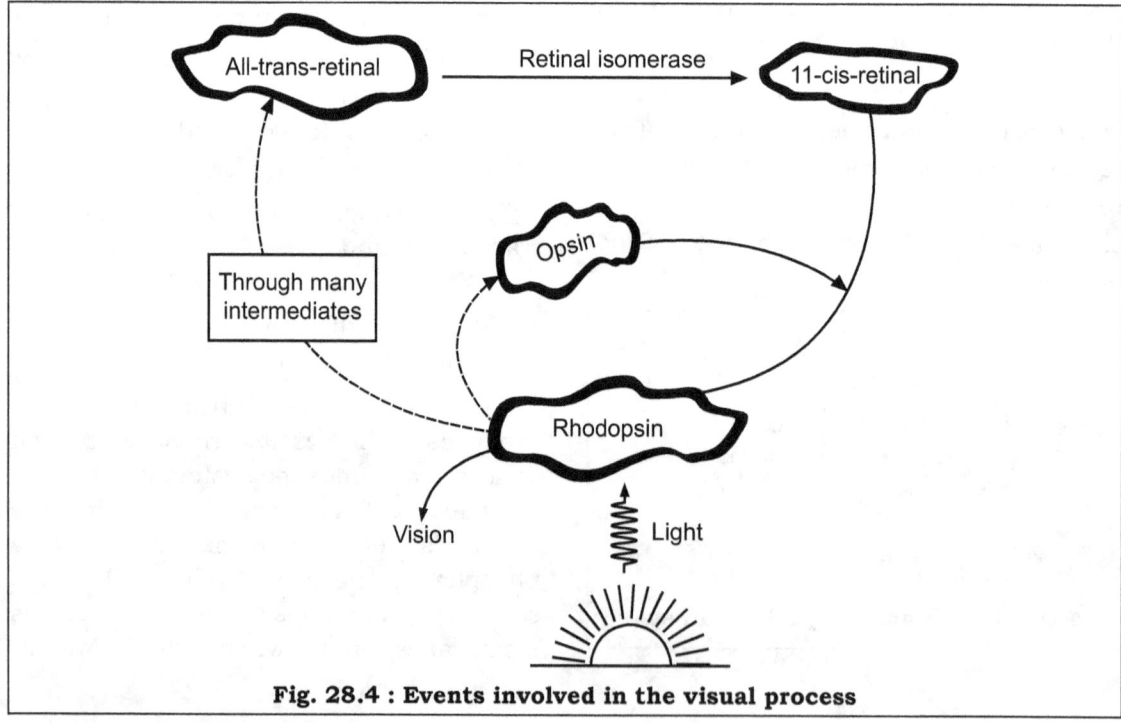

Fig. 28.4 : Events involved in the visual process

Deficiency Symptoms :

(a) Vitamin A is needed for the proper functioning of goblet mucous cells. It stimulates basal epithelial cells to secrete mucous. In the deficiency of vitamin A, the mucous secretion is suppressed, followed by proliferation of the basal cells. In the absence of mucous, the continued growth of epithelial cells results into the substitution of stratified keratinizing epithelium for the normal epithelium. This usually occurs in respiratory tract, alimentary tract, eyes and genitourinary tract. The external surface thus becomes dry and bacteria are not washed away. This leads to irritation and infection. The dryness and scaliness may be due to impaired formation of tissue glycoproteins.

(b) Vitamin A stimulates mucous secretion and suppresses the proliferation of the epithelial cells. The effects of vitamin on mucous secretion, cell proliferation and on the synthesis of proteins (e.g. keratin) were reported to be propagated by gene modulation. Vitamin A was found to exert its actions through intracellular receptors. Due to its suppressant effect on cell proliferation, its deficiency may decrease the patient's resistance to carcinogenesis. The antiproliferative activity of vitamin A may be of clinical importance in the treatment of tumors. One such metabolite of vitamin A having both vitamin A activity and anti-proliferative effect is 5,6-epoxyretinoic acid.

5, 6-epoxy retinoic acid

(c) Vitamin A is involved in the mucous and tear secretions in the eye that normally lubricate and moisten the eyes. In the vitamin deficiency, the cells become keratinized and mucous and tear secretion almost stops. The drying (xerosis) is followed in severe cases by softening of cornea. The keratinization may extend to conjunctiva, iris and lens. The external surface becomes dry and bacteria are not washed out easily. Eyelids may become sticky and scaly. The infection and ulceration may lead to frequent bloody exudates. The partial or complete blindness may result due to permanent opacity of the cornea.

(d) Vitamin A plays an important role along with vitamin D in the tooth and bone formation. Since the enamel layer is an epidermal structure, vitamin A deficiency may lead to abnormalities in tooth formation reflected in defective enamel.

(e) Vitamin A deficiency leads to histological changes in taste buds and surrounding tissues resulting into changes in the taste perceptions.

(f) Vitamin A deficiency may result into diminished production of corticosteroids, growth failure and foetal malformations.

(g) In the vitamin A deficiency, the susceptibility to respiratory tract infections increases due to decreased mucous secretion coupled with keratinization in broncho-respiratory epithelium. In intestinal mucosa however, keratinization does not occur but mucous secretion declines. The structural changes in intestinal epithelium may sometimes leads to diarrhoea.

Pharmacokinetics :

The dietary vitamin is usually in the form of retinyl palmitate which undergoes hydrolysis in the intestine by pancreatic enzymes to release free retinol. The concentration of retinol in the intestine remains in equilibrium with retinyl esters. Its absorption from intestine is facilitated by lipids and bile. The absorption occurs through active transport process utilizing the carrier proteins. Liver is the site for storage of absorbed vitamin in the form of palmitate ester. Liver has a good capacity to store vitamin A in large amounts. This capacity is further increased by using low doses of vitamin E. Thus, vitamin deficiency signs do not appear readily in patients deprived of dietary vitamin mainly because of the slow release of vitamin from these hepatic stores. Even after a prolonged period of inadequate intake, the plasma level of vitamin remains constant until liver store is completely depleted. From liver, the vitamin is carried over to other tissues by retinol binding protein (RBP). The retinyl palmitate undergoes hydrolysis in liver to release free retinol, which then forms a complex with retinol binding protein. The latter is also biosynthesized in the liver. Vitamin enters into the circulation in the form of this complex which is biologically inactive.

The RBP-retinol complex breaks when it reaches to the cell membrane of various target tissues. The free retinol released then migrates into the cell cytoplasm and exerts its action by intracellular receptor mechanism.

Retinal undergoes exhaustive metabolism in body. Retinal and retinoic acid are the active metabolites resulting from its oxidation. Many other metabolites are excreted in urine in free form and in the form of their glucuronoids. Neither vitamin nor provitamins are excreted unchanged in urine. Vitamin A does not cross placenta and passes into foetus very readily.

Daily Allowance :

The recommended daily allowance of vitamin A is 1000 µg (5000 international units) for an adult male and 800 µg (4000 international units) for an adult female. During pregnancy and lactation the level should be raised to 1000-1200 µg respectively. Children should receive 400-800 µg depending upon age and sex.

Toxicities :

The toxicity symptoms depend upon the age of the patient, dose and duration of administration. Since the rate of excretion of excess quantities of retinol is relatively slow, overdoses of vitamin A may result into acute toxicity. The symptoms include drowsiness, severe headache, vomiting and bone fragility. Some newly developed vitamin A analogues (e.g. isotretinoin and etretinate) are comparatively less toxic and more effective agents.

Therapeutic Uses :

(i) Vitamin A elevates mucous secretion and suppresses the keratin synthesis. Hence, it may be useful in the dermatological diseases and in the treatment of skin lesions.

(ii) Though it possesses anti-proliferative effect, its use in the cancer prophylaxis is greatly hampered by its toxicity.

(iii) It can be used as treatment regimen in persons suffering from xerophthalmia.

(iv) Its routine use is recommended during infancy, pregnancy and lactation.

Presently vitamin A is marketed in the form of retinol, tretinoin (i.e. all-trans retinoic acid) and isotretinoin (13-cis-retinoic acid).

Hypervitaminosis :

The deficiency symptoms of vitamin A do not appear readily in patient deprived of dietary vitamin for prolonged period mainly because of huge hepatic reserves of vitamin A in the body. Hence any extra supplements of vitamin A readily results into toxicity symptoms. Usually hypervitaminosis develops when 15000-50,000 µg of vitamin is consumed daily for long periods. Excess provitamin intake however remains non-toxic except appearance of yellowish discolouration of the skin (i.e. carotenemia). The symptoms of hypervitaminosis include headache, anorexia, fatigue, edema, irritability, bone fragility and hemorrhage. Hypervitaminotic mothers usually deliver offsprings with congenital abnormalities. The symptoms of hypervitaminosis gradually disappear after the withdrawal of retinoids.

28.4 VITAMIN K

Vitamin K, a fat-soluble vitamin is not a single entity but occurs naturally in the form of at least two distinct substances. Vitamin K_1 (isolated from alfalfa leaf) and vitamin K_2 (from putrefied fish meal and also synthesized by bacterial flora in the intestine). Both are derivatives of naphthoquinones.

Dam, a Danish investigator in 1936 gave the name vitamin K (K for koagulation, a German word) because its deficiency leads to blood clotting defects. Vitamin K_1 (phytonadione) is the only naturally occurring form of this vitamin. Many other closely related compounds possess vitamin K activity. These include menaquinones which are synthesized, particularly by gram-positive bacteria. They possess side-chain having 2-13 prenyl units in place of a phytyl side-chain. Menadione is a clinically used synthetic analog of vitamin K, usually administered in the form of water-soluble tetra sodium salt of the diphosphate ester. It is converted in body to menadione.

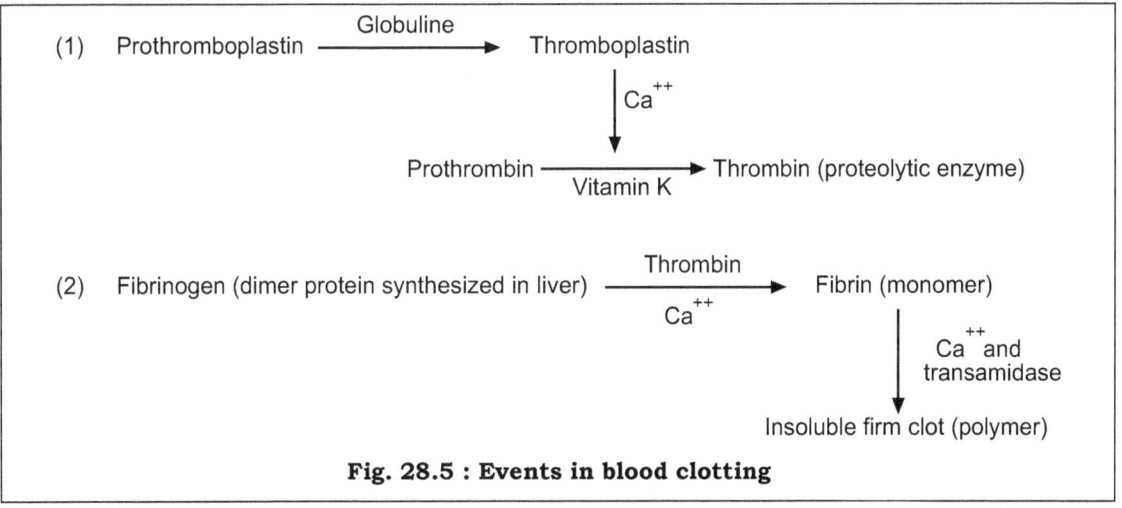

Fig. 28.5 : Events in blood clotting

Dietary Source :

Green vegetables, tomatoes, many vegetable oils and alfalfa leaves.

Physiological Functions of Vitamin K :

Liver is the site for the biosynthesis of various blood clotting factors like, prothrombin (factor II), proconvertin (factor VII), plasma thromboplastin component (factor IX) and the Stuart factor (factor X). These clotting factors are involved in the blood clotting phenomenon as shown in Fig. 28.5.

The above mentioned blood clotting factors remain biologically inactive in the absence of vitamin K. It is clear from the figure that in the clotting phenomenon, Ca^{++} ions play an important role. γ-Carboxyglutamyl residue within the prothrombin structure is necessary to produce strong binding sites for Ca^{++} ions. Vitamin K hydroquinone is a coenzyme in the conversion of glutamyl residue of the prothrombin precursor protein to γ-carboxyglutamyl residue which participates in the complexation of necessary Ca^- ions.

$$HOOC-\underset{\underset{NH_2}{|}}{\overset{\overset{H}{|}}{C}}-CH_2-CH\begin{matrix}COOH\\ \\COOH\end{matrix}$$

γ-carboxyglutamic acid

Vitamin K hydroquinone is produced by the reduction of vitamin K. Thus, reaction needs the presence of $NADPH_2$.

It is also significant that γ-carboxyglutamic acid has been found as a residue in all vitamin K dependent clotting factors.

Daily Allowance :

The vitamin K is synthesized in body by microbial flora present in intestine. Moreover it is adequately present in the normal diet. Hence, under normal conditions, humans do not need the vitamin supplement. However, if intestinal microbial flora is destroyed due to prolonged oral antibacterial therapy then vitamin deficiency may result. Under such conditions, daily allowance of 2.5 - 50 mg for an adult male will be sufficient. Since the natural vitamin K and menadione are lipid soluble, the bile salts or dietary lipids elevate their absorption from intestine. Hence if there is a deficient bile flow, a bile salt preparation should be administered. Both the bile salts and natural vitamins irritate the GIT membrane. Menadione may be used in the form of sodium bisulfite salt or tetra sodium salt of its diphosphoric acid ester due to their rapid absorption. They are usually preferred when there occurs any obstruction in bile ducts. Administration of vitamin A and E interferes with the absorption of

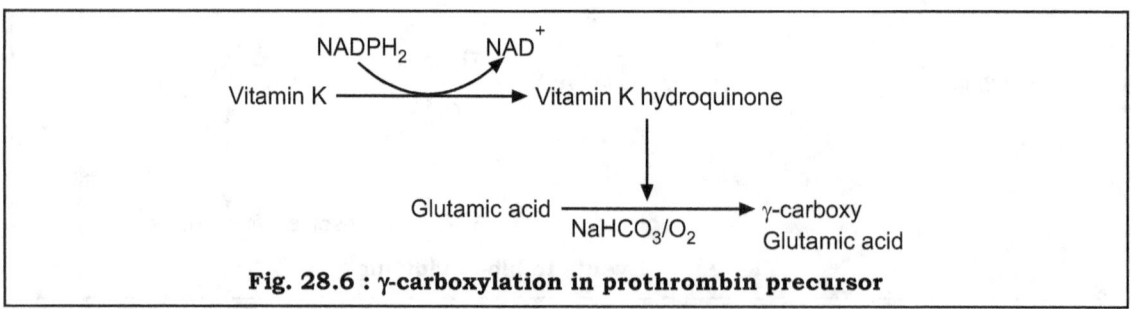

Fig. 28.6 : γ-carboxylation in prothrombin precursor

vitamin K. Vitamin K undergoes rapid metabolism to yield more polar metabolites which are excreted as sulfate and glucuronide conjugates. Adverse reactions are rare after oral administration. Large doses of synthetic menadione usually produce hemolytic anaemia due to increased breakdown of erythrocytes. Menadione competes with bile salts in the blood which results into jaundice. The overdose of vitamin results in an increased bleeding time. Certain vitamin antagonists can be used to treat poisoning from overdoses of vitamin K. These antagonists include heparin, bishydroxy coumarin and salicylates.

Therapeutic Uses :

(i) Vitamin K is used in the treatment of obstructive jaundice. However vitamin supplement is ineffective if prothrombin synthesis gets hampered due to excessive liver damage.

(ii) Vitamin K and its synthetic analogs can be used in the treatment of oral anticoagulant toxicity. Even ingestion of green leafy vegetables will minimize the intensity and frequency of such toxic symptoms.

(iii) Administration of vitamin K to mother prior to delivery can assure an adequate supply and safeguard against haemorrhage in infants.

28.5 VITAMIN D

The term, vitamin D is applied to a group of related steroids which have a common property of preventing and curing rickets. Atleast, ten different but chemically related compounds have vitamin D activity. They are all steroid alcohols.

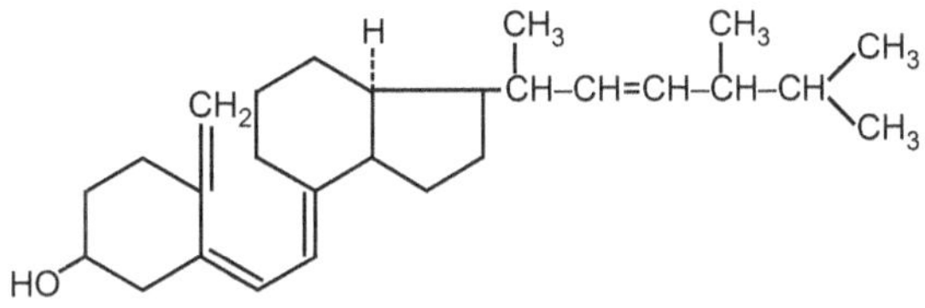

Ergocalciferol (Vitamin D_2)

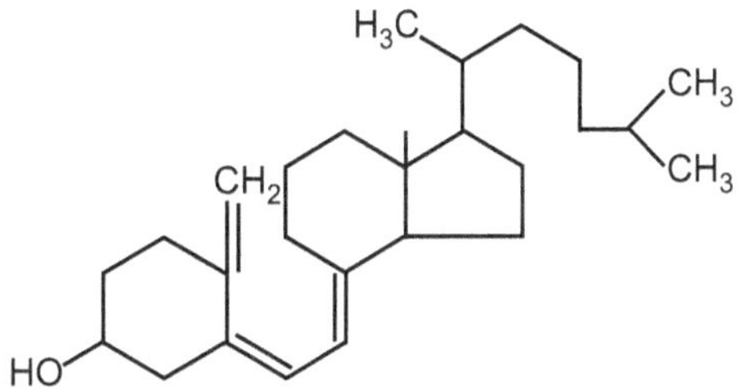

Cholecalciferol (Vitamin D_3)

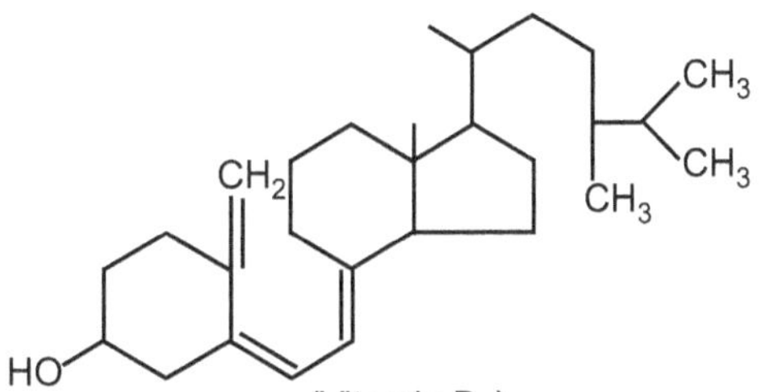

(Vitamin D_4)

Several other vitamins of this group are also known such as D_5, D_6, D_7 etc., but only vitamins D_2 and D_3 are of greater importance. They are usually obtained in the form of esters. The antirachitic properties seen due to direct exposure of body to sunlight was first reported by **Sniadecki** in 1822. Many compounds having vitamin D like activity were then obtained by ultraviolet irradiation of a variety of sterols. For example, ergocalciferol or vitamin D_2 was obtained as U.V. irradiation products of ergosterol which is present in yeasts and fungi. The reaction product, designated as vitamin D_1 was later found to be a 1 : 1 molecular complex of ergocalciferol and lumisterol and is no longer used.

7-dehydrocholesterol which originates from cholesterol, exists in the secretion of sebaceous glands of humans and animals. On exposure to solar U.V. irradiation, especially at 290 - 320 nm, it gets converted to vitamin D_3 (cholecalciferol). The rate of conversion is mainly regulated by the colour of skin (extent of pigmentation) and keratinization in the layer of stratum corneum. Vitamin D_3 is 50 - 100 times as active as ergocalciferol. It has also been isolated from other fish liver oils. Vitamin D congeners formed from plant steroids bearing varied side-chains are biologically inactive or less active than cholecalciferol. The side-chain is therefore of vital importance.

Dietary Source :

Vitamin D is present in egg yolk, butter, milk and fish liver oils etc.

Physiological Functions :

Calcium and phosphate are required for normal mineralization of bones and for maintenance of neuromuscular activity. For proper absorption of calcium and phosphate from the diet, vitamin D is needed along with parathyroid hormone (PTH) and calcitonin.

Vitamin D deficiency in infants causes rickets which results from an inadequate absorption of calcium and phosphate from the intestine and an impaired uptake of the minerals by the bony tissues; consequently the matrix fails to calcify and skeleton becomes deformed. The bones become soft and bend easily under the pressure of walking or standing. Enlargement of the ends of long bones occur particularly at the wrists and ankles. The muscle tone is reduced resulting into inability of the child to sit or to walk properly. In rickets, there is commonly a delay in dentition. The ricket children are more susceptible to respiratory infections. The disturbed neuromuscular activity may result into sleeplessness, convulsions or tetany. The disease usually attacks during the first two years of a child's life when the demands for calcium and phosphate are unusually high due to rapid skeletal growth in the body.

Certain forms of rickets in children were found to be resistant to the vitamin therapy. Some of these vitamin D-refractory rickets are hereditary and are characterized by a low serum phosphate level and elevated serum alkaline phosphatase level. The resistance to vitamin D therapy occurs usually due to hereditary defect in enzyme system involved in the conversion of 25-hydroxy cholecalciferol to 1, 25-dihydroxy-cholecalciferol in kidney. The latter acts as calcium mobilizing hormone.

The impaired calcium absorption from digestive tract is due to the lack of transport protein for calcium, which is not present in the patient but is formed on administration of the vitamin. Vitamin D_3 is converted in animals to 1α, 25-dihydroxycholecalciferol, now consi-dered to be the calcium and phosphate mobilizing hormone. The rate of conversion of vitamin D to calcitriol is regulated by plasma levels of calcium ions and parathyroid hormone (PTH). The calcitriol formation is increased by PTH through c-AMP system. Calcitriol then acts directly in the intestine to increase intestinal Ca^{++} absorption. The extent of reabsorption of calcium and phosphate by proximal tubules is also increased. The resulting increase in the blood calcium level suppresses further PTH release and hence further calcitriol synthesis. Calcitriol acts on the nuclear chromatin material of the target cells and stimulates transcription of messenger RNA to promote the synthesis of calcium binding proteins and alkaline phosphatase in the intestinal mucosa. It also promotes the renal reabsorption of calcium and phosphate. Nuclear chromatin is the site of action of calcitriol where it acts at m-RNA level. This is confirmed by an antagonistic effect of actinomycin D which is known for its inhibitory action for protein synthesis at the RNA level.

Calcitriol increases the rate of synthesis of calcium binding protein in the intestinal mucosa. Since duodenal mucosa is the primary site for Ca^{++} absorption, this protein accumulates more at this site with relatively lesser quantities in jejunum and ileum.

In the case of inadequate supply of dietary calcium, the vitamin D given, causes mobilization of calcium from bones. Such a decalcification of bones may occur during times of increased needs for calcium e.g. during pregnancy or lactation. Such mobilization of calcium from bones, if not prevented, results into osteomalacia or adult rickets.

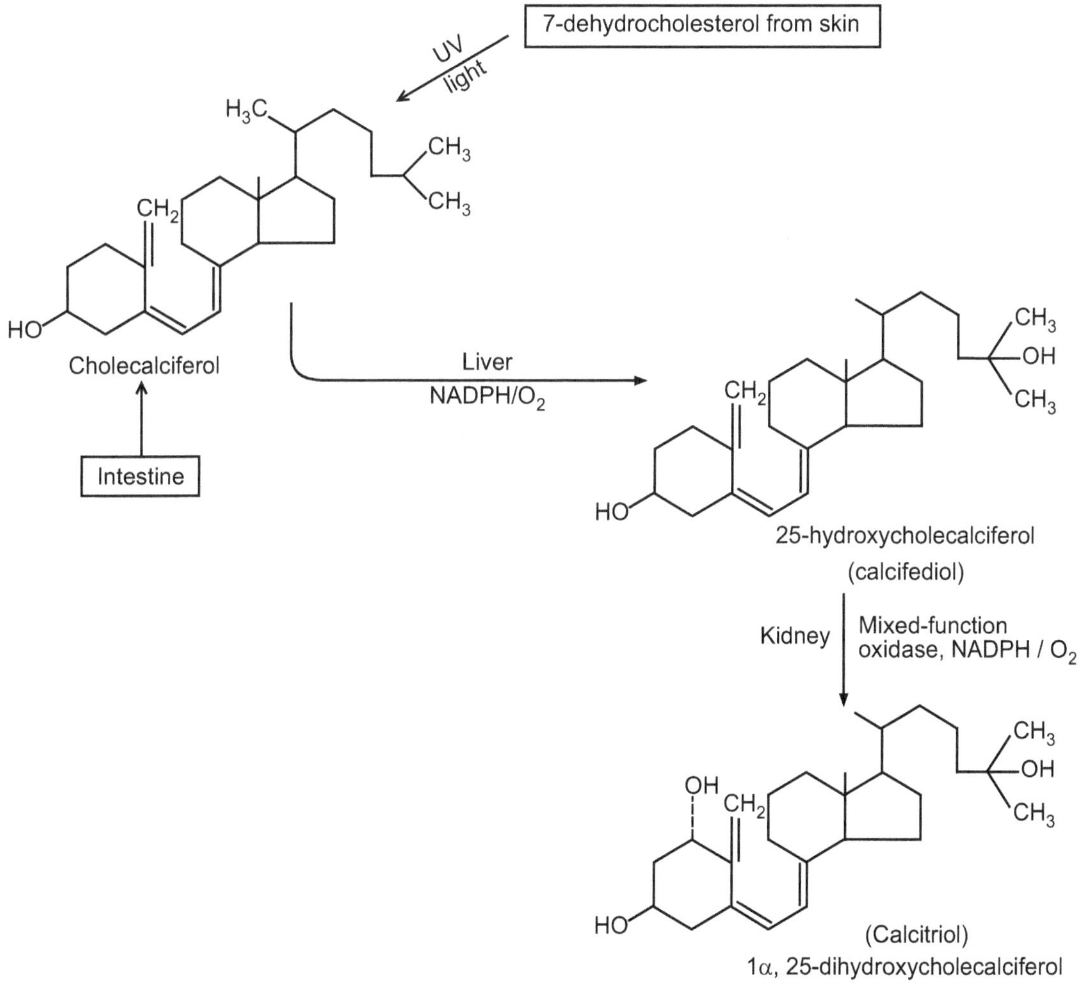

Fig. 28.7 : Conversion of vitamin D to bioactive hormonal form

Calcium and phosphate ions are essential for maintenance of :
(i) Normal neuromuscular activity
(ii) Mineralization of bones, and
(iii) Number of other calcium-dependent functions.

Vitamin D acts through intracellular receptor mechanism in order to maintain adequate plasma calcium level. The plasma concentration of calcium is maintained by,
(i) Calcium absorption from the intestine,
(ii) Mobilization of calcium from bones, and
(iii) Promoting renal reabsorption of calcium.

Parathyroid hormone and calcitonin work together with calcitriol in the execution of all above functions.

Pharmacokinetics :

Small intestine is the principal site for absorption of dietary vitamin. Vitamin D_2 is less readily and incompletely absorbed than vitamin D_3. Liver and kidney act as sites for activation of vitamin D where the vitamin is converted to biologically active metabolites like calcifediol and calcitriol. Hence, hepatic and renal dysfunction may lead to vitamin deficiency even if adequate dietary vitamin is absorbed. For example, in renal osteodystrophy, a diminished ability of kidney to convert calcifediol into calcitriol is exhibited, the rate of this conversion is also regulated through feedback mechanisms by plasma Ca^{++} level and parathyroid hormone activity. In patients having renal dysfunction, synthetic vitamin analogues like 1α-hydroxy vitamin D_3 and dihydrotachysterol (DHT) can be used.

It does not need renal hydroxylation. On activation in liver, DHT acts in a manner similar to calcitriol. In comparison to calcitriol, it is more potent and has a rapid onset of action. Other less active metabolites includes 1, 24, 25 trihydroxy vitamin D_3 and 24, 25-dihydroxy vitamin D_3. In some cases oxidative cleavage of side-chain has also been reported. These metabolites are mainly excreted through bile.

Deficiency symptoms for Vitamin D appear due to inadequate dietary supply and inadequate absorption of vitamin from intestine. For example, repeated diarrhoea or a diet rich in cereals, prevent absorption of vitamin D in intestine. Phytic acid content of cereals is responsible for this inhibition. Similarly hepatic and renal dysfunction, hypoparathyroidism and prolonged administration of anti-convulsant drugs are some of the factors responsible for deficiency of vitamin D. Due to enzyme inducer ability, phenobarbital increases the rate of vitamin D metabolism. In children, the deficiency of vitamin mainly results in faulty mineralization of bones and teeth. In adults, the low plasma calcium level caused by vitamin deficiency is normalized by mobilization of calcium from bones. This results into osteomalacia or adults ricket. It is more evident during times of increased demands for calcium e.g. during pregnancy or lactation.

Daily Allowance :

The average daily adult requirements for vitamin D is 400 I.U. or 0.01 mg of cholecalciferol or ergocalciferol. Pregnancy or lactation increases the demand for calcium and vitamin D, which if not met, results in mobilization of calcium from bones of mother. It is used in the treatment of rickets and hypoparathyroidism.

Toxicities :

Vitamin D is slowly excreted in the form of its metabolites mainly through bile. Since the rate of elimination of vitamin metabolites is very slow, the un-utilized vitamin remains circulated in the body for several months which accounts for adverse reactions. Excess vitamin D causes nausea, fatigue, headache, loss of appetite, thirst and elevation of calcium and phosphate blood levels, resulting in calcium and phosphate deposition in the heart, lungs and kidneys. Hypercalcemia results into inhibition of action of antidiuretic hormone, reflected into polyurea, polydipsia and proteinurea.

28.6 VITAMIN E

The term 'Vitamin E' refers to a group of closely related compounds which occur naturally and which are, to different degrees possessing fertility or antisterility property. **Evans** gathered an evidence about its existence in 1922 and 14 years later, isolated it from wheat germ oil. The generic name 'tocopherol' (Greek : tokos - for child birth; phero - to bear) was adopted when it was evident that more than one compound possessed the activity. The most wellknown tocopherols include α-tocopherol (vitamin E), β-tocopherol, γ-tocopherol and Δ-tocopherol. Dextro-forms are more active than laevo-forms.

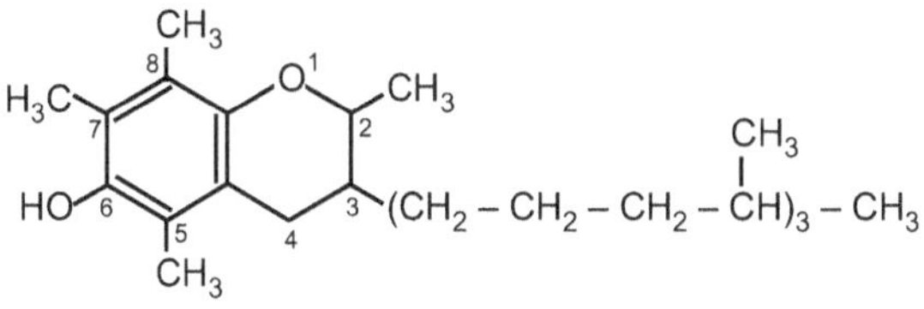

α-tocopherol (5, 7, 8-trimethyltocol)

β-tocopherol (5, 8-dimethyltocol)

γ-tocopherol (7, 8-dimethyltocol)

Δ-tocopherol (8-methyltocol)

Out of these, α-tocopherol is the most active and abundant form of vitamin E. Besides the tocol-series, another series, the toco-trienols also occur in nature which exhibits vitamin E activity.

The vitamin deficiency causes sterility in male rats while abortions in the female rats. However, deficiency symptoms of vitamin E in humans are not established.

Dietary Source :

The richest sources of vitamin E are wheat, germ oil, vegetable fats, eggs, cotton seed oil etc.

Physiological Function :

Most of the actions of vitamin E can be explained on the basis of their antioxidant properties. One of the primary functions of vitamin E is that, it prevents the oxidation of lipids, particularly unsaturated fatty acids. The latter are important constituents of cell membranes. Hence, vitamin E along with glutathione peroxidase, catalase and superoxide dismutase plays an important role in maintaining the integrity of the cell membranes. At the cost of which, vitamin E gets oxidized to durohydroquinone.

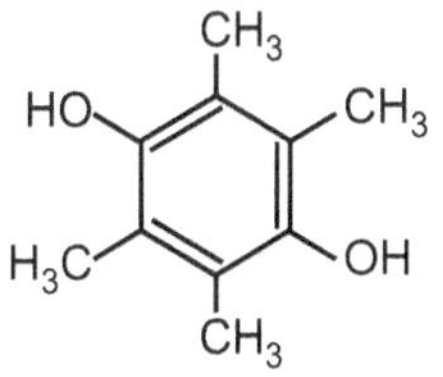

Durohydroquinone

Lipid peroxidation, i.e. the formation of harmful peroxides from the interaction between oxygen and highly unsaturated fats, needs to be controlled in the body. This otherwise results in serious damage to various body proteins. For example, oxidative destruction of erythrocyte cell membrane may result into hemolysis of the cell. Vitamin E is thought to be the leading agent for prevention of peroxides and free radical production. Hence, diet rich in fatty content increases the requirement for vitamin. Selenium was reported to act synergistically with vitamin E to protect the cell membrane from oxidative damage.

Vitamin E plays an important role in the maintenance of structural and functional features of smooth muscles, cardiac muscles and skeletal muscles. It also facilitates better utilization of available vitamin A by preventing its oxidative degradation.

Recently it has been postulated that, atherosclerosis, appears to be due to a deficiency of prostacyclin (a naturally occurring prostaglandin, derived from arachidonic acid. It is a potent vasodilator and is an inhibitor of platelet aggregation). This deficiency is caused by inhibition of prostacycline synthetase by lipid peroxides or by free radicals that are likely to be generated during hyperlipidemia or vitamin E deficiency.

Vitamin E also plays an important role in induction of essential cofactor in steroid metabolism. In GIT, the vitamin is poorly absorbed (about 20-40%). The presence of bile elevates the per cent absorption of vitamin. In different tissues, the vitamin is distributed through lymphatic system. The urinary metabolites are glucuronides of tocopheronic acid. Several quinone like metabolites result in intracellular metabolism.

Deficiency of vitamin E usually results in muscular dystrophy and morphological changes in various tissues. This is reported to be due to the action of lysosomal enzymes released during fatty acid peroxidation.

Hemolysis of erythrocytes is observed in deficiency of the vitamin. The polyunsaturated fatty acids present in the erythrocyte membranes are attacked by peroxides and the membrane gets destructed. The deficiency of vitamin also leads to axonal degeneration in posterior cord resulting into neuropathological lesions.

In reproductive system, the degeneration of germinal epithelium leads to sterility in male while abortion occurs in female due to similar degeneration process.

Daily Allowance :

As such no deficiency symptom has been revealed in human beings. However for good health, 5-30 mg of α-tocopherol per day are considered adequate. The large amounts are needed by individuals on a diet having high content of unsaturated fats. While diet containing selenium or anti-oxidants will lower the amount of vitamin needed.

Toxicities :

Overdoses of vitamin E may lead to nausea, vomiting, diarrhoea or intestinal cramps. The intensity of action of anticoagulant drugs can be increased.

WATER-SOLUBLE VITAMINS

29.1 INTRODUCTION

Eijkman (1897) found that birds developed polyneuritis when fed with polished rice and were cured, when they were given rice polishings. Later on **Grijns** (1901) observed that rice polishings cured beriberi in man (beriberi in man corresponds to polyneuritis in birds). Grijns suggested that the cause of this disease was some deficiency in the diet and this was confirmed by **Funk** (1911) who prepared a concentrate of the active substance from rice polishings. Funk believed that this active substance was a definite chemical compound. Later on it was confirmed to be 'vitamin B'. The term B-complex usually represents a group of about 11 different essential substances namely, thiamine, riboflavine, pyridoxin, nicotinic acid, pantothenic acid, biotin, cyanocobalamine, folic acid, choline, inositol and p-amino benzoic acid. Though p-amino benzoic acid does not play a vital role in human metabolism, it has growth promoting effects in certain bacteria. The class, water-soluble vitamins consists of vitamin B-complex and vitamin C or ascorbic acid. Unlike fat soluble vitamins, the members of this class are structurally altogether different from each other. The reason for grouping them in a single class was their solubility in water. Ascorbic acid was differentiated from vitamin B-complex by designating it as vitamin C. This is probably because the dietary sources of ascorbic acid are quite distinct from the dietary sources of members of B-complex series.

Many of the water-soluble vitamins have one feature in common and that is their ability to take part in reversible oxidation-reduction processes. Thus, they form a part of various coenzyme systems. However, in order to function as coenzyme in specific enzyme system, they have to undergo either phosphorylation (e.g. thiamine, pyridoxine) or coupling with nucleotides (e.g. riboflavin, niacin).

Unlike fat-soluble vitamins, the duration of stay of water soluble vitamins is very limited due to poor facility of their storage or accommodation. The administration of excessive amount of these vitamins usually is without pronounced toxicity due to rapid rate of their elimination through urine. Considerable toxicity may however appear if huge amounts are chronically administered.

Certain conditions if remained untreated may result into deficiency of these vitamins. Such conditions include, fever, chronic alcoholism, diarrhoea, injury, hyper-thyroidism etc. Since the coenzyme forms of different water-soluble vitamins tend to occur together and some of them regulate different stages of the same metabolism, dietary deficiency of any one of the member is commonly coupled with deficiencies of other members of the group. Hence, treatment with B-complex preparation as a whole, is usually indicated to treat the deficiency symptoms of any member of the class. In rare cases, the reason for deficiency of water soluble vitamins may be traced to the deficiency of some fat-soluble vitamins. Such a multiple deficiency symptoms can be treated with mixed-vitamin preparation.

[I] Thiamine (Vitamin B_1, Aneurin) :

Thiamine was the first water-soluble vitamin to be discovered. **Jansen** reported its isolation (1926) which was followed by determination of its structure by **Williams** in 1936. Thiamine consists of a thiazole and a pyrimidine ring which are bridged together through a methylene group.

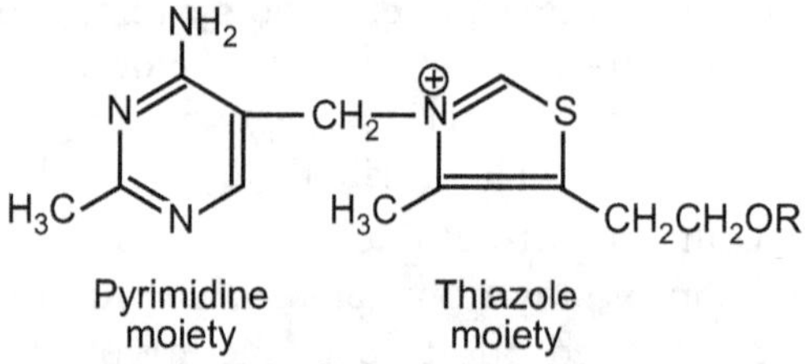

Pyrimidine moiety   Thiazole moiety

Thiamine; R = H

Thiamine pyrophosphate; R = $P_2O_6^{--}$

Dietary Source :

It has a widespread occurrence in nature either as a free vitamin or in the pyrophosphate form in many plant and animal foods. The rich dietary sources of thiamine include, rice polishings, yeast, egg yolk, vegetables and fruits. In medicines, the vitamin from synthetic origin is usually employed.

Physiological Functions :

(1) The thiamine pyrophosphate (TPP), the physiologically active form of the vitamin, constitutes the prosthetic group of decarboxylases involved in maintaining the operation of citric acid cycle. Each coenzyme requires a protein apoenzyme. TPP is found to be involved in transketolation (i.e. transfer of acetyl groups) reactions. For example, formation of acetyl CoA from pyruvic acid or the synthesis of acetyl choline involves TPP. The body's demand for thiamine is interlinked with the rate of carbohydrate metabolism. Hence, patients having diet of high carbohydrate content usually require higher quantity of thiamine.

(2) Thiamine pyrophosphate is involved in the synthesis of acetyl choline. The movements of skeletal muscles are controlled by transmission at neuromuscular junctions where acetylcholine acts as a principal neurotransmitter. Hence, in the deficiency of thiamine created naturally or by the use of thiamine antagonists (e.g. pyrithiamine), the neuromuscular transmission is impaired. Some of the symptoms of peripheral neuritis are due to decreased synthesis of acetylcholine.

(3) Polyneuritis : This is a condition characterised by deficiency of thiamine in birds. The muscular paralysis occurs resulting into inability of birds to fly, walk or even stand. It was proposed to be due to altered metabolic pathways in the brain. This is probably because of increased influx of pyruvic acid in the brain due to alterations in the blood-brain-barrier function. The neuritic symptoms seen in polyneuritis are inhibited by thiamine. Hence, the vitamin is also known as 'antineuritic factor or aneurin'.

(4) Beriberi : The disease is due to thiamine deficiency in man and is characterised by polyneuritis, muscular atrophy, cardiovascular changes, edema and GIT upset. The symptoms include, weakness, fatigue, headache, insomnia, dizziness, loss of appetite, constipation, sensory disturbances. (i.e. local anaesthesia type), paralysis of limb, palpitation, tachycardia, edema, confusion and depression. Depending upon the nature of the symptoms, beriberi sub-types have been recognized. These include,

(i) Dry beriberi : It is characterized mainly by predominance of symptoms of nervous origin, which include peripheral neuritis and muscular atrophy in adults.

(ii) Wet beriberi : The major symptoms are related to cardiovascular system and include edema and high output cardiac failure.

(iii) Infantile beriberi : This occurs within the first few months of the life. The main symptoms are high output cardiac failure, tachycardia, convulsions, vomiting, greenish stools and sometimes sudden death.

(iv) Cerebral beriberi (Wernick's encephalopathy) : It is a severe thiamine deficiency syndrome characterized by convulsions, tremors and peripheral neuropathy.

Due to effectiveness of thiamine in the treatment of beriberi, it is also termed as antiberiberi factor.

Pharmacokinetics :

Thiamine is well absorbed from GIT by Na^+-dependent active transport process which is assisted by passive transport if thiamine is administered in larger amounts. Usually thiamine exists in equilibrium with thiamine pyrophosphate content of the blood. Chronic alcoholism results in decreased absorption of thiamine leading to decreased activation of thiamine pyrophosphate. Like for all other water-soluble vitamins, the tissue-storage ability for thiamine is also limited. Once the tissue stores get saturated, the excess vitamin is excreted through urine in an unchanged form without any significant adverse effects. However, repeated intravenous injections of thiamine may lead to anaphylactic shocks.

Daily Allowance :

The normal daily requirement for the vitamin is 0.5 mg per 1000 calories to 3000 calories and then 0.3 mg for each additional 1000 calories. In pregnancy and lactation, about 0.6 mg may be sufficient for each 1000 calories. Under certain conditions like hyperthyroidism (increased metabolic rate), chronic diarrhoea, alcoholism and diuresis, extra amount of vitamin is needed. Thiamine has a limited distribution in the nature. Hence sometimes a fairly good diet may also be deficient in thiamine content. The chronic administration of glucose (or dextrose type carbohydrates) or chronic dependence on tea (contains antithiamine elements) may create vitamin deficiency.

Therapeutic Uses :

The vitamin B_1 can be used in the treatment or prophylaxis of :

(i) Alcoholic neuritis.
(ii) Cardiovascular disease due to nutritional deficiency.
(iii) GIT symptoms due to nutritional deficiency.
(iv) Neuritis of pregnancy, and
(v) Beriberi.

Thiamine Antagonists :

Oxythiamine and neopyrithiamine are the potent antivitamins which have been useful in studying thiamine actions. It is believed that oxythiamine competitively inhibits thiamine pyrophosphate whereas neopyrithiamine prevents the conversion of thiamine to thiamine pyrophosphate.

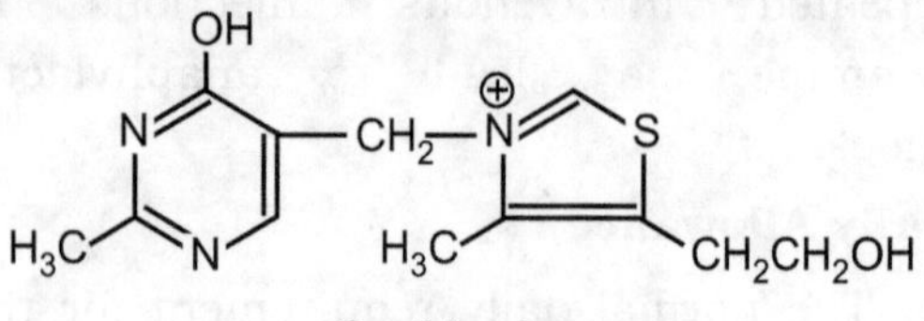

Oxythiamine

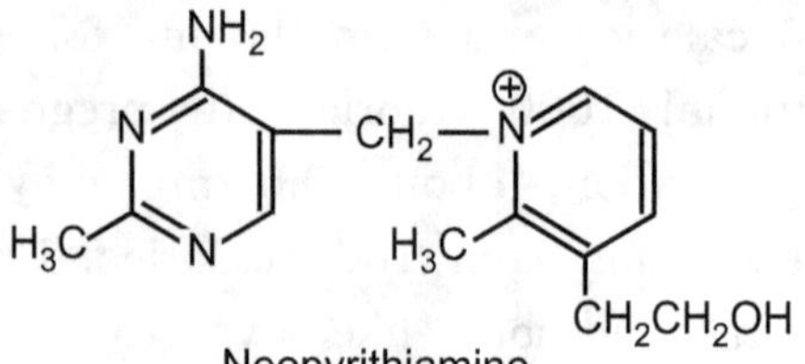

Neopyrithiamine (Pyrithiamine)

[II] Riboflavin (Lactoflavin or Vitamin B$_2$) :

In yeast, the presence of a yellow respiratory enzyme was reported in 1932 by **Warburg** which led to the isolation of the yellow pigment of the enzyme in 1933. The yellow pigment was characterised as vitamin B$_2$. Chemically vitamin B$_2$ is closely related to the yellow water-soluble pigments known as 'flavins' and since it was first isolated from milk, vitamin B$_2$ is also known as 'lactoflavin'. It is required because of its growth promoting activity. The name riboflavin was adopted when it was shown that a sugar alcohol (ribitol) or ribotyl moiety is the part of the structure.

Dietary Source :

The vitamin is widely distributed in nature as the free pigment or as a constituent of flavoproteins. The main dietary sources include, liver, kidney, meat, eggs, milk, yeast and green or yellow vegetables.

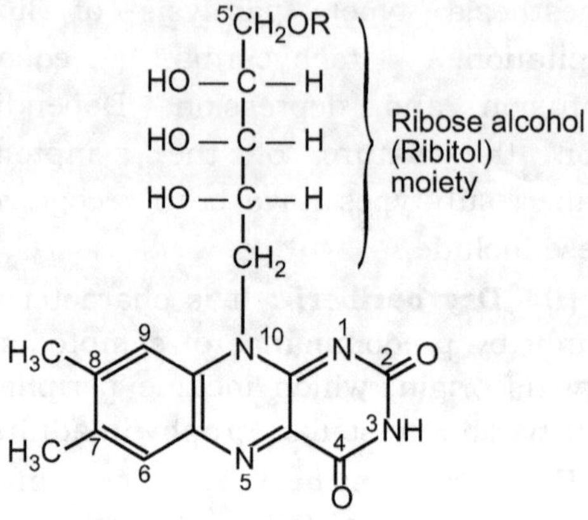

(Flavin nucleus)

Riboflavin; R = H

Riboflavin -5'- Phosphate; R = PO_3^{--}

Of the glycotyl derivatives tested, the L-ribityl, L-arabityl, D-xylityl, and D-lyxityl derivatives were inactive whereas D-arabityl and D-dulcityl (or galactoflavin) compounds were found to be antagonists.

Physiological Functions :

(1) In the body, riboflavin is found largely in the form of a dinucleotide, i.e. Flavine Adenine Dinucleotide (FAD). It is the coenzyme of a class of dehydrogenase enzymes known as 'flavoproteins' which function in biological oxidations as components of the electron transport system. Also a little amount of riboflavin is present as flavin mononucleotide (FMN).

Riboflavin + ATP → FMN + ADP ... (1)

FMN + ATP → FAD + PP ... (2)

Metals may also be present in some of the respiratory flavoproteins. In the reactions catalysed, the coenzymes never leave the enzyme and remain tightly bound to the parent enzyme throughout the reaction.

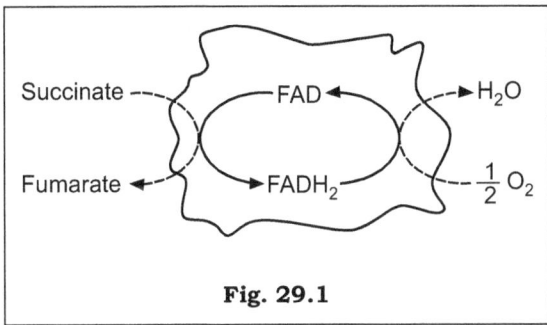

Fig. 29.1

(2) In different biological oxidation reactions, the flavoprotein coenzymes also assist several other enzymes (like, amino oxidases, xanthine oxidase and cytochrome 450 enzymes) to carry out their functions. For example, oxidation by liver microsomes, is a fate by which most of the drugs are metabolised. The key enzyme in these oxidation-reduction processes is cytochrome P-450. The enzyme cytochrome P-450 is present in the microsomes of liver and kidney (and in few other tissues in which microsomal oxidation occurs).

(3) The flavoproteins also play an important role in transfer of hydrogen and in oxidation of carbohydrates, amino acids and other products of metabolism. Thus, it is required for building and maintenance of body tissues.

Deficiency Symptoms :

The vitamin is devoid of any pharmacological effects. Riboflavin deficiency (araboflavinosis) is frequently complicated by the simultaneous presence of other dietary deficiencies. The symptoms include inflammation of mouth, inflammation of lips (cheilosis), inflamed pharynx, sore throat, anaemia and neuropathy. Ocular disturbances may also occur which are characterized by photophobia, redness of conjunctivas and corneal inflammation. The deficiency usually accompanies alcoholic pellagra.

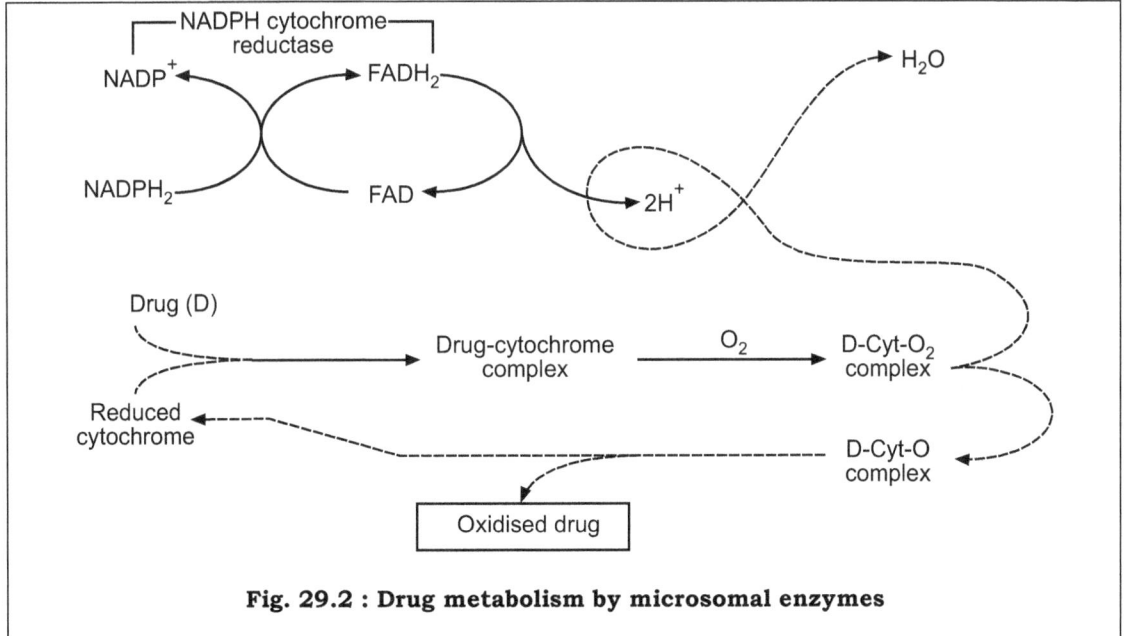

Fig. 29.2 : Drug metabolism by microsomal enzymes

Pharmacokinetics :

The vitamin is well absorbed from GIT, specifically from the upper segment by active carrier transport system. Like all other water-soluble vitamins, riboflavin saturates the storage sites at very low concentration and excess will appear in urine largely in unchanged form. Faeces also carry significant amount of the vitamin either in the free form or as its phosphate ester. Uroflavin is one of the urinary metabolites.

Daily Allowance :

Riboflavin is required for building and maintenance of body tissues. About 0.6 - 1.0 mg is needed for children. While 1.6 mg for adult male and 1.2 mg for adult female are the usual daily allowance. However increased amounts of the vitamin are needed during pregnancy and lactation.

Microbial synthesis of vitamin B_2 by bacteria *(Clostridium acetobutylicum)*, by yeasts *(Candida flaveri)* or by fungi *(Eremothecium ashbyii)* are some of the synthetic pathways of commercial importance.

[III] Niacin :

The term niacin is collectively used to represent both, nicotinic acid (niacin) and nicotinamide (niacinamide), which have been shown to be the human pellagra preventing (P.P.) factor. Nicotinic acid was first prepared by the oxidation of nicotine, a major alkaloid from tobacco. In humans, tryptophan in part, also gets *in-vivo* converted to nicotinic acid. The presence of nicotinamide in the coenzyme in the red blood cells of horse was reported in 1935 by **Warburg**.

Dietary Source :

Liver, meat, eggs and milk are relatively rich sources of the vitamin. It is also present to a smaller extent in potatoes and in vegetables. In general, the vegetarian diets do not contain considerable amounts of vitamin.

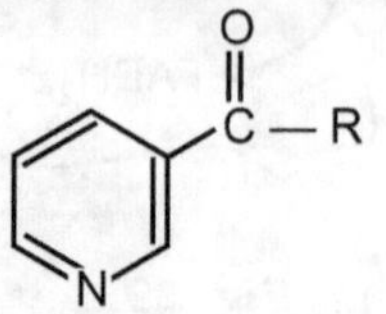

(i) Nicotinic acid (Niacin) :
R = – OH
(ii) Nicotinamide (Niacinamide) :
R = – NH_2

Tryptophan also serves as an important dietary source for niacin. Kynurenine is an intermediate in the conversion of tryptophan to hydroxyanthranilic acid. This conversion takes place in the liver and kidney and is catalysed by pyridoxine dependent enzyme. Hydroxyanthranilic acid has similar range of biological actions to that of niacin. In mammalian species, niacin can be formed from tryptophan in the intestine and in the tissues in the form of nicotinic acid nucleotides.

Physiological Functions :

(1) Niacin constitutes the coenzyme I (nicotinamide adenine dinucleotide, NAD) and coenzyme II (Nicotinamide adenine dinucleotide phosphate, NADP). In collaboration with flavoproteins, the niacin coenzymes are involved in biological oxidation reactions as the components of electron transport system.

Hydrogen liberated during Kreb's cycle is taken up by NADP which is thereby reduced to $NADPH_2$. This chain of reactions enables molecular oxygen to bring about oxidative change and it also plays an important role in the biosynthesis of fatty acids and various steroids. The reduced niacin nucleotides get deoxidized back to original forms by flavoproteins.

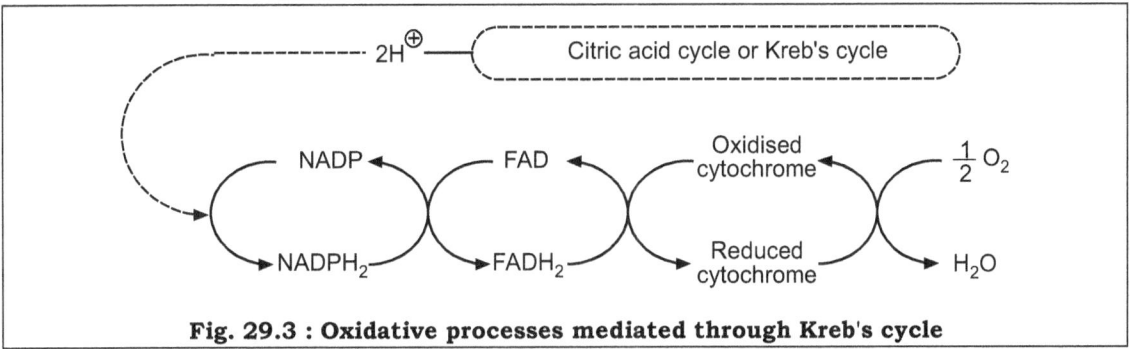

Fig. 29.3 : **Oxidative processes mediated through Kreb's cycle**

(2) NAD^+ and $NADP^+$ and their reduced forms are involved in many dehydrogenase reactions in the mitochondria, cytosol and endoplasmic reticulum of the cell which are essential for tissue respiration. Adequate level of niacin is therefore necessary for fat synthesis, growth and maintenance of healthy skin. The niacin nucleotide coenzyme forms are water-soluble and are usually free to diffuse away from enzyme surface to take part in another dehydrogenase reaction catalyzed by another enzyme.

(3) Though niacin and niacinamide are identical in their functions as vitamins, niacinamide is devoid of any pharmacological actions. While niacin, upon oral or parenteral administration causes peripheral vasodilation by the relaxation of vascular smooth muscles and causes flushing. The vitamin-induced release of histamine is suspected to be responsible for this action. Niacin also lowers the serum cholesterol levels and activates fibrinolysis, and thus is therapeutically effective as a lipid lowering agent in the treatment of certain cases of hyperlipidemia. Nausea, gastrointestinal disturbances, activation of peptic ulcers, glucose intolerance and hyperuricemia are some of the pharmacological actions of nicotinic acid.

(4) Pellagra : The name itself (pella-skin, agra-rough) is of Italian origin. Pellagra is usually remembered as the three D's disease. The three D's represent dermatitis, diarrhoea and dementia. In several cases, nervous dysfunction and mental disturbances may also appear. Other symptoms include, pigmentation of the skin, especially in the regions exposed to sunlight, anorexia, lethargy, mental confusion and hallucinations.

Though nicotinic acid deficiency is the major cause of pellagra, the deficiencies of riboflavin and thiamine also play an important role because they are necessary for the conversion of tryptophan into nicotinic acid.

The ability of individual foodstuff to prevent or to precipitate pellagra is not strictly determined by its content of nicotinic acid. Thus, milk has a low nicotinic acid content but effectively prevents pellagra because milk contains much tryptophan which is *in-vivo* converted to nicotinic acid. On the other hand, maize contains nicotinic acid in a form, that can not be absorbed from GIT.

Deficiency Symptoms :

The first deficiency condition was reported in dogs by **Chittenden** in 1917 which was termed as black tongue. In humans, under deficiency condition, the tongue becomes very red and may become ulcerative. The deficiency state usually occurs in chronic alcoholism and malnutrition and is termed as pellagra. Excessive salivary secretions are seen during this stage. Motor and sensory disturbances of peripheral nerves may also occur. The sex hormones e.g. estrogens present in the oral contraceptive pills, upon chronic administration may lead to vitamin deficiency in women.

Daily Allowance :

The minimum daily requirement for nicotinic acid is about 20 mg. The diet of high protein content may require higher amounts of the vitamin. In the treatment of pellagra, doses of 50-500 mg of nicotinamide are usually used. One niacin equivalent is equal to 1 mg of niacin which is considered equivalent to 60 mg of tryptophan.

Pharmacokinetics :

This vitamin is readily absorbed from the GIT and gets distributed to almost all tissues. The principal metabolites include, nicotinuric acid, N - methyl nicotinamide and N - methyl - 4 pyridone- 3 - carboxamide. The vitamin also appears in an unchanged form in the urine when higher amounts of the vitamin are administered.

Niacin is usually used for prophylaxis and treatment of pellagra. The symptoms rapidly disappear in certain cases by giving additional supplements of riboflavine and vitamin B_6.

[IV] Pyridoxine (Adermin; vitamin B_6) :

The name, vitamin B_6 is the generic name given to a group of structurally and functionally similar bioactive compounds. The group includes an aldehyde (pyridoxal), an alcohol (pyridoxol) and an amine (pyridoxamine). The structure of vitamin B_6 was first reported in 1939. The term pyridoxine is collectively used to represent all the three forms of the vitamin which are interconvertible and have the same biological activity.

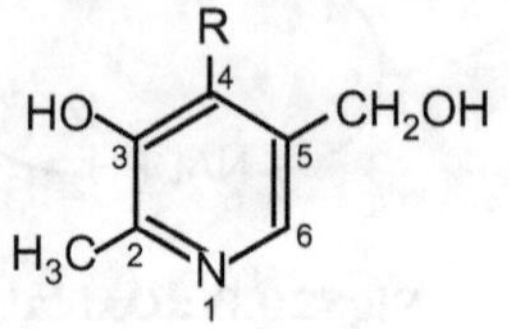

(i) Pyridoxal; R = – CHO
(ii) Pyridoxol; R = – CH_2OH
(iii) Pyridoxamine; R = – CH_2NH_2, and
(iv) 4-carboxypyridoxine; R = – COOH.

Dietary Source :

Yeast, milk, meat, liver, eggyolk and potatoes.

Physiological Functions :

(1) Esterification with phosphate at 5 position in pyridoxal occurs to give pyridoxal phosphate which is the physiologically active form of the vitamin. This reaction is found to be catalyzed by pyridoxal kinase enzyme. Pyridoxal phosphate acts as a coenzyme of a large number of important enzymes involved in the biosynthesis of niacin, coenzyme A and haemoglobin.

(2) Pyridoxal phosphate is responsible for a variety of enzymatic activities particularly related to nitrogen metabolism. Enzymes containing pyridoxal phosphate coenzymes catalyze a variety of reactions that include, transaminations, amino acid decarboxylations, amino acid dehydrations and desulphuration and metabolism of unsaturated fatty acids. Some of these reactions play regulatory role in the production of histamine, serotonin, catecholamines and γ-amino butyric acid in nervous system where these substances act as neurotransmitters.

(3) Vitamin B_6 is involved in the metabolism of tryptophan where it acts as a coenzyme in the conversion of tryptophan to serotonin. It also facilitates peripheral decarboxylation of levodopa. Its presence is also necessary for getting cysteine from methionine.

(4) It has also been employed for relieving from vomiting in pregnancy. Pyridoxine also interferes with the actions of steroidal hormones.

(5) Vitamin B_6 lacks pharmacological actions and exhibit no significant toxicity when administered in larger amounts either orally or parenterally.

Deficiency Symptoms :

Since pyridoxal phosphate acts as a cofactor in the biosynthesis of niacin, haemoglobin and various neurotransmitters, the main deficiency symptoms are related to skin, erythropoiesis and nervous system. They include depression, mental confusion, a decreased haemoglobin content and altered tryptophan metabolism. The biosynthesis of GABA (an inhibitory neurotransmitter) is catalyzed by glutamic acid decarboxylase enzyme which is dependent upon pyridoxal phosphate. Hence, failure of GABA production due to deficiency of vitamine B_6 leads to convulsions. Symptoms due to decreased production of norepinephrine and serotonin may also be seen.

Pharmacokinetics :

The vitamin is well absorbed from the GIT and is distributed to all tissues. The principal inactive metabolite include 4-carboxy-pyridoxine that is formed by the action of hepatic aldehyde oxidase on the vitamin. The metabolites along with unchanged vitamin are excreted mainly through urine.

Daily Allowance :

In infants and children a daily intake of 0.3 to 1.5 mg of the vitamin is sufficient. While a daily allowance of 2.2 mg for adult male and 2.0 mg for adult female is recommended. An increase in the dose is required, during pregnancy and when isoniazid is taken. Similarly extra supplement of vitamin B_6 is needed during chronic alcoholism and in women taking oral contraceptive pills.

The vitamin may be given prophylactically to the patients suffering from a deficiency of other members of B-complex. For example, beneficial effects of vitamin B_6 administration are seen in the treatment of rebound scurvy. The vitamin is also used in the treatment of premenstrual syndrome which is characterized by headache, depression, irritability and weight gain.

Vitamin Antagonists :

Isoniazid, cycloserine and hydralazine are the drugs which are found to antagonize actions of vitamin B_6. Isoniazid combines with the body pyridoxal to form pyridoxal hydrazone which has no coenzyme activity. Steroidal contraceptive agents also reduce the effectiveness of pyridoxal phosphate.

4-deoxypyridoxine, a structural derivative of the vitamin also exerts antivitamin properties. Its *in-vivo* conversion to pseudo coenzyme results into impairment of activity of several pyridoxal phosphate dependent enzymes.

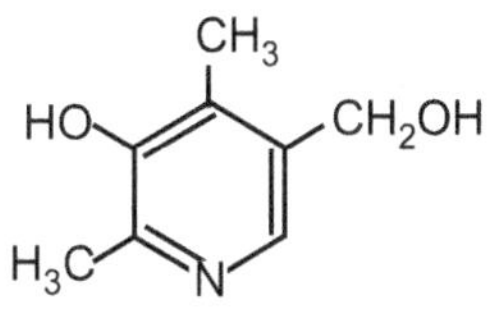

4-deoxypyridoxine

[V] Pantothenic Acid (Vitamin B₃):

A chick antidermatitis factor which is also capable of promoting the growth of the yeast and bacteria, when added to a simple medium of sugar and salts was recognized by **R. J. Williams** and his associates in 1938. As its occurrence was wide spread, it was called as Pantothenic acid from the Greek word meaning "from everywhere". Due to its wide spread occurrence, its deficiency in humans is rarely possible. However the symptoms of deficiency of pantothenic acid in human can be studied by developing the deficiency by using vitamin free diet along with the use of thiopanic acid. (i.e. vitamin antagonist).

Dietary Source:

The vitamin is synthesized by most of the green plants and microorganisms. The precursors are γ-ketoisovaleric acid and β-alanine. Yeast, wheat, peanuts, milk and liver contain large amounts of pantothenic acid.

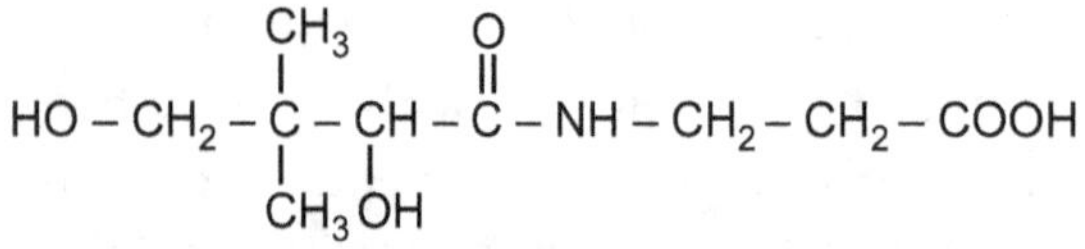

$$HO-CH_2-\underset{\underset{CH_3}{|}}{\overset{\overset{CH_3}{|}}{C}}-\underset{\underset{OH}{|}}{CH}-\overset{\overset{O}{\|}}{C}-NH-CH_2-CH_2-COOH$$

Pantothenic acid

This organic acid exists as a racemic mixture; out of which only dextrorotatory form is biologically active. This vitamin is a viscous oil and is best handled as the calcium salt.

Physiological Functions:

The coenzyme form of pantothenic acid is coenzyme A (i.e. coenzyme for acetylation). Coenzyme A is required for the enzymatic acetylation of aromatic amines. In acetyl CoA, the thioester linkage can activate the methyl carbon as well as the acyl carbon. It participates as an acyl donor in many metabolic processes like gluconeogenesis, oxidative metabolism of carbohydrates etc. It also acts as a precursor in the biosynthesis of acetyl choline, porphyrins, steroid hormones and fatty acids. Some detoxification reactions also involve acetylation.

Besides its participation in acetylation reactions in the form of coenzyme A, pantothenic acid is devoid of any pharmacological action as well as toxicity in therapeutic doses.

Deficiency Symptoms:

The cytoplasmic fatty acid synthesizing system utilizes a protein analog of coenzyme A which is called as 'acyl carrier protein', and the importance of this pantothenic acid derivative explains the reason for the presence of the vitamin in all cells of the body. Due to the widespread occurrence of the vitamin in the nature, its deficiency in human beings under normal circumstances is not known. In animals, deficiency may result into dermatitis, arrest of growth, depigmentation of hair and neuromuscular degeneration. In artificial deficiency produced in man, symptoms like, fatigue, headache, nausea, vomiting, abdominal cramps, flatulence, upper respiratory tract infections, cardiovascular disturbances, mental depression and muscle inco-ordination have been seen.

Pharmacokinetics:

The vitamin can be given orally in the form of calcium pantothenate which is readily absorbed from GIT. Vitamin then diffuses to almost all body compartments. No appreciable metabolism is found to occur and a major part of administered dose of the vitamin appears in urine in unchanged form.

Daily Allowance :

Calcium pantothenate has been employed in streptomycin toxicity and as a nutritional supplement. Panthenol (Dexpanthenol) is the alcohol analog of pantothenic acid, considerably more stable and is readily converted to the parent compound on administration. It has been employed topically for various skin lesions including burns, wounds and ulcer. The daily human requirement of pantothenic acid is estimated to be around 10 mg.

Pantothenic Acid Antagonists :

Pantoyltaurine and ω-methyl pantothenic acid are vitamin antagonists that have been used to block pantothenic acid utilization.

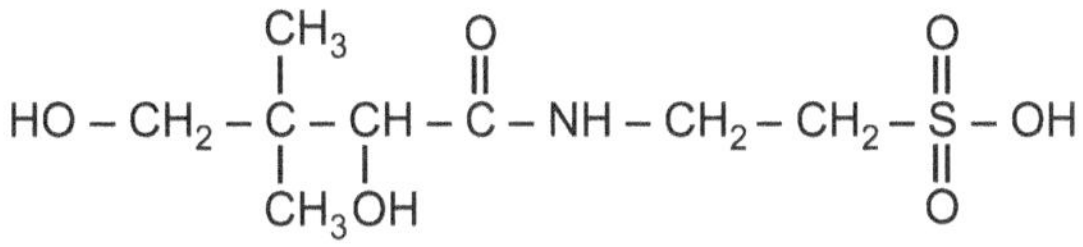

$$HO-CH_2-\underset{\underset{CH_3OH}{|}}{\overset{\overset{CH_3}{|}}{C}}-CH-\overset{\overset{O}{\|}}{C}-NH-CH_2-CH_2-\overset{\overset{O}{\|}}{\underset{\underset{O}{\|}}{S}}-OH$$

Pantoyltaurine

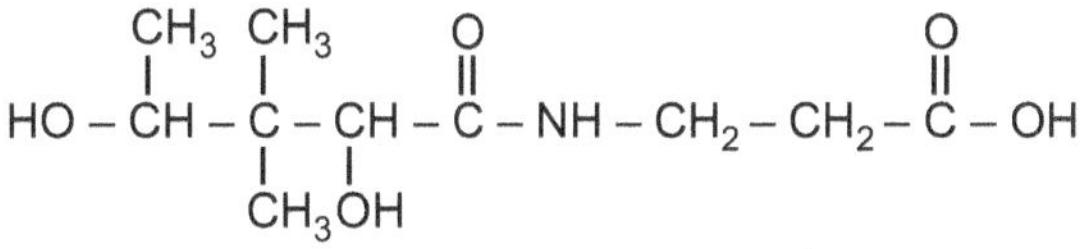

$$HO-CH-\underset{\underset{CH_3OH}{|}}{\overset{\overset{CH_3\ CH_3}{|\ \ \ |}}{C}}-CH-\overset{\overset{O}{\|}}{C}-NH-CH_2-CH_2-\overset{\overset{O}{\|}}{C}-OH$$

ω-methyl pantothenic acid

[VI] Biotin (Vitamin B_7 or Vitamin H) :

The presence of this vitamin in the egg yolk was first reported by **Kogl** and **Tonnis** in 1936. Bios, an extract of yeast was shown to be necessary for the growth of yeast. Later on, it was found to consist of three substances. They were Bios I (myoinositol), Bios IIA (pantothenic acid) and Bios II B (biotin). The structural formula of biotin was presented by **du Vigneaud** in 1942 that was followed by its route of synthesis. Subsequently other factors present in bios have been isolated e.g., pyridoxine and nicotinic acid.

The raw egg white contains avidin, a protein that binds with biotin with great affinity. This binding results in inhibition of biotin absorption, thereby depriving the animal from this vitamin. It is therefore an extremely effective inhibitor of biotin requiring systems. Its isolation in the pure form (glycoprotein) was first reported in 1940 by **Eakin**.

Animals feeding only on the raw egg white, soon develops deficiency symptoms (egg white injury) for biotin which include, nausea, anorexia, scaly skin, muscle pain and anaemia. However the binding ability of avidin to biotin can be destroyed by denaturation of the protein by heating the egg white.

Biotin is an organic acid that exists as recemic mixture, the dextro form is a biologically active form of the vitamin. It acts as a coenzyme for a large number of metabolic reactions that involve either addition or transfer of carboxyl groups. It is widely distributed in nature and large amounts are also produced by microbial flora present in human intestine.

Dietary Source :

The principal sources of biotin include liver, kidney, egg and yeast.

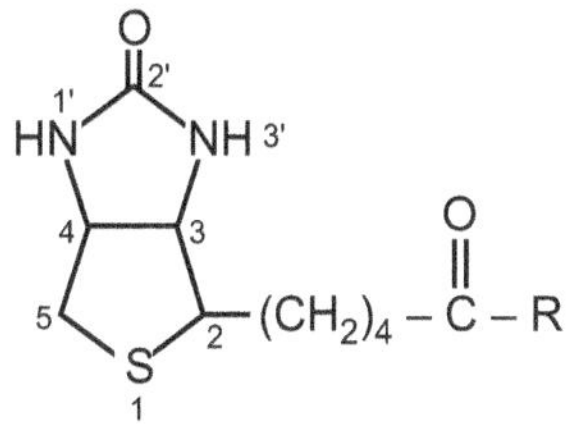

Biotin : R = – OH

Biocytin : R = –NH(CH$_2$)$_4$ – CH – COOH
                                      |
                                      NH$_2$

Table 29.1 : Formation of coenzyme A and acetyl CoA

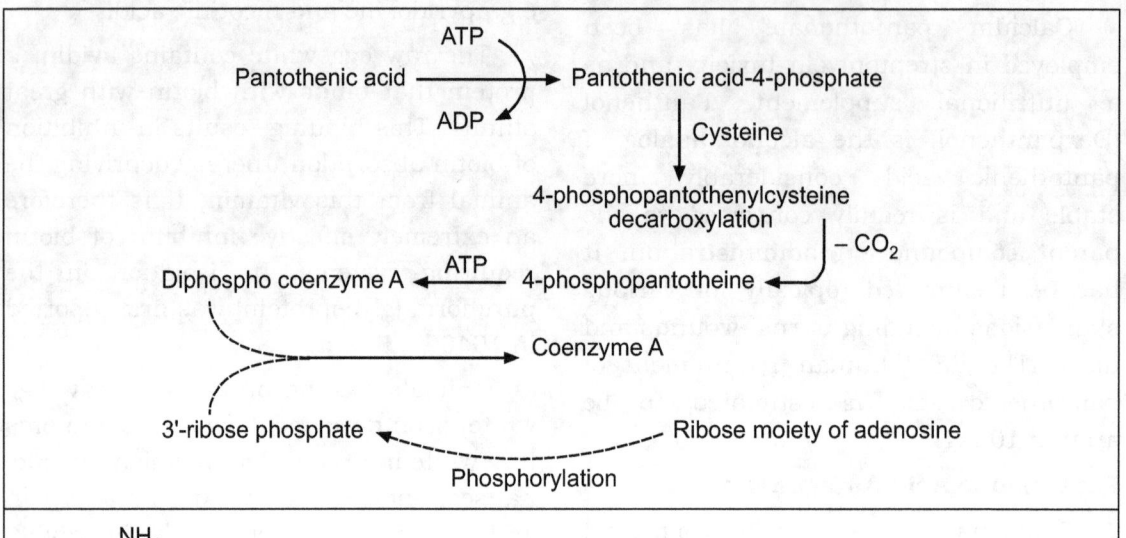

(i) Coenzyme A; R = H
(ii) Acetyl coenzyme A; R = $-\overset{\underset{\|}{O}}{C}-CH_3$ (thioester linkage)

Conversion of CoA to acetyl CoA

Pyruvic acid $\xrightarrow{\text{Thiamine pyrophosphate and lipoic acid}}$ Acetyl dihydrolipoic acid

Pyruvate decarboxylation

CoA → Acetyl CoA

Lipoic acid

Biocytin is the bound form of the vitamin present in the food.

Of the biotin analogs that have been prepared, desthiobiotin is of special interest because it can have vitamin activity, no activity or act as an antagonist, depending upon the micro-organism under study. Other biotin analogs having significant vitamin activity include, oxybiotin and biotin sulphoxide (dextro form only).

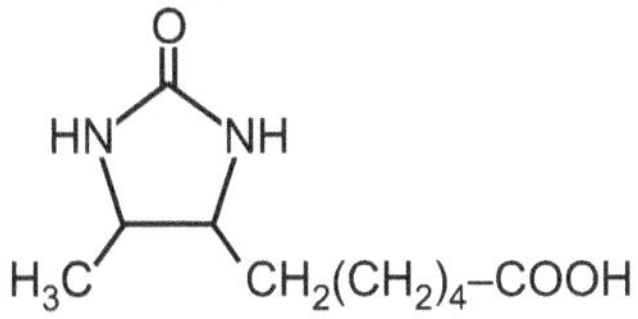

Desthiobiotin

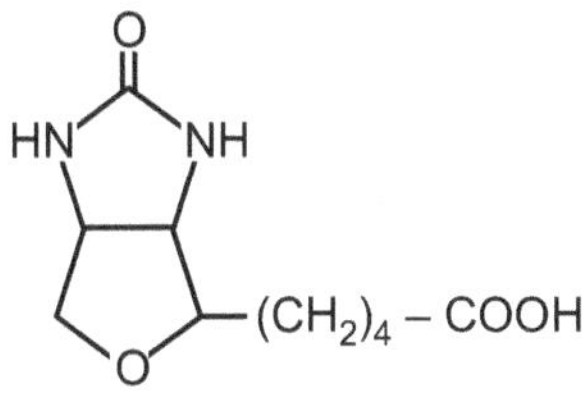

Oxybiotin

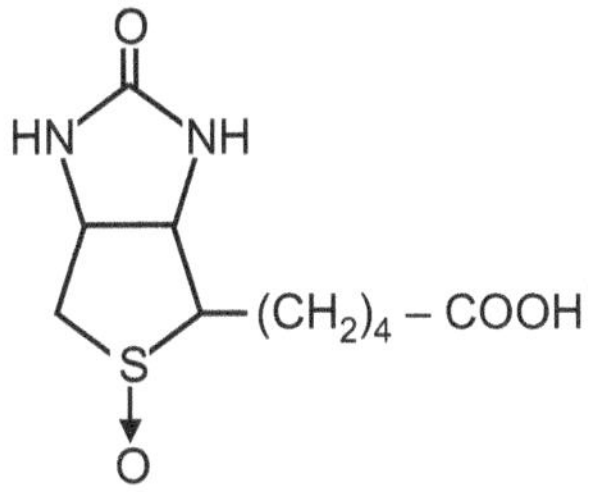

Biotin sulphoxide

Physiological Functions :

In the therapeutic doses, biotin neither exhibits any pharmacological activity nor any toxicity signs. It plays an important role in the metabolism of both carbohydrates and fats. The biological function of biotin is concerned with,

(a) the non-photosynthetic fixation of carbon dioxide by enzymes called as carboxylases.

(b) the transfer of carboxyl groups by transcarboxylase enzymes, and

(c) decarboxylation reactions.

Activation of carbon dioxide occurs resulting in its attachment to one of the ureidonitrogen atoms of biotin. The carboxybiotin thus formed, then transfers the carboxyl group to the substrate as shown in the figure 29.4. Other enzymes with which biotin appears to be intimately associated in carboxylation are,

(1) β-Methylcrotonyl-CoA-carboxylase (in leucine degradation).

(2) Acetyl CoA carboxylase (in fatty acid synthesis).

(3) Pyruvate carboxylase (in synthesis of oxaloacetic acid).

(4) Propionyl CoA carboxylase.

(5) Methylmalonyloxaloacetic transcarboxylase.

(6) Biotin containing enzymes are also involved in the synthesis of carbamoyl phosphate which further participates in amino acid metabolism and some nucleic acid synthesis.

Pharmacokinetics :

The vitamin is readily absorbed from GIT and is rapidly distributed to all tissues. No appreciable metabolism occurs. Excess amount of the vitamin is excreted through urine in an unchanged form with the traces of its metabolites like bis-norbiotin and biotin sulfoxide.

Deficiency Symptoms :

In humans, the deficiency of this vitamin rarely occurs. Symptoms of deficiency include, mild dermatitis, muscle ache, lethargy, anorexia and nausea.

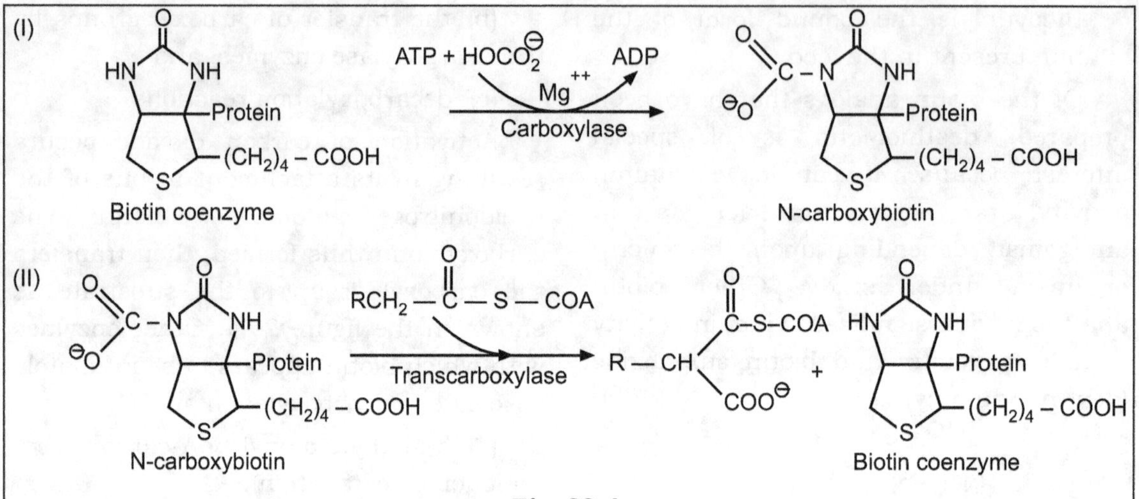

Fig. 29.4

Daily Allowance :

The minimal nutritional requirement has not been established because it has been difficult to quantify the amounts of the vitamin made available by intestinal flora of microorganisms. A daily dose of about 150 µg seems to be sufficient.

Biotin Antagonists :

Variation in the length of the side-chain affects the activity. Norbiotin (with three methylene groups in the side-chain), homobiotin and others with larger side chain are vitamin antagonists.

[VII] Hemopoietic Vitamins :

Folic acid and cyanocobalamin (vitamin B_{12}) collectively are called as 'hemopoietic vitamins' because these vitamins are involved in the development of blood cells. For the proper production of erythrocytes, many factors are needed. Principal amongst them are hematopoietic hormone, erythropoietin, folic acid and vitamin B_{12} (maturation factor). Other vitamins like ascorbic acid, pyridoxine and niacin are also required along with iron salts, copper and cobalt. Under the deficiency conditions of any one of the principal factors, abnormality in the erythrocyte production occurs resulting into decreased haemoglobin count. The oxygen carrying capacity of the blood is reduced leading to anemic condition. Anemias may thus result due to any of the following reasons :

(a) structural or functional changes in the bone marrow induced by chemicals or by pathogenic conditions; sometimes certain symptoms (e.g. renal dysfunction) or disease condition (e.g. rheumatoid arthritis) may create favourable situations for anemias.

(b) Loss of blood from the body.

(c) Increased destruction or abnormalities in blood formation. Pernicious anaemia and aplastic anaemia are the examples of this category.

Pernicious (i.e. deadly) anaemia is an example of megaloblastic anaemias. It results mainly due to unavailability of an intrinsic factor (a glycoprotein) which is secreted by the parietal cells of gastric mucosa. The glycoprotein deficiency is linked with failure to secrete pepsin and hydrochloric acid by gastric mucosa (i.e. achlorhydria). This intrinsic factor was found to be essential for the absorption of cyanocobalamin (extrinsic factor) from

GIT into the circulation. The inadequate or decreased absorption of vitamin B_{12} results into impairment of DNA synthesis specifically of the cells having rapid turnover e.g. red blood cells and epithelial cells of GIT mucosa. As a result, the erythrocyte formation in bone marrow is altered and a small number of abnormally large erythrocytes (megaloblasts) having a shorter life-span are produced instead of a large number of small erythrocytes. Since the biological activation of folic acid is dependent upon vitamin B_{12} availability, folic acid deficiency also occurs. Both these vitamins in their coenzyme forms, are essential for the synthesis of purine and pyrimidine bases, which are building blocks for DNA synthesis. The impaired DNA synthesis is then reflected into diminution in the formation of erythrocytes. The plasma iron and bilirubin level are increased by the unutilized haemoglobin. The macrocytic (megaloblastic) anaemia is usually accompanied by achlorhydria, leukopenia, thrombocytopenia and overall deficiency of haemoglobin. Under the deficiency of vitamin B_{12}, well marked neurological changes (i.e. peripheral neuritis, atrophy of optic nerves, mental deterioration and degeneration of spinal cord) are also seen. Since folic acid does not prevent the development of these neurological and lingual changes seen in pernicious anaemia, vitamin B_{12} deficiency seems to be responsible for these changes.

In megaloblastic anemia, the accompanied thrombocytopenia may sometimes become severe resulting in life-threatening hemorrhage. Such patients are immediately treated with platelet transfusion.

Thus pernicious anaemia is characterized by decreased absorption of cyano cobalamin due to less secretion of intrinsic factor in gastric mucosa. It is subcategorized into adult (addisonian) pernicious anaemia and juvenile (inherited) pernicious anaemia. Weakness, faintness, fatigue, palpitation and cardiovascular disorders (e.g. angina) are the usual symptoms of anaemias. Though folic acid fails to correct the neurological symptoms of pernicious anemia, it is effective in the treatment of anaemic phase of macrocytic anaemias.

[A] Folic acid (Pteroylglutamic acid) :

It is a group of vitamins for which folacin is a generic term used. The first member is folic acid. Its presence in green leaves was first detected by **Mitchell** in 1941 who then named the vitamin as folic acid (Latin; folium = leaf).

Other members of folic acid group are pteroyldiglutamylglutamic acid and pteroylhexaglutamylglutamic acid which are obtained by increasing the glutamic acid units in the chain.

Dietary Sources :

The main dietary sources of folic acid include, mushrooms, liver, kidney, yeast, bone marrow, soyabean, fish meal and green leafy vegetables. Most of the folic acid in vegetables is present in the conjugated polyglutamate forms where one or more glutamic acid molecules are incorporated into the structure. These are usually triglutamic and heptaglutamic acid conjugates.

Physiological Functions :

(1) Before folic acid can bring about its biochemical effects, it must undergo a chemical change to form more active form, which was originally thought to be folinic acid.

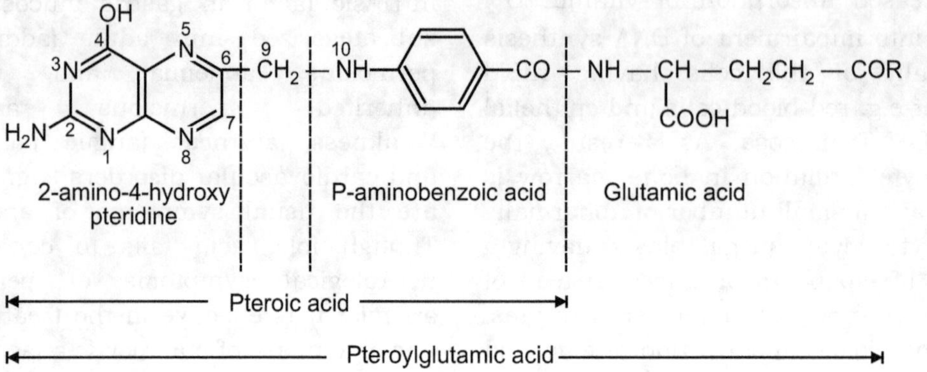

[Structural diagrams of folic acid and folinic acid]

Folic acid components: 2-amino-4-hydroxy pteridine — P-aminobenzoic acid — Glutamic acid
Pteroic acid = 2-amino-4-hydroxy pteridine + P-aminobenzoic acid
Pteroylglutamic acid = Pteroic acid + Glutamic acid
Folic acid : R = OH

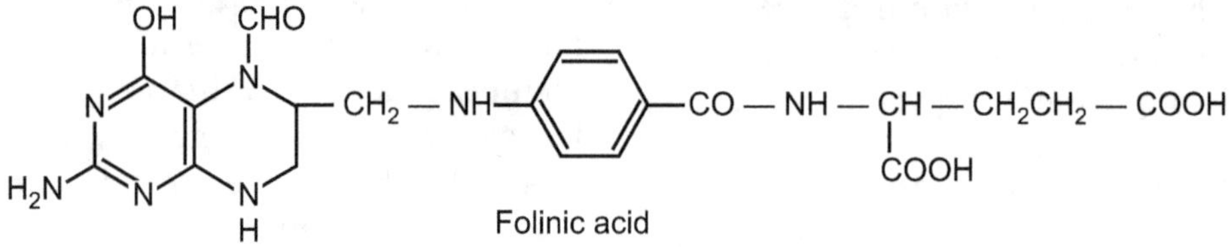

Folinic acid (structure shown with OH, CHO groups on tetrahydropteridine ring)

But the active factor is N^5-methyltetrahydrofolic acid. The reduction of folic acid and its derivatives to the tetrahydrofolic acid form is catalysed by folate reductase and dihydrofolate reductase enzymes. The reactions require the presence of NADPH and vitamin C.

Vitamin C protects tetrahydrofolic acid from oxidative destruction, at the cost of which ascorbic acid itself gets oxidised to dehydroascorbic acid.

(2) Various one carbon fragments are formed during metabolic oxidative reactions. The principal function of tetrahydrofolic acid (THF) is that of a carrier for these one carbon units. THF is actively involved in both, transport and transfer of these units at appropriate places in various biochemical reactions. The various coenzyme forms of folic acid perform the function of carriers for units such as methyl, hydroxy methyl, formimino (–CH=NH) and formyl (–CHO).

These one carbon units can be placed at positions N^5 or N^{10} of the molecule or may be bridged between N^5 and N^{10} to form a new 5-membered ring.

(3) The formyl (–CHO) unit is used in the biosynthesis of purines, pyrimidines, serine, methionine, thymine and glycine. Thus, the folate coenzymes are involved in the following important reactions :

(a) Biosynthesis of purine and pyrimidine nucleotides.

(b) Interconversion of certain amino acids. e.g. homocysteine is converted into methionine. Here vitamin B_{12} acts as a cofactor. Serine is converted to glycine using vitamin B_6 as a cofactor. Similarly folate coenzymes are also involved in the conversion of histidine to glutamic acid.

(c) THF is involved in both, generation and utilization of formate units e.g. incorporation of formate into purine ring.

Since all the above biochemical reactions are important for nucleic acid synthesis, folic acid plays an important role in cell division process.

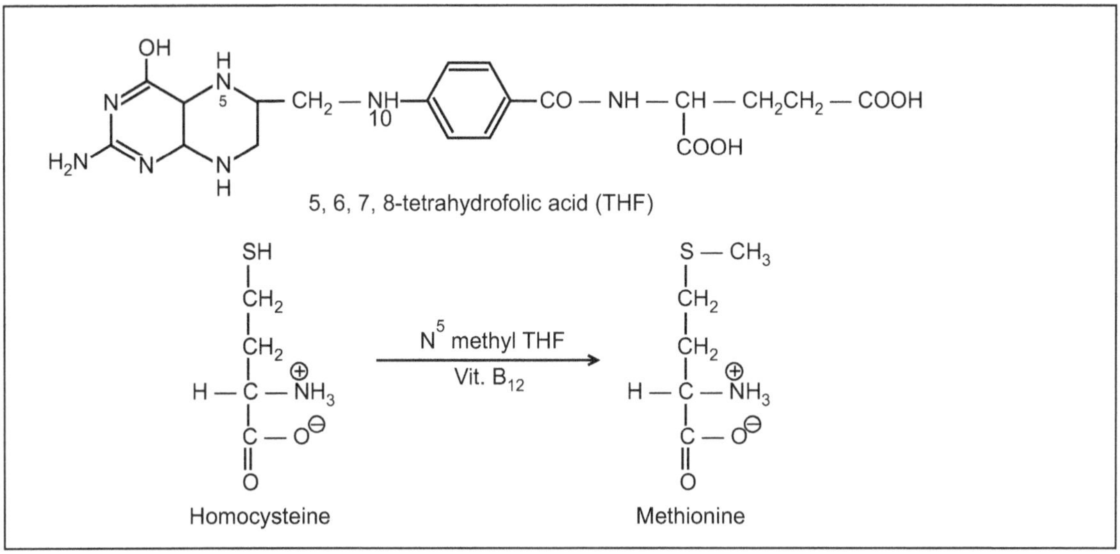

5, 6, 7, 8-tetrahydrofolic acid (THF)

$$\text{Homocysteine} \xrightarrow[\text{Vit. B}_{12}]{N^5 \text{ methyl THF}} \text{Methionine}$$

(4) The role of folic acid in cell-division is well reflected in the cell-types having rapid turn-over. Erythrocytes and epithelial cells of GIT mucosa are such examples of rapidly proliferating cells. Hence, folic acid effectively relieves anaemic phase of macrocytic anaemia by controlling the production of erythrocytes. However, folic acid does not prevent the development of neurological changes seen in pernicious anaemia. A possible explanation may be that folic acid is the essential factor required for proper development of erythrocytes while cobalamin may be responsible for maintaining the normal nervous function.

Pharmacokinetics :

In food, folates are mainly present in the polyglutamate form which are mainly absorbed from proximal part of small intestine by active transport process. Besides food, folate can also be given orally or parenterally. The latter route is preferred when oral administration becomes troublesome due to nausea or vomiting. In circulation, folate extensively binds with plasma proteins. It is circulated in the body mainly in the form of N^5-methyl tetrahydrofolate which then acts as a source of THF to various biochemical reactions in the body. In the form of polyglutamate, the folate is stored in the cells. Folic acid along with its metabolites are mainly excreted through urine. Some folic acid is also excreted through bile which is again reabsorbed from the gut. This enterohepatic recirculation is an important mechanism involved to avoid losses of body folates. Adverse effects of folate are rare and include fever and skin rashes.

Deficiency Symptoms :

The deficiency of folic acid may arise due to inadequate diet, chronic alcoholism, pregnancy or due to malabsorption of the vitamin. In alcoholism, the deficiency of folic acid may occur due to impaired enterohepatic reabsorption. The concurrent, administration of certain drugs like analgesics, adrenocorticoids, estrogens, pyrimethamine, trimethoprim etc. may also result in malabsorption of the vitamin. The deficiency symptoms include glossitis, weight loss, diarrhoea and megaloblastic anaemia (devoid of neurological signs).

Antiepileptic drugs may interfere in the biochemical functions of folic acid. Similarly, folic acid may also antagonize their antiepileptic activity. Hence, patients receiving anticonvulsant therapy when concurrently given folic acid for prolonged time, may develop megaloblastic anaemia and at the same time possess a low threshold of epileptic seizures. This is specifically true in the case of children.

Daily Allowance :

The minimal daily requirement in adults is estimated to be 50 - 100 µg of folic acid. However during pregnancy and lactation, the dose can be increased upto 200 - 400 µg per day as per the requirement.

Folate Antagonists :

Aminopterin and amethopterin (methotrexate) strongly inhibit the reduction of folic acid to dihydrofolic acid by the NADPH - linked enzyme, L-folate reductase.

These drugs thus prevent the formation of one carbon carrying coenzymes and inhibit normal synthesis of DNA molecules. These drugs hence, are used in the treatment of leukemias but the possibility of a megaloblastic anaemia developing under these circumstances must obviously be borne in mind.

[B] Cyanocobalamin (Vitamin B_{12} or antipernicious anaemia vitamin) :

The pernicious anaemia, one of the deficiency symptoms of vitamin B_{12} results mainly due to deficiency of an intrinsic factor (a glycoprotein of molecular weight of about 50,000) which is normally secreted by the parietal cells of gastric mucosa cells. The glycoprotein deficiency is linked with the failure of gastric mucosa cells to secrete pepsin and hydrochloric acid (achlorhydria). **Castle** in 1932, postulated the hypothesis that this glycoprotein is necessary for the transport of an extrinsic factor from the luminal side of the mucosal cells into the circulation. The transport is governed by extracellular Ca^{++} ion concentration and pH of the distal ileum region. **Smith** and coworkers, soon after showed that the extrinsic factor is nothing but vitamin B_{12}. Cyanocobalamin (vitamin B_{12a}) upon exposure to light is converted to hydroxycobalamin (vitamin B_{12b}), while hydroxycobalamin, in the presence of a cyanide ion, gets converted back to cyanocobalamin. Other cobalamins of physiological importance are nitritocobalamin (vitamin B_{12C}), nitrocobalamin, methylcobalamin and 5'-deoxy adenosine cobalamin.

Intestinal bacteria also synthesize cobalamin which is then stored in the liver. However an ideal absorption from GIT can not take place unless the vitamin combines with the intrinsic factor.

Dietary Sources :

Good sources include muscle, liver, kidney, eggyolk and milk. The vegetables are very poor in their vitamin B_{12} content. Vitamin B_{12} was first discovered in 1949. Commercially this vitamin may be obtained as a side product of streptomycin industry where it is synthesized by the microorganism, Streptomyces griseus. The molecule of vitamin B_{12} has a modified corrin ring (quite similiar to tetrapyrrole ring structure in porphyrins like heme and chlorophyll). The ring is nearly planar, co-ordinating a trivalent cobalt ion in its center. A cyanide ion is also co-ordinated to cobalt. Cyanide ion is a product of isolation method and can be replaced by a hydroxide, chloride, nitrite or another ion. An optically active aminoalcohol, R-1 amino 2-propanol is ester-linked to the phosphate group attached to α-ribazole moiety and amide-linked to propionate residue of the corrin nucleus. Various analogs of the vitamin have been isolated in which 5, 6-dimethyl benzimidazole moiety has been replaced by 5-hydroxy-benzimidazole, adenine, 2-methyladenine, hypoxanthine and other groups.

The closed system of the four pyrrole nuclei (joined through bridged carbons) have been named corrin and compounds containing this nucleus are called as 'corrinoid compounds'.

The simplest known corrinoid natural product is cobyric acid which is used as the starting material for the partial synthesis of vitamin B_{12}.

Physiological Functions :

(1) The two types of cobamides that participate as coenzymes in human metabolism are,

(a) Methylcobamide and
(b) 5'-deoxyadenosyl cobamide.

These coenzymes result through the replacement of cyanide ion in the cyanocobalamin by a methyl group or by a 5'-deoxyadenosine moiety, as shown in Fig. 29.6.

Methyl cobalamin is the major form of the coenzyme in the plasma while 5'-deoxyadenosyl cobalamin is the major form of the coenzyme in the liver and other tissues.

(2) The physiological functions of both, folic acid and vitamin B_{12} are interdependent on each other. For example, N^5-methyl tetrahydrofolate is the form in which folic acid is circulated and supplied to the tissues. However in the tissues, it is converted to bioactive form, tetrahydrofolate by transfer of N^5-methyl group to cyanocobalamin. The latter is thus converted to methyl cobalamin which is a bioactive form of vitamin B_{12}.

(3) Methyl cobalamin acts as a methyl group donor in a number of methylation reactions. For example, the conversion of homocysteine to methionine takes place by utilizing the methyl group of the coenzyme. Similarly the methyl group at position 5 in thymine is introduced with the help of methylcobalamin in the body. Thiamidine is a nucleoside. Thus, cobalamin plays an important role in the biosynthesis of DNA.

(4) Vitamin B_{12} in the form of 5'-deoxyadenosylcobalamin acts as a coenzyme for the mitochondrial mutase enzyme that catalyses the conversion of methylmalonyl CoA to succinyl CoA, which is the major pathway of propionyl metabolism. Propionyl CoA from lipid metabolism proceeds through this pathway via succinyl CoA in order to enter Kreb's cycle.

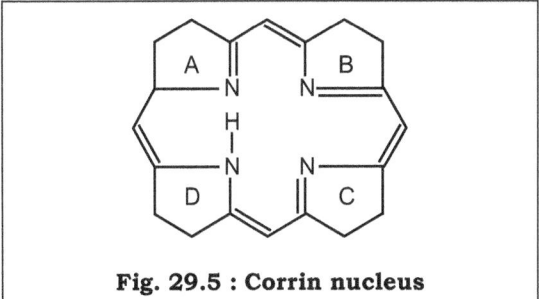

Fig. 29.5 : Corrin nucleus

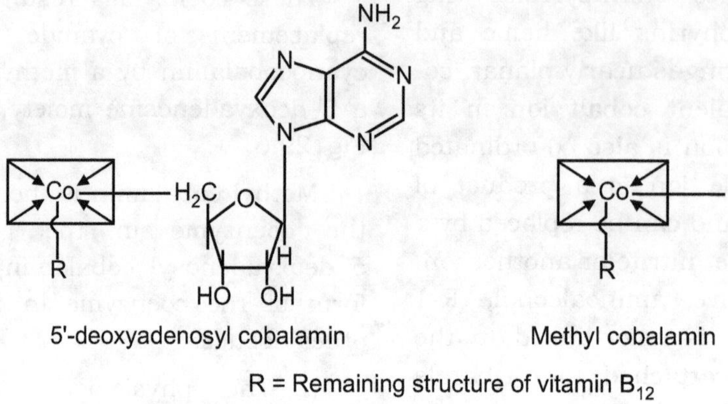

Fig. 29.6 : **Coenzyme forms of vitamin B_{12}**

(5) Vitamin B_{12} is concerned with the maintenance of sulfhydryl group (–SH) in reduced form which is necessary for the function of many SH-activated enzyme systems, e.g. glutathione. It reacts with many electron deficient compounds through its sulfhydryl group and forms S-substituted glutathione adducts and thus protects vital cellular constituents.

(6) Vitamin B_{12} plays an important role in the folate storage in erythrocytes. It is essential for normal red cell formation, for the formation of normal epithelial cells in the mouth and GIT and has growth promoting effects.

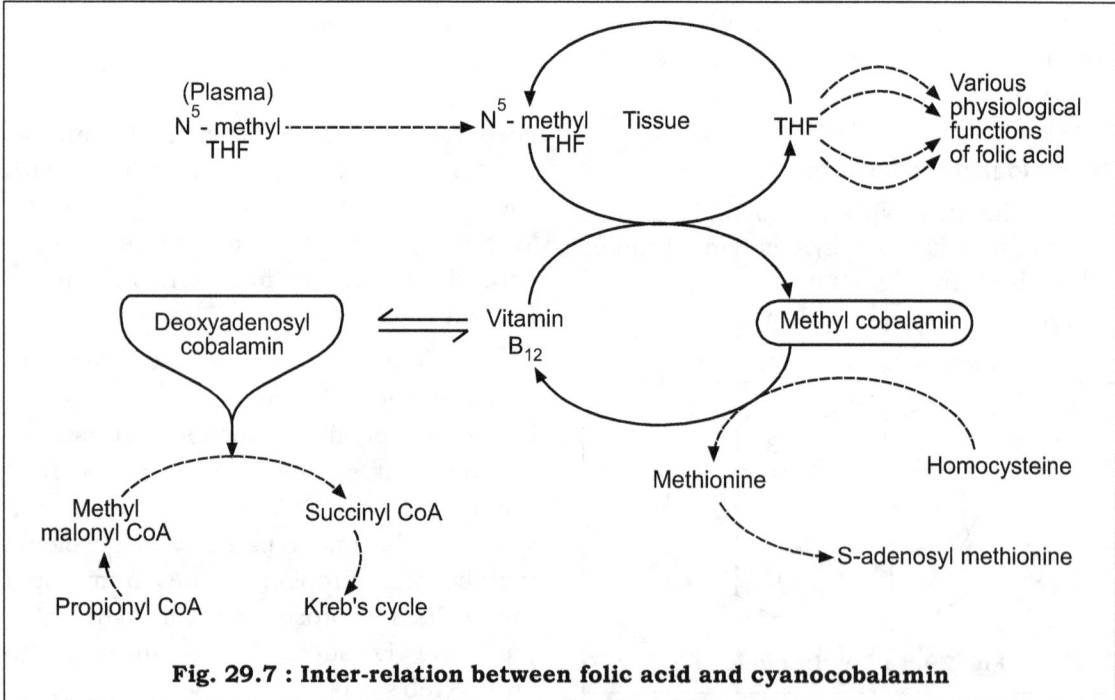

Fig. 29.7 : **Inter-relation between folic acid and cyanocobalamin**

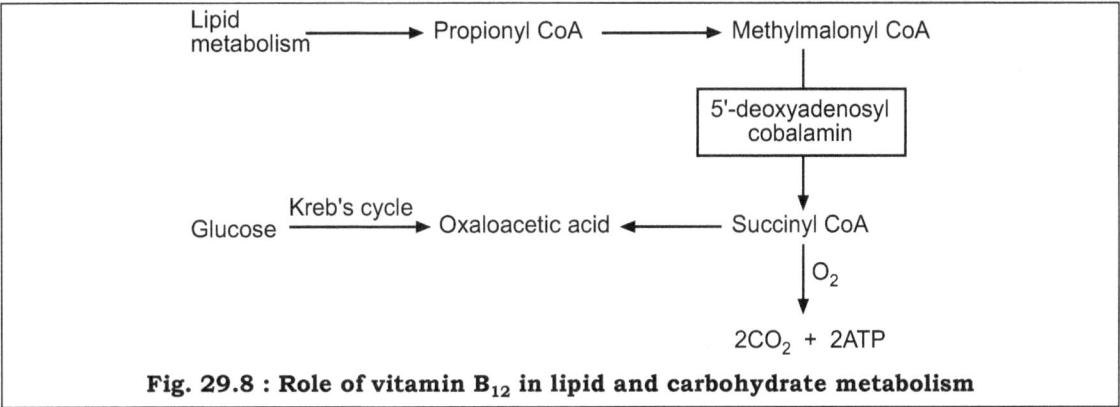

Fig. 29.8 : Role of vitamin B_{12} in lipid and carbohydrate metabolism

Pharmacokinetics :

A normal level of secretion of intrinsic factor (glycoprotein) from the parietal cells of gastric mucosa is necessary for the proper absorption of vitamin B_{12} from GIT. Vitamin then forms a complex with glycoprotein. In the form of this complex, the vitamin is then transported across the ideal mucosal cells to reach into the circulation. Here the complex dissociates to release free cobalamin which is then picked up by carrier globulins (transcobalamins I and II). These transcobalamins then transport the vitamin to the liver and other storage sites. The hepatic parenchymal cells serve the principal storage site for cobalamin where about 50% of the total body content (about 3-5 mg) of vitamin is stored.

Part of the absorbed cobalamin is secreted into the bile which is reabsorbed into the circulation from the gut. This enterohepatic reabsorption mechanism helps to conserve the vitamin content of the body.

Deficiency Symptoms :

(1) Inadequate dietary intake, chronic alcoholism, pregnancy and malabsorption are the basic reasons in the vitamin deficiency. However, dietary causes are rare and malabsorption of the vitamin is the prominent cause in the vitamin deficiency. The deficiency of the vitamin mainly affects the functioning of :

(a) Erythropoietic system,

(b) Gastrointestinal system, and

(c) Nervous system.

Since folic acid and cobalamin, both are involved in the nucleic acid biosynthesis, where their roles are interdependent upon each other, deficiency of either of these vitamins greatly influences the maintenance and functioning of tissues having high proliferative rate.

(2) N^5-methyl THF is the main circulating form of the folic acid. It is converted to the physiologically active form THF, by donating the methyl group to cobalamin resulting into methylcobalamin. The bioactive form, THF is involved in the synthesis of DNA. Hence, the deficiency of cobalamin results into derangement in DNA synthesis causing morphological abnormality of precursor cells in the bone marrow. This

is reflected in the formation of abnormal macrocytic erythrocytes having short life span. The patient becomes severely anemic due to ineffective hematopoiesis. The related deficiency of bio-active form of folic acid further contributes to the development of megaloblastic anemia. Since the folic acid and iron remain less utilized during cobalamin deficiency, the patient usually has an elevated plasma levels of iron and folate.

(3) The epithelial cells of gastric mucosa are also an example of rapidly proliferating cells. Hence, the deficiency of cobalamin may result into gastrointestinal symptoms that include, anorexia, indigestion, atrophic glossittis (i.e. sore and abnormally smooth tongue) and diarrhoea.

(4) Vitamin B_{12} is utilized in the form of methyl cobalamin and 5'-deoxyadenosine cobalamin. The methyl cobalamin acts as a coenzyme in the formation of methionine from homocysteine. Both, methionine and s-adenosyl methionine are involved in the protein synthesis, synthesis of polyamines, and methylation reactions (e.g. synthesis of phospholipids and myelin sheath). Deficiency of cobalamin may result into impairment of production of lipoprotein in myelin sheath. This demyelination of nerves may be a probable cause of neurological lesions seen in vitamin B_{12} deficiency.

Similarly 5'-deoxyadenosine cobalamin acts as a coenzyme in the conversion of methylmalonyl CoA into succinyl CoA. In the deficiency of the vitamin, methylmalonyl CoA appears in larger amounts in the urine. Similarly the normal fatty acid synthesis is impaired due to this interference in lipid metabolism. This is mainly reflected into abnormal functioning of the brain and nerve tissues. The main neurological abnormalities include, swelling of myelinated neurons, demyelination followed by degeneration of the nerve cells specifically in the spinal cord and cerebral cortex, mild irritation, instability of gait, loss of memory, confusion, hallucinations or even psychosis.

Daily Allowance :

About 3-4 µg per day is considered adequate. This much amount of vitamin B_{12} can be easily obtained from the diet or from the intestinal microbial flora. Besides its use in the treatment of megaloblastic or pernicious anaemia, it can also be used in the therapy of various psychiatric disorders.

Lipotropic Factors :

The fat content of many tissues (e.g. adipose tissue, liver etc.) and muscles is quite high. In muscles, particularly striated and cardiac muscles contain higher quantity of phospholipids due to their high energy requirement. Liver is the principal site for,

(I) the biosynthesis of fatty acids,

(II) formation of triglycerides, and

(III) synthesis of apoproteins.

For the proper control of hepatic lipid transactions, the presence of several lipotropic factors is needed. These factors include, vitamin E, pyridoxine, pantothenic acid, phosphocreatine, ATP, choline, myoinositol and coenzyme Q.

They are involved in the mobilization of excess fat from liver (lipotropic action). Hence, they are usually incorporated in the treatment of diseases characterized by disturbances in transport and metabolism of fat.

The lack of these lipotropic factors, specifically that of choline and myoinositol causes impairment of triglycerides from liver, mobilization of fatty acids from adipose tissues and accumulation of fatty acids in the liver. The accumulation of the fats in the liver may result into fatty liver syndrome. It is to be immediately treated which otherwise leads to enlargement of liver, cirrhosis and hepatic dysfunction. An elevated plasma level of free fatty acids is one of the important feature of fatty liver syndrome. Besides the lack of lipotropic factors, other reasons like nutritional deficiency or chronic alcoholism also favour its occurrence.

(a) Choline :

Since choline does not function as a coenzyme in any of the biochemical reactions in humans, it can not be considered as a true vitamin. Moreover unlike vitamins, it is required in quite larger amounts to exert its effects. In body, it is present as a constituent of lecithins (i.e. phosphatidyl choline and sphingomyelins).

Dietary Source :

It is mainly present in egg yolk, vegetables and in animal fat.

Physiological Functions :

(1) Pharmacologically it is a weak agonist of acetylcholine with mild toxicity reactions. In the body it acts as a starting material for the biosynthesis of acetylcholine.

(2) In the body, methionine and choline are good examples of methyl group donors. Reactions involving such a transfer of methyl groups (transmethylation) are involved in fat metabolism. This probably explains the lipotropic action of choline that is beneficial in the treatment of fatty liver syndrome.

(3) It is an important component of many biological membranes and that of plasma lipoproteins in the form of phosphatidylcholine.

Deficiency Symptoms :

In humans, no deficiency symptoms are yet reported. In animals, deficiency of choline may result into dysfunctioning of nervous system, motor inco-ordination and fatty liver syndrome.

Daily Allowance :

Since enough amount of choline is available to human from diet as well as endogenous metabolic sources, there is no daily requirement. However, in the fatty liver syndrome or dysfunctioning of nervous system that is characterised by decreased acetylcholine activity, the patient has to be treated with preparations containing choline.

(b) Inositol (myoinositol) :

The lipotropic action of inositol was first reported in 1942 by **Clavin**. Though it was found to be necessary for human life, it is not considered as a true vitamin. Chemically, inositol is hexahydroxycyclohexane and can be considered as an isomer of glucose. Out of the several isomeric forms of inositol, myoinositol is a physiologically active form that is mainly present in brain, erythrocytes, liver and in eyes.

Dietary Sources :

Fruits, vegetables, grains, nuts, milk and yeast are some of the good dietary sources for inositol. Its presence in nature has been recognized as free inositol, phytin (salt of inositol hexaphosphate), phosphotidylinositol and a water-soluble non-dialysable complex.

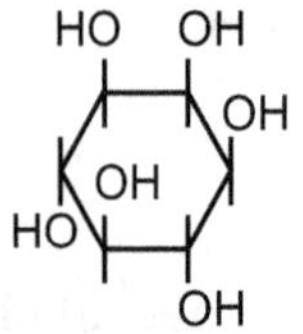

Inositol

Physiological Functions :

(1) It resembles choline in most of its physiological functions. Just like choline, it is present as phosphatidylinositol in the phospholipids of biological membranes and that of plasma lipoproteins. Unlike choline, it is devoid of pharmacological actions.

(2) It has a lipotropic action and it mobilizes the excess fat from the liver in fatty liver syndrome.

(3) Like c-AMP, inositol also acts as an intracellular second messenger, in its triphosphate form and regulates the Ca^{++} ion fluxes.

Deficiency Symptoms :

Enough amounts of inositol is provided to the body by diet as well as by intestinal microbial flora. It may also be biosynthesized in the body. Hence, no deficiency symptom has ever been reported for inositol in human body. In mice, its deficiency results into retarded growth and peculiar hairlessness. Due to the availability of inositol from various sources, its daily human requirement is difficult to establish.

(c) Coenzyme Q (Ubiquinones) :

It is a lipid soluble hydrogen (electron) carrier present in mitochondrial membranes. The name ubiquinone is given because of ubiquitous occurrence of this benzoquinone in the nature. The value of 'n' in the structure varies from source to source. Due to the presence of isoprenoid units in the side-chain, coenzyme Q possesses some degree of structural similarity with vitamin E and K. In fact, it offers some sort of protection to the animals deficient in vitamin E by governing the oxido-reductive biochemical processes in animals. It plays an important role in electron transfer chain by accepting the hydrogens from the reduced flavoproteins. As a result, the oxidised form of flavoproteins is regenerated. Coenzyme Q returns to its original quinone form by transferring these two protons to cytochrome system.

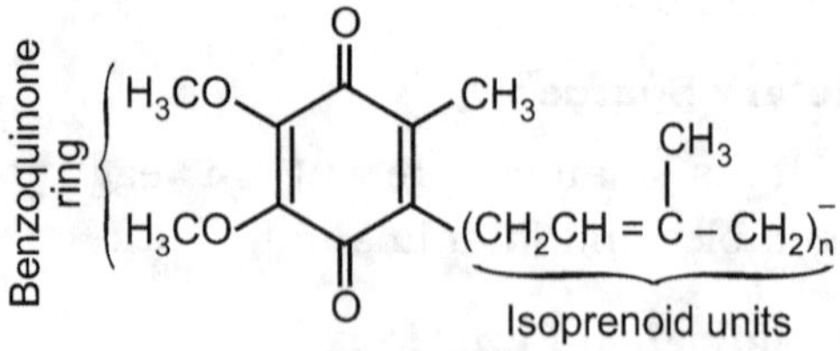

Fig. 29.9 : Coenzyme Q

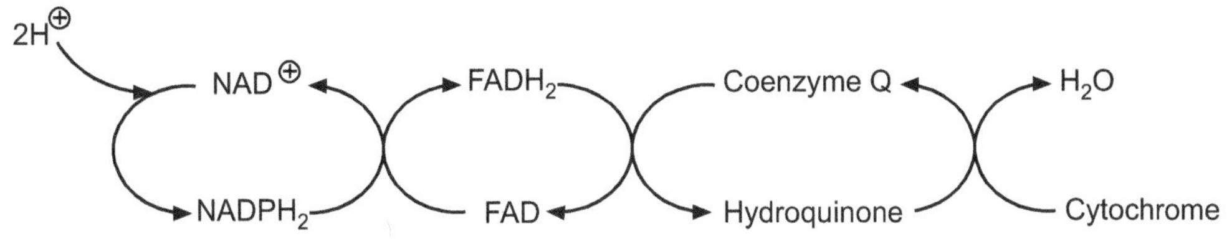

Fig. 29.10 : Role of coenzyme Q in electron transfer chain

Para-amino Benzoic Acid (PABA) :

It is not essential for the maintenance of human. Life like inositol, it is also not a true vitamin. However unlike choline or inositol, it is not a lipotropic agent. Its main metabolic role is in the bacterial cell where it participates in some biochemical reactions essential for bacterial cell life. In humans, PABA if taken, is devoid of pharmacological actions and adverse effects. The only significance of PABA in human metabolism is that it forms a part of the folic acid molecule.

[VIII] Vitamin C (Ascorbic Acid or Antiscorbutic Factor) :

The first attempt to detect the presence of ascorbic acid in human body was made by **Szent Gyorgi** in 1928 when he isolated a hexuronic acid with high reducing power from cabbage and from adrenal gland. The vitamin was later isolated from lemon juices in 1932. It was identified as 3-keto L-glucofuranolactone. This vitamin is synthesized by most of the mammals except monkey, man and guinea pig.

Ascorbic acid as it is called, is very readily oxidised (so it can act as a strong reducing agent) to dehydroascorbic acid, which is an active vitamin as ascorbic acid itself.

This reversible oxido-reduction system accounts for most of the biological activities of the vitamin. The vitamin contains an asymmetric C-atom, and the laevo isomer is the bioactive form of the vitamin. Yet another isomer, D-isoascorbic acid (erythrobic acid) also has a similar redox potential to that of ascorbic acid but does not exhibit good antiscorbutic activity due to its rapid rate of elimination from the tissues.

Dietary Sources :

The good dietary sources of the vitamin include, citrus fruits, tomatoes, potatoes, orange and lemon juices and green vegetables.

Physiological Functions :

Ascorbic acid exhibits few pharmacological actions at relatively higher concentrations in normal individuals. While no specific coenzymatic role of vitamin C in the body could be established, the following information about its biochemical function is available.

(1) Ascorbic acid along with its oxidised form, i.e. dehydroascorbic acid is intimately involved in biological oxido-reduction reactions. In cellular respiration, it may be a part of one of the important respiratory system, where it protects the functional integrity of sulfhydryl group (glutathione) of enzymes.

(2) Collagen is the supporting lattice of the bone. The presence of ascorbic acid is required for the formation of normal collagen where it causes direct stimulation of collagen peptide synthesis. Besides this, ascorbic acid is also essential for the activity of enzymes proline hydroxylase and lysyl oxidase which catalyse the formation of hydroxyproline and hydroxylysine from proline and lysine respectively. Both these hydroxylated amino acids are utilized to form collagen precursor peptides. Ferric ions and ascorbic acid appear to be required in this reaction.

(3) The greater part of the teeth is dentin. Dentin protein is largely collagen. Vitamin A, C and D are required for the proper development and classification of tooth. Deficiency of vitamin C affects formation of organic matrix of dentin, as it does in bone. Thus ascorbic acid is necessary for the formation of inter cellular supporting material that is being continuously biosynthesized by the body. The lack of vitamin E may lead to deficiency of this intercellular supporting matrix that may extend to cartilage, bone, teeth, muscles, capillary endothelium and symptoms like bone fracture or delayed wound healing may be seen.

(4) It is involved in the biosynthesis of epinephrine from dopamine in adrenal glands and in the brain.

(5) It facilitates the gastrointestinal absorption of iron. It influences the formation of haemoglobin, erythrocyte maturation, the conversion of folic acid to tetrahydrofolate and is also involved in certain immunological reactions of the body. A recent study provided some evidence that it helps the organism to recover from viral infections by acting through an indirect mechanism of body's immune system.

(6) It is involved in the carbohydrate metabolism and in the oxidation of phenyl alanine and tyrosine. Scorbutic animals exhibit hyperglycemia, lowered glucose tolerance and resistance to insulin.

(7) The adrenal glands contain highest concentration of ascorbate which is necessary for hydroxylation reactions in the biosynthesis of adrenocorticoid hormones. It is also involved in the conversion of cholesterol to cholic acid.

(8) Ascorbic acid is also involved in the microsomal drug metabolism.

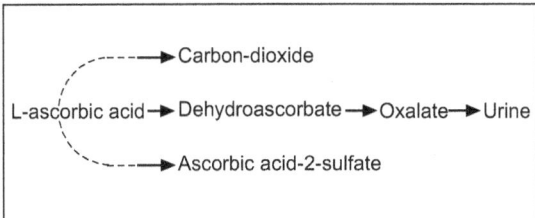

Fig. 29.11 : Metabolism of ascorbic acid

Pharmacokinetics :

Ascorbic acid is readily and almost completely absorbed from the intestine and is then distributed to various tissues of the body. The vitamin exists in plasma and tissues, in the form of both, reduced form (L ascorbic acid) and oxidized form (dehydroascorbic acid) usually in the ratio of 15 : 1. Adrenal cortex, leukocytes and platelets contain relatively higher concentration of the vitamin.

Ascorbic acid is metabolized in the body by different metabolic pathways resulting in formation of carbon dioxide, oxalates and ascorbic acid 2-sulfate.

Vitamin C does not appear unchanged in urine until the saturation of body tissues occur. This usually occurs when the daily intake of ascorbic acid is increased above 100 mg.

Deficiency Symptoms :

The prolonged and severe deficiency of vitamin C results into development of scurvy in humans. Frank scurvy is occasionally seen in infants, in older people on restricted diet and in alcoholics. Certain pathological conditions may lower down the plasma ascorbate level. These conditions include, infectious, diseases, kidney and liver diseases, gastrointestinal disturbances, cardiac dysfunctioning and endocrine cases. The plasma level of the vitamin is also lowered down by cigarette smoking and the use of oral contraceptive agents.

During the deficiency of ascorbic acid, initially loosening of teeth, gingivitis (inflammation of gums), delayed wound healing and perifollicular hyperkeratosis (accumulation of epidermal cells around hair follicles) may be seen. Since ascorbic acid is involved in the formation of intercellular supporting matrix, its deficiency may affect the calcification of bones, teeth and rupture of capillaries. The latter effect is due to defective formation of pericapillary fibrous tissue resulting into inadequate support to the capillary.

More severe deficiency of vitamin C leads to scurvy which is characterised by,

(i) Weakness and fatigue with muscle and joint pain, breathlessness and tachycardia.

(ii) The gums bleed, become spongy and inflamed and teeth get loosen in their sockets.

(iii) Haemorrhages (rupture of capillaries) then occur in the skin and elsewhere (mouth, GIT etc.) with a consequent anemia.

(iv) Resistance to infection is much reduced and this may become the cause of death.

Daily Allowance :

The daily requirement of vitamin C for various age groups is indicated below :

    For infants - about 35 mg
         children - about 45 mg
         adults   - about 60 mg
During pregnancy - about 80 mg, and
         lactation - about 100 mg

Besides use in the treatment of scurvy, claims about usefulness of ascorbic acid against the common cold condition have also been made. During long term use, sudden withdrawal of vitamin C from the therapy may result into rebound scurvy and bleeding of gums with loosened teeth may occur. Hence in such cases, the dose of vitamin C should be gradually lowered down instead of stopping the administration suddenly.

Megadose of Vitamin C :

The vitamin should not be administered in quite larger amounts (1 - 3 g daily) to the patient for long period of time. Since oxalate appears as vitamin C metabolite in urine, such megadose administration of vitamin may lead to kidney stones. Other severe side-effects of higher doses of vitamin C include, diarrhoea, excessive absorption of iron, destruction of erythrocytes, immunological disturbances, uricosuria and interference with anticoagulants. The uricosuric effect of vitamin C may cause precipitation of gout-like conditions.

IMMUNO-MODULATORS

30.1 INTRODUCTION

Diseases in man are caused by a variety of reasons. Most of the pathological diseases in man are caused by three most important groups of microorganisms namely, bacteria, rickettsia and viruses. The skin provides a barrier for the easy entry of microorganisms in the body, which is virtually impregnable to microorganisms and only when a tissue injury occurs, microorganisms enter the blood circulation.

A continuous chain of natural defence barriers exists in our body that restricts microorganisms to areas where they can be tolerated. Bactericidal action is exerted by many of the body secretions such as, tears, nasal secretions and saliva contain the enzyme lysozyme; hydrochloric acid is released from the gastric mucosa or a basic polypeptide like spermine is present in the semen. These non-specific endogenous antimicrobial systems are operative at all times against the entry of pathogenic microorganisms. Besides this, phagocytosis is an important tool for the engulfment and digestion of microorganisms.

In fact, the first line of body defence mechanisms consists of phagocytes and lymphocytes. Polymorphonuclear leucocyte is a short-lived, non-dividing white blood cell derived from the totipotent bone marrow stem cell. It is an actively phagocytic, motile cell that can pass through capillary walls and ingest foreign material, microorganisms or antigens. The foreign material is ingested and is fused with lysosomal granules present within the cell. Destruction of infectious agent usually occurs after the release of lysosomal enzymes from the lysosomal granules. It provides the major line of defence against pyogenic (pus-forming) bacteria. Thus, polymorphonuclear leucocytes are the mobile phagocytes while macrophages are the long lived tissue-fixed phagocytes. Though macrophages are scattered throughout all body organs, they are present in higher concentrations mainly in lung, liver, spleen and lymph nodes. They have an ability to take up and concentrate inert particulate matter, including microorganisms and tissue debris. In these organs macrophages function as filters to remove foreign material from the circulating lymph and blood. The macrophage system is also known as reticuloendothelial system.

When polymorphonuclear leucocytes fail to inhibit the entry of bacteria in the body, bacteria escape into blood vessels and lymphatics, and are carried to lymph nodes and spleen. At this place they are trapped by macrophages.

When micro-organisms escape from the attack of both the tissue-fixed phagocytes and mobile phagocytes, they enter the tissues which are normally inaccessible. This results into failure of the primary defences and development of infection. If remains untreated, a pathological condition may arise because of invasion and multiplication of microorganisms in the body organs. The term, *virulence* is used to indicate the degree of pathogenicity of a given strain of microorganism. In presence of virulent bacteria species, phagocytosis alone, is inadequate and the second line of defence including antibody and complement must act in concert to exert antimicrobial action.

This combination of phagocytosis (i.e. non-specific) and antibody-complement system (i.e. specific) constitutes body's natural defence mechanism, known as 'immunity'. The word immunity is derived from a latin word *immunis* which means 'exempt from'. Immunity is usually defined as 'a state of relative resistance to an infection'. Substances capable of stimulating immune mechanism are known as 'antigens'. Chemically they are mostly proteins, polysaccharides and complex lipids having molecular weight greater than 5000 deltons. Immunological mechanisms are found to be more pronounced in certain disease conditions like cancer and several genetic disorders. Many allergic and autoimmune disorders develop due to functional impairments in the immunological mechanisms.

Polymorphonuclear leucocytes (neutrophils), macrophages, and lymphocytes are the important categories of immune cells present in the human body. They are all obtained from the stem cells present in the bone marrow which is a site of continual proliferation and turnover of immature blood cells. Formation of particular immune cell occurs through differentiation of stem cells. This depends upon the demand for cells in peripheral immune organs. A sort of co-ordination and interconnection is seen between all these types of immune cells. For example, one of the types of monokines secreted from macrophages is interleucin-1 (IL-1) which, in the presence of antigen induces T-lymphocytes to proliferate.

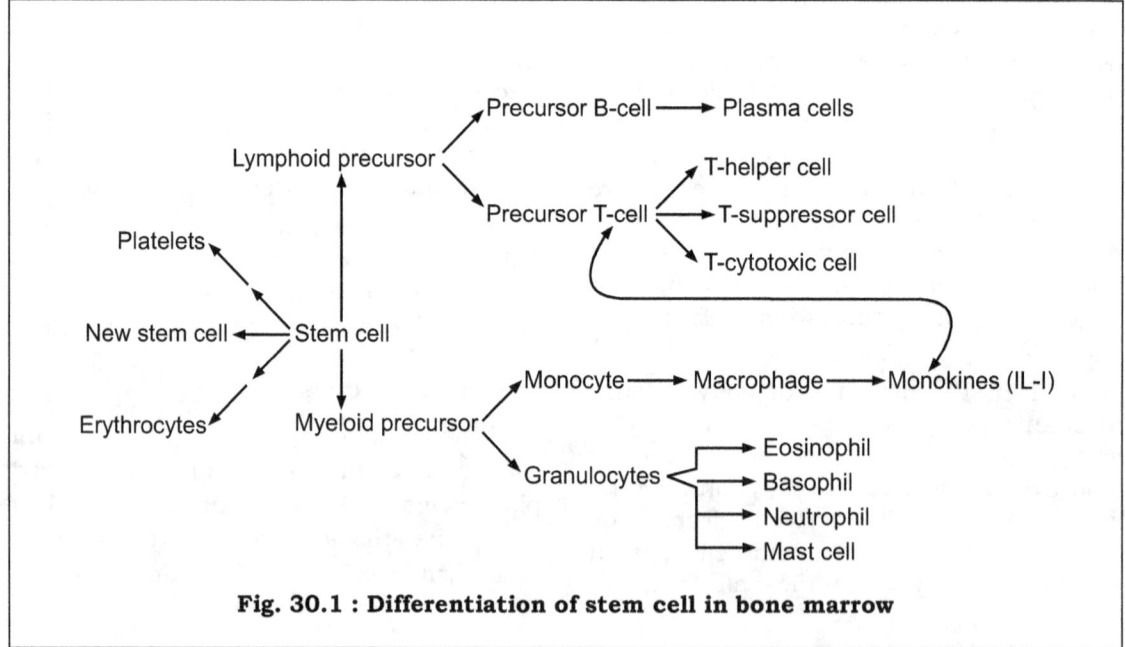

Fig. 30.1 : Differentiation of stem cell in bone marrow

30.2 COMPONENTS OF IMMUNE SYSTEM

(a) Lymphocytes :

They are an integral part of specific immune mechanisms and are mainly formed in the bone marrow through proliferation and differentiation of stem cells. Some stem cells also migrate to thymus gland where they proliferate to give lymphocytes. Thus, depending upon the site of formation, they can be classified into two major types, namely T-lymphocytes (thymus-derived) and B-lymphocytes (bone marrow-derived). Both types are found in the blood. T-lymphocytes are concerned with cellular immunity (i.e. phagocytosis) while B-lymphocytes are concerned with humoral immunity (i.e. antibodies production). Under certain conditions like stress or administration of corticosteroids, production of lymphocytes is inhibited.

(b) Cellular Immunity :

The effector substances in cell-mediated immunity include lymphokines, interferon and monokines. T-lymphocytes protect the tissues from intracellular diseases and cellular neoplasms. These lymphocytes are responsible for the immunity to those micro-organisms that have an ability to live and multiply within the cells of the host, e.g. tubercle bacillus, viruses and protozoal parasites. They react directly with foreign material. This interaction leads to the production of lymphokines by lymphocytes. These lymphokines either destroy the foreign material through phagocytosis or react with receptor sites present on B-lymphocytes to induce humoral immunity. The cellular immunity (T-lymphocytes) plays an important role against bacterial, fungal and viral infections, in transplant rejection, in neoplasms and in some autoimmune processes.

(c) Humoral Immunity :

Humoral immunity involves the production of specific antibodies from B-lymphocytes upon antigenic stimulation. Small population of B-lymphocytes are specifically concerned with retention of memory of antigens. They are known as 'memory cells'. Re-exposure to same antigen at a later time causes activation of memory cells to proliferate and secrete antibody at much faster rate. Upon antigenic stimulation, B-lymphocytes proliferate and differentiate into protein molecules having specific antibody activity. These molecules are known as immunoglobulins (Ig) or gamma globulins. They are categorized into five major classes like

(i) Immunoglobulin G

(ii) Immunoglobulin M

(iii) Immunoglobulin A

(iv) Immunoglobulin D, and

(v) Immunoglobulin E

For every antigen, there is a specific clone of B-lymphocytes that secretes an antibody capable of neutralizing only that antigen. Since the secreted antibodies circulate throughout the body, the immune responses associated with antibody production are called 'humoral immune responses'. The high specificity of antigen-antibody interaction is due to differences in the chemical composition of the outer surfaces of the microorganisms.

(d) Immunoglobulins (Antibodies):

Synthesis of various immunoglobulins occurs after the primary antigenic stimulation. The antibodies are polymers of five four- peptide subunits. They are extremely effective agglutinating agents that appear early in the response to infection.

Immunoglobulin G is the most abundant immunoglobulin synthesized during antigen activation. It contains 4 polypeptide chains (i.e. two heavy chains and two light chains) which are joined together by disulfide bonds. It has a molecular weight of about 150,000 daltons. These type of antibodies are found throughout the body and are effective against a large variety of antigens. Most virus antibodies and antitoxins belong to this class of immunoglobulins. Because of their ability to cross the placenta, they are effective against infections seen in new-borns.

Immunoglobulin A appears mainly in saliva, tears, nasal secretions, sweat, colostrum and in secretions of the lungs, urinogenital and gastrointestinal tracts where it protects the surface of mucosal cells from microbial attack. In all these secretions, it appears as a dimer.

Immunoglobulin D does not have any precise function. However it's role in the control of lymphocyte activation and suppression is suspected. It may serve as lymphocyte antigen receptor.

Immunoglobulin E sensitizes the mast cells after its interaction with antigens present on the surface of mast cells. As many as 500,000 IgE receptor sites are present on each mast cell. Thus, this type of antibody is involved in degranulation of mast cells resulting into release of histamine, serotonin, plasmakinins, platelet activating factor, eosinophil chemotactic factor and slow releasing substance of anaphylaxis, while immunoglobulin M participates in agglutinating and cytolytic reactions.

(e) Lymph Nodes:

Lymph has same composition of salts as interstitial fluid and plasma. The lymph vessels possess numerous valves and the flow of lymph from the periphery to thoracic duct is brought about in the same way as the flow of blood in the vein. Lymph contains large number of lymphocytes, mainly T- lymphocytes. Particulate matter which is being collected by the lymph, is brought into close contact with these lymphocytes in the lymph nodes. This results into fixation of particulate matter with the lymphocytes.

(f) Spleen:

The slow circulation through the spleen, enables macrophages to sequester and ingest the aged red cells or other foreign substances. Beside this, foreign particles are brought in close contact with lymphocytes resulting in their fixation.

(g) Thymus:

It is a 'master' lymphoid tissue which controls other lymphoid tissues (like, lymph node and thymus). This control is mediated through the release of hormones. Thymus consists of a peripheral cortex densely packed with lymphocytes and a central medula containing less lymphocytes. After adolescence, thymus becomes less active. This results into decrease in the effectiveness of cell-mediated immunity in old aged persons.

30.3 TYPES OF IMMUNITY

Immunity may be either of natural or of acquired origin. Because of body temperature or certain biochemical differences, man is susceptible to diseases to which other animals are immune. Because of same reasons, man is protected against the attack of some diseases which are quite common in other animals. This is known as 'natural immunity'. It is usually affected by age, sex, hormonal balance and health of the person.

Acquired immunity on the other hand is a state of induced immunity and is further subdivided into :

(a) Active Immunity :

It can be imparted either naturally by means of a clinical or subclinical infection or artificially by injection of appropriate antigen in the form of a vaccine or toxoid. These vaccines contain microbial strains of abnormally low pathogenicity. Their administration leads to antigenic stimulus and formation of antibodies at much faster rate. This type of immunity is normally long-lasting.

(b) Passive Immunity :

This type of immunity can be imparted either naturally by placental transfer of mother antibodies to her child (and also through breast milk) or artificially by means of administration of antibodies preformed in another actively immunized human being (e.g. human gamma globulins) or in an animal like horse. Examples include antitoxic sera such as tetanus, diphtheria etc. Human gamma globulin thus may be used in the prevention of infectious hepatitis. Passive immunity offers protection immediately but such protection is usually of short duration. Horses are chiefly used for the production of immunosera but cattles, goats and sheeps are alternative sources. Responses to vaccines against poliomyelitis and small pox have markedly reduced impact of these diseases on mankind.

30.4 HYPERSENSITIVITY REACTIONS

Antigen recognition leads to activation of immune mechanisms. This results into clonal proliferation of specific B-lymphocytes or T-lymphocytes. The interaction of antigen with the immune system can give rise to two types of responses.

(1) During the interaction, the antigen may damage immune system functionally. An immunodeficiency thus develops. Body's natural resistance to infection is decreased and person can easily be affected by infections. The immuno-suppression may or may not be reversible. The immunosuppression leads to an increased susceptibility to bacterial, fungal or a viral infection. For example, patients under a long-term cortisone therapy are more prone to certain diseases including rheumatoid arthritis, Hodgkin's disease etc.

(2) During the interaction, the antigen provokes the typical manifestations of allergy. Under certain conditions, the antigen-antibody interaction may provide an unusual and exaggerated reaction, damaging the host body tissues. This altered response of the host tissues is known as hypersensitivity or allergy. The details about types of antibodies that are found to be involved in immune reactions are tabulated in table 30.1.

Table 30.1 : Antibodies present in human immune system

Type of antibody	Molecular weight ($n \times 10^3$)	Half-life $t\frac{1}{2}$ (days)	Normal serum concentration (mg)
IgA	170	6.0	275
IgD	150	2.8	5
IgE	196	1.5	0.03
IgG	150	23	1200
IgM	890	5.0	120

Based upon the mechanism of immunological involvement, the allergic responses have been divided into four types, as shown in table 30.2. Type I reactions include anaphylactic reactions or immediate hypersensitivity reactions. These are mediated by humoral antibodies and depend primarily on the interaction of antigen with IgE antibodies (reagin antibodies) and some by a certain IgG subclass of antibodies. The term, anaphylaxis (which means 'removal of protection') was first coined by **Richet** and **Portier** in 1902 to describe a hypersensitivity reaction which was in exaggerated form. It leads to an intense systemic and general reactivity resulting into urticarial rash, swelling of the soft tissues, broncho-constriction, pulmonary airway obstruction, laryngeal edema, diffuse erythema, hyperperistalsis, cardiac arrhythmia and hypotension. It is a sudden and life-threatening reaction which may lead to the death of a patient due to broncho-constriction and cardiovascular collapse.

Chemical mediators which play an important role in anaphylaxis include, histamine, SRS-A (i.e. slow releasing substance of anaphylaxis), plasmakinins, prostaglandins, heparin, ECF-A (i.e. eosinophil chemotactic factor of anaphylaxis) and platelet activating factor. Hence, adrenergic agonist (e.g. terbutaline, salbutamol which induce bronchodilation), antihistaminic agents (e.g. ketotifen, cromolyn sodium), theophylline, diethylcarbamazine and corticosteroids may be used to reduce the frequency and severity of anaphylactic attacks.

Table 30.2 : Classification of allergic responses

Type	Antibody involved	Target tissues	Symptoms
Type - I (Anaphylactic reaction or immediate hypersensitivity)	IgE	Respiratory tract (asthma), vasculature (anaphylactic shock), skin (urticaria)	Edema and vasodilation
Type - II (Cytotoxic reactions)	IgG and IgM	Circulatory system	Hemolytic anaemia Granulocytopenia
Type - III (Immune complex reactions)	IgG	Vascular endothelium	Urticaria, arthritis, lymphadenopathy, fever, serum sickness
Type - IV (Delayed hypersensitivity)	These reactions are mediated by sensitized T - lymphocytes and macrophages		

Acute anaphylactic shock may be treated by giving epinephrine s.c. (0.3 - 0.5 ml aqueous epinephrine in dilution of 1 : 1000) every 20 minutes for several doses. Prophylactic antihistaminic agents may be useful in preventing serum sickness and other mild allergic manifestations.

Anaphylactic shock attacks almost all vital organs of the body and can be considered as a state of systemic anaphylaxis whereas in atopic diseases, the functioning of only restricted areas of the body are affected. Hence, atopic diseases, in simple words can be considered as state of local anaphylaxis.

A strong hereditary predisposition, eosinophilia (i.e. an increase in the blood eosinophil count) and a natural tendency to disappear with time are some of the characteristics of atopic diseases. Examples include asthma, hay fever, and urticarial dermatitis. Hapten-specific activation of T-lymphocytes results in the activation of B-lymphocytes. This leads to antihapten antibodies formation.

(i) Asthma :

It is characterized by paroxysmal attacks of difficult respiration. The symptoms include bronchoconstriction, oedema of bronchial mucosa and cyanosis.

Table 30.3 : Mediators of anaphylactic reaction

Mediator	Responses
1. Histamine	**H_1-receptor mediated responses :** Smooth muscle contraction, vascular permeability, pruritus and prostaglandin release. **H_2-receptor mediated responses :** Gastric acid release, mucus secretion, vasodilation and inhibition of lymphokine release.
2. Prostaglandins and Thromboxanes	Vasodilation (PGE), increased pain sensation (PGE), mucus secretion (PGD_2, $PGF_{2\alpha}$, TxA_2), bronchospasm (PGD_2, $PGF_{2\alpha}$, TxA_2) and bronchodilation (PGE_1 and PGI_2).
3. Acetyl choline	Mucus secretion and bronchospasm.
4. Heparin	Anticoagulant and modulator of complement activation.
5. Bradykinin	Bronchospasm, vasodilation and vascular leakage.
6. Eosinophil chemotactic factor of anaphylaxis	Eosinophil chemotaxis.
7. Leukotrienes (SRS - A)	Mucus secretion, bronchospasm and vascular leakage.
8. Unspecified inflammatory factors	Neutrophil chemotaxis followed by mononuclear infiltration.
9. Chymase	Chymotrypsin - like activity.
10. Acetyl glycerophosphoryl choline (PAF)	Platelet aggregation, bronchospasm and vascular leakage.

(ii) Hay fever :

It is a type of hypersensitivity that occurs in persons sensitive to a variety of pollens. Symptoms of hay fever include sneezing, running nose, itching and irritation of the nose and eyes, perfused lacrymation and photophobia.

(iii) Urticaria :

It is one of the commonest adverse drug reaction which is characterized by localized patchy or generalised erythematous lesions. These lesions are accompanied by an intense itching. This reaction is short-lived and disappears within few hours. Lesion is dose-dependent and high incidence of rash, fever, eosinophilia and other blood dyscrasias is associated.

In type II reactions, antigen-antibody interaction not only results in the destruction of antigen but also that of host cells.

These immunological reactions may be directed to a target organ or tissue like blood, skin, lungs, liver, kidney, heart and peripheral nerves. Therefore type - II reactions are known as 'cytotoxic reactions'. For example, hypersensitivity reactions, if occurred during blood transfusions, can be categorised under type - II reactions. Similarly, hemolytic anaemia is also sometimes reported to occur due to such cytotoxic reactions. Depending upon the quantity of antigen or antibody involved, type - III reactions are classified into :

(i) reactions in which antigen is in excess. Examples include serum sickness, and

(ii) reactions in which antibodies are in excess. Examples include Arthus reaction.

Serum Sickness :

In this reaction, antigen in excess, leads to the production of soluble type of immune (i.e. antigen-antibody) complexes. These complexes fix on the complement and get deposited during their circulation, in the blood vessels. This results into acute inflammatory and tissue damaging type of responses. Symptoms vary according to the severity. They include fever, urticaria, maculopapular eruptions, painful and swollen joints, nephritis, neuritis, lymphadenopathy and glomerulonephritis with albuminuria. The myocardium is also vulnerable to attack of inflammatory origin. The symptoms develop after a latent period of 6 days or more following initial exposure to drug. The latent period reflects the time required to synthesize an adequate amount of antibody. The immunoglobulins, IgM, IgG_1 and IgG_2 have ability to produce serum sickness, in the descending order.

Type - I, Type - II and Type - III reactions occur immediately after the introduction of an antigen. All these reactions are mediated by humoral antibodies. On the contrary, type IV reaction is mediated by sensitized lymphoidal cells (specific T-lymphocytes). As this reaction is provoked after a longer time lag, it is also called as a delayed type of hypersensitivity response (DHR) or tuberculin type hypersensitivity. Examples of this type include, contact dermatitis, transplant rejection etc.

Interleukins :

These are the lymphokines released from lymphocytes during immune activation process. The important interleukins released during immune mechanisms include :

(a) Interleukin - 1 (IL -1) : It is a protease-sensitive molecule having a molecular weight of 12000 – 16000 dalton. It mainly acts by induction of interleukin - 2 production.

(b) Interleukin - 2 (IL - 2) : Interleukin-2 is also known as T-cell growth factor as it induces proliferation of T-lymphocytes in response to stimulation by antigens. It is a protein having a molecular weight of 14500 daltons. Interleukin-2 is also suspected to play a role in the regulation of growth of B-lymphocytes.

(c) Interleukin - 3 (IL - 3) : It is a lymphokine that induces mast cell proliferation *in-vitro*. It also offers resistance to T-lymphocytes from the action of corticosteroids, by inducing 20 α - steroid dehydrogenase enzyme.

(d) Lymphotoxins (LTs) : It is a strong inducer of influx of Ca^{++} - ions. Its lytic effects on the cell are produced within minutes by rapid shrinkage of the cells.

30.5 IMMUNOMODULATORS

The important components of immune system are :
(i) Granulocytes,
(ii) Complement synthesis and antibody formation,
(iii) Cellular immunity, and
(iv) Mucocutaneous barriers

The overall immunological pattern may be influenced either by the administration of certain drugs, by infection with viruses or because of inherited disorders of immune system. Under such conditions, defects may be seen in the essential components of immune system resulting into immunomodulation.

Since, neutrophiles are synthesized from granulocytes, as the total granulocyte count falls below 1000 cells/mm^3, the rate of bacterial infection increases. The common organisms affecting granulocytopenic patients include *E. coli, Pseudomonas aeruginosa, Klebsiella, pneumoniae* and *Staphylococcus aureus*. The chances of fungal, viral or protozoal infections are also significantly high.

An increase in the infection rate is also seen when the defect occurs in complement synthesis and antibody production. Such defects are usually encountered through the chronic treatment with chemotherapeutic agents.

Cellular immunity provides protection against fungal, bacterial, viral and protozoal infections. Certain drugs (e.g. corticosteroids, cyclosporine etc.), neoplastic diseases (e.g. Hodgkin's disease, lymphoma) and organ transplantation procedures paralyze cellular immunity.

Mucocutaneous barriers present in our body prohibit pathogenic organisms from taking entry into the internal vital organs. However these barriers are damaged by a number of medical devices, procedures, endotracheal tubes or chemotherapy. This leads to easy access of pathogens to the internal organs resulting into infectious state.

Important immunomodulators used clinically are summarised below :

(a) Antihistaminic Agents :

Histamine-binding lymphocytes have immunosuppressive activities. By inhibiting the activation of these lymphocytes, antihistaminic agents improve cell-mediated immune responses.

(b) Indomethacin :

It is a non-narcotic analgesic agent that relieves pain sensation by inhibiting prostaglandin biosynthesis. The impairment of prostaglandin production results in the significant improvement in the functioning of T-lymphocytes. It may be used to improve immune response in leishmaniasis, coccidioidomycosis and mycobacterial infections which cause deficient cell-mediated immunity.

(c) Interferons :

These are the endogenous substances having immunopotentiating activity. They have potent antiviral and antitumor activities. Interferon specifically has a potent macrophage-stimulating activity. Beside this, bestatin and lentinan are other natural products having immuno-potentiating activity.

(d) Isoprinosine :

Chemically it is a complex of inosine and an organic salt. Though it was originally developed as an antiviral agent, later it was found to possess stimulant activity on a number of immunological and inflammatory processes. It enhances T-cell proliferation, phagocytosis and chemotaxis through unknown mechanism.

(e) Levamisole :

It improves chemotactic responses and immune mechanisms in patients with diseases associated with immunodeficiency. It probably acts by inducing the release of c-GMP.

(f) Lymphokines :

Only two lymphokines known as IL-1 (i.e. T-lymphocyte activating factor) and IL-2 (i.e. T-lymphocyte growth factor) were found to stimulate the patient's cellular immunity.

(g) Thymic Hormones :

These are the polypeptides isolated from epithelial cells of thymus gland. They induce formation of mature T-cells by unknown mechanisms. They may be used to improve immunity in patients with immunodeficiency. These preparations consist of thymic humoral factor, thymosin fractions, serum thymic factor, a non-apeptide secreted by thymic epithelium, a dialyzable fraction of calf thymus extract and a protein with molecular weight of 5260 daltons. They are usually given in saline intramuscularly in doses between 0.5 mg/kg and 1.0 mg/kg per day for 2 - 3 weeks and then reduced to 1 - 3 doses per week.

(h) Transfer Factor :

This is a low molecular weight peptide (molecular weight is less than 6000 daltons) isolated from blood leucocytes of the patient with delayed hypersensitivity. It has stimulant effect on the cell-mediated immunity. It may be used in the treatment of immune deficiency syndromes such as chronic mucocutaneous candidiasis, in prophylaxis of varicella in children with leukemia and in the treatment of recurrent *Herpes simplex* infections.

Muramyl dipeptide (BCG vaccine), azimexon, glucan, tufstin, polynucleotides and thiobendazoles are used as adjuvants to stimulate cellular and humoral immunity responses in variety of conditions.

30.6 DRUGS AFFECTING IMMUNE RESPONSES

Immune response is not a single step process. It involves various phases which are as follows :

(1) antigen recognition and/or processing,
(2) amplification,
(3) antibody formation, and
(4) immune effector responses

Many drugs on chronic administration influence body's immune responses by affecting these vital elements of immune mechanisms. Depending upon the suppressant and stimulant effects exerted by these drugs on immune system, they are categorised as :

(I) Immunosuppressants, and
(II) Immuno enhancers.

(I) Immunosuppressants :

During organ transplantation, certain complex antigens or allografts activate the cytotoxic T-lymphocytes. Their activation results into development of cellular (and in some cases, humoral immunity also) immunity that rejects organ transplants. Immunosuppressive agents exert beneficial effects in such conditions by suppressing the cellular immunity. They are also used to treat some autoimmune disorders like, myasthenia gravis, polymyalgia rheumatica, rheumatoid arthritis, systemic lupus erythematosus, cranial arteritis, membranous glomerulonephritis and ulcerative colitis. Most of these agents are primarily used as antineoplastic agents. Since these drugs also possess anti-inflammatory activity, they are useful in conditions where inflammation accompanies exaggerated immune response.

On the basis of mechanism of action, immunosuppressants can be classified as :

(a) Corticosteroids : Betamethasone, Prednisolone
(b) Alkylating agents : Cyclophosphamide, Cytimun
(c) Antimetabolites : Mercaptopurine, Cytarabine
(d) Antibiotics : Cyclosporin A
(e) Enzymes : L-Asparginase
(f) Antibodies : Antithymocyte globulin, and
(g) Miscellaneous agents

Table 30.4 : Drugs affecting immune responses

Phases of immune response	Suppressants	Enhancers
1. Antigen recognition and processing	Corticosteroids Cyclophosphamide Cytimun	BCG vaccine C. parvum Tetramisole
2. Amplification	L-Asparaginase Corticosteroids Cyclophosphamide Cytimun 5-Fluorouracil 6-Mercaptopurine	Concanavalin A Tetramisole
3. Antibody formation	Corticosteroids Cyclophosphamide Cyclosporin A Cytimun	Lipopolysaccharide Tetramisole
4. Immune effector responses	Corticosteroids Cyclophosphamide Cyclosporin A Cytarabine Cytimun Methotrexate	C. parvum Tetramisole

(a) Corticosteroids :

Betamethasone, dexamethasone, hydrocortisone, paramethasone, prednisolone, methylprednisolone, and triamcinolone are some common examples of immunosupressive corticosteroids. They all possess antiallergic, antiinflammatory and immunosuppressive activities. They affect almost all phases of immune response. T-lymphocytes are more susceptible to the action of corticosteroids resulting into lymphopenia (i.e. reduction in blood lymphocytes). They also interfere with binding of antibodies to target cells and affect humoral immune responses by inhibiting antibody synthesis.

Adverse effects usually result from the use of high doses and include osteoporosis, hyperglycemia, ulcer formation and increased susceptibility for fungal infections. By using combination therapy, one can lower down the dose of the drug and hence the frequency and intensity of these adverse effects.

Corticosteroids are used either alone or in combination with other cytotoxic agents in the treatment of autoimmune disorders and for the prevention of allograft rejection. They are usually given in the dose range of 2 - 10 mg/kg per day for few weeks or months.

(b) Alkylating Agents :

Alkylating agents are the examples of cytotoxic drugs that kill the components of immune responses of the body. Since bone-marrow is a tissue, having a high rate of proliferation, their immuno-suppressive action results due to their toxic effects on rapidly proliferating cells. They exert cytotoxic effects to lymphocytes by alkylating their nucleic acids. Examples include cyclophosphamide and cytimun.

(i) Cyclophosphamide : It is a nitrogen mustard having broad spectrum of antineoplastic and immunosuppressive activities. Though it affects all phases of immune response, it is more effective suppressant of humoral immune mechanisms. It exerts cytotoxic action on both T-cells and on B-cells. However, its effects on B-cells are more pronounced. Its many active metabolites (e.g. 4-hydroxycyclophosphamide, acrolein and nornitrogen mustard) are responsible for its antineoplastic and immuno-suppressant effects.

It is usually used in combination with corticosteroids in the treatment of several autoimmune diseases, including Wegener's granulomatosis, idiopathic thrombocytopenia purpura, childhood nephrosis and severe rheumatoid anthritis. For these purposes, it is used orally in the dose of 2 mg/kg per day.

(ii) Cytimun : It is an analog of cyclophosphamide having better therapeutic index. It is specifically effective against B-cells.

(c) Antimetabolites :

These drugs act by exerting cytotoxic effects on rapidly proliferating cells like, those of bone-marrow, myeloid tissues, gonadal tissues and gastrointestinal tract. Hence, they can be used as immunosuppressants. Methotrexate, 6-mercaptopurine and azathioprine are the examples of phase-specific cytotoxic drugs which are more toxic to S-phase, when DNA synthesis is occuring. Their non-selectivity of action leads to appearance of serious side-effects including bone marrow suppression, more susceptibility to infection and sterility. Azathioprine and mercaptopurine are the most extensively studied immuno-suppressive agents.

(i) Azathioprine : It is an imidazolyl derivative of 6-mercaptopurine, having antirheumatic activity along with cytotoxic effect. It is an orally effective drug having plasma half-life of about 16 hours. It is metabolised to 6-mercaptopurine. Xanthine oxidase enzyme converts much of this active drug in liver and erythrocytes to 6-thiouric acid, thioinosinic acid and various other metabolites. Thioinosinic acid competitively inhibits the synthesis of inosinic acid, the precursor of adenylic acid and guanylic acid. This results into inhibition of DNA synthesis. Thus, on metabolic activation, azathioprine suppresses both cell-mediated and humoral immune responses and depresses antibody proliferative responses. It also possesses powerful anti-inflammatory activity.

Azathioprine is thus the most effective suppressant of phase II of immune responses. It is used orally in the treatment of acute glomerulonephritis, systemic lupus erythematosus, Wegener's granulomatosis, temporalcranial arteritis and polymyalgia rheumatica. It is also used in the management of organ transplantation and delayed hypersensitivity reactions. Adult oral dose is 2 - 3 mg/kg per day.

(ii) Methotrexate : It is an orally active folic acid analog having antineoplastic, antipsoriatic and mild immunosuppressant activity. It has a plasma half-life of 7.2 – 9.0 hours. It acts by inhibiting folate metabolism and affects phase II of immune responses. It however does not block the expression of established delayed hypersensitivity reactions but may alter the intensity of these reactions. It is used to treat severe psoriasis, dermatomycositis and rheumatoid arthritis. It is also used in organ transplantation procedures.

Other cytotoxic immunosuppressant drugs include chlorambucil, mercaptopurine, thioguanine, azaribine, cytarabine and 5-fluorouracil.

(d) Antibiotics :

Cyclosporine A is a drug belonging to this category. It is a cyclic undecapeptide having immunosuppressive activity and is isolated from the soil fungus, *Tolypocladium inflatum*. It is an orally effective antibiotic having plasma half-life of 10 - 27 hours. It possesses more marked immunosuppressant effects than its antibiotic potential.

It specifically inhibits generation of effector T-lymphocytes without affecting expression of suppressor lymphocytes and impairing B-cell activity. It impairs proliferative response of T-cells to antigens. Once T-cells are stimulated by antigens, they synthesize interleucin - 2 that exerts growth promoting effects on T-lymphocytes. Hence to be effective, cyclosporine must be administered before proliferation of T-cells occur.

Cyclosporine possesses specificity and low toxicity profile. Commonly associated adverse effects include gum hypertrophy, tremor, hirsutism, neurasthesia, depressive psychosis, nephrotoxicity and benign breast tumors.

It is used alongwith glucocorticoids for prophylaxis and treatment of organ rejection specifically in patients with kidney, liver, pancreas, bone-marrow and heart transplants. It also exerts beneficial effects when used in the treatment of autoimmune diseases like rheumatic arthritis, psoriatic anthropathies etc.

Adult oral dose is 10 - 15 mg/kg per day. Intravenously 50 mg diluted with normal saline may be given by slow infusion.

(e) Enzymes :

L-Asparaginase is a drug of choice in the treatment of acute lymphoblastic leukemia. It has a plasma half-life of about 11-23 hours. The enzyme is usually given either intravenously or intramuscularly. When combined together with methotrexate, it lowers down the adverse effects and intensifies therapeutic effects of the methotrexate.

(f) Antibodies :

These are produced in significant concentration in an appropriate recipient, usually a horse by repeated injection of human cells. This results in formation of specific antibodies against lymphocytes or thymocytes. These antibodies are then used in the form of antiserum to produce immunosuppression. These monoclonal antibodies have great potential to be used against lymphocytes. Example of this category includes antithymocyte globulin (ATG).

ATG is used alone or in combination with azathioprine and corticosteroids in the prevention of renal allograft rejection in the dose of 1-5 mg per day. However in some patients, allergic reactions have been reported to occur leading to serum sickness and nephritis.

(g) Miscellaneous Agents :

(i) Adenosine deaminase inhibitors : The immunosuppressive examples from this category include, erythro-9- (2-hydroxy-3-nonyl) adenine hydrochloride and 2'-deoxycoformycin (pentostatin). The former agent selectively exerts toxic effects against T-lymphocytes while pentostatin has synergistic effect with vidarabine and is used as antimetabolite in treatment of certain neoplastic diseases. Pentostatin causes a pronounced lymphoidal depletion, especially in spleen. It has a plasma half-life of 25 - 30 hours.

(ii) Bredinin : It is an imidazole nucleoside having antimetabolite antineoplastic activity and is used as an immunosuppressant in human kidney transplantation.

(iii) Cycloimmune : It is an analog of cyclosporine, undergoing clinical trials for its immunosuppressant activity. It has shown promising activity to suppress tissue rejecting ability of patients in organ transplantation procedures.

(iv) Niridazole : It is an orally active nitrothiazole derivative having anthelmintic, antibacterial (against a variety of anaerobic bacteria) and immunosuppressive activities. It is used to suppress cell-mediated immunity responses.

(II) Immunoenhancers :

This category of drugs is used to overcome immunodeficiency or immunosuppression arising as a result of either inherited or acquired disorders of immune system. Agammaglobulinemia and severe combined immune deficiency syndrome (SCIDs) are the examples of inherited disorders of immune system. Chemotherapy, therapy with immuno-suppressive agents, radiation or viral infection (e.g. AIDs) may cause immuno-suppression. Besides this, certain autoimmune disorders and some types of fungal infections may require therapy with immunoenhancers. This category of drugs may either cause a generalised, non-specific stimulation of immune mechanisms or may enhance only specific phases of immune responses. Examples of this category include -

(a) Bacillus Calmette Guerin (BCG) Vaccine :

It is used as an immunological enhancer to stimulate intact immune system (i.e. a non-specific immunoenhancer) of the body. BCG and its methanol extracted residue (MER) contain muramyl dipeptide as an active immunostimulant ingredient.

T-lymphocytes are the principal target cells for the action of BCG vaccine. It causes stimulation of macrophage functions, phagocytic activity, lysosomal enzyme activity and chemotaxis mechanisms. It induces the production of lymphocyte-activating factor resulting in stimulation of phase I of the immune responses.

Because of its reactivity against tumor cell antigen, its use is beneficial in the treatment of malignant melanoma, acute lymphocytic leukemia, lung cancer, breast cancer, acute and chronic myelogenous leukemia, lymphomas and colorectal cancer. It is available either as live unlyophilized, live lyophilized or in killed lyophilized form. It may be administered by oral, intradermal, intrapleural, intralesional or intravenous route. Adult dose depends upon the route of administration chosen.

Table 30.5 : Bacterial vaccines used in prevention of human infections

Vaccine	Source materials
BCG	Living BCG cells grown on solid or in liquid medium, Cells of *Vibrio cholerae* of Inaba and Ogawa serotypes grown on solid medium.
Cholera	
Diphtheria (plain)	Diphtheria toxin from liquid cultures of *Cornybacterium diphtheriae*.
Diphtheria (adsorbed)	Diphtheria toxin from liquid cultures of *C. diphtheriae*..
Neisseria maningitidis Type A or Type C	Polysaccharides of type A and of type C from cultures of *N. meningitidis* Type A and Type C in liquid medium.
Pertussis (plain and adsorbed)	Cells of *Bordetella pertussis* grown in liquid or on solid medium
Pneumococcal polysaccharide	*Str. pneumoniae* serotype
Pseudomonas aeruginosa	*Ps. aeruginosa* serotype
Tetanus (plain)	Tetanus toxin from liquid cultures of *Clostridium tetani*.
Tetanus (adsorbed)	Tetanus toxin from liquid cultures of *Clostridium tetani*.
Typhoid	Cells of *Salmonella typhi*.

Table 30.6 : Viral vaccines used in prevention of human infections

1.	Influenza (inactivated)	Allantoic fluid from fertile hen's eggs infected with a naturally occurring or laboratory derived culture of influenza virus.
2.	Influenza (live)	Allantoic fluid from fertile hen's eggs infected with avirulent strain of influenza virus.

3.	Measles	Fluid from cultures of chick embryo cells infected with vaccine strain.
4.	Poliomyelitis (oral)	Fluid from culture of monkey kidney or human diploid cells infected with attenuated virus of each of the three serotypes.
5.	Rabies	Fluid from cultures of human diploid cells infected with rabies virus.
6.	Rubella	Fluid from cultures of rabbit kidney, duck embryo or human diploid cells infected with attenuated virus.
7.	Small pox	Dermal scrapings from infected calves, sheep or buffalo.
8.	Yellow fever	Aqueous homogenate of chick embryos infected with attenuated 17 D strain of yellow fever virus.

Table 30.7 : Immunosera used in the prevention and treatment of human infection

Immunoserum	Minimal potency (iu ml^{-1})
Botulinum antitoxin	500 type A 500 type B 50 type E
Diphtheria antitoxin	1000 if from horses 500 if from other species
Gas gangrene (novyi)	3750
Gas gangrene (perfringens)	1500
Gas gangrene (septicum)	1500
Gas gangrene (mixed)	1000 of novyi 1000 of perfringens 500 of septicum
Rabies antiserum	80
Tetanus antitoxin	1000 for prophylaxis 3000 for treatment

Table 30.8 : Human immunoglobulins used in prevention and treatment of human infections

Immunoglobulin	Minimal potency (iu m)$^{-1}$
Measles	50
Normal	Measurable amount of any one bacterial and any one viral antibody for which there are international standards
Tetanus	100
Vaccinia	500

(b) Tetramisole (Levamisole) :

Levamisole is orally active S (–) isomer of tetramisole. Besides anthelmintic agent, it is used as immunostimulant in the therapy of certain infections, rheumatoid arthritis and in immunosuppressive conditions.

It has a plasma half-life of 4.0 hours. Upon hepatic metabolism, it is converted to DL-2-oxo - 3 (2-mercaptoethyl) - 5 - phenylimidazolidine, an active metabolite and several other inactive metabolites.

It mainly acts by raising the c-GMP levels through interaction with thymopoietin receptor sites. This leads to decrease in metabolic inactivation of c-GMP accompanied with increased breakdown of c-AMP. This increase in c-GMP level induces lymphocyte proliferation and augmentation of chemotactic responses. This reflects into increased antibody production, lymphokine production, proliferative responses of lymphocytes and increased phagocytosis by macrophges. Tetramisole is also a potent inhibitor of mammalian alkaline phosphatase and diamine oxidase enzymes.

Tetramisole is used in the treatment of :

(i) Certain chronic and recurrent bacterial and viral infections including acute hepatitis, herpes labialis, herpes genitalis, recurrent furunculosis, influenza, upper respiratory tract infections, acne conglobata and chronic pyogenic skin infections,

(ii) Certain diseases with immunodeficiency like, Wiskott-Aldrich syndrome, chronic granulomatous disease, lazy leucocyte syndrome, ataxia telangectasis, Job's syndrome (i.e. hyperimmunoglobin E syndrome) and cyclic neutropenia, and

(iii) Autoimmune diseases like, rheumatoid arthritis, Crohn's disease, aphthous stomatitis and systemic lupus erythematosus.

(c) Corynebacterium parvum :

It has pronounced stimulatory effect on phase I of immune responses. The humoral immune response is intensified by an increase in the antibody production against both, the T-cell dependent, and independent antigens. This reflects into increased macrophage proliferation, accumulation of lysosomal enzymes, activation of phospholipase A and accelerated phagocytosis.

Adverse effects include chills, fever and changes in blood pressure. It is used as adjuvant in cancer chemotherapy, and can also be used to depress allograft rejection. It may be administered intravenously, intraperitoneally or intralesionally.

(d) Tilorone :

It is a synthetic immunoenhancer that stimulates T-lymphocytes originating in the thymus. It also possesses antiviral activity because of its ability to induce interferon production. Adverse effects are few and include nausea, vomiting, epigastric discomfort, dizziness and headache.

(e) Inosiplex :

Chemically it is the p-acetamidobenzoic acid salt of inosine dimethylaminoisopropanol. It is orally active synthetic drug that activates the cellular immunity through stimulation of interleucin-2 (i.e. T-lymphocyte growth factor). This results in an increase in macrophage activity and population of T-lymphocytes. It also has an ability to inhibit replication of both RNA and DNA viruses. Since on its metabolism, uric acid is formed, it induces gouty arthritis upon chronic administration.

It is used as immunoenhancer to treat cancer-induced immunosuppression in the dose of 50 mg/kg per day in divided doses. Because of its antiviral property, it may also be used in the treatment of infections due to herpes virus, rhinovirus, influenza virus and chronic measles virus.

(f) Lipopolysaccharides (LPSs) :

The lipopolysaccharides possess antitumor and immunostimulant effects. They mainly activate phase III of immune response.

(g) Dialyzable Leukocyte Extract (Transfer Factor) :

It is obtained from peripheral leukocytes of individuals who have been sensitized or are immune to certain pathogens. The extract contains ascorbic acid, chemoattractants for monocytes and neutrophil immobilizers, thymic factors, nicotinamide, serotonin, histamine and prostaglandins alongwith several moieties composed of proteins and RNA.

The extract contains polyribonucleotides which are known as 'transfer factors'. These factors potentiate antigen-specific cellular immunity responses. However minimum required number of T-lymphocytes need to be present in pateint receiving the treatment with transfer factor.

Adverse effects are few and include transient fever, occassional pain or erythema at the site of injection. Transfer factor is used in the treatment of sarcoidosis, Hodgkin's disease, mycobacterial infections, fungal infections, viral infections and autoimmune diseases. The solution of transfer factor is prepared in saline. Each one ml of this solution is equivalent to the extract obtained from $1 \times 10^8 - 1 \times 10^9$ leukocytes. Adult dose is 1 ml either s.c. or i.m. weekly or monthly.

30.7 DISORDERS OF IMMUNE SYSTEM

(a) Immunodeficiency :

In immunodeficiency due to certain inherited or acquired diseases, the natural immune response gets paralyzed. Besides this, a variety of factors such as malnutrition, metabolic disorders, malignancy and cytotoxic drugs may lead to immunodeficiency. Defects may be seen in particular phase of immune mechanism or when immune system as a whole gets impaired. There may be a failure of humoral (antibody) immune response or a failure of cellular immunity or a combination of both.

(b) Myeloma (excessive production of immunoglobulins) :

This condition arises because of an increase in immunoglobulin (antibody) production. This occurs specifically in patients in whom malignant change in the clone of plasma cells is reported. As the number of immunoglobulins increases, their metabolic turnover also gets increased. This results in appearance of light chains (Bence -Jones protein) in the urine of the patient.

(c) Autoimmune Diseases :

In normal person, complex network of feedback loops exist to make a smooth co-ordination between different components of immune responses. However, under certain conditions, this control is lost and the aberrant immune reaction results in a disease. Antibodies are secreted against a component of an individual's own immunoglobulins. These circulating immune complexes (e.g. DNA-anti DNA antibodies) fix with complements and lodge in certain tissues (e.g., skin, neuromuscular junction, joints of affected individuals and kidney). Autoimmune diseases of thyroid gland, stomach (pernicious anaemia) and adrenal gland are also reported.

Prominent examples of autoimmune diseases include -

(i) Myasthenia gravis : In this, antibodies are produced against cholinergic nicotinic receptors present in neuromuscular junctions. The breakdown of these junctional cholinergic receptors makes the patient weak and unable to move voluntary muscles.

Table 30.9 : Classification of primary immunodeficiency syndrome

(A) Disorders of specific immunity :	(B) Disorders of complement :
(I) Humoral immunodeficiencies (B-cell defects)	(a) Hereditary angioneurotic edema
(a) X-linked agammaglobulinaemia	(b) Paroxysmal Nocturnal hemoglobinuria
(b) Selective immunoglobulin deficiencies (IgA, IgM or IgG)	(c) Pulmonary vascular leukostasis
(c) Immunodeficiencies with hyper-IgM	(d) Pancreatitis
(d) Transcobalamin II deficiency	(e) Severe trauma
(II) Cellular immunodeficiencies (T - cell defects)	(f) Pulmonary distress syndrome
(a) Thymic hypoplasia (Di George's syndrome)	(C) Disorders of phagocytosis
(b) Chronic mucocutaneous candidiasis	(a) Neutropenia
(c) Purine nucleoside phosphorylase (PNP) deficiency	(b) Chediak - Higashi syndrome
(III) Combined immunodeficiencies (B and T cell defects)	(c) Chronic granulomatous disease
(a) Cellular immunodeficiencies with abnormal Ig synthesis	(d) Myeloperoxidase deficiency
(b) Wiskott - Aldrich syndrome	(e) Leucocyte G6PD deficiency
(c) Immunodeficiency with thymoma	(f) Job's syndrome
(d) Severe combined immunodeficiency e.g. Adenosine deaminase (ADA) deficiency	(g) Lazy Leucocyte syndrome
	(h) Hyper-IgE syndrome
	(i) Actin-binding protein deficiency

(ii) Rheumatoid arthritis : In this disease antibodies are secreted against a component of body's own immunoglobulins. These antibody-immunoglobulin complexes get deposited in the joints of affected persons. The local tissue necrosis and inflammation of joints are caused by lysosomal enzymes released during phagocytosis process.

(iii) Systemic lupus erythematosus (SLE) : In this disease, many organs are affected because of the production of autoantibodies. It is a chronic multiorgan inflammatory disorder that affects skin, lungs, joints, kidneys, heart and brain. The characteristic symptoms include fatigue, fever, weight loss, skin lesions, dyspnea, joint pain and swelling, renal damage (i.e. nephritis, proteinurea, hematuria, hypertension), abdominal pain and neurological manifestations.

The immune complexes after fixing with complement, get deposited into various organs and produce tissue damage by inflammatory reactions. Patients show B-lymphocyte hyperactivity and impairment in T-cell immuno-regulation.

Aspirin like drugs (e.g. aspirin, sulindac, ibuprofen or naproxen) may be used orally in the dose of 3.5 g per day to treat systemic lupus erythematosus.

(iv) Pernicious anaemia : The disease involves appearance of two types of auto-antibodies. One type of antibody causes achlorhydria and atrophic gastritis by affecting the functioning of gastric parietal cells, while second type of antibodies bind with gastric intrinsic factor thus inhibiting its uptake by intestinal mucosa. This results into inhibition of absorption of vitamin B_{12}.

The probable mechanisms involved in autoimmune diseases are as follows :

(a) The breakdown of feedback inhibitory loops of immune system leads to emergence of forbidden clones of antibodies. These antibodies then evoke immune responses against self antigens.

(b) Under physical, chemical or biological influences, antigenic alterations are reported to occur. Such altered antigen may then evoke immune responses by inducing the release of antibodies, and

(c) In some pathogenic conditions, defects are incorporated in a variety of T-lymphocytes. (e.g. enhanced helper T-cells and decreased concentration of suppressor T-cells) and B-lymphocytes. These defects may then lead to autoimmune responses. Besides this, defects in stem cell development, thymus and macrophage functioning may also contribute to the occurrence of autoimmune diseases.

Depending upon the organs involved, autoimmune diseases can be categorized as :

(i) Localized or organ specific autoimmune diseases : These include Addison's disease, Graves' disease, idiopathic polyneuritis, lymphadenoid goitre, myasthenia gravis, pernicious anaemia etc.

(ii) Systemic or non-organ specific auto immune diseases (collagen diseases) : These include rheumatoid arthritis, polyarteritis nodosa, systemic lupus erythematosus, dermatomyositis and scleroderma.

(iii) Haemocytolytic auto immune diseases : These include autoimmune leucopenia, autoimmune hemolytic anemias, autoimmune thrombocytopenia, etc.

(iv) Transitory autoimmune diseases : These diseases appear because of certain infections or drug treatment. These autoimmune diseases are of transitory nature and disappear as the underlying cause is brought within control. Examples include anaemia, nephritis and thrombocytopenia.

30.8 ACQUIRED IMMUNODEFICIENCY SYNDROME (AIDS)

AIDs is the end stage disease representing the irreversible breakdown of immune defence mechanisms. The immune competence of the patient is completely lost. As a result chemotaxis, antigen identification and the functioning of monocytes and macrophages are gradually diminished. The patient is susceptible to the attack of infections with relatively avirulent microorganisms as well as to lymphoid and other malignancies. The commonly seen infections in AIDs patients include oral candidiasis, herpes zoster, hairy cell leucoplakia, salmonellosis, P. carinii pneumonia, toxoplasmosis or tuberculosis. Lymphoid and other malignancies may also be present.

The first case of AIDs patient was identified in 1981 in New York. Thereafter efforts were directed to isolate the infecting agent of AIDs. The first report about isolation of infecting agent appeared in 1983 from the Pasteur Institute, Paris. It was isolated from West African patient. It was found to be a retro virus and was named as

Lymphadenopathy Associated Virus (LAV). This was followed by many reports describing the isolation of aetiological agents in AIDS. All these agents were described under the term, AIDS-related viruses (ARV). In 1986, the International Committee on Virus Nomenclature had coined the term Human Immunodeficiency Virus (HIV) for these infective agents, in order to avoid confusion.

The virus, HIV belongs to the Lentivirus subgroup of the family Retroviridae. It is an example of a thermolabile enveloped virus having a diameter of 90 - 120 mm. It survives for about 7 days at room temperature. It withstands lyophilization. Structurally it is a nucleoprotein core that contains a single stranded RNA genome alongwith proteins. Minor antigenic differences in both core and envelope antigens are reported between isolates from different patients as well as from the same patient.

The HIV virus can remain silent over a long period of time. Under favourable conditions, viral replication occurs by increased rate of synthesis of viral RNA and other components. Since HIV virus affects the functioning of immune system, the symptoms associated are mainly due to the failure of immune responses rather than due to viral cytotoxicity. The T_4-lymphocytes serve as suitable host cell for HIV viruses. The major damage occurs to T_4-lymphocytes. T-cells decrease in number which results in a lack of secretion of activating factors from T-lymphocytes. This is a contributing factor for the failure of immune system.

In an infected person, HIV viruses can be detected into saliva, tears, urine, cervical secretions, semen, breast milk, blood, lymphocytes and cell-free plasma.

It can be transmitted by following possible routes.

(i) through sexual contacts in both homosexuals and heterosexuals,

(ii) through the transfer of blood, blood products or other body fluids,

(iii) through the donation of tissue or organ,

(iv) through certain infections and/or injuries and

(v) from infected mother to baby. About half of the number of babies born to infected mother's are infected with HIV virus.

However HIV viruses are not transmitted through air, water or insect bite.

Within a few weeks of infections with HIV virus, the patient experiences mild symptoms like fever, malaise, headache, rash, arthropathy, lymphadenopathy etc. Due to the paralyzed immune system, patient may get attacked by many infections and malignancies like lymphomas, Kaposi's sarcoma, Hodgkin and non-Hodgkin types. AIDS is the last stage in the wide spectrum of clinical features of HIV infection.

Depending upon the type of infection and the organ most affected, different patients may complain about different symptoms. The prominent organs affected involve -

(i) Gastrointestinal Tract :

It is most susceptible for the attack of organisms like *Mycobacteria, Salmonellae, Cryptosporidium, Adenoviruses* and *Isospora*. Prominent symptoms include mouth thrush, dysphagia, abdominal pain, diarrhoea, gingivitis, herpetic stomatitis, and hairy leukoplakia. Chronic colitis is seen mainly in male homosexuals.

(ii) Cutaneous Signs :

These include candidiasis, impetigo, herpes lesions, prurigo, xeroderma, folliculitis, seborrhoeic dermatitis and mulluscum contagiosum.

(iii) Respiratory System :

This system becomes vulnerable for the attack of *P. carinii, M. tuberculosis* and *M. avium* intracellulare. Major symptoms include fever, dyspnoea, dry cough and pneumonis.

(iv) Central Nervous System :

Dementia and impairment of CNS functions are reported to occur because of the ability of HIV virus to enter into CNS. Besides this toxoplasmosis, cryptococcosis and lymphomas of CNS are also known to occur.

Treatment of HIV infection consists of four important phases. The first phase deals with control of infections and malignancies associated with the patient. The treatment is infection specific. For example, in AIDS patients with *Pneumocystis carinii* infection, cotrimoxazole is given orally. Pentamidine may also be used either i.m.ly or i.v.ly in the dose of 4 mg/kg body weight per day. *Toxoplasma gondii* is a protozoal organism that affects mainly head, lung, liver, spleen and CNS. Drugs of choice include pyrimethamine (25 mg/day) and sulfadiazine (2 g per day) orally. Folinic acid may be used in the dose of 10 mg per day to prevent hematologic abnormalities. Besides this, *Mycobacterium aviumintracellulare* is found in 50 % patients with AIDS. It affects mainly GIT, lung and other tissues.

To correct most of these infections, interleukin-2 is commonly used agent. It is a potent lymphokine responsible for the activation of various components of immune system.

The second phase of the treatment consists of employing general measures to cool down imaginary anxiety and fear experienced by the patients. The infected person must be reassured that he can resume a normal life if proper precautions and treatment are taken. The high risk factors must be identified and eliminated. This is to be supported by health education.

The third phase of the treatment deals with measures to improve the functioning of immune system. A large number of antiviral agents (e.g. α-interferon, ribavirin, suramin etc.), can be supplimented by administration of immunoenhancer like interleukin-2, thymic factor, leucocyte transfusion or by the transplantation of bone-marrow.

The last phase of the treatment consists of administration of anti-HIV agent. Zidovudine (azidothymidine) is the only drug available. It is an orally effective antiviral agent beneficial in the treatment of AIDs and AIDs related syndromes. Adverse effects include headache, leukopenia and macrocytic anaemia.

Efforts are being continued to develop a vaccine effective in the treatment of AIDs. However, prospects for such a vaccine in the near future are unfortunately dim.

ANTIMICROBIAL AGENTS

PENCILLINS

(1) Amdinocillin	**Adult:**	PO

1. 10 mg/kg every 4 hours when used alone (IM).
2. 10 mg/kg every 6 hours in conjunction with other antibiotic (IM).
3. 10 mg/kg 3 or 4 times daily, Moderate to severe renal function (IM).
4. Same as above (IV).

Pediatric: 10 mg/kg every hours (IM or IV).

(2) Amoxicillin   **Adult:** 250 - 500 mg every 8 hours.   PO

Pediatric: Drops (50 mg/ml).

Under 6 kg → 0.5 - 1 ml every 8 hours.

6-8 kg → 1-2 ml every 8 hours.

Suspension (125 mg/5 ml or 250 mg/5 ml).   PO

8 - 20 kg → 20 - 40 mg/kg/24 hours in divided doses every 8 hours. Over 20 g → follow adult dosages.

(3) Ampicillin   **Adult:** 250 - 500 mg every 6 hours → Respiratory tract and skin infections and soft tissue infection and 500 mg every 6 hours for GIT and urinary tract-infections.   PO/IM

Same as PO. Septicemia or Bacterial meningitis → 8 - 14g/day at a rate so faster than 100 mg/min. in divided doses every 3 - 4 hours.   IV

Pediatric: Neonates → first 7 days after birth, 25 mg/kg/12 hr.   IV

After 7 days, 33 - 50 mg/kg/8 hr.

After 30 days, 33 - 50 mg/kg/6 hr.

Children under 40 kg → 50 - 200 mg/kg/24 hr in divided doses   PO

As above   IV/IM

Children over 40 kg → 1 - 2g/24 hr in divided doses.   PO

For severe infections 8 - 14 g/24 hr in divided doses.   IM/IV

(4) Potassium clavulanate   **Adult:** 250 mg of Amoxicillin and 125 mg of potassium clavulanate every 8 hr.   PO

Severe infections → 500 mg of amoxicillin and 125 mg of potassium clavulanate every 8 hr.

Pediatric: Children less than 40 kg → 7 mg/kg given every 8 hr.

Tablets: Severe infection → 13 mg/kg every 8 hr.

Children more than 40 kg → Usual adult dose

(5) Az locillin	**Normal renal function**:	
	Adult: 2 g every 6 hr → Uncomplicated urinary tract infection.	IV
	3 g every 6 hr → Complicated urinary tract infection	
	3 g every 4 hr or 4 g every 6 hr. → Lower respiratory tract, skin bone and joint infections	
	4 g every 4 hr → Impaired renal function	

Impaired renal function:

Urinary tract infection (uncomplicated)   IV

Creatinine clearance:
- (a)   < 10 ml/min. → 1.5 g every 12 hr.
- (b)   10 - 30 ml/min → 1.5 g every 12 hr
- (c)   > 30 ml/min → As normal renal function

Urinary tract infection (complicated)

Creatinine clearance:
- (a)   < 10 ml/min. → 2.0 g every 12 hr.
- (b)   10 - 30 ml/min → 1.5 g every 12 hr.
- (c)   > 30 ml/min → As normal renal function.

Systemic infection:

Creatinine clearance:
- (a)   < 10 ml/min → 3 g every 12 hr.
- (b)   10 – 30 ml/min → 2 g every 8 hr.
- (c)   > 30 ml/min → As normal renal function

Peadiatric: Neonates:

Children: 75 mg/kg every 4 hr. not to exceed 24 g/day over 30 min.

(6) Bacampicillin	**Adult:** 400 - 800 mg every 12 hr.	PO
	Pediatric: 25 - 50 mg/kg/day in equally divided doses every 12 hr.	
(7) Carbenicillin, indanyl sodium and disodium	**Adult:** Indanyl sodium salt 382 - 764 mg 4 times daily	PO
	Disodium salt not more than 2 g.	IM
	Disodium salt 250 - 50 mg/kg/day to 20 - 30 g/day for Proteus or *E. coli*. 30 - 40 g/day for Pseudomonas.	IV

Pediatric: Neonates:

(1) Under 2 kg   IM/IV Infusion
- (a) First 7 days after birth 100 mg/kg/ 12 hr.
- (b) After 7 days 100 mg/kg/8 hr.

(2) Over 2 kg
- (a) First 7 days after birth 100 mg/kg/ 12 hr.   IV

　　　　　　　　　　(b) After 7 days 100 mg/kg/6 hr.
　　　　　　　　Children:
　　　　　　　　(1)　400 - 500 mg/kg/24 hr in divided doses for severe *Pseudomonas* infection.
　　　　　　　　(2)　300 - 400 mg/kg /24 hr for severe *E. coli* or *Proteus* infection.

(8) Methicillin　**Adult:**　1 - 2 g every 4 - 6 hr (500 mg/ml)　　　　IM
　　　　　　　　　　　　1 - 2 g every 4 - 6 hr (1 g/50 ml)　　　　　IV
　　　　　　　　Pediatric: Neonates: Under 2 kg: 25 mg/kg every 12 hr. for the first 2 weeks of age, every 8 hr. after 2 weeks. Over 2 kg: 25 mg/kg every 8 hr. for the first 2 weeks of age, every 6 hr. from 2 - 4 weeks of age.
　　　　　　　　Infants and older children → Administer 50 mg/kg every 6 hr.

(9) Meflocillin　**Adult:** (1) Normal renal function
　　　　　　　　(a)　Urinary tract infection (uncomplicated) → 1.5 - 2 g　IM/IV
　　　　　　　　　　every 6 hr.　　　　　　　　　　　　　　　　　　　IV
　　　　　　　　(b)　Urinary tract infection (complicated) → 3 g every 6　IV
　　　　　　　　　　hr.　　　　　　　　　　　　　　　　　　　　　　　IM/IV
　　　　　　　　(c)　Lower respiratory tract infection 3 g every 4 hr.　　IV
　　　　　　　　(d)　Gonococcal urethetris: 1- 2 g with 1 kg probencide.　Infusion
　　　　　　　　Children: (1 month to 12 years) 50 mg/kg every 4 hr. over 30 min

(10) Penicillin G　**Adult:** 200000 - 500000 units every 6 - 8 hr.　　PO
　　　　　　　　300000 - 4.8 million units　　　　　　　　　　　　　IM
　　　　　　　　1 million to 80 million units　　　　　　　　　　　　IV
　　　　　　　　Pediatric: Premature and full term neonates　　　　　IM/IV
　　　　　　　　30000 - 50000 units/kg/12 hr.
　　　　　　　　Neonates with meningitis → 75,000 - 1,25000 units/kg　IV
　　　　　　　　/12 hr.　　　　　　　　　　　　　　　　　　　　　　PO/IM/
　　　　　　　　Children 25,000 - 50,000 units/kg/24 hr in 4 - 6　　　IV
　　　　　　　　divided doses.
　　　　　　　　Meningitis → 200000 - 4000000 units/kg/24 hr.

(11) Penicillin V　**Adult:** 250 - 500 mg every 6 hr.　　　　　　　　PO
　　　　　　　　Pediatric: 30 - 50 mg/kg/day in 3 - 4 divided doses.　PO

(12) Piperacillin　**Adult:** (1) Normal renal function.
　　　　　　　　(a)　Urinary tract infection uncomplicated 6 - 8 g　IM/IV
　　　　　　　　　　every 6 - 12 hr.
　　　　　　　　(b)　Urinary tract infection (complicated) 8 - 16 g every　IV
　　　　　　　　　　6 - 8 hr.

	(c) Lower respiratory tract, intraabdominal, skin infections, IV septicemia - 12.189 every 4 - 6 hr.	IV
	(d) Gonococcal urethritis uncomplicated: 2 g IM with 1 g PO probenecid	IM
(13) Ticarcillin	**Adult:** (1) Normal renal function 200 - 350 mg/kg/day in divided doses for systemic, respiratory and soft tissue infections 1 g, every 6 hr for urinary tract infections.	IV
	Pediatric: Neonates:	
	(a) < 2 kg → initially 100 mg/kg or 100 mg/kg as 10 - 20 min.	IM/IV
	Follow every 8 hr. with IV infusions of 75 mg/kg during the first week after birth then increase to 75 mg/kg every 4 - 6 hr.	Infusion
	(b) > 2 kg: initially 100 mg/kg.	IM
	100 mg/kg as 10 - 20 min. follow every 4 - 6 hr. with IV infusions of 75 mg/kg during the first 2 weeks after birth then increase to 100 mg/kg every 4 hr.	
	Children: Respiratory, soft tissue and systemic infection as adults Urinary tract infection → 40 kg → 50 - 100 mg/kg/day in divided doses every 6 - 8 hr.	IM/IV
	> 40 kg administer as for adults.	
(14) Ticarcillin di-sodium Potassium clavulanate	**Adult:** (1) Normal renal function	
	(a) 60 kg or more: 3.1 g every 4 - 6 hr.	IV
	(b) 6 kg or less: 200 - 300 mg/kg given in divided doses.	IV infusion
	Pediatric: As above for age 12 and older.	

CEPHALOSPORINS

(1) Cephadenil	**Adult:** 1 - 2 g, 1 - 2 times daily	PO
	Child: 10 - 15 mg/kg 3 - 4 times daily	PO
(2) Cefanandoic	**Adult:** Normal renal function: 0.5 - 1 g, every 4 - 8 hr not to exceed 12 g/24 hr. at a rate of 3 - 5 min. Impaired renal function: loading dose: 1 - 2g	
	Pediatric: Over 1 month of age 50 - 100 mg/kg/day in 3 - 6 divided doses may be increased to 150 mg/kg/day	IV
(3) Cefajolin	**Adult:** 250 mg - 1 g, every 6 - 8 hr.	IM
	250 mg - 1.5 g, every 6 - 8 hr	IV
	Pediatric: Children	
	(1) 25 - 60 mg/kg/2 hr in divided dose.	IM/IV

	(2) 100 mg/kg/24 hr in divided dose.	IM/IV
(4) Cefopeafone sodium	**Adult:** 1- 2 g every 12 hr.	
	Severe infections 6 - 12 g divided in 3 to 4 equal dosages	IM/IV
(5) Cefotanine sodium	**Adult:**	IM
	(1) Normal renal function: (not to exceed 12 g daily)	
	(a) Gonorrhea → 1 g.	
	(b) Respiratory and urinary tract infection → 1 g every 12 hr.	IM/IV
	(c) Moderate to severe infections → 1 - 2 g, every 6 - 8 hr.	IM/IV
	(d) Septicemia → 2 g every 6 - 8 hr.	IV
	(e) Life threatening infection → 2 g every 4 hr.	IV
	(2) Impaired renal function creatinine clearance (< 20 ml/min) Reduce dosage by one half.	
	Pediatric: Upto 1 week age 50 mg/kg every 12 hr.	
	Ages 1 - 4 weeks: 50 mg/kg every 8 hr.	IV
	Ages 1 month - 12 years (< 50 kg) 50 - 180 mg/kg/every 4 - 6 hr.	IV
	Ages 5 - 12 years (> 50 kg) - Adult doses	IM/IV
(6) Ceftafidine	**Adult:**	IV
	(1) Normal renal function 1 g every 8 - 12 hr.	
	(2) Urinary tract infection (uncomplicated) 250 mg every 12 hr.	IV
	Pediatric: Upto 4 weeks age → 30 mg/kg every 12 hr.	
	1 month → 12 years → 30 - 50 mg/kg every 8 hr. Not to exceed 6 g/day	
(7) Cefteianone sodium	**Adult:** 1- 2 g once a day. Not to exceed 4 g daily	IV/IM
	Pediatric: Serious infections → 50 - 75 mg/kg/day in divided doses every 12 hr. Do not exceed 2 g/day	IV
	Meningitis 100 mg/kg/day individual doses every 12 hr. Not to exceed 2 g/day. Loading dose 75 mg/kg	IV
(8) Cephalexin monohydrate	**Adult:** 250 mg - 1.0 g, every 6 hr.	PO
	Pediatric: 25 - 50 mg/kg/24 hr. in divided doses	PO
(9) Cephalothin	**Adult:** 500 mg - 1 g every 4 - 6 hr	IM
	Mild to moderate infections 500 mg - 1 g every 4 to 6 hr.	IV
	Lifethreatening infections 1 g - 2 g, every 4 - 6 hr.	
	Pediatric: 80 - 160 mg/kg/24 hr in divided doses.	IM/IV
(10) Cephapirin	**Adult:** 500 mg - 1 g, every 4 - 6 hr.	IM/IV
	Pediatric: 40 - 80 mg/kg/day in 4 divided doses.	IM/IV

(11) Cephradine	**Adult:** 250 - 500 mg every 6 hr.	PO
	500 mg - 1 g every 6 hr do not exceed 8g/day.	IM/IV
	Pediatric: 25 - 50 mg/kg/day in 4 divided doses	
	50 - 100 mg/kg/day in 4 divided doses.	IM/IV
(12) Cefaclor	**Adult:** 250 - 500 mg every 8 hr. do not exceed 4 g/day.	PO
	Pediatric: 20 - 40 mg/kg/day in 3 divided doses do not exceed 1 g/day.	PO
(13) Cefonicid	**Adult:** 0.5 - 1 g, once daily not to exceed 2 g/day.	IM/IV
(14) Ceforamide	**Adult**: 0.5 - 1 g, every 12 hr. do not exceed 4 g/day.	IM/IV
	Pediatric: 20 - 40 mg/kg/day divided into doses every 12 hr.	IM/IV
(15) Cefoxiline	**Adult**: 1 - 2 g every 6 - 8 hr. do not exceed 12g/ day.	IM/IV
	Pediatric: 80 - 160 mg/kg/day in 4 - 6 divided doses do not exceed 12 g/day.	IM/IV
(16) Cefuroxine	**Adult:** 0.75 - 1.5 g every 8 hr do not exceed 9 g/day.	IM/IV
	Pediatric: 50 - 100 mg/kg/day in 3 - 4 divided doses. Do not exceed 240 mg/kg/day.	IM/IV

THIENAMYCINS

(1) Imipenem cilastatin sodium	**Adult:** Mild infections 250 mg every 6 hr. Severe infections 1 g every 6 hr. Max. total dose → 50 mg/kg/day or 4 g/day whichever is lower.	IV

AMINOGLYCOSIDES

(1) Amikacin sulfate	**Adult:** (1) Normal renal function → 15 mg/kg/day in 2 - 4 equally divided doses.	IM/IV
	Pediatric: (1) Neonates: loading 10 mg/kg, maintenance 7.5 mg/kg every 12 hr. over 1 to 2 hr.	IM/IV
	(2) Older infants and children 15 mg/kg day in 2 - 4 equally divided dose over 30 - 60 min.	IM/IV
(2) Gentamicin sulfate	**Adult:** Normal renal function (1) Urinary tract infection 3 mg/kg/24 hr. (2) Other infections: 3 - 5 mg/kg/24 hr. (3) Life threatening infections 5 mg/kg/24 hr.	IM/IV

	Pediatric: Neonates:	IV
	(1) First 7 days, 2.5 mg/kg/24 hr.	
	(2) After 7 days, 2.5mg/kg/'8 hr.	IV
	Children: 2 - 2.5 mg/kg/8 hr.	
(3) **Kanamycin sulfate**	**Adult:** 8 - 12 g/day in divided doses.	PO
	7.5 mg/kg/12 hr or 15 mg/kg/24 hr in equally divided doses, 3 - 4 times daily.	IM
	Pediatric: Neonates	

Birth weight (g)	≤7 days of age	> 7 days of age	
≤ 2000	1.5 mg/kg every 12 hr.	10 mg/kg every 12 hr,	IV
> 2000	10 mg/kg every 12 hr.	10 mg/kg every 8 hr.	

	Children as adults.	
(4) **Neomycin sulfate**	**Adult**:	
	(1) Hepatic coma → 4 - 12 g/day.	PO
	(2) Infectious diarrhoea → 50 mg/kg/day in divided doses.	
	(3) Preperative bowel sterilisation 190 mg/kg in gradually divided dose for 2 - 3 days.	
	Adult: 15 mg kg/day in 4 divided doses total daily doses not to exceed 1 kg.	IM
(5) **Paromomycin sulfate**	**Adult:** Amebiasis 25 - 35 mg/kg in 3 divided doses 5 - 10 days.	PO
	Tapeworms: 1 g every 15 minute for 4 doses. Hgmenolepis nana: 45 mg/kg once for 5 - 7 days.	PO
	Pediatric: Amebiasis and Hynenolepic nana-asaduts tapeworm → 11 mg/kg every 4 hr. for 4 doses.	PO
(6) **Tobramycin sulfate**	**Adult:** (i) Normal renal function.	IV
	(a) Serious infection 1 mg/kg/8 hr.	
	(b) Life threatening infection 1.66 mg/kg/8 hr.	
	As above diluted in 50 - 100 ml ojdenteose 5% saline over 20 - 60 min.	IV
	Pediatric: Neonates (Above 1 week)	IM
	Upto 2 mg/kg/12 hr.	IV
	As below	
	Children and older infants (normal renal function)	
	(1) Serious infection → 1 mg/kg/8 hr.	IM
	(2) Life threatening infection → 1.66 mg/kg/8 hr. 1 mg/ml.	IV
	Diluted 1 mg/ml over 20 - 60 min	

SULFONAMIDES

(1) Sulfamethoxazole	**Adult:** Moderate infections → 2 g initially followed by 1 g 2 times daily. Severe infections → 2 g initially followed by 2 g, 3 times daily.	PO
	Pediatric: Cover 2 months of age. Initially 50 - 60 mg/kg followed by 25 - 30 mg/kg/24 hr. in 2 divided doses. Do not exceed 75 mg/kg/24 hr	PO
(2) Sulfasalazine	**Adult:** Initially 4 - 12 g daily in 4 - 8 divided dose maintenance 500 mg 4 times daily	PO
	Pediatric Over 2 months of age Initial 40 - 60 mg/kg/24 hr in 36 doses maintenance 30 mg/kg/24 hr divided in 4 doses.	PO
(3) Sulfisoxazole	**Adult:** 2 - 4 g initially followed by 1 - 2 g every 4 - 6 hr. 4 - 5 g every 12 hr.	PO IM/IV
	Pediatric: 75 mg/kg initially followed by 150 mg/kg → 24 hr in 4 - 6 divided doses. Total daily dose not to exceed 6 g.	PO
	50 mg/kg initially, followed by 100 mg/kg/24 hr in 2 - 3 divided dose.	IV
	As above (IM) divided in 4 equal doses	
(4) Co-trimaxazole	**Adult: Urinary tract infections and shigellosis:** 800 mg of sulfamethoxazole and 160 mg of trimethoprim every 12 hr.	PO
	8 - 10 mg/kg gives in 2 - 4 equally divided dose every 6, 8 or 12 hr for 14 days for UTI and 5 days for shigellosis.	
	Pediatric: Children 40 mg/kg/24 hr of sulfamethoxazole and 8 mg/kg/24 hr trimethoprim given in 2 divided doses.	
	Adult and pediatric for *P carnii* pneumonitis	
	100 mg/kg/24 hr. of sulfamethoxazole and 20 mg/kg/24 hr of trimethoprim given in equally divided doses every 6 hr.	PO
	15 - 20 mg/kg given in 3 or 4 equally divided doses every 6 - 8 hrs. for upto 14 days.	IV
	Creatinine clearance 30 ml/min - As above 15 - 30 ml/min → Give half the dose < 15 ml/min → Do not administer.	
(5) Trisulfapyridine	**Adult:** Initial: 2 - 4 g maintenance dose, 2 - 4 g every 24 hr. divided into 3 - 6 equal doses.	PO
	Pediatric: (Over 2 months of age) Initial dose: 75 mg/kg, Maintenance dose: 150 mg/kg /24 hr, divided into 4 - 6 equal doses. Maintenance dose: 6 g/ 24 hr.	PO

(1) Cholramphe-nicol	**Adult:** Normal renal and hepatic function: 50 mg/kg/day in 4. equally divided doses at the interval moderate infection - 100 mg/kg/day.	PO
	Impaired renal or hepatic function: 25 mg/kg/day in 4 equally divided doses.	PO
	As above properly diluted.	IV
	Pediatric:	
	(1) Newborns and children 25 mg/kg/24 hr in 4 equally divided doses.	PO
	(2) Infants over 2 weeks of age 50 mg/kg/24 hr in 4 equally divided doses.	IV
	As PO over 1 minute.	
(2) Clindamycin	**Adult:** Mild to moderate infections → 150 to 300 mg every 6 hr. Severe infection → 300 - 450 mg every 6 hr.	PO
	600 - 2700 mg/24 hr	IM
	600 - 2700 mg/24 hr	IV
	Pediatric: Suspensions	PO
	(1) Mild infections 8 - 12 mg/kg/24 hr in divided doses.	
	(2) Moderate infections 13 - 16 mg/kg/24 hr in divided doses.	
	(3) Severe infections: 17 - 25 mg/kg/24 hr in divided doses.	
	Capsules: (a) Mild to moderate infections 8 - 16 mg/kg /24 hr in divided doses.	
	(b) Severe infections → 16 - 20 mg/kg/24 hr in divided doses.	IM
	(1) Mild to moderate infections 15 - 25 mg/kg/24 hr in 3 - 4 divided doses	
	(2) Severe infections → 25 - 40 mg/kg/24 hr in 30 divided doses.	
	As IM but diluted to less than 6 mg/ml less than 3 mg/min.	IV
(3) Erythromycin	**Adult:** 250 mg, 4 times a day for 10 - 14 days 100 mg, every 4 - 6 hr.	PO IM
	15 - 20 mg/kg/day.	IV
	Pediatric: 30 - 50 mg/kg/24 hr in 4 divided doses,	PO
	15 - 20 mg/kg/24 hr in 3 divided doses.	IV

(4) Metronidazole	**Adult:**	
	Trichomonias's: (1) 250 mg 3 times daily for 7 days	PO
	(2) 2 g or 2 doses of 1 g each administered same day.	PO
	Gardrenella Vaginitise: 2 g (Females)	PO
	Amebicadysentry: 750 mg 3 times daily for 5 - 10 days	PO
	Amebic liver abscess: 500 - 750 mg 3 times daily for 5 - 10 days	
	Giardiasis: 250 mg, 2 - 3 times daily, for 5 - 10 days	
	Anaero bacterial infections: 7.5 mg/kg every 6 hr.	
	Anaerobic bacterial infections:	
	(1) Loading dose: 15 mg / kg over 1 hr.	IV
	(2) Maintenance dose: 7.5 mg/kg over 1 hr. every 6 hr.	
	Pediatric:	
	Trichomoniasis → 35 - 50 mg/kg/24 hr in 3 divided doses for 7 days.	IV
	Amebiasis → 35 - 50 mg/kg/24 hr in 3 divided doses for 10 days.	
	Giardiasis → 35 - 50 mg/kg/24 hr in 3 divided doses for 7 days	
(6) Spectinomycin hydrochloride	**Male:** 2g (5 ml)	IM
	Female: 2.4 g, 5 - 10 mgl divided into 2 sites	
(7) Vaxomycin hydrochloride	**Adult:** Staphylococcal enterocolitis → 500 mg every 6 hr or 1 g every 12 hr.	PO
	Pseudomembranous colitis 500 mg every 6 hr for 7 - 10 days or 500 mg every 6 hr or 1 g every 12 hr.	IV
	Pediatric: Neonates: Administer 12 - 15 mg/kg/day in 2 divided doses	PO
	Children: 40 mg/kg/day in 2 - 4 divided doses as above	IV

TETRACYCLINES

(1) Tetracycline	**Adult:** 250-500 mg every 6 hr.	PO
	250 - 300 mg every 8 - 12 hr.	IM
	250 - 500 mg every 6 - 12 hr over 30 minutes	IV
(2) Chlortetra-cycline	**Adult:** 250 mg every 6 hr.	PO
	250 - 500 mg every 6 - 12 hr.	IV
	Pediatric: Neonates 100 mg/kg/day in 2 divided doses	PO
	10 - 15 mg/kg/day in 2 divided doses	IV
	Children: 25 - 50 mg/kg/day in 4 divided doses	PO
	10 - 20 mg/kg/day in 2 divided doses.	IV

(3) Deme-clocycline	**Adult:** 600 mg daily in 2 - 4 divided doses.	PO
	Child: 6 - 12 mg/kg/day in 2 - 4 divided doses.	PO
(4) Methacycline	**Adult:** 600 mg daily in 2 - 4 divided doses	PO
	Child: 6 - 12 mg/kg/day in 2 - 4 divided doses	PO
(5) Minocycline	**Adult:** 200 mg initially; 100 mg every 12 hr	PO/IV
	Child: 4 mg/kg initially; 2 mg/kg every 12 hr	PO/IV
(6) Oxyte-tracycline	**Adult:** 250 mg every 6 hr	PO
	100 - 250 mg every 12 hr	IV
	250 - 500 every 6 - 12 hr	IV
	Pediatric: Neonates: 100 mg/kg/day in 2 divided doses	PO
	10 - 15 mg/kg/day, 1 to 2 divided doses	IV
	Child: 25 - 50 mg/kg/day in 2 - 4 divided doses	PO
	15 - 25 mg/kg/day in 2 - 4 divided doses	IM
	10 - 20 mg/kg/day in 2 divided doses	IV
(7) Doxycycline	**Adult:** 100 mg every 12 hr first day; Maintenance 100 - 200 mg/day	PO
	200 mg - first day; maintenance 100 - 200 mg/day	IV

URINARY ANTIMICROBIAL AGENTS

(1) Cinoxacin	**Adult:** (1) Normal renal function 1 g daily in 2 - 4 divided doses for 7 - 14 days.	PO
(2) Methenamine mandelate	**Adult:** 1 g, 4 times daily.	PO
	Pediatric: Under 6 years of age 250 mg/kg, 4 times daily.	PO
	6 - 12 years of age → 50 mg, 4 times daily.	PO
(3) Nalidixic acid	**Adult:** 1 g, 4 times daily for 1 - 2 week.	PO
	Pediatric: 55 mg/kg/24 hr initially in 4 divided doses.	PO
(4) Nitrofuran-toin	**Adult:** 50 - 100 mg, 4 times daily for 10 to 14 days.	PO
	180 mg, every 12 hr. rate of 2 - 3 ml/min.	IV
	Pediatric: Over 1 month of age → 5 - 7 mg/kg/24 hr in 4 divided doses.	PO
	3 mg/kg/every 12 hr at a rate 2- 3 ml/min.	IV
(5) Phenaxopy-ridine hydrochloride	**Adult:** 200 mg, 3 times daily.	PO
	Pediatric: 100 mg, 3 times daily.	PO

ANTIFUNGAL AGENTS

(1) Amphotericin B	**Adult:** 250 mg/kg over 6 hrs slowly increased upto 1 mg/kg daily or 1 - 5 mg/kg on alternate days.	
	25 - 50 µg (diluted), 2 - 3 times per week. Gradually increased to 500 µg to 1 mg.	Intrathecal
	2 - 4 times daily.	
(2) Candicidin	1 applicator or tablet, 2 times daily.	Topical
(3) Ciclopiox olamine	**Adult:** Apply 2 times daily.	Inter vaginal
	Pediatric: As above	Topical
(4) Clotrimazole	2 times daily - 5 times daily for 14 days.	
	100 mg - once daily for 7 days	Inter vaginal
(5) Econazole nitrate	Once daily	Topical
(6) Flucytosine	50 - 150 mg/kg/day at 6 hr interval.	PO
(7) Griseofulvin	**Adult:** 500 mg - 4 g in single or divided doses daily.	PO
(8) Ketoconazole	**Adult:** 200 - 400 mg once daily.	PO
	Pediatric: Under 20 kg 50 mg once daily.	PO
	Between 20 - 40 kg: 100 mg once daily.	PO
	Over 40 kg: 200 mg once daily.	PO
(9) Miconazole nitrate	2%, 2 times daily.	Topic_
	1 applicator once	Intra-vagnal
	Coccidioidomycosis 1800 - 3600 mg divided into 3 doses.	IV
	Cryptococcosis 1200 - 1400 mg, divided into 3 doses daily.	
	Candidiasis 600 - 1800 mg, divided into 3 doses daily.	
	Paracocci diodimycosis 200 - 1200 mg, divided into 3 doses daily.	
	Pediatric: 20 - 40 mg/kg divided in 3 or more equal doses.	
(10) Nystatin	**Adult:** GIT → 500,000 to 1 million units 3 times daily.	PO
	Oral cavity → 400,000 - 600,000 units of suspension 4 times daily.	PO
	Pediatric: Infants 200,000 units 4 times daily	
	Premature and low birth weight infants 100,000 units 4 times daily.	
	Children: as for adults	
(11) Tolnaftate	1%, 2 times daily for 2 - 3 weeks	Topical

ANTITUBERCULAR AGENTS

(1) Ethamibutol hydrochloride	15 mg/kg as a single dose every 24 hr. Retreatment 25 mg/kg as a single daily dose. After 60 days reduce the dose to 15 mg/kg as a single dose every 24 hr. CCR < 10 ml/min 6 - 10 mg/kg.	PO
(2) Isoniazid	**Adult:** 5 mg/kg to maximum of 300 mg daily. Prophylactic therapy 300 mg daily, in single or divided doses.	PO
	As above	IM
	Pediatric: 10 - 30 mg/kg 24 hr in single dose or divided	PO
(3) Rifampicin	**Adult:** 600 mg once daily.	PO
	Pediatric: 10 - 20 mg/kg/24 hr with max daily dose of 600 mg.	PO

ANTHELMENTIC AGENTS

(1) Mebendazole	Pinworm 100 mg once	PO
	Roundworm, whipworm and hookworm 100 mg, 2 times on 3 consecutive days.	
(2) Piperazine citrate	**Adult:** Roundworm 3.5 g, a single daily dose for 2 days.	PO
	Pinworm 65 mg/kg a single dose for 7 days.	PO
	Pediatric: (1) Roundworm → 75 mg/kg for 2 days.	PO
	Pinworm: As adult dosage.	
(3) Pyrantel pamoate	**Adult + Pediatric:** 11 mg/kg once only.	PO
(4) Pyrvinium pamoate	**Adult + Pediatric:** 5 mg /kg a single dose.	PO
(5) Quinacrine hydrochloride	For tapeworm	PO
	Adult: 4 doses of 200 mg 10 min apart and 600 mg of $NaHCO_3$	
	Pediatric: Ages 5 - 10 years: 2 doses of 200 mg, 10 min apart followed by 300 mg of $NaHCO_3$.	
	Ages 11 - 14 years → 3 doses of 200 mg, 10 min apart, 300 mg of $NaHCO_3$.	
	Over 14 years of age → Adult dosage.	PO
	Giardiasis: Adult: 100 mg 3 times daily for 5 - 7 days.	PO
	Pediatric: 7 mg/kg daily in 3 divided doses.	
(6) Thiabendazole	**Adult:** 25 mg/kg (< 70 kg) 1.5 g (> 70 kg)	PO
	Pediatric: 22 mg/kg	PO

ANTIPARASITIC AGENTS

(1) Benzylben-zoate	28% and 50% solution.	External
(2) Gamma benzene hexachloride	1% Cream, lotion or shampoo	External use

ANTIPROTOZOAL AGENTS

(1) Pentamidine isethionate	**Adult and Pediatric:** 4 mg/kg once daily for 14 days	IM
	4 mg/kg once daily for 14 days	IV

ANTIVIRAL AGENTS

(1) Acyclovoir	**Adult:** 5% ointment, every 3 hr, 6 times daily.	Topical
	Initial 200 mg every 4 hr, 5 times daily for 10 days.	PO
	Chronic suppressive therapy for recurrent disease → 200 mg, 3 times daily for 6 months.	
	Intermittent therapy → 200 mg, every 4 hr, 5 times for 5 days.	IV
	CCR < 10 mg/min/1.73 m^2 200 mg capsule every 12 hrs. Normal renal function 5 mg/kg every 8 hr for 5 - 7 days.	
	Pediatric: Under 12 years of age → 250 mg/m^2 every 8 hr for 7 days.	
(2) Idoxuridine	1 drop every hour during the day and every 2 hr after bed time.	Opthalmic Solution
	Reduce to 1 drop every 2 hr during the day and every 4 hr at night.	Opthalmic Ointment
	Apply 5 times daily every 4 hr.	
(3) Ribavirin	20 mg/ml for 12 - 18 hr per day for 3 - 7 days	Aerosol
(4) Trifluridine	**Adult:** 1% solution → 1 drop every 2 hr.	Opthalmic
(5) Vidarabine	Encephalitis: 15 mg/kg daily for 10 day over 12 - 24 hr.	IV
	Keratitis 3% ointment 5 times daily at 3 hr interval.	Topical

ANTIHYPERLIPIDEMIC AGENTS

(1) **Chole-styramine** Adsorbent resin	About 4 g, 3 or 4 times daily.	PO
(2) **Clofibrate** Antilipemic agent	2 g daily, divided into 2 - 4 doses.	PO
(3) **Colestipol** hydro chloride Adsorbent resin	**Adult:** 15 - 30 g daily divided in 2 - 4 doses.	PO
(4) **Gemfibrozil** Antilipemic agent	**Adult:** 600 mg, 30 min before morning and evening meals. Dosage range 900 - 1500 mg daily.	PO
(5) **Niacin**	**Adult:** 500 mg, 3 times daily. Initially doses may be increased in 4 - 7 days increments up to 9 g daily. Dosage range 1.5 - 6 g daily in 3 - 4 divided doses.	PO
(6) **Probucol**	500 mg twice daily administered with meals.	PO

MISCELLANEOUS AGENTS

(1) **Atropine sulfate** Anti-cholinergic	**Adult:** 0.3 - 1.2 mg.	IM
	3 - 1.2 mg may be repeated in 4 - 5 minutes.	IV
	Pediatric: 0.01 mg/kg may be repeated every 2 hr as needed.	PO+
	Maintenance dose is 0.4 mg.	SC + IM
(2) **Benztropine** (Anticholinergic)	Parkinsonism 1 - 2 mg daily increased in increments of 0.5 mg.	PO
	Drug induced extrapyramidal disorders. 1 - 4 mg; 1 - 2 times daily.	PO
	1 - 2 mg, Acute drug induced extrapyramidal disordes. Repeat the dosage if needed. After parentral doses 1 - 2 mg; 2 times daily PO As above.	IM IV
(3) **Calcium chloride**	2.5 - 5 ml of 10% at a rate of 1 - 2 ml/min.	IV

(4) Cimetidine	300 mg 4 times daily.	PO
	As above	IM
	300 mg every 6 hr.	IV
(5) Cyclosporine	**Adult + Pediatric:** 15 mg / kg / day as a single dose 4 - 12 hr daily for 1 - 2 weeks.	
	Maintenane level 5 - 10 mg/kg/day.	
(6) Diphenoxylate hydrochloride	**Adult:** 10 ml liquid 4 times daily.	PO
	Pediatric: (2 - 12 years of age)	
	Ages 2 - 5 years: 4 ml, 3 times daily.	PO
	Ages 5 - 8 years: 4 ml, 4 times daily.	PO
	Ages 8 - 12 years: 5 times daily.	PO
(7) Disulfiram	Initially 500 mg, 1 time daily for 1 - 2 weeks	PO
	Maintenance dosage 250 mg daily.	
(8) Hetastarch (plasmaexpander)	**Adult:** 500 - 100 ml/24 hr.	IV
(9) Ipecac (emetic)	15 - 30 ml.	PO
(10) Lactulose (laxative, Annonia detoxicant)	**Adult: Laxative:** Initially 15 - 30 ml daily, may increase to 60 ml daily.	PO
	Portal systemic encephalopathy.	PO
	Initial 30 - 45 ml every hour.	
	Reduced to 30 - 45 ml 3 - 4 times daily.	
	300 ml with 700 in] water every 4 - 6 hour.	Recta
	Pediatric: Infants → 2.5 ml to 10 ml daily in divided doses.	PO
	Children and adolescants 40 - 90 ml daily in divided doses.	PO
(11) Loperamide Hydrochloride Antidiarrheal	**Adult:** Acute diarrhea: Initially 4 mg followed by 2 mg after each unformed stool	PO
	Chronic diarrhea: 4 mg followed by 2 mg after each unformed stool. Maintenance dosage 4 - 8 mg/day.	
	Pediatric: Recommendations for first 24 hr.	

Age	Weight	Dosage	
2 - 5 years	13 - 20 kg	1 mg; 3 times daily	PO
5 - 8 years	20 - 30 kg	2 mg; 2 times daily	
8 - 12 years	> 30 kg	2 mg; 3 times daily	

(12) Metoclopramide Hydrochloride (GI stimulant, antiemetic)	**Adult: Gastric disorder** 10 mg; 30 min before each meal. **Antiemetic:** Initial 2 doses: 2 mg/kg. If vomitting is suppressed follow with 1 mg/kg chemotherapy and repeat every 2 hr, for 2 doses followed by 1 dose every 3 hr for 3 doses. Small bowel intubation and Radiologic examination. **Adult:** 10 mg. **Pediatric:** Under 6 years of age 0.1 mg/kg 6 - 14 years of age → 2.5 - 5 mg (0.5 - 1 ml) as a single dose over 1 - 2 minute.	PO IV IV IV IV IV
(13) Naloxone hydro- chloride (Narcotic antagonist)	**Adult:** 0.4 mg. If required, repeat every 2 - 3 minute for 2 - 3 doses. As above. **Pediatric:** 10 µg/kg. May be repeated every 2 - 3 minute for 2 - 3 times.	IM IV or SC IM/IV/SC
(14) Oxybutyrin chloride (Urinary anti- spasmodic)	**Adult:** 5 mg, 2 - 3 times daily to a maximum of 20 mg daily. **Pediatric:** 5 mg, 1 - 2 times daily to a maximum of 15 mg daily.	PO
(15) Physostigmine salicylate	**Adult:** Therapeutic trial 2 mg slowly at a rate of 1 mg/min. Second dose of 1 - 2 mg may be repeated in 20 minute if no response. Theapeuti dose: 1 - 4 mg slowly as life threatening symptoms. As for IV administration. **Pediatric:** Therapeutic trial, 0.5 mg slowly over 1 min. Repeat at 5 min interval if necessary.	IV IM
(16) Ranitidine hydro- chloride	**Adult:** 150 mg, 2 times daily 50 mg every 6 - 8 hr. 50 mg every 6 - 8 hr. Renal impairment dosage CCR < 50 hr, 150 mg, every 24 hr. 50 mg, every 18 - 24 hr.	PO IM IV PO IM, IV
(17) Sodium bicarbonate Alkalinizing agent	Intitial 1 n eq./kg below (50ml) followed by 1 ampule every 5 - 10 min as needed.	IV
(18) Sucralate Anticulcer agent	**Adult:** 1 g, 1hr, before meals and at bedtime.	PO

CARDIOVASCULAR AGENTS

1. **Degoxin:**
   Adult:
   1. Digitalizing: 0.25 to 0.5 mg initially followed by 0.125 mg every 6-8 hours until adequate digitalization is acbieved.(PO)
   2. Maintenance : 0.125 - 0.25 mg daily for inotropic therapy. Some patients may require 0.375 - 0.5 mg daily for chronotropic effect. (PO)
   3. Digitalizing: 0.25 - 0.5 mg initially followed by 0.125 mg every 6 hours until adequate digitalization is achieved. Administer at a rate of 0.5 - 1 ml/min. (IV)
   4. Maintenance: as for PO adminitration.(IV)

2. **Digitoxin**
   Adult:
   1. Digitalizing: 0.6 mg initially followed by 0.4 mg and then 0.2 mg at intervals of 4 - 6 hours. (PO)
   2. Maintenance: 0.05 -0.3 mg once daily. The average dose is 0.1 - 0.15 mg daily. (PO)
   3. Digitalizing: 0.6 mg initially followed by 0.4 mg; 4 - 6 hours later and by 0.2 mg every 4 - 6 hours thereafter until therapeutic effects are apparent. These effects are usually observed within 8 - 12 hours. (IV)
   4. Maintenance: As for PO maintenance therapy. (IV)

ADRENERGIC AGENTS

1. **Dobutamine:**
   1. 2.5 - 10 µg/kg/min, but doses upto 40 µg/kg/min may occasionally be necessary of the diluted solution. (IV)

2. **Dopamine hydrochloride:**
   1. Begin administration at doses of 2 - 5 µg/kg/min. Increase gradually using 5-10 µg/kg/min increments upto 20 - 50 µg/kg/min. (IV)

3. **Epinephrine:**
   1. Cardiaresuscitation → Epinephrine 1: 1000, 0.2 - 1 ml. Epinephrine 1: 1000, 2 - 10 mg (0.2 - 1 mg) Inteacardiac: As above. (IV)

   Pediatric:
   1. Cardiac resuscitation: Epinephrine 1: 1000, 0.01 ml/kg/dose, Epinephrine 1: 10,000 0.1 ml/kg/dose. (IV)

4. **Isoproterenol hydrochloride:**
   Adult and Pediatric:
   1. 0.5 - 5 µg/min. Rate of infusion depends on the basis of heart rate, central venous pressure, systemic blood pressure + venous output. Rates over 30 µg/min have been used. (IV)

5. **Isoxsuprine hydrochloride:**
   1. 10 - 20 mg, 3 - 4 times daily, 5 - 10 mg (1 - 2 ml) 2 - 3 times daily. (PO) (IM)

6. **Levarterenol (Norepinephrine):**
   1. Initial dose: 8 - 12 μg of base/min, (IV)
   2. Maintenance dose: 2 - 4 μg of base/min. (infusion)
7. **Metaraminol:**
   1. 2 - 10 mg (IM)
      0.5 - 5 mg, (IV direct injection)
      Initially: 15 -100 mg in 500 ml of dextrose/saline IV (infusion)
8. **Phenylephrine Hydrochloride:**
   (Adult for mild to moderate hypotension)
   1. Usual dose: 2 - 5 mg (0.2 - 0.5 ml) Range 1 - 10 mg (0.1 - 1 ml) (SC of IM). Initial dose should not exceed 5 mg (0.5 ml).
   2. Usual dose: 0.2 mg , Range 0.1 - 0.5 mg, Initial dose (IV) should not exceed 0.5 mg.
   3. Initial dosage : 100 - 180 μg/min. After B.P. stabilises 40 - 60 μg/min IV (infusion).

Pediatric:
0.1 mg/kg.

(Adults for paroxysmal supraventricidar tachycardia):
0.5 mg over 20 - 30 sec. Doses may be increased by increments of 0.1 - 0.2 mg. Maximum single dose should not exceed 1 mg.

ANTIARRHATHMIC AGENTS

1. **Amiodarone hydrochloride:**
   1. Loading dose: 800 - 1600 mg daily in divided doses for 1-3 weeks until an individual therapeutic response occurs following this a dosage of 600-800 mg daily is given for 1 month. (PO)
   2. Maintenance: 400 mg daily (usually)
2. **Bretylium tosylate:**
   Ventricular fibrillation:
   1. 5 mg/kg. If conditions persist increase dosage to 10 mg/kg and repeated every 15 - 30 min. Maintenance total dosage should not exceed 30 mg/kg. (IV)

   Ventricular arrhythmia:
   1. 5 - 10 mg/kg over 8 - 10 min. If conditions persist repeat in 1-2 hour. (IV)
   2. 1 - 2 mg/min (IV continuous infusion)
   3. 5 - 10 mg/kg may be repeated, every 1-2 hour. If arrhythmia persists. Thereafter, repeat every 6 - 8 hour. (IM)
3. **Disopyramide phosphate:**

Adult:
   1. Normal renal functions (PO)
      (a) Initial 150 mg every 6 hour or 300 mg every 12 hour as the extended release

form.
   (b) Maintenance: 150 mg every 6 hour. Some patients may require 400 mg every 6 hour.
2. Moderately impaired renal function.
   (a) Initial 200 mg.
   (b) Maintenance: 100 mg every hour.

4. **Flecainide acetate:**

   Sustained ventricular tachycardia:

   Adults:
   1. 100 mg every 12 hours ; Increase in 50 mg increments twice daily every 4 hours Maintenance dose is 400 mg daily. (PO)

   (Non-sustained ventricular tachycardia):
   1. Initially 100 mg every 12 hours. Increase in 50 mg increment twice daily every 4 days. If patient is still symptomatic at 400 mg/day with plasma levels less than 0.6 mg/ml, continuously increase to a maximum of 600 mg daily. (PO)

   Renal impairement:
   1. Initially 100 mg every 12 hours. (PO)

5. **Lidocaine hydrochloride:**

   Adult:
   1. 200 - 300 mg (IM Detltoid muscle)
   2. Initial 50 - 100 mg (1 mg/kg) at a rate of 25-50 mg/min may be given to every 3-5 min till effect is achieved. Not to exceed 300 mg. (IV)

   Pediatric:
   1. Initial 1 mg/kg upto 15 mg if under 25 kg upto 25 mg if over 25 kg. (IV)
   2. Continuous infusion: 20 - 40 µg/kg/min (max 5 mg/kg).

6. **Mexiletine hydrochloride**

   Adult:
   1. 200 - 400 mg every 8 hour or 10 - 14 mg/kg/day. (PO)

7. **Phenytoin:**

   Adult:
   1. First day: 250 mg, 4 times. (PO)
   2. Second and third day: 500 mg daily.
   3. Subsequent days: 300 - 400 mg.
   4. Initially 250 mg at a rate so faster than 50 mg/min until the arrhythmia is abolished, a total of 1000 mg has been given or side effect appear.(IV)

   Pediatric:
   1. 1 - 5 mg/kg, slow IV push. Repeat as needed (IV).
   2. Maintenance total dose: 500 mg in 4 hr interval (IV).

8. **Procainamide hydrochloride:**

   Adult: Loading dose is 1-1.25 g

1. Second - 750 mg, 2 hr. after loading dose if the arrhythmia is still present. (PO)
2. Maintenance: 0.5 - 1 g, every 4 - 6 hour.
3. Enteric release tablets: Administer ¼th of the total daily dose every 6 hour. The usual dosage is 50 mg/kg.
4. 0.5 - 1 g every 6 hour (IM).
5. 100 mg every 5 min at 25 - 50 mg/min till condition persists. Afterwards 25 - 30 µg/kg/min continuous infusion. (IV)

Pediatric:
1. 50 mg/kg divided in 4-6 doses. (PO)
2. 2 mg/kg diluted in 5 % dextrose given over 5 min. (IV)
3. Repeat dose every 10 - 15 min until arrhythmias are controlled.
4. Mainenance total dosage: 1 g.
5. Normal sinus rhythm may be maintained at 20-80 µg/kg/min.

9. Quinidine:
Adult:
1. Quinidine sulphate 200 - 400 mg 3 - 5 times daily (PO)
2. Mainenance single dose should not exceed 600 - 800 mg.
3. Quinidine gluconate initially 600 mg, then 400 mg every 2 hour as needed. (IM)
4. Quinidine gluconate: 800 mg diluted to 40 ml with 5 % dextrose. Infused at a rate of 1 ml/min.

Pediatric:
Quinidine sulphate 30 mg/kg/24 hours divided into 4 - 6 doses. (IM)
As PO administration. (IM)

10. Tocainide hydrochloride:
Adult:
Initial - 400 mg every 8 hours. (PO)
Maintenance: 1200-1800 mg daily in equally divided doses every 8 hours.
Maintenance daily closes less than 2400 mg.

CALCIUM ION ANTAGONISITS
1. Diltiazem hydrochloride:
Adult:
1. Initially 30 mg 4 times daily before meals and at day time. The dosage is gradually increased to 60 mg 4 times daily at 1 - 2 day intervals. (PO)
2. Can continue glycerin therapy for acute anginal attack.

2. Nifedipine
Adult:
1. Initially 10 mg, 3 times daily. (PO)
2. Effective dose is 10 - 20 mg 3 times daily.
3. Doses above 180 mg not recommended.

    4. Sublingual nitroglycerin therapy may be continued.
3. **Verapamil**
Adult:
   1. Initial 80 mg 3 - 4 times daily. Increase daily to weekly under optimal clinical response is achieved. (PO)
   2. Sublingual nitroglycerin therapy may be contained.
      (a) Initial dose 5 - 10 mg over 2 - 3 min. (IV)
      (b) Repeat dose 10 mg, 30 min after first dose.
      (c) Administer over at least 3 min in elderly patients. (IV)

Pediatric:
   1. Birth — 1 year of age, 0.1 - 0.2 mg/kg over 2 min. (IV)
      1 - 15 years, 0.1 - 0.3 mg/kg over 2 min.
      Not to exceed 5 mg, repeat above doses 30 min after the 1st dose.

CORONARY VASODILATORS
1. **Amyl Nitrate:**
   0.18 ml or 0.3 ml (Inhalation)
2. **Nitroglycerin:**
   1. 0.15 - 0.6 mg (Sublingual tablets)
   2. 2.5 mg every 12 hours. (PO)
   3. 2 % ointment every 3 - 4 hour and at Bed time (Topical).
   4. 0.4 mg metered dose (Tongue spray).
   5. 50 mg. (IV)
3. **Erythrity tetranitrate:**
   1. 5 - 15 mg. (Subligual)
   2. 15 - 60 mg. (PO)
4. **Pentaerythritol tetranitrate:**
   1. 10 - 40 mg. (PO)
   2. 30 - 80 mg every 12 hour (sustained release). (PO)
5. **Sorbide dinitrate:**
   1. 2.5 - 10 mg (sublingual).
   2. 10 - 60 mg. (PO)
6. **Mannitol hexanitrate:**
   32 - 64 mg. (PO)
7. **Nitroglycerin:** 1 - 2 mg, 3 - 6 times daily (Transmucosal tablets).

INOTROPIC AGENTS
1. **Amrinone lactate:**
   Adult:
   1. Initially 0.75 mg/kg given slowly over 2 - 3 min. (IV)
   2. Maintenance infusion - 5 10 µg/kg/min. (IV)

3. After initial dosage 0.75 mg/kg may be given after 30 min.
4. Total daily dose should not exceed 10 mg/kg/24 hour.

DIURETIC AGENTS

1. Amiloride
Adult:
1. `Initially 5 mg daily. May be increased to 10 mg if necessary. If hypokalemia persists may be increased to 15 mg and then 20 mg. (PO)

2. Bumetanide
Adult:
1. Initially 0.5 - 2 mg once daily.(PO)
2. 2nd or 3rd dose: given at 4 - 5 hour intervals maximum upto 10 mg dose daily.
3. Intermittent doses may be given on alternate days.
4. Initial 0.5 - 1 mg 2nd or 3rd dose given at 2-3 hour intervals maximum daily dosage is 10 mg. (IM)
5. As same as above at a rate of 0.5 -1 mg over a period of 1-2 min. (IV)

3. Ethacrynic acid:
Adult:
1. Initially 50 - 100 mg followed by 50 - 200 mg daily. (PO)
2. 0.5 - 1 mg/kg. Add 50 ml of dextrose 5 % to 50 mg. (IV)

Pediatric:
1. `Initial 25 mg daily. (PO)
2. `Maintenance: Increase dosage in increments of 25 mg to desired effect.
3. `1 mg/kg dilute with dextrose 5 % and administer over 5 min. (IV)

4. Furosemide:
Adult:
1. 20 - 80 mg single dose in morning. (PO)
2. 2nd dose: 6 - 8 hours later.
3. 20 - 40 mg given over 1 - 2 min. (IV)

Pediatric:
1. 2 mg/kg initially. Increase by 1 - 2 mg/kg every 6 hour if necessary. (PO)
2. Initially 1 mg/kg. Increase by 1 mg/kg, every 2 hour to a maximum of 6 mg/kg. (IV)

5. Hydrochlorothiazide:
Adult:
25 - 200 mg/day. (0)

Pediatric:
1. Under 6 months of age.
2. 0.4 - 0.6 mg/kg/24 hour in 2 divided doses. (PO)
3. Over 6 months: Usual dose 0.4 mg/kg/24 hrs in 3 divided doses. (PO)

Indapamide:
Adult:
1. Initially 2.5 mg. Single dose in morning. After one week if necessary, dose is increased 5 mg daily. (PO)

Mannitol:
1. Oliguria + Acute renal failure:
   (a) Test dose 12.5 g in 50 - 60 ml (IV)
2. Over 3 - 5 min: 2nd dose may be given. (IV)
3. Prevention 100 g in 500 ml over 90 min to several hours. (IV)

Spiranolactone:
Adult:
25 - 50 mg 4 times daily. (PO)
Pediatric:
3 mg/kg/day. (PO)

Triamterene:
100 - 300 mg daily. (PO)

ANTICOAGULANT AND HEMORRHEOLOGIC AGENTS ANTICOAGULANT:

1. Heparin:
Adult:
1. Prophylactic 5000 units every 8 - 12 hour. (SC)
2. Therapeutic, initial 10,000 - 15,000 units.
3. Maintenance: 6000 - 10,0000 units every 8 - 12 hours. (IV)
4. Intermittent - initial 10,000 units bolus.
5. Maintenance 500 - 6000 units every 4 - 6 hrs.
6. Continuous infusion - Initial 5000 units hours.
7. Maintenance: 700 - 1200 units /hour.

Pediatric:
1. Intermittent: Initial 500 units/kg.
2. Maintenance: 50 - 100 units/kg, every 4 hour.

2. Warfarin :
1. 10 - 15 mg daily for 3 days, then 12 to 15 mg daily. (PO)
2. Maintenance: As above. (IV)

HEMORRHEOLOGIC AGENT

Pentoxifylline:
Adult:
400 mg, 3 times daily for at least 8 weeks. (O)

INDEX

A

Abortifacients, 16.23
Acetazolamide, 19.8
Acids, 2.6
Acriquine, 3.8
Acrisorcin, 10.13
Acromegaly, 14.11
Actinomycine D, 12.17
Acyclovir, 11.4
Addison's disease, 17.12
Adenohypophyseal hormonones, 14.1
Adrenal gland, 17.1
Adrenocorticoids, 17.1
Adsorbents, 20.17
AIDS, 30.20
Alcohols, 2.3
Aldehydes, 2.5
Aldosterone antagonists, 19.11, 27.24
Aldosterone, 17.10
Alkylating agents, 12.7, 30.12
Allergic responses, 30.6
Alpha interferons, 12.24
Aluminium compounds, 20.4
Amantadin, 11.4, 11.6
Amdinocillin, 6.4
Amethopterin, 29.18
Amifloxacin, 4.13
Amikacin, 7.2, 7.7
Amiloride, 19.13
p-Amino benzoic acid, 29.1
Amino caproic acid, 22.14
Amino salicylic acid, 13.7, 15.10
9-Aminoacridine, 3.8
Aminoglutethimide, 17.12

Aminoglycoside antibiotics, 7.1
Aminophylline, 19.7, 25.9
Aminopterin, 12.16, 29.18
Aminoquinolines, 3.5
Amiodarone, 26.15
Amodiaquine, 3.6
Amoxicillin, 6.5
Amphenone B, 19.13
Amphomycin, 6.19
Amphotericin, 8.3, 10.6, 10.10
Ampicillin, 6.5
Amrinone, 24.10, 24.14
Anaphylactic reactions, 30.7
Androgens, 16.13
Angina pectoris, 25.2
Angiotensin, 27.22
Anorexiants, 20.20
Anthelmintic agents, 20.22
Antiamoebic agents, 3.12
Antiandrogens, 16.15
Antianginal drugs, 24.15, 25.1
Antiarrhythmic agents, 24.11, 26.1
Antibiotics, 5.1, 6.1
Anticoagulants, 22.1, 22.6
Antidiarrhoeals, 20.17
Antiemetics, 20.12
Antiestrogens, 16.9
Antifungal agents, 10.1
Antifungal antibiotics, 10.9, 10.13
Antihypertensive agents, 24.16, 27.1
Antihypertensive agents, 27.3
Anti-leprotic agents, 13.9
Antimalarial drugs, 3.2
Antimetabolites, 12.13

Antimonial compounds, 20.24
Antineoplastic agents, 12.1
Antispasmodics, 20.10
Antithrombotic drugs, 22.12
Antithyroid drugs, 15.10
Antitubercular agents, 13.2, 13.3
Antiviral agents, 11.3, 11.4
Apomorphine, 20.11
Aprindine, 24.14
Ascorbic acid, 29.25
L-Asparaginase, 12.19
Asparenomycins, 5.14
Aspirin, 22.12
Asthma, 30.7
Atenolol, 27.18
Autoimmune diseases, 30.18
Azacytidine, 12.14
Azathioprine, 30.13, 12.14
Azlocillin, 6.5

B

Bacitracin, 6.19
Bacterial cell-wall, 1.3, 5.2
Bacterial resistance, 4.7, 5.4, 6.10, 7.7
Balantidiasis, 3.20
BCG vaccine, 30.11
Benzalkonium chloride, 2.9
Benzaquinamide, 20.13
Benzoyl peroxide, 2.8
Benzyl penicillin, 6.3
Bephenium, 20.23, 20.27
Beriberi, 29.2
Betaine, 20.21
Biguanides, 3.9
Bile acid-binding resins, 22.24
Biocytine, 29.11, 29.13

Biotin, 29.11
Bisacodyl, 20.14
Bis-biguanides, 2.10
Bismuth antacids, 20.6
Bismuth subsalicylate 20.18
Bithionol, 20.23, 20.27
Bleomycine, 12.17
Bredinin, 30.14
Bretylium, 24.24, 26.16
Bumetanide, 19.7, 19.11, 27.26
Busulfan, 12.10
Butenafine, 10.8
Butoxamine, 27.17

C

Caffeine, 19.7
Calcitonin, 15.11, 15.13
Calcitriol, 28.13
Calcium antacides, 20.5
Calcium carbonate, 20.18
Calcium channel blockers, 25.6, 26.12
Calomel, 20.17
Cancer, 12.1
Candicidin, 8.3, 10.11
Canrenoate, 19.12
Canrenone, 19.12
Capreomycin, 9.3, 13.9
Captopril, 24.20, 27.23
Carbacephems, 5.14
Carbamide peroxide, 2.8
Carbapenem, 5.14, 6.17
Carbarsone, 3.15
Carbenicillin, 5.13, 6.5
Carbenoxolone, 20.8
Carbimazole, 15.10
Carbomyin A, 7.14

Carbonic anhydrase inhibitors, 19.8
Carboplatin, 12.23
Carboxypyridoxine, 29.8
Carbutamide, 15.10
Cardiac glycosides, 24.1
Cardiovascular diseases, 23.6
Carminatives, 20.21
Carmustine, 12.10
Cationic surfactants, 2.3, 2.9
Cephalosporins, 5.13, 6.11, 6.14
Cephamycins, 6.12, 6.18
Chalcomycin, 7.14
Chaulmoogric acid, 13.12
Chenodiol, 20.22
Chiniofon, 3.13
Chlolecalciferol, 28.11
Chlomerodrin, 19.5
Chlorambucil, 12.9
Chloramphenicol, 7.12
Chlorhexidine, 2.10
Chlormadinone, 16.11, 24.4
Chloroguanil, 3.9
Chloroquinaldol, 3.13
Chloroquine, 3.6, 3.15
Chlorothiazide, 19.9
Chloroxine, 2.5
Chlorpropamide, 18.17
Chlorthalidone, 19.10
Cholestyramine, 22.24
Choline, 29.23
Chorionic gonadotropin, 14.14
Ciclopirox, 10.4, 10.11
Cimetidine, 20.6
Cinchona alkaloids, 3.5
Cinoxacin, 4.12
Ciprofloxacin, 4.12
Cis-platin, 12.22

Clavulanic acid, 6.18
Clindamycin, 7.17
Clioquinol, 3.13
Clofazimine, 13.11
Clofibrate, 22.12, 22.25
Clomiphen, 12.20
Clonidine, 24.20, 27.11
Clopamide, 19.10
Clotrimazole, 10.3, 10.6
Cloxacillin, 6.4
Coagulants, 22.1
Cobalamin, 22.18
Coenzyme A, 29.12
Coenzyme Q, 29.24
Colchicine, 12.23
Colestipol, 22.24
Colistin, 8.1
Collagen diseases, 30.20
Compactin, 22.27
Concanavalin A, 30.11
Congo red, 21.11
Corrin, 29.19
Corticotropin, 14.14
Cortisone, 17.8
Cortol, 17.8
Cortolone, 17.8
Corynebacterium parvum, 30.17
Co-trimoxazole, 4.11
Coumarin, 22.9
C. parvum, 30.11
Cretinism, 15.9
Cushing's syndrome, 17.11
Cyanocobalamine, 29.18
Cyclizine, 20.13
Cycloguanil, 3.9
Cycloimmune, 30.14
Cyclophosphamide, 12.9, 30.11, 30.12

Cycloserine, 6.21, 13.8
Cyclosparine, 30.13
Cyclothiazide, 19.9
Cyproterone acetate, 16.25
Cytarabine, 30.11, 12.15
Cytimun, 30.12
Cytosine arabinoside, 11.6

D

Dacarbazine, 12.12
Dactinomycine, 12.17
Danazol, 16.9
Danthron, 20.14
Dapsone, 3.10
Daunorubicin, 12.18
Deglycyrrhizinated liquorice, 20.8
Dehydrocholic acid, 20.22
4-Deoxypyridoxine, 29.9
Desonide, 17.10
Desthiobiotin, 29.13
Dextran, 22.13
Dextrothyroxine, 22.24
Diabetes, 18.1, 18.3
Diacetyldapsone, 3.10
Diagnostic agents, 21.1
Diaminopyrimidines, 3.5, 3.8
Diatrizoate, 21.3
Diazoxide, 24.20, 27.20
Dibromoquin, 3.13
Dibromsalan, 2.10
Dichlorisone, 17.10
Dichloroisoproterenol, 27.8
Dichlorophen, 20.23
Dicloxacillin, 6.3
Dicoumarol, 22.9
Didanosine, 11.6

Diethyl stilbestrol, 16.6, 16.21
Diethylcarbamazine, 20.23
Diethylpropion, 20.20
Diflucortolone, 17.10
Digestants, 20.21
Digitalis agonists, 24.3
Digitalis intoxication, 24.9
Dihydrofolate, 3.9
Dihydrotachysterol, 28.14
Diisopyramide, 24.14, 26.6, 26.10
Diloxanide furoate, 3.13
Diltiazam, 27.19
Diphenidol, 20.13
Diphenoxylate, 20.18
Dipyridamole, 22.12
Diuretic agents, 19.1
Diuretics, 27.25
Docusate, 20.15
Doxorubicin, 12.18
Drug resistance, 3.11, 12.5
Durohydroquinone, 28.15
Dyes, 2.3, 2.9
Dysmenorrhea, 16.18

E

Econazole, 10.4, 10.8
Emetics, 20.11
Enalapril, 27.24
Encainide, 26.13
Endometriosis, 16.19
Enemas, 20.17
Enoxacin, 4.12
Epsom salt, 20.16
Ergocalciferol, 28.11
Erythromycin, 7.15
Erythrosine, 21.11

Estramustine, 12.21
Estrogens, 16.5
Ethacrynic acid, 19.6, 27.26
Ethambutol, 13.5
Ethamoxytriphetol, 16.9
Ethionamide, 13.6
Ethisterone, 16.21
Etoposide, 12.22
Eugenol, 2.4
Eulicin, 10.14
Evans blue, 21.11

F

Famciclovir, 11.6
Famotidine, 20.6
Fat-soluble vitamins, 28.2
Fenfluramine, 20.20
Fibrinolytic agents, 22.14
Flecainide, 26.13
Floxuridine, 12.15
Fluclorolone, 17.10
Fluconazole, 10.4
Fludarabine, 11.6
Fludrocortisol, 17.10
Fluocinolone, 17.10
Fluorescein, 21.11
5-Fluorocytosine, 10.5
5-Flurouracil, 10.5, 12.15
Flutonidine, 24.20
Folate antagonists, 29.18
Folic acid, 12.16, 22.18, 29.15
Folinic acid, 29.16
Foscarnet sodium, 11.6
Ftorafur, 12.15
Fungal infections, 10.2
Furan derivatives, 2.3

Furazolidone, 2.7
Furosemide, 19.7, 19.11, 27.26
Fusaric acid, 24.19
Fusidic acid, 9.4
Fusidin, 9.4

G

Ganciclovir, 11.6
Glutaraldehyde, 2.5
Giardiasis, 3.19
Gramicidin, 6.21
Gentamicin, 7.3, 7.6
Griseofulvin, 10.3, 10.4, 10.9, 10.12
Growth hormone, 14.12
Goiter, 15.8
Grave's disease, 15.9
Gyaneological diseases, 16.9
Glypizide, 18.17
Glucagon, 18.18
Gastric antacids, 20.1
Gefarnate, 20.9
Gemfibrozil, 22.26
Guanabenz, 24.20, 27.12
Guanafacine, 24.20, 27.12
Guanethidine, 27.12, 27.7
Gelatin, 22.13

H

Haematinics, 22.15
Haemopoietic vitamins, 22.18, 29.14
Halogen-containing compounds, 2.3, 2.6
Haloprogin, 10.13
Harnycin, 10.11
Hay fever, 30.8
Heavy metals, 2.3, 2.8
Heparin, 22.7

Hetastarch, 22.13
Hexachlorophene, 2.4
Hexamethylmelamine, 12.23
Hexylresorcinol, 2.4, 20.23
HMG CoA reductase, 22.27
Homobiotin, 29.14
H_2-receptor antagonists, 20.6
Humoral immunit, 30.3
Hydnocarpic acid, 13.12
Hydracarbazine, 24.20
Hydralazine, 24.20, 27.19
Hydrochlorthiazide, 19.9
8-Hydroxyquinolines, 2.5, 3.13
Hydroxystilbamidine, 10.4
Hydroxyurea, 12.22
Hyperlipoproteinemia, 22.25, 22.22
Hyperparathyroidism, 15.13
Hyperpituitarism, 14.9
Hypersensitivity reactions, 30.5, 6.8
Hypomenorrhea, 16.19
Hypopituitarism, 14.9

I

Idoxuridine, 11.5, 11.12
Imipenem, 6.17
Immune globuline, 11.11
Immunity, 30.3
Immunodeficiency, 30.18
Immunoenhancers, 30.14
Immunoglobulins, 30.4
Immunomodulators, 30.9
Immunosuppressants, 30.11
Indacrinone, 19.14
Indanyl carbenicillin, 6.5
Indapamide, 19.10
Indigotindisulfonate, 21.10

Indocyanine green, 21.10
Indomethacin, 30.9
Indoramin, 27.7
Inosiplex, 30.17
Inositol, 29.24
Insulin preparations, 18.13
Insulin, 18.2, 18.6
Interceptives, 16.23
Interferons, 11.9
Interleukins, 30.8
Inulin, 21.10
Iocetamic acid, 21.3, 21.5
Iodine, 2.7
Iodipamide, 21.3, 21.5, 21.8
Iodochlorohydroxyquin, 10.13
Iodohippurate, 21.3
Iodoquinol, 3.13
Iodoxamate, 21.3
Iohexol, 21.8
Iopanoic acid, 21.3
Iophendylate, 21.3, 21.7
Iopronic acid, 21.5
Ioxaglate, 21.8
Ipecacuanha, 3.15
Ipodate, 21.3, 21.5
Isatin-β-thiosemicarbazone, 11.6
Isoniazid, 13.4
Isoprenaline, 27.16
Isoprinosine, 30.10
Isosorbide, 19.4
Isothalamic acid, 21.3, 21.5, 21.7
Itraconazole, 10.2

J

Josamycin, 7.14, 7.17

K

Kanamycin, 7.2, 7.6
Kaolin, 20.18
Ketoconazoke, 10.4, 10.7

L

β-Lactam antibiotics, 5.13, 6.1, 6.4
β-Lactamase inhibitors, 5.13, 6.18
Lactulose, 20.16
Lamivudine, 11.6
Laxatives, 20.14
Leishmaniasis, 3.16
Leucomycine A, 26.11
Leuprolide, 12.21
Levamisole, 30.10, 30.16
Levonorgestrel, 16.25
Lidocaine, 24.14, 26.11
Lincomycins, 7.17
Lipid lowering agents, 22.19
Lipoproteins, 22.19
Lipotropic factors, 29.22
Lipotropins, 14.15
Liquorice, 20.8
Lithium carbonate, 15.11
Lomustine, 12.10
Loperamide, 20.19
Lorcainide, 26.13
Lucanthone, 20.25
Lymphocytes, 30.3
Lymphokines, 30.10
Lynestrenol, 16.21

M

Macrolide antibiotics, 7.14
Magnesium antacids, 20.5
Malaria, 3.2
Mandelic acid, 2.11
Mannitol, 19.4
Matenide, 4.10
Mebendazole, 20.25
Mechlorethamine, 12.9
Mefloquine, 3.10
Melarsoprol, 3.18
Melphalan, 12.9
Menadione, 28.9
Menometrorrhagia, 16.19
Menopause, 16.18
Meralluride, 19.5
Merbromin, 2.8
Mercaptomerin, 19.5
6-Mercaptopurine, 12.13
Mercurophylline, 19.5
Merethoxyline, 19.5
Mersalyl, 19.5
Mesalamine, 20.10
Mestranol, 16.20
Metaraminol, 24.18
Metformin, 18.15
Methenamine, 4.13
Methicillin, 6.4
Methimazole, 15.10
Methisazone, 11.6, 11.8
Methotrexate, 12.16, 30.13
Methyl pantothenic acid, 29.11
Methyl paraben, 2.6
Methylcobamide, 29.19
α-Methyldopa, 24.18, 27.10
Methyloctopamine, 24.19
Metoclopramide, 20.8, 20.13
Metolazone, 19.10
Metrifonate, 20.25
Metrizamide, 21.7
Metronidazole, 3.14

Metrorrhagia, 16.19
Metyrapone, 17.12, 19.13
Mexiletine, 26.5, 26.12
Mezlocillin, 6.5
Miconazole, 10.3
Microorganisms, 1.2
Milrinone, 24.10
Mineralocorticoids, 17.10
Minoxidil, 14.7, 14.11, 24.20, 27.20
Mithramycin, 12.17
Mitomycin C, 12.18
Mitotane, 17.12
Mitoxantrone, 12.23
Monobactam, 5.14, 6.17
Monoclonal antibodies, 12.23, 12.7
Moxalactam, 6.14, 6.16
Myasthenia gravis, 30.18
Myeloma, 30.18
Myocardial cell, 23.2
Myxedema, 15.8

N

Nafcillin, 6.4
Nalidixic acid, 2.11, 4.13
Natamycine, 10.11
Neomycin, 7.3, 7.5, 22.28
Neopyrithiamine, 29.4
Netilmicin, 7.7
Niacin, 29.6
Niacinamide, 29.6
Niclosamide, 20.26
Nicotinamide, 29.6
Nicotinic acid, 22.25, 29.6
Nifedipine, 24.20
Nifuroxime, 2.7
Nifurtimox, 3.18

Niridazole, 20.26, 30.14
Nitrofurantoin, 2.7, 4.12
Nitrofurazone, 2.7
Nitrogen mustard, 12.8
Nitroglycerin, 24.16
Nitromersol, 2.8
Nitrosoureas, 12.10
Nizatidine, 20.6
Nocardicins, 5.14, 6.17
Norbiotin, 29.14
Norethisterone, 16.11
Norethynodrel, 16.21
Norfloxacin, 4.12
Nortestosterone, 16.10
Nystatin, 8.4, 10.11

O

Oleandomycin, 7.14, 7.16
Oligomenorrhea, 16.19
Omeprazole, 20.7
Oral anticoagulants, 22.9
Oral contraceptives, 16.20
Oral hypoglycemic agents, 18.1
Organomercurials, 19.5
Ovulation stimulants, 16.9
Ovulation, 16.8, 16.15
Oxacephem, 5.13, 6.17, 6.18
Oxacillin, 6.4
Oxamniquine, 20.26
Oxiconazole, 10.4
Oxidising agents, 2.8
Oxtriphylline, 19.8
Oxybiotin, 29.13
Oxychlorosene sodium, 2.6
Oxythiamine, 29.4
Oxytocin, 4.15, 14.11, 14.15

P

Pamaquine, 3.7
Pancreatic extract, 20.22
Pantothenic acid, 29.10
Pantoyltaurine, 29.11
Papaverine, 20.10, 25.9
Parabens, 2.4
Parasitic diseases, 3.1
Parathyroid hormones, 15.11
Pargyline, 24.19
Paromomycin, 7.2, 7.6
Pathogenicity of micro-organisms, 1.5, 5.5
Pearl index, 16.26
Pectin, 20.18
Pellagra, 29.7
Pencillin-binding proteins, 5.3
Penicillins, 6.1
Pentagastrin, 21.11
Pentamidine, 3.17
Pepsin, 20.21
Peptide antibiotics, 6.19
Pernicious anemia, 30.19
Phendimetrazine, 20.21
Phenformin, 18.15
Phenol coefficient, 2.2
Phenolphthalein, 20.14
Phenols, 2.3
Phentolamine, 24.20, 27.15
Phenylbutazone, 22.12
Phenytoin, 24.14, 26.11
Phytonadione, 28.9
Piperacillin, 6.5
Piperazine, 20.23, 20.27
Pirenzepine, 20.7
Pitutary hormones, 14.6
Plasma expanders, 22.12

Plicamycin, 12.17
Plummer's disease, 15.9
Pluracidomycins, 5.14
Polycarbophil, 20.18
Polyene antibiotics, 10.9, 8.3
Polymenorrhea, 16.19
Polymyxin antibiotics, 8.1
Polyneuritis, 29.2
Potassium iodide, 10.12
Practolol, 27.8
Prazosin, 27.7, 27.15
Prednisone, 17.9
Premenstrual syndrome, 16.19
Primaquine, 3.7
Probenecid, 6.11
Probucol, 22.23
Procainamide, 24.14, 26.9
Procarbazine, 12.12
Progestins, 16.10
Prolactin, 14.10
Pronethalol, 27.17
Propranolol, 27.16, 26.14, 27.17
Propyliodone, 21.5
Prostaglandins, 20.7
Prothionamide, 13.6
Prothromboplastin, 28.9
Providone iodine, 2.7
Pteroylglutamic acid, 29.15
Purgatives, 20.14
Pyrantel, 20.23, 20.27
Pyrazinamide, 13.7
Pyridoxine, 29.8
Pyridoxol, 29.8
Pyrimethamine, 3.8
Pyrrolnitrin, 10.14
Pyrvinium, 20.23, 20.26

Q

Quinacrine, 3.8, 3.19
Quinazoline, 27.15
Quinestrol, 16.24
Quinethazone, 19.10
Quingestanol, 16.24
Quinidine, 24.14, 26.7
Quinocide, 3.7
Quinolines, 3.5

R

Radioactive iodine, 15.9
Radiopaque agents, 21.2
Ranitidine, 20.6
Renin, 27.9
Resepine, 24.20, 27.13
Resorcinol, 2.4, 15.10
Retinal, 28.4
Retinoic acid, 28.4
Retinol, 28.4
Rheumatoid arthritis, 30.19
Rhodopsin, 28.6
Ribavirin, 11.6
Riboflavin, 29.4
Rifampin, 9.1, 13.6, 13.11
Rimantadine, 11.6
Rose bengal, 21.11
Rosoxacin, 4.12

S

Saralasin, 27.23
Schueler hypothesis, 16.6
Scurvy, 29.26
Semustine, 12.10
Serum sickness, 30.8
Sex hormones, 16.1

Sialagogues, 20.19
Siccanin, 10.14
Silver sulphadiazine, 4.11
Simethicone, 20.21, 21.8
Sisomicin, 7.7
β-sitosterol, 22.25
Sodium acetrizoate, 21.3
Sodium nitroprusside, 27.20
Sodium stibogluconate, 3.16
Somatostatin, 14.10
Sotalol, 27.16
Spectinomycin, 9.3
Spiramycin I, 7.14, 7.17
Spiranolactone, 19.11, 27.28
Stibamin, 3.16
Streptomycin, 7.2, 13.4
Streptozocin, 12.10
Sucralfate, 20.9
Sucrose, 19.4
Sulbactam, 6.18
Sulconazole, 10.3
Sulfapyridine, 4.11
Sulfasalazine, 20.9, 4.10
Sulfisoxazole, 4.9
Sulfobromophthalein, 21.10
Sulfonylureas, 18.16
Sulfur, 20.17
Sulpha drugs, 4.1
Sulphaclomide, 4.4
Sulphadiazine, 4.10
Sulphamethoxazole, 4.11
Sulphones and sulphonamides, 3.10, 4.1, 13.10
Suramin sodium, 3.17, 20.26
Surrainfection, 5.15
Synthalin, 18.15

T

Tamoxifen, 12.21

Teniposide, 12.22

Terbinafine, 10.8

Terconazole, 10.4

Testolactone, 16.14

Testosterone, 16.13

Tetrachloroethylene, 20.24

Tetracyclines, 7.9

Tetrahydrocannabinol, 20.13

Tetramisole, 30.16

Theophylline, 19.7

Thiabendazole, 20.24

Thiamine, 29.2

Thiazide diuretics, 19.9

Thienamycins, 6.16

Thioacetazone, 13.8

6-Thioguanine, 12.14

Thiomersal, 2.8

Thiouracil, 15.10

Thorium dioxide, 21.4

Thyroglobuline, 15.2

Thyroid gland, 15.1

Thyrotropin, 14.13

Thyroxine, 15.2

Ticrynafen, 19.6

Tilorone, 11.10, 30.17

Timorazole, 3.14

Tinidazole, 3.14

Tioconazole, 10.4

Tobramycine, 7.6

Tocainide, 26.12

Tocopherol, 28.15

Tolamolol, 27.17

Tolazamide, 18.17

Tolazoline, 24.20, 27.15

Tolbutamide, 18.17

Tolnaftate, 10.11, 10.3

Tolonidine, 24.20

Tomoxifen, 16.9

Topical anti-infective agents 2.1

Toxoplasmosis, 3.20

Tranexamic acid, 22.14

Transfer factor, 30.10, 30.17

Triamterene, 19.13

Tribromsalan, 2.10

Trichomoniasis, 3.18

Triethylene phosphoramine, 12.11

Trifluridine, 11.5

Triiodothyronine, 15.2

Trimazocin, 27.7, 27.15

Trimethobenzamide, 20.13

Trimethoprim, 3.8

Troleandomycin, 7.14

Trypanosomiasis, 3.17

Tryparsamide, 3.18

Tuberculosis, 13.1

Tylosin, 7.14

Tyropanoate, 2.13

Tyrothricin, 6.21

U

Urticaria, 30.8

V

Vaginitis, 16.19

Vancomycine, 6.20

Variotin, 10.14

Vasodilators, 27.18
Vasopressin, 14.15
Verapamil, 26.17
Vidarabine, 11.6
Vinblastine, 12.19
Vincristine, 12.19
Viomycin, 9.3, 13.9
Vitamin A, 28.3
Vitamin B_1, 29.2
Vitamin B_2, 29.4
Vitamin B_3, 29.10
Vitamin B_7, 29.11
Vitamin C, 29.25
Vitamin D, 29.11
Vitamin E, 28.15
Vitamin H, 29.11
Vitamin K, 28.9

W

Whitfield's ointment, 10.12

Z

Zalcitabine, 11.6
Zidovudine, 11.6

❖ ❖ ❖

www.ingramcontent.com/pod-product-compliance
Lightning Source LLC
Chambersburg PA
CBHW082224010526
44113CB00037B/2389